THE HOUSE *of* HOPE SERIES

Where Do I Go?
Who Do I Talk To?
Who Do I Lean On?

NETA JACKSON

Thomas Nelson
Since 1798

NASHVILLE DALLAS MEXICO CITY RIO DE JANEIRO

Other Novels by Neta Jackson

The Yada Yada Prayer Group Series

The Yada Yada Prayer Group
The Yada Yada Prayer Group Gets Down
The Yada Yada Prayer Group Gets Real
The Yada Yada Prayer Group Gets Tough
The Yada Yada Prayer Group Gets Caught
The Yada Yada Prayer Group Gets Rolling
The Yada Yada Prayer Group Gets Decked Out

The Yada Yada House of Hope Series

Where Do I Go?
Who Do I Talk To?
Who Do I Lean On?
Who Is My Shelter? available March 2011

where do i go?

BOOK 1

A

yadayada

HOUSE *of* HOPE

Novel

This series is dedicated to
the amazing staff of
Breakthrough Urban Ministries
and its "Joshua Center"
a shelter for homeless women in
Chicago, Illinois
who have literally created a "House of Hope"
for their many guests

❋ ❋ ❋

In memory of
Dottie Rambo
whose song "I Go to the Rock"
provides both the theme for this series
and the titles of all three books
1934—2008

prologue

The two American coeds stood at the apex of the tree-lined Esplanade, heads bent over their guidebook. Male passersby turned for a second glance, eyeing the youthful female bodies with lusty smiles. Tank tops, shorts, and Birkenstocks did little to cover the long, shapely legs and tan skin. Some slowed, hoping for a glance at the faces hidden by the straight, corn-silk hair of one and the rippling chestnut curls of the other, both worn long and whipping about in the wind coming off the large, open square sprawled before them.

"This is it—Place de la Comédie. See the fountain up there?" The young woman with the red highlights sparking in the sun pointed to the far end of the square. "Let's go up that way and find a café. It's after one already."

"But Gabby! The Polygone is right over there. It's like an American mall." The leggy blonde tugged her friend's arm, pulling her to the left of the Esplanade and away from the square.

Gabby jerked her arm free. "Linda! You and your malls. I didn't come all the way to France to *shop*. Come on. I'm hungry." She ran forward a few steps, then turned around but kept walking backward. "Come o-on! I'm going with or without you!" Then she ran on, laughing, backpack bumping on her back, threading through the other pedestrians filling the square.

Within moments she heard running footsteps and Linda's whine. "Wait up, Gabby!"

Laughing, Gabby locked arms with her companion as they walked to the far end of Place de la Comédie and approached the Fountain of Three Graces. They stopped, staring. The three graceful female figures stood atop a rocky mound of moss and green plants, with waterspouts pouring water into first one shallow basin surrounding the fountain, and then another. Several families with children sat on the smooth paving stones around the fountain, eating sandwiches and tossing crumbs to the pigeons that strutted about. A bald guy seated on a canvas stool nearby played a guitar, his guitar case open for the occasional francs. But the majority of warm bodies milling about the square or sitting on the ground around the fountain were young—late teens, early twenties—and multinational. University students.

"*Mmm*," Linda said.

"I know. It's beautiful."

"I meant those two guys over there. Sitting by the fountain. Do you think they're French?"

Gabby slapped her friend's arm. "*You* are impossible!" She laughed. "Come on. There's an empty table over there, see? At that café. We'll have a great view of the Opera House and we can watch the fountain—oh! Oh wait! Look!" Gabby clapped her hands. "It's a carousel!"

Linda rolled her eyes. "So?"

"I want to ride it! I've never ridden a carousel before!"

"Gabby! Don't be silly! Those things go up and down *and* around. You get dizzy riding a stupid escalator . . . Oh, brother."

A pair of eyes shaded by sunglasses followed the two young women as the curly-headed one ran up to the ticket booth, pointed at herself and her friend, paid their francs, and climbed onto the prancing carousel horses. The young man, sporting a loose shock of dark hair, poked his companion seated on the ground, his nose in a book, near the Fountain of Three Graces. "Hey, Cameron. Check out those girls."

"Where? The carousel?" His light-haired companion shaded his eyes and watched as the carousel started up, the horses lifted up and down, and the girls' laughter sailed over the square. "Silly Americans," he snorted. "Present company excepted, of course, Philip." Cameron went back to his book.

That got a laugh. "Stuffy Brit. Maybe we should go ride it too. Be good for you, my man. Too much studying can ruin your youth!" But Philip's eyes stayed on the young woman with the long, curly hair as she came around, up and down, on her prancing mechanical horse, her head back, laughing . . . disappeared . . . and came around once more. But this time the American girl clung to the pole, eyes tightly shut.

The carousel finally stopped and the girl climbed off unsteadily, almost falling. Her friend grabbed her and for a moment seemed to be holding her up. Philip started to his feet. Was she okay? But at that moment the young woman straightened and tossed her hair back, brushing off her friend's attention with a laugh. The eyes behind the sunglasses followed as the girls headed for the outdoor seating of the café between the carousel and the Fountain of Three Graces.

"Hey, Cameron. Let's get something to eat, okay?" Philip snatched the book out of the other's hands. "Come on."

His companion sighed, got to his feet, and grabbed for the book. By the time he repacked the book in his backpack and slung it over his shoulder, Philip had already picked out an outdoor table at the same café.

Gabby sucked on the straw in her lemonade and then sighed happily. "I could sit here forever watching people in this square. It's like . . . so international!"

Linda took a sip of her iced coffee and frowned at the menu. "Yeah, well, I wish you'd sat *here* fifteen minutes ago, rather than ride that silly carousel. I thought you were going to throw up back there . . . . Hey! Where'd the sun go?" Linda squinted upward as a shadow moved across the open square. "Better not rain," she grumbled. "We haven't ordered yet."

"So what? If it rains this afternoon, we can go to a movie at the theater over there." Gabby pulled the straw out with her teeth and pointed the dripping end at the domed building that said *Cinema Gaumont*.

"Gosh!" Linda rolled her eyes. "Do you always have to be so cheerful?"

Gabby giggled. "Yes. And I'd be even happier if Damien, the jerk, could see me now—*in* France, having a ball, with only one year to go getting my BA. Without him actually *being* here, I mean." She tossed her hair back and snorted. "*That* would be a bummer."

Linda raised her frosty glass. "To Damien, king of the jerks—"

Gabby clinked her lemonade on Linda's glass. "—may he get seasick on that fishing boat with the captain's daughter, who no doubt smells a bit *fishy* by now."

The two young women collapsed into laughter, which stopped abruptly when a male voice said, "*Excusez-moi, ma'amselles?*"

"Ohmigosh," Linda said under her breath. "It's them."

Gabby looked up, startled. A tall young man with dark hair and sunglasses stood beside their table, accompanied by another young man with sandy hair. "Yes?" *Oh, dear. I should've said, "Oui?" or something. He sounds French.*

"May I introduce myself? *Je suis Philippe* Fairbanks, and this is Cameron Brewer, my housemate. Graduate students at La Faculté des Lettres." He pointed at himself. "Business." Then at his companion. "History." He flashed a smile revealing perfect white teeth. "And you are—?"

His French accent rolled off his tongue like melted chocolate. Gabby cleared her throat, hoping her mouth hadn't been hanging open. "Oh! Uh, I'm Gabrielle Shepherd—most people call me Gabby—and this is Linda Banks. University of North Dakota." She had never seen such a beautiful man. Tall, dark, and handsome. Literally! And French to boot!

"*Pardonne*. May we sit?"

"Uh . . . of course! Please. Sit down. Right, Linda?"

Linda nodded, eyelashes fluttering, licking her lips.

"Have you ladies ordered yet?" The dark-haired one pulled over another chair. "The lamb kebobs here are superb."

"*Mmm*," the other seconded, sounding decidedly British. "Absolutely scrummy."

Linda snorted. "*Humph*. Gabby needs a salad or something light. She nearly lost it on the carousel back there—ow!" She glared at Gabby. "What did you kick me for?"

The two young men laughed. Gabby flushed. "I am *fine*. Just a momentary dizzy spell. The lamb kebobs sound great."

"Excellent." The dark eyes gave an approving wink. "Lunch is on us—right, Cameron?"

And so they talked and laughed over succulent lamb kebobs and freshly baked bread. Gabby was aware that the dark eyes seemed to feast on her, and she flushed at the attention. His English was perfect—unlike her French—and his lovely French accent gave her goose bumps . . . until Cameron pulled the plug. "Aw, ladies, don't be fooled by this bloke. His name is Philip, not '*Philippe*,' and he hails from Virginia in the US of A. I, on the other hand, am London born and bred."

Gabby's mouth dropped. Then she laughed, grabbed a cloth napkin, and playfully whipped Philip's arm with it. "You imposter!"

He threw up his hands and grinned. "Ah, well. Fun while it lasted."

She was actually relieved at the joke. It would have been charming to be romanced by a Frenchman, but her small-town roots in Minot, North Dakota, were so . . . so *provincial*. She'd married her teenage sweetheart right out of high school, but a divorce two years later made her determined to get out of Minot and do something with her life. Until this junket through Europe with Youth Hostels International, the farthest she'd been was the University of North Dakota in Grand Forks. Big deal.

However, an *American* in Paris—or, Montpellier, in this case—put this charming looker on more equal footing. She tossed her curls back confidently. "So, why did you decide to study in Montpellier, *Philip?*"

Philip's grin was half grimace. "Oh, you know the story. Family business. Dad's got my life planned, wants me to follow in his footsteps." He shrugged. "It's a good business, but I want to broaden my horizons, explore some new ideas to bring the business into the twenty-first century."

Intrigued, Gabby leaned forward, chin resting on her hand as Philip talked. A slight shadow of a beard lined his strong jawline. His dark brown hair had a boyish way of falling over his forehead—though Damien had been drop-dead gorgeous, too, she reminded herself, and look where *that* got her. But . . . Philip was different. Damien was just a local pretty boy who'd swept her off her feet with empty promises. But this man . . . he had roots. A solid Southern family. (How romantic was *that?*) Heir to a family business. And he had new ideas. Vision. She liked that. He seemed so self-assured—the type of guy who would go places and do things—and that excited her.

"—been to Paris yet?" he was saying. "You must see the Eiffel Tower."

Gabby let slip a wry grin and an exaggerated sigh. "Probably not. Uh, heights don't agree with me . . . nor carousels, it seems."

"Oh, nuts." Linda jumped up, bumping the table and nearly spilling their drinks. "It's starting to rain." The leggy blonde joined the throng surging toward the inside tables of the café.

Gabby was feeling giddy and bold. "So, what's a little rain?" Instead of going inside, she ran into the square, laughing and twirling around slowly in the warm shower, arms outstretched, letting her damp hair twist up tighter, like a crown of curly ribbons.

Standing under the awning of the café, Philip Fairbanks watched the sprite from North Dakota swirl, laughing, in the rain. "I'm going to marry that girl," he murmured.

"Don't be barmy, Philip." Cameron hunched his shoulders against the damp breeze. "She's just a ditzy yank from North Dakota. What would your mum do if you brought home a girl named *Gabby*?"

Philip laughed. "Probably have a hissy fit. I'll tell her the girl's name is Gabrielle—that sounds French, don't you think? And I think she's charming. A free spirit. Different."

Cameron snorted. "Different, all right. Look at that hair. Little Orphan Annie grown up."

Philip *was* looking at Gabrielle's hair. The sun broke through the light rain, and raindrops sparkled on the mop of chestnut curls flying around and around. "Mm-hm," he murmured to himself. "I'm going to marry you, Mop Top. You wait and see."

chapter 1

Looking thirty-two floors down was almost enough to bring up my lunch. Philip *knew* I had trouble with heights. So what kind of sadistic joke made him buy a penthouse, for heaven's sake! Not to mention floor-to-ceiling windows that curved around the living room, like putting a glass nose on a Boeing 747.

I groaned. It'd take me a week to wash the inside of those windows. And who in the world washed the *outside*—?! My knees wobbled. Uh-uh. Couldn't go there or I'd lose my lunch for real.

But the view . . . oh my.

I stood in the middle of our new living room and tried to take it all in. Trees dotted the park along Chicago's Lake Shore Drive, wearing the fresh new wardrobe of spring. On the other side of the Drive, the western edge of Lake Michigan lapped at the miles of beaches separated by occasional rocky retaining walls and disappeared southward amid the misty skyscrapers of Chicago's Loop. Tall, billowy thunderheads caught the late afternoon sun. Earlier that day, cars had hurried along the Drive, like toys zipping along a giant track some kid got for Christmas. But now, at the height of rush hour, the far lane was packed solid as commuters headed for the northern suburbs.

O-kay. Looking *out* at the view wasn't so bad. I stepped closer to the window, keeping my chin up, refusing to look straight down. Near the beach, cyclists whizzed along a bicycle path, swerving around joggers. Dogs with their masters chased Frisbees or dashed into the water after a ball. No one was in the water—too early in the spring, I guessed. But the sand sparkled in the late afternoon sunshine. What I wouldn't give to—

"Is that all, Señora Fairbanks?"

I jumped. The sweet face of the maid, who'd been setting up the catered buffet in the dining room the past hour, looked at me expectantly. Dark hair. Dark eyes. Plain white blouse with a name tag that said "Camila." Black skirt hugging her chunky legs. A wedding band on her left hand. Obviously hoping to go home and take care of her own family.

"Oh. Yes, yes, I'm sure it's fine, Mrs. . . . Mrs. . . . ?"

She reddened. "Just Camila, señora. *Gracias.*"

"Well, then, call me Gabby." I glanced at the Fairbanks' heirloom grandfather clock patiently ticking away in the corner of the large room. Almost six o'clock. Philip had said to expect him between seven and eight. "What do I need to do when the guests arrive?"

The short, stocky woman smiled with relief. "No problem. Cold salads in the refrigerator. Beef tips and saffron rice in the warming oven set at one hundred fifty degrees. Will be safe. Just take them out." Picking up her bag, she disappeared quickly into the entryway—called a "gallery" in the Richmond Towers brochure—and out the front door of the penthouse.

Still standing in the middle of the living room, I suddenly felt bereft. I was alone. Again. Philip had been gone since seven that morning. The boys were still in Virginia at boarding school. Philip wouldn't hear of taking them out so close to the end of the school year. And so we'd moved, lock, stock, and oriental rugs, to Illinois so Philip and his new partner could hurry up and dream big dreams in their luxurious office in downtown Chicago. And here I was, not only alone, but stuck up here in the sky, like an eagle impaled on a flagpole.

I imagined Camila in the elevator, riding down, down, nodding at the doorman, going outside. Free.

Stepping close to the curved window, I steadied myself with my hand, daring myself to look down, hoping to see her emerge. The glass was thick and cool to the touch. Probably leaving a grubby handprint on the glass. Huh. I'd have to clean it before Philip's guests arrived. Had to have a clean prison wall, right?

Stop it, Gabby.

A jogger caught my eye as she ran through the park below, ran past the trees, did a sharp turn, and then suddenly disappeared. *Wait a minute. What just happened?* I squinted . . . then a movement on the other side of Lake Shore Drive caught my eye. The same jogger was now running on the path by the beach!

There must be a pedestrian tunnel under Lake Shore Drive. My eyes widened. Why hadn't I seen it before? We'd been here five days already, and all this time I thought the ubiquitous Drive cut us off from the sand and water unless we got in the car and drove somewhere.

I cast another furtive glance at the clock. Ten after. Philip wouldn't be here for another fifty minutes at the earliest—maybe longer. I was already dressed in a white pantsuit and gold-strap sandals. The temperature was almost eighty—warm for April. *What if—*

On impulse I grabbed my keys from the wooden bowl on the table in the gallery and headed out the penthouse door. I felt slightly giddy as I stepped into the elevator and pushed the button for the ground floor, like the time I'd ditched classes in middle school back in Minot, North Dakota. When the elevator doors opened, I pushed open the security door into the lobby and breezed past the African-American doorman, not wanting to chat, and found myself on the narrow frontage street that gave limited access to several high-rise condos besides Richmond Towers.

But beyond the street, beyond the park, beyond the pedestrian tunnel was sand and water. *Sand! Sand between my toes. Splashing in the miniwaves.* The desire drove me on like an urgent hunger. How long, how long had it been since I'd even been barefoot?

I burst out of the pedestrian tunnel under Lake Shore Drive like a runner carrying the Olympic torch. *Oh Gabby, you are so bad.* I laughed out loud. Kicking off my sandals, I ran barefoot across the grass and stepped down a low concrete wall to the sand, sending a flock of seagulls hopping into the air and landing a short distance away. Delighting in the feel of the warm sand on my bare feet, I ran at the birds, sending them scolding and hopping again.

I giggled, turning around and around, arms outstretched to catch the wind off the lake, wishing I was wearing a princess skirt to whirl. Hardly anyone was on this strip of beach, so who cared if I looked stupid? No one knew me anyway.

On a whim, I rolled up my pant legs and waded into the water—and screeched. *Ay ay ay.* That was *cold*. Hurting cold! I splashed back onto the warm sand, but now wet sand clung like chiggers between my toes and up my legs. I sat down on the concrete bench to brush off the sand when I felt the first drop. And the second. I looked up. The clouds now hung low and heavy and looked about ready to dump.

Grabbing my sandals, I climbed back up to the grass and started running toward the pedestrian tunnel, hoping the grass would clean off my feet. By the time I emerged on the other side, the rain had become a chilly shower. Forgetting the paved path, I made a beeline across the grass and between the bushes toward Richmond Towers—and the next moment pitched forward on my face.

"Hey!" A raspy voice shot out of the bushes two feet from my head. "Whatchu go kickin' my cart for?" This pronouncement was followed by several hacking coughs.

I was more startled than hurt—except for my toe, which was sending stabs of pain up my leg. I rolled over and grabbed my foot, even as the rain soaked into my clothes and hair. *Cart? What cart?* I squinted in the fading light toward where I'd taken my fall and vaguely made out something metal sticking out from under the bush. "Sorry," I mumbled. "Didn't see it . . . where are you, anyway?"

The bushes parted, and a head poked out, half covered with what looked like a black plastic garbage bag. "Keepin' dry is where I'm at, tha's what." More hacking. "Leastwise I was till Orphan Annie came along . . . uh-oh. That foot's bleedin', girlie. Here, lemme see it."

To my astonishment, an old woman crawled out of the bushes, holding the thin protection of the garbage bag around her shoulders like a Superman cape, and grabbed up my bare foot in a thin, sinewy hand, even as the rain steadied into a moderate shower. "Aiya. Gotta stop that bleedin' . . . hang on a minnit." The woman dropped my foot and pulled out a metal cart from under the bushes, set it upright, and began digging through whatever was stuffed inside, her cough grinding away like a waterlogged car motor.

I scrambled up, standing on one leg, holding up the offending foot. "Oh, don't bother," I protested. "I really have to get . . ." *Home?* I couldn't yet say the word.

She hauled out a long rag. "Oh, don't get your mop in a knot. Siddown." The woman practically pushed me down, grabbed my bleeding foot, and began wrapping the rag around it. I shuddered. How long had *that* been in her cart, collecting germs and vermin and who knew what—

"It's clean, if tha's wha's botherin' ya." *Hack, hack.* She dropped my foot. "Now git on with ya, an' leave me be."

"Wait!" The absurdity of the situation suddenly loosened my tongue. Me go home to my sky-high penthouse while she crawled back under that bush? "This is ridiculous. It's raining, and you've got a terrible cough. Come on with me. I can get you dry clothes and some cough syrup." What she probably needed was a doctor.

The old lady snorted, sounding more like a bullfrog than a laugh. "Nah, I'm okay . . ."

But she hesitated just long enough to bolster my nerve. I took her arm. "Please, I mean it. Come on. Just until the rain stops, at least."

Rheumy eyes gave me a long stare, then she turned, grabbed the handle of her cart, and started across the wet grass. I caught up, steering her toward Richmond Towers. "My name's Gabby Fairbanks. Yours is . . . ?"

She didn't answer, just plowed on, with me hobbling along on my rag-wrapped foot. We crossed the frontage street and somehow wrestled her cart through the revolving door of the high-rise. And stopped.

The doorman loomed in front of us. His normally pleasant expression had evaporated, replaced by an enormous scowl that would have done justice to a bouncer at a skin joint. "Hey! Get that rickety cart outta here. Lady, you can't come in here. Residents only."

I waved timidly from behind the old lady. "Uh, she's with me, Mr. Bentley . . . Mrs. Fairbanks."

"Fairbanks? Penthouse?" The man's eyes darted between us. "Whatchu doin' with this old bag lady?" He suddenly became solicitous, though I noticed he kept a wary eye on my companion. "Are you all right, ma'am? What happened to your foot?"

"It's all right, Mr. Bentley. I, uh, we just need to get up to the, uh, apartment and get into some dry clothes." I beamed a smile that I hoped conveyed more confidence than I felt, took the "bag lady's" arm, ran my ID card that opened the security door, and headed for the elevator.

I let out a sigh of relief as the doors slid closed behind us, and the elevator quietly hummed its way upward. Closing my eyes, I started to shiver. I really needed to get out of these damp clothes, get cleaned up and changed before—

My eyes flew open. *Philip!* Philip and his guests were due at any time. *Oh Lord, oh Lord,* I pleaded silently. *Keep Philip out of here until at least eight o'clock.* A new absurdity was standing right in front of me. For the first time I took a really good look at the woman from the bushes. Matted gray hair . . . wrinkled, mottled skin, hanging loosely like a beige mask over her facial bones.

17

Several layers of clothes topped by a shapeless shirt or blouse, hard to tell, hanging out over faded navy blue pant legs, rolled up at different lengths. And here in the elevator, she smelled . . . stale.

Oh God. What in the world am I going to do with this, this—

"Lucy." The old woman's eyes were closed, and it didn't seem as if she had spoken at all, except for the raspy voice.

"Lucy," I repeated stupidly. "Oh! Your name. Thanks."

The upward motion stopped. The heavy doors glided open to reveal the glistening ceramic tile of the top floor foyer. Our apartment door was the only one to be seen, flanked by two enormous pots of silk flowers. "Well, come on, Lucy. Let's get you into some dry clothes and do something about that cough." *And get you out of here—quick,* I thought desperately.

I pulled out my keys and shoved one into the lock. Good. Got the right one on the first try. The lock clicked, and I pressed the brass latch to open the door. It swung wide and I hobbled into the gallery, Lucy huffing right behind me . . . and stopped.

There, through the archway, in the middle of the enormous living room stood my husband, tall, dark hair, easy good looks even at forty-one, a glass of wine in one hand, talking in a big voice to a strange man and woman, gesturing as though showing off the penthouse view.

In the same instant, they must have heard us, because all three turned, staring straight at me. Silence hung in the air for a split second. Then Philip took several strides in our direction, his eyes wide. Horrified, actually. "Gabrielle!" he hissed between his teeth. "What's the meaning of this?!"

chapter 2

I opened my mouth—but a bump from behind nearly knocked me over.

"Hey, wha's the holdup?" growled Lucy. "Ya gotta bathroom 'round here? I gotta pee."

"Uh, uh . . ." I cast a pleading grimace at my husband, whose face had turned a decidedly unpleasant purplish red. "Be right back," I whispered frantically at him. I peeked around Philip and tossed a weak smile at his guests, who held their wine glasses like startled statues frozen by the wand of the White Witch in Narnia. "Sorry!" I sang out. "A little emergency here. Be with you in a minute."

I turned and hurried Lucy in the opposite direction. Shoving her inside the powder room in the hallway just outside the kitchen, I made a beeline for the master bedroom. Could I take a quick shower, hop into something presentable, and get back to our guests before Lucy—if that was really her name—made it out of the half bath?

Philip was right on my heels, shutting the bedroom door behind us firmly. "Gabby!" He grabbed my arm. "Are you trying to ruin *everything* before I even get things off the ground?" He gaped at my feet. "Wait . . . what's wrong with your foot? Is that blood?" His voice changed. "Are you okay?"

I pulled my arm away. "Yes, I'm *fine*. And no, I'm not trying to ruin your evening. I just got caught in the rain and cut my foot, and she . . . never *mind*. Let me clean up, and I'll be with you in a few minutes." I pushed him away. I'd forgotten about my bloody toe. "Go *on*. Go back to your guests. I'll be there."

He ran a hand through his hair, still frustrated, and sighed loudly. "All right. But that . . . that—" He flung his arm toward the hallway where I'd penned the old woman. "Get her out of here, Gabby. *Now*."

With a final glare, he opened the bedroom door—only to catch a raspy voice floating our way. "Now, ain't this nice. Real nice. But say, now, this here cheese'ud be good wit some sandwich makin's . . . hey Gabby! Where are ya? Ya got some bread an' stuff?"

Both Philip and I flew down the hall toward the dining room—where Lucy was helping herself to the fruit and cheese platter on the buffet and stuffing handfuls of nuts into the pockets of her baggy pants.

"Out! Out *now*," Philip hissed—meaning the old woman, but directed at me—before heading back toward the living room where I heard him say with fake cheerfulness, "Please forgive our little interruption, ha-ha . . . must've followed my wife home when she got caught in the rain . . . have it straightened out in a few minutes . . . oh, here, let me freshen that for you."

I turned my attention to our other "guest," who popped a

green olive into her mouth, then immediately spit it out into her hand, followed by a disturbing cough or two. "Come on, Lucy. I'll get you some real food to eat."

The old woman followed reluctantly, as though she wasn't sure she should leave a sure thing for the mere promise of something more. But I quickly served a plate of the pasta salads in the refrigerator, topped with some of the beef tips and rice from the warming oven. She refused to climb onto the barstool at the granite counter, choosing to stand and shovel the food hungrily while I grabbed a phone book and looked up "Homeless Shelters." I couldn't just send her back out into the rain, Philip or no Philip, not with that cough.

No luck. Surely Chicago had at least one homeless shelter in this area! Grabbing the cordless off the wall, I dialed 01 for the lobby. "Mr. Bentley? . . . Yes, it's, uh, Mrs. Fairbanks. Top floor. Do you know the whereabouts of a homeless shelter for women in the area? . . . uh-huh . . . uh-huh . . . Is that nearby? . . . All right. Thanks—no wait. Could you call a cab for my, uh, friend? . . . Thanks."

I put down the phone. Lucy had stopped chewing and was looking at me under disapproving brows. "Did anyone ask *me* if I wanna go to some homeless shelter? Whatchu think I am, chopped liver?" Without waiting for a reply, Lucy turned her attention back to the rice and beef tips, mumbling under her breath.

Deciding that she was still occupied for another sixty seconds, I hustled into the master bath, pulled open the mirrored medicine cabinet, and grabbed a bottle of cough medicine. As I closed the cabinet, I raised my eyes—and saw for the first time the disaster pretending to be Gabrielle Shepherd Fairbanks.

I nearly screeched. My dark chestnut hair, already naturally curly, looked like it had been stirred up by an overzealous egg beater and left dripping. My "waterproof" mascara had smeared and left dark smudges under both eyes—complemented by a muddy streak that started in the middle of my forehead, ran straight down my nose, and skipped to my chin. Oh, right. Where my face had plowed into the muddy grass. My white pantsuit was rumpled and damp with grass stains in front and muddy splotches at knee level, and my feet were still bare—except for Lucy's rag, which was stained red around my big toe.

Tears sprang to my eyes. What had I been thinking?! I *knew* my husband was bringing guests, that he was eager to impress his new partner-to-be. So what do I do? I go on a fling out to the beach like an irresponsible ten-year-old! I come back looking like something the dog drug in, with a smelly old bag lady in tow, who hadn't even wanted to come anyway. And—

Lucy! I'd only meant to leave her for half a minute. What if she'd wandered into the living room, scandalizing Mr. and Mrs. Whatzit—what did Philip say their names were?—Fenton, or Fenchel, something like that. Clutching the cough syrup, I dashed out of my bedroom, through the hall and into the kitchen . . . only to slow down in relief.

Lucy the bag lady was leaning on her hand and elbow on the counter, eyes closed, snoring.

I felt a bit hysterical, unsure whether I was going to laugh or cry. *Oh God, this is too crazy! . . .* Was that a prayer? It'd been a long time since I'd really prayed, other than lonely prayers heavenward, asking God to protect my boys and bring them back to me soon, or to give me patience when Philip made me feel like a ball-and-chain around his life. Little did he know that I'd long ago become used to wearing the ball-and-chain that went along with the Fairbanks name. No, take that back. I never got used to it . . . which is why I was in the mess I was in today.

"Lucy?" I gently shook the old lady's shoulder. "Lucy, wake up. We've got to go. Here, take a spoonful of this . . . ." I poured some purple syrup in the plastic cap that came with the cough medicine. She gulped it meekly, only half-awake, and let me lead her down the hall. I hesitated at the gallery but heard voices in the den. Smart man, my Philip. Sequester the guests so they don't have to see me looking like Cinderella *before* the ball, shooing out one of the Sisty Uglers. I stifled a giggle as Lucy, her cart, and I rode down the elevator to the ground floor. *Sisty Uglers.* That's what I used to call the "Ugly Stepsisters" when I was five.

Thankfully, the taxi was waiting when we got downstairs to the lobby. I handed Mr. Bentley a ten for the cabbie and let him take over, getting the muttering old woman and her cart into the Yellow Cab, giving the driver the address of the shelter, and waving good riddance.

A quick shower, a long simple dress in royal blue, a quick blow-dry to my damp curls, a touch of mascara and blush, and I finally felt able to present myself to our guests. Philip looked me up and down with a hint of approval. I relaxed. "I apologize for that little snafu."

Philip's new partner threw back his head and guffawed. "Haven't heard that one in a while."

Philip grinned, as if they shared a private joke.

Whatever. I extended my hand to his wife, who looked like the prototype for white female actors on all the cop shows:

blonde hair to the shoulder, "pretty" features, business suit with short skirt, willowy legs, high, pointy heels. "Guess I need to start at the beginning. I'm Gabrielle. Most people call me Gabby. And you are—?"

The woman laid long, limp fingers in my hand, her eyes drifting somewhere past my ear. "Mona. Mona Fenchel," she murmured. The manicured fingernails fluttered in the air. "Lovely penthouse. Really. Lovely."

Yeah, and your husband's going to get an earful on the way home. "Who do they think they are, these Fairbanks? Buying a penthouse along Lake Shore Drive! And they've been in Chicago all of one minute. Did you see her when she came in? And what kind of name is Gabby? She's nothing but a hillbilly from—"

"Well, I'm delighted," boomed a voice, cutting off my imaginary rant. Mona's husband, tie loosened, shirt collar unbuttoned, shook my hand firmly. He looked about Philip's age—forty-one—a little fleshy about the face. "Henry Fenchel. Don't you worry about your little, heh-heh, *snafu*." A wink in Philip's direction. "These things happen. Homeless people all over the city these days. But they don't do too bad now that the weather's warming up. Downright industrious, some of them, selling the *Streetwise* newspaper on every corner downtown. But others . . ." He shook his head. "You can take them off the street, but you can't take the street out of them."

I did my best to smile brightly and be the perfect hostess, whisking the cold salads Camila had prepared to the buffet and rescuing the hot food from the warming oven. I lit candles on the teakwood dining room table, Philip poured wine, and the men chatted. I tried to engage Mona Fenchel in conversation—*How long had they been in Chicago? Did they have family here? Would she like more of the beef tips and rice?*—but not once did she look me in the eye.

I was relieved when they left. The grandfather clock solemnly bonged out ten chimes as the door closed behind them. The apartment was suddenly silent. I turned and saw Philip standing in the middle of the marble-tiled gallery, hands in his trouser pockets, jacket open, looking at me. "Let's talk, Gabrielle."

Uh-oh. Now I was going to get it. I sat on a hassock in the living room and tried once more to explain that I'd thought I had plenty of time, I didn't know it was about to rain, the old woman seemed sick and had no shelter . . .

But Philip couldn't get past his bottom line. "You *knew* I was bringing my new partner and his wife home to dinner. You *knew* this was important to me!"

I nodded meekly. "You're right. I'm sorry, Philip."

But my apology only seemed to trigger a long list of my sins. Did I know how long he'd had to keep them in the den, refreshing their wine glasses while I did my little goody-two-shoes thing? . . . He was lucky Henry Fenchel had a sense of humor, thought the whole thing was amusing . . . But I had certainly offended the wife—something you just don't do in business partnerships . . .

Again I said I was sorry. And I was. The whole thing was inconsiderate of me, and my good intentions had certainly backfired. I assured Philip I wanted his new business venture to succeed, and I would make it up to him somehow.

But we still went to bed with our backs turned to each other.

As Philip's steady breathing turned into soft snores, I lay awake staring into the unfriendly darkness, trying not to think about the fact that we were lying prone, thirty-two floors above terra firma, like being levitated by an unseen magician. Instead, I tried to count the days until P.J. and Paul could join us here in Chicago. Mid-April now . . . middle school graduation at the academy near the end of May . . .

But in the darkness, a wrinkled face with alert, darting eyes kept appearing in my mind's eye.

Lucy.

Did she get to the shelter all right? Was she safe in a bed with actual sheets and blankets? What would happen to her tomorrow? She still needed to see a doctor for that awful cough. Would she go? Would someone take her? Or would she end up back out in the park under the bushes?

I felt a surge of anticipation. Once Philip went to work, I'd get on the phone and try to call the shelter. *No.* Even better. I'd take a taxi, go to the shelter, and find out for myself.

chapter 3

Daylight filled the muted Vienna shades like a bar of white chocolate. *Mmm. Chocolate.* My stomach rumbled. Must be time to get up. I flung out an arm . . . and realized Philip's side of the bed was empty.

What time was it, anyway? I squinted at the red digital numbers on our bedside clock. *Eight twenty?!* I tumbled out of the king-size bed and into the bathroom. I never slept this late! In fact, I was usually up before Philip, trying to make a decent breakfast and eat together before he left for work—though more often than not, he just took a couple of bites of scrambled eggs, grabbed his coffee and bagel, and dashed out the door after a peck on my cheek.

Gargling a shot of mouthwash and running a brush through my snarly hair, I grabbed my bathrobe from the back of the door and headed down the hall, hoping to find Philip before he was off for the day. But the house—*apartment? condo? flat? What in the world did one call this oversize tree house?*—was eerily silent. Padding into the living room, I pulled the cord on the floor-to-ceiling drapes. Drat. Cloudy and gray. But up here in the stratosphere, I couldn't even hear the traffic below. No treetops interrupted the sky. Only other tall, glitzy residential buildings and hotels to my right and left, standing at attention along Lake Shore Drive while life scurried along down below.

In the kitchen, a note was propped on the coffeemaker. "Gabrielle, remember we've got a theater date tonight, 7:00. And no bag ladies!" Then he'd added a PS: "Forgot to tell you the maid comes to clean on Fridays, 9 a.m."

What maid? Every Friday? Good grief, what else did I have to do except clean the house? The stove digital said 8:40. *Oh, great.* So much for a leisurely cup of coffee. I hopped into the shower and then pulled on a clean pair of white capris and a rose-colored cotton sweater. With an eye on the clock, I made the bed and plumped the shams. No way did I want some girl from Maids R Us thinking I couldn't even make my own bed.

The intercom chimed while I was drying my hair. I buzzed the security door downstairs, feeling smug that I'd accomplished so much in just twenty minutes. Two minutes later, the doorbell rang. I pulled open the door. "Oh! Camila!"

The round-faced Latina who had prepared our buffet dinner so expertly the night before stood beaming in the hallway, a snug gray cardigan her only wrap. *"Buenos días,* Señora Fairbanks." She held a bucket full of cleaning supplies in one hand and a mop in the other.

For some reason I felt like throwing my arms around her and giving her a hug. A familiar face! But I just grinned and let her in. "Please, just call me Gabby. We . . . I . . . uh, I'm not sure what to tell you to do. We only moved in last weekend. There are a lot of boxes still in the spare bedrooms." I laughed self-consciously. "We haven't been here long enough to get it dirty yet, but—"

"No problem, Señora Fairbanks. I cleaned for the people who owned the penthouse before you. And"—she hefted the bucket, chuckling—"I brought my own cleaning supplies today. In case yours are still packed. Where would you like me to start?"

"Uh . . ." My mind scrambled. "The kitchen, I guess . . . oh, no, uh, I still need to eat breakfast." For some reason, I felt my face flush. Camila had probably gotten up at six, eaten breakfast already, and traveled to Richmond Towers from who knows how far away, while the spoiled rich lady barely had her eyes open.

I felt like screaming at my husband. *Don't embarrass me like this!*

Camila started in the living room and the den, courteously giving me time to finish in the bathroom and make a fresh pot of coffee. As I perched on a kitchen stool, munching a toasted bagel at the marble counter, she bustled past me toward the bedroom. A moment later I heard her call out, "Oh, no, no, señora, you don't have to make the bed. I need to wash the sheets on Friday." I heard the muffled sounds of the bed being stripped.

So much for making the bed. So much for first names, too, I guessed.

I finished my coffee, put my dishes in the dishwasher, and wiped the counter, listening with frustration to Camila's happy humming coming from the other room. What in the world was I supposed to do with myself while she cleaned? I couldn't unpack boxes—that would get in her way.

At least back in Virginia, I'd been raising the boys, driving them to school and sports, helping them with homework, and volunteering at the League of Women Voters. And, oh yes, the

Petersburg Garden Club, thanks to a membership from my mother-in-law. A weekly cleaning lady seemed justified then . . . especially when I went back to school to complete my credits as a certified therapeutic recreational specialist—much to Philip's amusement, who thought a CTRS was a fancy name for fun and games.

But it stood me in good stead landing the job as a recreational therapist at the Briarwood Senior Center. Especially when Philip registered Philip Junior at boarding school two years ago. He'd only been eleven, going into sixth grade. And last fall, Paul had joined him, emptying the house of my heart.

At least I'd had my job, something that made me feel useful. Needed. Filled the long days and hours.

Hot tears rose up unbidden, thinking of P.J. and Paul. *Oh God, I miss them so much.* I grabbed a napkin, dabbed my eyes, and blew my nose. Good grief, they were still just *boys*, only thirteen and eleven. So what if the Fairbanks males "always" attended George Washington Preparatory Academy? They had Shepherd in them, too, and Shepherds went to school half a mile from home, like everyone else, wearing jeans with holes in the knee, and sporting a tie only at weddings and funerals, if then.

I slid off the stool. I had to get out of here. But go where? Do what? And then I remembered.

Lucy.

That's it! I was going to find that homeless women's shelter and see if they'd taken her in. Just inquire how the old lady's cough was doing. Tell the staff how we'd met in the rain. Laugh about it. Say hello and good-bye.

Grabbing my purse from the coat closet in the gallery, I ran down the hall and poked my head into the master bath, where Camila was scrubbing the shower. "Camila? I'm leaving now. Do you know how long you'll be? If I'm not back, can you just lock the front door behind you?"

She waved a hand ensconced in a yellow rubber glove. "No problem, Señora Fairbanks! *Sí,* you go. Everything will be fine."

Thankfully, Mr. Bentley was on duty again, though he pursed his lips and frowned when I asked if he would call a cab for me and find the address again for that same homeless shelter where he'd sent the bag lady last night.

"Now, what you want to go there for, Mrs. Fairbanks? Have you been to State Street yet? Or"—he glanced outside—"well, guess it's not the best day to go up the Sears Tower. Clouds too low. But how about North Michigan Avenue? Lots of shopping there."

I tried to keep impatience out of my voice. "Please, just call a cab, Mr. Bentley. And get that same address, if you would."

The cab pulled up in front of a brick church squeezed between other two- and three-story buildings. I peered out the window. "Is this it? Where—?"

"This is the address, lady." The cab driver pointed at the church. "Building burned down a couple of years ago. That one you see there is brand-new. Don't know why they put in that stained-glass window an' stuff. The old building hadn't been used as a church for years, much less this one. You want me to wait?"

I looked at the meter. $7.85. I handed him a ten. "No, thanks." I got out and stood on the sidewalk. Seemed like it had taken barely five minutes to get here. Must not be that far from Richmond Towers. Maybe I could walk back.

As the taxi pulled away, a stab of doubt weakened my resolve.

I didn't see a sign anywhere saying "Women's Shelter." Several broad steps led up to a set of double oak doors, flanked by stained-glass windows on either side. High above the doors, cradled by the peak of the building, the wooden beams of a cross stretched top to bottom and side to side inside a circular stained-glass window.

Not far away I heard the metallic rattle of the elevated train, catching my eye as it passed over the street a couple of blocks away. I craned my neck to see what else was on the block. Most of the buildings seemed to be two- and three-story apartment buildings, though to the right of the church building was a Korean grocery, a Pay-Day Loan, and a twenty-four-hour Laundromat, with apartments above.

A young couple with a baby in a stroller turned the corner by the Laundromat and walked briskly toward me. He was white; she was black. *Interesting.* That would raise a few eyebrows back in Petersburg. I stepped aside to let them pass, but they stopped.

"Hi." The young man spoke first. "Can we help you?"

"Oh. Well, yes, maybe you can. I'm looking for a"—*How dumb was this going to sound?*—"um, a women's shelter that's supposed to be around here."

The young black woman laughed as she bent down to pick up the baby from the stroller. "Well, you found it!" She tipped her chin toward the oak doors of the church, cradling the baby on her hip. "Come with us. We're going in."

She spoke with a Spanish accent, sounding like the cleaning woman, but Camila had creamy tan skin as I supposed most Hispanic-Americans had. This woman was dark skinned, with loose, black corkscrew ringlets caught back from her forehead by a broad, bright-orange cloth headband. And her whole face seemed to laugh—a wide, bright smile and dancing dark eyes.

"Josh, grab the stroller, will you?" The young mother skipped up the stairs. "Come, *niñita*, let's go find Auntie Mabel." She pulled open one of the oak doors and disappeared inside.

Was Josh the baby's father? He seemed so fair, sandy hair down around his collar, looking more like a college kid than any- thing else. The mother was definitely black, and the baby . . . hard to tell. Creamy tan skin, dark hair, but loose and curly. Well, daddy or not, Josh obediently folded the little umbrella stroller with a kick to the brace between the wheels, darted up the stairs, and caught the door before it closed, holding it open for me.

I followed, but only as I got to the top step did I see the simple brass plaque beside the doors that said Manna House.

chapter 4

❀ ❀ ❀

Inside, the stained-glass windows on either side of the double oak doors filled the foyer with prisms of color and light. Large plants standing on the floor softened the large square entryway. In the open doorway of an office to my left, the young mother, still bouncing the baby on her hip, stood talking to an older black woman in a black skirt and soft, lime green sweater.

"Hi, Mabel. We have a guest," the young man announced.

"Oh, I am sorry. I did not introduce myself!" The younger woman shifted the baby and extended her hand. "My name is Edesa Reyes Baxter"—she dimpled at the young man—"and this is my husband, Josh Baxter. And this is Mabel Turner, the director of Manna House."

The baby in Edesa's arms let out a squeal and grabbed her mother's ear for attention.

"Oh, hush, hush, *mi niña*." Edesa Baxter unhooked the baby's fingers, laughing. "I would not forget you! This is Gracie. God's miracle gift to Manna House."

What an odd thing to say, I thought. *Wait a minute. Does the baby belong to the couple? Or is she homeless and staying at the shelter? No, that couldn't be. But why—*

My thoughts were interrupted by the director, who shook my hand firmly. "Can we help you in some way, Mrs. . . . ?"

She must have seen the wedding ring on my left hand. "Gabby Fairbanks. Actually, um, I was looking for an older woman I ran into yesterday. She had a cough and was sitting under a bush in the rain. She said her name was . . . um, her name was—" For some reason, I totally blanked.

"Ah! You must mean Lucy." Mabel smiled. "So you're the mysterious person who sent her here by taxi. I think she's still here. Josh, would you check to see whether she signed out?"

Josh Baxter sauntered over to the receptionist's cubicle on the other side of the foyer—a glass-enclosed cubby with an open window into the foyer, and a wide ledge on which lay a big notebook. Suddenly I felt foolish. What in the world was I doing here? I half hoped the old woman had signed herself out. If she was here, what would I say? *How are you? . . . Fine. . . . How's your cough? . . . Fine. Or worse. Whatever.* And then our "conversation" would be over.

Oh, suck it up, I told myself. I was here now. Might as well just do it. I smiled, trying to look self-confident. "That would be nice. I was just concerned about her. Uh, do you have many women staying here?"

Mabel Turner shrugged. "It varies. We have beds for forty-eight residents—but that includes a few with kids, who we try to put in a room together as a family, if possible. Some stay for two weeks or two months. Longer than that, we try to find transitional housing. Sometimes they just disappear back onto the street. Especially when the weather gets warmer."

Residents. She called them residents. I needed to remember that.

"Lucy didn't sign out," Josh called over. "Guess she's still here."

"I'll find her." Edesa shifted little Gracie to her other hip. "I've got fifteen minutes until I lead Bible study. Would you like a tour of Manna House, uh—I'm sorry, I forgot your name already." She seemed genuinely flustered.

"Gabby. Short for Gabrielle." I smiled reassuringly. "That's all right. You've got your hands full." I followed her through the double swinging doors into a large room. "Gracie . . . that's a pretty name. How old is she?" I was fishing, I knew.

"Eight months. Or thereabouts." Edesa kissed the top of the baby's soft black hair. "Her mother was a drug addict, and she never actually told us a birth date. Josh and I are adopting her. Takes a long time, though." She made a face at me. "Too long."

Well, okay. That was a successful fishing expedition.

"This is our multipurpose room." Edesa swept a hand around the large, bright room. Several women of various ages and colors were looking at magazines or talking in "seating groups" created by overstuffed chairs and small couches draped with colorful covers. A large woman—Mexican maybe?—hovered over a cabinet by the wall, pumping hot coffee from a large carafe into an over-size Styrofoam cup. Two young women barely out of their teens played cards at a table along the opposite wall.

"Yeah," fussed a voice, lounging somewhere within the cushions of the closest love seat. "An' Edesa been sayin' for months we gonna rename this room. Sheeze Louise! What kinda name is 'multipurpose,' I axe you?"

Edesa laughed. "Okay, Precious. Show yourself. Have you seen Lucy?"

A dark face appeared over the back of the love seat, a woman I guessed was somewhere in her thirties. Rows upon rows of tiny braids clung tightly to her head and hung down to her shoulders. "Take a guess where Miz Lucy's at! Down in the kitchen, eatin' breakfast leftovers. . . . Oh, 'scuse me." The woman hopped up, came around the couch, and held out her hand to me. "Name's Precious McGill. Didn't mean to be rude."

I shook her hand. "I'm Gabby Fairbanks."

"What are you doing here?" Edesa asked her. "You don't usually come till three." She turned to me. "Precious is one of our volunteers. She and her daughter Sabrina help supervise our after-school program—such as it is—three days a week. We need more tutors."

I blushed slightly. I'd assumed she was one of the "residents."

"Girl, ain't no school today, an' ain't no after-school program, neither. It's Good Friday. An' Jewish somethin' too—oh, yeah, Passover. Wait till Gracie starts school. Then ya gonna be scramblin' for child care two, three extra times a month 'cause it's this or that holiday again. Equal opportunity religious holidays, ya know. Can't ya hear them kids downstairs?"

Now that she'd mentioned it, I did hear muted squeals, thumps, and the general hubbub that goes along with kids at play coming from below.

Edesa made a face. "Speaking of Good Friday, I'm supposed to lead a Bible study on those scriptures in a few minutes, and I was giving Mrs. Fairbanks here a tour. Could you . . . ?" She looked hopefully at Precious.

I almost said, *"Please. Just call me Gabby."* But I gave up. Did I have "Mrs. Fairbanks" tattooed across my forehead or something?

"Oh, sure. Got plenty of time till I need to throw lunch

together. Fillin' in for Estelle today." Precious reached for Gracie. "Gimme that baby too. She need changin' or anything?"

And so Gracie and I were both handed over to Precious McGill, who cheerfully chatted nonstop as she showed me the toddler playroom populated by two toddlers and one mother on a cell phone, a schoolroom with two computers (deserted), a small TV room with a news station blabbing away to no one, and a small prayer chapel, all on the first floor. On the second floor, six medium-sized bedrooms held four bunks in each, plus showers, bathrooms, and a small central lounge. I felt embarrassed peeking into the sleeping rooms when someone was there, even though the doors were open, and Precious didn't bother to introduce me to anyone. She just said, "Hey there," or "Say hi to Tanya, Gracie," waving the baby's hand.

My tour guide did a quick change of the baby's diaper, using a stash of disposables in the second-floor lounge. Then we headed for the basement, where we peeked into a large recreation room. A handful of kids ranging in age from maybe six to eleven were sprawled in the beanbag chairs, watching cartoons, though a teenage girl and a little boy were playing foosball. Precious poked me. "That's my Sabrina over there, getting whupped by little Sammy."

The lower level also boasted a well-equipped kitchen and dining room, and that's where we found the old woman I'd met yesterday, hunched over a paper plate, wiping up the last drips of syrup with a rolled-up pancake.

"Someone to see you, Miz Lucy . . . Nice to meetchu, Miz Gabby. I'm gonna go catch Edesa's Bible study while I have a chance. Don't get to sit in too often, 'cause I'm usually waitressin' at this café, but this week they give me Friday off. Come on up later, if you want." And Precious disappeared up the stairs with the Baxter baby.

Lucy looked up at me with her watery eyes. "*Humph.*" The old woman finished mopping up syrup, coughed a couple of times into a napkin, stuffed the last bite of pancake into her mouth, then looked up at me again. "You gonna jus' stand there? Go on. Siddown." It was the same raspy voice. "You hungry?"

"No, I'm fine." I pulled out a molded plastic chair and sat. "I . . . I just came to see if you made it okay to the shelter last night. I was worried about your cough. And . . ." I felt my face flush. "I wanted to apologize for my husband's rudeness yesterday. I didn't know he'd be home."

Lucy just stared at me again. She was wearing different clothes than yesterday, a pair of yellow pants, gym shoes with no socks, a large white T-shirt, and a brown, nubby-knit cardigan. Her frowzy hair looked as if it had been washed. Good. At least she'd gotten a bath and clean clothes. And food. I smiled inwardly.

Finally she spoke. "Yeah, well. He can't help it. I shoulda known better'n ta go up ta that fancy penthouse wit' you." She coughed and cackled a laugh. "Man, that was some highfalutin place you got there. Ain't never seen one o' them. An' that bathroom smelled mighty good. Didn't have no bathtub in it, though. You must be payin' through the nose for that place, an' they don't even put a bathtub in there?"

I laughed, feeling more at ease. "Don't worry. It has two more bathrooms with bathtubs *and* showers." I didn't mention the Jacuzzi tub. "But I'm sorry the situation was awkward. We just moved here to Chicago, and my husband was entertaining his new business partner. And then we come in, all drippy wet, and me barefoot, bleeding on the rug . . ."

Lucy grinned, showing a few missing teeth. "Heh-heh, gotta admit. The look on they faces was priceless." And then she laughed, a series of snorts and guffaws, punctuated by a few more raspy coughs. I couldn't help it. I started to laugh too. It *was* funny. I just hadn't had anyone to laugh about it with yet. Until Lucy.

After a few moments, she wiped her eyes with a well-used napkin and struggled upward out of her chair. "Well, I'm goin' upstairs to sit in somethin' more comfortable than this plastic chair. You comin'?"

I followed her up the stairs to the main level and into the multipurpose room. Edesa had pulled several of the couches and chairs into a bigger circle, where she sat with a Bible open on her lap, talking earnestly to a group of five or six women. The baby was nowhere to be seen; Josh neither. Maybe he had Gracie in the toddler playroom while Mommy taught the Bible study. *That's sweet.*

Lucy sank with a wheeze into an overstuffed chair outside the circle, feigning disinterest, but I noticed she sat close enough to hear what Edesa was saying. I did too.

". . . no accident that *Jesús*"—she pronounced it *Hesús*—"was celebrating the Passover feast with His disciples that night, the day we now call Good Friday. For centuries, this Jewish feast had commemorated their deliverance from bondage in Egypt, that old, old story when Moses told the Hebrew slaves to put the blood of a lamb on their doorposts, and the angel of death would *pass over* them when he saw the blood . . ."

Something stirred in me. *Good Friday.* I hadn't thought much about it for years—not since that knucklehead, Damien Spencer, superstar youth leader at Minot Evangelical Church, had married me right out of high school and then dumped me two years later.

I refused to go to church after that, even though it upset my parents. In fact, I'd been pretty mad at God all through college—until I met Philip. And then it seemed my storybook dreams were all coming true, and God just didn't seem important anymore.

Oh, sure, our names were on the membership roll of Briarwood Lutheran Church, and Philip and I took the kids to church on Christmas and Easter—even sometimes in between, especially when my parents came to visit—because that's what the good, solid, God-fearing Fairbanks family had done for generations.

But it'd been a long time since I'd thought much about Good Friday. Philip said he didn't understand people who acted all gloomy and sad, as if Jesus had just died that day, and I kind of agreed with him. Christians believe He'd risen from the dead two thousand years ago, right? Why not skip right to Easter, with its joyful resurrection music and traditional brunch and egg-rolling races on the church lawn? So that's what we did.

But all that was yesterday. Today we were in a new town, a big city where we didn't know anyone, didn't have anyone to impress, didn't even know where the churches were. Where would we go to church Easter Sunday? Did it even matter?

I almost wanted to laugh. Or cry. Here I was, sitting in the multipurpose room of a homeless women's shelter in Chicago, with the only "friend" I'd met so far, listening to a twenty-something black woman with a Spanish accent talk about Jesus and the angel of death and why the Jewish Passover was important to Good Friday—and for some reason I didn't understand, I was hanging on every word.

". . . and now Jesus, the Lamb of God, was about to sacrifice Himself and spill His blood to deliver *all* of us from death. He broke the bread that night and said, 'This is My broken body.' He filled the cups with wine and said, 'This is My blood,' fulfilling the true meaning of this Passover feast, once and for all."

"Sounds gory ta me," Lucy muttered loudly.

Edesa grinned. "*Sí.* You're right, Lucy. Jesus' death on the cross wasn't pretty. But He took the punishment for our sins so we don't have to be separated from a holy God, either in this life or when we die—oh, praise You, *Senōr!*"

To my surprise, the pretty young woman got choked up and had to grab a tissue and dab her eyes. After a moment she recovered and ended with a short prayer. The few shelter residents who'd attended the Bible study just got up and wandered away, although one pole-slim woman went up to Edesa and said, "That was good. Real good. Thanks." And then, "Is it time for lunch yet?"

"Lunch is in half an hour!" Mabel Turner's voice chimed in from the back. "Tina, Tanya, Carolyn, and Lucy . . . you're on setup and serving." She glanced around the room. "Where's Carolyn? Would someone remind her she's on setup? . . . Thanks, Tina."

I made a few mental notes: Tina was the big Hispanic, Tanya was the tall, skinny black woman who seemed to be Sammy's mother, Lucy was Lucy, didn't know who Carolyn was.

"Hey, I got this cough," Lucy growled. She hacked a few times to prove her point. "You don't want me coughing all over the food, do ya?"

"Hmm. All right. Cleanup instead."

"*Humph.*" Lucy made her way toward the stairs to the lower level without a backward glance at me.

I looked around for Precious, but she must have slipped out to start lunch. I made my way over to the director and smiled. "Like summer camp. Everyone has chores?"

Mabel arched an eyebrow. Her skin shimmered like polished oak, with just the right amount of blush and burgundy lipstick for a businesswoman. "No to summer camp. Yes to daily chores. One of the rules. Everyone needs to contribute in some way to their room and board while they're here."

I nodded in the direction of Edesa Baxter, who was gathering up her Bible and notes. "You have a Bible study and an after-school program . . . I didn't realize a homeless shelter had activities." I gave a self-deprecating laugh. "Guess I assumed it was just a bare-bones bed-and-breakfast for the homeless."

The director shook her head. "To tell you the truth, Mrs. Fairbanks—Gabby—we'd like to do more. Manna House has only been back in operation since last Thanksgiving. And it's a long way up from the streets to a productive member of society. Even when the women are getting off drugs, learning how to work the system, getting some job training . . . there's a lot of downtime. Hurry up and wait. What I'd really like to find is a program director to give our residents life skills and enrichment experiences. But . . ." She shrugged. "We can't pay much, so it's hard to find someone qualified."

I nodded my head and smiled like a robot. But all over my body, nerve endings jumped to life like a racecar with all pistons firing.

Program director? *That's me!*

chapter 5

I opened my mouth and then closed it again like a stupid gold-fish. *Don't be a nut, Gabby!* I told myself. *You don't know anything about homeless women or what they need. Not to mention Philip would never hear of it.* Ignoring the voices in my head, I opened my mouth and blurted, "Program director? I'd like to hear more—"

"Mabel? Mabel Turner! Phone!"

The young woman manning the reception desk overrode my tentative inquiry. Mabel headed swiftly for her office off the foyer, calling to me over her shoulder, "Please feel free to stay for lunch, Gabby. We enjoy visitors!" And she disappeared through the swinging doors.

I stayed, hoping I'd get a chance to speak to the director again. But I felt awkward, standing in the lunch line in my Calvin Klein capris and Esprit hooded sweater, along with women who had probably never seen the inside of Nordstrom's or Marshall Fields. I said hi and smiled at some of the kids, but they were more intent on filling their paper plates with taco salad and tortilla chips, and balancing large plastic glasses of Hawaiian punch. I noticed that most of the other women left one or two seats between them, eating without much conversation.

When I got to the counter, a middle-aged white woman, who was serving the taco salad—hairnet covering her hair, plastic gloves on her hands—looked me over, frowning. "You just come in today? Did you sign in with Ms. Turner?"

Precious, bustling back and forth behind the counter, came to my rescue. "This is Miz Gabby Fairbanks, Carolyn. She's a visitor. Friend of Miz Lucy's."

"Oh really."

I could tell she believed *that*. Lucy had been first in line and was already in a corner of the dining room, shoveling in mouthfuls of salad and washing it down with punch.

I bypassed the red punch for a glass of water instead, wondering where I should sit. Well, darn it, I came to see Lucy, so I was going to sit with Lucy. I sat. We ate. The silence was punctuated only by the sound of crunching chips, slurps of punch, and the occasional raspy cough.

Might as well try to get better acquainted. "The people here seem to know you, Lucy. Have you been here before?"

I got The Look. *Okay, dumb question.*

"Have you lived in Chicago most of your life?"

This time I didn't even get a look. Lucy got up abruptly and headed for the counter, returning a minute later with another glass of punch and a handful of oatmeal cookies, which she held out to me with just one word: "Nope."

"Nope?" Oh, right. Her reply to my question about living in Chicago.

"Thanks." I took a cookie and nibbled the edges.

Guess I wasn't going to get much with yes and no questions. I wanted so much to ask about her story. Lucy couldn't have been homeless her whole life! How did she end up on the street?—or to be more exact, under a bush in the park along Lake Shore Drive? I looked at her rough, wrinkled skin and wondered what she'd looked like as a girl. Had she been married? Did she have any children? If so, how could they let their mother end up like this?!

Lucy stood up, piling my paper plate on top of her own. "Huh. If ever'body cleaned up after themselves, wouldn't be no need for a cleanup crew. Well, thanks for comin' ta visit me. If I don't see ya again, been real nice." She turned away.

"Wait. Lucy. I'd, um, I'd like to see you again. If I came back—"

"Nah, don't bother. If it don't rain this weekend, I'll prob'ly be outta here."

Boldness took over common sense. "But what about that cough? You really ought to get medical help."

Lucy rolled her eyes. "Lady . . . Gabby . . . whatever you wanna be called. I been takin' care of myself 'fore you came along, and I intend to do just that after you leave. But if it makes you feel any better, the nurse comes here ever' Wednesday, an' I'll probably let her fill me up with that red stuff an' a bunch o' pills, if it ain't gone already by then. Satisfied?" And she stalked off with our paper plates and plastic glasses.

My face burned. I felt like shouting after her, *"Well, good for you!"* But it was obviously time for me to leave. Mabel Turner hadn't shown up during lunch, and asking about the program director job was a dumb idea anyway.

I waved good-bye to Precious behind the counter and scurried upstairs as quickly as I could, now eager to be gone. I'd overstayed my welcome as it was. Should I call a cab? Or just walk? It hadn't seemed that far. Maybe the receptionist had a map and I could figure it out . . .

Luckily for me, she did. But while the receptionist—who looked slightly Asian to me, but mixed, yes, definitely mixed—was pointing out the location of Manna House on the map, in the neighborhood just north of Wrigley Field, a male voice said, "You leaving now, Mrs. Fairbanks?"

I turned. Josh Baxter stood behind me, holding the baby. "Yes. I'm trying to figure out if I can walk back to Richmond Towers without getting myself lost. It's not that far, is it?" I pointed out the area on the map.

"Mm-hm, about two miles straight up Sheridan Road. But I was just outside; I came back to get an umbrella. Could rain any minute. Hey, Gracie and I are going to catch the northbound El up to Rogers Park. If you don't mind riding the El, I could tell you where to get off. It's just a couple of stops north." He grinned and waved the umbrella. "Besides, we've got cover."

Which is how I found myself walking two blocks to the Sheridan El Station, pushing a baby stroller, while Josh Baxter held the umbrella against the light drizzle. "You're going home without Edesa?" *Obviously.* I might as well have asked *why*, as if it was any of my business.

He laughed. "Okay, you're not going to believe this, but she's staying to study. She'll come home later, in time for Good Friday service tonight. But it's easier for her to find a quiet corner to do her homework at the shelter—the chapel usually works—than it is in our tiny studio apartment with Gracie. She's trying to get her MA in public health, but Gracie kind of interrupted that last fall . . . didn't you, kiddo?" Josh bent down to tickle Gracie's neck, making her giggle, but in the process, the open umbrella nearly knocked me into the gutter. "Sorry!" he said, and grabbed me back onto the sidewalk.

At the El station, Josh showed me how to buy a CTA pass in the machine, insert the card into the turnstile, and grab it when it came popping out while pushing on the bar. He handed the stroller to me over the top of the turnstile, then came through carrying Gracie. I followed them up the stairs to the El platform, which stood eye to eye with the second-floor windows of nearby buildings.

My stomach got queasy as I glanced over the edge of the platform and realized how easily one could stumble (or be pushed) off the platform, down onto the tracks in the middle with no way to get back up. I backed as far away from the edge as possible, though that didn't help much. Behind me, only a short wall stood between me and the two-story drop to the street below.

An elevated train rattled and squealed its way into the station, stopped, and the car doors slid open. People got off. People got on. "This is ours. Red Line," Josh said, beckoning to me. Feeling foolish for my wobbly knees, I stepped gingerly into the car across what seemed like a big, wide crack and grabbed the nearest pole. Josh and Gracie swung into one of the molded plastic seats. "Come on. Sit down. It's safer."

I sank into the seat beside them as the elevated train jerked and picked up speed. I blushed. "Sorry. Heights are sometimes a problem for me."

"That's all right. Is this your first time on the El?"

I repeated my story about just moving to Chicago a week ago, we didn't really know anyone, we had an "apartment" in one of the high-rises, my husband was going into business here with a partner . . . while Gracie pulled herself up on her foster daddy's lap and stared at the people in the seats behind us.

"What about you, Josh?" I cocked my head so I could see his face. Nice-looking kid. College age, if you asked me. Sandy hair, a bit shaggy, but that seemed to be the style these days. "How long have you and Edesa been married?"

He laughed. "Since Christmas! Let's see . . . almost four months."

"Four months! But . . . how long have you had Gracie?" Didn't these kids know it made sense to wait awhile before starting a family? Even a honeymoon pregnancy would've given them nine months to get used to each other.

He grinned again. "Five months. She's the reason we got married. *When* we did, I mean. We were engaged but planning to wait till we both finished school."

"And Edesa? She speaks such fluent Spanish! What is her background?—Oh, I'm sorry, Josh. I know I'm asking too many personal questions."

Josh laughed. "It's all right. She's from Honduras. Came to Chicago on a student visa. Just like there are African-Americans, there are African-*Central*-Americans—oh. This is your stop, Mrs. Fairbanks. Berwyn, see? When you get down to the street, just walk two blocks over to Sheridan, then turn left—that'll be north. Should only be a block or so to your high-rise. You'll be all right? The rain doesn't look too bad."

I nodded, shoring up my confidence. "Thanks, Josh. I appreciate it. Best wishes with Gracie's adoption." I stood and was swept out the door with other disembarking passengers. A moment later, the train was gone.

Down on the street level, I walked the two blocks to Sheridan Road, crossed the street and turned left. Sure enough, I saw Richmond Towers up ahead, jutting into the air like a giant glass tube that had been fast frozen. But Josh was wrong about the rain. I managed to get downright soaked by the time I pushed through the revolving doors of the Sheridan Road entrance into the lobby.

Mr. Bentley looked up from behind the half-moon counter that gave him full view of both entrances. I'd already figured out that the true urbanites—the ones with no cars, who walked everywhere or used public transportation—used the Sheridan Road entrance. Those with cars used the frontage road entrance, near the parking garage. I felt proud of myself, going out and making it back again *sans* car.

The bald doorman with the wiry gray beard rimming his jawline peered at me over the top of the reading glasses he'd been using to read the newspaper. "Mrs. Fairbanks." *Not hello or good afternoon. Just saying my name, the way a teacher might if I walked into class late.* "You are wet again. You seem to have a knack for getting caught in the rain without an umbrella."

I didn't have the guts to say, *"So? None of your business."* Besides, maybe the man was just joking with me. I chose joking. "Yep. Except this time I have my shoes on, and I'm not bleeding." I tossed him my best grin.

The eyebrows went up. "Uh-huh. *And* you did not bring home any strays today. Mm, three out of four isn't bad for a new-comer." He grinned at me. "You'd better get into some dry clothes, Mrs. Fairbanks, before you catch a whopping Chicago spring cold."

I left him chuckling and headed for the elevator. But he had it wrong. I'd managed to avoid *four* out of *five* of yesterday's "sins." Today I was getting home *before* my husband, and I had plenty of time to get out of my wet capris and sweater, take a long, hot bath, and get gussied up for our theater date tonight.

chapter 6

Philip was pleased that I was dressed and ready to go when he got home. I freshened my makeup while he showered and changed clothes, watching as he dressed in dark gray wool slacks, a black silk shirt, and a light gray two-button sport coat. At forty-one, he was still incredibly good looking, no paunch, with a hint of that boyish glint in his eye that had first attracted me.

"Did the cleaning woman work out today?" he said, pulling on a pair of Gucci loafers.

"Yes, fine." I decided not to mention that I'd left her alone a good portion of the time she was here on her first day. Would he mind? Good grief, cleaning services had to be bonded or something, didn't they? "Her name is Camila."

"Oh. Got the tickets?"

I could tell he wouldn't remember her name. He might never meet her. Even her check would go to the cleaning service, not to her personally.

As Philip drove our Lexus through the wet streets, I was captivated by the way each drop on the windshield briefly captured glints of streetlights before it was swiped away. My thoughts drifted with each swipe . . . how had Camila ended up in Chicago in the first place? Had she always cleaned other people's houses? Did she have a husband? Kids? Uncles and cousins living in the same house? That was the stereotype, anyway—

"What's that address again?"

"What?—oh." I squinted at the ticket packet. *Blue Man Group. Briar Street Theater.* "North Halsted . . . there, isn't that it? Wow, I didn't know it'd be so close." We'd only been driving ten or fifteen minutes. Could this be near the Manna House shelter? For a moment I felt as if I'd come through a time warp. I'd spent a good part of the day at a shelter for homeless women, eating taco salad off a paper plate with a crusty old woman named Lucy . . . and now here I was, attending a popular show on Chicago's hip north side, if the number of restaurants, good-looking folks in late-model cars trolling for parking spots, and people in evening dress, dashing about under umbrellas on a rainy Friday night, meant anything.

Parking was terrible. Philip finally let me out in front of the theater and told me to look for the Fenchels while he parked . . . which was crazy, given the crowd inside the foyer, waiting for the doors to open. The chatter sounded like a false-teeth convention—not exactly the opera crowd, which was okay by me. Finally I spotted Henry Fenchel at the bar, flirting with the barista while she twisted the cap on a bottle of Sam Adams and handed it to him along with a glass of white wine.

As he turned, Henry's eye caught mine. "There you are! Philip parking the car? Say, would you like a drink? You can have this one. I don't know where Mona disappeared to."

"Right here, darling." Mona Fenchel seemed to appear out of

nowhere and took the glass of wine. "But we can get another one." She smiled sweetly. "Chardonnay?"

I shook my head. A glass of wine with no food in my stomach, and I'd be loopy enough to dance on the piano if they had one. "Thanks anyway. Philip will be here shortly." I hoped. I wasn't sure I could handle two Fenchels by myself.

Mona raised her glass happily. "Good thing it's Holy Week or whatever they call it. Otherwise I don't think we could have gotten weekend tickets at the last minute. Thank God for keeping the Christians and Jews occupied elsewhere." She giggled.

It was all I could do to keep my mouth from dropping open. If God wanted to strike her dead right then, it would be all right with me. Although if I remembered my Bible stories correctly, the earth opening up or fire falling from heaven usually consumed a good many bystanders too. *Forget it, God,* I muttered silently. *Do it when I'm not around.*

To my relief, Philip finally showed up, a bit damp. Mona looked him over and then glanced at my outfit—silk mauve blouse, contrasting fawn-colored slacks and jacket, and sling-back heels. "You're both so dressed up," she purred. "We should have told you to come casual."

For the first time I noticed that both she and Henry were wearing jeans—designer jeans, but denim nonetheless. She giggled and sipped her wine. "Sometimes the audience gets a bit splattered during the performance. But . . ." She fingered the material of my jacket. "If you get it dry-cleaned right away, any stains should come out."

I could feel my back arch. *Get your hands off my jacket! Did it occur to you to tell us how to dress for this show?* But I said nothing, slipped my hand through Philip's arm as the doors opened, and followed an usher to our seats.

I had no idea what to expect from the Blue Man Group, but the stone-faced trio, covered head to foot in blue paint, put on a freewheeling performance that left us feeling giddy and breathless—a circus of wacky percussion, banging on drums, and "making music" with PVC plumbing tubes. We couldn't help but laugh until our sides ached.

It felt good to have a good time. I was aware of Philip's arm resting across my shoulders and the occasional squeeze he gave me as we shared laughter. We'd laughed a lot before the boys were born . . . before the business started to take up more and more of Philip's time. Or more of his heart.

I was starving by the time we were seated at Jack's on Halstead after the show, and I ate more than my share of the crab cakes we ordered for an appetizer. I knew better. Should have eaten something before we left home. Even after fifteen years of marriage to money and nightlife, I wasn't used to eating dinner at ten o'clock at night.

I'd genuinely enjoyed the show—bizarre as it was—but after the four of us rehearsed all our favorite acts through asparagus-tips-and-spring-greens salad, my gas ran out and I barely ate the grilled lemongrass-encrusted salmon I'd ordered. Talk turned to business, and I tuned out, suddenly feeling bushed. Philip didn't seem to notice, as long as I added a seemingly alert "Mm" or "Uh-huh" from time to time.

Mona's comment about Holy Week still bothered me. The

young couple I'd met today—Josh and Edesa Baxter—said they were attending Good Friday services tonight. And Edesa's little Bible study at the shelter had actually been interesting. I'd never thought about how the Jewish Passover fit hand in glove with Jesus and what happened on Good Friday so many years ago. *What was their Good Friday service like?* I wondered. A far cry from the Blue Man Group performance, I was sure of that! Which had been a lot of fun . . . but I squirmed inside, thinking maybe it wasn't the most appropriate thing on the night Christians were remembering the terrible crucifixion of the Son of God.

You hypocrite, I scolded myself. I'd parked my Christianity on a backseat years ago. Why should it bother me what we did on a weekend night, Good Friday or not? Still, just being at the Manna House shelter today had touched a nerve—touched something— that felt a little tender.

"You're awfully quiet," Philip said on our way home. The rain had stopped, and we actually had the windows down, breathing in the cool, damp air.

I tried to read his tone. Just commenting? Asking why? Annoyed? *Whatever.* "Mm. Just tired." Then I added, "I enjoyed the evening." *In spite of Mona Fenchel.*

He looked at me sideways. "Good. I'm glad. I know the move happened pretty fast, Gabby, but I think you'll like it here. Chicago's an exciting city. Henry was telling me . . ."

Hm. Philip was certainly being pleasant tonight. Should I tell him about finding my way about the city on my own today? Of course, then I'd have to mention that I ended up at the homeless shelter to see Lucy. But maybe that was okay. At least she was at the shelter and not in our penthouse! I smiled to

myself, remembering how Lucy had laughed at the little scenario when we two drowned rats had come barging in on Philip
and the Fenchels . . .

"I think 'Fairbanks and Fenchel Development Corporation'
will make a good name for the business, don't you?" Philip was
saying. "Has a nice alliteration. 'Fairbanks and Fenchel' . . . We're
going to sign the partnership papers on Monday. Just . . ." He
paused and looked at me sideways. "Just don't do anything stupid,
Gabrielle. Like, you know, the business with the bag lady. Things
like that can sour a business relationship in a hurry."

I pressed my lips together. I wanted to shout, *Her name is Lucy!*
But decided, no, this wasn't exactly the time to tell my husband
I'd eaten lunch with the bag lady.

I called the boys Saturday morning—the second weekend my
boys were spending their weekly break from the academy with
their grandparents in Petersburg, Virginia, instead of with their
father and me. I tried to be upbeat and positive on the phone.
"Hey, how'd your Latin test go, P.J.? . . . You're going to try out
for lacrosse next year? That's neat, kiddo! . . . Yeah, yeah, I know
you gotta go. What are you and Granddad doing today? . . . Oh,
wow. Virginia Beach! Sounds like fun. What are you going to—the
aquarium? Yeah, I heard it was great . . . Wait a minute, P.J. Put
Paul on for a sec, will you?"

As I waited for my youngest to get on the phone, I started to
bristle. What was wrong with this picture? Sure, *one* weekend
with the grandparents now and then, doing special things, was
great. But was this the way it was going to be for the next six
weeks? The senior Fairbanks pulling out all the stops to entertain

my sons, while I got a two-minute report on the phone, like a parent who'd lost custody?

"Hi, Mom." My eleven-year-old's plaintive voice rattled my cool. "I miss you."

"I miss you, too, kiddo." It was all I could do to keep my voice from quivering. "Only six more weeks, right? We'll come to P.J.'s eighth-grade graduation and bring you back with us to Chicago."

A short silence. "But what about my friends here?"

"I know, hon. It's . . . it's hard to move away. But you'll make good friends in Chicago too."

Another silence. "Guess I gotta go. Granddad's calling us to get in the car."

I wanted to hug him so badly. But I put on a bright voice. "Sure, honey. Have a good time at the aquarium. Happy Easter tomorrow! You going to church with Nana and Granddad?"

"I guess. They haven't said anything about it. I . . . I gotta go, Mom. Say hi to Dad for me, okay?"

The phone clicked in my ear.

Hitting the Off button on the handset, I sank back into the deep cushions of our wraparound couch. Philip was in the den, working on his laptop. I probably should have gotten him on the phone too. But right now I didn't want Philip's company. I just wanted to remember P.J.'s and Paul's voices in my mind . . . in my heart . . .

All too soon, their voices faded. I tried to get the sound back—P.J.'s confident prattle, Paul's pensiveness—but I couldn't. Hot tears squeezed out of my eyes, and I grabbed a tissue from the end table. *Oh God! I am so lonely . . .*

After a few minutes, I blew my nose and went into the bathroom to repair my face. Seemed like I'd been talking to God a lot more since we moved here to Chicago. Huh. Not sure if He was listening, though. It'd been a long time since I'd done any praying, and the connection was probably pretty rusty.

I took a long, hard look at myself in the bathroom mirror. Dark reddish-brown hair—"chestnut" sounded better—a naturally curly mop, best worn short or it got out of hand. Oval face. Minimal makeup. Philip used to say my hazel eyes were my best feature—long lashes, dark eyebrows, nicely shaped. Even at thirty-nine, I knew I could turn a few heads. But for some reason I felt as if I were looking at a stranger. Who *was* this person? Did I know her? Who in the world was the real Gabrielle Shepherd Fairbanks?

I felt frozen in time, staring at the stranger in the mirror. Then, like a dog coming out of the water and shaking off every last drop, I mentally shook myself and got out of the bathroom. *Watch it, Gabby,* I told myself. *You could easily end up a basket case, and what good would that do? Get busy. Do something.*

Cookies. I'd make chocolate-chip cookies and send them to P.J. and Paul. Not exactly the same as coloring eggs and putting all sorts of goodies into their Easter baskets like I did when they were younger. I wished I'd thought of this sooner, so they'd have them for Easter, but . . .

I started pulling measuring cups and measuring spoons out of the drawer. Tomorrow was Easter. And I wanted to go to church. Might just go crazy perched up here on the thirty-second floor all weekend. But where in the world would I go?

Could always ask Mr. Bentley. Who else did we know? Camila, the maid? Well, I would, but I didn't have a phone number for her, only the cleaning service, and I was sure they wouldn't give out Camila's personal number.

Who, then? The Fenchels? I rolled my eyes. If Mona Fenchel were the last person on earth, I wouldn't ask her where to find a church.

So that left . . . the people at Manna House. Well, why not? They were familiar with the city. Someone would remember me from yesterday.

I peeked into the den. Philip was deep in thought, a spreadsheet on his computer screen. I picked up the bedroom extension, dialing the number Mr. Bentley had given me. A bright voice on the other end answered, "Manna House."

"Hi. This is Gabby Fairbanks. I visited Manna House yesterday—"

"Oh, yes, I remember. This is Angela. The receptionist."

"Yes, of course." The Asian-something girl. At least now I knew her name. "Uh, this might sound like a strange request, but we're new to Chicago, and I'm wondering if you could recommend a church for us. Tomorrow's Easter, you know."

"Well, uh . . ." There was a long pause. "I don't know where to begin, Mrs. Fairbanks. There are a lot of churches. Depends on what you want, you know, Methodist or Baptist or—"

"Where do you go, Angela?"

She giggled. "I go to a Korean-speaking church. I'm sure you'd be welcome, but I don't know how much you'd get out of it."

Oh, for heaven's sake. This isn't going anywhere. I tried not to sound exasperated. "What about Mabel Turner? Or that young couple, the Baxters. Do you know the name of their church?"

"Mm. Not sure about Ms. Turner. But Josh and Edesa . . . all I know is that some folks from their church are coming here tomorrow night to lead our Sunday Evening Praise. SouledOut something or other."

"Coming there?" Well, that was a thought. "In the evening, you said. Well, thanks, Angela . . . oh, what time?"

"Six o'clock," she said. I clicked the Off button. Not exactly Easter Sunday morning. But something inside me said, *Go.*

Maybe it was time to get the rust off that God connection.

chapter 7

To my surprise, Philip got up early the next morning—well, early for a Sunday—and said he was going for a run. "Henry goes to the gym," he grunted, tying his running shoes. "Might as well take advantage of the jogging path before those thunderheads get serious." He winked at me. "Send out the hounds if I'm not back in an hour." The door closed behind him.

I gave him two minutes to ride the elevator and cross the frontage road to the parkway; then I went to the wall of windows to watch his shiny blue warm-up jacket and matching shorts heading for the underpass. He reappeared moments later, a tiny blue dot, heading south along Foster Avenue Beach.

Maybe I should go for a walk too. But I had second thoughts when I saw the large thunderclouds piling up over the lake. Breathtaking . . . but I'd had my fill of coming home soggy and chilled to the bone. Besides, it was Easter Sunday and I really should call my mom. She'd been alone two years now since Dad died. That was another thing that made me mad at God. Why a heart attack at seventy-two, for heaven's sake?! Noble Shepherd had kept working at the carpet store he'd owned for over forty years until "Mama Martha," as the locals called her, put her foot down and said it was time for them to enjoy some retirement, buy a motor home, take the Alaska Highway, do something before they had to hang it up.

They never did buy that motor home.

I sighed and hunted for the cordless. At least my mom was young enough to manage on her own. I was the youngest of three, a "happy accident," Daddy used to tease—though they hadn't been very happy with me when I dropped out of college, got engaged to a man I met in France (whom they met for the first time at a lavish Virginia wedding), and settled in that foreign country called The South.

I finally found the phone in the cushions of the wraparound couch where I'd talked to the boys the day before. At least we were Central time now, same as most of North Dakota. I dialed.

The phone picked up on the other end. "Hello?"

"Happy Easter, Mom."

"Oh! Happy Easter to you too. I'm so glad you called, honey. I thought about calling you, but didn't know about the time difference in Alaska."

"Mom! It's Gabby. I'm in Chicago, remember?"

My mother seemed flustered. "Oh, well, that's right. You'll be leaving for church soon, I suppose."

Even though that's exactly what I'd been wanting to do, I felt a tug of irritation. "We just moved here, Mom. Haven't found a church yet."

"Well, sure. But I bet there're some good Easter services on the TV. How are the boys?"

That did it. I started to blubber and ended up having a good cry. Nothing like talking to your mama when you're feeling homesick and missing your kids.

When I hung up twenty minutes later, I picked up the remote to the plasma TV embedded in the wall and clicked it on. Sure enough, a large choir in white and gold robes was joyously singing, *"Christ the Lord is risen today-ay, Ha-ah-ah-ah-ah-le-eh-lu-u-jah!"* I got a fresh cup of coffee, tried two or three other channels, and finally settled on the Chicago Community Choir, taped earlier that week, singing Handel's *Messiah*. The choir looked like a ten-bean soup packet, all sorts of colors and shapes. The choir wore white blouses and shirts topping black skirts or pants—except for the occasional blue shirt or orange blouse of someone who forgot the dress code. I closed my eyes and just listened as the majestic music took over our living room.

Surely He hath borne our griefs, and carried our sorrows . . .
He was wounded for our transgressions, He was bruised for our iniquities. The chastisement of our peace was upon Him . . .
and with His stripes we are healed . . .

"Whooee. What a run!" Philip's voice broke into the choral music. "I'm starving. Is breakfast ready?" Flushed and sweaty, my husband stuck his head into the living room. "What's this?"

I held up my hand for quiet. I wasn't ready for Philip to return.

. . . All we like sheep have gone astray; we have turned every one to his own way; and the Lord hath laid on Him the iniquity of us all . . .

In the background, I could hear stuff being banged around in the kitchen, and minutes later the shower running in the master bath. Well, he could just wait for breakfast or get his own. Why did he expect me to jump up and take care of him? It was Easter Sunday, after all. And right now I was mesmerized by the familiar and yet strangely new words and music . . .

How beautiful are the feet of them that preach the gospel of peace, and bring glad tidings of good things! . . .

Humph. My own feet were tucked up under me, pretty much not caring if my husband got any breakfast or not.

"Bring glad tidings of good things?" Oh well, why not. I reached for the remote, turned down the volume, and pushed myself off the couch. By the time Philip got out of the shower, shaved, and appeared dressed in khakis and a sport shirt, I had batter sizzling in the waffle iron, frozen strawberries thawing in the microwave, and a fresh pot of coffee dripping.

He grinned and pecked me on the back of the neck. "Smells great. Say, what do you want to do today? I know I've been busy all week. What say we take in the Art Museum? Or the Museum of Natural History? Something indoors anyway. Day's going to get nasty."

That kiss on the back of my neck melted all my defenses. I perked up, practically purring. "Do you mind doing Natural History?" After all, I was a North Dakota girl, more at home with animals and geologic formations than great masterpieces. But this was perfect. Spend a quality day with Philip—and then tell him I wanted to attend the Sunday Evening Praise service at the Manna House Shelter for Homeless Women.

Getting out of the backseat of a taxi in heels and trying to get an umbrella up at the same time took more coordination than I was born with, but somehow I managed to get up the steps and into the door of Manna House just before a huge flash of lightning and a twin crack of thunder threatened to kill me on the spot.

Maybe Philip had been right, telling me I was stupid to go out in this storm. After that comment, my courage had faltered and I'd been rather vague about exactly where I was going. *"To this church nearby that has an evening service."* Well, the building *did* look churchy, didn't it?

"Mrs. Fairbanks!" Mabel Turner turned away from the group she'd been talking with in the foyer and extended a welcoming hand. "How delightful to see you. I didn't know you were coming tonight."

"Gabby, please." I returned her warm handshake. "Yes. I called Manna House wanting some suggestions of where to attend Easter services, and the receptionist—Angela?—kindly told me about the, uh, service here tonight."

"Yes, yes, of course. We have a Sunday Evening Praise service here every week, hosted by different churches. Our residents really enjoy it, and of course guests are more than welcome. Avis! . . . Avis and Peter, I'd like you to meet someone. And bring C.J. with you."

Mabel motioned to the attractive African-American couple she'd been talking to earlier, and they approached smiling, along with a sullen-faced black kid, maybe thirteen or fourteen. To tell the truth, I wasn't sure if the youth was a boy or girl. Hair braided tight to the head all over in a unisex style, jeans, sport warm-up jacket, and a heartbreaker face.

"Gabby, I'd like you to meet Avis and Peter Douglass and"—

Mabel pulled the youth into a hug—"this is C.J., my nephew. Say hello, C.J."

C.J. mumbled "hello" and shook my hand limply. Okay, *nephew*. That answered that.

"And this is Gabrielle Fairbanks, a newcomer to Chicago who stumbled on us by accident . . ." Mabel suddenly looked at me and then burst out laughing. "Oh! That was unintentional. But funny, oh yes, very funny."

By this time, Avis and Peter were looking a bit bemused. So I had to explain about tripping over Lucy in the park and coming to the shelter later to see her. We all laughed, and Mabel finally finished her introductions. "Avis comes with the worship team from SouledOut Community Church once a month to lead our Sunday Evening Praise, and Peter is one of our board members. Oh—I think we'd better let Avis go. The praise team looks like they're about ready to begin. C.J., go sit down."

We pushed through the double doors into the multipurpose room, following in Avis's wake, who excused herself with a whispered, "Nice to meet you, Gabrielle." The couches and overstuffed chairs had been pushed aside and folding chairs set up, though many of the residents were still milling around, getting coffee from the coffee urn, or chatting loudly in their seats. Several men and women with instruments—an electronic keyboard, saxophone, and two guitars—were looking around as if wondering how to get everyone's attention.

Another window-rattling crack of thunder did the trick. "Praise the Lord, sisters—and brothers too!" Avis called out in greeting. "It's Resurrection Sunday!"

Several people responded loudly: "That's right! Hallelujah!"

"We can't let the rocks cry out in our place—or in this case, thunder." Several residents snickered. "If Jesus Christ can sacrifice His own life so that we can live, we can bring Him a sacrifice of praise."

Turned out that was the title of the song, but I didn't know the words, so I just hummed along as best I could. It was hard to make out the words over the saxophone, anyway. I wasn't alone. Only about half the shelter residents sang along, and many of those were mumbling. *Sacrifices of thanksgiving? Sacrifices of joy? Hmm.* If the only bed I had was a bunk in a shelter, I might be able to drum up a sacrificial "thanks." But joy?

When was the last time I felt joy? A smile tickled the corners of my mouth. Running barefoot in the sand a couple of days ago, sending the gulls fluttering like dancing girls with gauzy white scarves. *Yes, that was joy.* My prelude to that strange encounter in the park with a metal cart belonging to a bag lady under a bush—

Lucy. I glanced quickly around the room but didn't see her. *Oh Lord, she's not out in this storm, is she?* No, no, surely not. She'd find shelter somewhere . . . wouldn't she? But I did see lanky Josh Baxter and his cute wife, Edesa—a poster couple for racially mixed marriage. A white man and woman stood next to them, the woman holding baby Gracie and nuzzling her affectionately as the singing group launched into a new song. Josh's parents, if I had to take a guess.

Interesting. Did the Baxter clan go to this SouledOut Community Church too? If so, this church certainly had a mixed group of people. The praise team had both blacks and whites too.

The next hymn was more familiar. "Up from the grave He arose!" I wasn't used to singing without a hymnbook, but I'd sung this one many times growing up, and it was also a staple when we made our Easter appearances in Petersburg. The guitars and sax gave it a rather funky flavor, though. Even the tinny piano at my home church in Minot, North Dakota—not to mention the majestic organ at Briarwood Lutheran—seemed more appropriate somehow.

We finally sat, and the woman who'd seen right through my claim to buddy-ness with Lucy in the lunch line two days ago—Carolyn, I think Precious had called her—stood up and read from a paperback Bible. "For we died and were buried with Christ by baptism. And just as Christ was raised from the dead by the glorious power of the Father, now we also may live new lives." She read several more verses, which basically said the same thing in more words, then lifted her head. "That's from Romans, chapter six. Amen." And sat down.

What was her *story?* I wondered. Pallid skin, middle-aged, thirty pounds too heavy, slicked-back brownish-gray hair worn in a ponytail, but quick on her feet, and she read smartly. Obviously not a high school dropout. But why homeless?

After the Bible reading, Avis Douglass gave what she called a short devotional on the meaning of "new life." She was certainly an attractive black woman—hair swept up into a sculpted French roll, black pantsuit, silk blouse, very professional looking. Her husband wasn't bad either. Salt-and-pepper hair cropped short, dark gray flannels, black open-necked shirt. I caught him eyeing his wife with a little smile.

"Jesus didn't rise from the dead just to prove He was God," Avis was saying. "There was one reason, and one reason only, that Jesus came to earth, went to the cross, and rose from the dead—and that was to take the death penalty for our sins, so that we might have new life. New life for me, new life for you."

Oh sure, I thought. *Easy for you to say. You have a good-looking husband, probably have a good job. You seem happy. But what about all these women here? No man, no family to take them in, no home . . . not much hope of a new life here.*

I was startled by my thoughts. Good grief. Who was I to pit this Avis Douglass person against these women? Look at me . . . Philip and I lived on a six-figure income, we just bought a penthouse, I arrived here tonight in a taxi. I didn't grow up rich, but we weren't poor either. Never missed a meal in my life. So what in the world was going on?

Only later, after the service was over, after I met Josh Baxter's parents—a friendly couple who seemed to kid around with each other and laugh easily, even though they had to be married longer than Philip and me—and after I was back in the taxi alone with my thoughts, did I realize why I had reacted so cynically to Avis's devotional.

Even though we had just moved to Chicago, it didn't feel like a new start or a new adventure or a new opportunity or a "new life" to me.

In fact, I wasn't sure I had any kind of life at all.

chapter 8

Philip was in the den with the phone to his ear when I came in. I could tell he was talking to his mother. I waved a hand to get his attention. *"Boys okay?"* I mouthed.

"Just a sec, Mom." He looked up with exaggerated patience. "The boys are *fine*, Gabrielle. Dad took them back to the academy this afternoon"—and then he turned back to the phone, his desk chair swiveling so that his back was to me.

What's wrong with this picture? I muttered to myself, stalking off to the bedroom. *We* should be telling the grandparents that our boys are fine—not getting the news from them. And why hasn't Mrs. Fairbanks talked to *me* about the boys? . . . though I knew perfectly well the answer to that. Philip's mother had been less than enthusiastic about his son's rash decision to marry "that girl from North Dakota." *"It was France,"* I overheard her tell a guest on our wedding day. *"Men don't think straight in France. The place is so quixotic, the first girl they meet, they think it's love."* And her friend had said, *"You'd think he would have fallen for a French girl. I love a French accent, don't you?"*

Well, howdy. I'd barely made it through France with my *Travelers' Guide to English/French Phrases*. So what? I was the mother of the Fairbanks grandchildren, and that ought to count for *something*!

I slammed the bathroom door on "something" and decided I needed a long soak in the tub. Running the water as hot as I could stand it, I found a bottle of bubble bath and shot a stream of golden liquid under the gushing faucet. Sliding under the bubbles until only my head and my knees poked out of the water, I wondered if this was how a crocodile felt, poking its eyes up out of the water and scoping out the territory. My eyes traveled around the room, the marble wall tiles, the glass-enclosed shower, the marble counter with two sinks—and no windows, thank God. I didn't need any reminders that *this* crocodile pond was thirty-two floors deep.

I flicked a bubble that floated past my knees, then another, bursting all that came within fingernail reach. *Story of my life . . . bursting bubbles.* First there was Damien . . . even now I got goose bumps remembering his dark lashes, lopsided grin, hair falling over his forehead like an Elvis clone. He was top banana of the pep squad at school, and had the same *rah-rah* attitude at the Minot Evangelical Church youth group. Even the mothers at church loved him, blushing when he paid attention to them. *"That color brings out the blue in your eyes, Mrs. Rowling"* or *"That's your grandson? You don't look old enough to be a grandmother, Mrs. Talbot!"* Oh, how puffed up I felt when he chose *me*—a mere junior—to go to his senior banquet. He used to love my curly hair, which I wore long in high school, twining it around his fingers, pulling my head back gently so he could kiss me . . .

I flicked another bubble. We got married the same summer I graduated high school. My dad even gave him a job at the carpet store as a salesman. I thought all my dreams had come true—married to the most popular guy at Minot High School's Central Campus, and his family went to our church, so my folks were happy. We had a little fixer-upper on the edge of town, with room for his hunting dog and my two cats. Damien said he'd take care of me so I didn't have to work, so I sewed curtains and mowed the lawn, joined the Junior League and impressed everyone with how I organized the Junior League Thrift Shop, and threw baby showers for my friends who were already starting families.

But Damien just kept flirting—old or young, it didn't matter. Women were like ice cream to him, his flattery dripping over their egos like thick chocolate sauce. And then one day he found a flavor he liked better than me, I guess. He decided we'd gotten married too young, quit the carpet store, and took a job on a fishing boat out of Puget Sound in Washington State.

I learned later that the boat was owned by Priscilla Tandy's daddy. Priscilla was the homecoming queen in the class before me. Damien's class.

I ran a little more hot water, then settled back into my pond. I'd been devastated. Cried for weeks. Married and *jilted*? Since when had they rewritten the fairy tales? My parents comforted me as best they could. "At least you didn't have a baby you're left to care for." *Humph*. Small comfort. Right then, I would have welcomed a baby to be mine, to love me back, to love me forever.

"Hey." Philip poked his head into the door, giving me such a start that I splashed water over the side of the tub. "How long have you been in there? You'll be a prune." He snickered suggestively. "Don't want a prune in bed. But clean is nice . . . very nice. Maybe I'll take a quick shower." He disappeared into the walk-in closet between bath and bedroom to strip.

I drained the tub, toweled off, and crawled into bed *sans* night-gown. I'd just have to take it off anyway. This had become Philip's intro to lovemaking. An announcement. "Hurry up and come to bed." Sometimes I got the feeling we made love because he felt the urge and I was the available female. But was he making love to *me*?

Philip was off early again the next morning, tossing down his orange juice, pouring coffee into a travel cup, and grabbing the plain whole-wheat bagel I toasted for him. "Oh, can you come by the office this afternoon, Gabby? Like two o'clock? Henry thought you and Mona could give some decorating ideas—window treatments, wall color, plants, that kind of thing. Needs to look professional, but we want our clients to feel welcomed. Just take a taxi to the Aon Center downtown. Here's the address if you need it. Okay?" He handed me a brochure with a picture of a ramrod-straight building on the front. Peck on the cheek. "See you at two." He disappeared into the gallery, and I heard the front door open. And close.

So Henry wanted my decorating ideas, did he? I groaned. I couldn't imagine anything I'd rather *not* do than decorate the offices of Fairbanks and Fenchel with Mona Fenchel. Maybe I'd call in sick . . . plead female troubles . . . a migraine . . . a death in the family. *Something!* Let Mona do it.

Sighing, I embraced the inevitable. *Stiff upper lip, Gabby,* I told myself, tossing dishes into the dishwasher helter-skelter and heading for the bedroom to get dressed. *Think of it as a way to support Philip's new business venture.* Besides, I had all morning to go online and familiarize myself with commercial decorating terms, ideas, and color schemes . . .

Which I did, feeling pretty smug as I gripped my briefcase and wheeled through the revolving doors of the Aon Center—second-tallest building in Chicago after the Sears Tower, the brochure had informed me. In the elevator I faced the bank of floor buttons. *Wait a minute. No button for the sixty-second floor.*

Noticing my bewildered expression, a woman in an oxymoronic "business" suit—tailored jacket, masculine tie, tight short skirt—said, "This elevator is only for odd-numbered floors. What floor do you want?"

Well, duh. I got off, feeling stupid, and found the even-numbered elevators. This one did have a button marked "62" . . . *and* "72" *and* "82." I felt dizzy even thinking about eighty-two floors. *Oh, Lord, help me, please.* "Sixty-two." I nodded to the person closest to the panel, and hummed like Pooh Bear trying to fool the bees until the bell dinged, the door slid open, and there I was.

Sixty-second floor. I followed the numbered signs pointing this way and that until I found the suite number Philip had given me. Company name wasn't on the door yet, but when I turned the knob, I could hear Mona Fenchel whining. "Well, of course, you have a *view*. But couldn't you get a suite facing east toward the lake? Or even south would give you more of a grand sweep of the city. North is so . . . well, not the best parts of the city." She turned as I closed the door, and the whine turned to sugar. "Don't you agree, Gabrielle?"

Philip, as usual, had a phone to one ear, finger in the other to shut out distractions. Henry stood in the middle of a mishmash of polished cherry office furniture, a plastic smile attached to his face. I ignored the question. "So this is it!" I said brightly. "Wow, right downtown. Very exciting. How many rooms do you have in the suite?"

Henry's smile widened. "Aha. I knew you'd be impressed. This is the reception area, natch. Two offices—that one's mine." He pointed. "Conference room is bigger than we need, but we're going to divide it, make half into a drafting room. Of course, heh-heh, it's a mess right now. But once we get painters in, finish ordering the furniture, and hire a secretary, we'll be in business."

Philip turned, flipping his cell phone shut. "We've got business right now, Henry. Robinson's people want to meet us at the Sopraffina Market Caffe in the lobby in half an hour." He gave me a nod. "Glad to see you made it, Gabrielle. You two okay for an hour or so? Give you time to come up with some ideas about the décor." He was halfway out the door. "Come on, Henry. Robinson could be a really big client. Oh, grab those sample spec sheets." And they were gone.

I stood face-to-face with Mona Fenchel, who seemed to be sizing me up, trying to make up her mind if I was a worthy opponent. I didn't blink. She wasn't a natural blonde, I decided, though the color was good. But I had her beat. My kid-red hair had darkened over the years to a nice auburn-brunette, all mine.

"Well!" she said, tossing her head. "They expect us to do something with this mess? What do they *want*, for crying out loud?"

I cleared my throat. "I think what they want is ideas. I came with a few color photo samples"—I snapped open my briefcase and withdrew the pages I'd printed out from the Internet—"but obviously I hadn't seen the space yet."

Clearing a place on the desk in the middle of the room, I spread out some of the color pictures of various office décors I'd found. Mona gave them a glance. "Obviously." She sounded bored.

I counted to ten. Then made it twenty. "All right. Where would you like to start?"

She didn't answer, just walked into the office Henry had indi-cated was his. She went room to room, then back to Henry's office. "A theme. An eye-catching theme, carried from room to room . . . something bold. Daring."

Oh brother. "Well, um, that's a thought. I was thinking of using neutrals, which can actually be very alluring if done right." *Ha. What did I know?* But I blabbered on, determined not to go down without a fight. "I'm not talking beige. Rather, sandstone, with browns and ochre reds—here, take a look at this photo." I pushed a sheet of paper at Henry's wife. "What I read suggested adding contrasting or seasonal colors with plants and fresh flower bou-quets. I think that would go well with the cherry furniture Philip and Henry already ordered."

She took the sheet of paper reluctantly. "Mm. Nice . . . if this was New Mexico. No, I'm talking seascapes, greens and blues. Not pastels, either. Emerald and azure, flowing in curves to rep-resent waves and movement . . ." She waved a hand to indicate a tsunami-sized wave rising from one side of a wall to another, ending at the windows—the very, very high windows—looking out over the north end of Chicago with the ever-present Lake Michigan far, far below.

My stomach lurched.

"Excuse me . . ." I bolted. I needed the bathroom . . . fast.

chapter 9

Philip glared at me over dinner that night—baked catfish, wild rice, steamed broccoli—which we ate in the formal dining room. The room was large enough to seat all Twelve Days of Christmas. Made me feel like the lonely partridge in the pear tree. At least we were eating at the same end of the table.

"Why didn't you override that crazy 'wave' idea, Gabby? For crying out loud, we'll look like an aquarium."

So this fiasco was my fault? "I tried, Philip. Really I did! I suggested neutrals—sandstone, with red ochre and brown accents. Mona just turned up her nose."

"Whatever." He attacked his fish. "Henry loves it, but it's not going to happen. Not if my name is Philip Fairbanks. My mother would throw a conniption . . ."

Let your mother do it, then. I swallowed my smart remark and adjusted my attitude. He needed encouragement. "Look, Philip. You need a professional decorator, an impartial third party. Don't pit Mona Fenchel and me against each other. We don't know each other well enough to buddy-buddy over decorating your offices. I backed off because I know it's important to you that we get along." *And besides, I had a sudden date with the toilet.* But I wasn't about to tell Philip I got seasick in his new restroom.

He brooded over his glass of chardonnay. Philip was not a drinking man, but he did love good wine with his dinner. However, I couldn't help but snicker at the glowing description of the Italian brand he'd brought home. *"The nose reveals bright pear, apricot, and fig aromas with hints of cinnamon, allspice, and vanilla."* Give me a break.

Finally he set down his glass. "Well, we'll just have to get a professional decorator. Henry was sure you two women would get a kick out of decorating the suite together. Would have saved us some big bucks too. I should have known you weren't up to it."

I strangled the hot words that flared up on my tongue. So the professional decorator was his idea now? Wasn't that what I just said? And did anyone ask *me* if I wanted to decorate the offices of Fairbanks and Fenchel?

Standing up abruptly, I stacked my dishes and marched into the kitchen, dumping my plate and silverware into the dishwasher without rinsing or scraping. The fancy-smancy dishwasher could clog up for all I cared. Clog up and spill soapy water all over the penthouse . . . out the door . . . down the elevator . . . flood the whole building . . .

The TV news came on in the living room. *"—attacked a Tel Aviv restaurant today, killing nine people and wounding many more. The group calling itself Islamic Jihad claimed responsibility for the suicide bomber, who . . ."*

I gripped the edge of the kitchen counter, suddenly feeling small and selfish. What was a spat with my husband over what color to paint his new offices compared to families who'd just gotten word that their son or daughter or husband or aunt had been blown to bits while eating out in a favorite restaurant? And what about the suicide bomber? Dead too. What would make someone do something so drastic, so utterly bloody and violent?

Glancing into the dining room, I noticed Philip's empty dishes still sitting there . . . and for a nanosecond, I felt an urge to do a little *jihad* myself. *Good grief!* Was it really too hard for the man to bring his own dishes to the kitchen?

How Philip talked Henry into hiring a professional decorator, he never said—and I didn't ask. But at least I wasn't the one who had to stand up to Mona Fenchel. Underneath all the tension of the past few weeks, I knew Philip was worried about the launch of his new business. He'd chafed at Fairbanks Brothers, Inc. back in Petersburg, frustrated when his fresh design ideas had been turned down by the conservative philosophy of his father and uncle, the "Fairbanks brothers" who'd started the commercial development company back in the late sixties. Mike Fairbanks had been twenty-nine then, was sixty-six now. His motto was, "If it ain't broke, don't fix it." The commercial buildings he and Matt Fairbanks had designed and built over the last thirty-odd years had a reputation for quality, durability, and function—and they weren't about to tinker with that formula just to stand out in the crowd with some funky design.

I knew leaving the security of a position in a stable family company was a risky leap for my husband. To his credit, he didn't want to start a competing company in Virginia, so he chose Chicago. But that left the question of who would inherit his father's share in the company when Mike Fairbanks retired. Philip's two sisters were married and settled elsewhere and had no interest in running the business. His father had threatened to sell out when the time came, ". . . since you don't want to help me build it up," he'd told his only son.

"Aw, he'll come around," Philip had boasted to me. "Then we can merge the two companies, and do twice the business." But after fifteen years of being married to the man, I suspected all that bluster hid a smidgen of insecurity, though he covered it up with all the fervor of a Rottweiler burying a bone.

On Tuesday, Philip went to work with no instructions for me to carry out, so I spent the day exploring the environs around Richmond Towers. Ohh, it felt good to walk. The sun was out, and the temperature hiked to a comfortable sixty-five . . . though at Mr. Bentley's suggestion, I went back for a small umbrella "just in case." Well, not a suggestion exactly. He just said, "Goin' out, Mrs. Fairbanks?" while turning the pages of his newspaper as if I wasn't standing there. "Chicago weather has a way of sneakin' up on you." I took the hint.

I spent the morning checking out the shops along Sheridan Road, asking if Tedino's Pizzeria delivered, chatting up the staff of Curves—though I felt a bit dizzy by all that spandex going great guns on those exercise machines—and familiarizing myself with the local Dominick's grocery store two blocks away, bringing home two top sirloin steaks and a movie I rented at their kiosk. Philip would like that.

After putting the steaks to marinate in some olive oil, balsamic vinegar, and minced garlic—lots of garlic—I topped off my day with a brisk walk through the pedestrian underpass to Foster Beach, took off my sneakers, and wiggled my toes in the damp sand. The soothing sound of waves lapping on the shoreline drained the last of yesterday's tension out of my spirit. I just needed to work harder to adjust to our new life here in Chicago, I told myself. Find ways to be supportive, take care of things so Philip could give his full attention to developing the new business. And after all, P.J. and Paul would be here in six weeks. There should be lots of fun things to do in the city during the summer. We'd explore, take in the ethnic festivals, go to the beach. I was just lonely for them, that was all.

That's what I told myself. I only wished I believed it.

I might go crazy before the boys even got here.

On the way home—my feet safely ensconced in my gym shoes this time—I passed the bush where I'd met Lucy . . . did she frequent this part of the park? I wandered up and down the jogging path both ways, but didn't see anyone except a few mothers pushing strollers and talking on their cell phones, and an older Asian man sitting perfectly still on a bench. The yuppie joggers must all be at work this time of day.

But this was Tuesday . . . didn't Lucy say the nurse came to Manna House on Wednesday? And that she might come to get her cough "checked out"?

I walked this time. Two miles straight down Sheridan to the north edge of Wrigleyville. Weatherman had said thunderstorms later in the day, but I could return by El if I needed to. I knew I was getting close to the shelter when I passed the Sheridan El Station, where the El crossed over the street, then passed Rick's Café, a few other eateries, and the Wrigleyville North Bar, which was obviously a sports bar for die-hard Cubs fans.

Took me forty minutes to walk the two miles, though. Turning the corner by the Laundromat, I gratefully dragged myself up the steps of the church-turned-shelter and pulled open one of the large oak doors. Man oh man, I couldn't wait to sit down.

"Hello again, Mrs. Fairbanks. Welcome!" Angela's sweet voice, carrying only a slight trace of a Korean accent, met me in the cool foyer. "Everyone is downstairs. Mrs. Enriquez the nurse is here." She laughed behind the open window of the reception cubicle and went back to her computer.

"Thanks." I smiled. For some reason, a sense of—*of what? well-being?*—settled over me as I headed into the multipurpose room. Maybe it was just familiarity. After all, this was the third time I'd been here in less than a week.

Well, *everyone* wasn't downstairs. A thin person, covered by a gray trench coat, was sacked out on one of the couches, a brown hand hanging limply over the side. The ponytailed woman named Carolyn and another resident with a big, loose Afro were hunched over a game of chess near the coffee carafes. I gave Carolyn a wave as I headed for the stairs, but her attention was obviously on how to slaughter her opponent with her knights and pawns.

Downstairs, the dining room resembled a Greyhound Bus Station waiting room. Fifteen or more women sat scattered around the tables, chatting or talking in a loud voice to someone across the room. Several were filling out forms, while two or three jiggled a young child on their knees. A bored-looking young black woman sat in a corner, leg crossed and swinging, filing her nails. Another, lighter-skinned, maybe Latino, tight-lipped and nervous, paced back and forth. She probably needed a cigarette.

I pulled out the closest chair, hoping to see someone I knew by name, but came up zero. A "privacy booth" had been created in one corner of the dining room with a simple room divider. Nearby, an array of medical supplies had been stacked on the closest table. A fifty-something African-American woman wearing a food worker's hairnet sat at the end of the table, knitting something blue and bulky from a bag of yarn at her feet, her elbow resting on a clipboard.

The pacing woman was making *me* nervous. They needed some activities going on while people waited. Something to entertain the kids . . . a "learn to knit" group . . . a nail salon . . . a book club . . .

A woman wearing typical blue hospital scrubs came out from behind the screen, pulling on a fresh pair of latex gloves. "Who is next, Estelle?" The nurse had dark, wavy hair and a round, pleasant face. A motherly look about her.

The knitting lady peered at the clipboard. "Aida Menéndez . . . Aida? You here?"

A young girl—she looked eighteen at the most—got up and let herself be trundled behind the screen by the nurse. The two began talking a rapid stream of Spanish.

"Hey! Miz Delores! You said I was next!" The loner in the corner waved her nail file.

"Pipe down, Hannah. She said no such thing." The woman named Estelle thumped the clipboard with a knitting needle. "I got your form right here . . . three more ahead of you."

The bored young woman shrugged and went back to doing her nails.

"Ya gotta fill out a form if you wanna see the nurse," a growly voice said in my ear. I jumped and turned. Rheumy blue eyes met mine.

"Lucy!" I couldn't help grinning. "Where'd you come from?"

"Question is"—the old woman squinted at me suspiciously—"where'd *you* come from? Seems like you poppin' up all over the place." She turned her head, hacking a few jagged coughs into a faded red bandanna.

I decided to make light of it. "Came to ask if you wanted to go out for coffee. Couldn't find you under the bush in the park, so I decided to try the next best place."

She darted a look sideways at me, bandanna still over her mouth, and a sudden pang clamped my mouth shut. What if she thought I was making fun of her? But before I could say anything, Estelle called out, "Lucy Tucker? Lucy! Get over here, darlin'."

Lucy shuffled off, muttering into her bandanna.

"Be sure to use the cream on that rash," the nurse was saying to the young girl as she left the makeshift examining room. Then her attention turned to Lucy. "About time you got yourself in here, Lucy. Still got that cough, don't you?" She shook her head and rolled her eyes behind Lucy's back. *"Obstinada."*

They disappeared behind the screen—but Lucy was anything but quiet. "All right, all right, don't rush me! . . . Get that thing outta my mouth, I'm gonna choke . . . whatchu mean, hold my breath? A person's gotta breathe, don't ya know . . ."

Estelle hollered over her shoulder, "Don't make me come in there, Lucy! You want lunch or don'tcha?" Several of the women waiting for a turn snickered.

After a while, Delores Enriquez came out alone, bent down, and talked in a low undertone to Estelle. Estelle frowned and scanned the room. "Anyone know where Miz Mabel is?"

"She's out," someone said. "Saw her leave a while ago."

I made my way over to the table. "Is something wrong? Can I help?" *And just how do you think you can help, Gabby Fairbanks?*

The nurse straightened up. "And you are . . . ?"

I held out my hand. "Gabrielle Fairbanks. I'm, uh, a friend of Lucy's."

"No she ain't!" a raspy voice hollered from behind the screen.

Estelle looked at me with a smile of recognition. "Oh, that's right! Precious told me about you." She turned to Delores. "This is the lady who found Lucy out in the rain, sent her here last week."

"She cut her foot an' I was helpin' *her*!" Lucy hollered.

"Actually, that's right," I admitted.

Delores raised her eyebrows hopefully. "Do you have a car?"

I shook my head. "Sorry. I walked."

The eyebrows fell. "Lucy needs to go to the clinic at Stroger Hospital. She's running a fever, could be pneumonia or bronchitis. And she needs someone to go with her." She lowered her voice. "To make sure she *goes*."

"That's all right. I'll take her. We'll get a cab or something."

I had no idea what I was doing. But it couldn't be that hard, could it? Just give the cabbie the name of the hospital, no sweat.

chapter 10

* * *

The clock on the clinic wall of the county hospital inched its way toward four thirty and Lucy's name still hadn't been called. I couldn't believe this! The waiting room still looked as full as when we came, though maybe half of those were family members of people waiting to see a doctor. A huge percentage of the people in the waiting room were Latino, if the swirl of Spanish going on around me was any indication.

"G'wan, Gabby," Lucy growled. "Get outta here. I don't need no babysitter."

It was tempting. If I left now and took a cab, I could get home before Philip . . . but I'd promised. And the fever must be sapping Lucy's strength. She'd been quiet for a long time—though this was the fourth time she'd told me to leave.

"Nope. I'm fine. They've got to call you soon—"

"Lucy Tucker!" a nurse barked from the doorway.

"See? What did I tell you?"

"Yeah. Whatever." Lucy hauled herself out of the molded

plastic chair and took her sweet time following the nurse. The door closed behind them.

I waited. The clock passed four thirty. Sighing, I realized I couldn't avoid the inevitable. Fishing for my cell phone, I walked out into the hall for some quiet and called Philip.

His voice mail gave me a beep. "Hi, Philip. It's me. Just wanted to let you know I might not be home when you get there and don't want you to worry. I'm at Stroger Hospital, just brought someone to the clinic down here. I can explain later. Sorry about supper. But maybe you could get some takeout or something, okay?"

I flipped the phone closed. *Whew.* Philip was not going to be a happy camper.

Well, so what. He left me alone all day to my own devices. He could manage a few hours by himself in the evening.

A few more people were called in, then a nurse came out and said, "I'm sorry. The clinic is closed. The rest of you, go on home and come back tomorrow." Her announcement met with groans and protests. "If you can't wait until tomorrow, go to the ER. That's it, folks. Go on home, now." I felt badly for the families who had been waiting several hours already. Some all afternoon. At least Lucy got in to see the doctor.

It was nearly five thirty when Lucy finally came out, clutching a sheaf of papers. "Bronchitis," the nurse said. "Make sure she follows those instructions."

"Any prescriptions?" *Anything to make her well instantly?*

The nurse shook her head. "No antihistamines, deconges-tants, or cough suppressants, either. She just needs an expectorant to get that mucus up. A vaporizer and hot showers will help. And drink plenty of water, Ms. Tucker. You can take Tylenol for the fever."

But as we walked the long halls toward the main entrance, the nurse's words to the other patients rang in my ears: *"Go on home, now."* Trouble was, Lucy didn't have a home. Hot showers? A vaporizer? Drink lots of water? That meant you had to pee a lot. Where was a sick homeless woman supposed to do that?

I thought of the two extra bedrooms in our penthouse, waiting for the boys, the unused bathroom . . . and quickly dismissed the idea. Philip would never stand for it. And he'd probably be right. You didn't just take homeless people off the street into your home. The police, the mayor—and surely Mr. Bentley!—would all say it wasn't wise. What did I know about this woman, anyway?

It had started raining while we'd been in the clinic. "You'd think we moved to Seattle," I muttered, holding my umbrella for Lucy as the taxi finally pulled up. I gave the driver the address of Manna House. I didn't know if they could put up someone who was sick. Lucy really needed a private room. But where else were we going to go?

The *swish-squeak, swish-squeak* of the windshield wipers and Lucy's sporadic coughs were the only sounds inside the cab for the next ten minutes, lulling me into a kind of stupor, so I was startled when Lucy poked me with her elbow. "How come you ain't praying for me 'bout this bronchitis? Ain't that what the Bible says to do when someone's sick?"

"Uh, sure, Lucy. I've been praying for you." That was a lie, but maybe I could send up a prayer now and make it retroactive.

Lucy turned her head toward the other window. "Huh. Ain't what I meant."

Good grief, what did she want me to do, pray out loud right here in the cab? The driver would think we were nuts!

Silence reigned until the taxi pulled up in front of Manna

House. I asked the cabbie to wait and tried to hustle Lucy into the doors of the shelter, though Lucy wasn't hustling. To my relief, Mabel Turner's office door was open, and she was talking to Estelle, the knitting woman. Estelle's hairnet was gone, revealing loose, kinky hair with streaks of silver, caught into a knot on the top of her head.

"Oh, thank goodness you're back." Mabel came quickly into the foyer. "Delores Enriquez said you'd taken Lucy to the clinic, but she didn't get your cell number, so we couldn't call." She turned to Lucy. "What's going on?"

"I'm hungry, that's what," Lucy snapped, but the coughs took over.

"Come on." Estelle took her arm. "They're serving supper downstairs. Meat loaf and baked potatoes tonight. How's that sound, Your Highness? You hungry too, Mrs.—? Sorry, I forgot the name."

"Just Gabby is fine. Thanks anyway, but I need to get home and the cab is waiting."

Estelle shrugged and followed Lucy, who was heading for the lower floor. "Hey, Aida. How ya doin'?" Estelle called out to the young Latino girl curled up in one of the overstuffed chairs. I'd seen her earlier in the shelter's makeshift clinic. The girl glanced at Estelle with dull eyes, but said nothing.

I wanted to ask about her—she seemed way too young to be out on the street, or even here in the shelter—but Mabel was looking at me expectantly. "So . . . ?"

"Nurse said bronchitis. No medication, but she's supposed to drink plenty of water. They said hot showers and a vaporizer would help."

Mabel frowned. "She needs a separate room. *Hm.* Can't do

that here right now. But maybe . . ." She turned back into her office, got on the phone, talked a little while, then came back out into the foyer, smiling. "The Baxters will take her for a few days. He's driving down to get her and Estelle."

I was confused. "Josh and Edesa Baxter? He said they lived in a tiny studio. How do they have room for—"

"No, no, not Josh." Mabel laughed. "His *parents*, Denny and Jodi Baxter. They were here Sunday night. You met them, I think. Josh told me on the sly to call them if I ever needed temporary space. With Josh married and his sister at college, they have a couple of empty bedrooms right now."

"Wow. That's generous."

Mabel laughed. "Well, Josh said his mom might not officially *volunteer* to take in somebody but would probably say yes if asked. And Estelle lives upstairs in the same two-flat. So she can look in on Lucy during the day."

I was glad . . . but at the same time felt a strange sense of loss, like something had died. The Gabby I used to know would've volunteered to take Lucy. At age seven, that Gabby had brought home a cardboard box with a litter of abandoned kittens. The mama cat had been run over in the road. My mom let me keep them out on the back porch if I *promised* to feed them six times a day. I was all over those kittens, feeding them with an eye-dropper, watching them get fat and spill out of the box until they were old enough to take to the pet shop. And then there was the dog with only three legs, and the box turtle with the cracked shell . . .

What had happened to that Gabrielle? Weren't people more important than kittens and box turtles?

I tried to refocus. "So Estelle is not a resident here?"

"She was, once upon a time. Ask her about it sometime." I noticed how Mabel's ready smile highlighted how attractive she was—smooth brown skin, straightened hair cut short but full and brushed off her forehead in a wave, simple gold loops in her earlobes, full lips colored with a creamy tangerine that matched her sweater. "Now she's licensed to do elder care, but between jobs she hangs out here and helps however she can." Mabel extended her hand. "Thank you so much, Gabby. I'm afraid I don't have the budget to reimburse you for the cab fare you spent today, but I want you to know how much we appreciate it."

I took her hand, afraid that if I spoke I might cry. Something was churning up inside me, and I didn't even know what it was. I just nodded and turned to go, then suddenly turned back. "Mabel." The words pushed out in a rush. "The other day you mentioned you were looking for a program director. I . . . well, I'm a CTRS—Certified Therapeutic Recreational Specialist—and I directed programs for seniors back in Virginia. I'm wondering . . . I think I'd like to apply for the job."

Mabel stared at me. "Well, well. If the Lord doesn't work in mysterious ways." She went into her office, consulted an appointment book, and then looked up. "Could you come back tomorrow, Gabby? We can talk about it then, and I'll have an application for you to fill out. Eleven?"

I nodded without speaking and dashed out to the waiting cab.

Oh Lord, Oh Lord . . . I didn't exactly know how to pray in the moment, but I knew I was going to need some supernatural help. *I'd really like this job. In fact, I need it. And if You help me get it, and pacify Philip, I promise I'll go to church more often. And read my Bible.* If I could find it. Packed somewhere. *And P.S., please be with Lucy and help her to get well.* There. That ought to cover my butt with Lucy.

But first I had to explain to Philip where I'd been all day.

"I just don't get it, Gabrielle." Philip was pacing. A bad sign. "What in the world were you doing at that homeless shelter in the first place? Then you volunteer—volunteer!—to take a perfect stranger who has pneumonia, or bronchitis, or whatever, something contagious anyway, to the county hospital, of all places, which is probably full of who-knows-what diseases flying around in the air. Sitting in a roomful of sick people all afternoon!" He stopped pacing right in front of me and shook a finger in my face. "You don't *think*, that's what wrong with you, Gabrielle. You . . . you just up and *do* things, willy-nilly, whatever comes to your mind. Did you think about how this would affect me? Affect *us*, affect getting this new business off the ground if you got sick? Not to mention that it's seven thirty, and we haven't had supper . . ." He spiked the air with an expletive, rolled his eyes, and flopped down on the plush sofa.

"I'm *sorry*, Philip. I didn't realize it would take so long. I thought we'd be in and out in an hour or two. I tried to let you know, left a message on your cell phone."

"Yeah, yeah, I got it. What was I to think? Maybe you'd been in an accident or something. All you said was you were at Stroger Hospital. Henry said it's the county hospital, over on the west side, not a good neighborhood."

"That's not true. I told you I brought someone to the clinic. Didn't you listen to the whole message?"

"Whatever." He pushed himself off the couch. "That's not the point. You still haven't explained what you were doing at this . . . this homeless shelter in the first place. Yeah, yeah, you ran into an old bag lady last week, you did the right thing and sent her to a shelter. *Period*. You don't need to go running over there to check up on her. Let them take care of the homeless. That's what shelters are for!"

I pressed my lips together. This was pointless. Telling him right now that I intended to apply for a job at this shelter would be like volunteering to be the human sacrifice in an ancient Aztec ritual.

chapter 11

The weather forecast still said rain, but today I didn't care. It was April, after all! The air was warm and moist, the kind of weather that sprung all the buds on the trees and sprinkled green kisses on the grass in the parks along Lake Shore Drive.

I allowed myself an hour to get to Manna House, but it was hard to wait until ten o'clock to leave. In spite of Philip's upset at me the night before, I woke up excited, my mind already spinning with ideas for activities and programs at Manna House. Job skills . . . word processing . . . parenting classes . . . cooking . . . maybe even field trips to the museums. Had Lucy ever been to a Chicago museum?

Well, probably. Surely she hasn't been homeless all her life.

I stood in the middle of our walk-in closet. It was a job interview . . . should I wear a suit and heels? But this was a homeless shelter; maybe that would be too spiffy. I finally decided to go with "business casual"—tan slacks, jade-colored blouse, black blazer, flats for walking, a bag roomy enough for a small umbrella.

And I'd take the El. If I was going to be working at Manna House, I'd need an inexpensive way to get back and forth. Might as well learn how to do it on my own now as later.

I was actually whistling as I bounced through the lobby of Richmond Towers and headed for the west-side doors spilling out onto Sheridan Road.

"Where are *you* off to, Mrs. Fairbanks, all twinkletoes today?" Mr. Bentley's bald dome and grizzled chin beard made him look as if his head was on upside down.

I laughed. "I'm interviewing for a job, Mr. Bentley. Wish me luck!"

He eyed me suspiciously. "What are you up to now, might I ask?"

I paused at the semicircular desk, eager to let the excitement within me bubble out. "That shelter you told me about needs a program director—and I'm it!" I giggled at my self-confidence. "Seriously, Mr. Bentley, I'm a qualified CTRS, and this job seems just right for me."

He peered at me over his reading glasses. "Oh, it does, does it?" He pursed his lips. "What do you know about homeless people, Mrs. Fairbanks?—no disrespect intended."

My confidence wobbled. "Well, good point. Not much. But I'd like to learn. And one thing I do know, Mr. Bentley—*everyone*, rich or poor, male or female, young or old, needs to feel useful, needs purposeful activities or work to occupy their time." I chewed on my lip. "Including me."

His expression softened. "Good luck then, Mrs. Fairbanks. I'll be lifting up a prayer for you today. Want me to call you a cab?"

For some reason, his blessing buoyed my confidence again. "No thanks. I'm taking the El. I did it once, think I can do it again." I waved and pushed through the revolving door for the three-block walk to the elevated station.

The Red Line. That's what Josh Baxter had told me. *Take it south to . . .* I squinted at the transit map on the platform at the Berwyn El Station, trying to keep my eyes from straying to the street below. *Sheridan. That's it. One . . . two . . . three . . . only four stations. Shouldn't take long.*

But I was still anxious once I was on the train, counting the stops, craning my neck at each one to be sure we hadn't passed it yet. The train bent around a big curve just before pulling into the Sheridan station. *Okay, that's my clue,* I thought, relieved to get out the door before it slid shut again.

Once back down on street level, I stood uncertainly, looking both ways. Did I turn right or left? Then I saw Rick's Café and the Wrigleyville Bar down the street to the right. *Aha. Back on course.* I glanced at my watch . . . only ten thirty. Good grief, I had a half hour to kill. Was there any place around here to get a cup of coffee?

I glanced around—and had to laugh. The Emerald City Coffee shop stood right under the El tracks next to the station, so close it could have bit me on the rear. Pushing open the door, I smiled at the decidedly casual décor. On one side, couches and comfy chairs circled around a beat-up coffee table. On the other, small tables were occupied by individuals busy at their laptops. At the counter I ordered a medium-size coffee with cream. The pro- prietor—a slender older woman with spiffy gray hair—looked at me oddly, as though trying to place me among her clientele as she poured the steaming coffee. "Just made a fresh pot. You want a muffin or anything with that?"

The lemon poppyseed muffins looked good. I took my coffee

and muffin to a comfortable chair near the front window, sank into the cushions, and sipped the hot coffee slowly. Now that I was safely back on the ground, uneasiness niggled at the edge of my excitement. *I shouldn't be doing this without telling Philip.* Especially after he'd made his feelings about me just visiting the shelter abundantly clear.

But, darn it, what else am I supposed to do? He took me away from a job I enjoyed back in Petersburg, left our boys in the academy there, hung me in a penthouse like a pair of panties on a clothesline . . .

I snickered at my mental image of the penthouse panties and pushed the problem of Philip into the recesses of my mind. I'd deal with that *after* the fact. No point getting him all stirred up if I didn't even get the job.

After enjoying a refill, I paid my bill and walked the few blocks to Manna House. It had started sprinkling, but not enough to need my umbrella. *10:55,* I noted smugly, grabbing the handle of the heavy oak door. Early but not too early.

The door didn't budge. I tried the other one. Locked too. *What in the world?* I hunted for a doorbell and found a white button beside the brass plate that said Manna House. I pushed and was rewarded by a shrill ring inside. But no one came to the door.

I pushed the button again . . . and finally the door cracked opened. "Oh, Mrs. Fairbanks!" Angela peeked around the door, her straight black hair swinging over her face. "Sorry the door was locked. I was on the phone and couldn't—oh, come on in. Did you want something?" She locked the doors behind me.

"Well, yes. I have an eleven o'clock appointment with Mabel Turner. Is she here?"

Angela grimaced. "Actually, no. I mean, she's not back yet. She had some kind of emergency with her nephew, C.J., at his school. But that was her on the phone. She's on her way. Do you want to wait in her office?"

Hiding my annoyance, I agreed to a seat in Mabel's office. I'd tried so hard to be on time, and Mabel Turner just blew me off. Did she go running to school every time her nephew had a problem? What about his parents? Couldn't they take care of whatever? Besides, I had a son about C.J.'s age and one even younger, and *we* didn't go running to school every time—

I stopped myself. I didn't even know if my boys *had* problems at school. Parents weren't supposed to call during the day, only in the evenings, before study hall, and weekends. But I no longer saw P.J. and Paul on weekends, either, because we'd moved a thousand miles away. *Admit it, Gabby, you're jealous of Mabel, that she can go to school and check up on her nephew.*

Reaching for a tissue box on Mabel's desk, I blew my nose, took a deep breath, and tried to think of something else. It wouldn't do for Mabel to walk in and find her new program director blubbering away.

Mabel Turner bustled in at eleven thirty. "I'm so glad you waited, Gabby." She dumped her bag and umbrella on the floor and hung up her trench coat on the back of the door. "I didn't forget you. Did Angela explain?"

"Just said it was something about your nephew, C.J."

Mabel nodded. "I'm his legal guardian, so when anything comes up at school . . ." She sat down at her desk, moved a few papers out of the way, and leaned forward, hands folded. "Now, tell me about yourself."

I blinked. That wasn't exactly the question I was expecting to start the interview. "You mean, my qualifications and work experience?"

"No, just tell me about yourself. Let's get acquainted."

Well, this was different. But I kind of liked it. Relaxing, I rehearsed the story of our recent move to Chicago from Virginia . . . the new business . . . two sons still in private boarding school back in Virginia until the end of the school year . . . I'd left college to marry my husband, but finished my BA degree and CTRS a few years ago, and had been working as activities director in a senior center in Petersburg . . .

"Did you always live in Virginia, Gabby? What about your parents?"

I squirmed a little. "No, actually, I grew up in Minot, North Dakota, a small town of about thirty-five thousand. My father owned a carpet store, but he, um, died a couple of years ago. My mom still lives alone in the home I grew up in." *Alone.* Kind of knew how she felt.

"Siblings?"

"Two older sisters. Celeste lives in Alaska, her husband works for the Park Service in Denali National Forest, one daughter in college. Honor has two kids, is divorced, and moved to San Diego so she wouldn't have heating bills." I skipped over my disastrous two-year marriage to Damien. What was the point? Water under the bridge.

Mabel put a hand to her mouth in an unsuccessful attempt to hide a smile. "Celeste? Honor? And Gabrielle? Your parents must have been very heavenly minded." The smile turned into a chuckle.

I grinned wryly. "It gets worse. My dad's name was Noble . . . Martha and Noble Shepherd. I think the names were my mom's idea. The three of us endured a lot of teasing at school and church when we were kids, but"—I shrugged—"we've all gone separate ways. It's mostly Christmas letters and birthday cards now." *Another sore point, but why go into it?*

Mabel studied me. I squirmed. What was she thinking? What did she want from me? What did all this have to do with applying for a job at Manna House?

The director leaned forward once again. "Gabby, as you're probably aware, Manna House is a privately funded, faith-based shelter for homeless women—which is a politically correct way of saying we are unabashedly Christian in our outreach and ministry. You say you went to church growing up . . . can you tell me about your own faith journey? Then and now?"

I stared at her, my hopes crumbling. Sure, I could tell her I grew up in the Minot Evangelical Church, attended Pioneer Girls clubs—a Christian version of Girl Scouts—from third through seventh grades, gave my heart to Jesus at age eight in my first summer camp, had memorized all the books of the Bible and my weekly Sunday school verse too. But she'd see right through my lame attempt to explain my insipid adult "spirituality" . . . *"Well, before we left Virginia, Philip and I were members of the Briarwood Lutheran Church all our married life, and we always took the boys to church on Christmas and Easter . . ."*

I studied my hands in my lap, twisting the tissues I'd been holding into tiny shreds. Finally I looked up. The compassion in Mabel's face brought tears to my eyes. There was nothing to do but tell her the truth.

"To be honest, Mabel, I gave up on God after . . ." I told her about Damien, about getting married right out of high school and dumped two years later by my supposedly "Christian" husband. When I'd married Philip, God had taken a backseat. After all, where had that gotten me with Damien? "But . . ." I twisted the tissues some more. "Ever since I walked in here last week, something has been stirring up in me. I . . . I've been praying again, though I have to admit I'm pretty rusty. Sitting in on Edesa's Bible study, and coming to the worship service Sunday night . . . well, I just wanted more. Almost like God tapping me on the shoulder and asking, 'Hey there, Gabby! Where've you been?'"

Mabel just looked at me, chin resting on her hands, elbows propped on the desk, as if trying to read my heart.

"I guess that sounds pretty dumb," I admitted. "Like I'm trying to say the right thing just to get this job."

"No. I believe you're being honest with me." Mabel sat back in her desk chair. "Now, I'm going to tell you something which may sound just as dumb. From the first time you walked in here, Gabby, I had the sense it was God who sent you. And He kept bringing you back. Maybe you don't see it this way, moving here because of your husband's business and all, but I believe *God brought you to Chicago* because He has a purpose for you"—she tapped the desk firmly with her finger—"right here at Manna House."

My lips parted. I blinked. What was she saying?

"But," she acknowledged with a small smile, "we do have to get approval by the board, and they are going to want to see this application." She pushed a couple of pages stapled together across the desk at me. "You fill that out, and I'll go get us some coffee. We still need to talk about what your job responsibilities would be as program director."

chapter 12

Mabel Turner made it clear that I didn't officially have the job yet. "But I'm going to bat for you, Gabby," she'd said, as we left her office and headed downstairs to see if there was anything left from lunch. "If this is God's doing—and I believe it is—we don't have to worry about it."

I thought about what she'd said all the way home on the El. I mean, I wanted the job, knew I had the right credentials, and was pretty sure I could put together a good program for the residents of Manna House . . . but what did she mean, *God* brought me to Chicago? And He had a purpose for me at Manna House?

"Bryn Mawwwr! Next stop is Bryn Mawr!" the loudspeaker squawked.

Wait a minute. I peered out the window. Was Bryn Mawr one of the stops before Berwyn, or had I gone past it? I stood up on the moving train, holding tight to the nearest pole, and scanned the row of advertisements and No Smoking signs running above the windows, looking for a transit map. *Not there . . . not there . . . rats!*

As the train slowed, I turned to the nearest person moving toward the door, a young black teenager with iPod plugs in his ears, nodding his head in time to some music in his head. "Berwyn!" I said loudly, trying to get his attention. "Up ahead?"

Without skipping a beat, the teenager jerked a thumb over his shoulder, back the way we'd come. The train jerked, stopped, and the doors slid open.

Oh, brother. I got off with the flow, finally found a map on the platform, and realized I'd only gone one stop too far. I decided to go down to street level and walk back—it only added a few more blocks.

But not even my stupid mistake could dampen my spirit today. Mr. Bentley peered at me over his reading glasses as I came through the revolving door. "Ah. There she is. Are you now gainfully employed, Mrs. Fairbanks?"

I simpered a little. "I'll find out Monday. But in the meantime, I'm going to work on my business wardrobe—shred a few of my jeans, forget to wash my clothes . . . what?"

Mr. Bentley's scowl stopped my spiel. "Homelessness is not a joke, Mrs. Fairbanks. If you don't know that by now, forget the job. They don't need do-gooders down at that shelter."

My face reddened. What was up with *him*? Wasn't he the one who didn't want me bringing Lucy into the building that first night? "I was just kidding around, Mr. Bentley." Miffed, I headed for the elevator, which, for some reason, took its own sweet time getting down to the ground floor. But as I waited, my irritation subsided. Next to Lucy and Mabel, Mr. Bentley was one of the few "almost friends" I had here in Chicago. I couldn't afford to let some minor comment become a wall.

I walked back to the lobby. Mr. Bentley was talking to another resident in the building who was upset because someone else had dared to park in the parking space he'd been guaranteed. I waited until Mr. Bentley had calmly assured him that he would contact the manager and get it taken care of immediately. The man went off in a huff, muttering about the hassle of having to park on the street.

I sidled up to the half-moon desk before the doorman could pick up the phone. "Mr. Bentley? You were right. My comment was inappropriate. I apologize."

The dark eyes studied me. "That's big of you, Mrs. Fairbanks. Maybe you'll do all right in that job after all." A grin escaped above his short, grizzled beard. "You've got guts, gotta say that."

Guts. I grinned as the elevator whisked me up to the thirty-second floor. When was the last time anybody had said that to me? Probably the time snotty Marvin Peters dared me to go up to the front door of "the old witch's house" on the outskirts of town when I was in fifth grade and still wearing my hair in braids. All the kids whispered about the old lady who lived there, saying she kept twenty cats and rode out on her broom at Halloween, and anybody who knocked on her door got a spell cast on them. I'd pooh-poohed the whole thing, marched up to the porch, and knocked on the door. The old lady invited me in, offered me cookies and hot chocolate, and we had a nice chat. Ruby was her name, and she invited me to come back anytime. But when I went out to the cluster of wide-eyed kids, I put my nose in the air and said. "You were wrong. It's twenty-*one* cats."

Marvin Peters never pulled my braids after that.

The answering machine light was blinking when I let myself into the apartment. I dumped my bag on a chair and touched the button. *"Philip, darling. Call home when you get a chance—oh. I'll try your cell.*" I rolled my eyes. "Call home" indeed. Why couldn't Philip's mother get it into her head that he wasn't her baby anymore? I felt like pushing the Redial button and telling Marlene Fairbanks that Philip's "home" was with his wife and children now and had been for fifteen years.

Except—my children were spending their weekends at *her* house, not ours. A mad that lay dormant most of the time popped out and burned behind my eyes. Well, that was going to stop! P.J. and Paul were *not* going back to George Washington Prep in the fall. If Chicago was our home now, that meant the kids too.

I was so busy fuming about the first message, I almost missed the second. "*. . . need your next of kin and emergency info. Please call ASAP so I can get copies of your application to the board before we meet on Saturday.*"

Had to be Mabel Turner. I fished in my purse for her card.

"Manna House."

Didn't sound like Angela. "Mabel? Is that you? This is Gabby returning your call. What are you doing at the reception desk?"

A laugh echoed in my ear. "Oh, we all cover for each other. Especially the front desk. Thanks for calling back. You forgot to fill in next of kin and that kind of thing. Your husband's name, I presume . . ."

I hesitated. Did I want Manna House to call my husband for some emergency? *Of course, you dodo-head,* I scolded myself. "Uh, his name is Philip Fairbanks, and you have our home number. But his cell is . . ." I rattled it off.

Mabel repeated his name and number absently as she filled in the information. "Gabby, what does your husband think of your application for this job?"

Good grief. The woman was as perceptive as Merlin the Wizard. I hesitated again, then realized there was no way around being straight up with her. I already had the sense that Mabel Turner didn't stand for any baloney. "He . . . doesn't know about it yet." I took a deep breath. "To tell you the truth, Mabel, his nose has been out of joint ever since I brought Lucy home. He's trying to establish a new business in Chicago and is very sensitive about our, um, 'connections.'"

"Gabby." Mabel's voice was firm. "You need to talk to your husband—now. Do it, girl. But, here, let's get God on the job." And Mabel began to pray right in my ear. I was startled. We didn't pray out loud in the Fairbanks household. In fact, even back in the evangelical church when I was growing up, people might say, *"I'll pray for you,"* and they probably did . . . later.

"—and Lord God, give Gabby the courage to share her heart with her husband. And prepare his heart to receive this direction You are leading her in. I pray for a blessing on both Philip and Gabby. Pour a blessing on Philip's new business, that it will flourish and prosper. And a special blessing on Gabby, as she seeks out Your purpose in her life. I believe You have sent her here, Lord . . ."

I barely heard the end of Mabel's prayer, because I started to cry, silently at first, and then shoulders shaking, my nose running, and tears messing up my makeup.

"I'm scared, Mabel," I finally hiccoughed. "Scared Philip will say no way. But if the board will have me, I really want—no, I need—this job."

"Girl, didn't we just give the whole thing to God? Now, you go pull yourself together, call up your husband, and take him out to dinner tonight. Ask him how things are going with his business . . . what did you say it was again?"

When I hung up with Mabel, the tears had dried with a flicker of hope. Take Philip out to dinner. What a good idea. For one thing, he couldn't yell at me in a restaurant. For another, she was right. I needed to take an interest in *his* business if I wanted him to support me in mine.

I picked up the phone again. "Okay, God," I murmured. "I hope You heard Mabel's prayer and that You're on the job."

The cab let me out in front of Bistro 110 on East Pearson Street just across from Chicago's historic Water Tower. The sidewalk outdoor eating area was empty—chairs stacked, tables glistening with the recent rain, flower boxes empty. *Would have been fun to sit outside,* I thought, pushing through the door into the restaurant. Another time, when the weather wasn't so iffy.

The restaurant was surprisingly full for a Thursday evening. Good thing I'd made a reservation. "Fairbanks for two, seven o'clock," I told the maître d' who looked at me questioningly. He consulted his list, smiled, and led me to a table covered with a white cloth. The fresh daisies tucked into a tiny vase were a nice touch.

A waiter appeared and handed me a menu. "Are you waiting for someone, or would you like to order?"

"I'll wait. He should be here soon. But hot tea would be nice. Thank you."

The tea soothed my jumpy nerves. Philip had been surprised when I'd called and suggested going out to dinner tonight. "Tonight? Why not the weekend?"

"Why not tonight?" I'd said sweetly. "You've worked hard all week, I'm sure you could use a break. I found a nice French restaurant downtown. We could meet there."

"I don't know, Gabrielle . . . I've got a five o'clock meeting with a new client, don't know how long it'll last."

My heart had sunk. Five o'clock meetings usually meant drinks and "unwinding." But I'd pushed forward. "I'll make the reservation for seven. Just the two of us," I'd added. No way did I want Henry and Mona to "just happen" to come along.

As my watch ticked closer to seven thirty, I was just about to change my mind and order some soup when Philip appeared, tie loosened, and sank into the cherrywood chair opposite me. "Sorry I'm late. Meeting went almost to seven. Whew! I need some coffee." He signaled a waiter and then leaned forward, a grin cracking his face. "But if we get *this* account? Oh baby! We're in. On our way."

"That's great, Philip!" My spirit rose. This was a good start. "See? This is a little celebration."

Philip shook his head. "Uh-uh. When we *sign* this account, *then* we'll celebrate—the four of us. We should know next week."

Next week? Hopefully I'd be working by then. But it shouldn't matter, although the staff and volunteers at Manna House seemed to be in and out all hours of the day and night. And I caught "the four of us." Well, I had a week to psych myself up for an evening with the Fenchels.

The waiter brought Philip's coffee, along with a pad to take our order. I selected the French onion soup, a romaine salad with apple *batonnet*—whatever that was—and roasted pecans, and the angel hair pasta with chicken.

"I'll have the *escargots en croute* . . . mm, skip the salad . . . and the roasted duck confit." Philip handed back the menu.

I laughed.

"What's so funny?"

"Your French! You're amazing. You do the accent so well."

Philip rolled his eyes. "Restaurant menus. That's about it for my French now. I was fairly fluent after two years at the university in Montpellier, though."

"I *know*, silly." My voice was flirty. "That's where we met, remember? You pretended you were French just to knock me off my feet."

He nodded, but I could tell his thoughts were still distracted by his meeting.

I gave up on the romantic angle. "So tell me about this new client. Is it a big project?"

"Huge." Philip seemed glad to talk. I nodded, trying to understand the jargon of commercial real estate development as we polished off our appetizers, and asked questions now and then until our entrées arrived along with a lull in the conversation.

"I'm excited for you, Philip." I was trying to eat the slippery angel hair pasta in a ladylike manner, but somehow more fell off my fork than got into my mouth. I should've ordered a steak. "Hopefully, I'll have some good news next week too."

The words were out of my mouth before I had time to think about how to bring up Manna House. For a moment, what I said didn't seem to register. Then Philip looked up from his roasted duck and potato ragout. "Good news? What do you mean?" His face paled. "Gabrielle. You're not—!"

I laughed. "No, no. Nothing so earthshaking." *Good move, Gabby. Scare him with a pregnancy, maybe he'll be relieved when I tell him about Manna House.* "I mean, I applied for a job, and I should know in a few days." I reached across the table and laid a hand on his arm. "I would be able to use my skills as a recreation therapist."

Philip dabbed his mouth with his napkin and then put it down, frowning. "I didn't know you were applying for a job. Shouldn't we have talked about this? We don't need the money, Gabrielle. You know that. Especially if this new client comes through."

"It's not the money, Philip. I had to quit my job at the senior center pretty abruptly to move to Chicago. Which is okay," I hastened to add, "but the boys are at the academy, you're busy with your work . . . I want to get on with my career too."

He threw up his hands. "Good grief. We've been here less than two weeks. I thought you'd appreciate time to get settled, finish unpacking, get familiar with the city. Mona knows downtown Chicago better than the cabbies. I'm sure she'd be glad to show you around, introduce you to some of the clubs she belongs to, that kind of thing."

I took a slow breath. In and out. Should I tell him I would absolutely *hate* to hang out with Mona Fenchel, and I'd be bored silly at her stupid clubs? . . . *Nope.* I sent up a desperate, *Help, Lord!* and hoped Mabel was still praying.

Philip wasn't through. "At least you could've waited until I've got this new business on a firm footing before jumping into your own game. There will be social events we're expected to attend . . . I don't know." He pushed his plate aside as if I'd ruined his appetite.

I tried to ignore his pouting. "I'm sorry, Philip. I hadn't planned to go job hunting yet—it just happened. Kind of fell in my lap. And it seemed so perfect, I jumped on it. But I should have talked it over with you before applying today. That's why I'm telling you now." I shrugged, trying to pass it off lightly. "For all I know, I might not get the job."

"So what is this job? Is it full-time? I sure hope not."

No way around it. "Um, I don't know about the hours yet. It might be part-time. The job would be program director at Manna House—you know, the homeless shelter in the Wrigleyville neighborhood just south of us. Where we sent Lucy last week."

Philip stared at me. "Lucy!" He spit the name out like a bone stuck in his teeth. "I should have *known* you'd do something stupid like this."

chapter 13

Now it was my turn to stare at Philip. I didn't care if we were in a restaurant. I wasn't going to just let him kick me into a corner. "Stupid? *Stupid?*" I kept my voice low, but I spat out the words with the intensity of a couple of knife jabs. "Philip Fairbanks, that's unfair. There's nothing stupid about a homeless woman—an *elderly* homeless woman, for heaven's sake!—and there's nothing stupid about admiring the people who run shelters and thinking I can make a contribution!"

Matter of fact, it was a good thing we *were* in a restaurant, because I felt like throwing something. My leftover pasta would have made a good weapon—*splat!*—right in the middle of his Fairbanks-perfect face.

Philip threw up both hands—almost as if he knew I was tempted to take aim. "All right, all right. I shouldn't have said 'stupid.' But admit it, Gabby. You've been *obsessed* ever since you tripped over that woman. I mean, you could have ruined our relationship with the Fenchels right then and there when you brought her in that night! The smell alone was enough to make me puke." He rolled his eyes. "Then you go checking up on her at the shelter and end up playing nursemaid, taking her to a clinic in the ghetto—"

He reached across the table and grabbed my wrist. "Look. We came to Chicago to start a business. I expect—I need—your support. To put Fairbanks and Fenchel first, to make decisions that will help ensure our success! For us, Gabby." Philip released my wrist and leaned back. "Sure, maybe a job in a few months would be all right. But a job that enhances our standing in the community, maybe gives us connections that could prove profitable. We've got to think about these things, Gabby."

I looked away, envying the other restaurant patrons, laughing, talking, enjoying their meal and the easy camaraderie of Bistro 110. Where did I go from here? Philip made it sound like I, personally, was about to bring down his hopes of making it here in Chicago by taking on this job.

Are you praying, Mabel? I hoped so, because I knew we couldn't leave the conversation here. I needed time to think, to approach with a different perspective . . .

The waiter appeared, like a God-inspired interruption. "Dessert, *monsieur? ma'moiselle?* We have crème brûlée, lemon and apple tarts, and if you like chocolate—"

Philip waved his hand as if brushing him away. But I spoke up. "The apple tart sounds good. And coffee, please." Didn't Mary Poppins say a spoonful of sugar helped the medicine go down? "Go on, Philip. You love chocolate cake."

He shrugged.

"Make that an apple tart and a slice of chocolate cake. And two coffees." For some reason, ordering dessert for both of us helped get my feet back under me. I had to steer down the middle lane here, or we were going to be barreling down the highway in opposite directions.

I made my voice bright. "Philip, honey, I do want to support you in this new venture. Tell you what, if Manna House offers me the job, I'll tell the director I'm only available part-time—and hopefully that can be flexible, so if you want me to be available, I can be." *Whew*. I was going out on a limb here. Would Manna House be open to a part-time program director? "But"—I didn't flinch—"I do want this job. *This* job."

The desserts and coffee arrived, once again giving us breathing space. The small talk about extra cream and dessert forks poked holes in the balloon of tension around our table. The waiter disappeared.

The Ping-Pong ball was on Philip's side of the table.

"Fine." He tackled the thick slice of dark chocolate cake. "You're going to do what you're going to do anyway. Just"—he waved his fork at me, loaded with chocolate—"just don't get any notions about bringing your homeless 'friends' home with you. And certainly not to the office. Never."

Could be worse, I told myself as the weekend loomed. At least Philip and I were still speaking. Agreeing to disagree, or something like that. And maybe it was all for nothing. I could get a call from Mabel saying, *"Sorry, Gabby. The board doesn't feel you're the right person."* Or, *"Wish we could, but we just don't have the money."* Huh, if it was just the money, I'd do it for free.

Camila had come again Friday morning, so the penthouse was sparkling. While she was cleaning, I'd tackled the boxes still stacked in the two extra bedrooms, doing load after load of sheets and towels. I made up the boys' beds—a bunk bed for Paul, and a single bed for P.J.—and stocked the second bathroom, even though they wouldn't be here until the end of May. "I can do that, Señora Fairbanks," Camila had protested, when she saw me making the beds. "It is my job, no?"

"No, my job." I'd laughed to make sure she knew I was teasing. "I want to do this for my sons, my—how do you say it?" I'd grabbed a photo of P.J. and Paul that had surfaced from one of the unpacked boxes.

"Ah. *Sus muchachos.*" She'd pointed to me, then to the photo. Then she held up two fingers. "*Dos muchachos.*"

This is good, I'd thought. I might learn a little Spanish. And by the end of the day, I'd unpacked most of the boys' bedrooms, had dinner ready when Philip got home, and decided it was worth wasting an evening watching TV just to sit together on the wraparound couch.

I was going to suggest we visit a church or two come Sunday, but when Philip said he had to go back to the office on Saturday, I scratched that. Doubted he'd want to spend his only free day of the weekend going to church. Besides, I'd gotten out of the habit of going to church every week. Was I ready to jump back into that discipline? Give up a lazy Sunday morning having coffee in bed, reading the paper, making crepes or omelets for brunch? At the same time, I felt a tug—a tug that was getting stronger. At Manna House, even homeless women had a chance to study the Bible and go to church on Sunday nights.

With no cleaning chores to do Saturday morning, I decided to make brownies for the boys and get them in the mail if I could find the closest post office . . . and tried not to feel too anxious about the Manna House Board of Directors meeting that morning to discuss my job application.

Mr. Bentley wasn't on duty in the lobby when I came out of the elevator and pushed through the security door just before noon with my packages. This doorman was practically a kid, a white guy somewhere in his twenties, shirt collar unbuttoned, cracking gum, and twirling in the swivel chair behind the desk as if bored out of his mind.

"Excuse me. Sir?" *Humph. "Dude" or "whippersnapper" would be more like it.* "Can you tell me where to find the closest post office?"

"Nope. Don't live around here." Another swivel.

Good grief. What good was a doorman who couldn't help the residents? I managed to finagle a Chicago phone directory out of him, but that was a dead end because I didn't recognize the street names and had no idea which one was close to Richmond Towers. Finally, I walked to the small branch bank down the street and asked for directions. Didn't sound like such a long walk to me . . . but I hadn't counted on the wind whipping off the lake. By the time I mailed the two boxes of carefully packed brownies and got back to Richmond Towers, I felt as though I'd run a marathon.

No messages on the answering machine. Should I call the boys? But what if Mabel called? Besides, it was already afternoon. The boys would probably be out and about . . .

That set off a good cry, realizing I had no idea what my sons were doing that afternoon. And Paul was only eleven! Still just a kid who should be watching Saturday morning cartoons or playing his PlayStation 3 or imitating the older boys on his skateboard. For that matter, Philip Junior was still a kid, too, though what thirteen-year-old didn't think he or she should have all the privileges (but none of the responsibilities) of adulthood?

I snatched up the phone. We had call waiting. If Mabel called, I'd just tell the boys I'd call back.

No luck. I just got Marlene Fairbanks' charming voice mail telling me to leave a brief message. *Beep.* "Paul and P.J.? This is Mom. Please give me a call as soon as you get in this afternoon. By the way, I sent you something special in the mail today. Should get to school by Monday or Tuesday. Love you!"

Mabel hadn't called by the time Philip got home from the office at eight. I didn't say anything—I was pretty sure I wouldn't get any sympathy if I wailed, *"Why hasn't she called?!"*—but I did wonder out loud why the boys hadn't called back.

"The boys? Oh, sorry, Gabby, I forgot to tell you. Mom called me at the office yesterday, no, maybe it was Thursday . . . anyway, she said she and Dad were taking the boys on a quick trip to Colonial Williamsburg and spending the night in a hotel. It sounded like fun."

My urge to send a book sailing at his head was stifled by a stronger urge not to sink the boat, not when I had his tacit permission to accept this job if it came through. (*"Use words to say you're angry, Gabby,"* my mother used to say when I was throwing a tantrum. *"You don't have to yell and slam doors."*)

"You *forgot*?! Good grief, Philip! I've been dying to talk to them all day, wondering if they're okay! You could have told me—better still, why doesn't your mother ever call *me* and talk to me about the boys?" By the end of my little rant, I'd worked up a decent mad.

"Calm down, Gabby. Good grief. I said I was sorry. Besides,

you worry too much. They're fine. They're probably having a blast with their grandparents."

That wasn't the point. I needed to hear my sons' voices, to tell them I loved them, to hear them say they loved me. But I dropped the conversation, went into the bathroom, and bawled silently into a towel.

I finally heard from the boys on Granddad Fairbanks' cell phone as he was taking them back to the academy on Sunday afternoon. They passed it back and forth, telling me all about Colonial Williamsburg, how they got to whittle a whistle, and the cool indoor swimming pool at the hotel. "So what did you send us, Mom? Our own cell phones?"

I shouldn't have told them I'd mailed something. Let it be a sweet, simple surprise.

It was all I could do not to call the shelter to see if Mabel was there after the call from the boys. I didn't want to seem too eager . . . though why not? It'd been twenty-four hours since the directors met. Surely she could tell me something.

Philip was watching baseball on the big plasma TV, kicking back with a bag of chips and a jar of mango salsa. I settled at the kitchen counter with a cup of chamomile tea to soothe my nerves and dialed.

"*Hola!* Manna House. Can I help you?"

Definitely not Angela. "Uh, hi. This is Gabby Fairbanks. Is—"

"Oh, hello, Señora Fairbanks! This is Edesa Baxter. How nice to hear your voice."

Edesa's lilting sunshine seemed to spark from the phone and

brighten the room. "Hi, Edesa. So they've got you on the desk this afternoon, I see."

She laughed into my ear. "Actually, I came to translate for the worship service this evening. Iglesia Cristiana Evangélica is doing our Sunday Evening Praise—the pastor is on the Manna House board."

I glanced at the clock. Ten past five. "It starts at six?"

"Give or take." She laughed. "Depends on when the band arrives. Are you coming? We'd love to see you."

Band? Maybe she just meant the musicians, like last week. "Thanks, Edesa. Maybe I will! But I called to see if Mabel is there. She around?"

"Mm, haven't seen her, but she usually shows up for Sunday Evening Praise. That woman doesn't know how to take a whole day off!—oh, must go, Mrs. Fairbanks." I could hear Gracie screaming in the background. "Precious is waving wildly. Where Josh is, I have no idea. Adiós!"

The phone went dead. But I was already making up my mind. I quickly changed into a black jersey dress, multicolored cinch belt, and dress boots, touched up my makeup, and grabbed my trench coat. "Philip?" I poked my head into the living room. "Mind if I take the car? I'd like to go to church tonight."

He half turned his head as a batter swung. When the ball sailed out of bounds, he looked my way. "Church? Now?"

No sense beating around the bush. "Actually, it's a worship service at Manna House. Different churches come in each Sunday evening. A Spanish church tonight. Could be interesting. Would you like to come with me?" *Did I really say that?* For a nanosecond, I panicked. *What if he said yes?*

"Honestly, Gabby. Isn't this a bit much? Good grief, if you

want to go to church that bad, I'm sure there are decent churches around Chicago—oh! Oh! Oh! That's a homer! Go, man! Go!" The action on TV grabbed his eyeballs and let me off the hook.

I crossed to the couch, kissed him on the cheek, and grinned. "I assume that's a no. Don't worry, I won't be late. I have my cell."

This would be my first time driving in Chicago, but I wasn't worried. Straight down Sheridan Road . . .

It was just the parking that was bad. I had to park the Lexus two blocks away from the shelter. The dense residential neighborhood, mixed with small businesses and eateries, had few garages, just street parking. Not a problem now, but it might be dark when I started home.

The band must have arrived in good time, because the music was already loud and joyous when I entered the foyer at six fifteen. From the doorway I saw a lively group of young Latinos playing guitars, tambourines, a trombone, and a conga drum. The multipurpose room was packed tonight, and everyone was on their feet, moving and clapping. I didn't recognize the song—they were singing it in Spanish—but my feet certainly felt like tapping.

To my left, the door to Mabel's office suddenly opened and she came out, followed by a stocky man in a dark suit and tie, clutching a Bible.

"Oh! Gabby!" Mabel said. "I didn't know you were coming tonight. But I'd like you to meet Reverend Carlos Álvarez, pastor of Iglesia Cristiana Evangélica, who is leading our worship tonight. Reverend Álvarez is a member of our board . . . we were just praying together before he speaks tonight. Reverend Álvarez, this is Mrs. Gabrielle Fairbanks."

A wide smile showed off two gold teeth hiding among his

molars. The pastor tucked his Bible under his arm and took my hand in both of his. "Ah! Señora Fairbanks. I'm delighted to meet you." Still holding my hand, he turned to Mabel. "So this lovely woman is our prospective program director?"

chapter 14

Prospective program director? My eyes darted to Mabel as the pastor took his leave for the multipurpose room. Did he mean—?

Mabel held me back a moment. "I was going to call you tomorrow morning and ask you to come in for a second meeting." Her tone was low, confidential. "But since you're here, can you stay a few minutes after the service? We can talk then, save you a trip." She smiled, gave me a little squeeze, and left me to find my own seat.

Now I was thoroughly confused. Rev. Álvarez acted like I had the job—or practically. *Prospective* was the word he'd used. But Mabel said we needed a second meeting. Was that why she hadn't called?

Precious, standing in the back row with her teenage daughter on one side, was waving at me, pointing to the empty chair next to hers. Josh Baxter was walking back and forth behind the last row, bouncing a wide-awake Gracie in his arms. He nodded hello and smiled as I slipped past him—stepping over the feet of

Hannah the Bored, who had confiscated one of the overstuffed chairs pushed against the back wall and was sitting on her tailbone, feet stuck out, arms crossed, eyes closed—and dumped my shoulder bag and coat on the chair next to Precious.

"Hey ya, Miz Gabby. Ain't this great?" Precious grinned at me, clapping along to the beat of the band and joining in on the occasional *aleluyas* that peppered the Spanish gospel song. "One of these days I'm gonna get Miz Edesa to teach me Spanish."

I nodded and smiled. But my mind was such a jumble, I didn't really pay much attention to the worship going on around me for the next fifteen minutes. Hardly any of the music was familiar, even the songs sung in English. But when Rev. Álvarez stood to speak and people settled into the odd array of folding chairs, I tried to focus. No sense getting myself stirred up. What was so unusual about two interviews for a job, anyway? Actually, it was usually a good sign when you got called back.

Rev. Álvarez called out something in Spanish as the band put down their instruments. Edesa Baxter, looking very American in her skinny jeans and nubby green sweater over a black tank top, translated. "How many of you have ever been hungry?" Murmurs and nods went around the room. Nearly all the residents held up their hands.

The pastor spoke again, and Edesa translated. "There are many kinds of hunger—hunger for food, hunger for love, hunger for God . . ."

Back and forth they went, first in Spanish, then in English. "Ever notice how what you feed on affects you? . . . If you eat junk food, your body suffers . . . If you're starved for love, your spirit dies . . . If you don't feed on God's Word, your soul shrivels up." Heads nodded, and a few *améns* popped around me.

Rev. Álvarez opened his big Bible, then nodded at the band members, who dug into a box and started passing out paperback Bibles. "These Bibles are a gift to you from Iglesia Cristiana Evangélica," Edesa translated, "so that we can all feed on the Word of God together. Some are in Spanish, some in English. Just say which one you want."

The teenager I'd seen on the nurse's visiting day—last name was Menéndez, I remembered that much—eagerly waved her hand until she got one of the Spanish copies. Precious leaned over at me. "You got a Bible, Miz Gabby?" she stage-whispered.

"Uh, at home, sure. Still packed, I'm afraid." Good excuse, anyway. To tell the truth, I wasn't sure where my Bible was—the one my parents had given me for high school graduation with *Gabrielle Shepherd* embossed in gold on the leather cover. Still in mint condition, if I could find it. It hadn't occurred to me I'd need a Bible tonight. Hardly anyone carried their Bible to church back at Briarwood Lutheran. The text was always printed right in the bulletin.

Precious caught the attention of the trombonist, who was still handing out English Bibles, and held up two fingers. She handed one to Sabrina, slouched in the seat beside her, and the other to me. I took the paperback, but my face heated up like a hot flash. Precious was just a bit too zealous looking out for me, as far as I was concerned.

The text was Psalm 103, verses 1 through 5. It took people helping each other or looking it up in the table of contents at least five minutes to find it. But Rev. Álvarez was patient, pointing out something in his Bible and talking quietly in Spanish to Edesa, who nodded eagerly. I sighed. *Why don't they just get on with it?*

But Rev. Álvarez never did preach a sermon. What happened next was more like a poetry reading plus prayer meeting plus therapy session. The pastor invited different volunteers to read each verse, after which he said we would turn the verse into a prayer—all of which Edesa translated for us.

"I'm with that." Precious stood up and read the first verse. "Praise the Lord, O my soul! All my inmost being, praise His holy name!"

The pastor prayed in Spanish, after which Edesa translated: "*El Señor*, sometimes I have to tell my heavy soul to praise You. Wake up, soul! Pay attention!"

Precious nodded vigorously. "Uh-huh. Got that right. Don't wait for Sunday to get your praise on!"

Volunteers among the residents were slow in coming, so Mabel Turner read the second verse. "Praise the Lord, O my soul! And forget not all His benefits."

The pastor lifted his face, eyes tightly shut, visibly moved as he prayed in Spanish. Again Edesa translated: "Oh God, how easy it is to look at all our problems and forget all the good things You have given each and every one of us."

I squirmed, unsure this would go over with women who had no home, no money, no health care, no—

"Who forgives all your sins—" someone read.

"Oh, *Jesucristo!* This is the greatest benefit of all! No matter how far we stray from You, You welcome us back and cover our darkest sins with Your blood of forgiveness!"

"—and heals all your diseases," the same person finished.

Ouch, I thought. *Most of these women aren't the healthiest specimens around. Thanking God for healing might come across a bit hollow.*

"*Señor Dios*, our bodies are broken, and we have abused

them," Edesa translated as the pastor prayed. "Give us the strength and wisdom to stop our bad habits, to take care of this holy temple where Your Spirit lives. We also ask healing for the diseases in our spirit—resentment, anger, bitterness, pride—which are the cancers of the soul."

I heard someone weeping . . . and then another.

The reading went on, back and forth, phrase by phrase. The weeping was getting louder. But the pastor pointed to another reader to read the last verse: "Who satisfies your desires with good things, so that your youth is renewed like the eagle's!"

His prayer in Spanish. Then Edesa's translation: "Oh God, we long to recapture the years stolen from us that we have so easily given to the enemy. Thank You, *Dios,* for all these benefits, wrapped like gifts at Christmas, just waiting for us to receive them. Amen and amen."

"Whew. That was quite a service." I sank into a chair in Mabel Turner's office. Some of the women were still in the multi-purpose room, crying and praying with Pastor Álvarez.

Mabel closed the door and sat down at her desk across from me. "Yes. Pastor Álvarez has led Sunday night service here before, but nothing like this." She seemed distracted, head averted toward the other room as if listening. But finally she looked back at me. "I'm sure you want to get home. Let's get to business . . ."

I sat up straight and crossed my ankles. Yes, this was business. She put on a pair of reading glasses and picked up my application. "The board was impressed with your credentials and experience, even though it hasn't been that many years—"

I flushed. "Yes, I finished my degree just a few years ago." I bit my lip. Should've finished it back in 1990 instead of marrying Philip so quickly—but I'd already plucked that chicken. No point shaving it again.

"Before finalizing the decision, the board would like to follow up on the references you provided, and get a chance to meet you—don't worry, nothing formal. Actually, you already met Peter Douglass—Avis Douglass's husband, who was here with her when she preached last Sunday night. And it was serendipity that Pastor Álvarez got to meet you tonight. But there are three other board members—another pastor here in the city, one of our social workers, and the former director, Reverend Liz Handley, who just retired." She smiled mischievously. "That's how I got *my* job."

My insides sank a little. So I still had to wait for an answer. How long would it take for these "informal meetings"? I'd been hoping—

"The main thing they recommended is that you spend a week just hanging out here at Manna House, getting to know the residents, talking to the staff and volunteers, and developing a sense of what the needs are. Then, if your references don't turn up a warrant for your arrest or that you've got a second job as a call girl"—she said this with a totally straight face—"we'll include this get-acquainted week in your first week's pay. So . . ." Mabel looked at me over the top of her reading glasses. "How would you like to start tomorrow?"

"Tomorrow!" I couldn't help the happy screech. So what if the first week was a trial balloon! "Absolutely—oh." I suddenly remembered my promise to Philip. "Uh, is it possible to start out part-time?" . . . and ended up explaining the whole tension with Philip starting up his business and wanting me to be "available." *Whatever that means.*

Mabel chewed on her pen. "Tell you what. We'll start at thirty hours and make the hours flexible." She smiled wryly. "We all work flexible hours anyway, Gabby. Manna House is a twenty-four-hour operation, remember?"

A knock interrupted our laughter. Josh Baxter stuck his head inside the door. "Edesa and I are about ready to leave, Mrs. Turner. Wondered if Mrs. Fairbanks wanted us to walk her to the train."

"That'd be great." I gathered my coat and shoulder bag. "Except I drove. Would you mind walking me to my car?"

The prayer meeting had dispersed. The band had packed up and gone home. The couches and chairs had been arranged back into their "conversational groups." A few of the shelter residents were playing cards, others stood around talking, while some slouched on the couches with unreadable expressions.

Excitement tickled my chest. Tomorrow they would have names. I'd have permission to talk to Carolyn, Tina, the Menéndez girl, and Hannah the Bored.

Gracie had fallen asleep in the stroller, her loose, dark curls peeking out from the blanket as we walked toward my parked car. Edesa was bubbling about the "church service" that evening. "Josh, did you see? I had a chance to pray with Aida, that *pobrecita* who came in last week. She wouldn't talk, just cried. But she let me pray for her."

I was curious. "She seems so young. How did she end up here at the shelter?"

"Don't know the whole story," Josh said. "But unfortunately it's not uncommon. Foster kid, in and out of foster homes, most lasting only a couple of months. But when a foster kid turns eighteen? The state washes its hands. Okay, kid, you're on your own. Aida literally had no resources, so she ended up at the shelter."

"Good grief," I murmured. "So young . . . and then there's Lucy, who's got to be in her seventies, at least. Still don't know her story. By the way, how is she doing at your parents' house, Josh? Lucy, I mean."

"Ha." He snorted. "She stayed two nights and then disappeared . . . what?"

I'd stopped short. The SUV was right where I'd parked it. The silver Lexus gleamed in the arching glow of a streetlight just above. But a beat-up two-door had squeezed into the parking space just behind and pulled up bumper to bumper. In front, an ancient Cadillac had backed up to Philip's pride and joy, packing it in like the baloney in a sandwich.

"Uh-oh." Josh walked from front to back of my parked car, as if measuring the inches. I looked around frantically, prepared to run house to house, knocking on doors, until I found the owners and got them to move their cars. But only the flat brick walls, locked doors, and dim windows of apartment buildings on both sides of the street stared back at me.

Josh shook his head. "This car isn't going anywhere tonight, Mrs. Fairbanks."

chapter 15

I could *not* believe this was happening to me! Pounding my fists on the car, I wailed, "I *have* to drive this car home, or Philip will shoot me!" Tears threatened to spill over, but I kicked the tires instead and muttered a few choice words under my breath, while Edesa and Josh stood there helplessly, letting me make a fool of myself.

Reality finally sank in, and I let the Baxters talk me into riding home with them on the El. "I'm sure the car will be fine till morning," Josh said as we settled into our seats on the northbound Red Line. "You can come back and get it then. A bit of a hassle, but at least it wasn't stolen or a window bashed in."

Oh great. Thanks a lot. He has no idea.

I leaned my head against the cool window, eyes closed, dreading the confrontation I knew was ahead of me.

"Gabby?" Edesa's soft accent tickled my ear. "Your stop is coming up. Would you like us to walk you home and pray together about the car?"

I didn't answer, letting the squeal-and-clatter of the train wheels fill up the space. I'd give anything for them to walk me home. It was already nine o'clock and dark, and even though Sheridan was a busy street, I'd feel so much better not walking the three blocks to Richmond Towers by myself. But pray? I hadn't thought about that.

I opened my eyes as the train slowed. "That's all right. You've got the baby and everything. You two need to get on home and get her to bed." I got up, grabbing a pole in the swaying train with one hand and clutching my shoulder bag with the other.

Josh and Edesa exchanged a glance. The train stopped and the doors slid open. "We'll come with you," Josh said, grabbing Gracie's stroller and helping Edesa, who was holding the sleeping baby, out of her seat. There was no time to protest. *Doors open. You get out. People get on. Doors close.* No time to diddle around.

Had to admit I was grateful for the company. The night was chilly, but Gracie was wrapped in several layers of blankets in the stroller. As we approached Richmond Towers, I started to thank them, but Josh was already wrestling the stroller through the revolving door. What were they doing? Again I expected to say good-bye in the lobby, but they waited with me as I opened the security door, then we all got on the elevator.

"Really, you guys. I'll be fine." I put on a smile.

"Mm," was all I got out of Edesa.

When the doors slid open on the top floor, they got out with me. Edesa looked around. "Only one door? Yours?" I thought she was making a comment about me living in a pampered penthouse, but her face lit up. "Good! Here we can pray." She grabbed my hand and one of Josh's and squeezed her eyes shut. "*Jesucristo,* we come to You with thanksgiving that no harm was done to

Gabby's car tonight. You are so good! We praise You, Lord and Savior! But we know it will be an inconvenience for her poor husband, who depends on it for work . . ."

I blinked my eyes open in astonishment at her prayer. Thanking God when our car was held captive miles from home? Praying for my "poor husband" who would be "inconvenienced"? I squirmed. What if Philip heard us out here?

Edesa's prayer, though intense, was quiet and short. I said thanks and unlocked the door, but realized they were still standing there. "Uh, do you want to come in?"

"No, no." Josh shook his head. "But maybe we can help explain."

"Gabby?" Philip's voice sailed from somewhere within. "That you?" He must have heard our voices, because he actually came to the door. "Oh. You have visitors." He stood there in his robe and slippers over sweats and a T-shirt, newspaper in his hand.

"Uh, yes. Um, Philip, this is Josh Baxter and his wife, Edesa, um, from Manna House. Volunteer staff," I hastened to add, remembering Philip's decree to never bring people home from the shelter.

Josh stuck out his hand. "Pleased to meet you, Mr. Fairbanks. We just wanted to make sure your wife got home safely. When we left Manna House tonight, cars had parked so tightly in front and back of your wife's SUV, she couldn't get it out. A real bummer! But that block empties out during the day, so she should be able to get it easily tomorrow morning."

Before Philip had a chance to react to this information, Edesa also shook his hand. "I am pleased to meet you, Señor Fairbanks. We have so enjoyed getting to know Gabby."

I wondered what my husband was thinking, seeing this tall,

white college kid and his dark-skinned wife—who looked African-American but spoke with a Spanish accent—at his door. Virginia born and bred, mixed couples were not "the usual" in Philip's world. Mine either, for that matter.

"And this," Edesa continued happily, pulling back the blanket from the baby's face, "is Gracie, who needs to get home and get to bed. So we will go now." She gave me a hug. "I'm so sorry for this *problema*, Gabby. But it will all work out. *Dios te bendiga*."

The young couple said their good-byes, got back into the elevator with a wave, and the doors slid closed behind them. Philip had not said a word.

We were still standing outside our front door in the large foyer of the top floor. Finally he spoke. "You mean . . . you didn't bring the car home."

I shook my head.

"It's parked somewhere down around that homeless shelter, jammed in like a sardine, and it's gotta stay there all night."

I nodded.

"Oh, for—" He whacked the doorjamb with the newspaper. "So what am I supposed to do in the morning, Gabby? Huh? Tell me that."

For some reason, my anxiety was gone. Sucked down the elevator shaft with Josh and Edesa. "Take a cab, I guess. Believe me, Philip, I'm really upset about this! But . . . I'm supposed to go back to the shelter tomorrow to begin my training, so I'll get the car first thing, park it where it won't get hemmed in, and bring it home tomorrow afternoon."

That got his attention. "Training?"

I nodded, and couldn't help the smile. "Yes. They offered me the job. Just waiting on references. And good news! They agreed to part-time. The hours are flexible too."

"Oh." He seemed confused by the turn in the conversation. "Guess you got what you wanted." He turned abruptly and disappeared inside the door. But a moment later a parting salvo flew back at me. "That car better be in one piece when you get back tomorrow!"

I lay in bed that night, thanking God for Josh and Edesa Baxter, who had somehow defused the whole situation . . . and I was still thanking God the next morning when I got off the El at the Sheridan station in bright sunshine, walked to where I'd parked the car the night before, and there it was. Still parked, but now lovely in its loneliness. And as far as I could tell, no scratches, bumps, or dings. Edesa would be squealing *"Gloria a Dios!"* or something like that.

I moved the Lexus and parked it in front of the Laundromat next to the shelter, making sure I was in the last parking space on the corner so I could back out. The sun warmed my back a few moments later as I rang the doorbell and was let in by a disgruntled Angela. "New policy. Doors always locked. Sure keeps me running."

"You need a buzzer or something you can push from your desk."

She looked at me, almond eyes widening, her mouth making an *O*. "That's it! I'll ask if we can do it at the next staff meeting." She gave me a playful poke with her elbow. "You're the bomb, Mrs. Fairbanks!"

There we go again. "If you're going to be so formal, I'll have to call you *Miss* . . . *Miss* . . . ?"

She laughed. "Kwon. Angela Kwon. But don't you dare. Angela is just fine."

"Then call me Gabby. Staff is on first-name basis, right?"

Angela nodded, then tilted her head. Soft, straight hair swung forward like a lady's silk scarf. "You working here now?"

I grinned. "Hope to be. This is my get-acquainted week, or something like that. In fact, do you mind if I hang out with you a little bit? Find out what you do?"

She laughed again. "Feel free! Here's the key to the staff closet—you can store your coat and purse in there if you want." She pointed. "Multipurpose room, far side."

I wanted to roll my eyes. *Precious is right. We've got to find a new name for the gag-awful "multipurpose room."* Mabel Turner's office door across the foyer was closed, but I knocked anyway, thinking I should check in. She might have other plans for me.

"She's not in," Angela sang out from behind the glass of the receptionist's cubby. "Out strong-arming local businesses to cough up funding for the shelter." The phone rang. "Manna House . . ."

O-kay. Guess when Mabel told me to come "just hang out," that's what she meant. I pushed through the double doors into the large sitting area, threaded my way around the couches and chairs and their occupants to the closet on the far side, stowed my stuff, and turned . . . suddenly realizing several pairs of eyes had followed me.

The woman closest to me peered up at me from the depths of an overstuffed chair, with small eyes in a rough, brown, leathered face. "Seen you here before, woman." Her accent was heavily Jamaican. "De city send you or someting?"

"No." I smiled and sat down nearby. I couldn't guess her age—somewhere between thirty and fifty. Wiry hair pulled back into a stubby ponytail with a rubber band. Fifty extra pounds encased in a sweatshirt and faded jeans. "I'm volunteering this week. My name's Gabby." I held out my hand. "Yours?"

She left my hand hanging in midair for a few seconds longer than was comfortable, but she finally shook it. "Go by Wanda . . . Gabby? What kind o' name is dat? You talk *jabba-jabba* or someting?"

I grinned bigger. "Something like that. Short for Gabrielle."

"Ah!" Recognition flickered in the tiny eyes. "Like de angel."

"Have you been at the shelter long, Wanda?"

She scowled. "Long enough. Waitin' to get me state ID so me can get a job. Dey get you coming an' going, ya know. Can't get a job witout an ID. Can't get an ID witout an address. Can't pay for a place to live witout a job. Dat's de drill."

I blinked, not knowing what to say. Getting an ID had never been an issue for me. Once you learned to drive and got your license at sixteen, that was it. "I'm sorry, Wanda. That's tough." I stood up. "See you around, I guess. I'll be here all week."

"Yeah, yeah. Me too. *Cha!*" She waved me off.

I wondered if I should introduce myself to the handful of women scattered around the room, but I'd already asked if I could hang around Angela's den and figure out how to work the front desk. So I just smiled, nodded, and said, "Hi," until I was back in the foyer with a folding chair I'd grabbed on my way.

The phone seemed to ring every few minutes. But during short lulls, Angela tried to acquaint me with the phone system. Extension one for Mabel Turner . . . two for the kitchen/dining room on the lower level, which supposedly also covered the rec room . . . another in the childcare room on the first floor . . . a fourth upstairs on the sleeping rooms level.

"Everybody who comes in or out needs to sign that day's log." She hefted the big notebook sitting on the shelf of the cubby's "talk-through" window.

"Oops." I grimaced. "I forgot." I signed my name and time in. A lot of names were signed out already that morning. Reason given: *job . . . job hunting . . . job interview . . .*

"Mrs. Fairbanks? I mean, Gabby. Would you mind taking over the phone for twenty minutes or so?" Angela stood up and squeezed past me. "I need to pick up some things at the drugstore on my break. Want me to bring you some coffee or something?"

"Uh, sure. Coffee would be great, a little cream. But answering the phone . . . I don't know people's names or where they are in the building."

Angela bent over the log, her long, dark hair flowing. As a kid I'd envied straight, silky hair like that. Mine was always a curly mop top. "Estelle should be coming in to make lunch today . . . lucky us. That woman is one good cook! As for the rest, maybe just take messages. I'll run them around when I get back."

The young woman grabbed her sweater and purse, and disappeared through the front doors with a wave.

And there I was, at the front desk of Manna House, without a clue what I should be doing. The phone rang. For Mabel. That was easy: took a message. Two more calls—one, a volunteer who couldn't come in to help with lunch that day, and the other for someone named Diane. I glanced at the log. *Diane . . . out.* I took a message on both.

The door buzzer rang at the same time as the phone. I

grabbed the receiver. "Manna House . . . Ms. Turner? I'm sorry, she's not in right now. Can I take a message?"

Blaaaaat. Someone was leaning on the buzzer. "All right, all right," I muttered under my breath as I scribbled the number for Mabel and hurried for the door. If that was Estelle—

It wasn't. A young woman stood on the stoop, a mass of tangled hair tucked up under a baseball cap, hands shoved in the pockets of her skinny jeans, and jiggling nervously. A ring pierced the side of her nose, and strings of hair streaked brown and blonde escaped the cap and fell around her ears and neck. Her gray eyes darted at me uncertainly.

"This the women's shelter?" Her voice had an edge. "They told me to come over here, I could get some help." She hunched her shoulders and shivered as if she were cold, although the day was mild and temperatures were supposed to head into the low seventies today.

What in the world was I supposed to do? Mabel wasn't here, and Angela was off who-knew-where. And who was "they"?

I swallowed and swung the door open wider. "Yes, this is Manna House Women's Shelter. Come on in. I'll try to find someone to help you." Where was Angela? *Oh God, send her back soon!*

The young woman followed me inside, slinking like a feral cat. *Get her name, something . . .* Glancing around Angela's desk for a pad of paper and a pen, my eyes fell on a clipboard with a folder that said "Intake Forms." I grabbed it, pulled out a sheet, and stuck it back in the clipboard. "Here, fill this out. You can sit over there." I handed her a pen and pointed to the folding chair now sitting just outside the reception desk.

The phone rang. Another message for Mabel.

"What if I ain't got no current address?" The woman was frowning at the page in her lap.

The door buzzer made us both jump. "Whatever . . . fill out what you can." *That better be Angela—or Mabel Turner. "Just hang out" indeed!*

Estelle Williams loomed in the doorway, plastic shopping bags hanging from both hands. "Here, take these quick," she huffed, slinging a couple of bags at me. "I need to get one of those little shopping carts on wheels—oh. Who do we have here?"

The fifty-something black woman glanced at the newcomer tapping her foot so hard she was making the chair shake, took in the clipboard, then looked back at me. "Lord have mercy, you're learning quick," she muttered under her breath. "That girl is high on somethin'. Amphetamines, likely. Keep her busy here till we can get someone to stay with her."

She trundled through the swinging doors, lugging her plastic shopping bags, then called back. "Oh, yeah. Sign me in, will ya?"

chapter 16

High? On what? Was she going to do something crazy? I wanted to call out, *"Wait! Don't leave me."* But Estelle was gone.

Oh great. I knew diddly-squat about the aftereffects of addictive drugs. Fortunately for me, Angela came back five minutes later while the newcomer was still tapping and frowning over the clipboard. "Good, you found the intake forms."

"What happens next?"

Angela shrugged. "Right now, just stay with her till Mabel comes in. Stephanie Cooper's our case manager, but she's usually only here Tuesdays and Thursdays."

I got another folding chair from the big room and set it up next to the tapping foot. The young woman handed me the clipboard. Most of it was still blank, but she'd filled in her name. "Naomi?" I tried a smile on her. "That's a pretty name."

"It's okay." She tucked her hands under her jean-covered thighs, as if sitting on them to keep them still.

"My name's Gabby. Sorry you have to wait. The director should be here soon."

As if on cue, the buzzer went off. I practically vaulted out of my chair to get the door. Mabel Turner, a bit more dressed up than usual in a pale green suit and heels, stepped in. I handed her the clipboard. "Thank goodness it's you. You have a new guest."

Mabel glanced at the intake form. "Naomi Jackson?"

"Yeah. That's me." *Jiggle, jiggle. Tap, tap, tap.*

"Come into my office. Let's talk, okay?"

The young woman followed Mabel into the office and the door shut behind them.

I looked at Angela back in her cubby. "Is Mabel going to be okay in there?"

"Oh, sure. Someone will stay with her while she comes off her high. Then she'll be assigned a case manager—Stephanie's good—she's a social worker, also one of our board members. Mabel does case management, too, but I think we could use a few more."

"So what's Mabel doing in there right now?"

"Probably getting more information out of her, then going over the rules for staying at Manna House. No drugs, for sure. It all depends on whether she actually wants to get help." The phone rang. Angela picked up. "Manna House . . . Yes, she's here, but she's in a meeting. Can I take a message?"

Messages! *I better tell Estelle her lunch volunteer isn't coming.*

I found her in the kitchen downstairs, putting away the groceries. "Guess that makes you my helper then," she grunted, dumping a ten-pound bag of flour into a large container. "You okay with that?"

"Sure." Making lunch would seem like a vacation in the Bahamas after manning the front desk.

"Here." She handed me a pair of latex gloves and an ugly

hairnet cap. "Better tuck that mop of yours under this. Don't want no hair spicin' up the soup. They gonna know the red ones are yours, for sure."

For the next hour Estelle kept me busy peeling and chopping vegetables for a vegetable-beef soup, while she mixed up several batches of biscuits and a large flat pan of brownies. But she caught me off guard when she said, "Mabel tell you I used to be homeless?"

"Just that you were once a resident here." I didn't admit I'd assumed she was homeless *now* when I first met her.

"Oh, yeah . . . before the fire took this place down." She laughed. "But, Lord, Lord, He is so good, because that fire turned out to be a blessing for *me*."

My knife paused in midair. "What do you mean?"

She chuckled. "This white girl, Leslie Stuart, kinda like you, 'cept she's got long blonde"—*wink, wink*—"California hair . . . anyway, she took me in after the fire. Turned out she was lookin' for a housemate and, knock me over with a cotton ball, we hit it off like the Odd Couple, so . . ." She laughed again, a big *hee hee hee*, while she slid the pan of brownies into the commercial-size oven.

"Did you know her or something?" I couldn't quite imagine the scenario. "Or did she just show up on the sidewalk the night of the fire and invite you to sleep over?"

Estelle scooped up my chopped carrots and potatoes, threw them in her soup pot, and handed me a bag of onions and a bunch of celery. "Nope. Didn't know her. But this church north of here, SouledOut Community, took all of us in the first night, then farmed us out to various church members till the city could find other shelters that had room."

"SouledOut?" The name was familiar. "Isn't that the church that did worship here on Easter? Avis Somebody preached. I think her husband is a board member here."

Estelle's shoulders shook with amusement. "That's the one. That's where I worship now. Not only that, I'm part of this prayer group called Yada Yada. Stu and me and about ten others, more or less. If you hang around here long enough, you'll meet most of them at one time or another. Edesa Reyes—I mean Baxter . . . she's a Yada too."

My eyes were swimming from cutting the onions. I grabbed a paper towel and dabbed. "Sounds weird," I sniffed. "Like a Greek sorority or something."

"Nah, it's Hebrew. From the Old Testament—uh-oh. Time creepin' up on us. Can you run upstairs and see if these two are around?" She pointed at names on a chore sheet. "They need to get down here to set up. And—*hee hee hee*—you better fix your face. You look like one of them raccoons we had back in Mississippi."

So much for waterproof mascara. As I repaired my makeup in the common bathroom, a thought popped into my head. *Funny. She didn't say anything about* why *she'd been homeless . . .*

I left at three o'clock, anxious to get the Lexus home and safely in the parking garage before I got tied up in traffic. Besides, I was exhausted. I'd helped serve lunch, which was fun, giving me a chance to chat with each resident and staffperson who came through the line, trying to memorize names and faces. Many were out for the day—Mabel said some of the residents at the shelter had jobs of one sort or another, or had appointments at public aid—so it didn't take long. Then I took my soup to a table and sat with Wanda, who turned out to be a lot more talkative the second time around while she polished off seconds on brownies. Took me a while to understand her patois accent, but it was fun trying to catch the gist.

I'd stayed for cleanup, along with Aida Menéndez and Tina, a large, good-looking Latina, but the two of them talked rapid Spanish to each other as they washed pots and pans, so I just concentrated on scooping leftover vegetable-beef soup into two large plastic containers and wiping down tables with a spray bottle of disinfectant.

As I drove north on Sheridan Road, Estelle's comment, *"You're learning quick,"* rubbed up against my spirit like a purring kitty welcoming me home. Even Mabel seemed pleased that I'd handled things at the front desk, though she'd apologized later for not letting me know what the intake procedure was. *"I didn't think you'd need it in the first hour!"* she'd laughed. *"Go ahead, call it a day. We'll see you tomorrow."*

I could see Richmond Towers and the other lakefront highrises coming up in the distance. But my thoughts were still back at Manna House. I'd noticed Mabel made a point to stick with Naomi at lunch, talking and laughing with others across the table even though the newcomer hunched silently over her food, still tapping her foot under the table. By the time I left, Naomi was zonked out on a couch in the multipurpose room while Tina sat nearby, flipping through a magazine, keeping an eye on her.

Had to admit, I was surprised they let someone who was high come into the shelter and sign up for a bed. I probably would have told her to come back when she's sober . . .

I parked the car in the Richmond Towers parking garage but bypassed the door directly into the secured elevator area in order to walk outside to the frontage street along the park. Such a beautiful afternoon! The time-and-temperature sign I'd seen on a bank coming home had said seventy-two degrees. Blue sky arched overhead with only a few wispy cirrus clouds to catch the eye. I couldn't see the lake from here—my view blocked by the trees in the park and Lake Shore Drive—but suddenly I had an urge to stick my toes in the sand and splash in the water again. Should I change? I was still in my slacks and cotton sweater I'd worn to work . . .

Nope. Once thirty-two floors up, I'd probably see stuff I needed to do and that'd be it.

On impulse, I pushed through the revolving door. "Mr. Bentley!" The bald-and-bearded doorman standing in the lobby, hands behind his back, was just the person I wanted to see. "Could I leave my purse with you for a little while? Half an hour, max, I promise."

"Now, Mrs. Fairbanks." He arched an eyebrow at me. "What would I be doing with a purse? What would people think?"

I giggled. "Didn't take you for a man who cared what people think. But, I mean, don't you have a drawer or something behind that desk I can put this in? Doesn't have to be locked. You'll be here, right?"

With a shrug, he took the bag, stuck it in a drawer behind the half-moon desk, and said, "Go on, get out of here. That purse ain't going anywhere."

Feeling free and lighthearted, I walked briskly through the park across from Richmond Towers, half-ran through the under-pass under the Drive, and in no time stepped onto the stone retaining wall. Slipping out of my flats and knee-high nylons, I walked through the warm, dry sand, then rolled up my trouser legs and waded into the lapping water. *Brrr.* Still numbing cold. Didn't Lake Michigan ever get warm?

Sitting on the two-level stone wall that made a convenient seat facing the lake, I let the sun warm my back and dry my feet. Something Mabel had said last week during my interview warmed me inside too. *"From the first time you walked in here, Gabby, I had the sense it was God who sent you . . . I believe God brought you to Chicago because He has a purpose for you, right here at Manna House."*

I wasn't sure what she meant. But it made me feel . . . wanted. As though God hadn't forgotten me, even though I'd ditched Him years ago. Even though the afternoon was slipping away, I felt reluctant to take the elevator to our sterile penthouse. Right now my heart felt full and I didn't know what to do with it. The staff and volunteers I'd met at Manna House—Estelle, Precious, Edesa, and even Mabel—seemed to so easily say, "Praise God!" or "Thank You, Lord!" That didn't come easily to me, but something deep inside wanted to tell God "thank You."

So I just closed my eyes and said it. "Thank You!"

"For what?" A gravelly voice behind me caught me off guard. I twisted around and found myself face-to-face with a beat-up shopping cart overflowing with bundles, bags, bits of carpet, plastic tarp, and assorted junk. Then a wrinkled face framed by flyaway, graying hair peered over the top and looked down at me. "You lost again or somethin'?"

I grinned up at her. "Hi, Lucy."

chapter 17

I scrambled to my feet. Lucy was dressed in yet more mis-matched layers of clothing, but her eyes seemed brighter. "You're looking better! Hope that means you're feeling better. How's the cough?"

She ignored my comment. "Put on your shoes."

"What?"

"Shoes. Put 'em on. Didn't your mama tell ya not to go bare-foot in the park? That's how ya cut your foot—an' I ain't got any more clean rags to spare mopping up blood after you."

"Yes, ma'am." I grinned, sat back down, and pulled on my nylons and flats. I patted the stone wall. "Sit down a minute. I'm glad to see you."

"Nah. Don't have time. I'm on my way somewhere."

I got to my feet again. "Where? Can I walk with you?"

"No, you can't. But turn around . . . now, see? Ya got a grass stain on the seat o' your good britches. Huh. Some people don't have the sense they was born with." She started off, pushing her cart ahead of her, shaking her head.

"Lucy! Wait." I ran after her. "When will I see you again?"

She shrugged and kept walking. "Maybe tomorrow. Maybe never. All depends."

"But I wanted to tell you something."

That got her. She stopped and cocked her head. "So tell me."

"I—I applied for a job at Manna House. I'm going to be there all week learning the ropes, then hopefully start next week. That's why I was saying 'thank You' to, uh, God."

Heavy-lidded eyes studied me. "What kinda job?"

"Program director. Planning activities for the residents." Why was I telling Lucy this? Why would she care? But I blathered on. "I used to do it for a senior center, but the shelter is a new situation for me. I could use some ideas."

She snorted. "Sorry. Ain't interested in bingo. Or shuffle-board. Big waste of time, if you ask me." She started off again.

"I *am* asking you, Lucy!" I called after her. "Think about it!"

She marched on as if she hadn't heard. Then she suddenly turned, marched back, and growled at me. "Now you git on home and take care o' that grass stain 'fore it sets. An' next time ya come to the beach, wear somethin' ain't goin' to get ruin't."

I chuckled at Lucy's bossiness all the way up the elevator to the top floor of Richmond Towers—but I took her advice, changed into my jeans, treated the stain on my slacks, and tossed them into the wash. I wanted to share the joke with Philip when he came home that night, but hesitated. Lucy's name might still be a sore point between us. Besides, he seemed distracted that evening, spending an hour on the phone, talking business.

"Is everything okay?" I asked when he finally got off the phone.

He flopped into an armchair that matched the curving couch. "I don't know. Maybe." He ran a hand through his hair. "Hope so."

I perched on the arm of the couch and waited . . . which paid off.

"It's this new account we bid on last week." He sighed in frustration. "Found out on the sly that another company is bidding for the contract. Big rep for underbidding on projects. Fenchel and I are trying to decide whether to lower our bid right now. We really need this deal. A big one."

"I'm sorry, Philip." I had a brief urge to say, *"Maybe we should pray about it."* But I was sure it would sound odd coming out of my mouth, as if I was trying to be superspiritual or something. "Anything I can do?"

He shook his head, sinking deeper into his thoughts. I left him alone, but fifteen minutes later brought him a cup of fresh coffee. I was pretty sure he'd be up half the night crunching numbers.

I never did hear him come to bed, and he was gone when I woke up. I still felt the urge to pray, but wasn't sure exactly for what. So I just prayed silently over my morning coffee. *"God, help Philip today. He'd really like to land this job to kick-start the new business."* I found myself adding, *"And I'd really like him to get this contract, so he won't be so tense and touchy."*

I set out for my second day at Manna House, but to my shock, the temperature had dropped thirty degrees overnight and it was misting again. I was definitely not dressed for cold and damp. When I got to the shelter at nine o'clock, I was shivering. And the hot water pot and coffee urn in the multipurpose room were cold and empty. *Well, I'm here to learn, so I might as well make the coffee.*

Wrapping my cold hands around a Styrofoam cup fifteen minutes later wasn't exactly down-home comfort, but at least the coffee was hot. The pungent smell seemed to draw people out of the woodwork, including Mabel and a woman I hadn't seen before, carrying a clipboard. White, medium height, a few extra pounds. Straight, light-brown hair hung just below her shoulders, bangs brushed to the side. Jeans, clogs, and a blue sweater. Not scary at all.

"Oh, good, you're here, Gabby." Mabel took the Styrofoam cup I handed to her. "I want you to meet Stephanie Cooper, our case manager. Stephanie, this is Gabby Fairbanks, who is applying for our new position of program director."

I shook Stephanie's hand. A nice grip. "You're also on the Manna House board, I've been told."

Stephanie laughed. "Yes, Estelle's housemate shanghaied me. Stu and I both work at DCFS. I'm glad to meet you, Gabby. We need some new blood around here. You're from Virginia, I hear?"

"Not if you asked my mother-in-law. I grew up in North Dakota, which cancels out the last fifteen years, I think."

Stephanie laughed again. "Now, that's an interesting vita. Wild West meets Old South."

I grinned. "Oil and water." I liked this woman.

"Sorry I can't talk more. I've got an appointment in a few minutes with a new guest who came in yesterday." She consulted her clipboard. "Naomi Jackson."

I nodded. "We've met."

"Really?" Stephanie looked at Mabel and then at me. "Say, would you like to sit in? It'd be good orientation. I'll have to ask her, of course."

Which is how I found myself in the TV room a few minutes later with Stephanie and the young woman who was still wearing her baseball cap, but not tapping. "Sure, fine. Whatever," she said, when Stephanie asked if she minded me sitting in. I parked myself in a corner and tried to be invisible as Stephanie got down to business. Fast.

"Naomi, we're here to help you any way we can. But to do that we need some help from you. Do you have a picture ID?"

A shake of the head. Stephanie wrote something down.

"When was your last TB test?"

"Can't remember . . . last year maybe?"

"Hm. All right. The nurse comes in tomorrow. You need to see her and get the test. No ifs, ands, or buts. Understood?"

Naomi nodded sullenly.

Stephanie handed her a couple of sheets stapled together. "These are the house rules. Read over them, and if there's anything you don't understand or have a question about, just ask. But let's go over some of the highlights, okay?"

Whew. As I listened, I realized I needed to know the rules too. *If you are assigned a bed, you must be here by 8 p.m. . . . all guests must have a physical and a mental health assessment within one week of being assigned a bed . . . must meet weekly with your case manager . . . must be actively working on goals as determined by your case manager . . . must take a shower daily . . . laundry is available on a sign-up basis . . . no profanity, no violence, no drugs, no smoking inside the building . . . personal belongings may be searched at any time . . . staff may conduct random drug tests . . .*

Stephanie set aside her copy of the rules. "What are your goals, Naomi? I don't mean way off in the future. I'm talking about this week. This month."

Naomi scrunched up her face. "Get a job so I can have my own money. And stay here till I can get my own place."

Stephanie leaned forward. "Naomi, we don't have time to play games here. Staff says you showed up here yesterday high on something. Amphetamines? The first question is: are you at a place where you want to stop?"

"Guess so."

I thought that answer would shoot the whole interview. Who was this Naomi person fooling? Even I could tell she wasn't ready to give up whatever her addiction was. But to my surprise, Stephanie's voice softened. "Naomi, I'm not here to judge you. But I'm not here to enable you either. If you can set some realistic goals for the next few weeks, and you make progress toward those goals, I'm willing to be here for you 24/7. You can call me any time you want—here's my cell number." She handed the young woman a card. "But first you need a plan. What are you going to do later today when you get a craving for those pills?"

The bill of the cap hid her eyes. "Try not to use."

"Wrong answer."

I half expected Naomi to walk out. But she seemed to reach deep somewhere, as if facing her own reality. A few seconds passed. She sighed. "Get into detox. Right away."

"That's right. I can help you with that. We'll try outpatient first, and you can stay here. If you can't handle that, then it'll have to be inpatient. You good with that?"

Naomi nodded.

"If you stay clean for two weeks, then we can work on getting you a job. But you'll need a picture ID. So . . . what's the plan?"

Naomi's mouth tipped into an almost-smile. "Get into detox. Get an ID."

"Good plan." Stephanie smiled. "I'm starting to hold you accountable as of right now. You and me, okay?"

The interview was over in thirty minutes. After Naomi left the room, Stephanie sat back and turned to me. "We'll see what happens in the next twenty-four hours. If she's still here by curfew tonight, we'll have a good chance of taking a few steps forward. But"—she shrugged—"it's up to her."

The days passed so fast, I almost felt dizzy by the end of the week. I dressed for the chilly weather on Wednesday, but by late afternoon the temp was back in the sixties and stayed there the next several days. Mr. Bentley teased me almost every morning on my way out. "Got your bathing suit? Umbrella? Snow boots? Might need 'em all before evening." At the shelter, I had the sneaking suspicion that Mabel was making sure I got a good feel for the place, because I ended up doing a bit of everything, from cleaning toilets to supervising the rec room after school— and somewhere in there, getting a chance to talk to some of the women in residence.

Like Carolyn. Gray cells popping beneath that brownish-gray ponytail. "Know what this place needs?" She had just whipped me at chess in thirty minutes, and I used to think I was pretty good. "Books. I like to read, but all they got here are a bunch of old magazines. And the Bible, of course. Heck, I cut my teeth on Dostoevsky."

Dostoevsky! She must have seen the shock on my face, because she grinned. "My ma fell for a door-to-door salesman selling Great Books. One gullible woman. Kicked him out but kept the books, which was fine by me."

I laughed and made a note. *Start a library. Maybe a book club?*

And Tina. The woman was big boned and carried her weight well, and she had a classic Latina face with golden skin. She'd taken the teenage Aida under her wing, and I saw her going over the house rules with the teenager, helping her with the English words.

"Tina, would you be interested in teaching an ESL class? English as a second language?"

"Who, me? A teacher?" But her eyes lit up.

I added another note. *Get basic ESL materials.*

Even Precious, who was a volunteer, not a resident, had hidden talents. She showed up three afternoons a week to supervise homework in the minimal after-school program, but I heard rhythmic music coming from the rec room and went to investigate. Precious had all five of the Manna House kids, ages six to eleven, on their feet, dancing in perfect rows and steps—stepping forward, back, to the side, half turn, do it again . . .

I clapped in the doorway.

"All right, back to the books!" Precious yelled, turning off the CD player. "We're busted!" The kids giggled and scurried back to their chairs around the single table. "Gets the blood goin' to their pea-brains—ain't that right?" She laughed and high-fived the eleven-year-old.

"That looked like a lot of fun. Why don't you teach it to everybody? You and the kids? For a Fun Night or something."

"For real?"

Another note. *Plan a Fun Night, with dancing and games.*

Thursday was another case management day for Stephanie Cooper, who showed up again in jeans—and I realized I hadn't seen Naomi Jackson since her meeting on Tuesday. I sidled up to

Stephanie in the lunch line. "What's happening with Naomi? Did she go to detox?"

Stephanie shook her head. "Walked out of here Tuesday, haven't seen her since."

"Oh no!" I'd felt a connection to Naomi, since I'd been the first one to meet her at the door, and I'd been hoping for the best.

"Just pray for her," Stephanie said. "She knows we're here. One of these days she'll be back. And she'll be ready to do business. But . . . it might get ugly between now and then. A lot of these young women are turning tricks for their drugs. She's going to need our prayers."

Pray for her. Funny. As soon as Stephanie said she'd skipped out, I assumed there was nothing Manna House could do until she came back. But these people actually prayed for the women who came to the door—whether they stayed at the shelter or not.

Another note. *Start a prayer list.* This one just for me.

On my way out the front door later that afternoon, Mabel called me back. "Oh, Gabby. Two of our board members you haven't met yet are going to drop in about lunchtime tomorrow. They'd like to meet you. Clyde Stevens is pastor of New Hope Missionary Baptist, and Liz Handley was—"

"Former director of Manna House. I know." I smiled. "I promise I'll be on my best behavior. What's for lunch?"

Mabel laughed. "Who knows? But Pastor Clyde has a weakness for macaroni and cheese and fried catfish, and Estelle knows it."

I walked toward the El smiling to myself. My first week at Manna House had almost come to an end. After tomorrow, hopefully I'd hear that I had the job. I was excited to get started, to sort through the ideas I'd been collecting and see which ones were viable.

Friday. Wasn't that the day Edesa Baxter led a Bible study in the morning? I smiled even broader. Tomorrow was going to be a good day . . .

The "William Tell Overture" erupted in my bag. I fished for the cell phone, flipped it open, and glanced at the caller ID. *Fairbanks, Philip.* I had a sudden ominous feeling. He'd been tight-lipped and silent most of the week, working late at the office or at home in the den, not wanting to be bothered. I'd given him a wide berth, not wanting the cloud over his head to rain on my parade. I almost let the call go to voice mail, but caught it on the fourth ring.

"Hello? Philip?"

"Gabby? Where are you?"

His voice was upbeat. My spirit inched upward a notch. "On my way home from work. Where are you?"

"Still at the office. But I've got great news. We sign the Robinson deal tomorrow morning, eleven o'clock!"

I squealed. "You got the contract! Oh, Philip, I'm so happy for you."

"You better believe it, Mop Top. That's why I'm calling. The Fenchels and Fairbanks are going to celebrate! How about that neat little bistro you took me to last week? Can you make a reservation for the four of us for lunch tomorrow?"

chapter 18

I stopped dead on the sidewalk. *Lunch?! Tomorrow? This can't be happening!* No way did I want to call Mabel and tell her I couldn't show up to meet the last two board members on Friday. My mind did a quick spin. "Ah . . . sounds great, Philip. But, uh, why not make it tomorrow night for dinner, make a real night of it?"

"What are you talking about?" Philip sounded irritated. "The signing is at eleven, Mona is bringing a bottle of champagne to the office to celebrate, and then what . . . we diddle our thumbs till six? Besides, the Fenchels have tickets to something or other tomorrow night. Just do it, Gabby. Make it one o'clock. Gotta go."

I flipped the phone closed and felt like throwing it. *Unbelievable!* I stalked into the Emerald City Coffee Shop near the El station and ordered coffee to calm my nerves. Thoughts collided like pinballs behind my eyes. Should I go back and talk to Mabel? What would it look like if she had to call the board members and tell them, sorry, our prospective program director can't make it? On the other hand, if I told Philip about my dilemma, he'd just use it as ammunition as to why this job at the shelter wasn't going to work out. All he needed was an excuse to be down on it.

"You want another, miss?" the owner called from behind the counter. I shook my head absently.

Weren't things supposed to fall into place when God was on board? Mabel seemed to think God had sent me to Manna House—and I was glad to accept her view of it, since the job seemed perfect for me, though I had to admit her take sounded a bit *hocus-pocus*. But if I missed showing up at the shelter tomorrow, my dependability rating might skydive before it'd even gotten off the ground.

Wait a minute. I corralled my thoughts into a neat little row. If Philip wanted a reservation at Bistro 110 for one o'clock, why couldn't I do both? Lunch at the shelter was usually noon, straight up. I'd go to the shelter in the morning, let Mabel know my little conflict, meet the reverends at twelve for half an hour, make my apologies, catch a cab at twelve thirty, and be at the restaurant before Philip and the Fenchels even arrived.

Perfect.

I settled back into the chair, downing the last of my coffee in its "tall" cardboard cup with the plastic sippy lid. Maybe God had a way of untangling these little *snafus* anyway.

Only when I was on the El, watching the wall of buildings and windows fly by, did a nagging thought step out of line. Philip had said Mona Fenchel was coming to the *office* with a bottle of champagne . . . did he expect me to be there for the signing too?

By the time I let myself into the penthouse, I was pretty sure I knew the answer. This was a big deal for Fairbanks and Fenchel, and I should be glad Philip wanted to include "the wives," shouldn't I? He and Henry could just go out to celebrate and come home with a hangover.

But, I argued with myself, kicking off my shoes and flopping onto our king-size bed, getting this job at the shelter was a big deal for me too. Maybe I should just tell my husband I had an appointment at noon, but I'd be at the bistro with bells on at one. Get it all out on the table. After all, there was no reason both things couldn't happen, right? Except . . . it was hard to reason with Philip once he decided things should happen in a certain way. He'd see it as making my petty agenda more important than his big moment. By wading straight into the water, I risked getting sucked in by the undertow that swept so many of our communications out to sea. If not setting off an actual tsunami.

Okay, maybe I wouldn't say anything, just do it and deal with the fallout later. After all, Philip didn't actually *say* he wanted me to come to the signing. Just asked me to make a reservation at that cute little bistro I'd taken him to before. Why not leave it at that?

I got off the bed. I'd feign innocence. Tonight, I'd raid the freezer—there should still be a package of king crab legs in there—make a lovely dinner, light the candles, rub all the tension from last week out of his neck. Tomorrow, I'd go to the shelter, meet the board members, show up for the celebration at the restaurant. And cross my fingers.

But first, I better make that reservation, or my name really would be mud.

Unlike most weekdays, Philip didn't dash out of the house at seven thirty the next morning. In fact, he was still there when

Camila arrived to clean at nine, trying to choose between his gray Armani suit, white shirt, and conservative maroon tie, or a tan suit with blue shirt and tan and brown striped tie.

I was glad for the interruption—anything to distract Philip from going over his plans for the day with me. We'd made it through dinner and the evening the night before, mostly because I kept asking questions at the table about the new job—a combination residential-office multiplex with more than one hundred one- to three-bedroom condos, twenty-five work studios, ten high-end shops on the first level, and underground parking. "Everything from the design to managing the construction, Gabby! Robinson Inc. is primarily an investment firm, putting up the money." Philip had happily picked his teeth with a toothpick after sucking out the meat from the last crab leg. Then he'd excused himself from the table and spent the next two hours on the phone.

I poked my head into the bedroom. "Camila's here, Philip. I'll get her started at the other end of the house. Mm, the tan and blue looks nice." I closed the bedroom door and steered Camila toward the living room. "Can you start up front? My husband is still dressing for an important day at work." I gave her an apologetic smile. "Sorry. We'll both be out of your way in a few minutes."

"*Sí*, no problem, Señora Fairbanks." Camila gave me a nervous smile. "But I have a favor to ask, *por favor*. Next Friday is Cinco de Mayo, fifth of May, a big celebration in my country. I would like to take the day off to be with my family . . . if that is okay with you and Señor Fairbanks?"

I tipped my head curiously. "Cinco de Mayo? What holiday is that, Camila?"

Camila must have taken my question as hesitation, because her words came out in a rush. "If it is a problem, I could make it up to you by coming to clean Thursday or Saturday after my regular—"

"No, no, it's fine." As little time as we spent in the penthouse, we could easily skip a week. I hoped it was okay with the cleaning service, but who cared. We were the employers, weren't we? "Tell me about this holiday—"

"What are you going to wear, Gabby?" Philip appeared in the archway between gallery and living room in the gray Armani. "How about that purple outfit I bought you?" He glanced at his watch. "Oh—gotta run. Don't be late, Gabby."

"Go on, go on, I'll be there." I pushed him out the door, at the same time pushing down the niggling suspicion we were talking about two different times. I leaned against the door and closed my eyes. The purple outfit. *Plum* would be the fashion word. A clingy, long-sleeved top with soft folds falling around the scoop neckline, and flowing pants that could pass for a long skirt. It was lovely . . . and completely wrong for my chestnut hair. Not to mention it would be totally out of place at the women's shelter.

But the purple outfit it would be. I'd have to shave off another five minutes to change in Mabel's office. And forget the El. I picked up the phone and dialed 01. "Mr. Bentley? Would you call a cab for me? . . . Twenty minutes would be fine."

I got to the shelter at ten wearing casual slacks (I decided against jeans today, even though most of the staff—except Mabel—dressed down) and carrying a bulging bag with the purple outfit and dressy shoes. Colorful prisms reflecting from the stained-glass windows on either side of the oak doors splashed over the tile floor of the entryway and decorated the walls. I drank in the colorful welcome. The sun was out. All should be well.

Mabel wasn't in her office, so I went hunting—and found her comforting a sniffling Edesa in the toddler playroom behind the multipurpose room. Gracie was on the floor, rocking on all fours, as if trying to get hands and knees coordinated for The Big Crawl.

"Oh. Excuse me." I started to back out of the room.

"No, no, you're just in time." Mabel waved me in. "I have an appointment soon, but I don't want to leave Edesa alone. She needs some help pulling herself together before leading the Bible study at ten thirty. Can you . . . ?"

"Of course." Except it was Mabel I needed to see, and she was disappearing down the hall. I turned my attention to the young mother. "What's wrong, honey?"

Edesa sank into a molded plastic chair, leaned over to place a squeaky toy in front of the baby, and then blew her nose into a well-used tissue. I fished in my bag and handed her an unused travel pack.

"I . . . I . . . I just got a call from our . . . our . . . social worker," she hiccoughed. "She says someone claiming to be *el papá del bebé* has come forward and . . . and . . . and wants to stop the adoption and take . . . take . . . take Gracie." A flood of fresh tears shook her body, and she buried her face in her hands.

"Oh, Edesa." I pulled over another chair and put my arm around her. I could only imagine how she must feel. "Oh, honey." I had a dozen questions—Who was he? Why was he only coming forward now? Where was he when the baby was born?—but I just hugged her to me and let her cry.

After a few minutes, Edesa blew her nose again and looked at me with a wry twist to her full lips. "And I'm supposed to—*hic*—lead a Bible study on trusting God this morning! Me! I'm a mess . . . and I don't have time to call Yada Yada."

She must have caught my funny look. "S-sorry. That's my prayer group." She hiccoughed again. "We meet every other week. I'll e-mail them later, and I know they'll shake heaven with their prayers. But I—*hic*—need prayer right now—and . . . and Josh doesn't even know. He has a test today, trying to test out of a class for next semester." Her dark eyes lifted and met mine. I'd hardly ever seen Edesa Baxter without a sparkle in her eyes, but even wet with tears, her eyes struck me as alive, honest, open—as though they were truly windows to her soul. "Will you pray with me, Gabby?"

"What?"

"Will you pray with me? And then, I hate to ask; but could you take care of Gracie for the next hour? Josh couldn't come today . . ."

"Of course." I meant, take care of Gracie. The Bible study only went to eleven thirty. But Edesa took my hand in both of hers, our light and dark fingers entwined, and she bowed her head. I realized she was waiting for me to pray.

I suddenly felt like an adolescent at my first Spring Fling, standing against the wall, terrified somebody would ask me to dance. And then someone did. And now was the moment of truth. "God . . ." I swallowed. I couldn't remember the last time I had prayed aloud. I used to pray, "Now I lay me down to sleep . . ." with the boys when they were small. But people around here didn't pray memorized prayers. They just talked to God.

I tried again. "God, Edesa's pretty broken up over this news about a relative showing up. But if anyone I know trusts You, God, it's Josh and Edesa. And they love this baby so much . . ." I stumbled on for a few more sentences and then said, "Amen."

Edesa gave me a hug. "Thank you so much, Gabby. I . . ." She grinned shyly. "I'm so glad you're going to work here. Nobody's married on staff except me. It will be *muy bueno* to have someone around who's been married a while to talk to about . . . well, you know." She grabbed her Bible. "Gotta go. Bye, Gracie, honey." She blew the baby a kiss and was gone.

My skin prickled. Me? Have marriage advice for those two lovebirds? Fat chance. Though . . . once upon a time, Philip and I were in love too. Smiles and glances across the room, hilarious pillow fights, finding a single rose on my pillow. One time I'd talked him into driving to Virginia Beach on the spur of the moment—at ten at night!—just to wade in the ocean by moonlight. He had laughed and told me I was good for him, good for their "proper" Southern family. I still remembered his strong arms around me as the tide swirled around our feet, his fingers in my "mop top" and his kisses soft on my lips, my eyes, my hair.

But that was then. This was now . . .

Now. *Yikes*. I still needed to find Mabel and tell her about my crunch. I scooped up the eight-month-old and cuddled her on my hip, smelling the softness of her dark hair as I glanced at the clock on the wall.

Ten forty. The signing at Fairbanks and Fenchel was in twenty minutes.

Just to be safe, I fished for my cell phone and turned it off.

chapter 19

Except Mabel was not to be found. "Oh, she went out," Angela informed me from her cubicle. "Had a hair appointment or something. Taking an early lunch."

I felt like rolling my eyes. Flexible schedules was right! Was she even going to be here when the two board members came? What if she came sauntering in at twelve forty, thinking there was no big rush for this meeting with the "reverends"? After all, she didn't know I had to leave at twelve thirty. But scooting out when she expected me to be here would be worse than telling her I couldn't make it at all.

Gracie started to squirm and squeal, annoyed at my inattention. I jiggled her in my arms and made absentminded cooing noises as I paced around the foyer, wondering what to do. Too late to make the eleven o'clock signing at Philip's office. No one here knew about the split-second timing needed to enable me to get to my second rendezvous . . . *Drat!* My coy conniving had lit a fuse burning at both ends, and I'd be apologizing for the mess in two directions.

Dear God, if I haven't totally blown it, I could use some help—"Ouch!"

Gracie had grabbed a handful of my hair. She kept her grip at my outburst, but the rest of her body pulled back in my arms, and the giggle on her face slid down to a quavering pout of her bottom lip.

"Aw, sweetheart, it's all right." Suddenly the baby in my arms came into focus. This little girl was oblivious of the storm swirling around her—her birth mother dead, a fight brewing between her loving foster parents and the supposed father over her adoption. And here I was, acting as if juggling my tight schedule was the linchpin of a Middle East peace proposal. And nothing had even gone wrong yet! I was getting carried away, praying about such trivial stuff.

"Come on, Gracie," I whispered in the baby's ear. "Let's go play. But we gotta be quiet, 'cause Mommy's leading the Bible study." I squeezed through the double doors and was heading quietly toward the toddler playroom when the lilt of Edesa's accent from the circle of chairs on the other side of the multipurpose room became actual words . . .

"The psalmist said, 'When I am afraid, I will trust in God.' And then, in the same psalm, he turned it around and said, 'I trust in God, why do I need to be afraid?' And do you know what, *mis amigas*? Those are God's words to *me* today!" Edesa caught sight of Gracie and me slinking out of sight and blew a little kiss. "Because today I learned there is a big problem in the way of Gracie's adoption . . ." Her voice caught, but she blinked, smiled, and went on. "So I have to admit, *sí*, I am *asustada*, but I will trust in God."

The women slouching in the sloppy circle of chairs and old

couches seemed to straighten, lean forward. A few murmurs reached my ears, and then a voice spoke up belonging to Diane, with the big Afro. "An' if you trust in God, you don' *need* to be afraid, girl. We gon' keep you covered in prayers, so we got your back, 'Desa. Know what I'm sayin'?"

Nods and murmurs of "Got that right."

I slipped out of the room with Gracie, my eyes blurry with sudden tears. Destitute women without homes and family, some separated from *their* children, praying for one of the volunteers and her child . . .

Whew. Manna House was certainly an upside-down place. In fact, maybe God heard my piddly prayer after all, because Rev. Liz Handley popped in at eleven thirty as the Bible study was breaking up—all five-feet-two of her, a stocky white woman in her sixties, wire-rimmed glasses, salt-and-pepper hair cropped so short it might have passed military muster. As I returned Gracie to her foster mom, several of the residents gave "Reverend Liz" big hugs, and they laughed when she blustered, "Where's Estelle? I hope she's cooking."

Mabel still hadn't shown up, so I stuck out my hand. "I've been looking forward to meeting you, Reverend Handley. I'm Gabby Fairbanks, hopefully the new program director."

"Liz is fine, Gabby." The former director of Manna House cocked her head. "So you want to get mixed up with this crew?" She laughed and we sat.

We chatted about the typical stuff—where I was from, past experience, how I stumbled upon Manna House. She seemed genuinely interested in some of my ideas for life enrichment— setting up a library, getting ESL materials, field trips to museums, even the occasional Fun Night for starters. "But I'm so new to

Chicago, I'm not sure how to find resource people, or even resource materials." I hoped my confession wouldn't disqualify me.

"You'll learn. Start with putting the word out to the board, the staff, and the volunteers. We all go to different churches. Who knows what we can come up with!" She peered over her wire frames. "And don't forget to look under your nose, Gabby. Some of these residents have talents and connections you wouldn't believe. Talk to them. Find out what they like to do."

"I can do nails!" Hannah the Bored popped her head up over the arm of a nearby chair and waggled her long, purple nails.

I gave her a smile—but lowered my voice. Why were we having this conversation in the multipurpose room, anyway? "But . . . aren't the residents here temporarily? I mean, people like Lucy Tucker come and go like will-o'-the-wisps. Others stay here, what—a few weeks at most?"

Liz shrugged. "Some. But many stay the full ninety days allowed. And some, when they get on their feet, come back to volunteer. Look at Precious and Estelle. Both were residents at Manna House before the fire, and now look at them. Giving back. I'd start with them. Pick their brains for ideas too—oh, hey, Angela. What's up?"

The receptionist appeared waving a couple of sticky notes. "Sorry to interrupt, but Mabel just came in, said to tell you she'd be here in a minute. And Pastor Stevens's secretary called. He can't make lunch today because a teenager in their neighborhood got shot this morning—he's with the family. Oh, and there's a taxi waiting outside for you, Mrs. Fairbanks."

I leaped up. "Oh no! What time is it?" I glanced at my watch . . . 12:32! How had the time gotten away from me? "Tell him to wait! I need five minutes." I turned to Rev. Liz and blurted out

that I needed to run, I was so glad to meet her, and please let
Mabel Turner know I'd explain later . . . and suddenly realized I
had no idea where I'd left my bag with the purple outfit.

By the time I found my bag in the toddler playroom, wiggled
into my outfit in a toilet stall and freshened my makeup, I'd kept
the taxi waiting ten minutes—with the ticker ticking. And by the
time the taxi pulled up in front of Bistro 110, it was five after.

Late.

But I put on a brave face and breezed into the restaurant. No
familiar faces waiting to be seated. I started to relax. Maybe they
weren't here yet.

"Name please?" The maître d' looked at me inquiringly.

"Fairbanks, party of four, one o'clock?"

"Oh yes. Come this way, please."

My chest tightened. They were already seated! They even
had drinks and a bread basket. Henry Fenchel leaped up as I
approached the table for four tucked in a front corner with windows. "Gabrielle! Now this party can get started." Philip's partner
gave me a flirty grin and pulled out the empty chair for me.

No such grin from Philip. My husband took a long drag from
a stein of beer and leveled a long gaze at me over the top.

I'd rehearsed a little speech in the taxi. *"So sorry I'm late . . .
had a meeting with the board at my new job . . . you know how that
goes!"* But a glance at Mona Fenchel's simpering face changed my
mind. I was not going to grovel in front of this woman for only
being five minutes late.

Instead I laughed. "You won't believe what I had to do to get
here! Had a meeting with the board this morning at my new

job—had to practically walk out. But I told them this was important." I turned a bright look on my husband. "How did the
signing go? I want to hear all about it!—oh. Waiter? Can I have a
lemonade please?"

Philip still held me with his gaze. "You'd know how it went if
you'd been there, Gabrielle."

"If I'd—?" I managed to look astonished. "Honey, you didn't
say anything about coming to the signing. Just asked me to make
a lunch reservation for one o'clock to celebrate." I made a puppy-
dog face. "Oh, dear. I'm sorry . . . one of those communication
snafus." I turned to Henry and Mona. "You two never have those,
right?"

Henry guffawed. "Never. Ha-ha." He slapped Philip on the
shoulder. "See? I told you it was just a mix-up. A little *snafu*, the
lady said. Heh-heh. I like that. Besides . . ." He winked at me.
"Mona made sure your glass of champagne didn't go to waste.
Ha-ha-ha."

Mona Fenchel rolled her eyes. "Oh, pipe down, Henry." She
took a sip of her double martini. "You didn't miss much, Gabrielle.
Boring, actually. The bigwigs from Robinson wanted some last-
minute changes to the contract, so I had to sit around for forty
minutes while they argued, with nothing to do in that—how do I
say it kindly?—*provincial* waiting room. So . . . suburban. And not
even one magazine to read." She shook her head at the offense to
her sensibilities.

I couldn't believe it. Mona Fenchel had unwittingly let me off
the hook. But I turned to my husband. "Changes to the contract?"
My concern was genuine. "Is everything all right?"

Philip shrugged. "Just last-minute nonsense was all."

"Don't you believe it, Gabby." Henry shook a finger at me.

"Philip, here—he's the man. Philip refused to budge on the main points, and they backed down." He raised his stein of beer. "Here's to Philip. He saved our hides."

My lemonade had arrived. We each hefted our glasses in acknowledgment. I could tell Philip was starting to thaw. I got brave and laid my hand on his arm. "So everything's okay? You signed the deal?"

He nodded and broke into a smile. My heart squeezed as the tension evaporated. Gosh, he really was handsome.

"I'm so glad, honey." And I was. Very, very glad. I lifted my glass again. "Here's to Fenchel and Fairbanks!"

My husband stiffened. Three pairs of eyes stared at me. Philip paled. Then Henry threw back his head and guffawed. "'*Fenchel and Fairbanks*' . . . I like that. Yes, indeed. I like that!"

chapter 20

My face heated like a hot flash. Never had I so desperately wished a hole would open up and swallow me. *"Fenchel and Fairbanks"* . . . How could I have turned the names around like that?! In front of my husband! Worse, in front of my husband *and* the Fenchels!

Henry would never let Philip forget it. Worse, Mona would probably never let Henry forget it. *"You jerk! I told you not to let Philip bully you into putting the Fairbanks name first! Well, if Gabby Fairbanks can call it Fenchel and Fairbanks, so can I!"*

My tongue felt like cotton candy. I couldn't look at Philip. I knew my husband saw me as a traitor . . . and I felt like one too. *Oh God,* I moaned inwardly. *If only You'd rewind the last few minutes and let me do them over.*

Huh. While I was begging, might as well rewind the past twenty-four hours and take another shot.

The waiter—that God-sent apparition in black pants, white shirt, and black tie—penetrated my misery with his notepad. "How are you folks doing? Ready to order?"

I grabbed the menu, but the words swam before my eyes. I heard Henry order the bistro steak and *frites*. Mona went for the baked artichoke and arugula chicken salad. Philip was forced to speak. "Shrimp cocktail. Spinach salad. The salmon." He flipped the menu closed like a snap judgment.

I'd lost my appetite. "Just the quiche, thank you."

Somehow we made it through the "celebration lunch." Henry tackled his steak and fries with concentrated attention. Philip drank too much and avoided talking to me. Mona Fenchel dripped sweetness into the chasm. "I didn't know you started a job, Gabby. Can you tell us what you're doing, or is it a deep, dark secret?" She simpered at me over a second double martini.

I did not want to talk about Manna House after my faux pas. It might feel like sticking Philip's nose in it. So I mumbled something about doing a program for a nonprofit and let it go at that.

But Mona had the subject in her teeth. "And what nonprofit is that, dear?"

I counted to ten while hiding behind a long glug of lemonade. "Manna House. A shelter for homeless women."

"Well." I could feel Mona's pitying eyes on me. "That's sweet."

Philip and I walked to the car in total silence. As the doors closed and the locks clicked, I knew I needed to say something.

"Honey, I am so sorry."

He started the car and revved the engine like a sixteen-year-old.

"I know I put my foot in my mouth, Philip, but it was totally unintentional. I'm so embarrassed."

"Whatever." Philip pulled into traffic, stone-faced.

I plunged on. "When I realized what I'd done, I didn't know how to make it right! It was so awkward. I was afraid saying something would just make it worse. Give it more attention than it deserved. I . . . I was hoping it'd just blow over."

Philip snorted. "Oh, right. Just blow over." He swiveled his head toward me, eyes dagger slits, pinning me to the passenger side door. "Awkward for you? What about me, Gabby? You know Fenchel will goad me about this, my own wife putting his name first—as if you were disagreeing about the decision to name the company Fairbanks and Fenchel."

A horn honked. Philip jerked his eyes back to traffic, hit the steering wheel with his hand, and cussed out the other car. Or maybe me.

"I'm . . . I'm really sorry, Philip."

Silence stuffed the car like an inflated air bag the rest of the way to Richmond Towers. And the rest of the weekend passed pretty much the same way . . . two bodies taking up physical space in the same condo, but not *sharing* it in any real sense. We went through the motions of Saturday—calling the boys at separate times, Philip talking to his mother in the den, me running clothes through the laundry, shopping for groceries at Dominick's a few blocks away, Philip taking the Lexus for an oil change.

Sunday was much the same. Gray clouds had dampened the climate outside, as well as in. Philip went for a run between sprinkles, came home, showered, went out again for hours, and then came home and holed up in the den.

I thought I might scream if I had to stay inside this tomb another hour. But where could I go? The on-again, off-again drizzle made a walk along the lake a soggy prospect. I didn't have anyone to talk to, to vent, to let off steam. Even Mr. Bentley was off duty until Monday.

As the hands on the grandfather clock inched toward four o'clock, my spirit lifted. The Sunday evening worship at Manna House . . . I'd go there, just to have *somewhere* to go. But when I called the shelter, a voice I didn't recognize picked up, then yelled to someone else, "Lady wants to know if there's a church service here tonight! . . . Oh, yeah. Okay." The voice came back on the phone. "Sorry, it's the fifth Sunday this month. They ain't having nothin' tonight."

I slammed the phone into the charger, pulled my hoodie and a windbreaker out of the closet, and headed for the elevator. Rain or no rain, I had to get out of here!

Lake Michigan was calm in spite of the gloomy day. I walked along the jogging path, hands jammed in the pockets of my windbreaker, letting built-up tears mix with the light rain on my face. "Oh, God . . ."

My moan escaped out loud. Well, so what? I pretty much had the path to myself, save for the occasional die-hard biker zipping around puddles at breakneck speed. "God, what am I going to do? I really let Philip down! I tried to tell him I'm sorry, but . . . I don't know how to fix it! I can't live with his mad forever. Help me, please."

I'd reached a stretch of large boulders creating a retaining wall between lake and park. Carefully climbing up the slick rocks, I stood huddled inside my hoodie and windbreaker, listening as the sprawling lake licked gently at the craggy rocks.

"*When I am afraid, I will trust in God . . . I trust in God, why do I need to be afraid?*"

Where did *that* thought come from? Oh, yeah. Edesa's Bible

study at the shelter Friday morning. And she had bigger troubles than I did. If she could trust God under the threat of losing little Gracie, could I trust God to take care of this mess with Philip?

I snorted. Looked like it was my only option.

"... *why do I need to be afraid?*"

Exactly! If Philip wanted to sulk, well, let him. I blew it. I said I was sorry—really sorry. What more could I do?

Let God handle it. If He could.

Philip took himself off to work early Monday morning, much to my relief. The weekend from hell was over—I hoped. The TV weather guy said it was still drizzly, but temperatures were supposed to climb back into the seventies this week.

Perfect for the month of May. For some reason, turning the kitchen calendar to a new month made me feel positively giddy. Today I would know if I had the job or not . . . the sun was bound to come out . . . and in three and a half weeks we'd drive to Virginia to pick up P.J. and Paul. "And if I have anything to say about it," I growled at the mirror in the gallery as I headed for the front door, "they aren't going back either!"

The African-American doorman was back at his post as I came through the main lobby. "You can relax, Mr. Bentley," I sang out, patting the large tote bag over my shoulder. "I've got an umbrella."

"*Humph.*" The bald-headed gentleman kept turning pages of the *Sun-Times*. "One of those itty-bitty collapsible things? How's that supposed to keep you dry if a thunderstorm rolls through?"

I laughed. "That's what I like about you, Mr. Bentley. You care what happens to me even if nobody else does."

He looked up sharply. My face reddened, and I quickened my step. "Have a good day," I called back, disappearing through the revolving doors that spit me out on the Sheridan Road side. *I'll be answering questions about that if I'm not careful.*

The commute by El was beginning to feel familiar. I even recognized faces on the El platform. Businessmen and smart-suited women of assorted hues carried briefcases, newspapers, and cell phones. A tall young woman with Caribbean good looks could, I decided, be a model. A short, round—okay, fat—woman with a babushka always lugged three or four plastic bags, puffing up the stairs to the platform one step at a time. I nodded and said hello to anyone standing nearby and usually got a nod or hello in return—except for the under-thirty-year-olds, who all had iPod buds in their ears.

Today I sat next to the babushka—well, she sat down next to *me* with a *whoomph*. I gave her a smile. She pulled a transit schedule out of her bag and fanned her face. "In ze old country," she said with a heavy accent, maybe Russian, "ze trains stay on ze ground. I tell you, *dyevushka*, those stairs will be killing me one day."

I didn't have time to find out where she was going at this time each day, because by the time she arranged her bags, accompanied by several *oomphs* and wheezes, the train was rolling into the Sheridan El Station.

"Hi, Mrs. Fairbanks—I mean, Gabby!" In the receptionist's cubby, Angela tossed her black, silky mane off her face and pointed at Mabel Turner's door. "Mabel said to come on in when you got here."

Uh-oh. I'd meant to call Mabel on Friday and tell her where I'd disappeared to! And here it was Monday, and she had no idea where I had gone in such a hurry.

Might as well face the music. I knocked, opened the door, and peeked in. Mabel had the phone to her ear, but she motioned me in and held up a finger. I sat in the chair across the desk from her, feeling as if I'd been called to the principal's office. A moment later, the finger came down, and the phone returned to its cradle. She looked at me, puzzled. "What happened on Friday, Gabby? Liz Handley said you went running out to a taxi after a quick change to a fancy purple outfit. And you'd call to explain."

Once again my face heated, and the tops of my ears burned. "Oh, Mabel, I am so sorry I didn't call. Philip and I had a major meltdown—well, I guess more like a deep freeze. And I was so busy navigating the icebergs, I totally forgot to call." I suddenly teared up. "Seems like all I've done the past few days is apologize."

Mabel handed me a tissue . . . so I blew my nose and started at the beginning with Philip's phone call Thursday, just after I'd left Manna House. "Guess I handled the whole thing badly. I should have called you right away to explain my dilemma, not try to juggle things on my own." I wagged my head. "I let everybody down, didn't I? My husband, you, Reverend Handley . . ."

"Gabby Fairbanks, next time you get yourself in a pickle and need somebody to talk to, *call me.* Here's my card with my cell phone." She pushed a business card across the desk. "Day or night. I'm serious."

I looked at the card stupidly. "Does that mean . . . you haven't given up on me yet?"

A tiny grin tipped the corners of her mouth. "Honey, if we gave up on people that easily, we'd be in the wrong business. Besides, Liz Handley took a liking to you. And she may be the *former* director, but around here, what Liz says carries a lot of weight. And she told me, 'Hire that woman, Mabel. Don't let her get away.'"

Mabel held out her hand to shake mine. "So congratulations, Mrs. Fairbanks. Welcome to the Manna House staff." Then she waved me out. "Now, go find the office Josh Baxter set up for you off the dining room downstairs."

chapter 21

In a daze, I walked downstairs to the lower level. A couple of the shelter residents were still in the kitchen, cleaning up after breakfast. I recognized Diane—her big Afro was hard to miss—and waved hello. Carolyn, hairnet askew, ponytail sticking out the back, was wiping down tables. I stood uncertainly in the dining area. *Office? What office?*

"Hear you're movin' in." Carolyn grinned at me. "They put you in the broom closet." She snickered and pointed toward a door standing slightly ajar near the stairway, then squirted disinfectant on yet another table.

A sheet of orange construction paper was taped to the door. In childish bubble letters, it said Ms. Gabby's Office. I pushed the door open wider. The room was dark, no window. I pawed around for a light switch and clicked it on . . . and caught my breath. On my left, a lush bouquet of spring flowers—irises, tulips, and daffodils—sat on an ancient wooden desk in the tiny room. (Had it really been a broom closet? Big broom closet.

Small office!) Next to the bouquet, a computer monitor blinked at me, hiding a simple laser jet printer. Keyboard and mouse pad were in place, as was a padded office chair pushed into the chair well. A phone (my own phone!), a legal pad, and several pens had been arranged neatly to one side. There was just enough room beside the desk for another chair and . . . that was it.

"Look behind the door!" Carolyn yelled behind me. "I didn't help lug that thing in here for nuthin'!"

I peeked around the door. A beat-up file cabinet with four file drawers stood against the other wall, along with a wastebasket. On top of the file cabinet sat two boxes, one marked "Hanging Files" and the other "File Folders."

A lump caught in my throat. Josh Baxter had set up this office for me over the weekend? Not just Josh, either, if he rounded up Carolyn—and probably others—to help him move the stuff in. And the computer . . . I sat down at the desk and manipulated the mouse. Instantly a background of the Chicago skyline at night filled the screen, along with program icons—Microsoft Word, Internet, e-mail, dictionary, streets and maps, even a Bible search icon.

"Go on, try it out." Carolyn had leaned into the doorway. "Mr. Josh was here all day Saturday programmin' that thing. Signed you up for e-mail an' everything."

It was true. When I clicked on e-mail, my name came up, and several e-mails popped into the in-box. My eyes blurred as I read Mabel Turner's welcome *("We praise God for sending you!")*, Josh Baxter's helpful advice *("Don't forget to store our e-mail addys in your address list so you can contact us")*, and Edesa's encouragement *("Check out Proverbs 3:5–6")*.

Oh, great. She's making sure I dig out my Bible.

I had to laugh at Liz Handley's e-mail. *"Welcome to the broom closet, Gabby Fairbanks! My office was in a broom closet, too, before the place burned down. Hopefully nothing that drastic has to happen before you get a window. 'Beauty for ashes,' you know. On behalf of the Manna House board, welcome!"*

I sat at the desk a long time, staring at the delicate bouquet of flowers and sorting through my jumbled feelings. The Manna House staff, and even some of the residents, had been fixing up this office and getting me "operational" this weekend, while I'd been sitting up in my luxury penthouse surrounded by silence, being punished for all my sins. Even though I hadn't called Mabel to work out my dilemma . . . even though I'd run out on Rev. Handley with no explanation . . . even though I hadn't called Mabel afterward to explain, like I'd said I would . . . what did they do?

They gave me flowers.

It took me close to an hour to get past being blubbery and able to start thinking critically about my new job. I pulled the legal pad close and began to scribble notes. Recreational needs for homeless women were certainly different than for the residents of the retirement center where I'd worked back in Virginia. The elderly needed fun and stimulation to keep their minds and bodies active. But homeless women needed life skills, an expanded vision of what life could be beyond the streets, as well as stimulating activities to fill listless hours.

I feverishly jotted down every idea that came to me—*budgeting, etiquette, cooking, dressing for success, word games, ESL (Tina?), Fun Nights/dancing (Precious?), book club (Carolyn?), making jewelry (other crafts?)* . . . I paused, then wrote: *literacy? GED classes?*

Finally I put down my pen. Maybe I was getting out of my

depth. I was a recreational therapist, not an educator. Still, my title was "Program Director," not "Recreation." And a variety of educational classes certainly seemed needed. But . . . I should back up. What did *Mabel and the board* expect of me? So far, they'd left me on my own to just "get acquainted." But I needed to set goals, construct a balanced program, find resources . . . Good grief, did I even have a budget?

I flipped to a new page on the legal pad and wrote: *(1) Meet with Mabel! Job description? Responsibilities? Accountability? Budget? . . .*

A knock on the door made me jump. A brown face, damp with perspiration beneath a puffy hairnet, peeked in. "Door ain't locked, you know. You can come out and eat lunch now. We don't do room service." Estelle smirked at me and disappeared.

Sure enough, I heard the clatter of aluminum pans and plastic glasses, and the chatter of women moving through the serving line. I'd been oblivious to time passing. As I came out, Mabel was already sitting at a table with a few of the "day residents" who didn't have jobs or job prospects. But she stood up and started clapping, urging everyone around her to do the same. "Cheers to our new program director, Gabby Fairbanks!"

Several of the women clapped or waved. Back in the kitchen, Estelle banged on the bottom of a pot with a metal spoon. My face surely turned beet red, because I could feel my ears burning. "So if you've got ideas for activities we need here at Manna House," Mabel added, "see Gabby."

From a corner of the room, a familiar voice growled, "Already told her we didn't need no shuffleboard or bingo 'round here—hey, Estelle! You got any more of that 'noodle surprise' over there?"

Lucy. Swathed in the usual layers of sweaters, knit tops, and cotton blouses, and a new knit hat in purple yarn jammed on her head. I wanted to laugh. If Lucy was here, it must be raining. Well, good. I wouldn't have to chase all over the park to find her.

"Thanks, everybody. I'm excited to join the staff here at Manna House." I grabbed Mabel in a hug before she could sit down again. "Thanks so much for the flowers," I whispered in her ear. "You have no idea what they mean to me." Then I hustled to the counter for my own plate of "noodle surprise" and sat down next to Lucy.

"Nice hat, Lucy. Looks new." I meant it. The hat was stylish, with a slightly wavy knitted brim and a clever rose made of yarn on one side. Even on Lucy's grizzled head, it lent a certain charm.

"*Humph.* Estelle made it. Glad ya like it."

I glanced across the room at Estelle, still behind the counter. That's right. The first time I'd met her, Estelle had been knitting. I'd thought it was probably your basic long scarf—every beginner's first project. But this hat was the cat's meow. *Hmm . . .*

Mabel and I got our meeting, and to my relief, she had already worked on a job description and list of responsibilities. I was happy to see that the list was specific without being limiting: *"Assess resident activity needs through questionnaires and personal interviews" . . . "Establish attainable goals for weekly and monthly activities" . . . "Establish budget needs within overall operating budget" . . . "Oversee interpersonal interactions during group activities" . . . "Educate residents in resources in the larger community" . . .*

I was so excited about my new job, I was tempted to stay into the evening and meet the women who were usually out during the day, maybe even try a brainstorming session to get their ideas.

Decided against it. Staying late today probably wasn't the

wisest thing. I still had fences to mend at home and didn't want to build them higher. Besides, I should probably work on a questionnaire and talk personally to staff and residents before throwing the discussion wide open.

As I walked into Richmond Towers at four thirty, I tried to keep Edesa's psalm that had encouraged me yesterday in focus. *"When I am afraid, I will trust in God . . . I trust in God, why do I need to be afraid?"* "That's right, Gabby," I murmured to myself. "You don't have to be afraid. You made a mistake, you apologized, what Philip does with it is his problem—"

"Evening, Mrs. Fairbanks." Mr. Bentley tipped his cap at me with a wink. "You always talk to yourself like that? I'm thinking you've been hanging around our friend the bag lady too often."

"Sorry about that, Mr. Bentley. I was thinking out loud . . . but I've got good news. I've been hired by the Manna House Women's Shelter as their new program director. I even have an office!" I had to grin. "Used to be a broom closet."

He laughed. "Well, congratulations. Have to admit, not too many of the residents of Richmond Towers have such a, uh, colorful job." He winked again.

"That's exactly what I like about it, Mr. Bentley!" I could feel the excitement returning to my voice. "Homeless people on the streets seem so colorless, so . . . gray. Even our friend Lucy—you remember, the bag lady. But at the Manna House shelter, there's so much"—I searched for words—"so much *life*, so much *color*."

Even as I said it, I realized how true it was. Not just the multicolored population of staff and residents, but something indefinable I'd felt the first time I'd walked through the double oak doors. And suddenly I knew what it was . . .

"The color of hope, I guess."

chapter 22

Philip usually got home around six thirty, which gave me a couple of hours to fix supper. I pounced on the two sirloin steaks in the freezer and popped them into the microwave to defrost. *Perfect.* "The way to a man's heart is through his stomach," so they say—whoever "they" are. I snickered at the dorky cliché as I mixed a simple olive-oil-and-red-wine-vinegar marinade. "But a good steak dinner can't hurt—"

I stopped, holding in midair the fork I was using to tenderize the steaks. *Good grief, Mr. Bentley is right. I am talking to myself.* I blew a stray curl off my forehead. I needed a dog. Or a cat. Something to talk to.

My whole chest tightened. No, I needed my children home. With me. And a husband who didn't shut me out.

At six forty I heard the key in the front door and tensed. Philip called out from the gallery, "Smells good! What's for dinner?"

I slowly let out my breath. *Score one for the dorky cliché.* I turned and smiled as my husband came into the kitchen, loosening his tie. "Marinated steak," I said. "Roasted potatoes with garlic and rosemary. And some fresh veggies. Have a good day?"

"Mm-hm. Got another promising prospect, a smaller job, but this way we won't be putting all our eggs in one basket." He leaned his backside against the counter and popped a cherry tomato into his mouth. "You?"

I blinked. Philip was asking about my day? Like a normal conversation? Had God heard my prayer?—though it hadn't even been a prayer, just an ache. I took Philip's cue and relaxed against the counter, too, snagging a strip of raw red pepper from the veggie plate. "Yes, a very good day. In fact, Manna House offered me the job. They even gave me an office." I didn't mention it had a former life as a broom closet. "I have a new e-mail to give you, and a work phone number—though my cell is still the best way to reach me."

He pursed his lips, as if considering my news, then shrugged. "Okay. Glad it worked out, I guess. Just . . ."

I touched his arm. "I know. Philip, I'm really sorry about Friday. I'll try not to let this job interfere with things that are important to you."

"Important to *us*, Gabby. Us! See? That's what upset me on Friday. You didn't show for the signing, you showed up late at the restaurant . . . and then you—you flippantly rearranged the name of our company. That hurt." His voice held an edge. "Are you on my side, or aren't you?"

No, no . . . I couldn't let this conversation slip back into the chasm between us. But I heard something new. He was hurt. Hurt was different than mad. I grasped at it. "I am on your side, Philip. I was incredibly thoughtless. And that's what I'm sorry for. That I hurt you. Will you forgive me?"

My words hung in the air between us. Then he nodded. "Yeah, well . . ." He pushed off from the counter. "Do I have time to change before dinner?"

"Steak will take ten minutes max!" I called after him, turning the oven to Broil. While I waited on the steak, I squeezed my eyes shut. "God," I whispered, aware I was talking out loud again, but wanting to do more than just a vague "thought prayer." "God, thank You. For my job. And for Philip forgiving me." Well, he had, hadn't he? Not in so many words, but . . . "And, God, please help this to be a new day for us."

I woke early the next morning before Philip and wandered into the front room, my mind already spinning with program ideas for Manna House . . . and caught my breath. A stunning sunrise over Lake Michigan filled the wraparound windows. Feathery cirrus clouds flung streamers of brilliant pink fluff across the sky, as though a flamingo were shedding its winter down. Lake Michigan, smooth and glassy, captured a mirror image of the brilliant sky.

Oh my. Between rainy days and my fear of heights, I'd been keeping the drapes pulled in the front room. But the TV weatherman on the nightly news had said the next several days would be in the low seventies and mostly sunny. I might have to give the view from up here another chance.

Philip actually ate the eggs I scrambled for him and pecked me on the cheek before heading out the front door. I smiled as I loaded the dishwasher and got ready for my own exit. Maybe things *would* be different now that the business was getting a toehold here in Chicago.

At the front door I paused. My Bible . . . where *was* it? I'd been meaning to look up the verses Edesa had put in her e-mail. Most of the boxes had been unpacked. Maybe it was with the books, most of which were in Philip's den. It took me five minutes to find it, but there it was, with *Gabrielle Shepherd* stamped in gold letters on the brown leather cover.

I sniffed—the cover still had a leathery smell—and opened it to the presentation page. *"To Gabrielle, our angel . . . on your graduation from high school. Love, Mom and Dad."* On the facing page, my mother had written in her beautiful script: *"Only one life, it will soon be past. Only what's done for Christ will last."*

I shut the Bible and stuck it in my bag. Didn't really want to think about Mom's sweet little proverb right now. Life—at least for me—had turned out to be a little more complicated. After all, it hadn't been *my* plan to be divorced after only two years by my sweet-talking-youth-group-leader-supposedly-Christian husband, had it?! And my second marriage to Philip had seemed more honest at the time. Just enough religion to keep my foot in the church door, but without all the hypocrisy.

I hadn't counted on the big hole in my life, though.

Forty minutes later, I rang the bell at Manna House—9:00 a.m. on the button—signed my name on the in-and-out log, and smiled a greeting at the handful of residents lounging around the multipurpose room before heading downstairs. I unlocked the broom closet and flipped on the light. Flowers, computer, legal pad—everything was just as I had left it. Too bad about not having a window. The prisms of sunshine coming through the stained glass in the foyer upstairs had been a delightful greeting. But I was soon so absorbed in creating a questionnaire for the board, staff, and volunteers, I wouldn't have noticed anyway . . .

Name three activities you think would benefit Manna House residents. (List the resources needed to create those activities.)

What skills, hobbies, or interests do you have that might be shared with MH residents?

Would you be willing to conduct an activity (a) once a week; (b) every other week; (c) once a month; (d) a one-time event . . .

"*Hola.*" Edesa Baxter peeked into my office, her warm brown skin a contrast to the chubby latte cheeks of the Latina baby she held in one arm. Gracie rode her foster mother's hip like she'd been glued on, eyeing me shyly.

"Hey! Where's that handsome husband of yours? I want to thank him for setting up this computer for me—" I'd started blabbing before I noticed that Edesa's usual megawatt smile was missing, and the baby hiccoughed as if she'd been crying. "Um . . . are you okay?"

Edesa shook the little twists crowning her head. "I think the *bebé* has an ear infection. She kept tugging on her ear and screamed half the night." Her own dark eyes puddled. "Josh had to go out in the middle of the night for some infant Tylenol. None of us got much sleep—and he has classes at Circle Campus this morning."

"You're taking Gracie to the doctor today, right?"

The young mother nodded. "But we cannot go until later this afternoon. We have an appointment with the social worker at one o'clock. Josh is supposed to meet us there." She hugged the little girl a bit closer. "We need a lot of prayer, Gabby."

"Oh, Edesa." I pulled her into the office, crowded as it was, and shut the door. "Will the father be there?"

"No, *gracias a Dios*. But the social worker is going to go over the petition to stop our adoption"—her lip quivered—"and tell us

191

what must happen next. We have to go to court, I think. But . . . I have hope, Gabby. God brought Gracie to us, I believe that." A glimmer of smile returned. "I have a friend—one of my Yada Yada Prayer Group sisters—who told me, 'God didn't bring you this far to leave you, 'Desa.'"

"Of course not." No way was I going to dump my doubts on her. The courts always ruled in favor of a relative, didn't they? "I'll be sure to pray for you this afternoon."

At least Edesa didn't ask me to pray right then. I still wasn't comfortable praying out loud, especially on the spur of the moment. In fact, I wasn't sure my connection to the Almighty was all that reliable just yet.

During the next few days, I felt as if I accomplished a lot. I printed my questionnaire and passed out copies to as many staff and volunteers as came in that week, and I sent the rest by e-mail attachment to the board. I even got a few back, though Precious handed hers back blank. "I don't like forms ya gotta fill out. Too much like public aid." She rolled her eyes. "Just let me talk atcha, and *you* write it down."

I laughed and grabbed a pen. "Fire away."

"Okay, first, you gonna get a bunch of well-meanin' stuff from some people, doing cut-an'-paste crafts, which, let me tell ya, it's just busywork any three-year-old can do. Just 'cause these women ain't got homes, don't mean they ain't got brains too." She tapped her head, which was braided all over so tight it looked like it must hurt. "An' those pastors on the board, bless 'em, they probably gonna say we should be havin' group devotions at six a.m.—or maybe a Bible class from Genesis to Revelation."

I repressed a smile. The Bible class idea had already come back from Pastor Stevens, whom I hadn't met yet.

"Nothing wrong with that, I'm just sayin'. But take it from somebody who's been there—correction, somebody who's been *here*—that ya really need to ask the women themselves what kinda things they like ta do. An' don't dis ideas like doin' nails and fixin' hair—yeah, I heard Hannah harpin' at you ta let her do nails. But when you been living on the streets, a bit of pamperin' is pretty nice. Homeless women need ta *feel* like women, too, ya know."

I wrote down "Pampering—nails and hair," feeling duly chastened. I had indeed totally ignored Hannah's harping about doing nails. In fact, I'd basically been ignoring Hannah in general, because for some reason her bored mannerisms bugged me.

"What about you, Precious? Supervising homework for the kids a few times a week is great, but I know you've got more talents hiding under the rug that could perk up the lives of the residents."

"Hidin' under what rug? You talkin' 'bout my hair?" She patted her braided head.

I'm sure the color of my face clashed with my hair. "No, no, it's only a saying. I meant—"

Precious hooted. "Heh-heh! I'm just messin' with ya, Miz Gabby. I'll think about it. Meantime, didn't you say somethin' 'bout having a Fun Night where we could do dancin' an' stuff? How 'bout next Friday?"

"Next week? Uh . . . sure. Let me look at the calendar." I clicked the organizer icon on my computer, and a calendar popped up. "Week from Friday would be . . . oh, that's Mother's Day weekend. Maybe that wouldn't be such a good—"

"And why not?" Precious leaned both hands on my desk. "You think these women have someplace else to go Mother's Day weekend? Maybe fly to California, visit the grandkids? Huh." She snorted. "Them that still got their kids—ain't too many of them here anyway—are the lucky ones. Them that don't, a Fun Night might be a good way to dull some of the pain doggin' the holidays."

I bit my lip. *Mother's Day* . . . Last year, even though P.J. had been away at the academy, the school had scheduled a three-day leave for Mother's Day weekend. But this year, both boys were at the academy, and we were a thousand miles from Virginia. I wouldn't get to see either of them. Unless . . .

But I didn't say anything to Precious, just nodded my head and typed in "Fun Night."

chapter 23

I took Precious McGill's advice and asked for a gab session with the shelter residents on Thursday evening. This was the first time I'd met some of the women who were out during the day, some of whom had jobs or sold the weekly *Streetwise* newspaper. Others, I'd been told, spent their days standing in lines at public aid or the Social Security office, or trying to get their names on the long waiting lists for subsidized housing. "'Course a little panhandling on the side comes in handy now an' then," Precious said with a smirk.

I was disappointed when only a dozen or so showed up in the multipurpose room at seven o'clock, even though Mabel had announced it at both lunch and supper. She must have seen the look on my face. "I'm sorry, Gabby," she murmured. "We can't make them come. You'll just have to make do with the ones who show up."

"Why? Don't they want a say in what activities are offered here?" *Huh.* I'd left my husband to fend for himself that evening,

probably using up some of my capital in the "good graces" department. The least these women could do was show up to make it
worth my while.

The director shrugged. "Some are just tired, Gabby. They've
been pounding the pavement all day. And I'll admit, some don't
care. Food, shelter, clothing—that's the bottom line. The rest is
'whatever.'"

Okay, then. Whatever. I pulled some of the furniture into a
semicircle, hoping for a cozy chat, but a few of the women—
including Hannah the Bored—sat off to the side, arms folded. I
was determined to make this work. I introduced myself as the
new program director, thanked them for coming, and said I'd like
to hear their ideas for activities. "And please say your name when
you speak, since I haven't met several of you. This is a brainstorming session, so all ideas are welcome—"

"What she sayin'?" An old woman with a mouth so puckered
it looked as if she'd swallowed her teeth turned to the person
beside her and spoke loudly, drowning me out. "Can't hear a
word!"

"Pipe down, Schwartz!" someone muttered, accompanied by
several snickers. Mabel hustled over and sat down beside the old
lady, patting her on the hand.

"—and I'll, uh, list them here." I uncapped a black marker,
indicating the pad of newsprint propped on a chair.

Silence yawned. Not even the old woman spoke.

I could feel my underarms getting wet. I should have told
Precious to be here. She was so sure this was what I needed to do.
Huh.

In desperation I said, "Here are a few ideas to get us started.
Carolyn suggested a book club . . ." I wrote it down and under-

neath added *Fun Night/Dancing, Budgeting Your $, ESL (English as Second Language), Trip to Museum*, reading off each one. "We want a variety of activities—some just for fun, others to help with practical skills, even some outings. Obviously, we won't be able to do everything, but let's brainstorm."

It worked. A woman named Kim—slender, light brown skin, soft voice, neatly dressed—suggested "Typing Class." Hannah the Bored wanted a "Spa Day" (no surprise there). Soon other ideas flew about—"Movie Night" . . . "Can we go see Oprah?" . . . "I like to make jewelry"—and I wrote them all down, in spite of a few arguments among the group. ("Why just ESL? Why not Spanish for gringos?" "Because this is America, stupid, not Mexico." But I wrote down *Spanish for Gringos* and got a laugh.)

Kim timidly waved her hand. "Some of us work during the day but need more job skills. Can you do those on the weekend?" A few heads nodded.

Weekends. I'd been hoping to keep my part-time hours to weekdays, when Philip was at work. But her suggestion made sense . . .

By the time we wrapped up at 7:45, I had a pretty good list. "That was, um, interesting," Mabel deadpanned, offering to drop me off at the Sheridan El Station, even though it was still light outside. "But just so you know, tickets to see the *Oprah* show may be free, but you can spend a whole day on the phone trying to get a couple . . . let alone enough for a group."

I laughed. "Really? Drat. That was my favorite suggestion."

I showered quickly the next morning, eager to get back to work and sort through the ideas I'd been collecting, choosing a good balance of activities to start with and drawing up a possible calendar. Then I'd have a proposal to present to Mabel and could start to work on a budget.

Not bad for my first real week on the job.

As I was toweling my wet hair, Philip poked his head into the bathroom. "Gabby, tell the cleaning woman to be sure to wash the inside of the windows in the front room today. I deliberately specified inside windows on the contract with the cleaning service, but I don't think she's . . . what?"

I'd stopped toweling when he said "cleaning woman" and grimaced. "Uh, Camila isn't coming today. It's Cinco de Mayo—some kind of holiday for the Mexican community. She asked me about it last week. I'm sorry. I should have told you."

He gaped at me. "What kind of holiday? You agreed? Gabrielle, she only comes once a week! Did you arrange for her to come tomorrow? What if we want to entertain this weekend? The place is a mess!"

"Philip." I tried to keep impatience out of my voice. "The house looks fine. I thought missing one week wouldn't matter. Neither of us is here much during the week. If we entertain"—*Where did that come from? He hasn't said anything about entertaining this weekend*—"I'll do whatever needs to be done to be presentable."

"*You* thought . . . ! Did you remember I've already paid a month ahead?" He withdrew his head, but I heard him cursing in the bedroom. "Stupid Mexicans. They come here wanting jobs and then don't show up when you need 'em."

I pressed my lips together and turned on the hair dryer, staying in the bathroom longer than I'd intended to avoid getting into it any further with Philip. *What a jerk.* Good grief, Camila probably worked longer hours than both of us put together and undoubtedly deserved a day off, holiday or no holiday. Still fussing with my hair, I finally heard the front door slam. Good, he was gone.

But it was obvious *some* kind of holiday was afoot. As I walked to the El, cars flying green, white, and red flags zipped past, their sound systems blasting Spanish music as young people hung out of the windows, waving and shouting. Now I was curious. I still didn't know what the holiday was all about. As soon as I got to my office at the shelter, I turned on my computer, called up Google, and typed "Cinco de Mayo" into the search box. Lots of Web sites. I clicked on one, then another.

"Not to be confused with Mexican Independence from Spain on 16 September, 1810" . . . *"Cinco de Mayo, the 'Fifth of May,' celebrates the victory of the 4,000 Mexican troops over 8,000 French forces in the Battle of Puebla in 1862"* . . . *"A minor holiday in Mexico, but celebrated in the U.S. by Mexican-Americans with parades and festivals with the same cultural pride as St. Patrick's Day by the Irish."*

Parades? Shoot! Wish I'd thought of this sooner! It would've been neat to take some of the women from the shelter to the parade today. Still browsing, I clicked on a site that said, "Cinco de Mayo Festivities, Chicago 2006." *Wait a minute* . . . The parade was on *Sunday?* Strange. I'd assumed Camila wanted the day off because the festivities were today.

My mind started spinning. If the parade wasn't until Sunday noon, I might have time to get it together after all! I'd need a car—no, a van. Didn't Josh Baxter say he used their church van sometimes? Maybe—

Excited, I went hunting for Edesa. I hadn't seen her since Tuesday, hadn't even heard how the meeting with the social worker went, but today was Friday, and she usually led the weekly Bible study. Sure enough, the young black woman was pulling chairs into a small circle with the help of Tina, who looked strong enough to pick up one of the overstuffed chairs and heft it over her head single-handedly. The two of them were talking rapidly to each other in Spanish as a few of the shelter residents started to straggle in.

"Edesa, I don't mean to bother you, but I need to get hold of Josh—" I suddenly realized she had no "papoose." "Where's Gracie?"

Edesa made a face. "Sick. Home with Josh. Double ear infection. But at least you'll be able to find him. *¿Qué pasa?*"

Quickly I shared my idea of taking some of the shelter residents to the Cinco de Mayo parade on Sunday, but needing a van. "How about you, Tina? Would you like to go? Maybe you could tell the rest of us what it's all about."

The big-boned Latina drew herself up, looked down her nose at me, and muttered something in Spanish. Edesa giggled.

"What?" I looked from one to the other.

Tina thumped her chest. "I am *Puerto Rican*, not Mexican. It is not *my* holiday."

I could feel my ears getting hot, and Edesa laughed right out loud. "Cut Gabby some slack, Tina. She's new to Chicago. Besides, I know you'd love to go, right?" She gave the larger woman a playful poke in the ribs, then scribbled a number on a scrap of paper. "Here's our phone number, Gabby. See what Josh says about the van. What a great idea! I'd love to go, too, but . . . well, depends on Gracie."

I skipped the Bible study to make my call. Thirty minutes later, Josh called me back and said the church van was available, but had I ever driven a fifteen-passenger van? "I could if I have to,"

I said. "I learned to drive on my dad's utility van in North Dakota—he owned a carpet store. But I don't know Chicago streets. I was hoping you'd drive." Talk about understatement.

"Can't promise," he said. "Gracie's pretty sick. We plan to lie low this weekend. I could probably get the van down to the shelter, but don't count on me to be the chauffeur. But for what it's worth, I think this is a great idea, Gabby. Be sure to take in the festival at Douglas Park after the parade. Lots of great food and bands. In fact, Delores Enriquez's husband will probably be there with his mariachi band. Don't miss it!"

Well, so be it. I'd drive if I had to. Maybe I'd take our car on Saturday and practice the route.

By the time Estelle banged on a pot, signaling lunch, the plan was falling into place. Josh Baxter would deliver the van and the keys to the shelter by Sunday morning. The first twelve residents who signed up would get a seat on the van. (I was still hoping for another staff person or volunteer to go along.) We'd leave at eleven, park as close to Douglas Park as we could, take in the parade along Cermak Road, then hang out for the festivities. I even printed out a map that gave me the best route from the shelter.

So far everyone I'd talked to had loved the idea. Even Mabel had given her somewhat dubious blessing to my seat-of-the-pants idea—"As long as you're back in time for Sunday evening service," she'd said. "It's Pastor Stevens's church"—and let me announce the outing at lunch. Aida Menéndez was especially excited, jumping up from her chair and throwing her arms around my neck. "Oh, *gracias,* Señora Fairbanks!"

Tina told me later that Aida's first foster mother had taken her to the parade when she was five, but the girl hadn't been to a festival since. "This is *muy bueno*. She needs to connect with her culture."

I spent the rest of the afternoon working on my proposal for the first set of activities and a list of resources needed. I was just getting ready to hit the Print button when my "William Tell" ringtone went off. Grabbing the cell out of my purse, I flipped it open. "Hello? Hello?" Only crackling on the other end. *Rats!* No signal down here. I looked at the caller ID . . . It was Philip.

I called him back on my desk phone. "Philip? Hi, honey. Sorry about that. Couldn't get a signal on my cell. What's up?"

"Don't plan anything for Sunday, Mop Top. We've been invited by a new client to go sailing on his new sailboat—a thirty footer! The weather is supposed to be great." His excitement oozed from the phone—an insidious gunk clogging up everything I'd been doing that day. Not Sunday . . . not Sunday!

I felt as if I might need electric paddles to jump-start my heart. "We who?" I squeaked.

"The Fenchels and us, of course. They said we'd need some good windbreakers and boat shoes—"

"But . . . but . . ."

"—and I offered to bring some good wine and cheese, that kind of thing . . . Gabby? You still there?"

"Uh, sorry, Philip. I've gotta go. Talk about it later, okay?" I hung up the phone. My head sank into my hands. Why didn't I just say, *"I'm sorry, Philip. I can't go. I have to work Sunday. Part of my job. I've already made a commitment to take—"* Oh, sure. After Philip's rant this morning about Camila taking the day off, he'd just love to hear that I couldn't go sailing—with his client, no less, which made it "business"—because I'd be taking a vanload of homeless women to the Cinco de Mayo parade. Not to mention the icy silence I'd had to swim through all last weekend when I didn't move heaven and earth to be at the contract signing. Did I want to go through that again?

"Argh!" I grabbed fistfuls of my hair with a sudden urge to pull curls out of my head, roots and all.

"Gabby? *¿Qué pasa, amiga?*" Edesa slipped into the room behind me and shut the door.

I rolled my eyes. I didn't even want to repeat the phone call, cementing my dilemma into reality. But I finally told her, hot tears sliding down my face. I grabbed a tissue and blew my nose. "What am I going to do, Edesa?! Go back out there and chirp, 'Sorry ladies, the outing's off, I'm going sailing?' Or tell my husband, 'Sorry, I'm going to a parade, see you later'?" I didn't bother to explain the edgy dance Philip and I had been doing around work issues.

Edesa was quiet for a long moment. "Gabby, did you look up the scripture I gave you in the welcome e-mail on Monday?"

I shook my head. "Sorry."

"Do you have a Bible here?"

I started to shake my head again—then remembered the Bible I'd stuck in my bag a few days ago. "Uh, yes, right here." I pulled it out.

She paged through it and stopped someplace in the middle. "Here it is. Third chapter of Proverbs, verses five and six. Here. You read it." She shoved the Bible at me.

"You read it." I shoved it back. I knew I sounded petulant, but I didn't feel like reading "Obey your husband" or "Thou shalt not lie" right now.

"Okay." She picked up my Bible and read with her Spanish accent. "'Trust in the Lord with all your heart and don't lean on your own understanding'—"

The words were familiar. Probably one of the verses I'd memorized in Sunday school as a kid.

"—'In all your ways acknowledge Him, and He will direct your paths.'" Edesa closed the Bible.

I sat silently, picking apart my soggy tissue, digesting what I'd just heard. *Trust in the Lord . . . don't lean on my own understanding . . . He will direct my paths . . .*

Finally I glanced sideways at Edesa and gave a snort. "You think?"

She smiled, the beautiful grin that seemed to stretch ear to ear. "*Sí,* I think. God is going to show you what to do, *mi amiga.* I will pray." She gave me a hug and slipped out of my broom closet.

Huh. Easy for her to say.

chapter 24

To my relief, no one was in the dining room or kitchen when I left at four o'clock, and I scooted through the multipurpose room without waving to the two women who sat sprawled in a corner, playing cards. I took a deep breath and stopped by Mabel's office . . . *Drat! Not in!* I wasn't sure if I was relieved or vexed. Just delayed the inevitable confession and flagellation.

I signed out and scowled my way home, going over my options. Not that I had any. I'd practically promised Philip—okay, I *had* promised—that I wouldn't let my job interfere with things connected to his work. But I hadn't anticipated having to break a promise to *my* "clients," after getting them all excited about our first outing.

Should I tell him my dilemma? If I told him I canceled an outing at the shelter to go sailing on his client's boat, maybe he'd quit harping at me about whether I was "on his side" or not. Or would he get ticked off that I'd even planned something on the weekend? Maybe "don't ask, don't tell" was a better policy. Just go, try to have fun . . .

I groaned inwardly as the buildings and shops along Sheridan Avenue slipped past the train windows. What was this going to look like to Mabel and the board? The new program director makes plans for an outing, gets everyone all excited, then turns around and *cancels* because she and her husband got an invitation to go sailing . . .

Argh! I felt like banging my head against the window of the El. Not the greatest way to kick off my program plans. Maybe I should write a book: *The Idiot's Guide to Starting a New Job—How to Get Fired the First Week* by Gabrielle Shepherd Fairbanks.

But instead of head banging, I leaned my cheek against the cool window. When was God going to show me *the* path I should go? Felt like I was in the soup either way—

"Thorndale! Next stop Thorndale!"

What? I scrambled for the door of the train car. I'd overshot my stop by two stations this time.

Sunday. Eleven o'clock. Sunny. Breezy and mild. Perfect day for a parade.

But instead of loading up the borrowed van with Manna House residents, I was walking behind Philip along a dock in Waukegan Harbor north of Chicago, carrying a picnic basket with two bottles of Shiraz, three kinds of cheese, and a couple of boxes of good crackers. We were wearing his-and-hers white deck pants, new navy windbreakers, "boat shoes" with good rubber soles, sunglasses, and white baseball caps—except my bushy chestnut curls stuck out from under the cap, making me look like Bozo the Clown.

I'd finally sucked up the courage to call Mabel on Saturday

morning and told her I had an unavoidable family conflict—something my husband had arranged—that put the kibosh on the Cinco de Mayo outing on Sunday, and would she please tell those who had signed up that I was so, so sorry. She'd been quiet on the other end for several beats, a yawning gap that made me want to crawl in a hole and pull dirt down over my head. But all she said was, *"Of course, Gabby. These things happen. I'll pass the word."*

I'd been hoping she'd say, "Oh, no problem, someone else can drive the van, we'll still go, don't worry about it." But she hadn't.

"What's wrong with you?" Philip had asked when he got home Friday night. "You practically hung up on me! Don't you want to go sailing? You can be such a wet blanket, Gabby." Keeping my voice even, I told him the sailboat invitation was very nice, but I'd been planning an outing for the homeless women at Manna House for Sunday, and now had to cancel, which put me in a very awkward position, thank you very much.

He'd just shrugged. "Just reschedule for another day. It's not like those women have corporate jobs they have to go to next week."

I'd decided to drop it. It wasn't going to help anything to point out that the Cinco de Mayo parade *only* happened on Sunday. He'd just ask, then why did Camila take Friday off?

I had a few dark words with God about the whole mess. Was this the right thing to do? Edesa had been so sure God would show me the "right path."

However, once I'd made the decision, a certain smugness settled into a corner of my spirit. The sacrifice I was making might come in handy when I brought up my idea for Mother's Day weekend . . .

As Philip hunted for the slip number he'd been given, I tried to take in the harbor in panoramic snatches: clubhouse with a nautical-themed restaurant, gift shop, and large restrooms with showers and dressing rooms. Rows and rows of docks with all kinds of power boats and sailboats lined up side by side, from glitzy yachts to weather-worn, chunky fishing boats, tied up in their individual slips. And beyond the harbor, Lake Michigan stretched blue-green and vast, broken only by small whitecaps like so much dotted-Swiss material.

A voice hailed us from the deck of a sleek sailboat bearing the name *Rolling Stone*. The man was a very tan fifty-something, dressed casually in shorts, windbreaker, captain's cap, rubber-soled shoes, no socks. No Fenchels to be seen, but a thirtyish brunette peeked out from the cabin and smiled a welcome. Introductions were made: Lester Stone, Sandy Archer. *Hmm. The boat and the owner have the same name, but not Sandy.* I didn't see any wedding rings.

Lester helped me cross from the dock to the fiberglass deck, and Sandy took me below to the cabin. Everything fit like a miniature puzzle—two-burner gas stove, fridge, sink, drop-leaf table wedged between two padded benches that supposedly made into a single bed on one side and a double on the other. Toward the bow, Sandy pointed out the "head"—a flush toilet and a vertical, coffinlike shower—and more bunks. Everything was trimmed in wood, the curtains royal blue. Taking my picnic basket, she lashed it to the counter with a bungee cord and handed me a sleeveless jacket-style life vest.

For the first time, it occurred to me sailing might be a bit different from putzing along on my uncle's outboard fishing boat on Devil's Lake in North Dakota.

"Ha-ha-ha. How are ya, Lester?" I heard Henry Fenchel's voice booming above deck. "Mona, this is Lester Stone, our new client . . . ha-ha-ha, *Rolling Stone*, I like that. Hey, Philip, where's Little Orphan Annie?"

Thanks a lot, Henry. Did he think I hadn't heard that old joke before?

"*I* think all those curls are pretty," Sandy whispered to me before going back up the three-step ladder. I followed, deciding Sandy was a friend for life. For the next fifteen minutes, I scrunched in a corner of the blue padded seat of the open cockpit, trying to stay out of the way while Lester gave instructions to Philip and Henry about casting off from the dock and how to unfurl the sails once we reached open water. Sandy seemed at home scooting around the boat, unsnapping the blue cover from the main sail and stowing it below, checking ropes and wires. Mona lounged opposite me, looking perfectly cool in a light blue jumpsuit and gold-strap sandals. I noticed she did not put on the life vest Sandy handed to her.

Well, so what if I looked like Winnie the Pooh with a bulletproof vest. Sandy was pulling the straps tight on hers, and I was going to take my clues from a sailor.

Sail untied but not raised, Lester stood at the wheel and effortlessly piloted us out of the harbor using an inboard motor. I relaxed, smiled at Philip, who was casually sitting on the slightly rounded deck above the cabin, feeling the warm sunshine kiss my face. Might as well just enjoy the day.

Once out on the lake, Lester shouted instructions, Philip pulled quickly on the line to raise the sail, the boom swung out, and as Sandy secured the line—*snap!*—wind filled the large sheet and the boat picked up speed. My stomach did a couple of flip-flops, but I tried to keep my eyes focused on the flat horizon. *Okay, okay, I can do this.* After a while, Lester yelled, "Coming about!" Laughing, the guys ducked, the boom swung to the other side, the sail snapped—and immediately Mona's side of the boat tipped up. *Wa-a-ay up!* My stomach leaped into my throat, and I tasted bile. I grabbed at the rail behind me, though the waves seemed dangerously close.

Lester grinned at me from behind the wheel. "When we heel up like that, Gabby, just move to the other side. Brace your feet on the opposite seat."

I was afraid to let go, but Sandy reached over and gave me a hand. Once on the high side, I sat sideways between Mona and Sandy, clutching at the rail, one leg straight out, foot planted against the fiberglass bench where I'd been sitting. Mona just lifted her chin and let the wind tousle her golden hair, but to my satisfaction, I noticed she did put on her life vest.

Every ten minutes or so, Lester changed direction, tacking back and forth, farther and farther from shore. The higher we "heeled up," the more Philip and Henry seemed to be enjoying themselves. "What a great day for a sail!" Philip shouted to Lester, and the "captain" grinned back at him.

But when we heeled up so far the opposite railing brushed the water, I had to fight a rising panic. My knuckles were white clutching the railing behind me. My ankles and thighs ached from pressing against the opposite bench. And finally my stomach rebelled, and I turned, retching over the side.

Mona recoiled. "Ohhh, *gross.* If I'd known you were going to be so much fun on the water, Gabrielle, I would've stayed home."

Sandy simply handed me a roll of paper towels.

I didn't dare look at Philip.

That sail was the longest, most miserable two hours of my entire life.

When we got back to the harbor, I excused myself, climbed onto the dock, and walked on wobbly legs back to the clubhouse, where I locked myself into a toilet stall, stuffed a few paper towels into my mouth, and had a good silent cry. What a wimp I was! I should have known. If I got queasy from heights, it was a straight jump across a checkerboard to being seasick-prone.

I finally pulled myself together, repaired my face, and went back to the *Rolling Stone*, where the others were passing around plastic tumblers of wine, the cheese and crackers, and sliced apples. Sandy made coffee and brought out a tin of rich, dark brownies. The men talked business, Mona and Sandy chatted about people and parties in Chicago, and I smiled and nodded, wishing I'd spent the afternoon with my feet on the ground, watching the Cinco de Mayo parade.

Once back in the car, Phillip and I rode in silence back down to the city, passing the occasional car with Mexican flags attached to the windows on either side. Finally I said, "That was really nice of Lester to invite us out on his boat."

Philip flipped on his turn blinker and moved into a faster lane.

"Sorry I got seasick. That was my first time sailing. I didn't know what to expect!"

Philip grunted and just kept driving.

I watched his profile—sculptured, handsome, smooth—but couldn't read his eyes behind the sunglasses. I decided this wasn't the time to bring up Mother's Day weekend.

But once we got back to Richmond Towers, showered and changed, and settled at the kitchen counter with hot roast beef sandwiches, I said casually, "You know what I was thinking, Philip. Next Sunday is Mother's Day, and the boys have a three-day weekend. Why don't we fly them here to Chicago, introduce them to their new home, and do something special all together as a family next Sunday? We haven't been to any of the museums yet. Best Mother's Day gift I can think of!"

Philip looked at me as if I'd just suggested climbing the Swiss Alps. "Gabby, that's silly! Philip Jr. graduates from eighth grade in a couple of weeks, and they'll be coming here for the summer. It doesn't make sense to spend the money to bring them now."

Unbidden, my eyes watered and I had to grab a napkin. "But I really miss them, Philip."

"Aw, Gabby, don't go crying. I miss the boys too. But it's only a couple more weeks! We'll fly down for his graduation, stay a few days with my parents, and bring them home with us then."

I stared at him. I'd just rearranged my whole weekend for him and humiliated myself getting seasick in the process. That should earn me *some* brownie points. "Is that a no?"

Philip rolled his eyes and got up from the kitchen stool. "Be reasonable, Gabby. You can wait another couple of weeks." He headed for the front room, and I heard the TV come on.

I sat at the kitchen counter for a long time, my thoughts and feelings so convoluted I hardly knew how to untangle them. I had to get out of this house! Go somewhere, do something . . . before I said—or did—something I'd regret later.

chapter 25

My ears pricked up as the grandfather clock in the front room bonged five thirty. Sunday Evening Praise at Manna House was at six . . . Mabel had said Pastor Stevens's church would be there, and he was the one board member I hadn't met yet. As for the shelter residents, I might as well face the music tonight and get it over with. Aida Menéndez and the rest deserved a personal apology from me, if nothing else. Never could tell who'd be around tomorrow.

Suddenly determined, I pulled on a sweater, grabbed my purse and the carry-all bag with my Bible, and headed for the front door. "I'm going to church!" I yelled into the living room, loud enough to be heard over the TV but not waiting for an answer. *Like I'm really dressed for church,* I thought wryly on my way down in the elevator, looking at my jeans and loafers. But I didn't care. And I knew the "church" at Manna House wouldn't care either.

Lively gospel music could already be heard clear out on the

street by the time I'd waited thirty minutes for an elevated train on its weekend schedule and walked to the shelter. Using my staff key to let myself in, I snuck into the multipurpose room and found a chair in the back. The room was surprisingly full, with quite a few unfamiliar faces, many clapping and shouting, "Glory!" or "Praise You, Jesus!" as the song came to an end. Many of the unfamiliar folks were wearing dresses and heels, even a few hats. Must be members of New Hope Missionary Baptist. I wished I'd taken time to at least put on a pair of slacks and a nice sweater.

A young African-American man with a few too many pounds for his age—this couldn't be Pastor Stevens, could it? He seemed too young!—bounced back and forth at the front of the room as an electronic keyboard and set of bongo drums filled in the lull. "C'mon now, church, c'mon," the young worship leader said, "let the redeemed of the Lord *say* so!"

More shouts, clapping, hallelujahs, and lifted hands. Couldn't say I was used to all this raucous enthusiasm during a worship service—so unlike the formal liturgy of Briarwood Lutheran back in Virginia, or even the more informal but still sedate services at Minot Evangelical Church growing up. But it was impossible to just sit there. I clapped with the others. Clapping for God— well, why not?

"Okay, now, you all heard our girl Whitney sing Dottie Rambo's song 'I Go to the Rock' on *The Preacher's Wife* sound-track—c'mon now, don't pretend you didn't see that movie." Laughter. "But even if you didn't, you'll pick it up mighty fast. On your feet, everybody! One-two, one-two—"

Right on the beat the keyboard player and drummer, both young black men barely out of their teens, struck up the lively gospel tune and the Missionary Baptist folks helped carry the words . . .

Where do I go . . . when there's no one else to turn to?
Who do I talk to . . . when nobody wants to listen?
Who do I lean on . . . when there's no foundation stable? . . .

I'd seen the movie, though couldn't say I remembered the song, but now it echoed in my head as if putting words to all the aches, confusion, loneliness, and anger sitting like crud in my spirit. *No one to turn to . . . nobody wants to listen . . . who do I lean on . . .*

Suddenly the tension in my spirit uncoiled like a live wire, unleashing a torrent of tears. I couldn't stop. Shoulders shaking, eyes and nose running, fishing for a pack of tissues, I sank back into my chair as the shelter "congregation" all around me kept singing . . .

I go to the Rock I know that's able,
I go to the Rock! . . .

A light hand touched my shoulder, then two thin arms went around me, and Aida Menéndez was whispering in my ear. "It is okay, Miss Gabby. We're not mad at you. Miss Mabel said you couldn't help it. Next time, maybe. *Sí?*"

I nodded, still mopping my face, and hugged her back. "Thanks, Aida. I am so sorry I had to cancel our plans to go to the parade."

As the song finally wound to a close and a middle-aged black man in a suit and tie got up to speak—this must be Pastor Stevens—Aida, the young girl who'd been kicked out of the foster-care system at eighteen, who'd probably been disappointed by people like me all her life, slipped back to her seat. Aida had presumed my tears were guilty ones—and maybe some of them were—but she had no idea how deep and dry the well was from which they'd sprung.

I liked Pastor Stevens. He made a point to introduce himself after the service. "You must be Mrs. Fairbanks," he said, shaking my hand and smiling, a slight tease in his deep brown eyes. "They said you had curly hair. Mm-mm. They weren't kidding." He laughed.

I only hoped my nose wasn't bright red after the crying spell during the service. We chatted, he apologized for missing our lunch date a week ago, and I assured him I understood. He said he appreciated the questionnaire I'd sent to the board and was sure several members of his congregation would be glad to sign up as volunteers. He didn't seem to know about the Cinco de Mayo fiasco, didn't mention it anyway, so I left it to Mabel to inform the board if she felt it necessary. But I was grateful it didn't come up in my first meeting with Pastor Stevens.

The pastor also introduced me to his wife, a sweet-faced woman who looked at least six months pregnant, and several members of his congregation who, Mabel explained later, enthusiastically showed up whenever their pastor had to speak somewhere else.

That kind of loyalty must be nice, I thought.

As soon as I was able to slip away, I went downstairs to my office, closed the door behind me, and booted up my computer. Then I called up the Internet, typed in the travel site we often used, and filled out the necessary information:

Departing from:	Chicago O'Hare Airport
Destination:	Richmond, VA
Date of departure:	Saturday May 13
Date of return:	Monday May 15
Number of passengers:	1

I didn't say anything to Philip when I got home later that evening, but the next morning as he was leaving for work, I handed him his travel mug of fresh coffee and a folded piece of paper.

"What's this?"

"My flight info. I'm going to Petersburg this weekend to see the boys. Wanted to let you know a week ahead of time so it doesn't interfere with any last-minute plans." I kept my voice light, matter-of-fact.

"What? Gabby, we should have talked about this!"

"I tried. Don't worry. I'm working now, so I can pay for the ticket. Have a good day." I smiled and walked out of the gallery back to the kitchen.

Behind me I heard, "Of all the—" and then the front door slammed.

My smile grew even wider.

There was something else I had to do before I could leave for work. I picked up the phone and called Philip's parents in Virginia.

"Hello, Marlene? This is Gabby . . . No, nothing's wrong. Philip's fine. I'm calling to let you know that I'm coming to Petersburg this weekend to see the boys—Mother's Day, you know . . . Yes, I *know* Philip didn't call to let you know. I thought I should call you myself . . . No, just me. We'll both be coming in a couple of weeks for P.J.'s graduation, but I thought—"

I repressed a sigh and listened while Philip's mother fussed for a full minute about having to change plans now and I should have let them know sooner. "Yes, I'm sorry about that, it was kind of a last-minute decision. I'd like to spend some time with just the boys since I haven't seen them for a whole month, but of course I'd love to see you and Dad Fairbanks too . . . No, don't worry about picking me up, I can rent a car . . . Of course, I understand. I'll get a room at the Holiday Inn Express . . . Yes, two nights, Saturday and Sunday. I'll fly to Chicago Monday after the boys go back to school . . ."

I was so exhausted after navigating the phone call with Philip's mother that I felt like crawling back into bed. But I drank a second cup of coffee, gathered up my stuff, and headed for the elevator. Hopefully Mabel would have had time to look at my program proposal and we could get started lining up volunteers and resources. *ESL materials—they shouldn't be too hard to find . . . and typing—Kim's idea is probably the most practical of all . . . the shelter already has two computers in the schoolroom . . . there are probably self-help programs available, but a teacher would be nice . . . probably more available on the weekends anyway—*

"Mrs. Fairbanks! Wait a moment . . ."

Mr. Bentley had been busy giving directions to a trio of Japanese men, who seemed to be having trouble understanding their Chicago map. But the men nodded and bowed and waved as they pushed through the revolving door to the sidewalk, where they stood in a huddle, looking at the map and pointing in different directions.

"They thought this was a hotel," the doorman explained, shaking his head. "I'm glad they have all day to find what they're looking for. They're going to need it." He looked me over, noting my khaki jeans, tooled leather belt, and ankle boots. "How's the job going? Is this Casual Monday?"

I laughed. "Pretty much. Manna House is casual seven days a week. Besides, my office is a former broom closet."

The house phone on the half-moon desk rang; he answered, but held up a finger for me to wait. I tried to stem my impatience. I really did need to get to work. But a moment later he came back. "I just wanted to tell you I saw your, uh, friend Saturday— you know, the old bag lady."

"Lucy?"

"Yeah, that one."

"Where was she? I haven't seen her for a while. I've been kind of worried."

He scratched his graying beard, which outlined his jaw and chin. "Behind the Dominick's grocery store, just south of here. My nephew works in the back unloading trucks, and I was supposed to pick him up. So I drove around back, and the old lady was picking through the Dumpster. The stuff they throw away could feed an army, I tell you! And she was stuffing her bags left and right."

"Was she all right? How did she look?"

He shrugged. "I guess she was all right. I didn't talk to her, didn't want to scare her. She kept lookin' around, like somebody was goin' to tell her to get out of there. Just thought you might want to know I saw her." His voice softened. "Ever since you brought her in here soakin' wet that day . . . well, wouldn't want that to be my mother, livin' like that."

"Is your mother still living?"

"Eighty-eight, goin' on ninety, and feisty as ever." Now he laughed.

"That's great." Would my own mother live to be ninety? She was only in her seventies, but my dad had died at seventy-two. And I had no idea how old Lucy was . . .

"I don't know why Lucy doesn't stay at the shelter! She could sleep in a bed, get three decent meals a day." I shook my head. "Anyway, thanks, Mr. Bentley. I better go. I've got a new program to implement and a Fun Night to plan for Friday night."

"A Fun Night! What's that?"

I laughed. "Just what it sounds like! Having fun, playing games, doing group dances . . . you know."

He grinned. "You mean, like the Mashed Potato, stuff like that?"

I grinned back at him. "I don't know about that. Wasn't that a sixties craze? You're showing your age, Mr. Bentley. But maybe you ought to come, show some of our residents a good time. Not all of them are old ladies, you know." I gave him an exaggerated wink.

The bearded doorman shook his head. "Nah. I'd be the only guy—"

"Oh come on. There'll be some other men there." I was sure Josh would come, and Mabel had said she was going to ask Peter Douglass to bring a few other "brothers" to give security. I laughed. "Just think about it."

But Mr. Bentley didn't look convinced.

chapter 26

The week seemed to fly by quickly. My spirits had lightened considerably—partly because I was going to see my boys in a few days, partly because I'd stood up to Philip and bought a plane ticket, whether he liked it or not. Was it that easy? I mean, it wasn't like I wanted to be at odds with my husband, but in this case, *he'd* been the one who hadn't been acting reasonable. Good grief! I hadn't seen my boys for a whole month! Mother's Day was coming up! I'd be gone all of two days.

It made perfect sense to me.

But for some reason I forgot to tell him I would be staying at work Friday evening too. Forgot? Or was some part of me still scared to upset him? He'd grumbled about me "going off and doing things on your own," but he'd seemed to accept that I was going to see the boys. I was reluctant to push my luck.

I'd busied myself all week putting the first few programs in place. Josh Baxter said his mother was an elementary teacher in the public school system and could probably get me some ESL materials. When I talked to her—her name was Jodi, and she sounded friendly enough on the phone—I found out that Avis Douglass, the beautiful black woman who spoke at the Sunday Evening Praise the first time I'd shown up, was the principal at her school, and between the two of them, they could surely come up with materials, both basic English and basic Spanish. Since she's a teacher, I got brave and asked Jodi if she might consider coming in on Saturday to teach typing to some of the women like Kim who wanted to increase their job skills. She said she'd pray about it.

That took me aback. I expected her to say she'd think about it. It made me feel funny. Had *I* prayed about anything this past week? Edesa had said she'd pray that I'd trust God and He'd show me "the right path." But had I prayed about the sailing-or-parade dilemma?

Maybe not. I did what I thought was right . . . or had I just gambled on who would be madder at me if I let them down—Philip or the shelter residents? To put it bluntly, would Philip have forgiven me like Aida did if I'd disappointed him?

There was no way I was going to disappoint the residents *this* weekend. I screwed up the courage to tell Philip on Friday morning that I'd be late getting home that evening because I'd organized a Fun Night.

"Tonight? Good grief. You're going to be gone clear till Monday, Gabrielle. The least you could've done was save tonight so we could go out to dinner or a movie or something."

"I'm sorry, Philip. That's just the way it worked out. I should have told you sooner." I felt like gritting my teeth. I was so sick of apologizing.

The intercom interrupted, and I hustled to open the front

door for Camila, leaving him muttering, "So what am I supposed to do all weekend while you're off gallivanting?"

A few minutes later, the short, squarish cleaning woman came into the gallery bundled up in a jacket, her head scarf and round face glistening and damp. "Good morning, Camila! Oh dear, you're wet. Is it raining this morning?"

"*Sí*, Señora Fairbanks. And getting colder again. Be sure to dress warm—"

"And where were *you* last week?" My husband's voice cut her off as he came into the gallery with his suit coat and briefcase. "I heard you asked for the day off because it was a Mexican holiday last week. But the parade and festivities weren't until Sunday!" He glared at her.

Her eyes rounded in fright. "No, no, *señor*, it wasn't for the parade. *Mi esposo* is a cook for a restaurant, good Mexican food, and I help him cook food in the restaurant booth during the whole festival—Thursday to Sunday! I did not even get to see the parade."

I smiled smugly. I knew she'd have a good reason.

"Well . . . don't expect me to pay you for work you didn't do." Philip grabbed a felt dress hat from the hat rack and huffed out the door.

Camila looked at me, her eyes frightened. "Oh, *señora*, I did not expect you to pay!"

"I know you didn't, Camila. Don't mind him; he's just in a bad mood this morning." I helped her out of her jacket and hung it up in the coat closet. "I wish I'd known you had a vendor's booth at the festival. I would have loved to come."

"Oh, you should have come! We would have cooked *carnitas* or *chamorros* for you special." As we chatted, I felt a little guilty and grateful at the same time. Her arrival had deflected Philip's rant at me and given him something else to be mad about.

Camila was right. The warm temperatures of the past several days had taken a dive, and it was barely in the forties again—and raining, to boot. Forewarned, I took along an extra pair of slacks, socks, and shoes to work, as well as my umbrella, and by the time I got to Manna House, I'd determined to forget about Philip and his infantile behavior. Which I did, because a pleasant surprise came walking through the door right after the morning Bible study . . .

Lucy showed up again.

"Lucy!" I gave the old woman a hug, though she was badly in need of a bath. "I see you decided to show up for our party!"

"What party? Who has time for a party?" But her eyes glittered.

The old woman's cough was back; otherwise, she was as feisty as ever. After lunch, Estelle Williams rounded up several of the other residents who were "in" that day to help make snacks for the evening, while Lucy poked her nose into their business and snitched a sample of everything. Precious McGill and her daughter Sabrina showed up after school and organized the after-school kids to twist crepe paper decorations and tape them to the walls of the multipurpose room. By the time supper had been cleared away—a simple affair of macaroni and cheese, sausage links, and applesauce on paper plates—excitement for the evening ahead had pumped up, and the multipurpose room was filled with chatter long before seven o'clock.

Josh and Edesa Baxter showed up with Gracie, who was always a hit with the shelter residents. I was surprised how easily they let the baby be passed from person to person. Wasn't Gracie just getting over ear infections? Estelle, who'd changed into a royal blue caftan she'd made herself and put on dangly gold earrings, finally stole Gracie and kept her. "You just want an excuse not to dance and get all sweaty," I teased.

She arched an eyebrow. "Exactly. This has to be dry-cleaned."

Peter Douglass showed up with another "brother" named Carl, and Josh said he thought his parents might come too. I felt good. This party was getting a lot of support.

To kick off our Fun Night, we started with a game of Steal the Bacon for anyone who wanted to play, and ended up with two teams of eight big-and-little people each. I numbered off each team, put them behind masking-tape lines at opposite ends of the room, tossed a dish towel tied into a knot into the center, then called a number—"Six!"—and the two "Sixes" ran toward the middle, danced around and around the knotted towel, trying to grab it and run back to their masking-tape line without getting tagged by the other "Six." The kids were better at this game than the adults, snatching the rag and darting back to their line to the hoots and cheers of the rest of us on the sidelines.

When one team was declared the winner with ten "steals," Precious put a CD on the Manna House boom box, turned up the volume, and within minutes, had nearly everyone in the middle of the floor doing the Macarena—even me. Right arm forward, then left. Right palm up, then left. Right hand to left shoulder, ditto left . . . right hand to neck, then the left . . . hands to hips, wiggle the pelvis, turn ninety degrees and start all over again . . .

I was laughing, getting lost, trying again, slapping the wrong hip at the wrong time, when I heard the door buzzer. Probably Peter Douglass and his friend Carl—they'd slipped outside a while ago—now wanting back in. I was closest to the foyer, so I ducked out of the multipurpose room and opened the big oak door. Peter and Carl came past me, but a third man stood on the steps, wearing slacks and a sport coat, with a dark open-necked shirt and a gold chain circling his neck. He nodded a polite greeting, revealing a familiar bald dome. Brown face, short gray beard running from one ear around his chin to the other . . .

My face burst into a grin. "Mr. Bentley!"

Flying was not one of my favorite activities. I avoided window seats—or closed the shade if I had no choice—squeezed my eyes shut during takeoff, and kept telling myself I was just inside a big, long, noisy building. But I couldn't help grinning to myself on the American Airlines flight to Richmond the next morning. Mr. Bentley had been a big hit at the Manna House Fun Night. Once I introduced him as "a friend of mine," he was dragged into the middle of the Macarena—and his popularity skyrocketed when he insisted on teaching us the Mashed Potato. "Who else knows this oldie but goodie?" he'd teased.

His gaze had zeroed in on Estelle, who protested, "Hey, I was only ten when that one came out!" But then the two of them cut the rug with such hilarity that everyone else jumped in, filling the multipurpose room with music and laughter.

Everyone said the Fun Night was a huge success. It made me wish I'd invited Philip to come. Maybe it would have changed his attitude about my job and given him a chance to meet the staff firsthand.

Or not. But I'd never know unless I asked him . . .

The flight landed on time at 1:55 Eastern time, but it was nearly three o'clock by the time I got my bag, picked up my rental SUV, and headed down Route 295 toward Petersburg. Four o'clock by the time I drove into the countrified hamlet of Briarwood just outside Petersburg and into the winding driveway of the Fairbanks home.

The red brick home was lovely, almost like a large bungalow, with a low front porch along the main part of the house and three dormer windows jutting from the roof on the second floor. An addition had been built at some point to accommodate a large family room with a loft, a stone fireplace, and an attached garage. The house nestled among two acres of trees and lawns . . . a wonderful play space for grandkids. No wonder my boys loved coming here.

The front door opened, and eleven-year-old Paul came running toward the car. "I knew it was you!" he yelled, jumping up and down as I got out of the car and enveloped him in a mama bear hug. Then Philip Jr. appeared, a bit more subdued, but I still got a hug. I held both boys at arm's length, drinking in the sight of them: Paul, still scrawny and short, his school buzz cut starting to grow out into the chestnut curls he'd inherited from me. And P.J., dark haired like his father, starting to add inches. He'd soon be looking me in the eye.

Marlene Fairbanks appeared, smiling benevolently. "Well, come in, Gabrielle. You can have dinner, can't you, before you have to go to your hotel? Mike will want to see you. He had to go into the office today."

Like father, like son. "Dinner would be lovely. Thank you, Marlene. And then . . ." I knuckled both boys on their noggins. "I wondered if the boys would like to come to the Holiday Inn with me for the night. My room has two queen beds. They have an indoor swimming pool and a game room—"

"Yes!" Paul pumped his arm. "Can we, Nana?"

His question grated on me. But Marlene, ever the Southern gentlewoman, said, "Well, of course, if that's what your mother wants, though I'd thought . . . well, never mind. Shall we go in?"

Our supper was pleasant enough, served by the live-in housekeeper, and delicious as always: country ham, smothered potatoes, cornbread, green beans, and peach cobbler. Mike Fairbanks welcomed me with a warm squeeze but kept saying, "So why didn't Philip come with you? Too busy to come see his family?"

I found myself defending my husband, saying our plan had been to come for several days the following week, when P.J. graduated from eighth grade, and this trip was "a little extra gift from Philip to me for Mother's Day." That seemed to pacify the senior Mr. Fairbanks, and I even wanted to believe it . . . until I saw Marlene's face, and knew she'd undoubtedly heard a different story from Philip.

Marlene called the Holiday Inn that evening and asked if we wanted them to pick us up for church. "Always something special on Mother's Day Sunday," she purred.

But the boys and I had already talked about picking up the boys' bikes—the reason I'd rented the SUV—and riding along the paths of the Petersburg National Battlefield Park. "And if I could borrow one of the other bikes Mike keeps around . . ."

"Oh dear." I could practically see my mother-in-law pout over the telephone. "Mike will be so disappointed. He just lives to see those boys on the weekend."

I pressed my lips together so hard, I practically bit them. *Who* hadn't seen them for the past *five* weekends? Good grief. Couldn't the Fairbanks give me just one day without whining about it?! I was sure the good Lord would understand if we didn't show up for church tomorrow.

But in the end we compromised. The boys and I would spend the day together at the Battlefield, and then we'd come back to the house in late afternoon for a barbecue if the weather held. And I had to admit later, I was glad we had a place to go by three that afternoon, because the boys were tired of riding their bikes, tired of seeing the monuments they'd seen half a dozen times before, and I was tired of their bickering and complaining. Besides, the fog that had started the day held a chill that began to seep beneath our windbreakers, and we were all glad to get back to the Fairbanks' home, where Grandad Mike had built a fire in the stone fireplace . . . though I soon found myself warming my toes alone as the boys scrambled to play their video games.

Only when I finally got back to my room at the Holiday Inn around nine o'clock did I realize Mother's Day was almost over, and I hadn't called my own mother. Terrible-daughter guilt threatened to undo my joy at spending the past twenty-four hours with my own sons. It was only eight o'clock in North Dakota . . . *Still time.* But the phone rang and rang. No answer. I tried at nine thirty, then ten. Still no answer.

Anxiety put my nerves on alert. Was something wrong? Wouldn't one of my sisters have called me? I tried the number I had for Celeste in Alaska, and all I got was a recording that said the number was not in service. I tried Honor in California—thank goodness, it was ringing!—but her answering machine kicked in. *"Not here. Leave a message. Peace."*

I finally crawled under the thick comforter of the Holiday Inn bed, worried sick. Had my mother heard from any of us? *How could I let this happen?* As I lay in the dark, kicking myself for my selfishness, I had an inkling of how some of the mothers at the shelter must feel, crawling into their bunks on Mother's Day and not hearing from a single child.

chapter 27

A phone rang . . . kept ringing . . .

I woke with a start and grabbed the bedside phone. The boys? Philip? But it was only the hotel's automated wake-up call. I fell back into the bed, feeling disoriented. I was here in Petersburg . . . had spent the weekend with the boys . . . the visit with Philip's parents had gone better than expected . . .

So why did I feel sad, like it had all gone wrong?

My mother. I still hadn't talked to my mother!

Opening the room-darkening drapes and gulping water to clear my voice, I found my cell phone and pushed the speed dial for Mom. One ring . . . two . . . three . . . and then to my relief, the phone picked up. A wobbly voice. "Hello?"

"Mom?! Oh, thank goodness! I tried to call you several times last night and got no answer. I was so worried!"

A pause. "Who is this?"

What—? "It's Gabby! I should have called you yesterday morning, but—"

"Oh. Gabby. You girls all sound alike, you know."

Sound alike? My mother had never said that before. "Mom, I'm so sorry I didn't call you first thing yesterday. I'm in Petersburg, visiting P.J. and Paul for Mother's Day. And we were running around all day—"

"Petersburg? Didn't you move to Chicago?"

"Yes, yes. But the boys are still in school here in Petersburg . . . Mom, are you okay? You don't sound so good."

"Oh, yes. I'm fine. Just tired is all. Didn't feel too well last night, so your dad told me to go to bed early . . . no, no, that's not right. I think I was at Aunt Mercy's house for dinner, and she brought me home because I didn't feel good . . ."

Now I was really worried. That was the first time my mother had slipped up, talking as if Dad was still alive. Aunt Mercy was my dad's sister, our only other relative in Minot. Maybe that's why Mom got confused. I tried to keep it light. "Oh, well, that explains why you didn't answer the phone. You must be a sound sleeper, Mom. But . . . are you sure you're okay?"

"I don't know, Celeste. This house is too big. I can't keep up. Do you have to live so far away in Alaska? Maybe you and Tom could come live in the house and I could go to the nursing home. After all, it's just me and Dandy now . . ."

My eyes blurred. I didn't bother to remind my mother again that I was Gabby, not Celeste. Dandy was my parents' dog, also aging, a sweet mutt somewhere between a sheltie and a cocker spaniel, with a lot of hair. But in spite of the dog, she sounded lonely. Shouldn't be a surprise after forty-eight years of marriage, now a widow living alone—but her confusion was what worried me.

The phone call with my mother unsettled me long after I

checked out of the Holiday Inn . . . after taking the boys to Aunt Sarah's Pancake House for breakfast . . . after reluctantly saying my good-byes and heading the rental car north to Richmond International. Should I have gone home to see my mother this weekend instead of insisting on seeing the boys? Maybe Philip was right; it was silly to make this trip when we'd be flying down there in another ten days for P.J.'s graduation!

I buckled myself into the aisle seat of the American Airlines plane, due to arrive in Chicago shortly after noon. Usually I loved to chat up my seatmate when flying alone, but my inner tussle took up all my attention.

That verse in Proverbs Edesa showed me . . . what does it mean to trust God with all my heart and He will direct my paths? Am I trusting God? Did I make the wrong choice this weekend? Surely there isn't anything wrong with wanting to see my boys after a whole month, is there? But . . . should I have given up what I wanted and done what was best for my mom? Who needed me more?

"Uh . . . coffee. Cream, no sugar. Thanks," I said the flight attendant, who'd had to ask me twice if I wanted something to drink. But the possibility that my decision to go see the boys had more to do with standing up to Philip than choosing "who needed me more" made me squirm. To be honest, I hadn't even thought about my mom, hadn't even called her until Sunday night . . .

As the plane squealed to a wet landing at O'Hare International—Good grief, was it still raining in Chicago?—I blew out a long breath. What was the point of second-guessing myself? I did go to Petersburg, and I was glad I got to see P.J. and Paul. The question now was what to do about my mom. I probably needed to see her too—and soon.

I called Philip's cell from the taxi and got his voice mail. "Hi, Philip! I'm back; my flight was on time in spite of the rain. Since it's still early, I'm going to Manna House to put in a few hours this afternoon. The boys send their love and can't wait to see you next week. See you tonight. I'll make dinner. Bye!"

I flipped the phone closed, once again wrapped in my thoughts as the taxi driver—foreign, dark, maybe Indian?—darted into traffic on I-90 heading into the city. *Has it really come to this?* Philip hadn't called me once while I was gone. I hadn't called him either. And just now I didn't say "I missed you" or "Love you"— those little endearments that marked our early years. I missed those little whispers in my ears. And yet . . . was I at fault? Was I the one pulling away?

"Oh, God, I need help here . . ."

Only when the driver glanced into his rearview mirror at me did I realize I'd spoken out loud. Then he grinned, teeth stark white against his dark skin in the mirror, and he made curlicue motions with his fingers around his head. *My hair.* It always went bonkers in the rain.

I rolled my eyes and laughed back. "Where are you from?"

"Pakistan, two years! English I like to practice." He seemed eager to talk, and I was glad for the distraction as the car crawled through heavy traffic.

When the taxi finally pulled up at Manna House, I rushed in and tapped on Mabel Turner's door and opened it. She looked up from her paperwork. "What are you doing here? I thought you were in Virginia!"

"I was. But my plane got in at twelve thirty, so thought I'd come in for a few hours. Thanks for giving me the time off."

She gave me a sly look. "Didn't give you time off. We have ways of filling up your time card."

"In that case, I already did it." I smirked back at her. "I was here until eleven cleaning up after the Fun Night!"

The director laughed and waved me off. But Carolyn accosted me as I pulled my suitcase across the multipurpose room. "Hey, Gabby. What about the books you promised? I found a bookcase in the alley, not too bad. We could put it right over there in that corner, or maybe in the TV room, make it a library instead. And we need a new chess set too. The one we got is missing two pawns, have to use checkers." Then she looked at my suitcase. "You movin' in or somethin'?"

"Not today." I laughed. "But you never know. Thanks for the reminder about the books. I'll work on it." That and a zillion other things. Donations. I needed donations of books. And a resource list sent out to supporters and volunteers . . .

The rest of the afternoon I worked on a *Manna House Needs Donations* sheet for board members, staff, and volunteers to hand out to their churches, friends, and coworkers. And mailing list. I needed access to the shelter's mailing list of supporters.

By the time I left Manna House at five o'clock, the "shelter kids"—about five of them school age—were ricocheting around the rec room, letting off steam. A crew of people I didn't recognize—volunteers?—were banging around the kitchen, making supper. On the main floor, a couple of toddlers and their mothers were making use of the playroom, while the TV room bleated some kind of sitcom laugh track. Aida Menéndez yelled at me from across the multipurpose room, "The Fun Night was awesome, Miss Gabby! Can we do it again this Friday?"

"Not this week, Aida! Maybe—" I caught myself just before I said, *"Maybe next month."* No way did I want to set up expectations I couldn't make good. "Maybe we can do it again sometime, though."

Since I had my suitcase and it was still drizzling, I broke down and called a taxi for the ride home. And somewhere between Manna House and Richmond Towers, I came to some direction about my mother. First of all, I needed to call her more than once a week. Maybe even every day for a while, to keep an ear on her situation. And I really needed to be in contact with my sisters about our mother, if nothing else. Last but not least, I needed to plan a visit—maybe even a trip to North Dakota with the boys this summer. They'd only been to Minot twice—when they were about five and seven, and later to my dad's funeral two years ago. The outdoor community swimming pool had been a favorite, plus all the comic books they'd found in my parents' attic from when we were kids. Even better . . . what if Honor and Celeste came too, and we had a family reunion?

As the taxi drove into the frontage road and pulled up in front of Richmond Towers, I made another resolution. I was going to start praying about my mom. And trust God to work something out.

With a lilt in my step, I pushed through the revolving door, then managed to get my suitcase stuck outside and had to back up . . . but finally I wrestled it through the door and crossed the lobby, in a hurry to get upstairs and see what ingredients might magically be on hand to make a nice supper for Philip. But I dreaded what I might find. Philip wasn't good at "baching it." An overindulgent mother and a live-in housekeeper had pretty much inoculated him from catching any domestic skills. But that was the way it was. So be it.

"Hello, Mr. Bentley!" I called out to the doorman. "Thanks for coming to our Fun Night at the shelter." I simpered at him. "You were definitely the life of the party."

Mr. Bentley gave me a little bow with a smile. "Thank you for inviting me, Mrs. Fairbanks. I looked for you this morning but didn't see you. Did you"—he tipped his head at my suitcase—"go somewhere this weekend?"

I smiled big. "Yes. I flew back to Virginia to see my boys for Mother's Day. They'll be coming next week. Afraid your job may never be the same. They're lively."

"Mm. Wonder who they get that from? . . . Oh, by the way." Mr. Bentley glanced into space, his voice super casual. "The woman named Estelle . . . I think she's a volunteer at the shelter. Seemed like a mighty fine woman. I was, uh, wondering if you happen to have her phone number. She said something about doing elder care, and I thought maybe sometime I could talk to her about my, um, mother, in case she, you know, needed some in-home care. Just in case."

I stared at him, listening to him stumble and blather, remembering how he and Estelle had cut the rug doing the Mashed Potato at the Fun Night—and ended up dancing or being partners for games the rest of the evening. And I burst out laughing. "Mr. Bentley! Elder care, my foot. I do believe you have a crush on Miss Estelle Williams!"

chapter 28

I chuckled all the way to the thirty-second floor. Mr. Bentley and Estelle . . . now, that would be a pair! I promised him I'd get her phone number—with her permission, of course—and somehow finagled his age out of him. ("I don't know, Mr. Bentley, she's just a young *chica*, and you—" "What do you mean? I'm still this side of sixty, got lots of miles left, and she's a mature woman, at least fifty.")

He'd wanted to know more about her, but I had to admit I didn't know much—just that she lived in the Rogers Park neighborhood up north, attended SouledOut Community Church, was licensed to do elder care, and volunteered at the shelter. I didn't tell him she herself had been a Manna House resident at one time. I didn't know that story, didn't know how she became homeless, and I didn't want to speculate. She could tell him if he got brave enough to ask her out.

I unlocked the door to the penthouse, wondering if I'd have time to pick up the house, clean the kitchen, *and* cook supper before Philip got home—but to my surprise, the house was as tidy as when I left Saturday morning. Kitchen counters clear . . . bed made . . . no dirty clothes on the floor. In fact, the only evidence that my husband had even been there all weekend was a used towel in the bathroom, hanging over the shower door.

"What do you know?" I said to my reflection in the bathroom mirror as I dried my damp hair with the blow dryer. "Guess old dogs *can* learn new tricks." I'd have to really thank him for the nice welcome-home surprise.

The answering machine light was blinking. *Eight messages?* That was a lot for a Monday . . . unless Philip hadn't bothered to answer them all weekend. I touched the Play button to listen as I opened the refrigerator to scout our meal possibilities. The first two were telemarketing recordings. I hit Delete twice and kept rummaging in the fridge.

The third was Henry Fenchel. *"Philip? You still there? Mona says she wants to stay Sunday night too, okay with you? We can get back to the office by midmorning Monday . . . Philip? Pick up if you're there, buddy. Okay, guess I'll try your cell. Bring plenty of Horseshoe money! And clean shorts. Ha-ha-ha."*

I stood stock-still with the refrigerator door wide open. Stay *where* Sunday night?! What did he mean, "Sunday *too*"? Had Philip been gone all weekend without telling me? Was he doing that to spite me? And where did they go? Henry said bring plenty of "Horseshoe money" . . . what did he mean by that? I'd seen billboards advertising a Horseshoe Casino but had never paid any attention where it was. Indiana maybe . . .

I pushed Play to listen to Henry's message again, a shaky mad building in my gut. Maybe Philip didn't agree with me going to Petersburg this past weekend, but at least I'd told him! After the third time through, I let the answering machine run through the other messages: a call from his mother . . . two more telemarketing reps . . . then my spinning mental wheels did a U-turn as I heard my name.

"Gabby dear? Please give me a call. This is Aunt Mercy. Your mother had a fall this morning at home. Didn't break anything, thank God. Good thing I was picking her up to go to church. I heard Dandy barking, so I let myself in. I took her to the ER just to be sure she's all right, then brought her to my house. Just wanted to let you girls know where she is if you call her today."

Now I was really upset. My mother had fallen yesterday? She hadn't said anything about that when I talked to her this morning!

The last message was from Aunt Mercy, too—6:10 last night. *"Gabby? I don't know if you got my other message, but I'm taking your mother home now. I wish she'd stay overnight, but she wants to go home to take care of the dog. I'll check in on her on Monday. Please call me. We need to be able to get in touch with you in an emergency. Do you have a cell phone? All right. Guess you're not there. Good-bye."*

I forgot all about making supper for Philip and used the caller ID to return my aunt's call. I apologized all over the place for the missed communication, told her I'd been out of town, gave her my cell number, told her to call me at any time day or night, told her I'd tried to call my mom on Sunday and finally got her this morning, but Mom hadn't said anything about a fall . . .

I held off crying until I hung up with Aunt Mercy, and then I had a good bawl on the living room couch, feeling like the proverbial no-good, rotten, terrible daughter. And that's how Philip found me when he came in the door at six thirty, surrounded by used tissues. And I yelled at him. "Where were *you* this weekend, Philip Fairbanks?! My mother had a fall, and, and Aunt Mercy called here, and if you'd been here, you could have let me know! Why didn't you *tell* me you were going to be away too?! What did Henry mean, bring Horseshoe money? Did you and those, those Fenchels go gambling at one of those casino hotels?" I pulled my knees up to my chin and sobbed some more.

Philip just stood there, tight-lipped. Then he said, "Is your mother all right?"

I nodded, hiccoughed, and blew my nose again.

"Good. Then let's talk about this when you get control of yourself." He stalked out, then returned. "Did you make anything for dinner?"

I shook my head. "I . . . I was going to, but—"

"Never mind." A moment later I heard him on the phone, ordering something to be delivered.

Philip had been unapologetic when we finally talked over Chinese takeout. "It came up at the last minute, Gabby. Henry tossed me the idea on Friday, and I said I'd think about it. But you didn't get home till late that night, remember? After I dropped you off at the airport the next morning, I realized it was going to be a long, lonely weekend until you got back on Monday, so, heck, why not? I called Henry; we drove to Indiana and had a great time. Snazzy hotel, great food, a good show . . . If you'd been here, they'd have invited you too."

"But . . . gambling, Philip? It's a big racket! People lose money. And it can be terribly addictive, as bad as a . . . a drug addiction or alcohol."

"Good grief, Gabby. What do you take me for? I didn't take any more than I could afford to lose—but the fact is . . . I won."

His boyish grin widened. "Seventeen hundred bucks. Not bad for a weekend's work."

I'd been floored. What could I say?

The whole fiasco troubled me for days, but I tried to drown my worries at work. Josh Baxter showed up on Tuesday to drop off a packet of ESL materials from his mother and Avis Douglass. I wanted to ask him how Gracie's adoption process was going, but he seemed to be in a big hurry, so I let it go. I passed the ESL materials on to Tina and told her to look them over. "They're geared more toward kids than adults, but it'd be a start," I told her. She nodded, came back to me the next day, and said she'd give it a shot. She seemed both nervous and excited. We set up an ESL class to start the next Tuesday at 5:00 p.m.

I talked Estelle into bringing as much leftover knitting yarn and extra needles as she could muster and encouraged her to teach knitting to women on Wednesday morning while they waited their turn to see the nurse. At least five women took a pair of needles and labored on and off for two hours learning how to "cast on" and do simple "knit and purl" stitches before and after their turn behind the nurse's room divider. Even Hannah the Bored picked up a pair of needles and tried a few rows—though it was a bit awkward with her long nails. Today they were decorated with flourishes and tiny rhinestones. Where did she get money to do *that*?

But I swear, when I told Estelle that Mr. Bentley had asked for her phone number, the woman deepened at least two shades to raspberry chocolate. But she gave it to me, muttering, "*Humph*. I need a business card."

Lucy hadn't been at the shelter when I got back on Monday, but she showed up again Wednesday morning to see the nurse about her cough and to get something for her "rheumatiz" . . . and signed up for a bed when a thunderstorm cracked overhead, unleashing a torrent of spring rain. The woman was still a mystery to me, but she usually rebuffed my attempts to get her to talk. But I took my lunch tray on Thursday and pulled out a chair at her table. "Mind if I sit?"

"Free country." She stabbed a forkful of kielbasa, potatoes, and cabbage.

I took a bite. "Mm. This is good." I was surprised how tasty the stew was. "Wonder what's in it?"

Lucy gave me her "dumb question" look. "Whatever ya got on hand is what's in it, missy. Ain't your ma never made stuff like this? Cabbage, taters . . . some kinda meat if you're lucky."

"Hm." I swallowed my mouthful. "I don't think so. We kids didn't like cabbage."

"Humph." Lucy shoveled in another mouthful. "That didn't make no difference at our table. Head o' cabbage went a long ways. Sometimes that's all it was. Cabbage soup . . . cabbage stew . . . rice rolled up in cabbage leaves . . . Used to grow the things on our two-bit farm down in Arkansas 'fore the drought drove us out."

My ears pricked up. Lucy grew up on a farm in Arkansas!

"Drove you out?" I tried to keep my question light, not prying.

Lucy eyed me up and down sideways for half a minute. "Huh. You too young to know anything 'bout the big migration. Where'd you grow up anyway? Chicago? . . . Nah, you just moved here."

I could hardly contain my excitement. Lucy and I were having an actual conversation! "Yes, from Petersburg, Virginia. My husband's home. But I grew up my first twenty years in a small town in North Dakota." I laughed. "Most of the farms around us were wheat and cattle ranches. But not my family. My dad owned a carpet store."

Lucy just looked at me with her rheumy blue eyes as she chewed on cabbage and sausage. To my disappointment, she didn't say any more.

As I went back to my office, I tried to put together the bits of information she let drop. *A two-bit farm in Arkansas . . . "the drought" drove them out . . . the big migration . . .* Lucy was likely in her seventies, at least. Which probably meant her family was hit hard by the Dust Bowl and the Great Depression. But where did the Tuckers "migrate" to? And what brought her to Chicago?

I shrugged, dug out my cell phone, and hustled upstairs where I got better reception. Lunch seemed a good time to catch my mom, and it was already one o'clock.

Philip and I had been civil but distant most of the week. Thursday night I suggested we make plans for our trip to Petersburg for P.J.'s graduation and work out the details for bringing the boys to Chicago. Philip said he'd already made plane reservations for next Wednesday so we could be present for the academy's award night, as well as the graduation ceremonies the next day.

"Oh. Well, that's good." I looked at the computer printout. Return flight was scheduled for Saturday. *Drat.* I'd been hoping we could return on Friday, but . . . oh, well. At least we'd be with the boys.

"Their bicycles," I said. "How are we going to get them here? They'll want them, I'm sure. There are a lot of bike trails along the lakefront. In fact, that'll be fun if the four of us—"

"Leave them."

"Leave them?" I was startled.

"Of course. It doesn't make sense to ship them here when they'll want to have their bikes on weekends next school year."

"*Next* school year?" Dismay and panic fought with a familiar anger. I wanted to scream, *"Over my dead body!"* But instead I said, "Philip! We *moved* to Chicago, remember? It's one thing for the boys to finish out this school year, but we need to find a school for them here in the city. I'm sure there are plenty of good private schools—"

"I already checked it out. The enrollment for most decent schools closed months ago. Besides, Fairbanks males have always gone to George Washington Prep. It's family tradition."

I was speechless. When I finally found my voice, it was shaking with anger. "No! I will not be a thousand miles away from my sons for a whole school year! That wasn't part of the deal! They're just *boys*, Philip! They need their parents!" *And I need them*, my heart cried. I'd never realized how much the boys had filled up the cracks in Philip's and my marriage . . . until we came to Chicago.

"Oh? If they need their parents so badly, why did you get a job that's going to take you out of the house during the summer while they're here? Who's going to take care of them during the day while we're both at work? Did you think of that, Gabby?" He snorted. "Of course you didn't. You never do."

chapter 29

I woke Friday morning with a ferocious headache. The same headache that started during the fight with Philip the night before. Philip had nailed me. In the past few weeks, my mind had conveniently separated into two tracks, job and family. When I was at work, I got excited about all the possible activities for Manna House residents that summer. I'd also imagined doing all sorts of fun things with the boys once they got here—swimming at the beach, exploring the lakefront bike trails, getting family passes to the museums, taking in the ethnic festivals that went on all summer . . .

I'd stammered, "I—I'm sure I can work something out . . ." but before I could finish my sentence, Philip drove in another nail. "Never mind. I've already signed them up for sailing camp the second week of June. You'll just have to take time off from work until then." And that was that.

Dragging myself out of bed the next morning, I downed a couple of extra-strength Tylenol and brewed a strong pot of coffee. I stayed at the penthouse long enough to get Camila started on the housecleaning, then ducked past Mr. Bentley in the lobby on my way out the door. The man was too perceptive. One kind word from him, and I'd be blubbering my mascara down to chin level.

I decided to walk the two miles to work. I needed the exercise to help clear my head. The sky was cloudy, the air damp, but at least it wasn't raining. When was Chicago going to dry off, for heaven's sake?! No way did I want the boys to arrive and be stuck in the penthouse five days a week, or we'd have mutiny on our hands.

My insides clenched. Rain was the least of my worries. I dreaded the boys getting caught in all the tension Philip and I seemed to generate like static from walking over a wool rug.

At the shelter, I somehow managed to sign in and make it down to my cubbyhole without getting caught in any conversations. *Turn on the computer . . . call up e-mail . . . go over Mabel's staff notes and announcements . . .* But all the words on the screen seemed to run together and reformat in my brain: *"Fairbanks males have always gone to George Washington Prep. It's family tradition."*

I grabbed fistfuls of my hair. *No, no, NO!* I'd go crazy if the boys went back to school in Virginia next fall, leaving their father and me to navigate rough waters alone. It took too much energy trying to keep an even keel when Philip's "gusts" hit my sails. My life kept tilting off balance like Lester Stone's sailboat—"heeling up," he'd called it—and it was my side that kept skimming dangerously close to those choppy waves. One more gust, and I'd be in the drink.

Drowning.

Okay, I needed to get a grip. The Bible I'd set on the back corner of the desk caught my eye. Hadn't I promised God I'd start reading the thing again if He answered my prayers and helped me get this job? Well, God had kept His end of the bargain. I pulled the book toward me. But where to start? Too many times as a girl I'd made a New Year's resolution to read the Bible straight through and started with Genesis 1, only to get bogged down in Exodus and never get any further.

Suddenly my eye caught something on the computer screen. Mabel's staff announcements included Edesa Baxter's topic for her Bible study today: "Isaiah 54—The Barren Woman." That seemed like a curious topic. But maybe it was as good as any to read today. I could go to the Bible study prepared.

I found Isaiah 54 and began to read—and within moments the tears I'd been holding back all morning flooded over. *"Sing, O barren woman,"* the chapter started. *". . . burst into song, shout for joy . . . because more are the children of the desolate woman than of her who has a husband . . ."* I groaned. The verses seemed to be talking about *me*. I had a husband, I had children—but I was the one who felt desolate.

Grabbing a ready supply of tissues, I kept reading through blurry eyes and came to verse six. *"The Lord will call you back as if you were a wife deserted and distressed in spirit—a wife who married young, only to be rejected, says your God . . ."* The flood of tears spilled over again. Oh, yes, I'd married young—and been rejected. But that was then. I should be over it now. Why did I still feel so . . . so deserted?

I backed up and read the first several verses again, reading and rereading the fourth and fifth verses. *"Do not be afraid; you will not suffer shame. Do not fear disgrace; you will not be humiliated. You will forget the shame of your youth, and remember no more the reproach of your widowhood . . ."* Except it wasn't true. Even though I had married again and had thought I'd be living the fairy tale of my dreams, if somebody asked me right now, I still felt afraid. Humiliated. But mostly, I felt . . . alone. Like a widow.

So what in the world did verse five mean? *"For your Maker is your husband—the Lord Almighty is His name . . ."*

I never did make it to Edesa's Bible study, because all I could do was sit at my desk behind a closed door . . . and weep.

I ran into Edesa in the line for lunch, Gracie riding her hip. "Gabby!" She gave me a hug. "I thought you weren't here today."

"I know. I missed your Bible study." I gave her a wry smile. "It's all your fault."

Her eyebrows went up.

"Yeah. I decided to read your Scripture passage before I came to the Bible study, and . . . well, it touched a few raw nerves."

Now her eyebrows came together, putting wrinkles of concern into her smooth, brown skin. She lowered her voice. "Do you want to talk about it, *Gabriela*? Or pray?"

I shook my head. "Not right now, but thanks anyway."

She smiled. "At least you are reading the Bible, *mi amiga*. That is good."

Gracie reached toward me. "Gaaa."

What a cutie. I leaned close to give her a kiss, and the eight-month-old grabbed a fistful of my hair.

"Ow!" I gently untangled the little girl's hand from my curls. "Uh, what's happening with Gracie's adoption? Any news?"

Edesa instinctively drew the child closer to her body and

nuzzled her soft hair. "*Sí y no*. Next week we go to a hearing about our petition to get guardianship of Gracie. This must happen before we can proceed with the adoption. But now this ex-boyfriend of the mama's—at least that's what he claims—says he's the daddy and wants to take her."

"But, didn't you get guardianship when you became her foster parents?"

"*Sí! Sí!* But now they say it is only 'temporary' guardianship—an emergency, because her mama died of a drug overdose while she was here at the shelter, and she needed *una familia* right away. But I know Carmelita wanted me to take care of Gracie, to bring her up! She left us a note! That is how we got custody of her in the first place."

We had stepped out of the lunch line in order to talk off to the side. "And other people witnessed this note?"

Edesa nodded, eyes determined. "*Sí*. Many staff members and residents here, they all knew. Reverend Handley, Mabel, and others will have to come to this hearing and testify . . . and even then, the judge will also talk to this man. The social worker at DCFS told us blood family usually has priority." The young woman's full lips trembled. "But I *know* God put Gracie into my arms! It is why Josh and I got married—"

She must have seen my startled look, because she quickly added, "I mean, it is why we got married *now* instead of waiting longer. Though . . ." She looked away. "Well, it is not so easy."

I pulled her farther away from the lunch line. "Are you two okay? I mean, you and Josh seem very much in love."

"Oh, *sí*, of course I love Josh. It's not that. It's just . . ." She sighed. "The apartment *es minúsculo*! Only two rooms and a bath. And the walls . . . like paper! The *familia* we are renting from must hear every time we *a-choo*, not to mention . . ." She rolled her eyes. "They are good friends—one of my Yada Yada sisters— which makes it worse."

"Oh Edesa." I wanted to hug her. "Have you looked for a bigger apartment?"

She shook her head. "We have no money. I mean, Josh works part-time, but we are both going to school. Money, so tight. Sometimes we fight." She sighed. "I wish—"

Heavy feet coming down the stairs caught our attention, and a second later Josh Baxter materialized from the stairwell, backpack slung over one shoulder, looking this way and that around the dining room. "There you are! Am I in time for lunch? My afternoon class got canceled, so I thought . . . hey there, Gracie girl, come to Daddy?" The overgrown college guy held out his arms.

Edesa surrendered the baby and grimaced at me behind his back. I gave a single shake of my head. I didn't think he'd heard us talking.

"Hey, you three!" Estelle's voice sailed across the room from behind the kitchen counter. "You goin' to eat or what? I gotta sit down. My feet are killing me."

We hustled over to the counter, where Estelle handed us plates of sliced ham, cooked carrots, and what looked like corn pudding. As Josh jiggled Gracie on his lap and hand-fed her bits of corn pudding, he said, "Oh, hey, Mrs. Fair—um, Gabby . . . my mom wants to know if you'll be at the Sunday Evening Praise this weekend. It's SouledOut's turn to do worship here, and she and my dad are coming. She'd like to meet you and talk to you. Something about a typing class?"

"Sure. I'll make it a point to be here. And I've been meaning to ask you two—do you know where I could get a CD of that song the New Hope worship team did two Sundays ago? The chorus went something like, 'I go to the Rock . . .'"

Josh scratched the back of his head. "I kinda remember. I think it's an old Dottie Rambo song. I don't know if it's been recorded lately . . . but I'll check around."

Saturday, I had to admit, was a perfect spring day—low seventies, sunny. I stood a few steps back from our floor-to-ceiling wraparound windows, drinking in the sun sparkles on the lake. *I might even like Chicago if there were more days like this.* But as tempting as it was to go out and play, I spent the weekend putting the finishing touches on the boys' bedrooms, making chocolate-chip cookies and freezing them, and shopping for groceries so we'd have their favorite foods on hand—boxes of macaroni and cheese, frozen hamburger patties, hot dogs, both kinds of buns (plain and poppy seed), and cans of spaghetti and meatballs. And frozen Pizza Bites.

At least they still preferred my homemade cookies.

When Philip went running Sunday morning, I got on the computer and searched online for Memorial Day activities in Chicago. We were bringing the boys home on Saturday, which meant we still had Sunday and the Monday holiday. I found lots of things going on—the Memorial Day parade, an Irish Fest, fireworks at Navy Pier . . . *whoa.* The Cubs were playing Atlanta at Wrigley Field next Sunday! Could I get tickets this late? Maybe Henry Fenchel could help me. Philip would be dazzled.

My spirit lifted. I was *not* going to let the fight with Philip over my job ruin the boys' homecoming. I'd work out something. After all, my job was part-time and the schedule flexible. I'd cut my hours if need be—which should be possible once I got a number of activities up and running. And if I did have to take some time off . . .

A tickle of an idea brought a smile to my face. Why not? I picked up the phone. What time was it in Alaska, anyway?

chapter 30

When I told Philip I'd managed to get four tickets to the Cubs game next Sunday—with Henry's help—he was elated. "No kidding! Good thinking, Mop Top."

Building on this goodwill, I asked for the car to go to the Sunday Evening Praise at Manna House, promising I wouldn't come home without it. Then, in a burst of good intention, I asked if he'd like to go with me. "You could see where I work," I said. "And we haven't been to church together since we came to Chicago."

Philip snorted. "You call that church? When you're ready to go to *church*, Gabby, we can talk about going to church."

My face burned. A quick retort rose to my lips. As if Sunday Evening Praise at Manna House was stopping us from going to church somewhere Sunday morning! But I decided to leave it alone. "Okay. Maybe when the boys come, we'll find a church."

He didn't answer.

Park it, Gabby, I told myself—and I didn't mean the Lexus, though I did find a parking space halfway down the block from the shelter, and I was able to leave two feet of room between me and the next car. It was still light at six o'clock, but might be dark when I came out. As I *beeped* the remote car locks, a couple came walking up the sidewalk, then stopped.

"Mrs. Fairbanks?"

They looked familiar—and I realized I'd met them once. "You're Josh's parents!"

The man laughed. "Gee, I thought when the kids moved out, we'd get our names back." He held out his hand. "Denny Baxter. And this is my wife—I mean, Josh's mother."

"Denny!" "Josh's mother" backhanded her husband with a smart left, then held out her right hand to me. "I'm Jodi—and don't mind him. You're Gabby, right? We talked on the phone."

I smiled and shook both their hands. "Yes, of course! Thanks so much for the ESL materials. We'll put them to good use." I wanted to laugh. Finally! "First name" people. I'd never seen a man with dimples as deep on both cheeks as this guy. They were both probably a few years older than I—early forties?—but both were pleasant looking. Denny had short-cropped hair, still brown but graying. Jodi wore her dark brunette hair shoulder-length, bangs swept to one side.

"I'm so glad we're getting a chance to meet you," Jodi said. "Josh and Edesa talk about you all the time—oh, there's Avis and Peter. Hey, you two!"

Another couple came from the opposite direction as we converged on the Manna House steps. I recognized Avis Douglass as the woman who spoke at Sunday Evening Praise the first time I'd come, and her husband, Peter, was on the Manna House board. The two couples seemed very cozy with one another, which was interesting, since the Baxters were white and the Douglasses black. But I remembered that about SouledOut the last time the church had come to Manna House—the praise team and others from the church were a rather diverse crew. Not a "black church" like New Hope Missionary Baptist, or a "Spanish church" like the time Rev. Álvarez spoke, or Rev. Handley's white suburban church that came on Mother's Day last week, the Sunday I'd missed.

As we all stood in the foyer and chatted, my thoughts drifted. If only Philip had come with me, I wouldn't feel like a fifth wheel . . . and it'd be good for him to meet men like Peter Douglass, who owned his own software business, and Denny Baxter, who said he was athletic director at a Chicago public high school. Respected people in the Chicago community who supported shelters like Manna House.

What was Philip's *problem?* The jerk.

"Gabby? Come sit with us." Jodi Baxter took my arm. "If you don't have to rush off afterward, maybe we can talk about that typing class you asked about—though I teach third grade, and they're not typing yet!" She laughed and hustled us into the multipurpose room, where the SouledOut instrumentalists and singers were starting on their first song.

My eyes blurred a little bit as the saxophonist pulled the words along. *"We bring a sacrifice of praise . . . into the house of the Lord!"* But it wasn't the song. Not even the rather poignant image that this homeless shelter was "the house of the Lord."

It was a longing deep inside I'd buried for a long time. I needed a friend. A *girlfriend.* Someone who wasn't a coworker, as friendly as all the volunteers and staff at the shelter were. Someone who wasn't half my age, as much as I adored Edesa. Someone married, with a husband near Philip's age, someone with the potential to have good times as a couple. Someone who called me Gabby and would like me just for myself.

Someone like Jodi Baxter.

On Monday morning, I asked Mabel Turner if I could take a week off the first full week of June, no pay, to take my sons to North Dakota to see their grandmother. With our trip to Virginia in a few days, and Memorial Day weekend coming up, that only left six working days in the next two weeks, but I promised I'd try to have a slate of activities up and running by then, which hopefully could function for a week without my oversight.

"Jodi Baxter is willing to do a Saturday typing class starting next week. And once school is out, she'll consider doing another on a weekday. Peter Douglass said he'll look into getting us a couple more computers. Carolyn wants to start a book club, as soon as we can settle on which book . . . and I've got a couple other ideas I'm pursuing."

I couldn't read Mabel's face. What if she didn't want to let me off? I'd already left messages for both my sisters suggesting a family reunion in Minot that week. I'd just assumed I could work this out with the job! And the more I'd thought about it, the more I realized I had to do this—for my mother, for the boys, for my marriage . . .

"I'm sorry to ask for time off again so soon after our trip this week to pick up the boys, Mabel. But I really need to check in on my mom. And the boys don't begin their summer camp until the following week. This would take care of both, and I'd—"

Mabel held up a hand. "Gabby, stop. You don't have to convince me. If that's what you need to do, we'll swing by somehow here. What concerns me is . . . what's going on at home? You seem to be juggling some delicate plates in the air, acting as if you're afraid they'll fall and break into a thousand pieces."

I wasn't prepared for that. But I couldn't answer either. I didn't want to paint Philip as some ogre before Mabel and others here had even met him. And Philip and I *were* going to work this out, weren't we?

"Sorry," I said weakly. "We're still . . . adjusting to our move, new jobs, boys coming home—you know how it is. Thanks for understanding about taking the week off." I fled downstairs to my office.

When I switched on the light, I realized someone had already been there. On my desk was the shelter's CD player and a plastic CD case. I picked up the plastic square. The soundtrack from *The Preacher's Wife*. I glanced at the list of songs, and there it was: "I Go to the Rock." But when I opened the CD case, it was empty. Already in the CD player.

I grinned. *Bless Josh Baxter.* I wondered where he'd found it. Clicking through the songs, I got to the number I wanted and pushed Play. The music pulsed and filled my cubbyhole . . .

Where do I go . . . when there's no one else to turn to?
Who do I talk to . . . when nobody wants to listen?
Who do I lean on . . . when there's no foundation stable?
I go to the Rock, I know that He's able, I go to the Rock . . .

I practically wore out that CD in the next few days. I even found one of the boys' old portable players with earphones and listened to it as I traveled to and from work on the El. The CD contained some other neat songs too, most of which I'd also never heard. How could I be so ignorant of really great gospel music? To tell the truth, my repertoire of "Christian music" consisted mostly of hymns and Sunday school songs I'd learned growing up, with a few contemporary songs and choruses that were popular with my youth group when I was a teenager. Twenty-plus years ago.

I had a lot of catching up to do.

I was soon caught up in the whirlwind of washing clothes Tuesday evening, packing, canceling Camila on Friday, trying to reach my sisters again and finally sending e-mails about meeting up in Minot in June, calling my mom and aunt ahead of time to let them know we were heading for Virginia . . . and finally Philip and I were on the plane Wednesday afternoon heading for Richmond.

Philip buried his attention in a copy of *BusinessWeek*, with the complimentary glass of wine provided in business class, leaving me to close my eyes and begin to relax. We were going to see the boys in a few hours . . . and then bring them home. *"Home"* . . . that wasn't a word I applied easily to the penthouse in Richmond Towers. But maybe with the boys there, we would begin to feel like a family again.

Oh Lord, please, make us a family again.

My thought-prayer bounced to my sisters, who still hadn't responded to either my phone messages or e-mails. What had happened to our family? The last time I'd seen either of my sisters was at my dad's funeral two years ago, and we rarely communicated. *Lord, can you make us a family again too?*

On the other hand, for the next few days I was going to be

wrapped once again in the tight-knit web of Philip's family—where I felt not so much included as caught. *Huh*. Could I pray the same prayer for the Fairbanks family?

We drove our rented luxury SUV directly from the airport to George Washington Preparatory Academy for the annual end-of-the-year award night, with plans to meet Mike and Marlene Fairbanks, who were getting a ride with another set of grand-parents so we four could return together. Philip was his charming self, joking with his parents and escorting me with a gentlemanly hand on my elbow. I warmed to his touch and started to relax, his self-assurance flowing to me. I suspected he felt good about return-ing home to Petersburg—and to his alma mater—on the upswing of a new business.

The stately auditorium with its dark wood wainscoting and pewlike seating was abuzz with proud parents, siblings, and grandparents as we found our seats, just before the academy's middle school students marched in, dressed in their maroon, navy, and royal blue school blazers, depending on the class.

"There's P.J.! Do you see Paul?"

The evening was long, but I felt like cheering when Philip Jr. received a second-place science award for his astronomy project on black holes, as well as a "team participation" trophy in soccer. But to my surprise and delight, Paul received a band award for original composition.

"Since when is Paul musical?" Philip stage-whispered.

"You knew he signed up to play trombone in the band."

"Yeah, well, every boy goes through a stage when he wants

to play the trumpet or trombone or something big and brassy. Usually doesn't last long."

A lump settled in my throat. I hated that I hadn't known he'd composed a piece for the band. What else didn't I know about my youngest son?

Afterward, amid congratulations and hugs and excited babble, we went out to eat—along with scores of other family groups. I wasn't really hungry, just kept sneaking peeks at my sons as they chattered. P.J.'s dark hair and Romeo lashes preempted the few pimples that had erupted on his chin. Paul's childish flush still bloomed beneath his chestnut curls trying to grow back. I could have soaked up their faces all night, but we had to have the boys back to the academy by eleven. The school expected all its students to be present for the graduation ceremonies, so report cards and room clearances were deliberately scheduled for the following day.

The SUV hummed its way back to the Fairbanks' "country suburban" home near Petersburg in the warm night air, still in the midseventies. Mike Fairbanks rode in the front seat with Philip, while Marlene and I chose our corners on the soft leather seat in back. Chatter about the award ceremonies and how proud we were of "our boys" turned to polite questions about Chicago. With a note of pride, Philip confidently described the accounts he and Henry had been able to land in the last six weeks.

"That's right," I chimed in. "I'm proud of Philip. Fairbanks and Fenchel has gotten a good footing in Chicago in a short time."

His father *harrumph*ed. "Well, that's good, Philip. I'm real happy for you. Just don't lose those accounts by getting cocky and trying designs that are more fluff than functional."

"Fluff!" A flash of anger hardened Philip's voice. "I don't do *fluff*, Dad. I do bold, I do cutting-edge . . . I just don't do old and tired."

"Watch your mouth, young man!" the senior Fairbanks snapped. "The Fairbanks name means something here in Virginia. Quality. Heritage and tradition."

Even in the dim interior, I saw Philip's mouth turn into a thin line and his eyes dart to the rearview mirror, where he caught his mother's eye. Marlene blew her son a silent kiss. "Don't you worry, Mike dear," she purred. "Philip is going to make a name for himself in Chicago."

"*Humph*. Make a name for himself . . . He already had a name here to live up to—if he could."

The tension in the car thickened until I thought I might suffocate. I pushed the button to roll down my window, inviting a snap from Philip. "Gabby. I've got the air on." I rolled it partway up.

We rode in silence through the winding roads. Then Mike Fairbanks growled, "I'm just thinking about the boys, Philip. It's one thing for you to have your fling, get some of these newfangled ideas out of your system—"

I saw Philip's hands tighten on the steering wheel at the word "fling."

"—but what are the boys going to do in a big city like Chicago? They've already got a good start at George Washington; they've got their friends *and* a family business to take over when the time is right."

Philip's mother took over. "Well, of course they'll continue their schooling at George Washington, darling. Philip knows the boys love it here, and he knows they're always welcome to stay with us."

Of all the—! How dare they talk as if I had no say in my sons' future! I opened my mouth, ready to blast them all. *"Forget it! The boys aren't coming back to Virginia in the fall. They're our sons, and they belong with us!"* But all I got out was, "I'm sorry. We haven't made that decision yet—" before Marlene interrupted, still purring, but more like a bobcat than a kitty.

"I'm not worried about Philip, darling. He'll do the Fairbanks family proud . . . if certain people don't tarnish the name with their own foolish ideas."

I stiffened in the darkness. *Wait a minute.* What did she mean by "certain people"? Did she mean Henry Fenchel? . . . or me?

chapter 31

Even after we unloaded our suitcases and squirreled away in the guest suite of his parents' beautiful home, Philip was still fuming. "The old fart! I thought he'd be over his little tantrum about me starting my own business by now. Well, he can just stuff his opinion up his you-know-where—"

It wasn't a conversation. I let him rant while I brushed the snarls out of my Orphan Annie hair, wishing I had the nerve to complain about his mother's little dig. I did suggest maybe we could change our tickets to leave Friday instead of Saturday, but he just rolled his eyes. "No way. I'm not going to let him run me off." He flopped on the bed, the steam dissipating. "Let's just make the best of it and enjoy the graduation tomorrow. I don't want to disappoint my mom. They do adore the boys, you know."

Argh! Now I was fuming. Why didn't he just stand up to his parents? His father goaded him, made him feel like a failure waiting to happen, while his mother dripped sweetness that stuck like flies on flypaper.

Only later in the darkness, listening to Philip's soft snoring, did I realize that the little interaction in the car between father and son was a mirror of how Philip treated me.

Summer temperatures settled over Virginia the next day like a wool blanket with no sheet. Hot. Sticky. Scratchy. We sweated in the ancient hall that still boasted no air-conditioning, fanned our way through the graduation ceremonies with our programs, and glared at the families who cheered when their son's name was called even after the headmaster requested that applause be held until *all* the graduates' names had been called . . . Then it was over, and the four of us stood outside under a shade tree, watching indulgently while P.J. and Paul tussled with their friends on the wide lawn, acting out because all the adults were watching.

Philip and I did the final room checks with the boys in their dorms. Good thing, since we found an overdue library book, a single dirty sock, and a wadded-up T-shirt under P.J.'s bunk, and Paul's suitcase wouldn't close because he'd just stuffed everything into it willy-nilly. But the resident assistant finally stamped their room inspection cards, which the boys and I had to have in hand at the registrar's office in order to pick up their report cards. When we got back to the car, waving cards that were mostly Bs sandwiched between an occasional A and C, Philip and his father had loaded the boys' suitcases, trunks, and sports equipment . . . and then we were off.

"Can I play lacrosse next year, Dad?" P.J. hollered from the third seat as we headed down the long drive that led off-campus. "Most of my friends are going to sign up for the Upper School's junior team."

"Don't see why not, son."

I turned in my seat. "What Dad means, P.J., is that we'd love to see you play lacrosse. But with the move to Chicago, we can't make any promises about anything just yet."

"But, Mom! Dad just said—"

"We'll talk about it, okay, P.J.? Just not now. Hey, I'm hungry. How about you boys? What would you like? This is a special day. P.J., you choose."

But P.J. had flopped back in his seat, arms folded, lips tightly pressed, glaring out the window.

"Pizza Hut!" Paul offered.

Philip groaned from the driver's seat. "At least let's do Sal's and Brothers pizza."

I tried to laugh off P.J.'s sulk. "Hey, did you boys know Chicago has the best pizza in the world?"

I let out a long sigh of relief once our American Airlines flight to Chicago was in the air on Saturday. Paul was in the window seat next to me in business class, playing with a handheld electronic game, a gift from his grandfather. Philip and Philip Jr. sat across the aisle. Finally it was the four of us. A family again.

I leaned my seat back and closed my eyes. The rest of our visit with the Fairbanks had gone reasonably well, I thought, with the exception of a conversation between Philip and his mother I'd overheard the previous night . . .

"Of course the boys will be returning to George Washington Academy in the fall, Philip! You said that was the plan before you moved to Chicago. They're already registered! I don't understand why Gabrielle—"

"I know, Mother. But she's their mother, and of course she misses them. Right now she doesn't want to think about them coming back. But things may look different after a couple of months. Give her time. And like you said, they're already registered. It won't hurt to look at the Chicago academies and consider our options."

I glanced across the aisle, where P.J. was plugged into his own iPod world—a graduation gift, also from his grandparents. Of course the boys were already registered at George Washington Academy, but so what? We'd done that last January, before moving to Chicago had even blipped onto the family radar. All we had to do was tell the school we'd moved out of state and get our deposit back . . .

A flicker of uncertainty licked at the edges of my thoughts. *What if it's too late to register for any of the Chicago-area private schools?*

No. I wasn't going to let doubt make me afraid. Didn't Philip say it wouldn't hurt to consider our options? Said it to his mother's face, in fact! But why hadn't Philip and I talked about this before? *Really* talked, and come to a decision. Decided who was going to check out the Chicago schools, make applications . . .

"When I am afraid, I will trust in God . . . I trust in God, why should I be afraid?"

I let slip a small smile. I wasn't used to thinking Scripture verses, but Edesa's Bible studies at the shelter seemed to stick on me. Okay, I was afraid. I wished I'd brought my Bible so I could look up those verses in the Psalms, but that was a habit I hadn't revived. *Yet.* I needed to get one of those travel-size Bibles I could tuck in my purse so I wouldn't look like some fanatic Bible-thumper . . . if that mattered. What was a "Bible-thumper" anyway? People like Edesa Baxter, who loved to study the Bible?

Mabel Turner, who always had the right scripture for me? Avis Douglass, the classy elementary school principal who preached at the shelter once a month, encouraging women on the down-and-out?

I felt a tad guilty. Okay, forget whether I'd look like a Bible-thumper or not. But a travel-size Bible would still be a good idea.

Paul seemed awestruck by the view from the penthouse's glass wall in the front room. "We *live* up here? Wow! Is that really a lake? It looks like the ocean!" Then my youngest turned eyes of concern on me. "Don't you get a little, you know, queasy up here, Mom?"

I nearly melted.

His brother was already staking out territory. "Awww-riight! My own room. Mom, I want a lock so I can keep Punkhead here out."

I delighted in all the noise and chatter, giving the boys time to explore while I started a "welcome home" dinner sure to please—Southern fried chicken, mashed potatoes, creamy gravy, buttered green beans. Philip called for a cart to get the boys' luggage up the elevator, then disappeared into the den to check phone and e-mail messages and go through the mail, which was fine by me.

"Hey, P.J.! Paul! Come set the table, okay? Supper's almost ready!"

Twin groans radiated from both bedrooms down the hall. "Aww, do we have to?"

Philip appeared, waving an envelope. "Oh, give 'em a break, Gabby. It's their first night in Chicago. But I think they'll like what Henry sent us . . ."

Philip handed the envelope to P.J. as we sat down to dinner.

Our oldest crowed. "Cubs tickets! Hey, look, Punkhead! Four tickets to a Cubs game at Wrigley Field!" P.J. squinted at the fine print. "Tomorrow? Against Atlanta? Aww-riiight. Thanks, Dad!"

"You're welcome, buddy. Now, how about passing some of that chicken over here?"

I flinched. The Cubs tickets were *my* surprise. Why did Philip take the credit? *Well, just say so, Gabby. It's not a big deal.* "Actually, boys, the tickets were my idea—but they're from both of us." Or *something.*

But the opportunity passed, and the more seconds that ticked away, the more awkward I felt bringing it up. *So let it go, Gabby.* I did, smiling as the boys poured too much gravy over everything. But a too-familiar crack tore wider in my spirit.

The boys were totally berserk with excitement as we joined the crowd of Cubs fans on the Red Line El Sunday afternoon. Ninety percent of the riders got off at the Addison El Station, where Wrigley Field towered just a block away. The weather cooperated, draping Chicago with a bright, sunny day and temps heading into the nineties. I smiled happily. Looked like Chicago's rainy season might be over.

I had brought a backpack full of water bottles and snacks, but a security guard wouldn't let us in unless I dumped it all. "No food or beverages allowed inside the park," he growled. "Club rules. You can buy it inside."

I started to argue, but Philip took the backpack away from me and dumped the offending contents into the nearest trash can. "Come on, Gabby. That's just the way it is."

It was all I could do to keep from diving back into the trash can to retrieve it. Dump perfectly good food and water just so we could pay twice as much for it inside? When there were people like Lucy digging through Dumpsters, hoping for something to eat? Felt downright sinful to me.

Let it go, Gabby.

The game was exciting, even though I didn't follow the baseball teams much. Wrigley Field roared with happy fans as the score nudged upward, first the Cubs ahead, then the Braves. Between innings, Philip and the boys put away three hot dogs each, plus nachos and peanuts, washed down with soft drinks and two large beers for Philip. Well, at least he wasn't driving.

At the close of the ninth inning, the Braves won by one measly run—13 to 12. But the loss didn't dampen the boys' gusto. Philip bought Cubs caps and pennants for them on our way out of the stadium, and Chicago suddenly had two new Cubby fans.

I felt pretty smug. A Cubs game was a perfect way to help our sons own the move to Chicago. Even the ride on the El was exciting to them, in spite of having to stand in the swaying car, jammed like human sardines. I tried to think . . . was this Philip's first time taking public transportation? Well, good. Now he had some idea of how I got to work each day.

As the train passed the Sheridan El stop, I nudged P.J., who was hanging on to the nearest pole. "This is where I get off to go to work."

He looked at me funny. "Where do you work?"

"At a homeless shelter. You know. I told you. I'm the program director."

He wrinkled his face. "That's weird."

"I'll take you sometime—so you can see where I work." I looked at my watch. Sunday Evening Praise would be starting in an hour or so. Pastor Álvarez's Spanish church would be there. I was halfway tempted . . .

No. One step at a time.

The four of us got off at Berwyn and walked toward Richmond Towers, which rose in the distance. My mind was tumbling over things Philip and I needed to talk about in the next few days. Sailing camp didn't start till mid-June, but then ran for four weeks. If I took the boys to see their grandmother in North Dakota next week, that just left the rest of this week—four measly days after the Memorial Day weekend—to juggle between us. But even before we planned the boys' summer, we had to talk about school—

"*Streetwise!* Get your new issue of *Streetwise* right here!"

Just ahead of us on the first corner, a black man in a knit hat and a few missing teeth was peddling the newspaper. "*Streetwise!* Only one dollar! *Streetwise!*"

I rummaged in the backpack for my wallet, pulled out a dollar, and got a copy of the newspaper and a "God bless you, lady!" in exchange. I hurried to catch up to Philip, who had already walked ahead several yards, then realized the boys had fallen behind. Turning, I saw P.J. mimicking the man, covering his teeth with his lips as if he were toothless and pretending to call out, "*Streetwise!*" while Paul snickered. Before I even thought about it, I grabbed my firstborn by the collar, practically jerking him off his feet.

"Ow!" P.J. yelped, trying to pull away.

I put my face nose to nose with his thirteen-year-old mug. "Don't let me *ever* catch you doing something like that again, young man!" I hissed.

chapter 32

Hustling the boys out of earshot of the *Streetwise* vendor, I turned both of them to face me. "That man has had troubles you can't even imagine, but he's working for a living and trying to make a better life. He deserves to be treated with respect. He has a *name*. It's on his *Streetwise* badge. Maybe he has kids your age he's trying to support. Did you ever think of that?"

"You don't have to yell." P.J. looked at me beneath sullen eyelids.

"You think this is yelling?" I had deliberately lowered my voice to avoid embarrassing the boys in public. "Yelling is what I'm going to do if you *ever* disrespect someone like that again." I turned on my heel and marched off to meet up with Philip, who had turned around, frowning.

Behind me I heard Paul mumble, "Gee, if that homeless guy has kids, I bet they don't want anyone to know *he's* their dad." I ignored it and marched on.

Philip didn't see what the big deal was. "Good grief, Gabby," he said when I told him what happened. "They were just goofing around. They're kids!"

"That's no excuse! Philip, I work with homeless people like that—not with men, but some of the women at Manna House sell *Streetwise* too. What if that had been one of the women I know by name, someone I've eaten lunch with, who's told me her story, someone who's excited about some of the program ideas I've started?"

Philip looked back to be sure the boys were still following, then started to push through the revolving door of Richmond Towers. "Ah. I get it. This is about you. You don't want the boys to embarrass you."

My mouth hung open as the door swallowed him and spit him out on the other side. I pushed myself through to make sure he didn't get away. "No! I just made it personal, because it's easy to mimic someone or laugh at them when you don't know them, don't know anything about them. It doesn't have anything to do with me being embarrassed."

We passed the weekend doorman—"door dude" was more like it—who ignored us as Philip swiped his security card for the inner door. As he held the door open, waiting for the boys to catch up with us, Philip leaned toward me and lowered his voice. "Maybe not, Gabby. But did it ever occur to you that your choice of company might embarrass your *sons*?"

The boys, being boys, forgot about our little spat by the time we got to the top floor. Philip rode above it as though it had nothing to do with him. But I was upset. Upset that the boys had behaved so rudely—P.J. in particular, with no apology—and upset at Philip's insinuation. It just made me determined: I was going to take the boys to the shelter this week, introduce them to the staff and residents, let them hang out, and find something they could do to contribute.

Memorial Day turned out to be a bust, holiday-wise. Big clouds rolled up over the lake, throwing lightning darts and growling thunder just as we were getting ready to go downtown to see the Memorial Day parade. The boys stomped off to flop in front of the TV, but Philip didn't seem too disappointed. "I've got a lot of catch-up work to do anyway. You and the boys do . . . whatever." He headed for the den.

"Philip, wait a minute." I followed him into the den and shut the door behind me. "We need to talk about school for the boys next fall. I don't want to send them back to Virginia, not with us so far away. So we have to do something *now*."

He was already booting up his computer. "So what's stopping you? You're the one who's hot to find an alternative. When you find something that compares to George Washington Prep, then let's talk."

That took me aback. I thought for sure Philip would want to be in the driver's seat when it came to choosing a school for any child of his carrying the Fairbanks name. I'd held back, not wanting to step into territory he'd already claimed. But I wasn't about to question this turnabout.

"All right. I will. Thanks, Philip."

He was already calling up his spreadsheets and opening files. "Mm-hm. Shut the door behind you, Gabby."

Oh my goodness. If I'd known it would be this easy, I would have started weeks ago, as soon as he'd set his sights on Chicago.

Today was a holiday, so schools would be closed. But at least I could get the phone directory and start making a list—

"Mom. I'm bored. There's nothin' to do." Paul drifted into the kitchen, right behind his whine.

"How about . . ." I racked my brain, then picked up the phone and dialed 0-1. "Mr. Bentley? Oh, good, you're here today. Be right down." I turned to Paul. "Where's P.J.? I have somebody I'd like you to meet."

I managed to pry P.J. away from the widescreen TV in the living room, which was televising the rather wet Memorial Day parade, and we rode down to the lobby in the elevator. Mr. Bentley was standing in front of the half-circular desk, spiffy as usual in his blue uniform. I gave him a wide smile. "Boys, I'd like you to meet my friend, Mr. Bentley. You'll see a lot of him. He *rules* this roost."

"Mrs. Fairbanks," he said, doffing his cap. "You're back from Virginia, I see. And this must be the young man who just graduated from middle school." Mr. Bentley held out his hand to P.J. "Congratulations, young man. And welcome to Chicago."

P.J. shook Mr. Bentley's hand with all the enthusiasm of a limp noodle. Mr. Bentley didn't seem to notice—or chose to ignore it. He turned to Paul. "What about you, young man? Do you have a name, or should I give you a street name? Like your mom." He looked side to side, as if casing the lobby for spies. "Her street name is Firecracker."

"Wha—what?" I giggled, feeling my cheeks flush.

Mr. Bentley leaned closer to Paul's eye level and patted his own bald head. "You know. The, um, hair."

Paul laughed out loud. "Nah. My dad calls her Mop Top. But

only when he's in a really good mood." He held out his hand. "I'm Paul. He's P.J."

Mr. Bentley's eyebrows went up. "Ah. Now, what would that stand for? Pearl Jam? Para Jumper? . . . I know. Peter Jackson! *Lord of the Rings—*"

Uh-oh. I saw P.J.'s eyes flash. "No. It stands for Philip Fairbanks, *Junior.*" P.J. turned to me. "Come *on*, Mom. I thought we were going to do something."

Mr. Bentley straightened. I wanted to apologize for my humorless son, but Mr. Bentley pulled a couple of coupons out of his pocket. "Well, then. Maybe these will come in handy. Good for free doughnuts or ice cream at the Dunkin' Donuts a couple of blocks north of here." He gave one to each of the boys. Paul's eyes lit up. P.J. gave a grudging nod of thanks. "And it seems to have stopped raining. Just in time."

The doorman smiled, put his cap back on, and turned to greet another Richmond Towers resident coming in. I headed for the revolving door, eager to get out of there to cool off my flaming cheeks. I had so looked forward to introducing Mr. Bentley to my sons. Why was P.J. acting like such a jerk?

Give them time, Gabby. Give them time. Right. They'd been in Chicago all of two days. They'd grown up in Deep South Suburbia. Had to be some culture shock.

We found the Dunkin' Donuts on Bryn Mawr and used the coupons to get ice cream for the boys while I splurged on an iced latte. As we came out of the shop, the sun was drying up the puddles, and the thunderheads were drifting westward. "Hey, guys. I know what let's do. Come on!" I headed for Richmond Towers once more—only this time, we skirted the high-rise for the park on the other side. Feeling a tickle of excitement, I started to run, leading the boys through the pedestrian tunnel beneath Lake Shore Drive . . . and introduced them to kicking off our shoes and splashing in the gurgling edges of Lake Michigan.

After all, I giggled as I chased first Paul and then P.J. along the wet sand, the boys and I were still dressed in the shorts and T-shirts we'd planned to wear to the parade. Even if we ran into Lucy Tucker—Miss Beach Police herself—she couldn't fuss at me.

Philip wasn't happy about my plan to take the boys to North Dakota for a week. "Good grief, Gabby, they just got here."

"Yes, but you said yourself sailing camp doesn't start for another two weeks, and you wanted me to take time from work to spend with them. So I'm taking that week off."

"I meant give up the stupid job, Gabby."

I tensed. The boys were finally in bed and we were heading that way, but I didn't want to fight with Philip. I chose my words carefully. "Don't be unfair, Philip. You've already got them signed up for sailing camp, and after that there'll probably be something else. It doesn't need to be either-or. Besides, I need to go see my mom, and this would be the best time to take the boys too. It all works out."

Philip pulled off his gym shoes and tossed them. "What about this week? You taking this week off too?" Socks came off, then his T-shirt, all ending in a pile with the shoes.

I bought time picking up his clothes and putting them into the laundry hamper. "No-o. But it's only four days. I thought I'd take them to work with me one day and show them around, then maybe do one of the museums for a half day. If you took them to work with *you* one day, why, that's three days already—"

"Take the boys to work with me?" Philip looked at me as if I'd suggested hanging the boys by their thumbs.

"Well . . . sure. I thought you'd want the boys to see your new office, meet your partner, and, you know, get a feel for what their dad does."

"Sure. But that would take, what, one hour? Why don't *you* bring them to the office one day, on your way to the museum or something. And let me know exactly when you're coming. I've got a busy week."

I kept back the tears until I was in the bathroom by myself, door locked, water running in the sink as I washed my face. *Oh God, why is this so hard?* I looked at my face in the mirror—snarly curls askew, cheeks sunburned from our afternoon at Wrigley Field, mascara smudged from tears. Was I being stubborn? Should I have taken the job at Manna House? It had seemed like such a God thing. Mabel even said as much. But maybe I *should* quit—

No. That made no sense. We only had four days to cover for the boys! A week to visit my mom . . . then they'd be gone all day to sailing camp for a whole month. It was a good plan. Philip was the one being unreasonable. If he'd just meet me halfway, we could work this out.

Burying my face in a towel, I wished I had someone to talk to. Or pray with. It seemed so much easier when Mabel or Edesa talked to God. But right now it was just me. *Jesus,* I started—but instead of a prayer, the gospel song on the CD Josh gave me filled my head. *"Where do I go . . . when there's no one else to turn to? Who do I talk to . . . when nobody wants to listen? . . ."*

I groaned into the towel. Good question.

chapter 33

Taking the boys to Manna House the next day went better than I expected. Of course, before we left the house, I threatened to take P.J.'s iPod away for the rest of his natural life if he showed the slightest disrespect to any living soul that day.

"O-*kay*, Mom, I get it. But what are we supposed to do all day while you're working? It's going to be so *boring*."

"So? Nobody ever died from being bored. But tell you what. If you're so bored you can't stand it at two o'clock, I'll knock off and take you home—but you'll have to cook supper tonight so I can get some work done at home. However, if you hang with me until four, I'll cook supper *and* even do your dishes tonight. Deal?"

The boys brightened considerably. I knew they liked to mess around in the kitchen—mile-high hamburgers and doctoring frozen pizzas were their specialties—so the whole deal probably felt like win-win to them. They even seemed to get a kick out of riding the Red Line again, choosing to hang on to the poles rather than sit as the train jerked and swayed around corners.

I'd called Mabel to ask if it was okay to bring the boys along, but I was surprised when she met us in the foyer when we arrived at nine thirty and presented the boys with orange and black "Manna House Volunteer" T-shirts, which said in small lettering beneath, "I'm part of God's miracle."

"Is that black lady the boss?" Paul whispered to me.

"Top dog." I grinned. This was going to be a good education for my sons. George Washington Prep had its small share of minority students, but except for the maintenance and grounds crew, the entire administration and teaching staff were white.

I was hoping we'd run into Lucy, but Mabel said she hadn't been in for about a week and a half—which meant my conversation with Lucy about growing up in Arkansas had been the last time anyone had seen her. But I did see several new faces in the multipurpose room, including a busty young woman still in her teens who was falling all out of her half-buttoned blouse. I hustled the boys to the lower level on the pretext of showing them my office. P.J. was unimpressed. "Gosh, Mom. Our bathroom at home is bigger than this."

I laughed. "Of course it is. This used to be a broom closet."

Just then Estelle Williams hollered at us from the kitchen. She'd whipped up a batch of chocolate-chip cookies in the boys' honor and gave P.J. and Paul the task of passing out the hot-from-the-oven cookies to everyone on the lower and main floors, which made them immediately popular with the current crop of residents. "Top floor is off-limits though," Estelle warned.

"What's up there?" Paul's eyes widened, as if he suspected hidden corpses.

Estelle chuckled deep in her chest. "Sleeping rooms. This is a *women's* shelter, son. No men allowed."

Between delivering cookies and playing Ping-Pong in the rec room, the boys managed to entertain themselves while I caught up on responses to my recent e-blast requesting donated supplies. Two boxes of books had come in from Rev. Handley to start the Manna House library, and Carolyn had already appointed herself Head Book Honcho and invented an honor-based "checkout" system. An e-mail from Josh Baxter's mom, Jodi, confirmed that she was all set to teach typing in the schoolroom this coming Saturday at eleven, and three people had signed up, including Kim, even though we only had two computers. And Tina left me a note saying she would try teaching the first ESL lesson tonight— Tuesday—from five to six, just before supper.

So far, so good.

When the bell rang for lunch, I went through the line with the boys and got them settled at a table, then caught Estelle by herself when I went back to the counter for napkins. "Did Mr. Bentley call you?" I whispered.

"Mm." Estelle didn't miss a beat refilling the bowl of butter pats.

"Well?"

"Well, what?"

"Estelle!"

"Well nothin'. We talked about care options for his mother."

"And . . . ?"

"And none of your business, Gabby Fairbanks." She flounced over to the heavy-duty refrigerator to replace the plastic container of butter pats.

Chuckling, I returned to our table, only to find Miss Bulging Blouse sitting across from the boys, talking loudly with someone at another table. But there was no mistaking the way the older teenager cut her eyes at P.J. or her sultry smile. P.J., on the other hand, wasn't looking at her smile . . .

With a start, I realized P.J. was going into *high school* in a few months, looking for all the world like a junior version of the dreamboat I fell in love with in France on that fateful day sixteen years ago in the Place de la Comédie.

I gulped. I wasn't ready for this!

Making a quick getaway after lunch, I let the boys watch a Spiderman movie in the TV room on the main floor, while I made up an activity calendar of weekly events so far: ESL on Tuesday late afternoon . . . Typing on Saturday morning . . . Knitting on Wednesday while the nurse was here . . . plus the Friday Bible study . . .

I still had a few more "life skills" ideas I wanted to get off the ground—basic cooking classes (Estelle?), basic sewing (Estelle again?), maybe a dance exercise class (Precious?). And Josh had suggested a sports clinic for the shelter kids on the weekend. Was he volunteering? His dad was athletic director for a high school in Rogers Park . . . *Hmm, that might be a good resource.*

Somehow I also managed to squeeze in a few calls to Chicago-area private schools, but the answers were all the same. "I'm sorry, registration is closed" or "We can put you on a waiting list." My heart was starting to sink. *Oh God, please help me find a good school for the boys . . .*

I sighed. Seemed like most of my prayers were still the *"Oh God, help!"* variety. How did Edesa and Mabel and that Avis woman learn how to pray? Seemed like the prayers of all those women were full of praise and thanksgiving, no matter what disaster was pending. *I need someone to teach me how to pray.* Funny thought, given that I'd grown up going to church until I gave it up in college. Correction: until Damien left me. But how could I go to church all that time and still not get it when it came to prayer?

I glanced at the clock. Almost four. We'd been here almost all day! The boys' movie should have been over an hour ago . . . what were they up to? Gathering my bags, I hustled up the stairs to the multipurpose room. Carolyn's ponytailed head was bent over a game board in the far corner, matching wits with P.J. and Paul in a game of Stratego.

"Time to go, guys," I called out. "Thanks, Carolyn."

"Aw, Mom, do we have to?" P.J. fussed. "We're right in the middle of a game!"

A smile started somewhere inside and popped out on my face. P.J. didn't want to go home yet? *God, You really do have a sense of humor.*

Somehow we made it through Wednesday and Thursday too. On both days I put in three or four hours of work, then took the boys to see the beluga whales at the Shedd Aquarium on Wednesday, and on Thursday we took the El downtown to the Aon Building so the boys could see the offices of Fairbanks and Fenchel—yes, there it was, a large nameplate beside the door—and have a late lunch with their father. My eyes nearly bugged out when I saw the professional décor: sandstone and fawn on the walls, tan leather couches with deep brown and ochre-red throw pillows, a rug that picked up the rich brown and sandstone colors, desert prints on the walls, and large, leafy plants.

My kind of room, exactly.

Uh-oh. Did Mona Fenchel think I pushed for my idea instead of hers? I was amazed she was still speaking to me. Or was she? Come to think of it, we'd been on Lester Stone's sailboat together all one Sunday afternoon, and I couldn't remember more than three sentences she'd said to me that day.

But on Friday the boys balked. "Can't we just stay here and play video games?"

"I wanna go to the beach," Paul whined. "Can't we go to the beach?"

Frankly, I'd run out of ideas. *Just one more day. One more day to juggle—*

The intercom chimed. That would be Camila. I buzzed the security door so she could come up and briefed the boys. The three of us were waiting in the gallery when she got to the door. "Camila, these are my sons, P.J. and Paul. Boys, this is *Señora* . . ." My glance pleaded with the woman to please provide a last name.

Blushing, she seemed to understand. "Sanchez. Camila Sanchez. I am very happy to meet your fine sons, *Señora* Fairbanks."

To their credit, both boys gravely shook hands before disappearing into their rooms. I ran a hand through my hair, which seemed to be getting frizzier as the June humidity hiked up. "I—I hope we won't be in your way, Camila. I had planned to go to work, but the boys want to stay home today, so I'm not sure what I'm going to—"

"Oh, you go. You go." Camila Sanchez flicked a hand at me, as though shooing a fly. "Your fine boys can stay with me. I am here until two o'clock. I will watch them. Just give me a phone number where I can call you. It is no problem. Go, go."

I gaped at her. "Oh, Camila—and please, call me Gabby—are you sure? I'd be happy to pay you extra." I couldn't believe how this answer had dropped from above right into the gallery, almost like that Bible story where a bunch of friends lowered their sick buddy right through the roof to get to Jesus. I grinned at the analogy. Camila Sanchez's generous offer felt like a little miracle.

The boys seemed okay with the arrangement, and agreed to stay out of Mrs. Sanchez's way in whatever room she was cleaning. I made them promise not to leave the premises until I got back, and if they behaved, we'd go to the beach as soon as I got home that afternoon.

I had to admit I felt relieved going to work without having to worry about entertaining the boys. Couldn't blame them, either, for not wanting to tag along with me every day. Had Philip given *any* thought to his kids when he bought the penthouse at Richmond Towers? Even if I wasn't working, what were they supposed to do every day? It'd be different if we lived in a neighborhood where they could ride their bikes or run outside to play with their friends any time they wanted . . .

One thing at a time, Gabby. Right. At least the boys would have a great time romping with their cousins for a week in my old hometown—which reminded me. Celeste and Honor still hadn't confirmed that they were coming home next week! The three-hour time difference in Alaska made finding a convenient time to call my oldest sister difficult. And Honor tended to view time on a sliding scale. "I'll call you tomorrow" might be tomorrow—or a week later.

Well, I'd try when I got to work. Celeste ought to be up by then.

But my first phone call after I dumped my bags on my desk was to the penthouse. "Camila? How are the boys? . . . Good. Good. Yes, I know it's only been an hour . . . But you'll call if there's any problem, all right?"

285

Well, that was silly. Of course they're all right. Those two could play video games for hours. I'd wait until noon to make the next call, and maybe just before I left at two.

Next I tried Celeste. She should be up by now, even with the time difference. But I immediately got a recorded voice saying, "That number is being checked for trouble." *Rats.* That usually meant a dump of snow had hit Denali National Park, disrupting their landline. And the geography made cell phone access spotty at best. I dialed her cell anyway and left a message.

At ten thirty I went upstairs to catch Edesa before the Friday Bible study, hoping to find out what had happened at the adoption hearing while we were in Virginia last week, but they'd already started. I tried to slip in quietly, but Edesa stopped midsentence and said, *"Hola!* Gabby's back!" She flashed her familiar megawatt smile as I sat down. "We missed you last week, Gabby. I was just telling the ladies that today we're going to ask the same question the disciples asked Jesus: 'Lord, teach us to pray.' Has everyone found the book of Matthew, chapter six?"

Well, this was ironic, given that I was wishing someone would teach me how to pray earlier this week. But . . . the Lord's Prayer? I'd memorized that as a kid, and it was a regular part of the liturgy at Briarwood Lutheran. But repeating a rote prayer wasn't exactly what I had in mind.

I considered slipping out, but that seemed rude after just sitting down. So I stayed put—and then forgot about leaving as Edesa Baxter broke down the prayer into tiny parts. "First, Jesus encouraged His disciples to give God praise! 'Hallowed be Thy name!' *Hallowed* means holy, sacred, blessed. When we come into the presence of the King of kings, this is the first thing we do. We worship Him!"

I listened in amazement as the young black woman from Honduras—who seemed too young to be so wise—went phrase by phrase through the Lord's Prayer, encouraging these women off the street to get familiar with the Bible, so they could pray *in* the will of God. "Because prayer is powerful, *mis amigas*. Prayer changes things. But that doesn't mean God's going to answer your prayer for security by sending you a smooth-talking pimp who's promised to take care of you if you'll just take care of his johns." Nervous snickers and a few guffaws consumed the room.

The discussion got a bit dicey when she got to the part about confessing our sins and asking God to forgive us. "Jesus said we also need to forgive people who sin against us."

"Man! I ain't forgivin' my daddy for what he done to me. He can burn in hell for all I care."

"What if the scumbags don't confess *their* sins? Do we still have to forgive 'em?"

"Jesus did," Edesa said simply. "While He was hanging on the cross, after being whipped and nailed through His hands and feet, He said, 'Father, forgive them, because they don't know what they're doing.' But that doesn't mean it's easy. I know." Her lip trembled. "I admit I'm very angry at the man who got Gracie's mother pregnant, probably got her hooked on drugs, too, and then abandoned her to die. And now he's trying to take Gracie away from us."

Suddenly everyone wanted to talk about the crackheads and slicksters in their lives who didn't deserve to be forgiven. I slipped out of the room. This didn't seem to apply to me. Nothing in my life matched what these women had suffered—not even Edesa's fight for Gracie.

But I decided to take another look at the Lord's Prayer.

Starting with praise . . . I was definitely weak on that one. *Asking God to meet my needs* . . . Yeah. When I got desperate. But it talked about "daily bread." Basic needs. Why not *before* I got desperate? *Confessing my sins* . . . Didn't do that too often. *Huh.* It was bad enough constantly having to apologize to Philip for all the ways I didn't measure up to his expectations. *Forgiving others—*

I stopped with my hand on the doorknob to my office.

Could I forgive Philip for making me feel like I was nothing more than sand in his shoes?

chapter 34

I phoned the boys at noon and talked to Paul. The natives were getting restless. "It's eighty degrees out there, Mom! I wanna go swimming."

"I know, hon. Hang in there. Let me talk to Mrs. Sanchez."

Camila said everything was fine, but she had to leave at two o'clock.

"That's fine, Camila. The boys can stay by themselves for a little while. I should be home by two thirty or so. I'll check in with them by phone."

I made a point to catch Edesa at lunch and ask about the hearing, but she just shook her head. "It got postponed, Gabby. Nobody said why." The anxiety in her large, dark eyes contradicted her wry smile. "Makes it hard to practice what I preach—you know, what I said this morning, about forgiveness. And patience!"

Frankly, it was good to know she was human. I gave her a sympathetic hug, told her to keep me posted, and went looking for Mabel. I hadn't seen the director at lunch, so I tapped on her office door, my list of current and proposed activities in hand.

"It's open!"

I peeked in. She and Stephanie Cooper, the case manager, had their heads together—beauty-shop-relaxed black coif and wash-and-wear light brown bangs—poring over a stack of manila file folders. "Oops, excuse me. I can come back later."

Mabel looked up. "That's okay. Just doing progress reports. What's up?"

I waved my list. "I can just leave this with you. There are some life skills I'd like to add to the program—and Estelle Williams could do it all. Sewing. Cooking. But she's already making lunch five days a week, and she's teaching some of the women to knit when the nurse is here. I hate to ask her to do more as a volunteer." I took a deep breath. "Have you thought about adding her to the program staff? Even part-time?"

The director cast an amused glance at Stephanie. "How did you know we were talking about adding to our staff? Stephanie needs another case manager too."

Mabel invited me to write a memo to submit to the board meeting in two weeks, listing the need and Estelle's qualifications. "Personally, I like the idea. What else is on that list?"

By the time I got back to my office and typed up the memo, it was already after two. I grabbed the phone and dialed the penthouse. The phone rang seven times and went to voice mail. "P.J.? Paul? Pick up! This is Mom." Nothing.

Oh, great. They probably have the TV on and can't hear the phone. But I knew Camila had to be gone by now, and I didn't like not knowing if the boys were all right. Grabbing my purse and backpack, I signed out and headed for the El. I tried again while I waited for the Red Line. Still only got voice mail.

An uneasy thought niggled at me as I paced on the platform.

What if the boys got tired of waiting in the house and decided to go swimming on their own? Did the beaches have lifeguards yet? Chicago schools weren't out, but it was after Memorial Day . . .

By the time the train finally opened its doors at my stop, I was that jumbled bag of nerves familiar to parenthood—furious that the boys hadn't answered the phone, plotting dire punishments if they had disobeyed me, and scared spitless that something had happened to my kids. I practically ran the three blocks to Richmond Towers, pushed through the revolving doors, heart pounding . . . and stopped dead in my tracks.

A chunky white man I recognized as another resident in the building had the shirt collars of both my sons locked in his grip, one in each hand, and—neck veins bulging—was spouting off to Mr. Bentley. "Call the police right now!" he was yelling. "If you don't, I will!"

P.J. was writhing like a wild feline. "Let me go, you jerk! I'll tell my dad."

The doorman patted the air with both hands as though trying to calm everyone down. "Now, no need to call the police. I know the parents. Just let me—"

Paul spotted me and burst into tears. "Mom! Make him let us go!"

Heart pounding, I finally found my voice. "Mr. Bentley! What's going on?"

Before Mr. Bentley had a chance to say anything, the red-faced man had let go of my sons and was shaking a finger in my face. "These your kids? You live here? What kind of parent are you, letting them run loose around the building, raising Cain?!"

"What—what did they do? . . . Mr. Bentley?"

But the man wasn't finished. "Snuck into the parking garage

and ran around rocking cars, setting off a dozen car alarms." He stabbed his finger at me again. "You better believe management is going to hear about this!" He stormed off, but he had one parting shot for Mr. Bentley. "If you can't keep hooligans like these brats from running amuck in our building, mister, I'll have your job!"

The man's words burned in my ears. *"Hooligans like these brats . . . I'll have your job."*

But I tried to focus on the real issue with P.J. and Paul when we got up to the penthouse. "He shouldn't have said that, but he was angry. With good reason. You boys know better than to create a ruckus like that! What were you thinking?!"

P.J. flopped on the couch, arms folded, face molded in an angry pout. "But, Mom, we got so bored! There's nothin' to do here."

"No excuses. I told you not to leave the house until I got home."

"Yeah, but you didn't come, and the whole day was almost gone."

That got me. It was so tempting to relent, pack a snack, grab our swimming suits, and let the sparkling waters of Lake Michigan wash this whole ugly incident into oblivion. But I braced myself to follow through. "I'm sorry I wasn't here when Mrs. Sanchez left. And I'm sorry you had to wait so long. But that's still no excuse for setting off car alarms, for heaven's sake! You have embarrassed your dad and me and . . . and you even put Mr. Bentley's job in jeopardy."

P.J. shrugged sullenly. That did it. I realized neither boy had so much as said, "I'm sorry."

"Both of you. To your rooms. You're grounded the rest of the day—and maybe longer. Depends on what Dad says when he gets home."

Twin wails went up. "Aww, Mom!"

"Go!"

I pressed my fingertips to my scalp as bedroom doors slammed. *Oh God. Please don't let this get Mr. Bentley in trouble too.* Heating water for tea to calm my nerves, I realized I was less concerned about us getting kicked out. In fact, I almost hoped it would happen. Maybe we could look for a house—on the *ground*—or even buy one of those charming row townhouses in one of the "gentrified" urban neighborhoods.

Get a grip, Gabby. Philip would blow a gasket—

Philip. I groaned as I steeped my chamomile tea. I'd give anything if I didn't have to tell Philip. But I had no doubt we would hear from management about this, and it would be even worse if he found out that way.

By the time my husband got home, I had a pot roast in the oven—I figured a heavenly "welcome home" smell never hurt— and had steeled myself to tell him right away what had happened. Personally, my own mad at the boys was over, and I was going to lobby that not getting to go swimming today was punishment enough for a first offense . . . but I should have known better.

Philip was furious with *me*.

Somewhere in the back of my mind, I had hoped the boys and I could pack Friday evening and take off for North Dakota on Saturday. But Philip insisted on taking the boys to Navy Pier for the day—"Since you kept them holed up here like moles yesterday," he'd hissed at me—to ride the enormous Ferris wheel, eat lunch at Bubba Gump's, and take a sail on one of the masted "tall ships" that gives rides by the hour to tourists.

My eyes burned with unshed tears as I washed and folded clothes, ordered a rental car for the trip—a minivan, no frills—and packed duffel bags for the boys. Nothing I'd done yesterday had been right according to Philip, from leaving the boys with Camila Sanchez in the first place, to not being there when she left, to not fulfilling my promise to take them swimming. Of *course* they got into trouble. What did I expect?

I'd said nothing. From his point of view, he made a good case. None of this would have happened if I'd been home with them instead of at work.

I argued my own case to the laundry basket. "Good grief! P.J. is thirteen, old enough to stay home a few hours by himself—*and* look after his younger brother! . . . Many families have working parents . . . I was home for years when the boys were small . . . Philip is the one who sent the boys off to boarding school nine months out of the year! . . . A job for me at this time in our life makes sense. My job is a worthy one, and I'm good at it . . . Since I do have a job, there will be times we have to pull together as a family and adjust. I can't just work a few months and quit, then start up again . . . Good grief! One day of boredom isn't going to kill the boys. And I *am* taking a week off to take them on a vacation trip . . ."

But it was no use. Philip's words continued to beat me over the head in the silent penthouse. *"Selfish"* . . . *"Pigheaded"* . . . *"My mother is right about you"* . . . *"Might as well send the boys back to Virginia right now"* . . .

I buried my head in a still-warm-from-the-dryer T-shirt. Was I just selfish and pigheaded? Was I the crazy one here?

Frankly, I was glad to be leaving for a week. We both needed time to cool off. By the time I got back, the heat would be off, the boys would be in sailing camp for a month, and we could settle into a workable routine.

But the silence in the empty penthouse was starting to give me jitters. I called Manna House at noon to ask how the first Saturday typing class went. I waited for several minutes while someone went to see if Jodi Baxter was still there, then she picked up.

"Checking up on me, are you, Gabby?" Her voice was teasing. "Actually, I was surprised you weren't here to make sure I showed up." Jodi laughed. "I'll have to tell you sometime about the first time I volunteered at Manna House. The place burned down." She chuckled again. "But seriously, the class was good, I think. That Kim is a real go-getter. She's still in the schoolroom practicing. A couple other people dropped by and asked if they could learn to type, too, which would be fine with me, but you'll need several more computers." She paused a mere nanosecond, as if shifting gears. "How are you doing, Gabby? Everything okay?"

The question took me by surprise . . . and for some reason I found myself telling this woman I barely knew about the juggling act all week, trying to entertain my boys *and* keep up with my job.

"Oh, boy, tell me about it. I've been teaching third graders ever since our youngest started school. At least Denny and I both work for the public schools, so when school is out, so are we. Well, technically. Except Teacher Institute Days. And athletic meets on weekends, ad infinitum. But if one of our kids got sick? There went all *my* sick days."

For some reason, I found Jodi's homily strangely comforting. Lots of families had to juggle schedules. I was not crazy. "The worst part is," I found myself saying, "I let them stay home yesterday since the woman who cleans for us was there until two o'clock, which was fine, but I didn't get home until three—which turned out to be just long enough for them to get into trouble."

"Oh dear. What did they do?"

Why was I telling her this? "It's so embarrassing. I guess they were exploring the building we live in, got into the parking garage, and started rocking cars to make the car alarms go off. Like ten or twelve all at once."

I heard a gasp at the other end, and mentally kicked myself for saying *anything*—now she thought I was a terrible mother!—but to my shock, Jodi Baxter started laughing. I mean, howling.

"Oh. Oh. Oh." More belly laughter. "That is so *funny!* I mean, I know it isn't right now, but it's the sort of thing you and your husband will tell on your kids and laugh about later. I mean, I'm sure they meant it as a prank, and there was no real harm done. But, oh dear. I can just imagine. *Yikes*. The noise! Just be sure you guys stuff a sock in your mouths so the kids can't hear you laughing behind closed doors. *They* can't know you think it's funny until they're at *least* eighteen."

Her laughter was contagious. I couldn't help it. Pretty soon I was giggling too. And that night, after the boys had come home, talking a mile a minute about their exciting day at Navy Pier with their dad and getting excited about our road trip to North Dakota, the world no longer felt like it was falling apart. Of course not!

What the boys did was naughty, yes. They had to be disciplined, yes. But it wasn't the end of the world.

As I lay in bed after Philip had fallen asleep, I wondered what it would be like to giggle in the dark with my husband about what had happened yesterday, and laugh so hard we had to stuff socks in our mouths.

chapter 35

A cloudless sky arched over the city Sunday morning, and the TV weatherman promised mild temperatures in the low seventies. Perfect travel weather. I sent up a heavenly thank-you. The weekend "door-dude" called the penthouse at eight to tell us Enterprise had delivered the rental minivan. While Philip rode down the elevator with the boys and the luggage, I did a last-minute sweep of the house. Good thing. I found the earphones to Paul's portable CD player, my cell phone still charging in the bedroom, and our damp swimsuits still in the washing machine where I'd washed them last night. I guiltily whisked them into a recloseable plastic bag. My name would be mud if I forgot those.

At the last minute, I also stuck my Bible into my bulging backpack. I'd been telling God I was going to start reading the Word more regularly. Maybe this week while I was on vacation I'd have time to actually make good on that promise.

Outside by the car, Philip gave me a peck on the cheek, smelling faintly like his Armani aftershave. Sea breezes and tropical forests. He'd already picked up a tan from the outing on Lester Stone's sailboat, our afternoon at Wrigley Field, and another layer yesterday. Gosh, he looked good. I had a sudden urge to slide my arms around his neck, feel his body pressed against mine, satisfy this hunger for skin touching skin . . . but the moment passed as he opened the car door and waited for me to get in.

"You're sure you know how to get out of the city?"

"I think so." I showed him the maps I'd printed out from the computer.

"Looks okay. Just be sure you get on I-90 to Wisconsin, Gabby, and not I-94, or you'll waste a lot of time." He leaned in a side window. "'Bye, guys. Don't give your mom any grief. Call me when you get there, okay?" Philip stepped back and waved us off. When I looked in my rearview mirror just before leaving the frontage road, he was gone.

It seemed to take forever to get out of Chicago's sprawl, even without major traffic delays. Finally we were zipping northwest on the toll road, past newly plowed fields, pretty farms, and the occasional oasis for gas, restrooms, and fast food. The day was so beautiful, I drove with my window down, the sunroof open, and no AC. The wind felt so good, I didn't even mind that my curls would probably end up a snarly mess. And the farther we drove away from Chicago, the lighter I felt.

My cell phone rang the "William Tell" midmorning just as we were entering Wisconsin. I snatched it up and recognized the area code for Alaska. "Celeste? Thank goodness you called! . . . What? . . . Yeah, the boys and I are on the road now, heading for Minot. Are you coming? . . . Can't hear me? I *said*, are you coming home?!"

I pressed the cell phone to my ear, my sister's voice fading in and out. But I got the gist of it. She wasn't coming. Late snow. Some stranded hikers. Tom needed her there. Maybe later in the year when their daughter Kristi was home from college . . .

I finally flipped the phone closed, fighting the lump in my throat. I knew it'd been a long shot, trying to get my sisters and their kids home all at the same time. But I'd been hoping . . . no, *needing* to try to tie up the loose ends in my life. We'd been distant too long.

I shook off my disappointment, stuck an *Eighties Faves* CD in the car player, and turned up the volume. It would've been great to have a family reunion, but the boys and I were going to have a good time anyway.

"What's love got to do, got to do with it . . ." I bellowed with Tina Turner.

"Mo-om! I can't hear my CD player!"

"Too bad. It's my turn."

"I'm hungry!"

I tossed the bag of snacks into the backseat and kept singing. "Who needs a heart, when a heart can be broken . . . !"

Nothing was going to stop me from enjoying every second of this trip.

We stopped just west of Minneapolis at a chain hotel for the night. *Eight hours on the road, not bad* . . . though it took a twenty-ounce Pepsi to keep me awake in the late afternoon, and I had to move P.J. to the front seat to end the jabbing and poking.

But once in a booth at a local Outback Steakhouse, I actually managed to get the boys talking. Well, Paul anyway. "Tell me about this piece of music you composed for the band, Paul. I wish we could have heard it."

"Aw, I was just horsing around with my trombone and came

up with a tune, and my band director showed me this really neat composition program on the computer, and, well . . ." As he prattled on, I mentally made a note to ask Philip about getting the software for our home computer.

The boys spent an hour in the hotel pool after supper, while I soaked in the Jacuzzi, watching them horse around, letting the forceful water jets coax the last of the tension from the past several weeks out of my body. I didn't think about Philip. I didn't think about Manna House. I didn't think about anything at all except how warm and relaxed and . . . and *safe* I felt, five hundred miles away from my life.

The next morning, we were on the road again by eight o'clock after a carbohydrate-heavy continental breakfast in the hotel lobby. P.J. elected to sit up front, and as the long miles clicked by on the odometer, I had a momentary hope he'd open up and tell me more about what was happening at school, but he pretty much kept plugged into his iPod.

However, both boys did reasonably well on the second leg of the trip, as long as I stopped every two hours and reloaded the snacks and drinks. Between Minneapolis and Fargo, we played the License Plate Game and called out thirteen different state plates plus two Canadian provinces, then ran Twenty Questions into the ground. Paul decided he'd annoy us by starting in on, "Ninety-Nine Bottles of Beer on the Wall," and was delighted when I joined in the old camp song. But at around sixty-five bottles left on the wall, P.J. hollered, "Enough already!" I couldn't have agreed more.

My heart was singing. I wanted to keep driving forever.

As we crossed into North Dakota around noon, the topography had definitely changed from compact family farms to sprawling prairie. Cattle dotted the slightly rolling grasslands, which were still reasonably green in early June, though miles went by without seeing a single tree—just shrubs, sagebrush, and occasional sandstone formations. Mega-acre fields sprouted the first mantle of spring wheat, looking like a military crew cut.

Both boys pronounced it "boring," but to me it was beautiful. The pungent smell of sagebrush made me feel slightly drunk, and my pulse quickened as we turned off I-94 at Jamestown and headed north on a two-lane highway. MINOT—170 MILES the sign said.

Home . . .

For the first time in months, that word formed in my conscious thought and rolled around on my tongue.

"There's Grandma!" I pulled into the driveway of the boxy beige house that had been my childhood home and beeped the horn. My mother, grayer than I remembered her, got up stiffly from the flower bed where she'd been weeding, turned, and shaded her eyes from the five o'clock sun. A four-legged bundle of wispy yellow hair erupted from the grass and charged the car, barking.

"Hey there, Dandy," I said, trying to keep the dog from jumping up on me as I crossed the yard and threw my arms around my mom. Had she always been this short? But she still smelled like lavender, the same soft smell I remembered from nighttime kisses when she'd tucked us girls in bed.

Paul was already tussling with the dog. I waved P.J. out of the car. "Hey, guys. Come give your grandma a hug."

"Hi, Grandma!" Paul ran over, gave his grandmother a noisy smack, and ran off again with the yellow mutt, who led him on a merry chase around the yard.

P.J. climbed out of the car and sauntered over to where we stood by the flower bed. He gave his grandmother a polite hug. "Whatcha doing—planting flowers?"

My mother looked at my oldest quizzically. "Is this Ryan?"

"No, no, Mom. This is P.J.—Philip Junior. You remember."

"Oh, yes, of course. Philip's boy. He's just grown so much. Looks so much like Ryan now."

P.J. rolled his eyes at me. His cousin Ryan was Honor's oldest, at least two years older than P.J. *An easy mistake*, I decided, since my mother hadn't seen any of the grandchildren since my dad's funeral two years ago. Except that even then, Ryan had been a beanpole, blond and freckled.

I made a quick call to Philip and left a message on his cell that we'd arrived safe and sound. Then we unloaded the car, and I had the boys put their stuff in the second-floor bedroom with the two dormer windows that Honor and I had shared for years until Celeste left home, at which time Honor inherited her bedroom.

P.J. made a face. "Aw, Mom. It's all full of, you know, girl stuff."

"I won't tell anyone." I laughed. "I'm going to help Grandma with supper. But I'll tell you a secret. Behind that little door into the crawl space, I bet you'll find a whole box of superhero comic books. Go for it."

I left the boys diving into the crawl space. To my surprise, the oven was cold, no supper makings in sight. In fact, the refrigerator was surprisingly bare. A half gallon of milk, half-empty. A carton of orange juice. A wilted head of iceberg lettuce. A bag of raw carrots. A package of shredded cheddar cheese. A carton of eggs—full. An array of condiments in the door. Several containers of leftovers. A partial loaf of wheat bread. And in the freezer, two TV dinners and a package of Mrs. Stouffer's Homemade Lasagna.

"Uh, Mom? Did you have any plans for supper? How about if I make some cheese omelets? We can eat at the kitchen table, make it easy."

"No, honey, we can't eat in the kitchen. I've got the dining room all set with the good china. Tonight is special, having you and the boys here."

I peeked into the dining room. Sure enough, the dining room table was covered with my mom's antique lace tablecloth. Her rose-patterned wedding china sat at each chair—six place settings in all. A silk flower arrangement graced the center of the table.

China on the table, but no supper? Six place settings? What was going on here?

I woke up in Celeste's old room the next morning, sunlight streaming in through its single dormer, and stretched. What a good sleep! And we'd had fun the evening before, eating our cheese omelets on china and lace, pretending to ignore the two empty place settings, and then all four of us had played a rousing game of Pit, yelling and trading and hoarding. My mother had laughed triumphantly when she *won*.

It felt so good to just lie in bed this morning, cuddled in the faded lavender-flowered comforter. *Funny* . . . Celeste had been the girly-girl of the family. Now she was married to a park ranger in Alaska with, I guessed, very few frills. Honor had always been the "wild child," doing things differently just to be different. She'd been born in '62 and came of age in the early seventies, and flower-power stuck to her like a permanent tattoo. As the youngest, I was the tomboy my parents never had, climbing trees, always running, never walking, living up to all the stereotypes of redheads with tempers, fighting for my place in the family.

Trouble was, I didn't fight for my place in the world. Got married right out of high school—even before Honor. Got divorced two years later—even before Honor. At least I got married again—unlike Honor. *But, oh God, look at me.* I hardly recognized the person I used to be.

Sudden tears blurred the sunshine, and I brushed them away. *Get a grip, Gabby. This week is your gift. Don't waste it on spilled milk.*

I grabbed a tissue, blew my nose, and reached for my Bible. Okay. Might as well put first things first. Trouble is, I didn't know where to start. Maybe one of the Gospels, the story of Jesus. After all, He was the main point. Right?

I'd read the first two chapters of Matthew about the birth of Jesus and was trying to imagine the headlines if that had happened today—PREGNANT TEEN DENIES HAVING SEX WITH A MAN or WORLD LEADER KILLS ALL INFANTS IN TOWN TRYING TO GET RID OF A POSSIBLE SUCCESSOR—when I heard the *click click click* of doggy nails on the stairs, and Dandy poked his nose into my room and cocked his scruffy ears quizzically. I smiled. The dog had a sweet face. "Hey, boy," I murmured. "Anybody else up? You need to go out?"

And then I remembered. I had planned to get up early and make a quick trip to the nearest Miracle Mart so we could have breakfast. My mom had obviously forgotten how much food two adolescent boys could pack away in a day, much less a week!

When I let the dog out into the backyard, I realized something else my mom had forgotten. Dog poops. The yard was full of them.

By late morning of our first day at Grandma Shepherd's, I was feeling that things were a little more under control. Old leftovers and expired food had been tossed out. The refrigerator and cupboards had been restocked with fresh food. I'd called Aunt Mercy and invited her to come over around four and stay for supper. And I'd corralled the boys into helping me do pooper-scooper duty. I sweetened the deal by saying we'd not only go swimming at the public pool after lunch, but I'd let them go to the movies on their own afterward if we got the yard clean.

The public pool I remembered as a kid—shallow end, deep end—had been replaced by a larger pool with a water slide. I bought the boys waterslide bracelets for unlimited trips through the curlicue and let them run off. As Mom and I looked around for a place to set up camp, I thought, *Odd. Everyone here is white.* Which wasn't that odd, given that Minot was in the heart of Scandinavian country. What was odd was that I even noticed. My reality had changed.

Both Paul and P.J. were good swimmers, so I let them horse around in the pool on their own, while I sat with my mom under a shade umbrella and talked. She seemed perfectly fine . . . except for the occasional long pause in the middle of a sentence, and then she'd say, "My, my, what were we talking about?" But mostly she smiled a lot and patted my hand, happy for company.

On the way home, I dropped the boys off at the neighborhood theater, which had a four o'clock showing of the latest blockbuster animated movie. "Pick you up at six!" I yelled after them. I watched them go. *Could I do this in Chicago?* Probably not. I'd have to go with them, which wasn't such a bad thing. But today I had a reason for getting them out of the house.

I needed to talk to Aunt Mercy about my mom.

Aunt Mercy was my dad's younger sister, ten years his junior and still working as a reference librarian at the Minot Public Library, even though she was nearing retirement age. "They won't let me retire." She laughed as we peeled potatoes and diced ham for scalloped potatoes. She tapped her head. "I know too much. That's what they get for letting me work as a reference librarian for thirty years."

I'd talked my mom into lying down for a nap, telling her not to worry about supper, Aunt Mercy and I would take care of it. Dandy curled up on the rug beside my mom's bed and gave me a look. *Dog on duty. Beat it.*

Aunt Mercy shrugged. "Even if they did, I need to work another two years to get my full pension. And I only have a one-bedroom apartment. Otherwise I'd invite Martha to come live with me until her name comes up on the list for assisted living. They said it would be another three to six months at least. Maybe longer." She shook her head. "I don't think your mom can wait that long, Gabby."

I stopped slicing and stared at my aunt. She was an attractive woman in her sixties, her short shag turning silver (or tinted, I couldn't be sure). And she was dead serious. "What do you mean?"

Aunt Mercy pointed a paring knife at me. "Gabby, we've got a problem. Your mom's still driving that old Ford Galaxy, but she had three fender-benders last fall. Drove into the birch tree in the front yard in December. But it's not just the driving—it's her memory. I come to pick her up for church and she thinks it's Tuesday. Gabby, she calls me Mary all the time—*her* sister." My dad's sister sighed. "The doctor says she's had a series of small strokes. Nothing major—yet. I try to check on her at least one other time during the week, but I live on the other side of town, Gabby. I can't do it every day."

I was silent as I stirred the white sauce for the potatoes. What was she saying? I'd been hoping we could get Mom moved into an assisted-living situation—but Aunt Mercy had already answered that. Waiting list.

Aunt Mercy broke the silence. "What about you girls? Have any of you considered moving your mom closer to one of you?"

Move Mom closer to—? I was sure Mom wouldn't want to leave Minot. Even getting her to sell this house would be tricky. But even if she did, I couldn't imagine moving Mom to Denali National Park in Alaska to live with Celeste! And moving her to Southern California with Honor was just as laughable. Honor lived in a trailer with two kids, for goodness' sake! It was some artsy trailer park for aging hippies, and she made jewelry for a living, more or less. Plus, I didn't know whose forgetfulness would be worse—Mom's or Honor's. I snorted to myself. Honor would probably call me back about my proposed "family reunion" next week. *"Oh, when did you say it was, Gabby?"* Yeah, right.

I stopped stirring and stared out the window at my mom's poop-free backyard.

That left me.

chapter 36

Oh, great. In my haste to grab my cell phone at the last minute, I'd forgotten to unplug the charger and take it too. *Well, no big deal.* I'd just turn it off and save it for the trip home. The boys could use the house phone to call their dad while we were here. And my mom's number was in our address book at home, if Philip bothered to look.

Besides, I had bigger problems. Aunt Mercy's question niggled at me all the next day, most of which we spent at the pool again since the weather forecast threatened rain at the end of the week. My thoughts bounced around like a pinball trying to find the right hole. What was I going to do? I couldn't just take my mom home with me! We didn't have an extra bedroom, not since we decided to give the boys their own rooms. And Philip . . . I didn't even want to go there. Maybe we could set up something like Meals on Wheels, so she'd at least get a decent meal once a day . . . find a housekeeper to come in once a week . . . hire a kid to walk the dog . . .

I tossed aside the magazine I'd been flipping through and scanned the bobbing heads in the pool until I found Paul's curly head and P.J.'s dark one. *How am I going to do all that in just two days? We have to leave on Saturday!* I suddenly felt like throwing something. *Grr! Celeste and Honor should have come home like I'd asked them to! Then we could talk about what to do together.*

I looked over at my mom in the other deck chair. She was asleep. Her hair looked as if it needed a cut and a perm. Definitely didn't get my curly hair from Mom. I sighed. One more thing to do . . .

I got up and dove into the deep end of the pool, letting the cool water slide over my body and black tank. In the underwater silence, a line from the gospel song on the CD Josh Baxter got for me floated through my head. *"Who do I talk to . . . when nobody wants to listen . . . ?"* I came up gulping for air, hearing the chorus in my ears: *"I go to the Rock of my salvation, go to the Stone that the builders rejected . . . !"*

I felt like yelling, "Okay, God, I'm listening!" But what I really wanted was a husband I could call who'd listen to the pain in my heart and help me decide what to do.

I called my aunt that evening to ask what she thought about Meals on Wheels. She sighed in my ear. "I tried that a few months ago, Gabby. Your mom would eat a little, then stick the leftovers in the refrigerator to 'save for another day.' I came over one weekend and found six or seven half-eaten containers and threw them all out. I was afraid she'd get food poisoning."

"Mom? Mom!" Paul was tugging on my shirt.

I frowned at him and held up a finger to wait.

"But Mom—"

I covered the phone receiver. "Just a minute. I'm talking to Aunt Mercy."

"But Mom! There's an empty pan on the stove, and the gas burner's turned up on high!"

Okay, that was it. The pan-on-the-stove episode scared me. What if she set the house on fire someday? I had to do *something* about my mom, and do it quick.

Since I woke up Thursday morning before working people were even out of bed, I dutifully turned on the bedside light and read chapters five, six, and seven of Matthew's gospel—three whole chapters devoted to Jesus' famous Sermon on the Mount. I skimmed most of it. Didn't want to deal with radical stuff like "turn the other cheek" and "love your enemies" right now.

But I skidded to a stop in the middle of chapter seven, where Jesus said, *"Ask and it will be given to you; seek and you will find; knock and the door will be opened to you. For everyone who asks receives; he who seeks finds; and to him who knocks, the door will be opened."* The verses were familiar. I'd probably even memorized them in Pioneer Girls club as a kid. But today, something about those promises felt like wide-open arms, and I wanted to fling myself into them.

Instead, I flung the comforter off. *Get a grip, Gabby*. I wasn't likely to get any answers about my mom until I got on the phone, knocked on some doors, and asked about services I could line up for her. I still had two days. Maybe I could put together something that would fill in the gaps until the assisted-living unit opened up. After all, Aunt Mercy said it *might* be only another three months—I hoped.

The temperature had dropped into the fifties under a gray cloud cover that matched my glum spirit as I served up old-fashioned oatmeal for breakfast. P.J. frowned at his bowl of oatmeal. "Doesn't Grandma have any instant stuff?"

"I want cold cereal." Paul plopped into a chair. "What are we gonna do today?"

I kept a watchful eye on my mother as she sorted her medications and vitamins into a plastic seven-day pillbox, while I heaped brown sugar and raisins on the boys' oatmeal. I'd have to double-check that pillbox later. "First, you're going to eat this hot cereal. Then Paul is going to walk Dandy, and P.J. is going to mow Grandma's lawn before it rains, while I make some important phone calls this morning—"

"Aw, Mom! I thought this was supposed to be vacation!"

"—And if we get that stuff done, then maybe we can go to the Dakota Air Museum this afternoon. I hear they've got a replica of the Wright Brothers' flyer."

That mollified them briefly. As soon as I heard the lawn mower start up, I got out the yellow pages and looked up Senior Services. A lot of listings . . . in other towns. Fargo. Bismarck. Burlington. The list for Minot was pretty short. I called one church group that had an "in-home companion" program and was told that their current volunteers were all assigned. But they'd be happy to put my mother on a list for when they got new volunteers. "We are usually able to assign a companion within a month or so who can give five to ten hours a week. How many hours a day does your mother need a companion?"

I thought about the pan on the stove. Twenty-four hours a

day would be about right. But I agreed to put my mom on their list. It was better than nothing.

I next tried the local Agency on Aging. The person on the phone explained their list of services, which included day care at the local senior center, transportation to medical appointments, home-delivered meals, and hot meals available at various sites around the city. "We'd be happy to set up a home visit to assess your mother's needs. How about next Wednesday at eleven?"

The piano in the living room tinkled a jazzy tune. Didn't sound like my mom. I stuck a finger in my ear so I could hear the phone. "Uh, I'm only in town this week. Could we do this today?"

"I'm sorry. The best we can do is a ten o'clock tomorrow here in the office."

Tomorrow?! I gritted my teeth. "Fine." What was I going to do between now and then?

I poked my head into the living room. Paul was sitting at the piano, playing with both hands, while my mother sat nearby, beaming. I listened. Not bad. "Where did you learn that, kiddo?"

Paul shrugged. "Made it up myself. Can we go to the air museum now? Are you coming, Grandma?"

I hesitated. I really should make more calls! But my mother was already getting her hat. "Just so we're back in time for prayer meeting tonight," she said.

Was she assuming we were all going to church? I opened my mouth to protest . . . and was surprised to realize I actually wanted to go. Maybe *needed* to go was more like it. I could sure use some help praying.

At the last minute, I tore out a page from the yellow pages and stuck my cell phone in my pocket. No way could I waste several hours wandering around a museum while there were still stones to be turned.

In spite of the change in weather, the boys had a great time at the air museum. The huge DC-3 World War II Troop Transport standing out in an open field, named *Gooney Bird* by its now-silent heroes, was the boys' favorite, while inside the museum a replica of the Wright Brothers' famous flyer and a two-winged, red-and-white aerobatic plane came a close second and third.

Mom tired fairly quickly, so I parked her on a bench while the boys ran their batteries down. Stepping away a few paces, I turned on my cell phone and dialed all the social service agencies I could find. But the answers all ended at the same place: zero. "We would need a doctor's referral" . . . "Why don't you call the Agency on Aging?" . . . "I'm sorry" . . . "Would you like to put her name on our waiting list?"

And then the battery died. *Drat!* Tomorrow's appointment was my last chance.

Trying not to be panicky, I picked up a pizza and a video for the boys on the way home, and let them stay home with Dandy and the TV remote while I drove Mom to church.

Only a smattering of people were at the prayer meeting at the little stone church, maybe fifteen max. I didn't know anyone there, for which I was glad. My parents had changed churches shortly after Damien dumped me nineteen years ago. The scandal of a divorce in a "no divorce—ever" church had been too much for them. A few people shook my hand and murmured, "That's nice," when my mom introduced me as "my daughter from Virginia." I didn't bother to correct her. Someone started a

song a cappella, and I was surprised how quickly the words came
back to me . . .

> *What a friend we have in Jesus,*
> *All our sins and griefs to bear*
> *What a privilege to carry*
> *Everything to God in prayer . . .*

A stack of prayer request cards were passed out. I got two—
someone's sister who had breast cancer, and another for a
husband who drank too much. I was surprised when everyone
got down on their knees along the wooden pews, and I heard
murmurings all around me as people prayed aloud. But I got
down on my knees, too, wishing I'd worn slacks instead of a
skirt, and dutifully prayed silently for the cards in my hand.

But Jesus' words kept rolling around in my mind. *Ask and you
will receive. Seek and you will find. Knock and the door will open.* I
squeezed my eyes shut even tighter. *Okay, Jesus, I'm asking. What
should I do about my mom?!*

I stayed on my knees, head buried in my hands, listening to
the rise and fall of the murmured prayers all around me. I kept
thinking about my mom living alone, thinking about having to
get the boys back by Sunday night so they could start sailing
camp, realizing there wasn't enough time to do everything I
needed to do to get my mom set up here and keep her safe . . .

"Come to Me."

The words were so clear, they seemed to echo in my head.
Where did that come from? Was that supposed to be God's
answer? What kind of answer was that? That's what I was doing,
wasn't it—coming here to prayer meeting to pray?

But I couldn't get the words out of my head. *"Come to Me."* Not even the next morning—the last day of our visit before heading back to Chicago—while I read another three chapters from Matthew. *"Come to Me."* I shook them off. What I needed to do was get up, get dressed, and get Mom and me over to the agency to see what my options were.

That was before my mom backed into Dandy, who was standing underfoot in the kitchen as we made breakfast, and tumbled backward over the dog and thumped her head on the floor.

"Mom! Mom! Are you okay?" I tried to get to her, but the dog still stood in the way, looking confused. "Dandy, get out of here, you stupid mutt." I grabbed the dog by the collar, pulled him across the kitchen floor, and shoved him outside. *Oh God, no . . . what if Mom broke her hip . . . I should call 9-1-1 . . .*

My mom sat up, rubbing her head. "Oh, it's nothing. Just a bump." She looked at me reproachfully. "Go say you're sorry to Dandy, Gabby. It's not his fault."

I blew out a relieved breath. "Okay, I will. Later." I helped my mother up from the floor. "Are you sure you're okay? Come on, I want you to lie down on the couch with an ice pack." After I checked her pupils to make sure she didn't have a concussion, she let me lead her into the living room, prop her feet up with some pillows, and make an ice pack for the back of her head. I told the boys to get their own breakfast, then went back into the living room to sit with my mom. Concussion or not, I decided I had my answer.

Mom was going back to Chicago with me.

I made my peace with Dandy, who wagged his forgiveness and promptly curled up on the couch with my mom. But the dog was a problem. I called Aunt Mercy at the library, told her I was taking my mom back to Chicago, and could she please keep Dandy?

"Oh, Gabby. I'm sorry. My apartment complex doesn't allow pets. But I've got a key to the house. I'll be glad to check on things and water her plants. You better have her mail held—on second thought, she has a slot in the door, so I'll just collect it and forward anything that's important. How's that?"

It would have to do.

I took the boys upstairs and told them Grandma was coming back with us. P.J.'s eyes narrowed suspiciously. "Where's she going to sleep?"

I'd steeled myself for that question. "In your room for now. Paul's still got a bunk bed. You can sleep there—"

"That's not fair!" P.J. yelled. "I'm the oldest. Let Grandma sleep in Paul's room."

"Keep your voice down," I hissed. "And don't give me that look, young man. You and Paul share a room at your Nana Marlene's house. It's not going to kill you for a few weeks." Who was I kidding? A few months was more like it. "Grandma just can't stay by herself right now."

P.J. flopped on one of the twin beds, his back to me. "Still not fair. You and Dad didn't ask *us* if we wanted to move to Chicago. Didn't want to come on this dumb trip, either." He buried his face in the pillow.

I almost snapped, *"Dad didn't ask me if I wanted to move either!"*—but P.J. suddenly rolled back over and faced me, his eyes challenging.

"How come Dad didn't come with us to Grandma's?"

"Well, uh . . . he had to work. You know, just starting the new business and all."

P.J. glared at me a long moment, then rolled back over. "Just go away. Leave me alone."

My eyes blurred. I pushed Paul out of the bedroom and started down the stairs. This trip wasn't turning out like I had hoped. I'd wanted to spend some special time with my sons, getting to know them again, just having fun together. But P.J. seemed so distant, hard to reach. The move had been tough on me . . . what else should I have expected from him? But now I felt so consumed trying to figure out how to care for my mom that—

Paul was tugging on my arm. "Can Dandy come too?"

"What?" I stopped on the staircase.

"You know, back to Chicago."

I hesitated.

"Mom, please! Grandma would cry without Dandy. I'll help take care of him. I can run him in the park. I'll even pick up his poops."

I pulled my youngest into a bear hug and rumpled his curly head. If only it were that simple. But what other choice did I have? My mom would never agree to leave her dog locked up in a kennel for a couple of weeks, much less three months. She'd fuss about the cost, anyway.

I canceled the appointment with the Agency on Aging and spent the rest of the day washing clothes, packing a suitcase for my mom, cleaning the house, and even packing a duffel bag for the dog: leash, brush, food and water bowls, sleeping rug, bag of dog food, plastic bags. "Guess that makes you official," I muttered to Dandy, who seemed quite anxious about the suitcase on my mom's bed.

The weather was still coolish, with occasional drizzles, so the boys didn't even beg to go to the pool. They discovered an ancient

Monopoly game with most of its parts, which helped kill the afternoon and kept my mom company in the living room while I made a quick trip to the Miracle Mart for trip food.

But I knew I was stalling.

I had to call Philip.

Tonight.

chapter 37

The car was a little crowded with four of us plus a dog in the minivan, but Dandy turned out to be a good traveler, curling up on the floor under Paul's feet, only getting up from time to time to check on Mom in the front passenger seat. Paul was true to his word, snapping on the leash and taking the dog for runs at rest stops, a plastic bag in his back pocket in case the dog did his business.

My mom still had a lump on her head, but otherwise she seemed fine, sitting quietly in the front passenger seat, taking in the scenery, a little smile on her face. Casting an occasional glance her way, I realized she probably hadn't been anywhere since my father had died two years ago.

"Did you tell Dad that Dandy is coming too?" Paul asked. "What he'd say?"

I glanced at my youngest in the rearview mirror. Did he have a sixth sense that his father was not going to be happy with this whole plan? "Ah . . . I had to leave a message." Which was true.

The house phone rang seven times last night, and then voice mail picked up. At first I thought God must be smiling on me, because I was able to leave a matter-of-fact message, saying my mom and Dandy were coming for a visit, even adding that my mom really couldn't stay alone any longer. But then I realized it just put off the inevitable: Philip's reaction.

Still, when he hadn't called back by the time I locked the house Saturday morning and got everybody into the car, I began to relax. My cell phone was dead. I had a whole day before I had to try calling again from the hotel tonight. I started to hum. Might as well enjoy the trip.

Funny thing, though. When I tried to call the penthouse that evening from our hotel room, I only got voice mail again. I sucked up my courage and tried Philip's cell. Same thing.

Odd.

We were a wilted bunch when we piled out of the minivan in front of Richmond Towers Sunday evening. I sent Paul over to the park with Dandy on a leash and asked P.J. to get a luggage cart from the weekend doorman while I helped my mother out of the car. P.J. was back in five minutes, holding the nonrevolving door open for Mr. Bentley, pushing a luggage cart.

"Mr. Bentley!" I was so happy to see him, I threw decorum to the wind and gave him a big hug. "What are you doing working on Sunday? I thought the door-dude—"

Mr. Bentley burst out laughing. "The 'door-dude,' as you so aptly call him, got himself fired. I have to fill in until they hire his replacement. And who is this lovely lady?" He tipped his head in a little bow toward my mother, who stood beside the car trying to juggle her sweater, pocketbook, a plastic bag of car trash, and a magazine.

"Oh . . . This is my mother, Martha Shepherd, from North Dakota. Mom, this is Mr. Bentley. He's the doorman here at Richmond Towers, and also a good friend."

Mr. Bentley doffed his cap. "I'm very pleased to meet you, ma'am—"

A happy bark, followed by a breathless Paul, announced the rest of our crew. "And, uh, this is Dandy, my mom's doggy companion," I finished. The little yellow mutt danced and turned circles in front of my mother until he got his rump scratched and a pat on the head, then Dandy bounced over to Mr. Bentley and sniffed his shoes.

"I see. You've multiplied." Mr. Bentley replaced his cap and glanced at me with a twinkle. "Are you expected?"

I flushed. I knew what it must look like, Gabby Fairbanks bringing home more strays. *Mr. Bentley knows me all too well.* "Uh, I hope so. It was kind of a last-minute thing. I left a message . . ."

"Mm. A message." Mr. Bentley helped P.J. lift bags out of the rear of the minivan and pile them on the cart. Then he straightened. "Would you like me to call upstairs and tell Mr. Fairbanks you've arrived?"

My brain *cha-chinged* in light speed. Appear en masse at the penthouse front door . . . or have Philip meet us down here in public? "Uh, that would be great. Thanks, Mr. Bentley. We can load the rest of the bags."

The boys wanted to go right up, but I made them pick up all the trash in the car, brush out all the crumbs as best they could, and then wait with their grandmother while I parked the rental in a "Visitor" space until Enterprise could pick it up. When we finally pushed the luggage cart into the lobby, Mr. Bentley shrugged. "No answer upstairs."

A funny feeling prickled the back of my neck. Should I be worried?

We were sitting around the dining room table an hour later, passing around the makings for tacos, when I heard the front door open and close, then a bag being dropped in the gallery, and Philip appeared in the doorway. Tan. A stray wisp of dark hair falling over his forehead. Sunglasses. Open-necked silver-and-black silk shirt. Gray slacks. As if he'd just stepped out of *GQ* magazine.

"Dad!" Paul screeched, jumping up from the table and throwing himself on his father. Dandy immediately came to life, barking at this stranger.

"Dandy! You hush," my mom said. "Come here, boy. Lie down." Dandy obeyed, still rumbling throaty little growls.

I saw Philip's face twitch, but he hugged Paul and then walked over to P.J. and rumpled his dark hair. "Hey, guys. Good to have you home. Save any of those tacos for me?" He pulled out a chair by the empty plate and sat down, removed his sunglasses, and stuck them in his shirt pocket.

My husband did not look at me. But he nodded at my mother. "Mom Shepherd. You're looking well."

"And you." My mom gave him a smile. Then she stage-whispered to me, "You have a very handsome husband, Gabrielle."

I flushed, my eyes hot, afraid I was going to cry. But I smiled. "You bet." I forced myself to look right at Philip. "Hi, honey. Looks like we beat you home. I've been trying to call—"

"I got your message." His voice was even. Emotionless. "Tried to call your cell."

I grimaced. "Sorry about that. The battery died, and I forgot the charger." I forced brightness into my voice. "The boys are excited about sailing camp tomorrow. Couldn't wait to get home."

"Yeah, Dad!" Now even P.J. jumped in. "What kind of boats do we get to sail?"

Philip disappeared into the den after supper. I put clean sheets on P.J.'s bed and got my mom bedded down after promising to take Dandy out one last time. P.J. was still bent out of shape that he had to give up *his* bedroom, and I heard the boys squabbling over who was going to sleep in which bunk. Well, it'd take a few days to work out the kinks . . . maybe I could rearrange Paul's room so P.J. could have space for some of his own stuff . . . plus Mom would need a couple of drawers for her clothes and personal things . . .

On the way out of the house with Dandy, I saw Philip's leather overnight bag still sitting in the gallery. *Huh.* He had some explaining to do too.

It felt weird to take Dandy down the elevator and across the frontage road for his last "outing" in the dark. I saw a couple other Richmond Tower residents out with their dogs. A pit bull. A Pekinese with a bow in its hair. Come to think of it, most of the dogs I'd seen at Richmond Towers were actual breeds. Not another mutt in sight. But as far as I was concerned, Dandy was cuter than any of them. I wasn't sure how he related to other dogs, so I kept him on a tight leash and didn't venture far into the park, even though the night was mild. How did people do this in the dead of winter? Or in the rain?

Back in the penthouse, I put Dandy into P.J.'s room. The dog sniffed at my mom, then curled up on his rug beside the bed. "Good dog," I whispered and closed the door.

The light was still on in the den. Might as well face the music. I tapped on the door and peeked inside. Philip was at the computer, his back to me. I went inside, closed the door, and leaned against it. "Hi."

Thirty seconds went by. Then Philip slowly turned around in his swivel chair and leaned back. The desk lamp outlined his striking features with light and shadow. More seconds went by as he looked at me. Finally he said, "Just tell me, Gabby . . . Do you get a kick out of turning our household upside down? No warning, just showing up here with your mother. And the *dog* too! Good grief! What were you thinking?"

I held on to the doorknob behind me. "I didn't plan it this way, Philip. But when we got to Minot, it was obvious my mom shouldn't be living alone any longer. She—"

"That's what retirement homes are for."

"She's on a waiting list, Philip."

"What about your Aunt Grace, or Mercy . . . whatever. She lives right in town."

I shook my head. "I asked. She works full-time—"

"Like you don't?" His voice was hard.

"She doesn't have a spare bedroom, either. She lives in a—"

"And you think we do?"

I counted to five. "Look. Will you let me finish? I spent most of the week trying to line up in-home care for Mom—*something* to fill in the blanks until her name comes up for assisted living. But it wasn't like I had two or three weeks! I only took a week off, and I had to get the boys back here in time to start sailing camp. And then Friday morning she tripped and hit her head—"

"How long?"

"How long what?"

"Until her name comes up on the list for assisted living."

"Ah . . . maybe only three mon—"

"Months?! *Three months!*" Philip vaulted out of his desk chair. I flinched. But he just threw up his arms. "Uh-uh. No! There is *no way* this penthouse is designed to be a mother-in-law apartment!" He stopped and jabbed a finger at me. "You know what the trouble with you is, Gabby? You just up and do whatever you want to do without considering anyone else. You go off half-cocked to see a homeless bag lady and end up with a job. You pine for the boys to come here, then leave them alone to get in trouble. You say you're going to Minot for a visit, then you bring your mother *and* her mutt here, without even discussing it with me."

I pressed my lips together. He flopped into the chair again, one elbow on the armrest, rubbing his chin. After a few moments, I spoke. "I left you three messages—two here at home, one on your cell. Where were you this weekend?"

His face darkened. "What does that have to do with anything? Did you expect me to sit around babysitting the phone all weekend?"

"But I couldn't get hold of you."

"I wasn't *here*, Gabby. The Fenchels invited me to spend the weekend with them."

"At the casino again, no doubt." It was a stab in the dark. But I could tell by the way his eyes twitched that I'd hit the bull's-eye.

"And the problem with that is . . . ?"

"It's *gambling*, Philip. Is that what we're working for, to throw our money away like that?"

He started to laugh, a mirthless sound that was more like a sneer. "Good job, Gabby. Turn this around, make me the bad guy, just because I got to relax this weekend after putting in sixty hours at the office. But let's get down to the bottom line. Tomorrow morning. I go to work. The boys go to camp. You'll probably waltz off to work. So . . . just what are your plans for your mother—who, according to you, can't stay alone? Drag her to the shelter with you? They'll love that for sure."

"Exactly. For a start."

Philip rolled his eyes. "Of *course*. That's your plan. Well, get this, Gabrielle Fairbanks." He stood up abruptly and stabbed his finger at me again, making shadows on the wall that pierced the dim light. "You have one week to find another place for your mother and her mutt. *One week*. Or she goes back to North Dakota."

chapter 38

We spent the night with our backs turned to one another. I woke up at two and couldn't get back to sleep. Sliding out of bed and pulling on my robe and slippers, I felt around in my backpack for my Bible and tiptoed toward the living room, hoping I wouldn't wake up the dog. I hadn't kept up with my Bible reading the past two days, and I doubted the morning would be conducive, getting everyone up and out the door. On the way, I heated a mug of milk in the microwave, doctored it with honey, then curled up on the couch with just one lamp on.

So quiet. Peaceful.

Unlike the knot in my spirit.

I had to do something to get my mind off that disastrous conversation with Philip the night before. Even though I was only half-awake, I found my bookmark at chapter eleven of Matthew's gospel, and plodded through the verses—until suddenly three words leaped off the page. *"Come to Me . . ."*

There it was! That *was* God talking to me, after all. I feasted on the verses at the end of the chapter. *"Come to Me, all you who are weary and burdened, and I will give you rest. Take My yoke upon you and learn from Me, for I am gentle and humble in heart, and you will find rest for your souls. For My yoke is easy and My burden is light."*

A yoke. I knew enough about farm animals to know that a yoke was a wooden frame that harnessed two oxen together so they could pull a load. I read the verses again and again, wanting so much to know what they meant. But all I knew for sure was that I fit the description of someone who was "weary and burdened." *Oh, God. I am so tired. Tired of the tension between Philip and me. Tired of trying to keep the peace. Tired of trying to live up to Philip's expectations.* And now, a big load on my shoulders. My mom needed care—but what? It felt like it was all up to me. And Philip had given me *one week* to figure it out?

I turned out the light and pulled an afghan over me right there on the couch. *God, I sure could use some of that rest . . .* And I fell asleep, dreaming that a voice kept whispering in my ear, *"Come to Me."*

Philip took the boys to Burnham Harbor for the Youth Sailing Camp on his way to work the next morning, but he asked me to pick them up at four. "Call Enterprise and tell them we need the minivan for another week. Maybe we'll lease a second car for the rest of the summer so you can cart the boys around."

Philip's announcement both surprised and pleased me. I didn't mind taking the El to work, but we really did need a second car now that the boys were here. And if he was willing to take the boys to camp in the morning, I could work with that. Now all I needed to do was figure out what to do with my mother.

"Mom, would you like to see where I work? I plan activities at a shelter for homeless women. I know the staff would love to meet you—no, no, Mom. You already took your meds today. Those are for tomorrow, see? It has a *T* for Tuesday."

"Oh." She stared at the pillbox. "Would we be gone all day?"

"Well, yeah, pretty much." Especially by the time I picked up the boys.

She shook her head. "I can't. I need to stay with Dandy. I wouldn't want to leave him in a strange place all by himself."

She had a point. Could Dandy hold it all day? Would he get frustrated and chew up the furniture? But there was no way I was going to leave my mother alone all day either. Which is why the three of us ended up in the rental, heading down Sheridan Road toward Manna House, while I tried to devise some kind of brilliant excuse for showing up at work with a dog. *He's a therapy dog . . . I'm thinking of having a class in pet care . . . a watchdog would be a good idea for a women's shelter . . .*

In the end, I did what I always did—threw myself on Mabel Turner's mercy. We showed up in the foyer of Manna House and I introduced my mother to Angela in the reception cubby, while making soothing noises to Dandy.

"Oh, what a sweet dog!" Angela came out of the cubby and bent down, letting Dandy lick her face. Instant friends. The Asian-American girl stood up. "And how nice to meet you, Mrs. Shepherd. Gabby keeps things interesting around here." She laughed.

I could have kissed her. A perfect welcome.

Mabel heard the commotion and came out of her office. She looked professional as always—black slacks, tangerine short-sleeved sweater that brought out highlights in her warm, brown skin. Her eyebrows went up at the sight of the dog, but I hastily introduced her to my mother and then said, "We, uh, have a situation. I'll explain later. But for right now, can I keep Dandy down in my office?"

Mabel gave a slight roll of her eyes but waved us off with a tolerant smile. The woman had the patience of Job—though I figured she'd used half of it up just on me in the past two months. So far, so good. I'd park Mom in the multipurpose room, take Dandy down to my office, and—

What I hadn't figured on was the terrified screech that met us when we walked into the multipurpose room. "Eeek! Get that dog out of here! I'm scared of dogs!" A heavy-chested black woman I'd never met before jumped up, grabbed the nearest person, who happened to be Carolyn, and hid behind her, still yelling, "Go 'way! Go 'way!"

I don't know who was more upset—the new resident, my mother, or Dandy. I expected Mabel to come bursting in any second and order us out.

"Oh, gimme a break, Sheila." Carolyn untangled herself from the woman's grip and came over to us, bending down and stroking Dandy's head. "Atta boy. Good dog." She called over her shoulder, "See? This dog's a sweetie pie. What's his name?"

Carolyn, bless every hair in her ponytail, chatted with my mom and glared at Sheila every time the woman started to freak out again. We finally made it downstairs, where I shut Dandy into my office, got two cups of coffee—black for my mom, cream for me—and tried to wrap my mind around catching up on the activity program after a week away while I had a dog underfoot, a list of senior facilities to call, and two boys I was supposed to pick up at four o'clock at Burnham Harbor, wherever that was.

As it turned out, Burnham Harbor was a straight shot down Lake Shore Drive, just beyond Soldier Field, the Chicago Bear's "remodeled" football stadium. I snickered when my mom murmured, "Oh my. Looks like a flying saucer landed on top of a Roman coliseum," because that's exactly what it looked like. But at least there was no way I could miss my turnoff, and I managed to get to the harbor at ten after four.

The boys bragged all the way home about their new "expertise" handling a two-man 420 sailing dinghy. "And then we get to try a one-man Pico all by ourselves!" Paul was excited that Dandy had come along to pick them up, and immediately took the dog to the park for a good run when we got back to Richmond Towers.

I'd had a good long talk with Mabel before I left work, trying to bring her up-to-date on my latest crisis. She gave me her blessing to bring my mom to work that week and make calls to various senior facilities. I needn't have worried about entertaining my mom. She seemed content to read or watch television or just sit, playing audience to the comings and goings at the shelter—much like many of the residents did between their case management meetings and trips to public aid. That is, until Carolyn the game-meister discovered that "Gramma Shep," as the younger residents soon dubbed her, liked to play Scrabble and old card games, like Rook. My mom started to look forward to "going to work" each day.

As for the dog . . . I really needed to find another solution. So far we'd had no major problems at home except for an excess of dog hair and Dandy's tendency to growl when Philip first got home. But the dog was developing a real attachment to Paul. I even discovered Dandy on Paul's bed one night when Mom's door wasn't tightly closed.

On Wednesday, the dining area outside my office clucked like a henhouse since the nurse was there. I put my mom's name on the list and kept my office door cracked to hear when her name was called. Dandy kept wanting to nose the door open to check out all the excitement, but I finally got him to lie down and stay under my desk.

Estelle had a regular knitting club going with several of the women as they waited for their turn with the nurse. My mom's eyes glittered, and she ended up helping two or three of the residents untangle the messes they made and pick up their stitches. But she was surprised when Delores Enriquez called out, "Martha Shepherd? You are next."

I shut the door on Dandy and went behind the makeshift privacy booth with my mom, watching as Mrs. Enriquez gently did a brief workup—heart, breathing, reflexes, weight and height, eyes, organs. "You seem in good health, Señora Shepherd." The sweet-faced nurse smiled encouragingly. "But your daughter says you had a fall last week?"

"Oh, that." Mom seemed embarrassed. "It was nothing. Dandy didn't mean to."

Mrs. Enriquez eyed me curiously.

I nodded. "The dog was in the way, and Mom fell backward, hitting her head."

"Mm. Probably should have had her checked out, but—"

"Hey!" a familiar voice croaked on the other side of the

privacy divider. "What does a lady gotta do to see the nurse around here?"

I didn't have to peek to know who it was, but I did just the same, and grinned.

Lucy Tucker, purple knit hat and all. And wet. It must be raining.

"That lady with the purple hat is interesting."

"What?" I'd been thinking about the calls I'd made that day as we drove down Lake Shore Drive, windshield wipers on, to pick up the boys. All the retirement homes had waiting lists. Huh, big surprise. I did have a couple of good leads for in-home care, as well as elder day care—*if* Philip would back off his one-week ultimatum. Big *if*.

"That lady with the purple hat is interesting," she repeated.

"You mean Lucy?"

"Yes. Her real name is Lucinda. Isn't that a pretty name? She ran off with a boy when she was only sixteen because she got tired of moving from place to place every few months. I think they were migrant farm workers back in the thirties and forties. But she said Romeo—isn't that funny? That's what she called him, 'Romeo'—dumped her when they got to Chicago. Never did find her family again, poor soul."

I stared in astonishment at my mom as we pulled up to the clubhouse at Burnham Harbor. How did my mom know this? She'd only met Lucy this morning, yet she knew more about my favorite bag lady than I'd managed to discover in two months!

I wanted to ask if Lucy said anything about how she ended up on the street, but just then P.J. and Paul jumped into the minivan, grousing about not being able to go out on the boats because of the rain. They'd spent the day tying sailors' knots, learning how to pack sails, and touring some of the big yachts moored at the harbor. Don't know what they were complaining about. A day at the docks sounded like fun to me.

Fortunately for the boys, the sun was out again the next day . . . but I was surprised to see Lucy still at the shelter. "Why shouldn't I stick around, Fuzz Top? *Somebody* 'round here needs ta spend time with your mother, her bein' a guest an' all. Respect your elders, ya know? Come on, Martha, we can watch us some TV."

I kept a straight face. Respect your elders? If I figured right, Lucy was at least five years older than my mom, maybe more. I peeked into the TV room an hour later, and the two of them were trying to outguess each other how the TV judge was going to rule in one of those civil courtroom shows. Correction: *uncivil,* by the tone of the plaintiff.

That day was the warmest we'd had so far, mid-eighties. Too nice to be inside all day. I let the boys take Dandy *and* their grandmother for a walk in the park before supper, as long as they took my cell phone and promised to call if Grandma got too tired.

I was just about to call them to say supper was almost ready when the front door opened. "P.J.? Paul? That you?"

Philip appeared in the kitchen door, loosening his tie. "No, it's me. Where are the boys?"

"Out in the park with my mom and the dog. I was just going to call—"

"Don't." My husband parked his briefcase on the counter. "We need to talk. It's not that easy, you know, with a houseful of other ears."

"O-kay." I turned off the stove under the pan of pasta water and leaned against a counter. I had a feeling what was coming.

Philip sat on one of the counter stools. "So . . . have you found a retirement home for your mom?"

I felt like rolling my eyes. "You have to know they all have waiting lists. But I did find some good possibilities for in-home care—or, if we want, elder day care. I could drop her off every morning and pick her up after work. Really, Philip, she's coming up on the list back in Minot. All we have to do is fill in a few months until her name—"

"No!" He got up and paced. "You said it might be three months. *Might.* I know how that goes. Three if we're lucky, but probably six or eight or, who knows." He stopped pacing and threw an arm wide. "Have you *looked* at this penthouse lately, Gabrielle? Dandy underfoot. Dog hair on the couch. More bickering because the boys have to bunk up when all could be solved if they had their own rooms again. And coming home to peace and quiet? Forget it. Everywhere I turn, there's a warm body! Dog on the couch. Your mom watching some lame rerun on the plasma when I want to relax and watch TV." He sat down again on the stool. "No. She's got to go back."

"Go back to what? She still shouldn't be alone. She's had two falls, Philip!"

"I don't know. Get her a live-in companion. Whatever."

"And how am I supposed to do that from Chicago? I'm already taking time from work to make calls. My boss has been very patient."

"So *quit* the job already, Gabrielle. How many times do I have to tell you?"

I could feel my spine stiffening. "Why? According to *you*, my mom has to be out of here *this week*. The boys are perfectly happy at sailing camp for the next month. What am I supposed to—"

He snorted. "That's just it. They're not."

I blinked. "They're not what? Not happy?"

"Not going to sailing camp next week." Philip's jaw muscles tightened. "Some goofball got our application mixed up and put the boys down for only a one-week camp. Now they tell me the four-week camp is filled. There's not another one until late July."

I stared at him, speechless. Finally I licked my lips. "And you were going to tell me this when?"

"I'm telling you now. Good grief, Gabby. I just found out this morning."

I felt like I was gasping for breath. "But . . . I can't quit work just like that. I'd need to at least give two weeks' notice, find people to cover my responsibilities, give them time to find some-one else."

"Oh. Well, then"—his tone was sarcastic—"maybe I'll just have to send the boys back to Virginia where there *is* someone who wants to take care of them."

chapter 39

As I lay awake in bed that night, I kept telling myself Philip didn't really mean it. Sometimes he threatened stuff just to bully his point. But the news about sailing camp was a huge blow. *Humph.* Was it really some administrative "goofball" who messed up? Maybe Philip had filled out the wrong application and didn't want to admit it.

Does it matter, Gabby? Whatever happened, come Monday, the boys had no activities scheduled. Not to mention I was under the gun to find a place for my mom, or send her back to North Dakota . . . no, I couldn't just send her. I'd have to take her. *Oh God,* I groaned. *What am I going to do?* I felt as if walls were closing in on me, pressing in, no windows, no light, and I only had a fraction of airspace left . . .

In the bright light of day, as Mom and I drove to Manna House the next morning with Dandy sitting in the backseat, pressing his nose to the two-inch window opening, I realized I only had one choice. I would have to quit my job—or at least take several weeks off, maybe even the whole summer, until I got my family stuff squared away. Would Mabel hold my job for me? They'd been looking for a program director when I fell into the job. If I took off too much time, they might have to get someone else.

For some reason, the thought of not returning to Manna House was almost a physical pain, like a stab wound to my gut. *Get a grip, Gabby. It's just a job.* I blinked away the tears before I ended up blubbering in front of my mom. *Just do it, Gabby. Sit down with Mabel and tell her what you have to do. See what she says.*

Except . . . Mabel wasn't in. Again. "What?" I said to Angela at the front desk. "But I have to talk to her! Today!"

Angela shrugged, her black silken mane falling over one shoulder. "Sorry, Gabby. She's at the hospital. Something about her nephew."

"Her nephew?" I'd almost forgotten about the boy she was raising. She called him C.J., or something like that. "Was he in an accident?"

Angela shrugged again. "She didn't say. Just said she wouldn't be in today and couldn't use her cell at the hospital."

Oh, great. Now what was I going to do? Philip was in no frame of mind for me to tell him I couldn't quit because my boss wasn't in. But I couldn't just not show up next week without talking to Mabel first! How unprofessional was that?

"*Hola,* Gramma Shep! You too, Dandy dog." Aida Menéndez hopped off a chair as we came into the multipurpose room and gave my mother a hug. "Would you like some coffee? Black, right?"

My mother beamed.

"There she is!" hollered Lucy. "Carolyn's been buggin' the daylights outta me to play her some Scrabble, but them word games ain't my thing. C'mon over here, Miz Martha, and take her down a peg or two."

In spite of feeling like my life was spinning out of control, I had to laugh. You'd think my mother was a regular fixture at Manna House, the way the residents had taken her under their wing. And Lucy, of all people! Here it was, hiking into the nineties today, and Miss Disappearing Act was still hanging around the shelter. *Thank You, God. That's all I can say . . . thank You.*

Estelle was banging around the kitchen, already working on lunch, when I came downstairs. I tried to sneak into my office with Dandy without her seeing me, but no sooner had I shut the door and got Dandy settled than it opened again, and Estelle stuck her head in. "I know when I'm being avoided. What's goin' on, girl?"

I shook my head, but all that did was slosh out the tears that I'd been holding back for the past twelve hours, and the next thing I knew, I was bawling into Estelle's broad bosom, her warm, brown arms around my shaking shoulders. When I finally got hold of myself, I told her about the catch-22 I was in. ". . . And even if I—*hic*—quit my job here," I added, "I still don't know how I'm going to take care of the—*hic*—boys *and* take my mom back to North Dakota. I mean, it might take me a week or more back there to line up the care she needs until her—*hic*—name comes up on the list for assisted living."

"*Mm-mm-mm.*" Estelle brushed my hair back off my damp face, tucking a misbehaving curl behind my ear. "Now listen, Gabby Fairbanks. I don't believe God brought you this far to leave you now. He's gonna make a way, just you wait an' see. *Mm-hm.* But I sure would like to give that man o' yours a piece o' my mind. Or . . ." She started to chuckle. "Maybe I oughta sic Harry on him. Now, *there's* a man."

I sniffled and blew my nose. "Harry? Who's Harry?"

I could swear Estelle blushed, though it was hard to tell under her creamy brown skin. "You know. Harry Bentley. The doorman at your place who—"

My mouth dropped open—and then I started to laugh. "His name is Harry? *Bald* Mr. Bentley's first name is *Harry*?" My shoulders started shaking again, but this time it was laughter draining all the tension from my body. And before I knew it, Estelle was laughing too, laughing so hard *she* had to wipe away the tears.

I was glad I'd spilled my guts to Estelle and got that out of the way. By the time Edesa Baxter came flying in the door to teach her Friday morning Bible study, her hair enveloped in a multicolored head wrap and Gracie riding in a sling made from a long length of cloth on her hip, I was able to give her a warm hug without falling apart. But I felt a pang as I held out my arms to the baby. Would this be the last time I'd see Edesa and Gracie for a while?

"Where has your mama been keeping you all week, *chica*?" I said, smooching Gracie's cheek and neck until she squealed with laughter. I turned to Edesa. "I haven't seen you, 'Desa, since I got back from North Dakota. Did you finally have the hearing while I was gone? What happened?"

Edesa nodded, her expression tentative. "*Sí*. Mabel Turner and Reverend Handley both came to the hearing to testify about the note Carmelita left me before she died." Strain crept into her voice. "The honcho's DNA test came back positive, though. As far as they know, he *is* Gracie's father. The caseworker at DCFS tried to encourage us. He's on parole and has no income right now, though the judge gave him a month to get his life together, and then she'll make a ruling." She swallowed. "But we are still praying. We . . . have to trust God."

"Oh, Edesa. I will keep praying too." I wrapped my arms around her and gave her a long hug. Then . . . "Hey, come on. There's someone I want you to meet. The residents have dubbed her Gramma Shep, can you believe it?"

I left my mom in Edesa's Bible study but didn't stay, and I didn't offer to look after Gracie either. I had too much to do. I tried Mabel's cell several times that day, but only got her voice mail. I didn't leave a detailed message, just asked her to call me at her earliest convenience, even on the weekend. I still had a few leads to call about my mom—one was like a "group home" for senior adults, only five other residents, and yes, they had an opening for one more. My heart beat faster. Was this our answer?

I made an appointment for tomorrow—Saturday—at eleven o'clock.

At the end of the day, I didn't say good-bye to anyone. I couldn't tell others I was resigning before I had even told Mabel. I would just have to come in on Monday. Philip would have to grant me that much, especially when he saw I had decided to resign. And to be honest, I still needed a couple of days to leave the program—such as it was so far—in good shape for someone else to pick up.

I was surprised, however, when I picked up the boys and they talked as if they were going back to sailing camp next week. Didn't Philip say anything to them? Well, I wasn't the one who was going to break the news to them . . . and I told Philip as much when he got home that evening.

"Don't break into a sweat, Gabby." Philip actually seemed in a good mood. "I've got a surprise for the boys that ought to make up for sailing camp. I was telling Lester Stone about the boys learning how to sail, and he invited me and the boys on a two-day sail this weekend—perfect for Father's Day, eh? He said they'd learn more in two days of sailing his yacht than in four weeks on a dinghy."

I flinched. P.J. and Paul on a sailboat all weekend? "But what about the weather? Isn't it supposed to rain this weekend?"

"Don't worry about it! You know Chicago weather—a thunderstorm rolls through, and then the sun comes out. Besides, Lester says if the lake gets too choppy, we'll just pull into the nearest harbor."

I wasn't convinced, but told him I had news too—a group home that might work out for my mom. "And I've decided you're right. I need to resign from my job, or at least take an extended leave. But I couldn't put in my resignation today. My boss had an emergency and was out of the office. I'll have to go back at least one or two days next week to finish up."

Philip narrowed his eyes. "And what's supposed to happen those days? You always do this, Gabby! Take a simple request and bend it like a pretzel to go your way."

"I'm trying, Philip! It's *not* a simple request, and I'm doing my best!"

"Yeah?" He snorted. "Well, as usual, your best just isn't good enough, Gabrielle."

I was so glad Philip and the boys left early the next morning for their sailing date with Lester Stone. Philip's words had stung,

343

and I really needed some time to get my head together. Or my heart.

Mom was still asleep, so I took Dandy out and then got another cup of coffee and curled up on the couch with my Bible. Hadn't cracked it even once in the past week . . . where was I? Dandy jumped up and rested his head in my lap. I found my place at chapter twelve and started reading. Good grief, Jesus really lit into the religious leaders who kept finding fault with Him, calling them a "brood of snakes." I laughed out loud. I'd have to remember that next time Philip criticized me. I mean, if Jesus could do it . . .

As I read further, Jesus said He couldn't expect anything else from them. Their hearts were evil. And, He said, the stuff that comes out of our mouths reflects what's in our hearts. I thought about that. I didn't think Philip was evil. Maybe that's why I felt devastated when he said hurtful things—I kept expecting him to be good. That's all I wanted, just to love my husband and be loved back, to be a family.

Which is why I teared up at the end of the chapter when Jesus' family interrupted what He was doing and wanted Him to come with them. Jesus basically said, "Who is my family? The people who love God and serve Him—that's my family."

I closed the Bible and hugged it to my chest. Dandy snuggled closer now that there was more room on my lap. I remembered that scripture from my Sunday school days. I always thought Jesus' reply was kind of rude. But it made more sense to me now.

"Oh, God," I moaned. "I don't want to have to choose between my husband and kids and the new family You've been giving to me!" But I knew which "family" had been feeding my spirit and bringing me closer to God.

chapter 40

Mom took forever to sort out her various meds and vitamins into the seven-day pillbox, but at least I still had the rental car, so we made it to our appointment on time. This time I left Dandy behind. We weren't going to be gone that long.

The "group home" was a Victorian three-story in Rogers Park, with a wraparound porch, wedged between two six-flats. The whole neighborhood was oddly incongruent—older, once-noble homes in various stages of upkeep left standing here and there as apartment buildings crowded in.

The houseparents seemed nice, a white couple in their mid-fifties, and the home was pleasant enough. Three meals a day and housekeeping. A social worker came once a week to assess needs and arrange transportation to medical appointments. But I was perturbed to learn that the other five residents were all men. "We'd be happy to accommodate your mother if she'd feel comfortable here," the husband said.

"What about Dandy?" Mom said. "My dog."

"I'm sorry." The woman smiled. "No pets."

I should have seen that coming. "Mom, any retirement home we find will have the same rule. Maybe"—I went out on a limb—"we can take care of Dandy for a while."

But my mom was still shaking her head. "No. I would be the only woman. That wouldn't feel right."

"Mom," I said, lowering my voice. "It's only for a few months. Then we can take you back to Minot when your name comes up on the list for the home there!"

"A few months?" The male supervisor shook his head. "I'm sorry. We require at least a twelve-month contract—which, of course, is void if the guest, um, passes before that time. We try to keep our guest list as stable as possible. Turnover is always an adjustment in a home this small."

My mind scrambled. Should I sign up anyway? This was the only choice I had! But if Mom's name came up back in Minot in three, or even six months, she might lose her place there if we didn't take it right away. And if we took her back there when her name came up, we'd be stuck having to pay the unused months here!

"Uh, thank you so much." I stood up. "We need to think about this a bit more."

But I hit the steering wheel in frustration when we got back in the car.

"I'm sorry, Gabby." My mom's lip trembled. "Why can't I just stay with you?"

"Oh, Mom . . ." How could I explain? "I wish you could." But the wistfulness in my mother's voice wrenched my heart. We were both in danger of losing it. "Hey. I've got an idea." I'd seen a Supercuts near the El stop where I got on the train. "Let's stop by the beauty shop and get your hair done. What do you say?"

As we headed down Sheridan Road, it suddenly occurred to me that my mom hadn't called me by the wrong name for a whole week. Maybe consistent presence and regular interaction helped her memory.

The answering machine was blinking when we finally got back to the penthouse around two o'clock. "Let me check this, and then I'll make some lunch!" I called out to my mom, who was laughing at Dandy's excited welcome-home dance in the gallery.

"Do you like my new hairdo, Dandy?" I heard her say. "You think it's too short?"

I punched the Play button. *"You have one new message"* . . . *"Gabby? Are you there? It's me, Henry. I just got off the phone with Bill Robinson, and we've got a problem. I know Philip's out on the boat with Lester Stone, but I really need to get him on a three-way with Robinson before Monday. Do you know how to reach him? I tried his cell, but it didn't even give me his voice mail. If he calls, or if Stone has a radio or something, just tell Philip it involves the Robinson deal and to give me a call ASAP—today if possible. Thanks, Gabby."*

Oh, great! Why did Henry have to leave this in my lap? Philip had said their cell phones might be out of range, and I could contact the Coast Guard in an emergency. The boat had a ship-to-shore radio. But I didn't think the Coast Guard would think a business call was an "emergency." All I could do was—

Wait a minute. I listened. The house was too quiet. "Mom? Dandy?" A quick look through the house confirmed my suspicion. Mom must have taken the dog down the elevator to do his business! I ran into the hallway and jiggled the Down button. *Oh, Mom, please don't get lost . . .*

But there she was, across the frontage road along the edge of the park, walking Dandy on his leash while the dog sniffed at bushes and lifted his leg. I laughed in relief and joined them until a light drizzle chased us inside. "My goodness!" Mom said as we rode back up the elevator to the thirty-second floor. "And I thought it was hot in North Dakota! But this humidity . . . I was already wet before the rain started."

By the time we ate our lunch, it was three o'clock, and Mom was ready for a nap. I took a peek out the windows in the front room—gray and rainy across the lake. *Oh, dear. Not the greatest day for a sail.* And then it occurred to me that I had a perfect excuse to find out how my kids were doing: Henry wanted me to contact Philip.

I grinned as I dialed Philip's cell. No one could accuse me of being an anxious mother. I had to deliver a message to my husband, right? But all I got was a funny beep. It didn't even ring. Just in case, I tried leaving a quick message for Philip to call Henry ASAP and hung up. Okay, plan B. Philip had left Lester Stone's cell number on the fridge along with the Coast Guard number. I dialed. It rang . . .

"Yeah? Stone here."

"Oh! Lester? This is Gabby Fairbanks! Sorry to bother you. I need to speak to Philip. It's business."

"Ha-ha. Knew we should've left our phones home. Your husband's a little preoccupied right now. He and the boys are trying to bring down the jib. We've got some waves here . . . Can I give him a message?"

My heart lurched a little at what "we've got some waves here" meant. But I said, "Sure! Tell him his partner, Henry, needs him to call ASAP. Something about the Bill Robinson deal."

"Hang on . . ." There was a lot of wind static in my ear, then Lester Stone came back on. "Did you say Bill Robinson?"

"Yes! But Philip should call Henry about it, not Robinson, okay?"

A slight pause. "Okay, got it. Gotta go."

I'd wanted to ask if they were going to pull into a harbor and get out of the weather, but the phone went dead. Oh, well. I delivered the message. That ought to earn me some brownie points with Philip.

I turned on the TV and kept it on the weather channel the rest of the afternoon. And tried to remember the psalm that said, *"When I am afraid, I will trust in God . . . I trust in God, why do I need to be afraid?"*

I swam up out of my dreams into consciousness the next morning, fighting off panic. Not about the boys. God had given me peace that they were going to be all right—wet, maybe, but not in danger. But I realized it was Sunday, Philip was coming home, and the only possibility I'd found for my mom had fallen through.

It was all so unfair!

I made coffee, rehearsing a speech in which I would ask Philip for more time. Begging for mercy was more like it. And I hated feeling that way.

My mom came into the kitchen dressed in a navy blue suit and a white blouse with the tag sticking out. "What time are we leaving for church, Gabby?" I started to tuck it in when I realized she had the blouse on inside out.

I put on a smile. "Uh, nine thirty. Church starts at ten." I knew my mom would expect to go to church. At work on Friday, I'd looked at the schedule and realized that SouledOut Community Church was on for Sunday Evening Praise this weekend. Of all the groups who led the weekly evening service, so far SouledOut had been my favorite. But it was likely that Philip and the boys would just be getting home from their sailing trip Sunday evening. Why not go to SouledOut in the morning? It was just Mom and me. At least we'd see some familiar faces—Josh and Edesa, Josh's parents, Avis and Peter Douglass, even Estelle!

The directions I'd gotten from Estelle took me straight up Sheridan Road to Howard, and then west about a half mile to a shopping center by the Howard Street El Station. I pulled the minivan into the parking lot at five minutes to ten.

My mother craned her neck. "I don't see any church."

I pointed to a sign on one of the large storefronts: "SouledOut Community Church." The air was still misty with leftover rain as we dodged puddles on our way across the parking lot. *Drat*. My hair would be totally frizzed by the time we got inside.

When we walked through the double glass doors into the large friendly room, however, I forgot to worry about my hair. "Mrs. Fairbanks!" Peter Douglass gripped my hand, his smile warm, his dark eyes delighted. "What a pleasure to see you here. And who is this charming lady?" The well-groomed businessman took one of my mother's pale hands in both of his brown ones. She seemed startled.

Smiling big, I introduced my mother and added, "Mr. Douglass is one of the board members at Manna House."

"Oh, that's lovely." Mom gave me a quizzical look. "What's Manna House?"

I barely had time to remind her that that was where I worked, when Josh and Edesa Baxter swooped down on us, and right on their heels, Josh's parents. Denny Baxter was carrying Gracie, his smile betraying the two large dimples in his cheeks. Edesa gave me a big hug. "Oh, *Gabriela!* I have good news! . . . Well, it's bad news in one way, but good—"

Just then the worship band launched into a song. and over the music a woman called out, "Good morning, church! Let's find our seats and begin our worship this morning with 'Shout to the Lord'!" I thought the voice sounded familiar and looked over Edesa's head. At the front of the room I saw Peter Douglass's wife, Avis, face glowing as the song began to roll: *"Shout to the Lord, all the earth, let us sing . . ."*

"Tell you later!" Edesa kissed my cheek and scampered off with Josh.

"This must be your mother!" Jodi Baxter whispered, giving my mom a warm hug. "Come sit with us." She found four seats, but everyone was standing, many arms lifting in praise as the music continued to swell . . .

". . . Nothing compares to the promise I have in You . . ."

Still trying to take it all in, my eyes swept the room. Dark faces, creamy brown, fair-skinned . . . African braids, brunettes, blondes . . . wow, what a diverse congregation. And there was Estelle, decked out in one of her roomy caftans that hid her extra pounds! I tried to catch her eye and then did a double-take as the bald African-American man next to her tilted his head and winked at me.

My mouth dropped open, and I tried not to laugh. Mr. Bentley!

By the time the service ended, I was so full, I felt like I'd just eaten a ten-course meal. The songs were a mixture of upbeat and worshipful—I really did love that saxophone wailing beneath the melody on some of them—and the sermon by one of the copastors, a tall, gangly white man with thinning hair, was punctuated by "Amens" and even an occasional, "Thank ya, Jesus!" from the congregation.

My head was in a whirl afterward as Jodi and Edesa and Estelle tried to introduce me to several women—"our Yada Yada Prayer Group sisters," they called them. Estelle's housemate was a stylish, slender blonde in a red beret she introduced as Stu. I could hardly imagine two people who looked more different. I was surprised to learn they lived upstairs in a two-flat over Josh's parents.

Edesa introduced me to the African-American family she and Josh rented their "studio" from. I'd seen Carl Hickman before—he'd come with Peter Douglass to our party at the shelter. His wife was a wiry woman named Florida. "How ya doin', Gabby?" She shook my hand in an iron grip. "We been prayin' for you at Yada Yada—'scuse me. Girl!" Florida's hand shot out and grabbed a youngster darting past. "You know better than ta be runnin' in the house of God!"

I was grateful when Jodi Baxter showed up with two cups of coffee and pulled me aside. Mr. Bentley, even without his uniform, had graciously taken my mom under his wing, keeping her company and her coffee cup refilled, so I sat down with Jodi, blowing out a big sigh. "This was quite a church service."

"Yes, praise God! I love the worship here." Jodi brushed her soft bangs back. She wore her brunette hair with its slight wave just skimming her shoulders. *Wouldn't mind hair like that for a change.* "We used to be two different churches, but we merged because God told us we needed each other . . . long story." She chuckled. "We're still in training, but we love it." Jodi cast an affectionate glance toward her son, who was holding little Gracie in one arm, the other draped around Edesa, talking to an excited knot of people. "And it's good for our kids, who don't have to give up their own culture to feel at home as a family."

I noticed Josh and Edesa seemed especially happy. "What's this bad news–good news Edesa was going to tell me?"

"She didn't tell you yet? Gracie's birth father violated his parole and landed back in prison. So his petition to take the baby got thrown out! I can still hardly believe it, after all the worry of the past few months—but God really answered our prayers."

"Oh, I'm so glad." That's what I said. But I felt a pang. *God really answered their prayers . . . why not mine?*

"Are you okay, Gabby? You look a bit strained. What's going on?"

And just like that I found myself telling Jodi Baxter my whole saga—moving, feeling adrift, finding the job at Manna House, tension with my husband, now triple complicated with needing to find a place for my mom and summer plans for the boys falling through. I shook my head. "I don't know what to do, Jodi. I was going to resign Friday, but Mabel wasn't there—"

"I know." Jodi's face clouded. "Her nephew, C.J., tried to commit suicide."

I gasped. "What?! That little boy? Oh, Jodi. I had no idea. Is he going to be OK?"

"I think so. We've been praying around the clock since we found out yesterday."

I looked at her. "Does God really answer prayer, Jodi? I've been praying and praying about my mom and about my job and about what's going wrong with me and Philip, and it seems like the only answer I got was, 'Come to Me.'"

Her hazel eyes got round. "'Come to Me?' God said to you, 'Come to Me'?"

I felt embarrassed. "Well, those are the words that popped into my brain while I was at the prayer meeting at my mom's church. It didn't seem to make a lot of sense—not exactly an answer to my prayer about Mom. But a couple of days later I was reading my Bible—I've been trying to read Matthew—and I came to those verses, you know, the ones that go, 'Come to Me, all you who are weary—'"

Smiling, Jodi chimed in. "'—and bearing a heavy burden, and I will give you rest. Take My yoke upon you and learn from Me, for I am gentle and humble in heart, and you will find rest for your souls. For My yoke is easy and My burden is light.'"

I gave her a wistful grin. "Yeah. That's the one."

Jodi Baxter took my coffee cup, set it aside, and took both my hands in hers. "Gabby, that *is* God answering your prayer! Don't you see? All these other things—your husband, your kids, even your mom—yes, they're important. And God really cares about them. But the thing God cares about most is *you*. I think . . . it sounds to me like God is calling you, Gabby. To come home."

chapter 41

"There were a lot of black people at that church, weren't there?" My mom was still watching people spill out of the doors of SouledOut as I snapped her seat belt in place.

Her comment took me by surprise, but I tried not to show it. "Mm-hm. All kinds of people. It was nice, wasn't it? Maybe that's what heaven's going to be like."

My mom nodded thoughtfully. "I didn't know there'd be so many nice people in Chicago. Mr. Bentley is very nice. And the lady named Estelle."

I pulled out of the parking lot. "We didn't have much of a chance to know many black people back home, did we?" In Petersburg, either, for that matter. Our own fault. Everybody tended to stay in their own little neighborhoods and their own churches.

"But they're not really black, are they? Brown. And all different shades too."

I felt a little impatient with Mom getting so chatty. It was nice that she was being observant, but what I really wanted was some time by myself to think about what Jodi Baxter had said—and get myself psyched up for the inevitable talk with Philip tonight. Maybe Mom would take a nap after lunch, and I'd have a few quiet hours to just think and pray before the sailors got home.

But to my surprise, the TV was on and the boys were sprawled on the wraparound couch, watching a *Pirates of the Caribbean* DVD when we got back to Richmond Towers. "Look who's here!" I gave them each a hug. "I didn't expect you back so early! The weather get too rough for sailing?"

P.J. shrugged, his eyes locked on the movie. "The weather was OK. Ask Dad. He's the one who called it."

The door to the den was closed. I hung up my coat, found the makings for tuna fish sandwiches and put my mom to work, filled the teakettle and turned on the burner . . . before tapping on the den door and sticking my head in. Philip was slumped in the leather armchair by the reading lamp.

"Hey. You guys are home early."

My husband looked up, eyes hard. "That's right. Thanks to you."

I tensed. "What do you mean?"

"Close the door."

I did but stood with my back against it, hand on the handle. *Déjà vu.*

Philip threw his hands wide. "You just cost Fairbanks and Fenchel our business with Lester Stone, that's what."

"Wha—what are you talking about?"

"The phone call to Lester? Dropping Bill Robinson's name into the conversation?"

"But Henry asked me to get a message to you! He said it was important!"

"Fine. Talk to *me*. But you don't tell my business to *anyone*, Gabrielle!" His voice was hard, clipped. "Do you understand?!"

I was totally confused. "I tried to call your cell. Henry tried too, but he couldn't get through. That's why he called me."

"Doesn't matter. You had no business talking to Lester Stone about Bill Robinson."

"But . . . I thought that was the message, so you'd know why Henry wanted you to call."

Philip pushed himself out of the chair. I flinched, but all he did was jab a finger at me. "Did Henry tell you to go through Lester? Huh? Did he?"

"Well, no, but—"

"I'm telling you! That phone call cost us our contract with Stone! And it's your fault!"

I gripped the doorknob harder. "But I didn't tell Lester anything! I just said what Henry told me, for you to call about the Bill Robinson project."

"'But I didn't tell Lester anything,'" he mocked in a high-pitched voice. "You told enough just dropping Robinson's name. Turns out Lester Stone is involved in a lawsuit with Bill Robinson, and he didn't like it one bit that Fairbanks and Fenchel are working with him. Said it was a conflict of interest for him to employ the same developer." Philip threw up his hands. "Zap. We're done. Just like that."

My heart was pounding now. "But I didn't know that! How could I—"

"You don't have to know it!" He was yelling now. "All you have to know is not to talk about my business with *anyone*! Do you understand me, Gabrielle?"

The teakettle whistled. Jerking the door open, I fled to the kitchen to silence it, catching frightened glances from the boys as I ran through the living room. I needed time to pull myself together—but I forgot my mother was still puttering in the kitchen, taking her sweet time making the tuna sandwiches. I flipped the burner off under the teakettle and kept going to my bedroom, where I flung myself on the bed.

Philip followed me, slamming the bedroom door behind him. "I'm not through with you, Gabrielle. You just don't get it, do you? Ever since we moved here, you've done everything you can think of to undermine my new business."

I sat up, hugging a pillow in front of me. "That's not true, Philip!"

"Shut up. That's the problem with you. You don't have any business savvy. You don't know what a corporate wife should be doing to help make her husband a success. You turn up your nose at Mona Fenchel's connections that would help us break into a business class social strata. You puke all over Lester Stone's sailboat. You bring your mother and her . . . her dumb mutt here just after the boys come home for the summer, turning this penthouse into a three-generation madhouse . . ." He stopped and glared at me. "Speaking of your mother, what's the deal with the group home? When is she moving in?"

I was too scared to speak. I shook my head slightly.

"I knew it!" he yelled. "This is the last straw, Gabby! The last straw!"

Philip stomped out without saying where, and the whole household felt like a graveyard the rest of that day. The boys holed up in their room. My mom shut herself and Dandy in her borrowed bedroom. Moving like a zombie, I finished the sandwiches my mom had started, set out fruit and chips on the kitchen counter, tapped on doors, told my sons and my mother they could get something to eat when they got hungry, and spent the rest of the day in my bedroom, blinds pulled, crying until I'd sucked out every drop.

Philip still wasn't back when I turned out the light at nine o'clock.

But I woke with a start when I heard Philip yell, "What the—!" followed by a string of curses. Then, "Where's that dog! Who didn't take the dog out?"

I grabbed my robe and went flying down the hall to the gallery. Philip was hopping on one canvas boat shoe, ripping off the other. A pile of dog poop had been deposited right beside the front door, now mashed and stinking where Philip had stepped in it.

"Oh no! Paul must've forgotten to take him out before bed . . . I'll—I'll get the dog and take him out now. Just give me a sec to get my clothes on."

"Just clean up this mess, Gabby," Philip said between clenched teeth. "I'm dressed. I'll take the stupid dog out. Just . . . just get my other gym shoes and take this one and clean it off."

I carried the stinking canvas boat shoe into the laundry room, got Philip's other shoes from the bedroom, then went for paper towels, a bucket, rag, and pine cleaner. When I got back to the gallery, Philip was trying to clip the leash onto Dandy's collar, who was pulling backward and growling.

"Let me do it."

"Forget it!" Dropping the leash, Philip grabbed the dog up under his arm and disappeared into the elevator. The doors closed.

I cleaned up the mess in the gallery, washed the entire marble-tiled floor with pine cleaner, and then tackled Philip's shoe. I got the poop off as best I could, then threw it into the washing machine. A half hour passed. Philip still wasn't back, so I went to bed.

I woke at three-something and realized the other side of our king bed was empty. Putting on my robe, I wandered through the dark penthouse. The gallery light, which I'd left on, was out. Philip was sacked out on the couch, snoring gently.

Well, fine. I didn't want to sleep with the big jerk anyway.

I woke the next morning, a dull headache throbbing above my eyes. I could hear the shower running in the bathroom. Philip was getting ready to go to work.

I put on my robe and dragged myself to the kitchen, feeling like Charlie Brown with a cloud of gloom over my head. I had no idea how to dig myself out of the pit I was in. I should go in to work today to drop the bomb on Mabel that I needed to take an extended leave of absence and offer to resign. Mom would probably be happy to go with me. But that left the boys hanging . . .

To my surprise, the pungent smell of fresh coffee greeted me. I stared dumbly at the coffeemaker, which was dripping merrily. Philip had made the coffee?

A tiny ray of hope broke through the gloom cloud. Maybe Philip was over his mad. Maybe I should call Mabel, tell her I have a family emergency, take the day off, try to work out plans for the boys and my mom with Philip, and go in tomorrow to have the face-to-face talk about—

"Celeste?" My mom's voice was plaintive. "Have you seen Dandy? He wasn't beside my bed when I woke up."

I frowned. That was the first time Mom had called me by the wrong name in over a week. Had she heard the dog-poop-in-the-gallery fiasco last night? "Oh, he's probably sleeping in Paul's bed. I'll get him." I needed to take the dog out soon, anyway.

I headed for the boys' bedroom and peeked in. Both boys were still asleep. But no Dandy. Picking up my pace, I did a quick search through the main rooms and was just heading for the master bedroom when Philip appeared in the hallway, clean-shaven, tan slacks, black silk short-sleeve shirt, smelling like his Armani aftershave.

I stood in his way, arms crossed, knowing I looked like a frowzy housewife in my robe and uncombed hair. "Where's the dog?"

He looked down at me, unperturbed. "I put him out. What did you think I was going to do after he crapped all over our floor?"

"He's been out since *last night*?"

Behind me, I heard a plaintive wail and felt my mother clutch my robe. "Oh no! No, no . . . he'll get lost! Oh, Celeste, we have to find Dandy! It's too cold in Alaska!"

"You rat!" I hissed through my teeth at my husband as he calmly squeezed past us and headed for the kitchen. I pried my mother's fingers off my robe and patted her hand. "Don't worry, Mom. He's probably hanging around outside, wanting breakfast. I'll get dressed and go right down, okay?"

I pulled on jeans and a T-shirt and was heading for the elevator when Paul came running after me in shorts, pajama top, and sockless gym shoes. "Mom! What happened? Where's Dandy? Why is Grandma crying in her room?"

I tried to be matter-of-fact as the elevator door dinged open and Paul followed me in. "Your dad, uh, took Dandy out last night, and I guess the dog got away. I'm sure he won't have gone too far."

It seemed to take forever as the elevator stopped again and again to pick up residents leaving early for work. In the lobby, Mr. Bentley was already on duty, passing out newspapers, whistling for taxis. But I shouldered in. "Mr. Bentley? Did you see Dandy outside this morning?" I pointed toward the frontage road exit. "We . . . lost him last night."

The doorman shook his head. "Sure haven't, Mrs. Fairbanks. I'll keep an eye out and let you know soon as I do."

But Paul and I were already flying out the revolving door toward the park, and we spent the next half hour running up and down the jogging path, calling the dog's name. We even went through the underpass and out toward the beach, barely noticing the calm blue of the lake under a perfectly clear sky. We stopped joggers, described Dandy, and asked them to keep an eye out, pointing back toward the high-rise where we lived.

But no dog.

chapter 42

Paul was in tears. We walked back to Richmond Towers with my arm across his shoulders. "I know, kiddo. But we'll keep praying, okay? Maybe somebody found Dandy and took him to the animal shelter. I'll call, okay? He has a tag on."

"But it has Grandma's North Dakota phone number!"

"Well . . . but if the shelter has him, we can use it to identify him."

Back upstairs, I tried to soften the bad news. "Mom . . . Mom. Don't cry. I'm sure we'll find him. Look, I'll stay home today with you and the boys, and we'll look for Dandy and—"

"Don't you have to go to work today, Gabrielle?" Philip broke in, coffee cup in hand. "To finish things up, talk to your boss?"

I glared at him. "Yes. But I can't leave now, can I? There's the boys and—"

"Yeah. Just like I figured. Look, you just go. I've got the boys."

I gaped at him, my thoughts ricocheting. Was Philip actually going to pitch in and take care of the boys? "What do you mean? Are you going to—"

"I *said*, I've got it covered." My husband turned on his heel and disappeared into the den. Not out the door. Into the den.

Well. This was an interesting turn of events. Maybe Philip felt guilty for throwing the dog out last night. Maybe he and the boys would go look for the dog while I was gone. If Philip was willing to stay home from work and cover for the boys while I took Mom to Manna House and finished business there, maybe there was hope we could work things out bit by bit.

Mom was reluctant to leave with Dandy still missing, but on the other hand she didn't want to stay there ". . . with that mean man," she whispered to me. I hustled to get ready before Philip changed his mind. On the way out, I fished in the wooden bowl in the gallery where we kept car keys but couldn't find the keys for the rental car. I poked my head into the den. "Have you seen the keys for the minivan?"

Philip looked up, all nonchalance. "Oh. Enterprise picked it up yesterday afternoon, or maybe early this morning. I left the keys at the front desk downstairs."

I counted to three. "You could have said something."

"I did. Last week we said we'd keep the rental another week. Week's over. And you can use the El today, Gabby, since you don't have to pick up the boys at camp." He turned back to the computer.

We'd also talked about leasing a second car. But . . . so be it. I wasn't going to get bent out of shape about this. The El was fine with me, though it meant more walking and stairs for my mom.

It took longer to get to the shelter, but we finally walked in at ten o'clock. I signed in, got my mom settled in the multipurpose room with a cup of coffee, and came back to the reception cubby to ask if Mabel was in. Angela shook her head. "Not yet. But she called. She'll be in around lunch." She stood up and peered over the counter. "Where's Dandy today?"

"Don't ask."

It was hard pretending that this was a normal day. I gave a wave to Estelle as I scurried for my office, but she leaned over the kitchen counter, hairnet covering her usual topknot, apron covering her roomy dress. "I hear you the one told the board I should get paid for all the cookin' I do."

"What? Oh! Estelle!" I'd totally forgotten that the Manna House Board was supposed to meet last Saturday and consider new staff. "They offered you a job?"

"Yep." A wide grin pushed her dark eyes into half moons. "Twenty hours a week. Which means I got a few extra hours left over for them cookin' and sewin' classes you talked to me about."

"That's wonderful! I'm so glad, Estelle." I leaned across the counter and gave her a hug. *And really, really awkward*, I thought, as I escaped into my broom closet office. *Now what am I going to do?*

I booted up the computer. Well, I would type up a proposal for the cooking and sewing classes, ask Estelle to list materials needed, suggest a time slot, and turn it in to Mabel with my resignation. Estelle could probably launch those classes by herself and wouldn't need me to look over her shoulder.

But first, I needed to type up my resignation. After addressing the letter to Mabel Turner and the Manna House Board, however, my resolve faltered. *If I quit this job, I'll wither up and die.* My head sank into my hands. It wasn't just the job. It was the living faith of the staff and volunteers. I'd lost my way, but I was beginning to find it again . . . here, in this unlikely place! Here I'd felt accepted, needed, appreciated. I'd made all kinds of mistakes, and they still loved me.

What was I going to do once I walked out of those doors tonight?

I got another cup of coffee from the kitchen to steady my nerves, punched the Play button on the CD player sitting on my desk to distract my thoughts, and started typing again as gospel music filled up my little office. But I flipped it off when the Dottie Rambo song came on. *"Where do I go when there's no one else to turn to . . . ?"*

It hurt too much.

My phone rang just before lunch. It was Angela at the front desk. "Mabel's here."

I took a deep breath, folded my resignation letter and the proposal for Estelle's classes, and went upstairs. A small circle of shelter residents were clustered around my mother, and I heard Lucy mutter loudly, "What kinda lowlife would kick out yer dog?"

I slipped through the room and through the double doors. Angela looked up from the desk. "She said go right in." I took a deep breath and opened the door.

Mabel Turner's eyes had bags under them, and I suddenly remembered what she'd been through the last few days. "I . . . heard about C.J. Is he okay?"

The director nodded wearily. "He's going to be all right. Physically. But . . . I don't know. You've met him, Gabby. He gets teased a lot at school, called 'pretty boy' and 'faggot'—all the cruel things kids say. He's had a real tough time—but I didn't expect this." She sighed. "He really needs your prayers. Me too." She was quiet a long moment, then seemed to remember I was there. "Anyway, Angela said you needed to see me. What's up?"

I sat down, though I was tempted to flee. Mabel didn't need more bad news. But I had no choice. I spilled it all . . . and used up thirty minutes and a whole wad of tissues in the process.

"I'm so sorry, Mabel. I wanted to tell you Friday, to give you more warning, but I don't know what else to do." I blew my nose, sure by now that I looked a sight. "In fact, even if I resign today, I'm still in a fix. Unless I find a situation here, I'll probably have to take my mom back to North Dakota, but—"

A loud commotion suddenly erupted in the foyer, and then Mabel's door burst open. Lucy Tucker stood there, purple knit hat crammed on her grizzled head, dragging my mother in by the hand. Several other residents crowded in behind them.

"So why can't Gramma Shep stay *here*, is what I wanna know. That scumbag Gabby's married to—don't mean no offense to you, Gabby—already kicked Martha's dog out, now he's sayin' Martha can't stay. She don't wanna go back there anyway, an' she don't have nowhere else to go right now. Don't that make her homeless? Ain't this a shelter for homeless ladies? Ain't I right, girls?"

"Yeah, that's right." . . . "They's a couple beds open upstairs." . . . "Uh-huh."

I looked in astonishment from Lucy, to my mom, then to Mabel. I practically stopped breathing. Had the answer to the dilemma about my mom been under my nose all the time?

"Oh, Mabel, if . . . if she could. Just for a few days, or maybe a few weeks, or—" What was I saying? This was my mother! I turned and looked at her. My mother had a triumphant look on her face. "Mom?"

"I like it here. They're my friends." She held up her hand, locked in Lucy's.

I went out the double oak doors into the late afternoon sun, my heart and my feet lighter than they'd felt in weeks, even though my backpack was heavy with stuff I'd cleaned out of my desk. I'd hunted high and low for the CD Josh had given me, but someone had borrowed the CD player from my office—must have had the CD still in it.

Didn't matter. I'd be back soon. Manna House was willing to give my mom shelter up to the usual limit—ninety days—as long as I was working on alternative solutions. Surely I'd find something before then, or maybe her name would come up on the assisted living list back in Minot.

I told my mom I'd be back later that night with her clothes, but just in case, Estelle rustled up the basic "kit" that was given to women just coming off the street: personal-size toiletries, new underwear, and pajamas. Estelle had even offered to stay a night or two to help get my mom settled, walk her through the routines, and make sure she took her meds, which Mom always carried in her purse, at the right times. She'd brushed off my profuse thanks. "Hey, might as well piggyback my jobs. I'm still licensed to do in-home elder care, ya know."

I had turned in my resignation letter, though Mabel said she was willing to consider it an "extended leave," depending on what happened at the Fairbanks household in the next few weeks. Just before I got ready to leave, Mom tugged on my arm. "Please look for Dandy, won't you, Gabby?" Her lip trembled a little.

I wrapped her in a hug. "Absolutely, Mom. I'm sure we'll find him." At least she'd used my right name. A good sign. "Where's Lucy? I want to say good-bye."

My mother shook her head. "I don't know. She went out. Said she had to do something. She'll come back, won't she, Gabby?"

Drat. After making that big show about my mom staying here, the least Lucy could've done was hang around! "I'm sure she will, Mom." Well, she always did—sooner or later. I would've felt better leaving my mom if her new buddy, Lucy, had been there.

Still, I felt eager to get home, impatient with how slowly the El rattled along during rush hour, loading and unloading scores of passengers at every stop. I'd tried calling home with the news, but only got voice mail. Philip and the boys were probably out doing a museum or something. Just as well. I wanted to see Philip's face when I calmly announced I'd found a place for my mom, he didn't have to worry about her staying with us anymore . . . *Where, you ask? Oh, a homeless shelter.*

The scumbag. Let him live with *that* on his conscience.

But that, and the news that I'd turned in my resignation, ought to calm things down on the home front. Give me time to focus on the boys. And find Dandy.

"Hello, Mr. Bentley!" I threw the doorman a smile. "Guess what? *Estelle*"—I winked at him—"is looking after my mother at Manna House for a while. Ought to ease things upstairs—oh, did Dandy show up?" I looked toward the glass doors that faced the frontage road and the park, hoping to see a mournful mutt tied to the bike rack outside.

"Haven't seen him, Mrs. Fairbanks. Your boys went out looking after you and the missus left this morning, but they came back empty-handed . . . and then they took off on their trip, so I kept a lookout for the dog whenever I could. Never did see him, though. Sorry."

I shrugged. "Well, thanks anyway. I'll go change my clothes and do another run through the park. Oh—the other big news. I quit my job at Manna House. Didn't want to, but I need to spend more time with the boys . . . long story."

A puzzled look crossed Mr. Bentley's face, but I really didn't want to go into detail right then. "Tell you more later, okay? Right now I've got to run." I gave him a wave, ran my card through the security door, and headed for the elevators. If Philip and the boys were still out, that would give me time to thaw something for supper and go outside to look for Dandy. Maybe make a few calls to nearby animal shelters. After all, a cute mutt like Dandy was sure to get someone's attention, and they'd see he had a collar and a tag, maybe even call the number. I should call my aunt, have her go to Mom's house and check any messages—

Ding! The elevator slowed its upward journey, and the door slid open on the thirty-second floor. I pulled my house key out, still lost in thought as I crossed the foyer, so that at first I didn't notice the pile of stuff beside the front door. I stopped in midstride. What was all this?

My mother's two suitcases were standing next to the door, bulging and presumably filled with her things. Had Philip packed her clothes already? But I hadn't called. How did he know—?

Wait. What was all this other stuff? An even larger pile of suitcases, boxes, and bags stretched on either side of the door. I opened a box and stared at the contents. Dandy's rug, bowls, dog food, and leash.

And then I saw my suitcases. The tan-and-green set my parents had given me when I finally graduated from college several years ago.

Starting to feel frantic, I opened each bag and box. My coats. My shoes. A box with all my personal stuff from our bathroom— toothbrush, deodorant, makeup . . .

I stared at the door. What was on the other side? Trembling, hardly daring to think, I stuck my key in the lock and turned.

Nothing happened. The lock didn't budge.

And then I knew.

When Philip said, "That's the last straw," he'd meant it.

My husband had thrown me out.

chapter 43

I just stood there, mouth agape, staring at my belongings stacked in the foyer. A growing fury gradually swallowed my disbelief. I pounded on the door. "Philip?" I screamed. "If you're in there, open this door right this minute!" I pounded until my fist was red, but no answer. Was he in there, pretending not to hear? "*Paul! P.J.!* Are you in there? Let me in! It's Mom, and this isn't funny!"

Silence.

I grabbed one of my clogs and threw it as hard as I could against the door. "You've gone too far this time, Philip Fairbanks!" I screamed.

My words ricocheted like echoes in the Box Canyon.

Dumping my backpack, I pressed my back against the wall next to the elevator and slid down until I was sitting on the floor, trying to catch my breath. *Think, Gabby, think! . . . Okay. Okay.* So he and the boys were still out. He wanted me to get home first, *wanted* to shock me. *Well!* If he thought I was going to sit here bawling like a baby and lick his shoes when he got home, that . . . that *snake* had another think coming. I'd sit right here and wait for the dirty rat to show up. And then he was going to get an earful, and I didn't care if the whole building heard me! He had to show up sometime. He couldn't keep the boys out all night—

Wait. My thoughts did a sudden tailspin. Mr. Bentley had said the boys had gone looking for the dog that morning, and then "took off on their trip." *What trip?* I thought he just meant some day trip around Chicago—

My mouth suddenly went dry.

Scrambling to my feet, I punched the call button for the elevator, which took forever to arrive and even longer to reach the ground floor. *No, no, no, no* . . . I burst through the security door into the lobby. Mr. Bentley was chatting amiably with one of the other building residents, but I ran up and grabbed his arm. "Mr. Bentley!" And with a wild look at the other man, "I'm sorry! It's urgent!"

The other man shrugged good-naturedly and caught the security door before it closed.

I was practically hyperventilating. "What did you mean, the boys took off on their 'trip'? *What* trip?"

Mr. Bentley gave me a strange look. "What did *I* mean? Don't you know? It just looked like they were going on a trip is all. Your man and the boys came out that security door each pulling a suitcase, you know, the kind with wheels—"

"*When?* When did they leave? Did they take a cab?"

He shook his head. "Didn't ask me to call a cab. But they came through the lobby, *mm*, maybe 'round two o'clock, and went out that door." The doorman jerked a thumb toward the frontage road exit. "Car must've been parked outside."

My heart was pounding so hard I could hardly get a good breath. *No, no, he wouldn't—!* But Philip's words a few nights ago stabbed me with vicious reality: *"Maybe I'll just have to send the boys back to Virginia . . ."*

I grabbed my purse off my shoulder, dumped the contents on the half-moon counter, and snatched up my cell phone. I had to catch them before they got on that plane! I punched Philip's speed dial . . .

"Mrs. Fairbanks. What's the matter? Are you—"

I held up my hand for silence. But even when Mr. Bentley stopped talking I couldn't hear any rings. I ran outside to the frontage road for a better signal and tried again. Still nothing. Dead.

I stared at my phone. Had he—? He had! Philip had cut off my cell phone too!

That's when I lost it. I threw the phone as hard as I could as a wail ripped from the bottom of my gut. *"No, no, no, nooo . . . !* Oh God, Oh God, he took my boys away!" I collapsed against the building, bent over, hands on my knees, sobs coming so hard I thought my lungs would turn inside out.

A few moments later I felt big hands lifting me up and pulling me into his arms. I struggled, beating my fists on Mr. Bentley's chest, but he held on, the fingers of one hand threaded through my mop of curls, holding my face to his chest, the other around my waist, holding me up until I went limp in his arms and just cried and cried and cried.

Finally spent, I pushed Mr. Bentley away and stumbled across the frontage road to the nearest park bench. *Oh God, oh God, what am I going to do?* A few minutes later, Mr. Bentley followed, handed me a bottle of water, my purse, and my cell phone, which had landed in the grass. I took a few gulps of water and then muttered dully, "He's gone. The boys too. I'm locked out. Can't get in." I lifted raw eyes to the kind, brown face. "You don't happen to have a master key or something?"

Mr. Bentley nodded slowly. "But don't get your hopes raised. A service guy came in this morning, said he had an appointment with Mr. Fairbanks. I didn't think anything of it, just called the penthouse and your husband buzzed him in. Honey, if your key doesn't work, I don't think mine will either. But come on . . . come on now. Let's check it out."

Reluctantly, I let Mr. Bentley lead me by the hand back into Richmond Towers and up to the thirty-second floor. Neither one of us spoke. I was embarrassed for him to see all the suitcases, bags, and boxes—the shreds of my life—piled up against the wall of the foyer. One lone clog lay on the sparkling ceramic tile floor where I'd bounced it off the door.

The doorman pulled out his master ring and tried several keys. None of them worked. He surveyed the piles, absently scratching the grizzled gray beard along his jaw line. "What are you going to do?"

"I—I don't know. I need to think."

"Well, come on now. Come down to the lobby and sit. You can have my chair at the desk."

"No, no . . . you go on." I grabbed both sides of my head. "I need to think!"

"You sure?"

I nodded. "Please. Just . . . leave me alone."

When the elevator door closed behind him, the suitcases and piles of bags and boxes began to taunt me. I paced back and forth,

unable to stay still. *Did the boys see Philip bagging my stuff and tossing it out here? . . . What did they think? . . . Did they try to stop
him? . . . What lies did he tell them? . . . Why didn't they call me to say
good-bye? . . . Are they on a plane heading for Virginia? . . . Do they
think I have abandoned them?*

I had to get out of there! Frantically, I pushed the elevator
button. On the way down, the elevator stopped at three other
floors and people got on. But I turned away, my back rigid, willing no one to speak to me—or I might lose it again right there in
the elevator. On the ground floor, I managed to slip through the
lobby and out the revolving door without Mr. Bentley seeing me,
then walked in a daze across the frontage road to the park and
along the jogging path until I found an empty bench out of sight
of Richmond Towers. I sank into it . . .

Joggers ran past, plugged into their iPods.

The evening air was sweet, still warm after washing Chicago
with sunshine most of the day.

A gentle breeze off the lake ran its fingers through my hair.

The only sounds were the drone of traffic on Lake Shore
Drive and the trill of birds darting here and there in the trees.

I felt as though I could sit there forever . . .

I might have to.

That thought jolted my numb brain and a hundred questions
crowded into my head. What was I going to do? My phone was
dead . . . Did I have any money? I fished in my purse, all a-jumble
after Mr. Bentley had stuffed everything back in. Thirty dollars in
my wallet. A couple of credit cards. A debit card to my household
account . . .

How much was in my household account? Philip and I didn't
have joint accounts. I was supposed to use a credit card for every-

thing from groceries to clothes, and Philip paid the bills. Other than that, he put a hundred dollars into a household account every week that was mine to use for anything that required cash. My paychecks from Manna House had gone into that account too— though I'd used a good deal of that for the trip to North Dakota.

I groaned. The checkbook for that account was up in the penthouse. *Okay, Gabby, don't panic. You have your debit card.* But if I remembered correctly, there was only a couple hundred left. And I'd just quit my job.

I fingered the credit cards. Had he frozen my credit cards too? I already knew the answer.

"Oh, God!" My head sank into my hands. "What am I going to do?!"

"Come to Me, Gabby . . ."

I looked up, startled. The words were so clear I thought someone had spoken them out loud. But the path in front of me was empty. That Voice in my spirit . . . Jodi Baxter had said it was God calling me. Just like that verse in the Bible, the one where Jesus said anyone who was weary and carrying a heavy burden could come to Him, and He would give them rest.

Pulling my feet up onto the bench and hugging my knees to my chest, I held on for dear life. "Help me, Jesus! I don't know what to do! . . . I can't lose my boys! . . . I'm so tired of fighting, trying to keep my life from unraveling . . . But I can't do it by myself! . . . I need You, God! *I need You!*"

A cold nose poked itself between my ankles and then nudged my arm. Startled, I looked up. A muddy yellow dog very much in need of a bath was pushing its muzzle into my lap, the rest of its body wiggling all over. I blinked in disbelief. The dog was now trying to crawl into my lap. I gasped. "Dandy!"

That's when I noticed a bandana knotted to the dog's collar—and another knotted to it, and another, making a rope. I followed the bandana rope with my eyes and found myself staring at a wrinkled face wearing a purple knit hat.

"You an' God havin' yourselves a private tête-à-tête, or can a body sit down on that there bench too? My feet are tired." Lucy Tucker plopped all six layers of her clothing down on the bench beside me.

"You found Dandy!" I croaked. By this time the dog *was* in my lap, and we were both a muddy mess. I pushed Dandy off and wiped my eyes and nose with the back of my hand. I felt like laughing hysterically. I'd just told God I needed Him—and He sent *Lucy*?

Lucy eyed me skeptically. "So what's wrong with you? You look worse'n the day I first found you in this park, wet as a drowned rat and bleedin' like a stuck pig."

Now I did laugh hysterically. *Who found who?* My shoulders shook from the sheer insanity of it all, the tears started again, and my story came out in little gasps. No penthouse. No husband. No kids. Locked out. Nowhere to go. Just a bunch of suitcases, bags, and boxes sitting in the foyer on the thirty-second floor of Richmond Towers.

"Hey, hey, hey," Lucy said, patting me awkwardly. "It's gonna be all right." She sat beside me for a while until the shaking and crying died down once more. Then she rose stiffly from the bench. "C'mon, let's go. You got enough for cab fare? My feet are killin' me."

"Go?" I blubbered. "Go where?"

"Manna House, of course. Nobody's ever locked outta Manna House."

Dandy's ears perked. He tugged on his bandana leash and barked.

I stared at her. But I didn't move. "What about my boys? I can't just let Philip take my boys!"

"That's right. But one day at a time, Missy. Them boys are all right. Now, you got cab fare or not?"

I nodded, stood up on wobbly legs, and let Lucy the bag lady walk me back along the jogging path toward Richmond Towers. Handing me Dandy's bandana leash, the old woman in her unmatched layers of clothes pushed through the revolving doors. I could see her gesturing to Mr. Bentley, who got on the phone. Within minutes, a cab pulled up on the frontage road. Mr. Bentley came out and opened the rear door.

"Hey!" the cabbie said. "I don't take dogs." I saw Mr. Bentley slip him a folded bill. "Well," the man grumbled, "maybe this once."

Mr. Bentley leaned into the backseat before shutting the door. "Don't worry about those suitcases and stuff upstairs, Mrs. Fairbanks. I've got a car. I'll bring it all later tonight when I get off work."

I nodded, not trusting myself to speak. The cab pulled away, and we rode in silence down Sheridan Road. Lucy rolled her window down, and Dandy stuck his head out, his mouth open in a doggy-smile. Within ten minutes, we pulled up in front of the shelter that had been my workplace for the past two months.

Now it would be my home?

I fumbled in my purse, paid the cab, and the three of us walked up the steps to the double oak doors. "I—I think I still have my key. Forgot to turn it in."

"Good," Lucy muttered. "What time is it, anyway? Did we miss supper?"

I turned the key and opened the door. Late evening light still shrouded the peaceful foyer with muted colors from the stained glass windows. The receptionist's cubicle was empty. Beyond the swinging doors, sounds of chatter and laughter came from the multipurpose room. And music. Turned up loud.

I stopped and listened. Someone was playing my CD! I closed my eyes as fresh tears slid down my face, but strangely, this time they felt like a spring rain washing out the crud as the familiar words sank deep into my spirit . . .

> . . . *The earth all around me is sinking sand*
> *On Christ the Solid Rock I stand*
> *When I need a shelter, when I need a friend*
> *I go to the Rock . . .*

reading group guide

1. The Yada Yada House of Hope series introduces a new primary character. Who *is* Gabby Fairbanks? Describe her as a person— her personality and character . . . her emotional strengths and weaknesses . . . her spiritual assets and debits. How do you *feel* about Gabby? What do you want to say to her?

2. What do you think has happened internally to Gabby between the time she first met Philip in the Prologue, and when we meet her sixteen years later in Chapter One? Are there ways *you* feel you've lost part of "who you are" or had to give up hopes and dreams while simply coping with life's circumstances? If you could get back that lost part of yourself, what would it be?

3. How would you characterize the tension in Gabby and Philip's marriage? In what way does Gabby feed into this tension? Do you see yourself or your marriage in their relationship in some way? What feelings does it bring up for you?

4. Mr. Bentley and "Mrs. Fairbanks . . . penthouse" are probably as different as two people can be. And yet, why do you think Gabby thinks of the doorman as her "first—and maybe only—friend" in Chicago? Who in your life has proven to be an "unlikely" but genuine friend?

5. In Chapter 10, Lucy the "bag lady" asked Gabby, "Why ain't you prayin' for me 'bout this bronchitis?" Gabby assured her that she, um, had been (intending to make it "retroactive"). What do you think Lucy meant by, "Huh. Ain't what I meant"? What is *your* usual response when someone asks you to pray for them?

6. Even though Josh and Edesa Baxter—whom you met in the original Yada Yada series—are quite a bit younger than Gabby, in what ways do they help open Gabby's spiritual eyes and heart? Even though they have a temporary reprieve in their efforts to adopt Baby Gracie, what challenges do you anticipate they may face in the future as a multicultural family?

7. Gabby is caught in the "sandwich generation"—parenting not only her two growing sons, but "parenting" her mother as well. In reacting to the crisis in her mother's life, how is she missing what her kids need? In what ways have you experienced (or are experiencing) a similar family squeeze? If you are discussing this question as a group, how can you encourage and support one another in times of family stress?

8. The setting of this story alternates between a *luxury penthouse* and a *homeless shelter*. In what ways do these settings symbolize what's happening in the story itself—with Gabby in particular, but also some of the other characters (Philip . . . Lucy . . . Estelle . . . etc.)?

9. In spite of what happens in the last chapter, what do you see as glimmers of hope for Gabby? Do you think there can be any redemption for Philip? Why or why not?

10. In what ways do Gabby's encounter with Lucy in the first chapter and their encounter in the final chapter act as "bookends" to this story? What are the similarities? What is the significance of the differences?

who do i talk to?

BOOK 2

A
yadayada
HOUSE *of* HOPE
Novel

To Brenda Williams,
outreach coordinator at the Joshua Center in Chicago,
who dispenses no-nonsense help, hope, and love
to women both on and off the street . . .
"Because," as she says, "I've been there."

prologue

Springs protested in the darkness as a lumpy body turned over on the bottom bunk. From another bunk—one of four lining the walls of the small bedroom—a pair of nearsighted eyes peered anxiously into the shadows, making out the dim outline of her roommate trying to get comfortable on the narrow mattress.

"Lucy?" The voice was tremulous, a cracked whisper. "Are you awake?"

"Mmph." The springs groaned again.

For several moments all was quiet. Then—

"Lucy?"

A long sigh. "Whatchu *want*, Miz Martha? It's late."

"Is Gabrielle asleep?" The anxious whisper poked the darkness.

"Fuzz Top? Think so. Ain't heard nothin' from her bunk. But if you don' stop talkin', you gonna wake her up."

"But she was crying. I could tell. A mother knows."

"Well."

"Why was she crying?"

A snort from the other bunk. "She got her reasons."

"But . . ." The unsteady whisper trailed off. The elderly woman reached a hand out from under the blankets provided by the homeless shelter until she touched thick doggy hair, newly washed and silky. A rough tongue licked her fingers. Now the voice choked up. "I was just so happy you and Gabrielle found Dandy, I didn't ask why she's sleeping at the shelter tonight with me. Shouldn't she be home with her boys?"

"Well."

The woman named Martha slipped her hand back under the covers, pulled them up under her chin, and closed her eyes. Her slight body made only a small ripple under the blankets. It was her first overnight at Manna House. She felt a little strange—but her daughter had come to stay with her a night or two, that's what she said. Martha was glad, even though she didn't know why Gabrielle was sad. And her new friend Lucy was "sleeping over," too, just like a slumber party.

Martha giggled. A homeless shelter! Noble would roll over in his grave if he knew where she'd ended up. But she wasn't lonely here, not like she'd been in the big old house in Minot. And Dandy was asleep on the little rug by her bed, just like always. He'd been lost all day . . . but she couldn't remember exactly why. Had he run away? No, Dandy never ran away. Well, it didn't matter. He was safe now, snoring gently beside the bunk bed. But . . .

Her eyes flew open, staring at the bottom of the upper bunk overhead. Somebody had said, *What's that dog doing here? Manna House don't allow no dogs!*

Oh dear. Would the shelter let her keep Dandy? Oh, she couldn't stay another day if Dandy wasn't welcome.

She rose up on one elbow. "Lucy! You still awake? Do you think—?"

"Miz Martha! If you don' shut up and go to sleep, I'm gonna come over there and bop you one." Martha's roommate flopped over, turned her back, and the springs groaned once more. "Wonkers!" The gravelly voice settled into a mutter. "I get more sleep out on th' street than I do in a roomful of talky wimmin."

chapter 1

A lawn mower rumbled through my dream, shredding it beyond remembering.

Semiconsciousness rose to the level of my eyelids, and they fluttered in the dim light. *Uh-uh. Not a lawn mower. Snoring.* Philip was snoring and popping like a car with no muffler. I reached out to roll him over onto his side—

My hand hit a wall. No Philip in the bed. Something was wrong. What was it? A heavy grief sat on my chest, like someone had died. *Had* someone died?

I struggled to come to full consciousness and half-opened my eyes. Above me, all I could make out in the dim light was a rough board. I stared, trying to make sense of it. Why was I lying underneath a wooden board? Was *I* the one who died? Was I inside a wooden coffin?

Coffin?! A surge of panic sent me bolt upright. "Ow!" I cracked my head on the board, and the snoring stopped. Rubbing the tender spot, I squinted into dimly lit space and made out three bunk beds, one against each wall of a small room.

Mine was the fourth.

No coffin.

Blowing out my relief, I swung my feet over the side of the lower bunk but was startled as a hairy face pushed its cold nose against my bare leg with a soft whine. I reached out and touched the familiar floppy ears. *Dandy*. My mother's dog . . .

And suddenly all the cracked pieces of my life came into focus.

I'd just spent the night at Manna House, a homeless shelter for women, where, until yesterday, I'd been on staff as program director.

The small lump in the bunk across from me was my mother.

The bigger lump in the bunk next to her, producing the high-decibel racket, was Lucy, a veteran "bag lady," who for some odd reason had befriended my frail mother.

Mom and I were "homeless" because yesterday my husband had kicked both of us *and* the dog out of our penthouse condo along Chicago's Lake Shore Drive, changed the locks, and skipped town . . . taking my two sons, P. J. and Paul, with him.

As reality flooded my brain, I fell back onto the bunk, bracing for the tears I knew should follow. But the well was dry. I'd cried every drop the evening before and long into the night. Now raw grief had settled behind my eyes and into every cavity of my spirit.

I must have dozed off again, because the next thing I heard was a ringing handbell and several raps on the door. "Wake up, ladies! Six o'clock! Morning devotions at six forty-five sharp,

breakfast at seven. People with jobs get first dibs on the showers."
The footsteps moved on to another door. "Wake up, ladies! . . ."

I groaned and sat up, being careful not to hit my noggin
again on the bottom of the top bunk. Should have gotten up
when I first awoke and jumped in the shower then. No telling
when they'd be free now.

My mother was stirring on the bunk next to mine, but Lucy's
bunk was empty. "Mom, you okay? Do you need help getting to
the bathroom?" I pulled on the same slacks I'd been wearing the
night before.

"I'm all right." She gingerly got out of bed, attired in a pair
of baggy, clean-but-used flannel pajamas the shelter had provided, then carefully spread out the sheets and blankets. "But I
don't have my clothes. Where are my clothes? I have to take
Dandy out."

Dandy! A quick glance confirmed that the dog was not in the
room. But neither was Lucy. "Don't worry, Mom. I think Lucy
took him out. Wasn't that nice? You can put on the slacks and top
you wore yesterday. Mr. Bentley said he'd bring our things when
he got off work last night." The doorman at Richmond Towers
had kindly offered to load his own car with the piles of bags and
suitcases my husband had unceremoniously dumped outside our
penthouse door, but Mr. Bentley didn't get off until ten o'clock
and still hadn't arrived when we'd gone to bed. Who knew how
long it had taken him to get all that stuff down the elevator from
the thirty-second floor!

But if there was one person in the world I could count on, it
was Mr. Bentley. Our stuff would be downstairs . . . if we ever got
there.

Clutching the shelter-issued "Personal Pak"—toothbrush,

toothpaste, soap, deodorant, comb—my mother managed to navigate the crowded bathroom with me hovering right behind her. She even smiled as several of the young residents called out, "'Mornin', Gramma Shep! How'd ya sleep?" and "Hey! Nice of Miz Gabby ta stay over with ya."

I wanted to die right there. If they only knew.

Good thing I had no time to linger in front of the mirror after brushing my teeth. I looked a fright. My hazel eyes were red rimmed and my frowsy, reddish-brown curls a snarly mess, and would probably stay that way until I got a chance to wash my hair and use some conditioner.

Back in the bunk room, I tried not to show my impatience as my mother slowly dressed. *Is it too early to try calling the boys?* I had to talk to them! It was already seven thirty in Virginia. I fumbled for my cell phone. *Not in Service* blinked at me.

I groaned. *Right.* I forgot. Philip had canceled my cell.

Okay, I'd use my office phone . . . wait, I needed to get a phone card first. Shelter phones had local call service only. "Mom, come *on*. You ready?"

My mother looked at me reproachfully. "Always in a hurry. Hurry, hurry . . ." But she put up her chin and headed out the door.

The night manager had told us last night we could use the service elevator—not available to most residents, but they made an exception for my seventy-two-year-old mother. But Mom had taken one look at the small cubicle and said she'd rather take the stairs, so this morning we went down, one step at a time, to the multipurpose room on the main floor, where the residents were gathering somewhat reluctantly for morning devotions. I realized that even though I'd been working at the shelter for two months,

I had no clue what the morning routine was like before 9 or 10 a.m. when I had usually arrived. "Guess I'm going to find out," I murmured, pouring two ceramic cups of steaming coffee from the big carafes on a side table, added powdered cream, and settled down beside my mother in one of the overstuffed love seats.

"Buongiorno, signores! Who will read our psalm this morning?" The same booming voice that had woken us up with a thick Italian accent, packaged in a sturdy body about five foot four, black hair pulled back into a knot, waved her Bible and "volunteered" the first person who made eye contact.

I'd met the night manager briefly at our Fun Night several weeks ago and again last night, but for the life of me I couldn't remember her real name. Everybody just referred to her as "Sarge." I'd been told she was a God-fearing ex-marine sergeant, just the sort of tough love needed on night duty at a homeless shelter. She knew my mother had been put on the bed list, but Lucy's and my arrival last night with a muddy mutt in tow had thrown her into a conniption. She and Lucy had gone nose to nose for a few minutes, but with my mother crying tears of joy over the return of her lost dog, to the cheers of half the residents, Sarge had the presence of mind to call the Manna House director to ask what to do with the shelter's former program director who'd just turned up with a muddy dog, distraught and needing shelter.

I could only imagine what Mabel Turner thought. How many times had the director graciously made exceptions for me in the two months I'd been on staff? I'd lost count.

But somehow Dandy had gotten a temporary reprieve, and we both got a bed.

But . . . Oh God? Now what?

"'. . . Better the little that the righteous have than the wealth of many wicked,'" one of the residents was reading. The psalm got my attention. "'. . . for the power of the wicked will be broken, but the Lord upholds the righteous.' Psalm 37, readin' verse 1 through—"

"Humph!" growled a gravelly voice coming up behind me. "Ain't seen it happen *yet*."

"Ha. That's 'cause ya gotta be *righteous*, Lucy," the reader shot back. Snickers skipped around the circle.

"Sit *down*, Lucy," Sarge barked. "If you are going to be late, at least do not interrupt. All right, who has a prayer request for today? Any job interviews? Wanda, did you get your state ID yet? . . . *Va bene*, we will pray about that. Anything else?"

Behind me, Lucy leaned over the back of the couch and whispered in my ear, "I put Dandy in your ol' office downstairs after he did his bizness, thinkin' it might be best ta keep him outta the way this mornin'. But there ain't much room for him in that ol' broom closet. It's all full of your stuff that Mr. Bentley musta brought last night. Suitcases an' boxes an' stuff."

I gave her a grateful nod over my shoulder. "Good idea, Lucy," I whispered back. "Thanks for taking him out this morning." It *was* a good idea. The familiar smell of our belongings would probably keep the dog pacified for a while. "And thanks for giving him a bath last night. Sorry I didn't say something earlier. I was a bit of a wreck."

"Humph. You *still* a wreck, missy. Didja look in a mirror this mornin'?"

I rolled my eyes and didn't care if she noticed. As if *Lucy* had a leg to stand on, in her mismatched layers of clothes, most of which could use a good wash. Better yet, tossed out for good. And her matted gray hair looked like she cut it herself . . .

A hairstylist. That's what we need at Manna House! I wonder if anyone knows a beautician who'd be willing to volunteer, come in a couple of times a month—

I caught myself. What in the world was I doing, thinking like a program director? *You quit yesterday, remember?* I reminded myself. And I had bigger problems to deal with.

Much bigger.

I was pacing back and forth in Mabel Turner's office when the director arrived that morning.

The attractive African-American woman, every hair of her straightened bob in place, opened the door and stopped, hand on the doorknob, her eyebrows arching at me like twin question marks. "Gabby Fairbanks."

"Um, Angela let me wait in your office." I jerked a thumb across the foyer where the receptionist busied herself behind the glassed-in cubby. "I'm sorry, Mabel. I just couldn't wait out there in the multipurpose room with people all around. I—" I flopped down on a folding chair and buried my face in my hands.

Mabel shut the door, dropped her purse on the desk, and squatted down beside me. "Gabby, what in the world happened?"

I thought the well had gone dry, but the concern in her rich-brown eyes tapped another reservoir of tears, and it took me half a box of tissues to get through the whole sorry mess. *Locked out. Put out. Boys gone. No place to go but here.*

"I-I didn't even g-get to tell Philip I quit my job here like h-he wanted me to, or—or that Mom was going to stay here at Manna House and be out of his hair . . ." I stopped and blew my nose for the fourth time. "B-but he was so *mad*, Mabel, 'cause I accidentally passed on a message from his business partner, you know, when he and the boys were out on a sailboat with one of his clients last weekend, and it caused him to lose that client. He blamed me, said I didn't want his business to succeed—but that isn't true, Mabel! He—"

"I know, I know." The shelter director patted my knee, stood up, and got her desk chair, pulling it around so she could sit next to me. "But he just locked you out? I mean, he can't do that! Go talk to the building management. Today. If both your names are on the purchase contract, he can't just change the locks and kick you out. That's your home too! And he can't just take the boys either. You have rights, Gabby. You—"

I held up my hand to stop her, staring at her face. *Both our names?* I felt confused. Had I ever signed anything to purchase the penthouse? I tried to think. Philip had come to Chicago four months ago to finalize things with his new business partner and find a place for us to live . . . and then we just moved.

"I . . . never signed anything," I croaked.

"But they require both spouses on a joint account to—"

"We don't have joint accounts." I swallowed. "I never really questioned it. Philip was always generous. I had his credit cards and a household account in my name . . . It never seemed important."

Mabel looked at me for a long minute. "Do you have *any* money, Gabby?"

I winced. "Probably a couple hundred in my household account. And I should have a week's salary coming from Manna

House still." Which we both knew wasn't much. The job had never been about the money.

I jumped out of my chair and began to pace once more. "I don't want to talk about money, Mabel. Or even the penthouse. Good riddance, as far as I'm concerned. It's the boys! I need to get my sons back!" My voice got fierce. "He . . . he just up and took them back to their grandparents in Virginia! I never even got to say good-bye." I shook a finger in her face. "I'm their mother! You said it yourself—I've got rights!"

Mabel grabbed my wrist. "Gabby . . . Gabby, stop a minute and listen to me. Sit."

I pulled my hand from her grasp and glared at her because I didn't have anyone else to glare at. But I sat.

She took a big breath . . . but her voice was gentle. "Gabby, you do have rights. But you need to understand something. No court is going to rule in your favor if you don't even have a place to live."

chapter 2

I wept and railed in Mabel's office for a good hour. It took that long for the full weight of my overnight calamity to sink in. She was right. By now the boys were probably cozily ensconced at their grandparents' home in Petersburg. Who in their right mind would ask them to come back to Chicago and sack out at a homeless shelter just to be with Mom?

Fury at Philip fought with gut-wrenching loss. How could my own husband *do* this to me?!

Mabel mostly listened. But once I was out of steam, my former boss gently but firmly insisted I needed to work on a plan. "Be realistic, Gabby. One step at a time. What do you need to do *today*?"

We made a list. Buy a phone card until I could get a pay-as-you-go cell phone. Call the boys to make sure they were all right. Go to the closest ATM and find out if my credit cards were still good. (Fat chance.) Use my debit card to assess exactly how much money I had in my personal checking account. Go back to

Richmond Towers and talk to the manager. What were my legal rights concerning the penthouse?

"Are you going to call Philip, Gabby? Maybe he got angry and just overreacted. He might be having second thoughts about what he did."

Oh yes. I'd love to call Philip and curse him to his face. But I shook my head. "Tried that already this morning from my office. He didn't answer. And I can almost guarantee he's not having second thoughts. The whole thing was too calculated. Deliberately losing the dog. Packing up all my stuff, and Mom's too, and clearing us out. Canceling my cell phone. Changing the locks. Taking the boys on a trip—probably back to Virginia."

"Then find a lawyer, Gabby."

"Oh yeah. And pay attorney fees with what money?" I stood up to go.

"Wait a moment. Two more things . . . no, three." Mabel went behind her desk, pulled a form from a stacker, and handed it to me. "First, fill this out when you can."

I glanced at the paper. *Intake Form for Manna House Bed List.* The questions were standard: "Are you currently using drugs? Alcohol? . . . Cause of homelessness? . . . Previous living situation? (Prison? Public housing? Non-housing/Street/Car?)" . . . I looked up at Mabel. "You've got to be kidding."

"Not kidding. Sorry. Just do it, Gabby. Second . . ." She reached for a file folder, pulled out a sheet of paper, and held it up facing toward me. I recognized the resignation letter I'd turned in yesterday. With a sly smile she tore it in half, crumpled the pieces, and tossed them into the wastebasket. "I'm giving you your job back. Also not kidding." The smile rounded her smooth, nutmeg cheeks and crinkled the corners of her eyes.

My throat caught, and I had to clear it a couple of times. "Thanks," I finally croaked. "And the third thing?"

She came around the desk and took my hands. "Let's pray, Gabby. All of this looks like a mighty big mountain, but the God I know is in the mountain-moving business."

I slipped through the multipurpose room, grateful to see my mother dozing in an overstuffed chair near a group of shelter residents gossiping loudly about who was the hottest guy on *Survivor*. She was fine for the moment. I headed for the stairs to the lower floor, which housed the shelter's kitchen, dining room, recreation room, and my office—a former broom closet. Literally.

I needed to check on Dandy and then get out of there. Get that phone card. Call the boys. It was frustrating that I couldn't just pick up my office phone, but I understood why all the shelter phones were "local calls only."

At the bottom of the stairs, I peeked around the corner, hoping Estelle Williams—the shelter's weekday lunch cook—hadn't come in yet. The fifty-something African-American woman had offered to stay overnight with my mom her first night, but when I showed up unannounced, offering the lame excuse that "Lucy and I found my mother's dog, so I thought I'd just stay the night," she decided to go on home.

"No sense all of us smotherin' your mama," she'd muttered. She didn't ask any questions but had given me a funny look. It was hard to hide anything from Estelle. The woman could read my face like an open book.

I heard pots banging. So much for Estelle coming in late. But her back was turned. Maybe I could just slip into the tiny office, get Dandy, and—

"If you're lookin' for a certain yellow dog, Gabby Fairbanks, Lucy already took him out." Estelle's voice stopped me before I even had my hand on the doorknob. I turned. The big-boned woman was coming around the wide counter that separated kitchen and dining room, a puffy, white hairnet perched on her head and a white apron covering one of the loose, handmade caftans she usually wore. She made a beeline for me and without ceremony gathered me into her arms. "Oh, baby. You don't have to pretend with me. I know all about it."

My eyes burned hot but stayed dry. "You know? How—?" My voice was muffled against her broad bosom.

"Mm-mm. I was still here when Harry showed up last night with his car crammed front to back with your suitcases and boxes. I helped him shoehorn all that stuff into this lame excuse for an office."

Harry Bentley. Estelle's new love. "He—he told you?"

"Humph. Not Harry. But, honey, I already knew your man kicked out the *dog*. Already knew he gave your *mama* an ultimatum. Why else is Gramma Shep here? When Harry showed up with all your stuff . . . It ain't exactly rocket science, Gabby." The woman held me at arm's length. "You want to talk about it, baby?"

I shook my head. "I will, though. I promise." Estelle meant well, but I had to get out of there! "I've got to find my boys. Know the closest place to get a phone card?"

She gave me another funny look, as if adding up all the bits and pieces. Without a word, she moved to the counter, grabbed her oversize bag, rummaged in it, and pulled out her own cell phone. "Take it. Use it. No fussin' at me either. Girl, you don't have *time* to go lookin' for someplace 'round here that sells phone cards."

Hunched over Estelle's cell phone on the front steps of the shelter, I punched in my in-laws' home phone number. I didn't know it by heart—we'd always had their number on speed dial—but I still had juice in my defunct cell phone, thank God, and was able to access my phone book. *I need to write down all the phone numbers before my battery's totally gone*, I told myself, as the phone rang in my ear.

One ring . . . two . . . three . . . four . . . and then the answering machine picked up. *"Y'all have reached Mike and Marlene Fairbanks—"* I flipped the cell phone shut. No way was I going to leave a whimpering message on their answering machine.

My spirit sagged. Were they out? Just not answering their phone? *Oh God! I need to talk to my boys!*

An elevated train squealed and screeched over the trestle that crossed the street a block away. I sat on the wide front steps for several more minutes, trying to think what to do. It was a perfect Chicago day, temperatures in the seventies, sunny blue sky above . . . well, somewhere up there above the three-story apartment buildings and storefronts that rose all around me. I closed my eyes. A breeze off Chicago's lakefront somehow found its way into the narrow streets of this tiny neighborhood just north of Wrigley Field, home of the Cubs. As much as I'd disliked living up on the thirty-second floor of a luxury high-rise along Lake Shore Drive, I missed the sweeping view of Lake Michigan. Today the water would be sparkling blue.

Maybe I *should* call Philip's cell again . . . No. I'd call his office. If he was there, he *had* to answer his office phone. And if he wasn't, maybe Henry Fenchel would answer. Philip would've told his business partner where he was, wouldn't he?

I flipped open my cell phone to get my husband's office number. The battery was already getting low! I let myself into the front door of the shelter with my staff key. "Angela, quick. I need paper and pen." I grabbed the pad and pencil the young Asian receptionist offered me and ran back outside—bumping straight into a woman coming in the door, wearing her baby in a sling on her hip.

"Edesa!" A sense of déjà vu swept over me. Edesa—a young black woman from Central America—and her husband, Josh Baxter, a white, still-in-college kid with gray eyes and a great grin, had been the first people I'd met on these very steps the first time I'd visited Manna House. It seemed years ago, but it had only been a little more than two months.

Edesa Baxter shifted the dark-haired baby on her hip, her wide, beautiful smile greeting me. "Gabby? I didn't expect to see you here today! I thought . . . I mean . . ."

I held up my hand. "Can't explain now. I'm sorry, Edesa." Feeling terrible at brushing her off, I scurried down the steps and ran to the building next door, which housed a twenty-four-hour Laundromat on the corner. I dropped into one of the ugly, molded-plastic chairs, flipped open my fading cell phone, called up the phone book, and scribbled down as many numbers as I thought I'd need right away: Philip's office; Philip's cell; Philip's parents; Philip's partner, Henry Fenchel. My aunt Mercy in Minot, North Dakota; my mom's home phone back in Minot, even though nobody was there. The Manna House number, Mabel's cell, Estelle's cell . . .

I finally flipped the phone closed. Maybe I could borrow a charger from somebody who had a phone like mine and get the rest. But I still had to find my kids.

A bald-headed dude, wearing a dingy sleeveless undershirt that showed off the tattoos covering both arms from shoulders to wrists, pulled a huge wad of wet clothes from a front-loading washing machine and stuffed the whole caboodle—jeans, a sweater, a bunch of whites, plaid boxers—into one of the humongous dryers and set it on High. *Huh. Who cares if he fries his clothes.* I turned my back and punched the office number of Fairbanks and Fenchel into Estelle's phone.

Someone picked up on the first ring. "Fairbanks and Fenchel, Henry speaking."

My mouth suddenly went dry, and my heart thudded so hard I could feel the pulse in my ears. "Uh, hi, Henry. It's Gabby. Is, uh, Philip there?"

"Philip?" Henry sounded surprised. "No. Aren't you—?" He seemed to catch himself. "Uh, Philip left a message for me yesterday that something came up, he had to take the boys somewhere and wouldn't be back till Wednesday. I just assumed you . . ." His voice drifted off.

I felt as if I couldn't breathe. Henry didn't know any more than I did. Less. He probably had no idea Philip had kicked me out.

I gulped some air and decided not to play around. "Henry, Philip left me. Locked me out, actually. And I have no idea where he is or where he's taken the boys. I *need* to find P. J. and Paul. If you know *anything*, or hear from Philip, please call me at . . . uh, my work number." I rattled off the Manna House number.

There was a long moment of silence on the other end of the

phone. "I'm real sorry, Gabrielle. I don't know what's going on. But, uh, I can't get involved in personal stuff between you and Philip."

"No, no, of course not, but—"

"I mean, he's my business partner. We've got a lot invested in this venture."

"I know. I'm sorry. It's just that . . . the boys—"

"I don't know anything about the boys, Gabrielle. Look, I need to go." The phone went dead in my ear.

I flipped Estelle's phone closed and pressed it to my forehead, feeling like a fool. Why was I apologizing? Why was I *always* apologizing?

And what was *up* with Philip's partner, anyway?! Henry and his snobby wife, Mona, had acted like best buddies when we first arrived in Chicago, getting tickets to the Blue Man Group, going out to dinner, all of us spending a day sailing with one of their clients. Now, suddenly, he was all business. Even my given name.

Tattoo guy looked over at me with a leer. I turned my back.

What now? I'd been assuming Philip had taken the boys back to their grandparents in Petersburg, Virginia. When Philip and I had moved to Chicago in April, leaving the boys in boarding school, P. J. and Paul had spent weekends with their grandparents until P. J.'s eighth-grade graduation. Both Philip and his parents talked as though the boys would go back to Virginia for their next school year—*"After all, Fairbanks boys have always gone to George Washington Prep"*—though I'd been contacting prep schools and magnet schools all over Chicago. And Philip had threatened to send the boys back when summer sailing camp fell through—which wasn't *my* fault, but Philip made it seem that way since I'd taken the job at the shelter and couldn't immediately pick up the slack.

But . . . what if he hadn't?

chapter 3

Panic flickered in my chest. My breath shortened. I was going to hyperventilate if I wasn't careful. *Breathe in slowly, Gabby . . . breathe out . . .*

As my heart rate slowed, I could almost hear Mabel's firm voice in my head. *"Be realistic, Gabby. One step at a time. Do what you need to do today. And pray. You can't do this on your own."*

Pray. Seemed like all my prayers were of the "Help!" variety lately. Before I came to Chicago, my prayers had gotten pretty rusty. But the staff at Manna House all seemed to be on a first-name basis with the Almighty, talking to God like He really cared about the mundane problems of homeless women. Mabel had even said *I* was an answer to their prayers for a program director and that God had a purpose for bringing me to Manna House after tripping over Lucy in the park that rainy day.

And the worship teams from different churches that came to the shelter each weekend to lead Sunday evening praise acted like worshipping God and studying the Bible were more exciting than . . . than watching the Cubs hit a homer.

The last two months had brought back a lot of what I'd been taught by my parents and our little community church growing up in North Dakota. A faith I'd pretty much tossed out when my starry-eyed marriage right out of high school hit the skids after only two years. In fact, meeting the charming Philip Fairbanks on a summer jaunt through Europe had all the earmarks of a "happily ever after" fairy tale, so why bother to pray?

That was before everything started to fall apart between Philip and me, and the only firm ground I had to stand on was my job at Manna House Women's Shelter, and the people there who made me feel that I *mattered*.

I stuck Estelle's cell phone in my shoulder bag, left the Laundromat—tattoo guy was still smirking at me—and started walking the few blocks toward the Sheridan El Station. "God," I whispered, "it's me, Gabby. Thanks for . . ." *Good grief, what do I have to be thankful for?* Well, lots, come to think of it. ". . . for a roof over our heads last night for both Mom and me. That Lucy found Dandy after Philip let him run loose all night and he got lost. That Mabel gave me my job back, so I'll have some income." I smiled to myself in spite of my predicament. Three whole sentences and I hadn't yelled "Help!" yet. But I was getting there. "But I really do need help, Lord. Please, please help me find out where P. J. and Paul are so I'll know they're okay."

Realizing I'd left the shelter without checking out or telling anyone, even my mother, where I was going—against shelter rules—I fished out Estelle's phone again and called. "Angela? It's Gabby. I forgot to sign out. I have some errands to do. Could you tell my mother I'll be back soon? . . . I don't know, maybe a couple of hours . . . Thanks. Oh! If you see Lucy, would you ask her if she can take care of Dandy? I'll make it up to her, promise."

The El tracks loomed overhead where the Red Line stopped at Sheridan Road. I crossed the street and pushed open the door of the convenience store that sat next to the station. Did they have phone cards? What about an ATM machine? The clerk, who looked Indian or Pakistani under a cap of straight, black hair, pointed to a circular rack of prepaid phone cards, then jerked a thumb out the door. "Bank! You have to go bank for ATM machine."

I quickly bought a twenty-dollar phone card with my debit card, knowing I had at least that much in my household account, and scurried out the door, looking up the street beyond the El station. Bank? I hadn't realized there was a bank close by, probably because I'd always walked straight from the El station to the shelter, going the other direction. But sure enough, a small bank sat on the corner half a block north—probably a branch of some big bank I'd never heard of.

An old man was using the ATM inside, and I fidgeted while he fumbled with his card and the push buttons. But finally he stuffed his money, card, and receipt in his pants pocket and shuffled out the door, tipping his hat at me on the way out. I was in such a hurry to find out the bad news, I had stuck my Visa card into the machine before his polite gesture even registered on my scrambled brain. And I hadn't acknowledged it.

Guilt joined the puddle of self-pity I was wallowing in. Would life ever be normal again? Would I ever wake up again with my children safely under the same roof, my husband in my bed—huh! Not that I wanted him there right now, maybe never—looking forward to an ordinary day, happily greeting the people who came across my path? After fifteen years of not having to think about money, was I now destined to live from paycheck to paycheck, counting every dime?

Get a grip, Gabby. I shook off the maudlin thoughts, tapped my PIN number on the pad, and tried to make a "credit loan" of a hundred dollars. The card came spitting out at me. The readout said, *Card Rejected.*

I tried my American Express. *Card rejected.* The only other credit cards I had were for Bloomingdale's and Lord & Taylor, and I was pretty sure what would happen if I walked into one of those stores and tried to use them.

The slimeball! Philip had canceled them all—which, frankly, was what I'd expected, though I'd hoped . . .

I had one last card, the debit card to my household account. I stuck it into the slot, tapped in my PIN number, and withdrew twenty dollars. A moment later, a twenty-dollar bill, my debit card, and the receipt whirred out of their slots. I focused on the receipt. How much was left?

The faded blue ink at the bottom said, *Balance: $187.23.*

Someone else came into the foyer and stood behind me, wanting to use the ATM. I stuffed the twenty, the debit card, and the receipt into my shoulder bag and stumbled out the door of the bank. That was it? That was all the money I had in this world?

The rich aroma of fresh coffee lured me into the Emerald City Coffee Shop under the El tracks. I flopped down in a chair at one of the small tables near the front window. A cup of coffee, that's what I needed to steady my nerves . . .

Wait. Could I afford a cup of coffee? My hands shaking, I grabbed a napkin and pulled a pen from my purse. Thirty dollars in my wallet—no, make that twenty after I paid for the cab last night that brought Lucy, me, and a bedraggled Dandy to the shelter. Add twenty that I just took out of my account, that's forty. One-eighty-seven still in the account, plus forty cash . . .

I had roughly $220 to my name. Plus a twenty-dollar phone card.

That was it.

So much for a mocha latte at three dollars a pop.

Wait . . . My last two-week paycheck from Manna House should come by Friday. I suddenly felt like laughing. I was rich! Well, maybe not rich. Not enough to live on, not enough to rent an apartment yet. But at least I could afford one cup of coffee.

I was relishing each sip of a medium regular coffee with cream when I heard a cell phone ringing close by. Didn't recognize the ring, so I ignored it—until I realized the ringing was coming from my shoulder bag. Estelle's phone! Was she calling me? Or was someone else calling her? Should I answer it?

I grabbed the phone, flipped it open, and looked at the caller ID. *Harry Bentley.* Eagerly I pushed the Talk button. "Mr. Bentley? It's me, Gabby!"

"Uh . . . Mrs. Fairbanks? Uh, I thought . . ."

"Oh, Mr. Bentley, I'm sorry. You were calling Estelle. She loaned me her cell phone." I felt guilty, as if I'd intercepted a note between two lovers. Shouldn't have answered the phone. "But she's still at Manna House. You could call the main number."

"Mm. That's all right. I'll catch her later. But . . . just a minute. Can you hold?" Without waiting for an answer, I heard Mr. Bentley turn from the phone and say something to someone in his polite doorman voice. "All right, all right. You have a nice day,

Mrs. Pearson, you hear?" His voice came back on, though speaking low as if not wanting others to hear. "Mrs. Fairbanks, are you still there?"

"I'm here, Mr. Bentley."

"Just wanting to know . . . are you all right?"

The kindness in the older man's voice nearly turned on the faucet again. I fished for a tissue. "Um, still in shock, I guess. Trying to sort things out . . . you know."

"Did you get hold of your boys? Don't mean to pry, but . . ."

"That's all right, Mr. Bentley." I had to swallow hard a couple of times. "I appreciate your concern. Haven't talked to them yet. No one answers at my in-laws'."

I heard the doorman mutter something on the other end that I didn't catch. But then he said, "Well, don't worry, Mrs. Fairbanks. I know you're upset—you've got a right to be—but I'm sure your boys are all right. Bad as it is, they're with their dad."

My reply came out in a choked whisper. "I know. Thanks."

"Well, now. Don't know if you plan on comin' back to Richmond Towers today or not, but thought I'd let you know I haven't seen Mr. Fairbanks, and I've been on duty since six this mornin'. Don't think he's come back. The manager is in the office, though. You might want to come up here and, well, you know, see what can be done about getting you back into your penthouse."

I sat up. That's right. That was still on my list of things I needed to do today. "Thanks, Mr. Bentley. I'm coming now. See you in thirty minutes."

I grabbed the napkin with the total of all my worldly finances scribbled on it and headed out the door of the coffee shop for the turnstile in the El station. That's when I remembered one other asset that was going to come in handy. I had a transit card in my wallet I'd bought just last week with twenty-five dollars in fares on it.

Should last me awhile—especially since the "commute" to my job from bedroom to office was now just down the stairs.

chapter 4

I rode the Red Line north to my usual stop, followed the other passengers down to street level, and started walking the few blocks to Richmond Towers. But when I turned the corner and saw the glass-and-steel building rising into the sky just ahead, I suddenly couldn't breathe. My hands started to shake.

I can't do this! Was it just yesterday that I'd come home from work, ready to tell Philip that I'd found a place for my mom to stay until I found something better? Ready to tell him I'd quit my job, just like he wanted, so I could supervise the boys this summer? Thinking these efforts would make everything all right that had gone wrong between us? Making a sacrifice worth the price of selling my soul.

Only to find that my sons were missing and I was out on the street . . .

The shock and rage of those first few hours threatened to boil up once again. *Steady, Gabby. Don't lose it right here on the street.* Besides, I encouraged myself, the first person I'd see when I walked through those doors would be Mr. Bentley. I forced myself to walk the last two blocks, each step a prayer for courage.

I pushed through the street-side revolving doors into the spacious lobby of the luxury high-rise, quiet and empty of building residents in the noontime lull. I'd always felt like an imposter pushing through those doors—as if someone would find out I was just a small-town girl from North Dakota—and today even more so. But like a familiar Chicago landmark, Mr. Bentley sat behind the half-moon desk, uniform cap tossed aside, bald head glistening like a brown bowling ball, and spearing what looked like Chinese takeout with a plastic fork. The knot in my spirit loosened a hitch.

I cleared my throat. "Mr. B."

Mr. Bentley jumped as if I'd said, "Boo!" spilling some of his lunch. "Don't sneak up on a body like that, Mrs. Fairbanks." He grabbed a napkin and dabbed at his pants.

"I'm sorry. Didn't mean to scare you." Hard to believe he hadn't heard me come through the revolving door. Mr. Bentley was usually aware of every squeak and puff of air that went through that foyer. "That must be some takeout you've got there."

"Humph. Nothin' special. I was just thinkin' about somethin'. . ." He grabbed his cap with the gold braid, buttoned his coat, and came around the desk. "You all right? I was afraid the manager might go out before you got here. But he's still here. You go on." The doorman gave me a push toward the glass door marked Building Personnel Only. "I'll buzz you in."

What I really wanted to do was hang out with Mr. Bentley for five or ten minutes before going in, but he was already leaning on the buzzer to the glass door across the foyer. I hurried over and pulled it open. "All right, all right!" I hissed over my shoulder. The doorman gave me an encouraging nod and flicked his hand as if shooing me in.

Several doors lined the short corridor: Sales Office. Lock Boxes. Security. Restroom—Staff Only. I stopped in front of the door marked Building Management, which was slightly ajar. What in the world was I going to say that wouldn't make me—or Philip, for that matter—look like a fool in front of a total stranger?

I knocked and peeked in. "Excuse me?" A fortyish white man in shirt sleeves and a loosened tie sat at his computer, papers spread over the desk. The nameplate on his desk said Walter Martin. "Mr. Martin? Do you have a moment?"

The man looked up. "Uh, certainly. Did you have an appointment, Miss . . . ?" He fished for his appointment book and frowned at it, as if wondering if he'd forgotten.

"Mrs. Fairbanks. Penthouse, thirty-second floor." Just saying the little refrain made me feel bolder, though I wished I'd found a dress and heels to wear and paid more attention to my hair and makeup. My head of natural red curls—though it had darkened to a chestnut color in recent years—had a tendency to get frowsy in humid weather.

"Fairbanks," he murmured. "Oh yes, your husband left a phone message on my answering machine. I'm sorry, I've been so busy I haven't called him back yet. Is that why you're here?"

I tried not to stutter. "Phone message?"

"Mm, yes. Something about canceling the penthouse lease early, needing to move suddenly. Said he'd have everything out by the end of the month. Of course, unless he can get someone to sublet, he will be responsible . . ."

I didn't hear the rest. My mouth went dry, my brain stuck on "lease . . . move . . . end of the month." *Lease?* I thought Philip had bought a condo! And he was moving out?

I tried to clear my brain. "Excuse me."

The man stopped his spiel. "Yes?"

"Could I see a copy of the contract?"

"Of course." The man rolled his chair, opened a file drawer, and after a moment of pawing through its contents, pulled out a file. He opened it, scanned the contents—then looked up at me. "I'm sorry. This is awkward. But only Mr. Fairbanks's name is on the lease. If you are his wife, of course you have a right to see it, but . . . do you have any identification?"

My cheeks flamed. What did he think I was, some hussy trying to pull a con? But my better sense told me to stay calm, play the game. He had to do what he had to do.

"Of course." I pulled out my wallet and slid my driver's license toward him. Still a Virginia license.

"I see. Do you have any identification with your current address? Or a current utility bill with both your and your husband's names on it?"

I flinched. We'd been in Chicago for barely three months. I hadn't applied for a new driver's license yet. The bills came in Philip's name—not that I had a copy of any of the utility bills on me anyway. The manager was probably wondering why I didn't just run upstairs and get a copy of the electric bill, or our marriage license, or something! But everything like that was on the thirty-second floor in Philip's study, behind a front door with a new lock, and my key did not fit that lock.

"Mr. Martin—" I hesitated. How much should I say? Should I just leave? But something inside me rebelled against rolling over and playing dead. "Mr. Martin, my husband left me yesterday and took our children. Not only that, but I can't get any of the ID you need because he changed the locks, so I can't get into my own home. I came here because I need to know what my rights are respective to—"

"Changed the locks? Did you say Mr. Fairbanks—?"

I nodded. "Yes, and—"

"But he can't do that! Not on leased property. Management needs to have a key to leased units in case of emergency."

I didn't know whether to laugh hysterically or scream bloody murder. I tried to keep my voice steady, but the sarcasm leaked anyway. "Maybe he *can't*. But he *did*. And this *is* an emergency, Mr. Martin. *My* emergency. I came here to ask what you can do about it."

Mr. Martin slumped back against his executive chair. He ran a hand over his military-short haircut, avoiding eye contact. Finally he picked up the file folder and busied himself putting it back. "I'm sorry, Mrs., uh, Fairbanks. My hands are tied. It is against Richmond Towers policy to get involved in domestic affairs. If you had some ID proving you have a spousal right to enter the penthouse . . ." He shrugged. "I'm sorry."

Again I had to fight the urge to get hysterical. Wordlessly, I retrieved my driver's license, put it back in my wallet, and stood up. I didn't trust myself to say anything, so I simply turned and left.

"Should sic Mr. Bentley on him," I muttered to myself, yanking open the glass door at the end of the corridor. "He'd vouch for me, tell Mr. Martin what he saw with his own eyes last night." But when I came out into the foyer, Mr. Bentley had the desk phone cradled in his ear, scribbling a message. *Forget it, Gabby. Don't drag Mr. Bentley into your mess. This is his job, remember?*

I was pretty sure he didn't see me as I slipped out the revolving door.

Barely noticing the squeals, rattles, and bumps of the El heading back to the Wrigleyville North neighborhood, I pressed my forehead against the cool window. *A lawyer. That's what I need.* Obviously I wasn't going to get anywhere trying to navigate the land mines of my situation by myself. I wasn't even sure I cared about getting back into the penthouse. Did I want to be someplace where I wasn't wanted? Not if my boys weren't there. I didn't even care that much about the furniture and stuff that filled the place, though there were personal things I did care about—photo albums, the boys' baby books, household items that had been wedding gifts from my parents . . .

But even those things seemed unimportant right now. Not until I talked to my sons and knew they were all right. And then . . .

"I'll get my boys back. Whatever it takes, Philip Fairbanks! You wait and see," I muttered, leaving steam on the window. In the window reflection, I saw the woman next to me give me a strange look. She got up and moved across the aisle as the train slowed.

So what? Let her think I was nuts. This was my stop.

I strode briskly the few blocks to Manna House. More focused now, I tried the number for Philip's parents again before I went inside the shelter. Still no answer. But this time I left a message. "Mike and Marlene, this is Gabrielle. If P. J. and Paul are there, tell them I need to speak with them as soon as possible. *Today*, not tomorrow. My cell phone is not working. They can call this number or . . ." and I rattled off the number for Manna House.

I felt proud of myself for not screaming or blubbering at my in-laws. I was firm. Clear. Concise. Surely they'd see I was a reasonable person and let the boys call.

Unless . . .

My stomach felt weak. What if Philip hadn't taken them back to Virginia?

I had to call Philip. No way around it. What was I afraid of? What more could he do to me that he hadn't already done?

Leaning against one of the double oak doors of Manna House, shaped to resemble the doors of the old church that had once housed the shelter before it was rebuilt, I dialed my husband's cell number on Estelle's phone. It went right to voice mail. "Fairbanks. I'm not available right now. Please leave a message . . . *Beep.*"

Just hearing his voice sucked the confidence out of me. But I tried. "Philip, it's Gabby. I need to know where you've taken the boys. I need to talk to them. Please." My voice started to crack. "Please. That's all. Just let me talk to my kids." I repeated the Manna House number and hung up.

I bent over, hands on my knees. "Oh God, please . . ."

The door beside me opened. "Sister Gabby? Oh, *mi amiga,* I am so glad you are back. Your mother is worried about you."

I recognized Edesa Baxter's voice but didn't look up. I remained bent over, just shaking my head. The next moment I felt the young woman's arms go around me. "I heard what happened, *mi amiga.* Mabel told me," she whispered in my ear. "God knows. He will help you be strong. We will all help you."

I was picking at the chicken stir-fry and rice that volunteers from a local church had brought for the evening meal, trying to shut out the constant fussing of two-year-old Bam Bam, whose mother had just signed up for the bed list, when Wanda motioned to me, waving the kitchen extension. She pointed to my office. "Better take it in dere!" she yelled over the general hubbub.

My chair tipped over in my haste to get to my broom-closet office. I set it upright so fast, it wobbled and almost toppled the other direction, but I didn't wait to see if it fell again. I tried to open the office door, but my mother's dog was standing in the way, trying to get out of his prison. "Dandy!" I hissed. "Back, back!" Finally closing the door behind me, I snatched up my office extension. "Hello? Gabby speaking!"

Silence. At first I thought the call was lost. Then I heard a small voice. "Mom?"

The room seemed to spin. I squeezed my eyes shut and sank into the desk chair. "Paul! Yes, yes, it's me. Are you okay, honey? Where are you?"

"I'm . . . we're at Nana and Grandad's house. Didn't Daddy tell you?"

"Well . . . sure, sure, I knew you'd be there." My brain scrambled, searching for the right words. How much did the kids know? What should I tell them? "Just asked 'cause I called earlier and you weren't there, thought maybe you were still out."

"Oh. Nana took us shopping for some shorts and stuff. But . . . Mom?"

The jealous monster squeezing my heart nearly cut off my breath. *I* should be taking my boys shopping for shorts and T-shirts, not Marlene Fairbanks! I took a deep breath. "What, honey?"

"What's wrong with Grandma? How come you hafta stay with her instead of us?"

I fought for control. "Is that what Daddy said?"

"Yeah. He said Grandma needed you real bad and you couldn't take care of us right now, so we had to go back to Virginia right away. He told us you and Grandma were movin' out, and we had to pack your stuff. But . . ." I heard Paul start to cry. "Why didn't you come say good-bye to us? I tried to call your cell, but you didn't even answer!"

chapter 5

I HATE you, Philip Fairbanks!

My emotions seethed as I tossed in my bunk that night, unable to sleep, listening to Lucy's heavy breathing across the room. How could the man I'd just spent fifteen-plus years of my life with let my kids think *I* was the one who wanted to move out so fast, I didn't even have time to tell them good-bye? Let them think I just wasn't answering my cell phone? Had them actually help pack up my things because Mom and Grandma were moving out?

You pig! I slugged the pillow I'd been clutching, wishing it was his face. *You slimy snake!* I threw in a few other dirty names, punching the pillow with each one.

I finally fell back, blowing out the dregs of tension. At least . . . at least Philip had said their grandma needed me "real bad" right now—not that I didn't love them anymore, or something equally devastating.

Still!

Lucy's heavy breathing hiked up a couple of notches into a rumbling snore. I flopped over on the skinny bunk and smashed the pillow over my ears. In the dark cocoon I created, the phone call with my sons played over and over again in my head . . .

Philip Jr.'s voice had been guarded. "Hey, Mom."

"Hey there, kiddo." It was *so* tempting to blurt out that their father had *stolen* them from me, and I was going to bring them back the very next day! But . . . back to what? I needed time!—time to figure out my options, to make a plan.

"Is Paul still there? Listen, both of you. I want to tell you something. Your dad and I . . . there's been a misunderstanding. I found a place for Grandma to stay, but your dad didn't know that. But I want *you* to know that I *never, ever* meant for you to go back to Virginia so suddenly, especially without saying good-bye. I—I want to be with you so bad." My voice caught, and I had to stop.

Paul jumped in. "Why can't Grandma and Dandy just live with us, Mom? I don't mind sleeping in P. J.'s room."

"Says you," his brother shot back. "I want my room back. I'm almost fourteen, you turkey."

"So? We have to share a room here at Nana's. Why not—"

"Boys!" I had interrupted. "It's . . . it's not possible for Grandma and Dandy to live with us right now." *Because your dad's a selfish pig,* I'd wanted to add, but bit it off. "But I want to get you back home with me as soon as possible."

"Gee, wish you guys would make up your mind!" P. J. had stormed. "Granddad just said he could sign me up for a summer lacrosse league! I'd be sure to make the spring team when I go back to GW if I could play this summer." GW . . . George Washington Prep, "where all the Fairbanks boys" had gone to school.

"So? Go ahead and stay here. I'll go back with Dad, and we'll *both* have our own rooms!"

"Stupid. Dad just left for the airport."

That news had hit me like cold water in the face. So Philip was on his way back to Chicago. Well, Henry Fenchel had said he'd be back in the office on Wednesday. *Tomorrow* . . .

I rolled out of the bunk. Rehearsing the phone call with my kids would never let me sleep. Usually when I couldn't sleep, I'd get up, make some chamomile tea, and read something for a while. What did one do in a homeless shelter?

Dandy popped up from his rug beside my mother's bunk and tried to follow me. "Stay, boy," I whispered. "Lie down. Stay." I squeezed out the door, shut it behind me, and padded quietly down the stairs. Or so I thought.

Sarge met me at the bottom step on the main floor. "*Mi scusi!* Back upstairs now—oh. It is you, Mrs. Fairbanks." The night manager folded her arms across her chest. "So, you do not abide by resident rules, no? And I know you still have that dog upstairs. Against *all* kind of rules, if you ask me."

I thought fast. "Uh, I need to go to my office for a minute. Sorry I disturbed you." I hustled down the next flight of stairs to the lower level, made my way by the dim EXIT-sign glow to my office, and flipped on its light. *Maybe I should do some work, give me something else to think about. Mabel rehired me, after all. Better start earning my keep—*

That's when I noticed the envelope propped against the computer, my name on the outside. Easing myself into the desk chair, I pulled a sheet of paper from the envelope. Edesa's handwriting . . .

Dear Sister Gabby,

My heart breaks for you, mi amiga, to have your children taken away so fast. But you are not forgotten! My Yada Yada sisters gave me this precious word from the Lord when it looked as if we might lose our Gracie:

"Can a mother forget the baby at her breast and have no compassion on the child she has borne? Though she may forget, I will not forget you! See, I have engraved you on the palms of my hands; your walls are ever before me. Your sons hasten back, and those who laid you waste depart from you." (From Isaiah 49. There's more. You might want to look it up!)

Dear Gabrielle, your parents gave you the right name! Live it!

¡Te amo!

Edesa Reyes Baxter

My heart beat faster as I read the note. I read the Bible verse again, and then again. ". . . *Your sons hasten back . . .*" Was this a promise for me? But it was from the Old Testament! Written thousands of years ago. How could it . . . ?

I pressed the note to my chest, turned out the light, and schlepped up the two flights of stairs to the bunk rooms, strangely comforted. "*Your sons hasten back . . .*"

Lucy was still snoring when I opened the door to the room we shared. Tiptoeing to her bunk, I felt for the old woman's body, put both hands under her side, and rolled. With a grunt and a groan, the "bag lady" heaved over onto her side, smacking her lips in her sleep. I waited, holding my breath.

Sweet silence.

Crawling into my own bunk, I slid Edesa's note under the pillow. As I drifted off to sleep, I wondered, what did she mean about *living* my name?

The six o'clock wake-up call grated on my nerves after my short night. Didn't homeless women *ever* get to sleep in? On the other hand, breakfast was ready at seven, prepared by the night staff— oatmeal and toast this morning—and the coffee was hot. I needed at least two cups to pry my eyelids awake.

I had just finished telling my mother I would get the rest of her clothes and personal things situated up in our bunk room, when Sarge rang the big handbell for attention. "Listen up, *signore!* Here is the chore list for today. Wanda and Gabby, break-fast dishes. Martha Shepherd and Tanya, wipe tables and sweep. Lunch . . ."

Drat! I'd forgotten about the chore list. How was I supposed to take care of my mother, put in my hours as program director, and start the uphill battle to get my kids back while washing dishes for thirty-some people? I sighed. Couldn't very well com-plain. All the residents helped with the daily chores in one way or another. At least my mother hadn't been saddled with heavy duty, like the dishes.

"Hey!" Lucy's crusty voice broke into my thoughts. "What if I don' wanna *be* here at lunchtime! Cheese Louise. A body's got things to do, places to go. Can't hang around all day just 'cause you put my name up there to push a broom after lunch."

"Trade with someone, then," Sarge shot back. "Just so it gets done."

Which was just as well, because Lucy ended up trading chores with Tanya, who had a nine o'clock interview at one of the housing agencies and wanted to get out of there. That put Lucy and my mom working together, so I just left them to it, while Wanda tried to teach me the ins and outs of the huge industrial dishwasher—though her Jamaican accent was so thick, I had a hard time understanding half of what she said.

"No problem, Sistah Gabby! You spray off de food, mi stack de dishes in de trays, slide dem in dis way, slide down de door, push dat button . . . see? All dere is to it!"

Except there was no such thing as "spraying off" cold oatmeal stuck inside the multiple bowls, which meant I did a lot of scraping and scrubbing before Wanda could load the trays.

By the time I'd dried and stacked the heavy coffee cups that came out hot and steaming from the dishwasher, my curly hair had frizzed up like a Brillo pad under the required white hairnet, and my hands were beet red. Delores Enriques, the nurse from the county hospital who came in once a week on Wednesday, was already setting up her makeshift nurse's station in a corner of the dining room. I gave her a wave as I hurried upstairs to check on my mom. She was sitting in a far corner of the multipurpose room chatting with Carolyn, the shelter's self-appointed "book maven," who'd been trying to set up a library with donated books. To my surprise, Dandy sat on his haunches, pressed close to my mother's knees, her hand lightly stroking his head.

I looked nervously about. "Mom! I don't think Dandy should—"

Carolyn put a conspiratorial finger to her lips. "Shh. We saw Sarge leave, so Lucy brought Dandy up. Nobody's gonna care for a few minutes." The middle-aged resident, who wore her long, brownish-gray hair slicked back from her pallid face in a straggly ponytail, grinned at me. "Say, Gramma Shep is the first person I've met at Manna House who's also read Robert Browning's poems. How come you never told me that?"

Just then Estelle breezed through the double doors from the foyer, loose orange caftan flying, carrying two bulging bags with yarn and needles sticking out of the top. Without breaking stride she called out, "Mornin', ladies! It's Wednesday—knitting club gonna be startin' up in a few minutes. Sure could use your help again, Gramma Shep." The colorful black woman disappeared down the stairs to the lower level.

I grinned. Looked like the knitting club I'd suggested Estelle pioneer was off and running for its second week, giving women something to do while waiting for the nurse to see those who signed up. Pleased, my mother struggled up out of the over-stuffed chair to follow. I started to help her, but Carolyn got there first. "Nah, let me. I'll get your mom downstairs and put the dog in your office. Just don't ask me to take him out and pick up his poopies. No sir. That's where I draw the line."

I tried not to laugh. "Thanks, Carolyn." I knew Lucy had already taken Dandy out once, and with Mom busy for the next hour or two, I should be able to get a few things done. First stop, Mabel's office.

As briefly as I could, I brought the director of Manna House up to speed on my visit to Richmond Towers yesterday, the status of my finances, and the phone call with my children, including the fact that Philip was probably back in town and expected at his office. "At least I know where to find him," I said wryly. "But I need a lawyer, Mabel—someone who does family law. Problem is, I don't have any money."

Mabel flipped her old-fashioned Rolodex and wrote down a number. "Legal Aid. Ask for Lee Boyer. He's done work for some of the shelter residents before. He's a good man."

"Thanks. Oh, before I forget . . ." I handed my boss the intake form I'd filled out. "Never thought I'd be checking off any of those boxes. Pretty humbling. Always thought homeless people were, well, like Lucy, bag ladies or winos living out on the street for years. But now look at me." I shook my head.

Mabel arched an eyebrow, the only wrinkle in her maple-smooth skin. "You're not the only person with a college degree we have in here. Look at Carolyn. She's got a master's degree in literature! Had a string of bad luck financially, lost a lucrative job, didn't have any close family, got evicted for some reason—"

"Yeah. That's me. Evicted by my own husband." I knew I sounded sarcastic. I stood up quickly. "Thanks, Mabel. I'm going to call Legal Aid and then get to work."

"One more thing, Gabby."

I paused. "Yes?"

"Sarge says we have to do something about the dog. She's right. What if every resident wanted to bring her dog or cat into the shelter?"

I groaned. "I know, I know. It's just . . ." I dreaded telling my mother she couldn't keep Dandy. "What am I going to do? He's been Mom's constant companion since Dad died! I'd keep him myself if I had my own apartment, but . . ." I shook my head in frustration. Dandy wasn't the only reason I needed to find an apartment—soon!

"Well, maybe we can find a foster home for him. I'll start asking around." A slow smile spread over Mabel's normally business-like features. "Lucy sure seems to have taken a shine to him."

"I know! She took him out three times yesterday and again this morning. Don't know where they go—there aren't any parks close by that I know of."

I started to leave when she called me back again. "Gabby?"

Now what? I tried not to roll my eyes.

"Don't be thinking about showing up at Philip's office today."

I gave her a look. I'd been toying with that very thought. Oh, how I wanted to give that man a piece of my mind, and do it in front of his partner and any clients who happened to be there too!

She jabbed a finger at me. "See the lawyer first. Know your rights. Until then, you'll just be acting the fool, and he'll feel justified walking out on you."

Now I did roll my eyes, jerked open her door, and let it close—hard—behind me.

chapter 6

I couldn't get an appointment with the Legal Aid guy until Friday. "But this is urgent!" I protested.

"Honey, they're all urgent," said the woman on the other end of the phone. "Mr. Boyer can see you Friday at two o'clock. You want the appointment or not?"

Frustrated, I said yes and banged my office phone back onto its base. Friday was two days away! Yeah, Mabel had told me to get legal advice before I confronted Philip . . . but two days?!

Outside my office door, the dining room buzzed with women waiting to be called by the nurse. Everything from bunions caused by ill-fitting shoes to mysterious rashes to a variety of STDs needing medication. Maybe Delores Enriques, the pediatric nurse from the sprawling county hospital on Chicago's near south side, had something that'd help the headache spreading over my skull like a cracked egg . . . or maybe I just needed to *do* something.

Like a steam-driven engine, I hauled the rest of my mom's

and my stuff two flights up to the bunk room we'd been assigned, put our necessities in the small dresser drawers provided for each resident, and stuffed the rest of the suitcases and boxes under our bunks. Not exactly the beautiful walnut bedroom set that had been a wedding gift from Philip's parents—and definitely not the spacious walk-in closet in the penthouse. At the same time, the Lord & Taylor pantsuits I'd just stuffed under the bed would make me stand out here at the shelter like a gold front tooth.

It took five trips, but by the time I shut the door on the bee-hive going on around the makeshift nurse's station in one corner and the knitting club in another, my broom-closet office seemed five times bigger. Even Dandy seemed happy with the new arrangement, coming out from under my desk and stretching along the wall next to the file cabinet.

For the next hour, I tried to get back up to speed with plans for the activities program here at Manna House—after packing it up on Monday, thinking I wouldn't be back and someone else would have to take over as program director. I focused on the activities I'd already put in place:

An ESL class once a week . . . Tina, one of the residents, a big-boned Puerto Rican who was fluent in both Spanish and English, had agreed to try teaching English as a second language to Aida Menéndez, a young Latina who'd been bounced around in the foster system until she was eighteen and dropped out of school because of language problems. Tina was good for a few weeks anyway, until she lined up some resources for alternate housing or found a job, and then I'd need to find someone more permanent. Edesa and Josh Baxter had rustled up some ESL materials from Josh's mom, a third-grade teacher on the north side. *I'll have to sit in on Tina's weekly session, see how it's going,* I thought.

Typing . . . Josh's mom, Jodi Baxter, had also agreed to teach a typing class on Saturday morning for residents who wanted to improve their job skills. The shelter had a schoolroom with two computers, but Jodi had said three people showed up for the first class a few weeks ago. I made a mental note: *Ask the board for another computer.*

And the knitting club . . . that had been easy. When I first took on the job, I'd noticed Estelle knitting something blue and bulky while managing the signup list to see the nurse. Now five or six women were knitting and purling away on Wednesday mornings, watching simple winter scarves grow longer, if not exactly symmetrical.

I chewed the end of a pencil as I studied the list of possibilities for more "life skills" for these women with precious few resources. Now that Estelle had been hired on a part-time basis, she was the obvious resource for basic classes in cooking and sewing. That proposal was already on Mabel's desk. And Edesa's husband, Josh, had casually suggested a sports clinic for the shelter kids on the weekend . . . *Hmm.* His dad was the athletic director at Rogers Park High School. Possible resource there.

I grinned to myself. Might as well get the whole Baxter clan involved here! They'd supported the Fun Night that Precious McGill and I had cooked up last month. Precious, a former resident and now a volunteer with the after-school kids—couldn't exactly call it a "program" yet—had managed to get all the residents and most of the staff off their duffs that night, doing the Macarena . . .

Precious! I suddenly realized I hadn't seen the livewire volunteer *or* her teenage daughter, Sabrina, since I got back from North Dakota with my mother almost two weeks ago. I doubted she knew I'd resigned on Monday, much less became a "resident" that same night. What was up with *her*?

I reached for the phone and my staff directory.

And I thought I had problems.

The first time I tried the number I had for Precious, I got her voice mail. *"Can't talk now, but leave a number an' I'll call ya back—if Jesus don't come back first, and if He do, it ain't gonna matter!"* I was a little taken aback, but managed to leave my name and a brief "Call me at Manna House when you've got a minute."

When Estelle banged on a pan for lunch, I went out and asked if she'd seen Precious lately. She shook her head. "It's goin' down tough for her an' Sabrina lately. Not sure she's in town." The big woman flounced behind the counter. "Line up, ladies! Who wants to ask God to bless this food?"

Going down tough? What did that mean? I decided I'd try calling again later.

Thankfully, the knitting club was putting away their projects in a corner of the dining room, so I didn't have to look far for my mother. But when I went to get her, I noticed her pale eyes were wet. "Mom? What's wrong?"

"I c-can't do it anymore, Celeste." Her lip trembled.

Uh-oh. Calling me by my sister's name was always a red flag. I gently took her knitting needles and the lump of pale green knitting attached. Dropped stitches and erratic knots were hopelessly tangled. "Oh, Mom."

One of the other knitters, a heavy-chested black woman named Sheila, shrugged sympathetically. "Last week, Gramma Shep was helpin' alla us. Today . . . dunno."

"It's all right, Mom. Let's put it away for now. We'll fix it later." *As in, ask Estelle to knit a few rows with the green yarn and let Mom start over when she wasn't feeling confused.* Steering my mother into the lunch line, I helped fill her plate with the fixings for tacos and was getting her settled at a table when I noticed Tanya's eight-year-old son sitting by himself at the end of our table, poking at his food. His usual shelter playmates—Trina and Rufino, seven- and six-year-old siblings—were throwing food at one of the other tables.

"Your mom not back yet, Sammy?"

Poke, poke. "Nah. Diane s'posed ta be watchin' me." He jerked a thumb in the direction of a dark-skinned woman with a big, loose Afro, like a throwback to the sixties. "But she say she gotta go out after lunch, even if my mama not back."

That was strange. Tanya had said she had an appointment at nine o'clock and she'd be back before lunch. The pole-thin young woman with the flawless caramel skin barely looked old enough to have a kid Sammy's age, but she'd always seemed to keep an eye on him. "Well, I'm sure your mom will be back soon. Come on and eat with Gramma Shep and me."

Sammy moved down a few chairs and grinned. "Yeah. Can't wait till she get back. Mama say we gettin' our *own* place now."

But Tanya wasn't back by the time the dishwashers started cleanup—and Tanya had traded her breakfast chore for Lucy's lunch assignment. "Hey, come on, Sammy, help me wipe these tables, okay? You start there while I get Gramma Shep settled for a nap." I winked at him. "Babies and grammas need their naps, you know," I stage-whispered. He giggled.

I didn't dare take my mom up to the bunk room, in case she woke up and tried to come down the stairs by herself, so I helped her stretch out on a sofa in the multipurpose room before I went back to the dining area. She'd be fine. My mom could sleep with a party going on, and it was better if there were people around anyway.

Still no Tanya. "Do you like to draw, Sammy?" I asked as we dried the last table. A smile lit up his face. So I found some scratch paper and a bunch of markers left over from the ad hoc "after-school program" Precious had supervised and let him color on the floor of my once-again-crowded office. At first he was a little timid to have Dandy curled up on the floor, too, but the next time I looked, dog and boy were nose to nose as if consulting how best to paint the Sistine Chapel.

My throat caught. What were my boys doing today? Should I try calling them now? No, more likely to catch them around suppertime. I tried Precious again—and this time she answered.

"Hey. Whassup, Gabby." Her voice was flat, tired. Didn't sound like the Precious I knew, ready to jabber about whatever trivia had caught her fancy in the paper that day, or—even more likely—never missing an opportunity to rib die-hard football fans that her Carolina Panthers had "whupped" the Chicago Bears in the divisional play-offs last season.

I decided against unloading my melodrama up front. "That's why I'm calling *you*, Precious. Haven't seen you around since I got back from North Dakota." I knew I'd told her I was taking my boys to see their grandmother—though she probably didn't know I'd brought my increasingly confused mother back to Chicago with me. "Are you okay?"

A pause. "I ain't gonna be frontin' ya, Gabby. I'm all tore up."

"Precious, what's wrong?"

I heard a long sigh in my ear. "Sabrina got all mad 'cause I wouldn't let her go to the prom with some baggy-pants gangbanger. That girl up and went anyway—an' *I* got so amped, I showed up at the hotel and dragged her out." She snorted. "Wasn't a good scene, know what I'm sayin'?"

My eyes were so bugged out, all I could do was make a strangled noise I hoped sounded like "uh-huh."

"Anyway, she up an' ran off, jus' disappeared . . . Didn't nobody there tell you this, Gabby? Estelle and Edesa and they Yada Yada Prayer Group cooked up an all-night prayer meetin' a week or so ago, prayin' God to protect my girl! You wasn't there?"

I gulped. "Sorry, Precious. I must've still been out of town." I didn't say that when I got back a week and a half ago, things got "all tore up" at the Fairbanks household too. If someone at Manna House told me that Sabrina had run away, it definitely didn't penetrate the fog in my brain.

"Yeah, well. Girl, I was goin' outta my mind! Then I get a call from the state cops—they picked up Sabrina hitchhikin' with some no-good hustler 'bout a hundred miles outside a' Greenville. Still got a slew o' cousins here. Jesus, help me! Don' know what Sabrina was *thinkin'*—"

"Did you say 'here'? Where are you, Precious?"

"Greenville. South Carolina. Where I grew up, girl! Now Sabrina sayin' she don' wanna come home with me, wants to stay with the cousins. So I gotta stay here awhile till we get things worked out. But . . . ." Her voice trailed off.

I waited a beat or two. "But what, Precious?"

Another long sigh. "That ain't the worst of it. She's pregnant."

I sat at my desk with my head in my hands for a long time. My heart ached for Precious. She was only thirty—which meant *she* had gotten pregnant at fourteen. I knew she wanted a different life for Sabrina. Look how far she'd come! Before the fire that had taken down the old Manna House building, Precious had been a resident here. Now look at her! She had a job waitressing—or did. No telling how long a restaurant would hold her job for a family emergency. She'd gotten her own apartment with a Section 8, worked the lunchroom at Sabrina's high school, *and* volunteered here at Manna House. And she was so smart! No telling how far she could go given half a chance.

Now this.

I felt a tug on my arm. "Miz Gabby? Is my mama back yet? I gotta go real bad."

"Oh, Sammy." I'd almost forgotten about the little boy. "Come on, I'll take you."

I stood outside the bathroom until he was finished, then sent him back in to wash his hands while I picked out a copy of *Curious George* from the bookcase in the rec room, which was usually noisy this time of day—or had been before school was out. The other four shelter kids must be out with their moms. "Come on, kiddo." We climbed the stairs to the multipurpose room on the main level. Good, my mother was awake, just sitting patiently on the couch, hands in her lap, watching people come and go.

"Mom, would you mind reading to Sammy? He's waiting for his mother."

She seemed delighted. But she crooked a finger at me. "Where's Dandy?" she whispered. "Does he need to go out?"

Oh brother. The dog had been shut in my office all day. How long had it been since he'd been out? The headache threatened to send tentacles snaking over my head again. But I assured Mom I'd take care of Dandy, then hurried into the foyer and knocked on Mabel's office door.

"Come in."

I poked my head in. "Um, we've got a situation. Tanya never came back from her nine o'clock housing appointment. My mom's reading to Sammy at the moment. But it's already two thirty. Should we be worried?"

chapter 7

Mabel pulled Tanya's file. "Hm. Stephanie's her case manager."
Stephanie Cooper was a social worker who volunteered two
mornings a week doing case management for Manna House. "Her
housing sheet says . . . here it is. 'Deborah's Place, Wednesday,
June 21, 9:00 a.m.'" The director looked up. "I'll make a call, see
if she showed up for her appointment this morning. We don't
normally go chasing after people, Gabby. If they're a no-show by
curfew, their bed goes to someone else. But leaving Sammy here
is a different story . . ."

I nodded and backed out. *Tanya better not be a no-show.* I had
too much on my own plate to take her kid under my wing too.
Slipping past my mother and Sammy, who were both giggling at
Curious George, I headed back to my office. I really needed to get
some work done . . . Oh, good grief! I'd just volunteered for dog
duty too.

Except my office was empty. No Dandy. The door was shut
. . . *How did he get out?!* I groaned. I did *not* have time to go looking

for the dumb dog! And if he did his business somewhere in the shelter, that was *it*. I'd send him to the pound myself! I'd—

That's when I noticed that Dandy's leash was gone too.

I sank down into my desk chair. Lucy had probably taken him out. Or somebody. Right now, I didn't care who. I was too close to losing it. I needed to get a grip.

Pray. That's what Edesa and Mabel and Estelle always encouraged when the devil grabbed life by the tail. And I wasn't the only one with heartaches. Look at Precious! And Edesa nearly lost the baby she and Josh were trying to adopt when Gracie's ex-con daddy showed up. And Mabel's nephew who lived with her—the kid couldn't be more than fourteen years old—got so much ragging at school because of his small size and effeminate ways, he'd tried to commit suicide.

In every case, seemed like the first thing they did was get people together to "pray up a storm," as Precious put it. And God seemed to answer their prayers.

Why not mine?

Wish I had someone to talk to. To help me pray.

Somehow I managed to get through the rest of the afternoon, checking on my mother and Sammy from time to time. Caught them playing checkers. The next time I checked, they were watching *Jeopardy* in the TV room. Well. That was one small blessing, anyway. Seemed to be doing as much good for my mom as for Sammy. Not to mention it gave me time to do some research online into museum fees and events going on in Chicago that summer that might make good outings for the residents. Two measly day trips a month. Was that too much to ask?

Printing out my proposed "day trip budget"—which included a fifteen-passenger van—I looked at my watch. Five o'clock. Virginia was an hour ahead . . .

I picked up the phone, using the calling card I'd bought yesterday, and dialed Philip's parents in Petersburg.

"Fairbanks residence."

My stomach tightened. Philip's mother. Probably the last person I wanted to talk to right now. "Uh, hello, Marlene. This is Gabby. May I speak to P. J. and Paul, please?" *Ugh!* It galled me to even say *please*. The woman had never liked me, never thought I was good enough for her charming son. It wouldn't surprise me if she and Philip had engineered the whole debacle of getting me out of the penthouse and spiriting away my kids.

"I'm sorry, Gabrielle—"

Yeah, I'll bet.

"—The boys are out with their grandfather right now. I'll tell them you called." The phone went dead in my ear.

I held the receiver at arm's length and gaped at it. The nerve of that woman! She hung up on me! She had to know the boys were at her house without my permission. If she didn't, she would have been more gushy, more chatty, filling in the blanks with what a *glorious* time the boys were having.

My thoughts smoldered like old electrical wires on overload. *Kidnapped.* That's what it was. Could I file kidnapping charges against my husband and his parents? Taking my kids across state lines without my knowledge or permission? But I had to wait two whole days before I could even talk to a lawyer! Maybe I should've just called the police last night. Could still call them. But . . . would they just think I'm crazy?

Oh, God. I buried my head in my arms. *I don't know what to do.*

I feel so alone! But even as *kidnapped* and *police* and *crazy* settled like jagged glass shards into my spirit, I suddenly remembered the words Edesa had written in the note I'd found last night . . .

"*I will not forget you.*"

I lifted my head. Where was that note? I searched my desk, then remembered I'd left it under my pillow in the bunk room. Didn't matter. I'd look it up . . . Isaiah, chapter 49. In fact, Edesa had said there was more I should read.

I reached for the Bible I'd found that morning when I sorted through all the stuff my husband had tossed out into the penthouse foyer. By the time I got done reading the chapter four or five times, I felt strangely comforted—and even vindicated.

If this chapter was meant for me, Philip should be worried. Very worried.

Lucy brought Dandy back just before supper, both of them soaked, caught in one of Chicago's late-afternoon thunderstorms. They'd been gone more than three hours, and Dandy wriggled his rear end like a rag mop on amphetamines when he saw my mom, leaving wet splatters everywhere and sending Sammy into giggles. When I casually asked Lucy where they'd been, the old woman gave me a look. "Out. Don't it look like it? Humph. Gotta get me some dry clothes. Here . . ." She tossed me a rag. "You can clean up the dog. An' if I was you, I'd put him up in the bunk room 'fore Sarge shows up."

Good point.

Supper came and went. I didn't feel like talking, but I sat with my mom and Sammy to be polite, picking at the tuna casserole on my plate. Tanya still hadn't shown up, and the shelter curfew was eight o'clock, unless a resident had prior permission. Sammy was getting very clingy with "Gramma Shep." Poor kid. If worse came to worst, I'd tell him he could sleep in our bunk room tonight.

When I still hadn't heard from P. J. and Paul by seven thirty, I slipped into my office and called again. This time P. J. answered.

"Oh, hi, honey. I'm glad I got you! Did Nana Marlene tell you I called earlier?"

"Uh, don't think so. Maybe she told Paul."

I doubted it. I tried to sound interested in what they'd done that day—trip to the pool, watching the baseball games at the local park—all the while trying to curb my jealousy that the Fairbanks had my sons.

P. J.'s voice got challenging. "So did you and Dad work out this 'misunderstanding' about where the heck we're supposed to be this summer? It's not fair, Mom! First we come to Chicago. Then Dad brings us back to Petersburg. Nana says we're staying here, but *you* say it's all a misunderstanding an' you want us back in Chicago. Will you guys just . . . just make up your stupid minds?"

It was all I could do not to rip the phone out of its jack and throw it against the wall. Fighting back tears, I managed, "I don't blame you for being upset, P. J. It *is* unfair. And it's not your fault. I . . . .Dad and I need a few days to work some things out. Please be patient."

"Well, what about the summer lacrosse league? Can I sign up or not?"

A sense of foreboding came over me so strong, I could almost taste it. If P. J. signed up for that lacrosse team in Petersburg, my sons were as good as lost to me.

I finally pulled myself together and went back upstairs to the multipurpose room—where a tearful Tanya was arguing with the night manager.

"But I got here before curfew, Sarge! Look. It's only 7:57!"

"So? This is not a babysitting service, Tanya. *Capisce?*" The night manager slapped the side of her head. "What were you thinking, leaving Sammy alone here all day while you were out? Rules are rules, no?"

"I know! I shouldn't a' done that. It—it was j-just . . ." The skinny young woman started to hiccough with fresh sobs. Sammy plastered his face against her side, his arms hanging on tightly. My mother was standing off to one side, wringing her hands.

"Uh, Sarge?" I'm not sure where the guts came from to speak up. "Why don't we leave Tanya's case till tomorrow when Mabel can decide what to do? If you want, they can move to our bunk room tonight. I'll take responsibility for the decision."

"Humph. *Some people* sure do feel free to bend the rules, if you ask me." Sarge moved off, grumbling. "Like a certain *dog* that is not supposed to be here. No?"

"Don't worry, Sarge. Mabel's looking for a foster home for Dandy."

Sarge headed for the foyer to check in the last few curfew-beaters—including Lucy, who was just coming in with Dandy after his evening walk around the block. "The dog better be gone by *Sabato!*" she tossed over her shoulder.

Tanya grabbed a tissue from a nearby box and blew her nose. "Thanks."

I waited until the double doors had swung shut behind Sarge. "I'm not your case manager, Tanya, but I think you have some explaining to do." The TV room was full of *CSI* fans, so I led her into the toddler playroom, empty at this time of night. Sammy wasn't about to be separated from his mother, and *my* mother followed right on our heels. Well, so be it. We all deserved an explanation.

Tanya sat on a preschool chair, knees together, feet splayed out, tearing her used tissue into little shreds. "Well, I had a"—*hic*—"appointment at Deborah's Place this mornin', an' . . . an' I was so sure I was gonna get a place for me an' Sammy this time. A studio, one-bedroom—I didn't care. 'Long as it was just us. Miz Gabby, I been puttin' my name on lists for six months! We was in two other shelters 'fore we came to Manna House—one place was jus' one big room for about thirty wimmins plus they kids. Manna House been good to let me an' Sammy stay here together, an' the bunk room's better'n nothin'. But I want my own place! You understand, don'tcha? What kinda mother has her kid livin' in a *shelter*?" Tanya's face went dark. "But this mornin' they sayin' I don't qualify. Somethin' about gotta be in they drug program. But I ain't done no drugs!" The tears threatened again. "Man! I felt so bad, I wanted to hurt somebody! Or . . . or get drunk or *somethin'*! So I . . . I just walked around, and, yeah, I drank a few beers. But that's all. Honest! I didn't get high or nothin'. And I never meant to leave Sammy. Aw, come here, baby. Mama's sorry." The two wrapped their arms around each other and rocked.

I shut my eyes, her story too painful to process. Here I was, wallowing in my private pity party, and I'd been homeless for all of *two days*. I felt like the spoiled princess who complained because there was a pea under the mattress.

"Am I wrong, Miz Gabby?" Tanya's voice broke into my stupor. "Sammy an' me, we just need a place. But it's like a dead-end road. Can't get an apartment. Don't wanna raise my kid in a shelter. Am I wrong for needing a little help to get on my feet?"

"No, no. You're not wrong, Tanya." I sighed. *And you're not the only one.*

chapter 8

Tanya and Sammy took over the fourth bunk in our room—the more the merrier, as far as Dandy was concerned. Lucy, on the other hand, muttered her disapproval the whole time we were getting ready for bed. "Howza body s'posed ta sleep packed up in here like a bunch a' sardines . . . Too many lungs usin' up all the air . . . Humph. Dandy an' me gonna go sit inna lounge till you all go ta sleep . . ."

Well, fine with me. Maybe I could get to sleep before Lucy came to bed and started her engines.

And I'd guessed right about Mabel the next morning. Since Tanya had shown up by curfew and hadn't broken an actual *written* rule—though leaving your kids unsupervised was about to become one—Mabel gave Tanya another chance, but with a stern warning that she was on probation. Probably to soothe Sarge's prickled sense of protocol as much as anything. I had to grin inside. Mabel and Sarge were like two sides of a kitchen sponge, one side soaking up people's blunders and good intentions gone awry, the other scratchy and rough to deal with the tough cases.

Having to wait another whole day to talk to a lawyer, though, almost killed me. This was ridiculous! Three days ago my husband had kidnapped my children—yes, that was the word for it—leaving me homeless and broke, and I wasn't supposed to confront him until I had my *facts* lined up in a row?

Bunk the facts. He needed to get a load of my *feelings*.

Twice I picked up the phone, dialed his office, and then hung up after one ring. The third time I steeled myself to stay on the line. Someone picked up. "Fairbanks and Fenchel. May I help you?"

The female voice took me by surprise. Since when did Philip and Henry have a receptionist? Sounded young too.

Okay. I can play this game. "Philip Fairbanks, please."

"May I say who's calling?"

I thought fast. "CitiCorp Business Accounts." It was a bald-faced lie, but she probably had instructions not to send through any personal calls.

"One moment." The line went blank. But a moment later the woman came back on the line. "I'm sorry. He's in a meeting right now. Would you like me to put you through to his voice mail?"

I almost slammed the receiver down—but caught myself. "Yes. Thank you."

Two rings in my ear, then Philip's voice message, pleasant and professional. No hint that he was a monster in a business suit. I heard the beep. "Philip. This is Gabby. You'll be hearing from my lawyer, and I'll see you in court." I hit the Off button.

There. No hysterics. No crying. No pleading. But now he knew I wasn't rolling over and whimpering like a kicked puppy.

And I had every intention of showing up at his office in person as soon as I had my facts in hand.

Better yet, what if the *police* showed up at his office? With a wicked sense of vengeance, I picked up the phone again. Voices in my head said, *"Wait, Gabby."* But I felt driven by an insatiable need to *do* something, to make something happen.

I dialed 9-1-1.

"9-1-1. What is your emergency?"

"My—my children have been kidnapped!"

"Ma'am? Can you give me your name and location?" The questions kept coming—name and ages of my children . . . when did I discover they were missing . . .

"You say they turned up missing Monday night?"

"Yes! I came home from work, and the doorman said they'd left with my husband—and I haven't seen them since!"

"Your husband." The tone of voice changed. "Ma'am, if your *husband* took your children—"

"Without me knowing about it! He took them! He kidnapped them!"

"I see. Mrs. Fairbanks, that was three days ago. Why are you only reporting them missing now?"

"I . . . I . . ." My confidence drained away as though someone had pulled a plug. "Please. Help me. Please get my children back."

"So you don't know where they are."

"Well, yes, I do . . . but I didn't at first. He took them to his parents' in Virginia."

I could almost hear the silence on the other end laughing at me.

"Look, officer!" I was angry now. "My husband took my

children away from me, without my knowledge or permission. He took them *out of state.* That's a federal offense, isn't it?"

Another pause. "Ma'am, do you have reason to believe your children are in danger?"

I felt pinned to the wall. "No," I whispered. "No. They're . . . they're all right. But they—"

"So you've talked to them."

"Well . . . yes. But—!"

"Mrs. Fairbanks. We'll send an officer out to take a report, but this is really a civil matter. It will need to be settled in court."

"Uh . . . no, that's all right. You don't have to send anybody. I'll . . . I'll talk to a lawyer."

I sat at my desk, burning with embarrassment and frustration. I'd made a fool of myself. So much for the cops barging into Philip's office and dragging him away in handcuffs. But I still knew I was right. Philip had kidnapped our children. And I was going to get them back.

Somehow I made it through that Thursday, trying not to feel like a fool. Even had a chance to sit down with Estelle and pull together ideas for the basic cooking and sewing classes we'd talked about before. We decided on Monday afternoon for Basic Sewing—threading needles, sewing on buttons, making repairs, hemming a skirt—while I worked on getting some sewing machines for the next level.

Huh. I have a sewing machine just sitting up in the penthouse. Maybe I should fight to get my stuff back.

"—Basic Cooking?" Estelle was saying. "You know I don't use no recipes. It's all in here." The fifty-something woman tapped the side of her head. I noticed she was wearing her hair down more often, her silver-streaked hair falling in kinky waves to her shoulders. And was that glow on her cheeks natural or a touch of golden blush?

"So Harry Bentley likes your hair that way?" I tried to keep a straight face.

She gaped at me. "An' since when is that any of your business? Humph."

"Since I'm the one who introduced you two. As for recipes . . ." I moved right on without blinking. "Just start with simple stuff—different ways to fix chicken, season vegetables, some healthy soups and salads. You know, using the basic food groups to create a balanced diet, stuff like that."

Estelle wagged her head. "Girl, you know I'll be goin' up against Fast Food City! Lot of these women think protein means a McDonald's burger, veggies mean a bag of potato chips, and fruit means a bowl of Froot Loops." Estelle started to shake with silent chuckles.

I suddenly had a burst of inspiration. "Hey. Maybe we ought to ask Edesa to show up at your class to teach good nutrition— she's working on her degree in public health. Poor nutrition has to be a big factor in many of the health problems we see in here."

"Yeah, well, you better sneak that stuff in between fried chicken an' chocolate cake. Ain't nobody goin' to show up for a whole class on *nutrition.*"

So it was settled. "Cooking with Estelle" on Thursday afternoon, served up with a sneaky side of "How to Eat Healthy and

Live Longer"—providing Edesa was available. But as Estelle got up to leave, she hesitated, looking me up and down. "How you doin', Gabby? I *know* you got more on your mind than cookin' an' sewin'."

It was so tempting to unload on Estelle, to bare the fragments of my heart, torn between wanting my sons back—*now*—and knowing I had nothing to offer. I needed somebody to tell me I wasn't a total fool for calling the police, for ignoring Mabel's advice and trying to contact Philip, but I knew if I opened my mouth, I'd be a wreck. I needed to keep going, keep working, keep my mind busy, or I'd never be able to hold on to this job. And I needed this job, for a lot of reasons.

I shrugged. "Hanging in there. I see a lawyer tomorrow at Legal Aid. Can't do much until then."

The older woman lifted an eyebrow, as if seeing right through my little charade. "Hm. Well, honey, seems to me one of these days you gonna want to do some screamin' at that man of yours. Just want you to know, I'd be glad to come with you so he don't bully you around. Might even do a little screamin' myself."

Friday. I woke up early, before the six o'clock wake-up bell by the ever-punctual night manager, and caught myself smiling at Estelle's offer. For some reason it made me feel good. It hadn't occurred to me to take someone with me when I did go see Philip with my facts. Well, if I did, Estelle would be the one. No one— not even Philip—would mess with her.

Sensing I was awake, Dandy padded over and nosed my arm. *Hmm. Why not take the dog for his morning walk?* Lucy saw me pulling on a pair of jeans and started to roll out of bed. "Let me," I whispered. "I need to get out. You can sleep in today. Where do you go—the cemetery?"

"Cemetery don't open till eight thirty," Lucy muttered. "Gotta go someplace else." She rolled over and was snoring again before I got Dandy's leash on, grabbed a couple of plastic grocery bags from her stash, and sneaked down the stairs. I heard someone—probably Sarge and her assistant—banging around in the kitchen, setting out breakfast. In the foyer, sunlight streamed in the stained-glass windows on either side of the oak doors, creating dancing prisms of colored light on the floor. I dutifully signed out, quietly opened the front doors, and slipped out.

Yes! Blue sky overhead. Cool, no hint of humidity. A beautiful day. I suddenly felt a pang of longing for the park and lakefront abutting Richmond Towers. I'd love to let Dandy run on the beach, kick off my sandals, and dig my toes in the sand. But here . . . I glanced up and down the neighborhood surrounding the shelter. Mostly two- and three-story apartment buildings. Brick, crowded together, several with storefronts on the ground level. The occasional Victorian house squeezed between them, with a six-foot wrought-iron fence in front as if holding the buildings on either side at arm's length with its iron bars.

How far was it to the lake? Maybe a mile. I quickly nixed that idea. Another time. Too bad Graceland Cemetery hadn't opened yet. Closest thing to a park I'd seen around here.

By the time we got back, morning devotions were just ending. Sarge hustled everyone downstairs for the usual weekday breakfast of cold cereal and milk, toast and jam, juice and coffee, giving Dandy and me the eye. "Saturday," was all she said.

I felt a flicker of panic. That was tomorrow. Had Mabel been asking around for a foster home for the dog? She hadn't said anything. And what about my mother? She was oblivious that Dandy's days were numbered.

But I determined not to let Dandy's fate get me down. Today was an important day. Today I had an appointment with a lawyer. Today I was going to get some answers.

chapter 9

A knock on my office door was followed immediately by a glowing brown face, brilliant blue headband, and bouncy hair twists. "Are you alone, *mi amiga?*" Without waiting for an answer, Edesa Baxter called over her shoulder in a stage whisper, "Coast is clear. Hurry!"

The next moment, Josh Baxter hustled into my office, carrying a large bakery sheet cake, followed by Edesa with Gracie on her hip. They shut the door behind them and stood there like the Three Bears, caught sneaking into Goldilocks's house instead.

"Can we hide this cake in here, Gabby? Josh, set it on top of the file cabinet, out of her way."

"Um . . . sure. What's going on?"

"Da-Da!" Gracie squealed, spying Dandy, who'd gotten up to sniff at our visitors.

"How d'ya like that?" Josh made a face as he carefully set the cake on top of the file cabinet. "She says 'Da-Da' and means 'doggy.'"

I had to smile. The young Baxter family made such an odd,

cute trio. The ten-month-old's creamy tan skin and loose, black curls made her look as if she could be their natural child—white daddy, black mommy—instead of a Latina child in the process of being adopted. "Are you going to tell me what all this hush-hush business is about?"

Edesa leaned forward, keeping her voice low. "*Sí! Sí!* It is Estelle's birthday today! But this is just the backup cake. Señor Harry is bringing—"

Oh no! Estelle's birthday! I slapped my forehead. "Drat! I forgot! I even mentioned it to Mr. Bentley last week, and then . . ." I shook my head. "With all that's happened this week, it totally slipped my mind. I don't have a card or a gift or—"

Edesa put a finger on my lips. "Hush, *mi amiga*. It's all right. Estelle thinks we've all forgotten. Which is good, since . . . why are you poking me, Josh?"

"Don't give it away, Edesa, my sweet. It's supposed to be a surprise, remember?"

"Sounds like a regular party." Had to admit my nose felt a little out of joint. Seems like somebody should have at least *told* the person in charge of shelter activities what was going on. But Edesa and Josh didn't seem to notice my little snit.

"*Sí!*" She giggled. "Estelle *might* guess that we'll celebrate her birthday Sunday night at Yada Yada, but she won't suspect anything today. Oh!" Edesa looked at her watch. "I've got to run. I'm teaching Bible study in ten minutes. Pray for me!" She handed the baby to her husband, blew them both a kiss, and disappeared out my door.

Yada Yada Sunday night. That was the prayer group Edesa and Estelle and Josh's mother, Jodi, were part of. Knowing each other so well, they celebrated birthdays . . .

457

I shook off my melancholy, aware that Josh and Gracie were still standing in my two-bit office. "Say, Josh, as long as you're here, I wanted to ask you about that sports clinic idea you once mentioned."

"Sure, Mrs. Fairbanks—I mean, Gabby—I'd be glad to talk about that. But . . ." The young man shifted the baby in his arms and cleared his throat. "Maybe it's none of my business, but Edesa said that you . . . uh, that your husband—"

"Josh. It's all right. Sit down." I indicated the metal folding chair leaning against the wall. As he flipped it open with his free hand, I went on. "If you mean, did my husband kick me out of our penthouse? Yes. That and he took the kids back to Virginia without my knowledge or permission. So . . ." I shrugged. "I'm staying here at Manna House for the time being. My mother too." For some reason, it was easier to be matter-of-fact with this young man than it was with Edesa or Estelle or Mabel. I even allowed a sardonic half smile. "Every staff person ought to be a resident of the shelter for a while. Gives one a whole new perspective."

Josh shook his head. "I'm so sorry, Gabby. I thought . . . well, guess I'd hoped Edesa and I could get to know you two better, you know, as an older couple who've been married a few years."

Now I did have to blink back a few tears. I nodded. "Yeah, I know. That's how it should be. But . . ." I bit my lip and glanced at my watch. Ten forty. Still three hours to go before I could meet with the lawyer. Philip and I were on a road I hoped Josh and Edesa never had to travel.

I'd intended to duck into Edesa's Bible study, but Josh and I ended up tossing around different ideas to meet the needs of kids who ended up at the shelter, while Gracie grabbed things off my desk. Now that his classes at UIC were over, he said, he'd have more time on the weekends. "Weekdays, though, I'll be working full-time for Peter Douglass till school starts again. He has his own business—Software Symphony. Edesa and I really need a bigger apartment, but that takes moola."

Huh. Takes moola to get one, period.

Currently, there weren't that many moms with kids at the shelter, but Josh talked about taking them to ball games this summer, finding a park where the preteens could shoot hoops and get some pointers, maybe starting a weekend league in this neighborhood for other kids. "My dad coaches some summer leagues. Maybe he could help us get started. We need a van, though. Can't keep borrowing the one from the church."

"Yeah, well, I just added a fifteen-passenger van to my program budget. We'll see if the board has a collective heart attack . . . Oh my. Is that the bell for lunch already?" Well, at least the rest of the morning had gone fairly quickly. Only two more hours . . .

Estelle had outdone herself on the lunch menu. A chicken pasta salad with walnuts and grapes and hot garlic bread. Maybe she was celebrating her own birthday by giving everybody a treat. She was certainly dressed brightly today—a long, blue tunic with silver filigree around neck and sleeves, worn over wide-legged pants, though the big white apron and food-worker's hairnet didn't do anything for the outfit. But nobody said anything about "birthday," so I kept mum, even when I went back for seconds.

While I was waiting my turn at the counter, I heard the doorbell ringing on the main floor . . . and then twice more, as if no one was around to answer. Darting up the stairs and through the multipurpose room, I reached the front door and pulled it open.

My friend from Richmond Towers and a young boy stood on the steps.

"Mr. Bentley! Mm. Don't tell me. You're here because—"

"Uh, you said this was Estelle's birthday, didn't you?"

I sighed. "Yeah, I did. But with everything that's happened this week, guess who forgot? Come on in." I held the door for them as they stepped inside, noticing the big, square box the youngster was carrying. "Who's your young helper here?"

Mr. Bentley grinned. "That's right, you two haven't met. This is my grandson, DeShawn. He's living with me now. DeShawn, this is Mrs. Fairbanks. She's, uh, from Richmond Towers, where I work. Here, let me take that." He took the cake so his grandson could shake hands.

The boy grinned at me. He looked about nine years old, recent haircut, caramel-colored skin, a tad lighter than Mr. B, firm handshake. "I didn't know you had a grandson." I felt like kicking myself. Why hadn't I ever asked Mr. Bentley if he had family? The boy was a little younger than Paul. If he'd just come to live with his grandfather, something must've happened to his mom and dad . . . like my boys, living with *their* grandparents now. But Mr. Bentley seemed tickled as all get-out. "I—I'm happy for you."

"You doin' okay? Your boys . . . ?"

"They're okay. Just trying to get them back is all." I managed a smile. "Look, you two can go on down. They've already started eating."

"Uh, is there a way I can sneak this in without Estelle seeing? We'd like it to be a surprise."

I peeked through the clear top of the cake box. Another cake—this one fat and round. "Wow. I guess we're gonna pig out on cake today. Here, let me carry it. She won't even notice what I'm carryin' when she sees you." I winked at Mr. B.

Sure enough, Estelle was so flustered to see Mr. Bentley, she didn't even notice me taking the cake box to the other end of the room. She filled two more plates of food and even sat down with her guests at one of the tables, seemingly delighted at the news that the boy had come to live with his grandfather. "Stu told me!" she exclaimed.

Stu? That's what she called her housemate, whose real name was Lily or Leslie Stuart or something like that. How did her housemate know Mr. Bentley? Now I was starting to feel left out. Everybody and their cousin seemed to know about Mr. Bentley's grandson except me. Wasn't he *my* friend first?

My disgruntled thoughts were interrupted by Mr. Bentley tapping a spoon on his glass for attention and announcing that this was a special day for a special lady—Estelle Williams's birthday. She tried to make him sit down, but everybody began singing "Happy Birthday" in two or three different keys while Mr. B brought the new cake and set it in front of Estelle.

Yells of "Make a wish!" . . . "Ohh, now, that's purty" . . . and "Cut it, Estelle! Don't wait all day!" greeted the end of the song. Mr. Bentley handed a kitchen knife to the "birthday girl" and sat down again.

"Oh, now. This cake is just too pretty to cut," Estelle protested sweetly, quickly taking off her apron and hairnet when Josh waved a camera.

"Cut it!" everyone yelled. I grinned. The residents were really enjoying this.

Estelle slid the knife through the frosting, thick with decorative pink and yellow sugar roses. Then she stopped, a puzzled frown pinching her forehead. She tried again in a different place. The knife only went one inch deep. "What?" she mumbled.

Behind Estelle, Edesa and Josh had hands over their mouths, trying to keep from laughing aloud. *What in the world?*

Estelle caught them. "Uh-huh. I get it now." Turning back to the cake, she lifted the knife over her head in both hands and plunged it into the middle of the cake. This time the knife went in, though it took an extra push on Estelle's part. Then she lifted the knife and the whole cake came with it.

The entire dining room was gasping with laughter. "What is it?" . . . "What? No cake?"

Estelle lowered the cake to the table, the knife still plunged into its heart, then took a big swipe of the frosting with her finger until she reached the "cake." "Uh-huh. Just what I thought. Foam cushions." I'd never seen Mr. Bentley laugh so hard.

"Ah, he gotcha good!" Lucy yelled.

Estelle wagged her head. "Harry Bentley! I oughta throw this whole frosted pillow in your face, but I'm too . . . I'm too—" And forgetting decorum, she picked up the bogus cake and dumped it right on his bald head.

Mr. Bentley's grandson was hopping up and down, pointing at his grandpa.

With perfect timing, Josh and Edesa brought out the real sheet cake from my office, giving Mr. B a chance to wipe frosting off his face and talk Estelle into letting him give her a birthday hug. I wanted to squeeze in my own hug and wish Estelle a happy birthday, but I glanced at the clock above the kitchen counter. *Ten after one.* My appointment at Legal Aid was at two! I needed to get out of there.

The prank Estelle's friends had played on her—"It was all Mr. Bentley's idea," Josh had said—left me feeling strangely hopeful. Estelle had once been a resident at Manna House—though I still didn't know why—but now look at her. Laughter. Jokes. New friends. Even a new beau . . .

"Mrs. Fairbanks?"

I looked up from the magazine I'd been flipping through in the waiting area of the Legal Aid clinic to see a man standing in the doorway, looking at me expectantly. *Wait a minute.* I'd been expecting some freckle-faced, idealistic law student in his twenties. Or maybe a fatherly type, retired, rich, doing pro bono work on the side. But this man was late thirties, probably five-eleven, wire-rim specs, brown hair with blond flecks brushed neatly to one side, nice tan, open-necked shirt tucked into a pair of jeans. Could've been Bill Gates for all I knew. Sure of himself. Decidedly casual.

And boots. I smiled, feeling a surge of familiarity. Maybe it was my North Dakota blood, but Lee Boyer—if this was indeed Lee Boyer—could've walked right off a cattle ranch into my father's carpet store.

I followed the man back to a small cubicle office and sat in the chair facing the cluttered desk while he shut the door. On closer look, those flecks in his hair were more silver than gold. Okay, maybe forty-something.

"What can I do for you, Mrs. Fairbanks?"

My mouth went dry. For some reason I felt embarrassed to tell my sob story to this man, who looked like someone I might've gone to school with back at the University of ND. But that's why I was here. To his credit, the lawyer took copious notes. He asked a few more questions about my mother. Did I have power of attorney for her? If not, was she rational enough to sign over power of attorney?

I felt frustrated by the direction of his questions. "Mr. Boyer, it's my *kids*—"

"I understand, Mrs. Fairbanks. But the fact that you currently have responsibility for your mother, who seems to be suffering from some kind of dementia, definitely strengthens your case." He handed me a set of power of attorney forms to fill out. "Talk to your sisters and your mother and get these filled out, all right? It's important. Now . . ." He leaned back thoughtfully, making a tent with his fingers. "Let's start at the beginning. Your husband is in violation of both Family Law *and* the Landlord-Tenant Law by changing the locks of your apartment without a court order. It doesn't matter if your name is not on the lease. Your husband can't evict you without proper legal procedures, and you can get a court order to return to the apartment."

"A court order? How long would that take? He's given notice that he's breaking the lease and plans to move out by the end of the month. That's next week!"

"Hm. That's tight. We could try to hurry that along, but maybe the main question is, are you prepared to take over the lease if your husband bails?"

Take over the lease? I shook my head slowly. "No way could I afford the penthouse at Richmond Towers on my own. Even if I could, I don't want it. Not now. Please. Just get my kids back. That's all I care about."

He jotted another note. "All right. We'll come back to this later. Now, the kids . . . P. J. and Paul, you said. If there is no order giving your husband custody—"

"Absolutely not!"

"—and if he has hidden your children in another state, you can call the police on the in-laws for kidnapping—based on the grounds that he can move *with* them, but he cannot move the kids alone and leave them in the care and custody of another, without your consent or a valid court order."

"But I already called the police." I'd left that part out, hoping to get a different answer from the lawyer—or that the lawyer would call the police when he heard my story. But now I rehashed what happened when I'd called 9-1-1.

The lawyer pulled a law manual from a stack on his desk and flipped through it. A minute passed, then two. Then he nodded. "Well, that's right. Since the kids aren't being hidden, and you're able to talk with them by phone, there would be no charge for kidnapping." Lee Boyer leaned forward, hazel eyes behind the wire rims sympathetic. "But no judge is going to take kindly to what your husband has done, Mrs. Fairbanks. At this point, our options are to file an unlawful eviction case *and* a custody case, and we can merge these into one. And divorce. You definitely have grounds to file for divorce."

Divorce? "Uh, wait a minute. Can't I get my kids back without a divorce?"

"Of course. But you should know your rights, Mrs. Fairbanks. Your husband has left you virtually penniless. If you successfully file for divorce, you are entitled to half of your husband's estate."

My eyes widened. "Did you say . . . *half* of what my husband is worth?" I almost laughed aloud. Oh, wouldn't that news spin Philip's clock!

Lee Boyer nodded. "And you have a strong case, though you

should do what you can to make it even stronger. Prove you can support your children. Get a higher-paying job if necessary. For goodness' sake, get out of the shelter and find an apartment with adequate room for two young teens! I have to warn you, Mrs. Fairbanks. We are Legal Aid. We do what we can. But someone like your husband, with a high-powered job and the money to retain an expensive lawyer, can keep throwing legal hurdles in the way to make life difficult."

His eyes were kind. "Just so you know . . . this might take awhile."

chapter 10

My head was spinning. I needed to think! Or . . . or talk to someone. But who? It was all so confusing!

I wandered the unfamiliar streets, looking for a café or coffee shop, trying to keep the closest El station within my frame of reference. All I could find was a tiny restaurant called Joe's Eats, with "Breakfast Special—Grits, Ham or Bacon, 3 eggs, Toast, $4.99" painted in red right on the window. I sat in a booth with a Formica tabletop and ordered a cup of coffee. It came in a thick, white mug and looked so strong I added twice the amount of cream I normally used.

During the meeting, Lee Boyer had been very encouraging about my rights, everything from getting the boys returned to me, to hope that I wouldn't be permanently destitute. And Philip! The jerk was in *big* trouble. The lawyer didn't say what the consequences might be, but he did say what Philip had done was illegal. *And* that a judge wouldn't take kindly to his disappearing act with our kids, which would give me an edge in any court case.

But the words *"This might take awhile"* cut off my hope at the knees. What did that mean? I wanted my sons back now!

Grabbing a paper napkin, I pressed it to my eyes, hoping to stem the tears threatening to well up and explode, right there in Joe's Eats. *Oh God, Oh God, what am I going to do?!*

"Refill, miss?" A thick-waisted waitress with flabby arms hovered over my cup with a coffeepot. "Got some good lemon pie too."

I shook my head, blew my nose in the napkin, and reached for my purse. "Just the bill." I had to get out of there.

Standing outside Joe's Eats a few minutes later, I realized I had no idea where to go or what to do. In the back of my mind, I'd imagined taking the El to the Aon Center after my meeting and showing up in the offices of Fairbanks and Fenchel, confronting Philip with my legal facts. But I knew Philip would just put another black mark on his ledger of my "sins" if I confronted him at his office, "ruining his business."

Maybe Estelle was right. I should take someone with me, someone who could keep me from being mowed down by Philip's spin on everything.

Still! It galled me to wait even one more day before confronting Philip face-to-face! The man had kicked me out and disappeared with my kids *four days ago*—and so far hadn't heard a peep from me except the cryptic message I'd left on his phone. He was probably laughing into his Chardonnay, thinking, *What a wimp.*

Well. He had another thing coming.

Gripping my shoulder bag, I headed for the El station. I'd just go back to Richmond Towers and wait till he came home. Six o'clock . . . nine o'clock . . . midnight. Didn't matter. He had to come home sometime. After all, I still had my security ID card that would get me in. Or I *could* just show up early tomorrow morning, when he'd be sure to be home . . . On second thought, bad idea. He could just refuse to let me in. No, I had to be in the penthouse foyer when he got off the elevator—

"*Streetwise* paper, lady? One dollar." A *Streetwise* peddler waved a copy of the latest issue at me, a friendly smile showing off a couple of missing teeth. I started to pass by, but the man beamed happily. "Got my name in here, an' a picture too! *Streetwise* Salesperson of the Month! I'll autograph it for you."

I had to smile. What was one measly dollar? If Mr. Lee Boyer was correct, I had a whole lot of money sitting in Philip's bank account.

A few minutes later, standing on the northbound El platform with my "autographed" copy of *Streetwise*, I started having second thoughts about confronting Philip at the penthouse. No telling when he would get home on a Friday night. I could wait for hours. But more than that, when he got off that elevator, we'd be alone, and no matter what my resolve, in two seconds he'd twist anything I'd say to make it be my fault.

A northbound train squealed into the station. I stood rooted to the platform as passengers jostled past me, reason and rage wrestling in my gut. Maybe I should get on and just get off at the Sheridan station and go back to Manna House. Or ride farther north and take my chances at Richmond Towers. Wait till he showed up and let him have it, both barrels, come what may.

No. I was tired of waiting. Now or never.

The doors closed. The train pulled out. I watched as it rattled out of sight; then I headed back down the stairs and up to the southbound platform.

At least I had dressed up a bit for my appointment at Legal Aid—boot-cut black slacks with a belted jacket over a teal silk blouse and low, sling-back heels. A pit stop in the women's restroom on the first level of the Aon Center to repair my makeup and tame my curly mane gave me confidence that I looked attractive. Sane.

I stuffed the voice whispering, *"Should you be doing this, Gabby?"* I didn't care. I had to quit running. I had to face my demons—in this case, my husband. The office was the most likely place to find him. The most likely place to guarantee that neither one of us would make a scene. I was going to march in there and—

A young woman looked up from the reception desk when I opened the door marked Fairbanks and Fenchel—Commercial Development Corp. She looked to be in her twenties. Short brunette hair. Conservative lavender blouse. Small pearl earrings. Attractive, but no fashion model. She smiled. "May I help you?"

"Yes. I'd like to speak to Philip Fairbanks."

She reached for the phone. "Your name, please?"

"Gabrielle Fairbanks." Her eyebrows went up. I helped her out. "His wife."

She picked up the phone and turned slightly aside. A moment later, Philip's office door opened, and Henry Fenchel stepped into view. The man was in his early forties, same as Philip, but a bit fleshy in the face, thinning hair. Tended to be a good ol' boy. He stopped. "Gabby." He sounded startled.

"Hello, Henry." My voice was calm. I did not smile.

The receptionist hung up her phone. "Mr. Fairbanks will see you. Go on in."

I pushed past Philip's partner, stepped into Philip's office, and closed the door behind me. My husband was standing at the wide window with his back to me, suit coat off, looking tall and slim in his pale green shirt sleeves. I said nothing, just waited. It was probably only five seconds, but it felt like five minutes. He finally turned, coffee cup in hand, expression mild, dark eyes and lashes framed by his beautiful tan.

I wanted to groan. *Oh gosh.* Did he have to look so gorgeous?

"Gabrielle." He waved his coffee cup at the mahogany chair on my side of the desk. "Sit. Would you like coffee?"

Would I like—? "No." I had no intention of acting as if we were just having a friendly little chat. But I did sit down, crossing my legs to keep them from shaking. Philip casually pulled out his executive chair and leaned back. Another five seconds went by. I got an inquisitive look, as if he wondered what I was there for.

Just do it, Gabby.

"I saw a lawyer today. What you've done, Philip, is *illegal*. You can't just kick me out without a proper order of eviction. You can't just take my children away from me and deposit them with your parents in another state."

Philip's eye twitched, and the corner of his mouth curved ever so slightly. I got the message loud and clear: *"But I did, didn't I?"* The anger that I had so carefully repressed threatened to surge right out of my gut in a seismic eruption.

Don't, Gabby, don't!

I waited until I could speak without screaming and took a deep breath to steady my voice. "My lawyer is filing an unlawful eviction case *and* a custody case. There's no question a judge will rule in my favor."

"Your lawyer?" His shrug felt like a slap in the face. "Tell me something, Gabby. Exactly how do you plan to *pay* for a lawyer?"

I stared at him.

"Ah." He smiled. "Legal Aid. Of course."

A glass paperweight sat on his desk within arm's reach of me. Oh, how I wanted to snatch it up and throw it at that smug smile. Or right through his picture-perfect window overlooking the city skyline. But even as I imagined glass shattering everywhere, I knew in my gut Philip was goading me. *"Go ahead, Gabby. Do something crazy."*

A hysterical giggle nearly escaped the emotions churning under my skin. Right. With my luck, the falling glass would probably kill somebody on the street below and I'd get sued. Or dragged off to jail.

I'd lost my upper hand. "Philip . . . why?" I couldn't help it. My voice shook. "Why tear our family apart this way?"

His eyebrows shot up and he threw his hands open. "Me! *Me?* I seem to recall *you* were the one who took this do-gooder job that started screwing everything up! The one who just showed up with her mother and her mutt, turning our household upside down. Without considering me at all in your decisions, I might add. Oh yes, the one whose idea of taking care of our sons was to drag them to a homeless shelter and expose them to all sorts of riffraff all day."

"But . . . but, Philip. I was trying! I came home Monday to tell you I'd quit the job and that I'd even found a place for my mom."

His eyes narrowed. "What place?"

"Why, Manna House. The shelter. They said they'd take her in, and she seemed happy with . . . What?"

My husband had started to laugh. He shook his head, shoulders shaking. "Listen to yourself, Gabby. The shelter! The *shelter!*

You're like a broken record. If you weren't so pathetic, this would be funny—"

His phone rang. Still chuckling, he picked up. "Oh, sure. Put him through." He glanced at me, then swiveled his chair so that his back was to me. "Oh, hey, Bill! What's up? . . . Saturday? What time? . . . Yeah, yeah, sure, I could make that . . . No, no, that's good . . . Gotta dig out my clubs, though. We just moved, you know. I might be a little rusty . . ."

I stared at the back of his head. Hot tears stung my eyes. I was so close to a meltdown, I was afraid to move.

Afraid not to move. I had to get out of there or I'd go crazy! Maybe I was already crazy.

Oh God, Oh God, Oh God . . . have You forgotten all about me?

I stood up on wobbly legs and somehow made it to the door as Philip chatted on the phone. But as I put my hand on the doorknob, a Voice seemed to be whispering in my ear: *Gabby. Gabby. Can a mother forget the baby at her breast? Though she may forget, I will not forget you!* I recognized the verses Edesa had written in her note. And there was more. Something about God engraving my name on the palms of His hands . . . and sending sons hastening back.

I couldn't remember it all word for word, but the turmoil surging through my veins suddenly lost steam, replaced with . . . what? A sudden stillness in my spirit. No hysterics. No hot anger. Just the return of a quiet confidence.

I lifted my head and waited at the door until Philip ended the call. He seemed surprised that I was till there. "My things," I said. My voice was steady. "I want the rest of my things. Like my sewing machine. I need it for a class at the shelter. I need to know when I can come get it."

chapter 11

Mabel had already gone home by the time I signed in at
Manna House at five forty. *Rats.* Was she gone for the whole
weekend already? I had to talk to somebody before next Monday!
Mabel was the one who'd steered me to the lawyer at Legal Aid.
I wanted to debrief what Lee Boyer had told me and figure out
what my next step should be.

Didn't immediately see my mom, so I headed upstairs to
change out of my pantsuit. Actually, what I really needed to do
was think through what had happened at Philip's office. Already
I was kicking myself for barging ahead. What had I accomplished? Nothing—except a flippant promise to let me pick up my
sewing machine sometime next week. We didn't talk about the
boys, about what he'd told them when they left, or how they felt
about being jerked back to Virginia so suddenly. Didn't talk about
when P. J. and Paul were coming back, or what was best for them
in the middle of our mess. The hundred and one important
questions.

I wiggled out of my pantsuit. *Ugh!* I didn't even get the satisfaction of making Philip squirm. Evidently, my husband was missing the squirm gene. Probably incompatible with the Fairbanks DNA, always right, always top dog—

Dog. Oh good grief. Dandy! Had Mabel found a foster home for Dandy? . . . No, of course not, or I'd have heard about it by now.

Quickly pulling on a pair of jeans, I scurried downstairs. What in the world was I going to do? Sarge usually showed up at seven, and she would no doubt ask when I'd have Dandy out of there. This weekend . . . I'd just have to work on that this weekend.

Several women in orange-and-black Manna House volunteer T-shirts—some church group, no doubt—were bustling around the kitchen, setting big pans of covered hot food into the steam table section of the kitchen counter. I found my mother and Carolyn sitting at one of the tables, sorting clean flatware from a dishwasher rack into their appropriate buckets—forks, knives, spoons. It was a good thing Carolyn was working with my mother, or she'd be there till midnight at the rate she was going. I peeked into my office . . . no Dandy.

"He's out with Lucy, if you're wondering," Carolyn called out. "Been gone most of the afternoon. Speaking of gone . . . I'm here filling in for you. You're supposed to be on setup with your mama here."

"Oh, Carolyn. I'm sorry. I had an appointment right after lunch and didn't even look at the chore list."

The book lady smirked. "Works for me. I just traded with you. You got my spot on supper dishes."

Oh great. That's when I usually tried to call P. J. and Paul. Maybe I should try during supper.

After making sure my mother was settled at a table with a plate of food, all the proper utensils, and Aida Menéndez nearby to look after "Gramma Shep," I took my own plate of sliced ham, scalloped potatoes, and chopped salad into my office. Using my phone card, I dialed the Virginia number for Philip's parents.

"Fairbanks residence." Male voice. Philip's father.

"Hello, Mike. It's Gabby."

"Oh. Hi there, Gabrielle." He sounded uncomfortable. Maybe at least one Fairbanks male had the squirm gene. "Guess you want to speak to the boys. They're outside riding their bikes right now. Can you call back, maybe an hour?"

I fought with my disappointment. "All right. Sure. But . . . Mike? Can I talk to you a minute?"

"Uh, sure."

"Mike, you know Philip brought the boys there without my knowledge and without my permission, right?"

His silence definitely squirmed. Then, "Yeah, yeah. I pretty much figured. But Philip told his mother you two are having some marriage problems. Maybe it's better if the boys are here right now, instead of, you know, in the middle."

The bald truth of it hit me square between the eyes. I shook off his words. "But that's kidnapping, Mike. Across state lines, no less." Not exactly true, but I wasn't ready to give up ground yet. "I don't want to press charges if I can get my sons back."

Now the silence at the other end stretched long and deep. Finally a heavy sigh. "Gabrielle, I don't want to get in the middle of stuff with you and Philip. You know I didn't approve of him moving up there to Chicago in the first place. As far as I'm concerned, the boys are Virginia born and bred and belong here. But I'm not their parent. What do you want? You want me to put the

boys on a plane back to Chicago? You feel okay with them traveling by themselves? Just say the word and I'll do it."

Now it was my turn to be speechless. Did I hear right? I could
have my sons back, just like that? Mike Fairbanks would go
around his son on my say-so?

"Mike, I . . . I appreciate that. But I don't have any money for
plane tickets right now. Long story."

"Don't worry about that. I'll pay for it, and you can pay me
back whenever."

My heart was beating so fast, I felt as if I'd just sprinted the
quarter-mile. This weekend?! I could have the boys back with me
by this weekend?

And then what, Gabby?

I finally found words. "Mike . . . thank you. But you're right.
It's not simple. Can I call you back? I need to think it through."

"All right. But call me tonight, or first thing tomorrow morning. If you decide to leave them here, P. J.'s chomping at the bit to
sign up for lacrosse summer camp the four weeks of July.
Tomorrow's the last day to get his name on the list."

My hand was shaking as I hung up the phone. *"If you decide
to leave them here . . ."* The decision was in my lap.

I joined the cleanup crew after supper in a daze. The church
group volunteers put away leftovers and took the trash bags out
the side utility door that accessed the gangway between buildings, and then they were gone—scuttling back to their own
homes and families somewhere in the 'burbs. Hannah the
Bored—my private name for the gum-chewing girl who was forever doing her nails—elected to wipe tables and sweep the floor,

the easiest after-meal cleanup. That put me on dishes with two of the new residents, which meant I had to show them how to run the monster industrial dishwasher, leaving me no time to *think*.

I finally escaped into a sink full of large serving pans that needed scrubbing. A one-woman job. My mind spun around Mike Fairbanks's offer with every swirl of the scrub brush. On one hand, a no-brainer! Of course! Send the boys back! I'd take the Blue Line out to O'Hare Airport and meet them myself.

And then what, Gabby? Bring them here to Manna House? That was the rub. Even if the boys were willing to stay here—big *if*—it wasn't even possible. The shelter only allowed mothers with boys up to age eleven, and P. J. was almost fourteen. *Well, what about someone else taking them until I find an apartment—but who? The only people I know here in Chicago I met here at the shelter . . . Wait.* An idea danced in my brain as I sloshed suds in the sink. Josh's parents—Jodi and Denny Baxter—had taken Lucy for a few days when she had that cough. Josh said they had extra bedrooms now that he and his sister were out of the house. Would they—?

This is ridiculous! Even if the Baxters agreed, would my boys? Leave their grandparents to stay with total strangers? Not a chance. And Philip would have a fit.

Oh God, what am I going to do?

I glanced at the kitchen wall clock. *Quarter to eight.* An hour later in Virginia. I had to call Mike back, soon! The rest of the cleanup crew had already finished. Draining the sink, I took off my apron, flipped off the kitchen lights, and started for my office—when I noticed my mother standing in the middle of the dimly lit dining room, wringing her hands. "Mom! You okay?"

"Dandy." Her lip trembled. "I can't find him."

"Oh, Mom. Lucy took him out." *Like hours ago.* "I'm sure

they'll be back soon. You know Lucy!" Yeah, but if "soon" wasn't the next few minutes, Sarge would lock the doors at eight, and that would be it.

As if on cue, we heard a commotion on the main level and a sharp bark. I gave my mother a hug. "See? There he is! Come on, let's go see him." I tried not to show my impatience. I needed to call the boys' grandfather—and I still had no idea what I was going to say. All I knew was that I wanted my boys back, *now*.

In her haste, my mother stumbled a bit going up the stairs, and I had to slow her down. But as we came into the multi-purpose room, she was rewarded with a dynamo of yellow hair jumping all around her, whimpering happily. "Oh, Dandy, good boy, good doggy. Are you hungry? You are? Oh, look at your red bandanna. Look, Gabby, Lucy dressed him up! . . . Yes, yes, good doggy. I missed you too."

But I was looking at Lucy's purple knit hat squaring off in the middle of the room with the night manager. Lucy planted her fists on her lumpy hips. Sarge folded her muscular arms across her bosom as the two women went nose-to-nose.

"That dog ain't goin' ta no pound," I heard Lucy say.

"Rules are rules, Lucy Tucker. No pets at the shelter. *Capisce?*"

"This ain't the army, and you ain't commander in chief."

"And this ain't no pet hotel. The dog goes—tomorrow."

Lucy shook a finger in Sarge's face. "Dandy's *family*. Miz Martha's family. Her mean ol' son-in-law already kicked the dog *an'* Miz Martha out. Ya gonna do it again? Huh? Huh?"

"'Course not. Miss Martha can stay. But the dog gotta go. *Sabato.*"

"Humph!" Lucy waved her hand in disgust and stormed past

us, heading for the stairs to the bunk rooms. "Over my dead body," she muttered.

My mother tugged on my arm. "Celeste? Celeste? What does the night lady mean, the dog has to go? Not Dandy. She's not talking about Dandy, is she?"

By the time I calmed my mother down, gave Sarge a piece of my mind for talking about the dog in front of her, and got my mom upstairs and ready for bed, it was almost ten o'clock. Eleven in Virginia! Was it too late to call? I ran down to my office and picked up the phone . . . and then put it back in its cradle.

What was I going to say?

Early tomorrow. Mike said I could call early in the morning. All right. I'd sleep on it and call first thing in the morning.

Except . . . I couldn't sleep. The bunk room felt stuffy and crowded. Tanya and Sammy took up the fourth bunk. Lucy's snoring grated on my raw nerves. And seeing Mom's tears as she'd hugged Dandy good night before crawling into her bunk was about the last straw. The next day loomed like a hangman's noose outside my prison cell. I had to decide one way or another about the boys . . . had to find a foster home for Dandy before the Battle Ax called the pound . . . and it was the weekend! No Mabel to talk to. Would Estelle be in to cook lunch? I had no idea. Edesa and Josh had no reason to come in, unless Josh just happened to drop by to hang out with the kids. Even Harry Bentley didn't work at Richmond Towers on the weekend.

Wait. Jodi Baxter was scheduled to teach a Saturday typing class at eleven. Maybe I could talk to her! Except . . . eleven o'clock would be too late.

I needed to talk to someone *now*. But who?

"Come to me . . . all you who are burdened and carrying heavy loads . . ."

I remembered the Voice in my spirit and the verse I'd read in Matthew's gospel. That left God. I'd have to talk to God.

Slipping quietly out of bed, I tiptoed to the door, opened it, and listened. All was quiet. Maybe I could sit in the tiny lounge here on this floor if no one was sleeping out there, which some-times happened. As I slipped out, Dandy squeezed out right behind me. "No, no, go back, Dandy," I hissed, trying to shove him back into the bunk room. But he wouldn't budge. I sighed. "Oh, all right," I whispered. "But if you alert Sarge, your name is mud."

The lounge was empty. Just a few stuffed chairs covered with cotton throws, a futon that had seen better days, and a table lamp. I wished I had my Bible, but it was downstairs in my office. Well, just as well. I'd keep the light off and just pray.

Curling up on a chair, I pulled the cotton throw around my shoulders. Dandy stretched out at my feet. *God,* I prayed silently, *You've been calling me to come to You. But it seems like I keep getting kicked off the path! Please . . . please lead me down the right path. I don't know what to do!*

My prayer drifted into rehearsing the options I'd already dis-carded. The boys couldn't stay at the shelter—and probably wouldn't want to. Probably wouldn't want to stay with the Baxters either, even if they were invited. Well then . . . the boys could stay with Philip! Except . . . he was moving out of the penthouse next week. But where? Would he have room for the boys? Or would he take them right back to Virginia?

God! I'm going in circles here!

And then the answer dropped into my spirit, like a flashing road sign. *Leave the boys in Virginia for the month of July.* I'd resisted the idea with every fiber of my being. It felt like I'd be giving in, letting Philip win! But . . . if I asked myself, *What's best for the boys right now?* given that I was living in a shelter and didn't know how soon I could get an apartment, or how quickly Lee Boyer could push through the custody petition—the answer was clear. Don't keep jerking Paul and P. J. around. Let them stay with their grand-parents. One month wasn't the end of the story. I still had two months to get them back here in time for school. And P. J. could go to lacrosse camp, like he wanted—

A low growl broke my concentration. "Dandy! Hush!" I hissed, kicking at the dog with a bare foot. But he was already on his feet, nose pointed toward the stairwell. I reached for him and felt his body tense. The rumble in his throat persisted, and he padded silently toward the stairwell.

Scrambling out of the chair, I tried to stop him. He probably heard Sarge or the other night assistant—a social work intern from a local college—doing their rounds. But I was too late. Dandy had already disappeared down the stairwell.

I followed as quickly as I could. *Good grief!* Just what I needed, for Dandy to tangle with Sarge in the middle of the night. Animal Control would be here at daybreak.

Aha . . . there he was, crouched at the staircase leading down to the lower level. One good grab and—

I stopped. Muffled noises and several thumps from below was followed by a voice snarling, "Shut up." My heart triple-timed. A *man's* voice!

At that instant, Dandy scrabbled down the staircase like a cougar after its prey. I tried to scream, "Dandy! Come back!"—

but nothing came out of my mouth. Instead I heard Dandy barking fiercely, and then—

"Call him off! . . . Umph!" *A man's voice!* "Get that dog off me—Ow! Ow! My hand! You—" A string of gutter words filled my ears as I stood frozen on the stairs. "Call him off, I tell you, or I'll cut him!"

And then a yelp of pain.

Dandy!

chapter 12

Without thinking, I burst into the open dining area in time to see a dark shape flying through the air and drop to the floor with another yelp as though in pain. "Dandy!" I screeched—and that's when I saw a stocky, dark figure whirl toward me.

"Watch out!" a woman's voice yelled. "He's got a knife!"

The dim room came into focus, as though time had stopped. Dandy lying on the floor . . . Sarge jerking her body back and forth on a chair . . . the blade of a kitchen knife gleaming in the glow of the EXIT sign . . .

But as the dark figure suddenly lunged toward me, Dandy scrambled to life and leaped, grabbing the man's wrist in his mouth. The man yelled. Man and dog fell to the floor. I heard, rather than saw, the knife clatter to the floor, skidding toward me.

"Grab the knife, Fairbanks!" Sarge yelled. "And untie me—now!" Adrenaline pulsing, I snatched up the knife.

Dandy still had the man's wrist gripped in his teeth, shaking it and holding on even as the man flailed about on the floor, hitting the dog with his other hand, trying to shake him off. A few feet away, Sarge half rose from the chair she was sitting in, but it came with her. That's when I saw that her hands were tied to the back of the chair with what looked like a dish towel.

"Fairbanks!" Sarge snapped. "Now!" Coming to life, I dropped the knife at her feet and loosened the clumsy knots. In two seconds Sarge was free. She snatched up the knife, breathing heavily. "Call 9-1-1. I've got it now."

I ran for my office phone. As I punched in the emergency numbers, I heard the man yell, "Call off the dog! He's tearing my hand off!"

"Lie still, buster. Then we'll call off the dog."

I quickly told the emergency operator we had an intruder with a knife at the Manna House Women's Shelter and gave the address. "Keep the line open," the operator said. "Cars are on the way. Do you need an ambulance?"

"No . . . yes!" *Oh God, what if Dandy really hurt that guy?*

Still clutching the phone, I stepped back out into the dining room. The night assistant clattered down the stairs, followed by Tina carrying a kid's plastic bat and several other residents who'd heard the commotion.

"Turn the lights on!" Sarge ordered. She had the knife pointed at the guy's chest. Even with the light on I couldn't tell his race or age beneath the scruffy, week-old beard and knit hat pulled low. He was moaning, wide eyes darting between his captor and Dandy, who crouched on the floor, mouth still locked on the man's wrist.

"Somebody tie his free hand to that table leg there. Tie his feet too. Get those dish towels or an extension cord—anything!"

Still holding the phone, I grabbed the dish towels the man had used to tie Sarge to the chair, and between the three of us—me, the college intern, and Tina, looking like a Puerto Rican Amazon carrying that plastic bat—we got the man's ankles tied and his free hand "handcuffed" to a table leg.

"Okay, Fairbanks. Call the dog off—and we better wrap something around this sucker's wrist. There's a lot of blood there."

I knelt down, my whole body shaking from the trauma of the past few minutes. "Let go, Dandy. Good boy . . . it's okay." Dandy let loose of the man's wrist, still crouching by his side. "Good boy. Come on, now . . . here, boy."

Dandy tried to rise, but let out a whine and sank back to the floor. Then, with an effort, he crawled away a few feet, using only his back legs and one of his front paws.

A wide smear of blood followed in his wake.

"No!" I cried, falling to my knees beside him. "He's hurt! Dandy's hurt!"

A dizzy hour later, I found myself pacing in the waiting room of a twenty-four-hour animal hospital, while somewhere behind closed doors a vet worked on the slashing knife wounds on Dandy's shoulder and chest. Lucy had appeared in baggy flannel pajamas just as the police were hauling the intruder to the ambulance outside, and she insisted on coming along when a nice young policeman offered to drive Dandy and me to the vet. He even put the siren on and raced through half a dozen red lights.

I barely remembered running upstairs to shed my bloody silk pajamas, pulling on a pair of jeans and a T-shirt, and grabbing bath towels to wrap Dandy in. Thankfully, my mother had slept through the whole thing.

In the police car, Lucy had held Dandy's head in her lap,

stroking his ears gently and murmuring encouraging words. But now she sat huddled in a corner, eyes streaming beneath the purple knit hat jammed on her head and swiping her nose with the back of her hand. I finally got a wad of toilet paper from a bathroom and stuffed it into her hand.

Before leaving us at the vet, the police officer—his name tag said Krakowski—had taken my statement of what happened. But the streetlights had dimmed and early morning fingers of light were tapping the rooftops by the time the vet came out. The good news was, the knife had not punctured any vital organs. The bad news was that the wound had torn muscles and tendons in the shoulder and chest, and might affect how well Dandy could walk in the future. The vet had to do about fifty internal stitches and twice that many external stitches. Did we want to leave him there for a day or two to rest?

Lucy emphatically shook her head. "Ain't gonna let that dog outta my sight. Miz Martha gonna want to see him, too, or she's gonna be mighty upset."

To my surprise, Officer Krakowski showed up to take us back to the shelter. "He's a hero, you know," the officer said, carrying a doped-up Dandy to the squad car and laying him carefully on the backseat. "The whole precinct is talking about him."

Lucy scrambled into the back from the other side, so I ended up in the front seat. "So, uh, the intruder guy," I ventured. "Was he hurt very bad?"

Officer Krakowski laughed. "The perp? Could've been worse. He's got some scratches and bites on his wrist, but if Dandy had been serious, his teeth could have punctured an artery. They got the guy patched up in the ER, and they're booking him down at the precinct."

Thank You, God. The way he'd been yelling, I was afraid Dandy had done serious damage, and, intruder or not, the guy would probably have sued us.

Officer Krakowski glanced sideways at me. "Just one thing. Dandy's up to date on all his shots, right? The hospital wanted to know."

Good grief! How would I know? My mom was so forgetful. I twisted in my seat belt. "Lucy. Does Dandy have a rabies tag on his collar?"

"Yeah. Somethin' like that."

"What's it say?"

Silence in the backseat. I twisted further. Lucy was glowering at me. "Can't see so good back here," she finally muttered.

"Don't worry about it," the police officer said. "We'll check it when we get him inside."

I glanced at my watch as we turned the corner by the Laundromat. Almost six thirty. I hadn't slept a wink all night. My eyes were so heavy I could barely keep them open. But it would be awhile before I got a chance to catch a nap. First thing I had to do was make a call to Virginia . . .

"See? What did I tell you? This city loves a hero." Officer Krakowski was grinning.

The squad car had pulled up in front of Manna House, and immediately we were surrounded by a flock of reporters and cameramen. Microphones were shoved in my face as we got out of the car. "Mrs. Fairbanks! Can you tell us what happened?" . . . "How badly is the dog hurt? How many times was he shot?" . . . "Why was the dog at the shelter? Is he homeless?"

I looked frantically at our police escort, but he was carefully lifting Dandy out of the car. Cameras clicked like little cap guns.

Dodging microphones and cameras as best I could, I scurried up the steps and rang the door buzzer, wishing I had my key—but of course I'd forgotten my purse, wallet, ID, keys. As soon as the door opened, I held it until Lucy and the officer had Dandy safely inside, then turned around to face the vultures.

"Uh, hi folks. It's been a stressful night, as you can all imagine. I'm sure Manna House will issue a statement as soon as possible. Please be patient." With what I hoped was a friendly smile, I escaped inside, pulling the big oak door shut behind me until I heard the lock click.

But inside the multipurpose room, another contingent crowded around Lucy and Officer Krakowski as the policeman gently laid Dandy on the closest couch. Even Mabel was there. No surprise. Sarge probably called her while the detectives were still taking statements. The excited residents in various stages of dress and undress were all talking at once. "Is he okay?" . . . "Aw, look, they shaved off all his purty hair on that side" . . . "How come I didn't hear nuthin'?" . . . "I wanna see!"

"All right, all right, back off, everybody," Sarge barked. "Let Miss Martha have a minute—it's her dog." The night manager ushered my mother, still in her nightgown, to the couch and got her settled beside Dandy, making sure she was comfortable.

I saw Mabel speak to Officer Krakowski, frown and nod; then the two of them headed in my direction. The officer handed me a card. "Checked the tag. The dog's good. Call me if you need anything." He jerked his head toward the front doors that held the media at bay and smiled. "Good luck. You're going to need it."

Mabel saw him out.

"Fairbanks?" The night manager showed up at my elbow. "You okay? Here—bet you could use some *caffe*, no? Just made it."

Sarge handed me a steaming Styrofoam cup. "Got someplace quiet you want to put Dandy so he can rest? Just say the word— I'll take him there."

If I wasn't so tired, I would have guffawed. Was this the same Sarge who'd been breathing threats about sending Dandy to the pound today?

"Thanks, Sarge." I took a sip of the hot coffee. Black, no cream. *Oh well.* "Guess my office is the best place for now, out of the way, if we can find some soft blankets or something. But first I need to—"

"Not to worry. Leave it to me." Sarge marched off on her search-and-recover mission.

My head ached. I wanted to go to my mother, who seemed bewildered by all the commotion. I really wanted to go to bed. But instead I made my way down to my office, flipped on the light, and pulled the pad with the Fairbanks' number on it toward me. I picked up the phone and dialed.

One ring . . . two . . . three . . . four—

"Mike? . . . It's Gabby. Sorry I didn't call last night. I needed time to decide what's best for the boys and . . ." I pressed my fingers against my eyes, willing the ache in my head and my heart to go away. "Anyway, I want to thank you for offering to send the boys back. But I've decided"—I had to push the words out—"I've decided they should stay there for the next few weeks. Let P. J. go to lacrosse summer camp. When camp is done, maybe things will be different here."

A moment later I hung up the phone, laid my head down on my arms, and wept.

chapter 13

A knock at the door made me grab for a wad of tissues and blow my nose. Lucy marched in with a tattered comforter that had seen better days, followed by Sarge carrying Dandy. Hovering behind them in the doorway, Tanya had an arm around my mother, who was still in her nightgown. "Tried to take her back upstairs to get dressed," Tanya whispered to me, "but she don't wanna leave the dog."

"That's okay." I slipped out of the tiny office so my mother could get in and supervise.

"He needs fresh water," she fussed. "And food in his bowl."

"Yeah, yeah," Lucy muttered, and marched out with the water bowl. We all knew Dandy wouldn't be eating or drinking anytime soon, but none of us were inclined to argue.

Sarge was next to leave. "Oh, Fairbanks, Mabel wants to see both of us soon as you get things squared away down here." She looked at her watch. "Breakfast stuff is on the counter. But I'd like to get out of here by eight if you—"

I nodded. "It's okay. I'm not hungry. Just let me get my mother settled and I'll be right up." *If I didn't fall over first.*

Tanya promised to get my mother fed and dressed when she was ready. Sammy eagerly said he'd "dog-sit," and I was surprised when my mother agreed. A lump caught in my throat. If my Paul knew that Dandy had been injured while protecting the shelter, he'd want to be the one sitting by the dog's "bedside."

Oh God! Did I make the right decision? Maybe I should have told the boys' grandfather to send them back here anyway and let the chips fall where they may!

Couldn't go there. I needed sleep. I needed . . . uhh, I was supposed to talk to Mabel. After pouring another cup of coffee from the carafe as I hustled through the multipurpose room, I knocked on Mabel's door and peeked in. Sarge was already hunkered on a chair, elbows on her knees. Mabel got up and gave me a quick hug. "Are you all right, Gabby?"

I offered a weak smile. "Been better. But I'll be okay." I sat down before my legs betrayed me.

Unlike her usual careful outfits, Mabel looked like she'd grabbed clothes off the floor without bothering to fix her face—a black silk headwrap still covered her hair—which wasn't surprising after getting a call from the shelter in the middle of the night. "We're all tired," she admitted, "so I don't want this to take long. Sarge already gave me a brief overview, but I'd like to hear again what happened from both of you, to get our facts straight." She jerked her head in the direction of the melee we knew was waiting outside. "I suppose we'll have to make a statement to the media before they'll go away."

I wagged my head. "How did they even know about this? We didn't call them!"

Sarge grunted. "Police scanners. Some reporters chase police stories like lawyers chase ambulances. If one of our residents had got cut up by the perp? The media couldn't care less. But a dog playing hero?"

My hackles rose. "Dandy wasn't playing! He knew something was wrong. I've never seen him act like that. He's usually a teddy bear!"

Sarge patted the air with her hand. *"D'accordo, d'accordo.* I am not blaming the dog. He saved my life, for all I know."

I stared at her. Frankly, I hadn't given much thought to what Sarge had endured during the night. "How . . . I mean, what happened before Dandy got there?"

"All right," Mabel interrupted. "Let's back up. Sarge, tell me again what happened."

The night manager shrugged. "The kid and I—Susan what's-her-face—"

"Susan McCall, your assistant," Mabel said.

"*Sí,* the kid. Anyway, we did rounds at midnight, everything was okay, *capisce?* Susan sacked out on a couch for a few z's, not a problem. I might have dozed . . . then I heard a sound downstairs. Didn't think much about it. Fairbanks, here, sometimes bends the rules and goes to her office in the middle of the night—"

I flushed but held my tongue.

"—but I decided to check. Made my way downstairs, and some tomfool is in the kitchen, rummaging around in the fridge. I thought it was one of the residents, helping herself to a midnight snack. So I yell, 'Hey!' Somebody turns out to be this big dude. He grabbed a knife—"

"Grabbed it?" Mabel asked. "He didn't have it with him?"

Sarge shook her head. "Saw him grab it out of the knife block. Definitely a Manna House knife. Then it happened so fast—that dude jumped over the counter and had that knife at my throat. Uh-uh, no way baby, not going to argue with a knife. Saw too many slit throats in Iraq . . ."

I gaped at her. I'd been so wrapped up in my own personal drama, I'd never given a thought to what Sarge had experienced in the military.

"Anyway, the perp found some dish towels and tied me to one of those plastic chairs. He was just about to stuff a gag in my mouth when"—Sarge broke into a laugh—"when all hell broke loose in the stairwell. Next thing I knew, that fur ball charges into the room, barking and snapping. It was dark, you know, so I am not sure exactly what happened. But the guy must have grabbed up the knife and cut him—kicked him too—because the dog yelped and went flying. That's when Fairbanks, here, showed up screaming bloody murder." Sarge volleyed the verbal ball at me. "Your turn."

I was so tired my memory felt blurry. But I admitted I couldn't sleep last night, so Dandy and I had been in the lounge upstairs. "Praying," I added. "Dandy heard something. I tried to stop him, but he was off like a shot . . ." I filled in the rest of the story as best I could.

Mabel had been listening intently and taking notes. When I finished, she jumped in. "Two questions. How did the intruder get in? And what did he want? Police said the side door off the gangway was unlocked when they arrived."

Sarge got defensive. "That door's always locked, except for deliveries. We don't let residents use it for any reason."

"Yes," Mabel shot back, "but it's your responsibility as night manager to check that *all* doors are locked every evening."

Ha. Part of me would have loved to let Sarge squirm after all the grief she'd given me about Dandy. But the night's events had been traumatic for her too—confronting the intruder alone, finding a knife at her throat, getting tied up.

"Uh, Mabel. I'm partly to blame as well. I saw the supper volunteers take trash bags out that side door and didn't think anything about it. I was on cleanup, the last one to leave, and I should have checked that door. But I had big problems on my mind and just wasn't thinking."

To my surprise, Sarge shot me a look that seemed almost . . . grateful.

Mabel finally leaned back. "Well, obviously, we need to tighten the security. When something like this happens, we all have to learn from it. We can't afford to make mistakes. We were fortunate this time. It could have been worse . . ."

I zoned out, impatient to talk to my mom, get some sleep, call the boys to tell them about Dandy, ask how they felt about staying another month in Virginia. But I tried to focus.

". . . a lot to be thankful for. We need to give God some serious praise around here! And no doubt about it, Dandy's the hero of the day. I'm so sorry he got hurt, Gabby. How's your mother taking it?"

I shook my head. "Haven't really talked to her. I'm not sure she understands. She gets confused when things get stressful. But I think she's doing all right for now. I just hope those reporters don't find out Dandy is her dog and shove those microphones in her face. She'd freak."

"Good point. Right now I think they assume Dandy is your dog, Gabby. Let's keep it that way."

Not that I wanted any microphones in my face either. "Uh, I

kind of promised we'd give them a statement soon, just so they'd let us get in the door." I looked at Mabel hopefully. "Would you . . . ?"

Mabel made a face. "All right. Hopefully, this will blow over soon. Most of our guests don't want—or need—media spotlight. Guess we should call a meeting of all the residents and make sure everybody has the straight story so we don't start a lot of rumors."

The three of us worked on a statement we hoped would satisfy the diehards still waiting outside. Finally Mabel stood up. "All right, while I'm giving our statement, would you two gather the residents in the multipurpose room? Sarge, can you stay a bit longer? Gabby, do we have anything scheduled this morning?"

I squeezed my eyes shut, trying to think. "Uh, yes, Jodi Baxter is coming to teach a typing class at eleven." I groaned inwardly. I'd had every intention of trying to talk with Jodi when she came this morning, thinking Mabel wouldn't be here. I still needed help sorting out the options the Legal Aid lawyer had presented to me. But now, all I could think of was sleep.

"Fine. We'll be done by then." Mabel started out of her office, then caught her reflection in the glass windows around the receptionist's cubby. "Oh, Lord, help me. You sure do have ways of keeping me humble." Our shelter director gave a short laugh, then gave a shrug and marched toward the front doors, crowned with her bedtime hair wrap.

I had to smile. Was that a prayer? Mabel talked to God like He was just another person sitting in on our conversation.

While Mabel was out facing the cameras, Sarge started rounding up the residents and I checked on Dandy—stretched out on his comforter, eyes closed, the bandages wrapped around his shaved chest and shoulder rising and falling with each labored breath. Eight-year-old Sammy sat patiently nearby.

"You okay, Sammy? You want a book to read? Or here . . ." I grabbed some blank paper and colored markers from my desk. "Would you like to draw?"

Tanya's boy nodded eagerly, took the paper and markers, and scrunched down on the floor. Then he looked up. "Some a' the other kids wanted ta come in, but I told 'em nobody s'posed ta be in your office but me. Ain't that right, Miz Gabby?"

"That's right, Sammy. For now, anyway." Smiling at his loyalty, I scurried back upstairs to the main floor, where residents were gathering just as Mabel came back through the double doors into the multipurpose room. I was glad to see my mother dressed in navy blue slacks and a clean—though wrinkled—white blouse, and her hair brushed. I slipped up to her, gave her a hug, and pulled a folding chair close.

Done with her statement, Mabel marched into the multipurpose room and clapped her hands. "Everybody here? Good. Ladies, quiet down . . . Hello! Ladies! We need to brief you about what happened last night, and—"

"'Scuse me, Miz Mabel!" Lucy's hand shot up.

"We'll have time for questions later, Lucy. First—"

"'Scuse me, Miz Mabel. We got somethin' ta say first, right, ladies?"

Murmurs all around. Mabel sighed. "All right, Lucy. What is it?"

Lucy poked Carolyn. "You go. They gonna listen to you, 'cause you got all that book learnin'."

"She would, *si te callaras la boca*, Lucy!" Tina hollered. Everybody laughed.

"Ladies, please . . ." Mabel looked frustrated.

Carolyn stood up. "Sorry, Mabel. We don't mean to joke. We've been talking—all the ladies here—about what happened last night, and we have a proposition to make."

Heads nodded all around the room. "That's right" . . . "Sí" . . . "Uh-huh" . . .

Lucy poked Carolyn again. "Get on with it."

"Lucy, if you poke me one more time, I'm—!" Snickers from the residents. "Anyway, we all know Dandy's been living here on borrowed time. Sarge has been saying he's got to be out of here by this weekend."

Sarge threw up her hands. "Well, not *today*. The dog's hurt."

"Exactly. Gramma Shep's dog got injured protecting all of us from an intruder. Hurt bad. So all of us here agree we owe him somethin'. We took a vote—"

Mabel's eyebrow went up.

"—and we all agree that Dandy should be made a resident of Manna House Women's Shelter as official watchdog."

The room erupted with cheers and claps from the residents, even Sheila, the big-chested woman who'd screeched like a banshee the first time I brought Dandy and my mom to the shelter for a visit. Carolyn handed Mabel a sheet of paper with a ballpoint pen clipped to the top. "See? We've all signed a petition."

Mabel glanced at the paper, a small smile tugging at the corner of her mouth, then handed it to Sarge. The night manager shrugged. "Humph. I'm overruled, no? City inspector might not like it, but tell you what . . ." Sarge grabbed the pen, laid the paper on the nearest end table, and signed it.

Now the residents did raise a cheer, laughing and slapping Sarge on the back. I saw Mabel turn her head toward the foyer as if listening to something, then slip out as Sarge passed the list of signatures to me.

I showed the paper to my mother, who had a fixed smile on her face, as if aware that something good was happening but not sure what it was. "Look at this, Mom! Everybody wants Dandy to stay here at the shelter as the official watchdog. Isn't that great?"

As I glanced over the list, I didn't see Lucy's name. But at the top, among the first few signatures, was a large, scrawled X.

My neck prickled. Was *that* why Lucy fussed about being asked to read Dandy's dog tag in the back of the squad car?

Lucy couldn't read!

A tap on my shoulder made me look up. "Gabby?" Mabel beckoned. "You've got a phone call. Take it in my office if you want to."

Strange. Who would be calling me? The boys? Maybe their granddad had told them they were staying in Virginia, and they wanted to talk to me. Or—

I picked up Mabel's phone. "Hello? Gabby Fairbanks speaking."

"Gabrielle!" My name was shouted in my ear like a cuss word. "What are you trying to do—ruin me?"

I recoiled from the phone in shock. *Philip!* But I took a deep breath and tried to collect my equilibrium. "What do you mean, ruin you? Why are you calling, Philip? This isn't exactly a good time. I've got a lot going on—"

"Yeah, I'll bet you do. Talking to reporters, splashing the Fairbanks name all over the news!"

I squeezed my eyes shut and pinched the bridge of my nose, trying to calm the voices shouting in my head. "Philip. I'm not—"

"Oh yeah? Turn on the TV! Of all the lowdown things to do,

making a spectacle of yourself. I'm supposed to play golf in an hour with one of our new clients today—now this!" He swore right in my ear. "Don't play innocent with me—I know what you're up to, Gabrielle. My mother always said you'd drag down the Fairbanks name someday!"

chapter 14

The phone went dead. Stunned, I stumbled through the multi-purpose room and into the TV room, turned on the set, and started flipping channels. *Cartoons . . . cartoons . . . home renovation . . . cooking show . . . news . . .*

There. Mabel Turner standing with the arched oak doors of the Manna House shelter at her back, camera lights bouncing off her maple-colored skin, finishing our carefully worded statement. *". . . grateful that no one was seriously hurt."*

Questions flew before she even had time to take a breath. *"Ms. Turner! Ms. Turner! You said the dog was treated by a vet—how badly was he hurt?" . . . "Who does the dog belong to?" . . . "Why was he at the shelter? Are you taking in homeless animals too?" . . . "Where's the dog now?" . . .*

"Oh brother," Mabel's voice breathed in my ear. I jumped. Where had Mabel come from? "The one time I'm on television and I look like I just fell out of bed."

". . . belongs to one of our staff," Mabel was saying on air, *"and just happened to be here last night. Fortunately."* She smiled into the cameras. *"Thank you. That's all."*

Aware that others were pushing into the small TV room and peering over our shoulders, I deliberately slowed my breathing. That was it? Mabel had been very careful not to give out any personal information. *What is Philip's problem?* But just then, the TV camera zoomed in on a perky blonde reporter with perfect makeup and a big microphone, saying, "Earlier this morning, a squad car brought back the shelter's hero, a mutt named Dandy . . ." The footage showed Officer Krakowski lifting Dandy out of the car, swathed in bandages, followed by Lucy Tucker in her pajama bottoms, sweatshirt, and purple knit hat—and me, running up the steps and leaning on the door buzzer, pulling it open until the trio got inside, then turning around while voices yelled, *"Mrs. Fairbanks! Mrs. Fairbanks! Can you—"*

Close-up of Gabby Fairbanks, bags under my eyes, snarly chestnut curls that hadn't seen a comb or brush (or a haircut) since who knew when, and chirping, *"Uh, hi folks. It's been a stressful night, as you can all imagine. I'm sure Manna House will issue a statement as soon as possible. Please be patient."*

Residents all around me babbled with excitement. "Hey, Lucy! You were on TV!" . . . "Didja hear that? They called Dandy a mutt! Stupid reporters." . . . "Me? On TV? Where?" . . .

But their chatter was drowned out by the TV voices echoing in my head—*"Mrs. Fairbanks! Mrs. Fairbanks!"*—and Philip's snarl on the phone: *". . . making a spectacle of yourself . . . always said you'd drag down the Fairbanks name someday!"*

I never did get a nap that morning. Jodi Baxter showed up to teach her class, along with Estelle, who flounced in like a mini tidal wave, muttering that leftovers—the usual fare for weekend lunches, I gathered—would not do after the trauma of such a night. She immediately set about banging pots and pans and cooking something that began to smell mighty good.

"We saw it on the news," Jodi told me. "Actually, Denny and I heard screeching upstairs, and the next thing we knew, Stu was pounding on our back door, telling us to turn on the TV."

It took me a few seconds to remember that "Stu" and Estelle were housemates, and they lived above Josh's parents in a two-flat. One day I'd get it figured out.

"But what's this Josh and Edesa are telling me?" Jodi reached out and rested her hand lightly on my arm. I was aware of her gentle touch, and for some reason I wanted to cry. "Your husband locked you out, and you and your mother moved into the shelter?" Her eyes were round with disbelief, as if saying the words aloud felt like telling a fib.

I gave a little nod, afraid my high water mark was ready to breach and I'd soon be a blubbery mess right then and there. "Yeah, well . . ." I grabbed a tissue from my jeans pocket and blew my nose. Wasn't sure how coherent I'd be on no sleep, but I really did want to talk to Jodi. "Um, if you don't have to run off right after your typing class, I'd . . . guess I would like to talk to you."

"Sure! Besides, I'd never hear the end of it if I left before Estelle's sacrificial lunch offering. Cooking and sewing—that's how she blesses people. Oh! Speaking of blessings! I need a few strong arms to carry in a couple of computers from our minivan. Software Symphony donated two more used computers to the schoolroom." Jodi eyed me slyly beneath the bangs of her shoulder-length brown bob. "Of course, I bugged Peter Douglass about it mercilessly when I realized more women signed up to learn word processing skills than Manna House had computers."

I couldn't help but grin. Jodi Baxter wouldn't exactly turn heads on the street, but she could turn a few hardheads into giving up what she needed. Sarge was gone, but I rounded up Carolyn and Tina to help Jodi and me bring in the computers, monitors, and keyboards. We made space for the equipment on the long table in the schoolroom that already held two computers, as Carolyn lifted the mass of wires and plugs out of a box. "Hm. Might be able to get these up and running for you," she murmured. "Not in time for today's class, though."

I raised my eyebrows. What other talents lay underneath Carolyn's scraggly ponytail?

Kim and Wanda showed up for Jodi's typing class, along with one of the new residents, named Althea, who seemed to be Mediterranean-something. Sicilian? Turkish? She spoke good English—easier to understand than Wanda's Jamaican patois. Jodi seemed comfortable, though, so I slipped down to my office to check on Dandy. Lucy was parked on my chair, leaning on the desk with her elbow, wrinkled hand holding up her head, which was still crowned in the purple knit hat, and snoring away.

"Lucy!" I shook her awake. "Go upstairs and get a nap. I'll take over."

"*Umph . . . gurkle . . .* huh? Whatchu want, Fuzz Top? I ain't sleepin'."

"It's okay. You had a short night." *Huh. Didn't we all.* "Besides, I need to use my office."

"Humph. Okay." The phone rang just as Lucy hauled herself up from my chair. "You want me ta get that?" Without waiting for an answer, she snatched up the desk phone. "Miz Gabby's office . . . Oh yeah? . . . Okay, I'll tell her." She hung it up. "You've got a visitor."

I stiffened. A visitor? Philip wouldn't . . . would he? "Did whoever's on the desk say who it is?"

Lucy shrugged. "Only one way ta find out. C'mon."

I followed meekly. If it was Philip, having Lucy pave the way wasn't a bad idea. She wouldn't take any guff from him. Or maybe it was just some reporter . . . Good grief. I'd almost rather talk to Philip. Didn't the media know they were stirring up a hornet's nest in my corner?

But my visitor was neither.

"Mr. Bentley!" I cried as Lucy and I came through the double doors into the foyer. The doorman from Richmond Towers— wearing slacks, a nice button-down shirt, and a tweed golf hat hiding his bald head, instead of his blue uniform and cap—stood holding a big bag of something. And next to him, carrying a couple of plastic store bags, stood his wide-eyed grandson. But the boy's name had slipped my mind. "Uh, hi, young man. What brings you guys here two days in a row?"

"We saw the story about your dog on TV!" the boy piped up. "Grandpa said it belongs to your mama."

Mr. Bentley looked a little embarrassed. "Yeah, DeShawn wanted us to bring something for the hero dog." He hefted the load in his arms—a twenty-five-pound bag of dog food. "DeShawn has some stuff too—rawhide bone, dog toy, you know."

"Yeah, but Grandpa! Who brought all that other stuff out there?" DeShawn tipped his head toward the front doors.

The boy had a beautiful face—large, dark eyes, smooth skin, an impish grin lurking beneath the surface. He looked up at Mr. Bentley with obvious respect. I stared, fascinated. Then what he said finally penetrated my brain. "Uh, what other stuff?"

Lucy was two beats ahead of me, already pushing the doors open. "Uh-oh."

"'Uh-oh' what?" I peered over her shoulder, then pushed the doors open wider.

The steps of the Manna House shelter were stacked with bags of dry dog food, towers of canned dog food, dog toys, dog chews, dog treats, and homemade posters in childish scrawls: *Dandy the Hero! Chicago loves Dandy! Get well, Dandy!*

And a plethora of stuffed toy dogs sat atop the doggy loot— big ones, little ones, yellow and brown and spotted ones, with cute faces and floppy ears—like a child's menagerie sprawled all over a lumpy bedspread.

chapter 15

I stared at the gifts piled high on the shelter steps, touched by the generosity of total strangers. But something felt out of whack. All this fuss over an injured dog—and I was grateful, I really was. But I felt embarrassed. Most homeless people in Chicago were invisible to the general population, except for the sleeping bodies here and there, dotting the parks or slumped in an out-of-the-way doorway. The *Streetwise* vendors were tolerated by most, even respected by some, but homeless families like Tanya and Sammy . . . who cared?

"Well, better get this stuff inside. Could rain this afternoon. C'mon, DeShawn." Mr. Bentley put his load down in the foyer, then started hauling bags of dog food and stuffed toys inside. I saw a couple of people with cameras lurking across the street, snapping pictures before the piles disappeared.

Lucy and I started picking up the toys. "Aw, this here dog is cute," Lucy said, holding up a floppy yellow dog with a big face and big paws.

507

"It's yours, Lucy," I said. "From Dandy. Next to my mom, you're his favorite person."

"Ya think so?" Lucy allowed a big grin, showing her missing teeth.

Once everything was inside the foyer, Mr. Bentley straightened, hand on his back. "Now, where do ya want this stuff, Mrs. Fairbanks? Seems like all I'm doin' lately is hauling your stuff around." He rolled his eyes—but then winked at me.

"You've done enough, Mr. B. I'll get some other volunteers to move this stuff once we figure out what to do with it . . . oh! There's the lunch bell. DeShawn, you and your grandpa are invited for lunch. Estelle showed up this morning, decided to wrap up our hair-raising experience with a good meal."

Mr. Bentley chuckled. "Sounds like Miss Estelle. Some woman."

I noticed I didn't have to ask him twice.

Estelle's lunch perked up everyone's spirits. She put Jodi to work after the typing class, and they served up teriyaki chicken, rice, fruit salad, and pineapple upside-down cake for dessert. A couple of the board members who'd seen the news clips showed up—Liz Handley and Peter Douglass with his wife, Avis—to make sure everyone was all right and to huddle with Mabel about how to deal with the media. Estelle must have anticipated extra mouths, because she made everyone eat and still had leftovers.

I tried to save a couple of seats for Mr. Bentley and his grandson at the table where I parked my mom, but when I looked up, they'd been hijacked to the table with the Douglasses. When Jodi finally got to eat, she and Avis got their heads together about something. Even Mr. B and Peter seemed to be talking like old times. Huh. I invite Mr. Bentley *one time* to our Fun Night here at the shelter, and suddenly he's everybody's best friend.

Still, Jodi did say she'd like to talk to me, so I tried to hurry my mother along, hoping to grab Jodi before she left. But Mom would not be hurried. "Mm, that upside-down cake is good. But I need coffee with something sweet. Gabby, would you—?"

I jumped up to get the coffee, thinking it was as good as any time to speak to Jodi. But Mabel got to me first. "Gabby, better ask for some volunteers to help you move the stuff in the foyer. Guess you can put it down here in the rec room for now. But you better keep checking the front steps—I don't think we've seen the end of it yet."

Oh brother. I'd almost forgotten about the glut of "dog stuff" upstairs. With a sigh, I got Mom's coffee, then caught Jodi Baxter on her way up to the counter with her dirty dishes.

"Jodi! I'd really like to talk to you, but I've got to do something about all the stuff total strangers have been leaving on the doorstep. And I don't want to keep you waiting . . ."

"Oh, that's okay. Let me help." She grinned. "Denny and Josh are doing some plumbing thing over at their apartment. The only thing waiting for me at home is a dirty kitchen floor and two baskets of laundry to fold. I'd rather play with those stuffed animals—oh." She dumped her dirty dishes and pulled me aside. "Actually, I'd really love to meet Dandy. Is he—?"

"In my office." I eyed the closed door. "But let's wait till the dining room clears out. I'll grab a few more people to help haul stuff, and maybe by that time—whoa! What's this?"

Tina clattered down the stairs, hefting a bag of dog food over her shoulder, followed by several of the other residents, arms loaded. "Where does this stuff go?" Tina demanded. "I got one more trip."

I pointed to the rec room. "Uh, Jodi, could you help organize stuff in there? I'll go upstairs and see what's going on."

Squeezing up the staircase past several of the kids coming down, arms full of stuffed animals and posters, I ran into Lucy at the top, who'd planted herself squarely in the way of anyone coming up from the dining room. "Two trips, missy. With as much as you can carry 'fore you go to the beauty shop or take a nap, whichever is gonna revive that fuzz top o' yours—hey! Hey, Sheila! Ever'body's gotta take two loads a' stuff outta the foyer and get it downstairs 'fore they do anything else! Means you, sister! You signed the official mascot petition, din'tcha? Well?"

I scurried to the foyer and got my first armload. "Thanks, Lucy," I said on my way back to the stairs.

"Huh. Don't thank *me*. Them that can run up an' down stairs get to carry stuff. Them that can't get to boss all the rest a' ya." But she allowed a grin for the second time that day—then hollered after me, "An' ya better check the front steps! Bunch more stuff showed up during lunch!"

Many hands did make light work, to prove the cliché, and Estelle was shutting down the kitchen as we deposited the last bag of dog food in the rec room. Jodi had done a great job, storing most of it out of the way under the Ping-Pong table, the rest in black plastic garbage bags in the corners behind the bean bag chairs. On the spur of the moment, I grabbed an armload of the cutest stuffed doggies and went hunting for young Sammy. "Here, buddy, I have a job for you. Give one to each of the kids here at Manna House, okay? And choose one for yourself."

I was rewarded with a high five.

"What are you going to do with all this?" Jodi asked as I unlocked my office.

I shook my head. "I dunno. Can't think yet. Well . . . there he is. The Manna House Hero."

Dandy lifted his head as I turned on the light. Jodi immediately got down on the floor beside him. "Hey there, Dandy, good boy." She spoke softly, crooning his name, gently stroking his matted neck hair. The dog licked her hand. "Aw, Gabby. He's so sweet." Dandy laid his head back down under her gentle petting. "We used to have a dog. A chocolate Lab. We named him Willie Wonka. He died a couple of years ago, just old age. I still really miss him . . ."

I sat quietly in my desk chair while she petted Dandy. Then she turned her head to me, still sitting on the floor. "Gabby, I still want to hear why you and your mom and Dandy here are staying at the shelter. But I've been thinking . . . would you like to come stay at our house for the weekend? We've got a couple of empty bedrooms right now—I mean, Amanda's home from college, but she went with the youth from our church on a mission trip and won't be back for another week."

"Oh, Jodi. That's so nice. But I can't leave Dandy right now. And my mom—"

"I meant all three of you! Actually, thinking about Dandy's injury gave me the idea. I mean, we've got a backyard, well, at least there's some grass, and it's only a few steps from the porch to the yard. We could make a bed for Dandy on the porch since the weather's decent, give him a few days to recover from his injury and a place to be outside when he's ready. Sheesh! Stay the whole week if you'd like."

I stared at her. The idea of sleeping in a room all to myself instead of a bunk room with four other people, one of whom snored like a chainsaw, sounded like an ad for a vacation in Tahiti. The media couldn't find me or Dandy . . . maybe they'd go away. *Huh.* Philip couldn't find me either—I needed another phone call like the one this morning like I needed a root canal. Mom wouldn't have to climb stairs . . . and what Jodi said about Dandy being able to recover away from hordes of admirers and curiosity seekers was downright brilliant.

"Oh, Jodi. Are you sure? I mean, I have to come to work Monday—"

"So?" She got to her feet and brushed dog hair off her slacks. "Take the El. Josh and Edesa do it all the time from Rogers Park. I'm off for the summer. Your mom and Dandy can stay with me."

Of course I could take the El. That's how I'd been getting to work before the fallout with Philip. I'd just have to allow a little more time. But leaving my mother with the Baxters during the day . . . that seemed like too much. Didn't Jodi have to check with her husband?

Still . . .

I grinned. "Okay . . . why not? At least for the weekend, I mean." I jumped up and gave Jodi a big hug. "Thanks, Jodi." I had to push the words past the lump in my throat. "Thanks so much. I can't begin to tell you what a gift this is."

It still took us a good hour to let Mabel know the plan and check out for the weekend, pack a bag for my mother and myself, gather up a garbage bag of laundry to do, and enlist Tina's help carrying Dandy out to the Baxters' minivan. We took him out the lower side door into the gangway and met Jodi and the minivan in the alley to avoid dozens of questions about why the official watchdog was suddenly leaving—making sure the door got locked again this time, of course. But I did make a point to let Lucy know what was happening.

She was not a happy camper.

"Why all a' sudden you think that other lady can take better care o' that dog than me, huh? Didn't you say next to Gramma Shep that I was his fav'rite people?" The scowl on her face was deep enough to hide a quarter in.

"That's not it at all, Lucy! It's just a quieter place for a few days. Fewer people. A yard where he can get up and walk around without attracting lots of attention—you know, out there." I pointed to the front doors. "And we'll be back in a few days."

Lucy turned and stomped off like Billy Goat Gruff across his wooden bridge. "Huh. Of all the dang-blasted . . ."

I didn't hear the rest of her muttering. Probably just as well.

My mother seemed bewildered by the sudden upset to her shelter routine, and I realized with a guilty stab that Martha Shepherd hadn't been outside the building the entire week—not since Mabel had agreed she qualified as "homeless" and could sign up on the bed list. But when Mom realized Dandy was coming along, she meekly submitted to me snapping her into the seat belt in the second seat of the Dodge Caravan.

"Wait!" I told Jodi as she started the engine. "Didn't Estelle come with you? Where is she? I didn't see—"

Jodi laughed. "Don't worry about Estelle. Harry Bentley and his grandson took her home."

Harry Bentley. Jodi and I looked at each other. "Ah. Young love," she said, and we both cracked up.

Jodi found a through street that took her to Lake Shore Drive and headed north. I leaned back against the headrest of the front passenger seat and watched the parkland next to the lake fly by, the paths full of joggers, people walking dogs, parents pushing strollers, and bikers in Spandex and helmets weaving in and out, somehow managing to avoid running over anyone. And beyond that, Lake Michigan, a peaceful, flat line against the far horizon.

The second wind that had kept me going so far that day started to fizzle, and I felt my eyelids getting heavy. *Oh God, thank You . . . It feels so good to just sit, to be taken care of just a little bit . . .*

chapter 16

"Gabby? We're here."

"What?" I opened my eyes. Jodi was pulling the minivan into a two-car garage, next to a candy-apple-red Hyundai. "Oh, I'm sorry! I must have fallen asleep." I glanced back into the second seat. "Good grief. We all slept like zombies—except you, I hope."

Jodi laughed. "Got you here, didn't I? Come on. I'll see if Denny's here to carry Dandy inside."

I shook my mom awake and helped her out of the car. "Nice car," I murmured as we threaded our way past the Hyundai. "Denny's?"

"Ha! Doesn't he wish. No, it belongs to Stu, our friend who lives upstairs. Estelle's housemate."

Denny Baxter, it turned out, was sprawled in a recliner in the living room, watching Saturday afternoon sports with two young cats parked on his chest, and he didn't seem the least bit fazed that his wife showed up with three extra warm bodies who were going to "stay the weekend," as she put it. "Hey, great," he said, dumping the cats. "And you brought Hero Dog? Ha! About time these two got dethroned." He jerked a playful thumb at the disgruntled cats. Two big dimples creased his cheeks.

Jodi got iced tea for Mom and me, while Denny brought up a large cushiony dog bed from their basement and put it on the back porch near the porch swing. "I knew we'd need this again someday," Jodi said. "Couldn't bear to throw it out after Wonka died."

Denny carried a whimpering Dandy from the backseat of the minivan and settled him gently on the dog bed while Jodi showed us to our "guest rooms." "Take your pick," she said. "Sorry about all of Amanda's stuff in here. Even Josh left some of his stuff here when he got married. Can't blame him, though—their apartment is no bigger than a postage stamp . . . Say, do you guys want to finish your naps? You've had a long day—hey! Patches! Peanuts! Get out of here." She snatched up the two cats—big kittens really, one calico and the other mostly black with white paws—and disappeared.

I was so tempted to crash. But it was already four o'clock. Told myself I should probably gut it out and just get a good night's sleep that night. But I encouraged Mom to lie down in Josh's old room—it had the least paraphernalia to trip over—with a light afghan over her, then made my way back through the Baxters' dining room and kitchen and out onto the back porch to check on Dandy.

Jodi was in the porch swing, husking corn on the cob. "I think the squeak of this old swing put Dandy to sleep." She grinned, stopped the swing, and patted the seat beside her. "Come sit. You okay?"

I sat. The Baxters' backyard was narrow, with straggly flower beds running along the fence on both sides. The neighboring buildings were a combination of similar two-flats—brick, tidy, their garages facing an alley running behind the houses—and three-story apartment buildings. Trees lining the next street over and the occasional backyard softened the cityscape. A bird feeder hung from the corner of the Baxters' garage, and flower boxes decorated the railings of the back porch.

A far cry from the Fairbanks' parklike suburban home in Virginia, the lush lawn spilling over with flowering bushes and flower beds. And yet this tiny urban yard felt like an oasis of peace. "Incredible," I murmured.

"Yeah, well, my family likes to pretend I have a green thumb. Denny made the flower boxes, and Amanda stenciled them—but the flowers would all be dead if Stu and Estelle didn't help me out."

I shook my head. "Didn't mean the flower boxes. You and your husband . . . I mean, you brought me *and* my mom *and* a sick dog home without even telling him, and he didn't bat an eye."

"Oh, Denny. He's pretty unflappable." She laughed—then stopped herself when she saw the tears sliding down my face. "Sheesh. I'm sorry, Gabby. Me and my big mouth . . . Do you want to talk about it?"

I mopped my eyes with a bedraggled tissue I pulled out of my jeans pocket and shrugged. "Don't even know where to start . . ."

Jodi laid a hand on my arm. "Try the beginning. When did you two meet?"

Jodi was a good listener, asking a question from time to time, but mostly just letting me talk. And once I started, I could hardly stop. Not sure how she put it all together, because I jumped all over the place. Even told her about getting jilted by Damien, my high-school Romeo who turned out to be Casanova instead. "But Philip was different. He never messed with other women. I thought he really loved me . . ." I bit my lip. "And I loved him. Still do, I guess. My heart used to do flip-flops every time he walked in the room. He used to hold me, whisper in my ear, tell me I added spice to his life . . ."

Jodi handed me a clean tissue and waited patiently through another torrent of tears.

"But then . . . I dunno. He and his dad didn't get along in the business. Philip started trying to prove himself or something. Now he . . . he's like a different person! Not overnight or any-thing—guess that's the problem. Not sure when things started to go south. I got used to feeling like I was in his way, started second-guessing everything I said or did, worried about how he might react. And then . . . then this move to Chicago. Suddenly I felt like I'd landed on Mars, gasping for air . . ."

It was hard telling Jodi about Philip refusing to let my mother stay with us, deliberately losing the dog, and then locking me out of my own home. Jodi with her "unflappable" husband. Kind Denny. Funny Denny. Easygoing Denny . . .

I blinked back the hot tears that seemed to lurk behind my eyeballs. *What did I do wrong to get treated like a dog?!*

I shook my head, trying to regain my composure. The *squeak, squeak* of the porch swing and birds flitting in the trees played like a simple melody against the far-off drone of traffic. I finally sighed. "Really, if I hadn't run into Lucy and ended up with the job at Manna House, I don't know what I would have done. Jumped off the roof or something."

"From what I've heard, Manna House considers you a blessing."

I looked sideways at Jodi. "Huh. Don't know about that. But . . . do you know what Mabel said to me when I applied for the job of program director? She said she believes God brought me to Chicago because He has a purpose for me at Manna House. Like that's the *real* reason God brought us here."

"Really?" Jodi's eyes went wide. "She said that?"

I nodded. "Sometimes that's the only thing I hold on to. That, and this note Edesa left for me the other night." I pulled the crumpled note out of my jeans pocket and handed it to her.

Jodi read it, absently tucking a strand of her shoulder-length brown hair behind one ear, a smile softening her pleasant features. She looked up. "Sounds like Edesa, all right. Isn't she something? She's older than Josh, you know—just a couple of years, but I think he fell in love with her while he was still in high school." She looked at the note again. "Hm. Isaiah 49. Yeah, I love that verse. 'See, I have engraved you on the palms of my hands . . .' Powerful stuff. Did you read the rest of the chapter?"

I nodded. "Like a dozen times. But I don't know what she meant by that." I pointed to the last line of the note.

Jodi read it aloud. "'Dear Gabrielle, your parents gave you the right name. Live it!'" Now her smile widened. "Well, let's find out!"

"Find out? What do you mean?"

She jumped up and pulled me off the swing. "Come on."

Two minutes later Jodi had booted up the computer in their dining room, which seemed to double as the family office, and was clicking through Web sites. I hunched over her shoulder, wondering what she was doing. "How do you spell your name?"

she murmured. "Gabrielle, not Gabby." She typed it into a search box as I spelled it out.

A moment later a page came up. *Feminine Names and Their Meanings*, it said. Jodi read it aloud: "'Gabrielle. Meaning: Strong woman of God.'"

She turned away from the computer and, to my surprise, took my face in her hands. "'Strong woman of God' . . . Yes, that's it, Gabby. Live your name."

A male voice sailed down the hall from the living room. "Jodi! When's supper?"

"When you fire up the grill so we can throw on some chicken!" Jodi yelled back. She looked at me sideways and snorted. "Men!"

I was glad for the interruption. *Strong woman of God?* Maybe somebody else. How was I supposed to "live my name" when right now I felt about as courageous as an overcooked noodle?

We had a pleasant evening, just hanging out on the Baxters' back porch. Denny donned a big apron and wielded a mean pair of tongs over the hot charcoal grill set a few feet from the porch. Stu and Estelle invited themselves for supper, thumping down the back outside stairs with a fresh fruit salad to go with the corn on the cob. My mom looked bright eyed, her cheeks pink after her nap, though she had a hard time keeping up with all the banter.

While we were eating, Dandy whined and struggled to get up, so Denny managed to get him into the yard, and the dog actually peed a little. Everyone on the porch clapped. "You go, Dandy!" Estelle yelled—and we all laughed at the pun.

And then I slept, curled up like a baby with one of Amanda Baxter's old teddy bears hugged against my chest . . . the first night I'd slept without nightmares or waking in panic since Philip locked me out of his life.

We went to church the next morning with Jodi and Denny. Estelle and Stu pulled out right behind us in the candy-apple-red Hyundai. As Denny drove into the parking lot of the shopping center that housed SouledOut Community Church, I felt as if I'd entered a time warp. Had it only been a *week* since Mom and I had come to church here while Philip took the boys on a sailing weekend with one of his clients? Only a week since he brought the boys home early, accusing me of losing that client over some dumb phone message I'd tried to deliver, and told me it was the last straw?

The longest week of my life.

I shook off the troubling thoughts. Didn't want to go there. Didn't want to lose the sense of peace that had surrounded me ever since Mom and I had walked through the Baxters' back door yesterday.

"Oh look, Gabby." Mom pointed shamelessly as we came into the "sanctuary" that had been created out of a large storefront. "That nice Mr. Bentley is here too. And he has his son with him. About Paul's age, isn't he?"

"Grandson, Mom. And he looks a little younger than Paul." Just the mention of my youngest wrapped coils of regret around my heart, but we smiled and waved at Mr. B, who was proudly introducing DeShawn to everyone who came within reach.

The music team started playing right then, and a young white man invited everyone to find a seat—"But don't sit down yet!"— and join in singing the first song.

"I thought Peter Douglass's wife was your worship leader," I whispered to Jodi.

"Avis? She's one of them. People take turns."

The young man did all right, I guess, but I'd kind of looked forward to the dignity and passion the middle-aged black woman had brought to the service the previous week. I had to smile as the keyboard, guitars, drums, and saxophone filled the room with music, inviting shoppers to peek in the glass windows along the large storefront. I'd been in Chicago for two and a half months, and in that time I'd gone to church more than I had in two and a half years—if I counted the Sunday Evening Praise at the shelter—and still hadn't stepped inside an actual church building.

Josh and Edesa Baxter came in late with Gracie in a back carrier as if they'd walked to church, and Edesa slipped me a hug before they found seats in the back.

The children up through middle school left for Sunday school classes before the sermon, but the African-American pastor—Pastor Cobbs, Jodi reminded me—asked Peter Douglass to come up and pray for the youth from the church who were in Mississippi with Habitat for Humanity, building houses for poor people. Then Pastor Cobbs announced that his copastor, Pastor Clark—an older white man, I remembered, tall and skinny—had been taken to the hospital last night, suffering from chest pains. Shock seemed to run through the congregation, and four or five different people prayed about that.

And then other people started to go up to the mike and mention things that needed prayer. Personal stuff. That surprised me. A nephew who'd been in a car accident. A daughter who had a miscarriage. A brother who was going to drink himself to death "if the Lord don't get hold of him." Pastor Cobbs reminded the congregation that Scripture says, "If two or three agree, we can ask anything in the name of Jesus, and He will answer!" A lot of people shouted "Amen!" After that somebody started praying, and then another. And another.

The pastor never did preach his sermon. And nobody seemed to mind.

But the impromptu prayer meeting made me squirm. Good grief, if anyone in that room needed prayer, it was me. But go up to that mike and ask for prayer? Admit that this college-educated mother of two had gone from luxury penthouse to a homeless shelter in one measly day? Admit that my life was screwed up big-time—and I didn't have a clue what to do about it?

Couldn't imagine it. It'd be like walking naked down Lake Shore Drive.

chapter 17

Never did open my mouth, but seemed like a lot of people at SouledOut must have seen the news clips about Hero Dog chasing off an intruder at the Manna House shelter. At least seven people came up to me and asked how Dandy was doing, and started in on the questions I was trying to avoid, like, "How did the dog happen to be at the shelter, anyway?"

Jodi had gone off to the ladies' room with my mother, leaving me standing by the coffeepot, holding on to my Styrofoam cup with a grip that threatened to splatter hot coffee in all directions. I was trying to decide what I could say—just enough to not be rude but not anything that might make its way into the media by accident—when Estelle swooped down on me like a brood hen, her dress of choice this morning being a billowy yellow number with black swirls. She wrapped me up like a chick under her yellow-and-black wing and hustled me off. "No questions! No questions!" she tossed back over her shoulder.

I didn't know whether to laugh or cry with relief. "How do

they even know it's me?" I complained when we were safely out of the crowd around the coffeepot.

"The hair, honey. The hair." Estelle patted my head full of frowsy corkscrew curls, which had sprung up like perky weeds after my fifteen-minute shower that morning. "Just don't commit no crimes, honey. You'll be caught within twenty-four hours—Hey! Florida! C'mon over here." Estelle waved her arm at one of the women I'd met last week. I remembered the interesting Zulu knots all over her head, looking like little tortellini noodles.

"How ya feel, Estelle? And this is Gabby, right? Girl, you all over the news—"

"Put a lid on it, Florida. Gabby's staying at the Baxters' for a little R & R this weekend—an' maybe till Mandy gets back. I'm just checkin' about Yada Yada tonight—we're s'posed to meet at your house, right? Gabby's got a mountain needs to be moved, and I'm thinkin' Yada Yada got some mountain-movin' experience."

I was totally bewildered. Mountains? What in the world was Estelle talking about!

"Estelle Williams!" Florida put a hand on one hip. "You know good an' well it ain't us that moves mountains. That's God's business. We just do our part 'bout gettin' two or three together an' agreein' in the name of Jesus, an' He'll do the rest in His own way an' His own time—Oh yeah! Glory! Mm!" And Florida danced a little jig right there in front of us.

"Humph. I'm just sayin'. Are we meeting at your house or not?"

Florida stopped her little dance long enough to say, "Uh-huh. An' thanks for the reminder. Works better if I kick Carl and the kids out during the meetin', so I better go give him a heads-up. Where he at, anyway?" The thin, brown woman craned her neck this way and that, scanning the room, then startled me by giving me a quick hug. "Lookin' forward to seein' you tonight, girl. If you got a mountain needs movin', Yada Yada's a good place to start." And she flounced off.

Estelle raised her eyebrows. "Like I said."

Which is how I found myself in the backseat of Leslie Stuart's candy-apple-red Hyundai with Jodi Baxter late that afternoon. Estelle sat in the front passenger seat, fussing about the big tin of chocolate-and-caramel turtles that Stu had insisted on bringing.

"Whatchu bringing that for? Sister who's hosting always provides the snacks—and if that was you, we wouldn't be drivin' now, would we?"

"Well . . . just in case she doesn't have something. I thought it might help."

"Now, why wouldn't she have somethin'? You show up with this fancy-smancy stuff, an' it's like you sayin' her food ain't good enough."

"Estelle! That's not fair. I just wanted to help out."

"That's the trouble with you, Leslie Stuart. You helpin' out people even when they don't need no help, didn't ask for no help, don't want no help."

"Is that so? Maybe *you* didn't need any help when the shelter burned down. Guess I should've kept my mouth shut about sharing the apartment since you didn't *ask* for my help."

"Humph. That's different."

"Hey, you two," Jodi piped up from the backseat. "Quit arguing. What's Gabby going to think? It's her first visit to Yada Yada."

"Arguing? We're not arguing, are we, Stu?"

"Who us? Nope." And they both laughed.

Jodi rolled her eyes at me. "Some people," she muttered, but couldn't help laughing too.

I started to relax. It felt good to be with people who could argue and then laugh about it.

My mother had elected to stay at the Baxters' with Dandy, who was more alert today. He'd eaten some food and was drinking more water, though he definitely needed help up and down the Baxters' back porch stairs to the yard. After making sure Jodi's husband would be there that evening, I agreed to go to this Yada Yada whatever with Jodi and the two single women upstairs.

They were definitely the Odd Couple. Stu was in her thirties, tall and slender, and still wore her dark-blonde hair long and tucked behind one ear, which boasted a long row of small, glittery earrings. Estelle, on the other hand, was as brown as Stu was white, fifty-something, big-boned and solid, her hair worn natural and streaked with gray, and caught up into a bun on top of her head. Every time I'd seen Stu, she was wearing pants, tall boots, and a jacket over a tank top. Estelle in pants? Couldn't imagine it. She made her clothes: big, loose-fitting caftans . . .

Which reminded me. Sometime this week I needed to get my sewing machine from the penthouse before Philip moved all our stuff to who-knew-where.

Stu found a parking spot on a street that boasted the occasional "Chicago bungalow"—little brick houses, mostly one story, or one and a half—scrunched in between three-story apartment buildings. We had to walk a block to Florida's brick bungalow, which actually had a front porch with two white wicker chairs. "A housewarming gift from one of our Yada Yada sisters," Jodi whispered to me. "Chanda won the lottery and rained gifts down on all of us until we told her to stop it."

Whoever Chanda was. I guessed I'd find out soon enough. The door opened just as Stu was about to punch the doorbell, and two kids came running out—a girl about twelve and a boy in his midteens—followed by Carl Hickman, whom I'd met once before when he came to the shelter to help with security at our Fun Night. Okay, so far I'd met three couples: Florida and Carl Hickman, Avis and Peter Douglass, Jodi and Denny Baxter. Hopefully this Yada Yada group wasn't just a bunch of happily married women. Wasn't sure I could take it—

"Oops, 'scuse me, ladies." Josh Baxter came hustling out the front door, little Gracie in a back carrier. "Hey, Carl, wait up!" he yelled and hustled out to the sidewalk.

Oh right. Edesa and Josh Baxter too. Young. In love.

Like I'd been. Once.

Wishing I'd stayed home, I meekly followed Jodi, Stu, and Estelle inside. The small living room area was already populated with women talking and laughing. To the left, Edesa was just coming down the stairs. I made a beeline for Josh's wife. "Ah, a familiar face!" I gave her a big hug.

"Gabby! *Hola!* I'm so glad you came to Yada Yada tonight. Josh told me his mom invited you and your mother to come for the weekend. We were late getting to SouledOut this morning. Gracie had one of those nights."

I peeked up the narrow stairs. "So this is where you guys live?"

She laughed. Even her dark eyes danced. "*Sí.* Only slightly bigger than your office at the shelter. Want to see?"

We slipped up the stairs, past two bedroom doors—"The

Hickman kids," she explained—then through a door that cut the hallway in half. She was right about the tiny apartment. One room served as kitchen and living space, plus a small bedroom and bathroom. But the bedroom held only a crib, three dressers, and a freestanding clothes rack.

"Where—?"

"—do we sleep?" Edesa pointed to the couch in the living area. "It folds out."

"Oh, Edesa." I gave her a sympathetic hug. "You do need a bigger apartment. No wonder you study down at the shelter!"

"You think?" She laughed. "We better get downstairs. They're starting to sing."

Oh great. Now I was going to walk in late.

But no one seemed to notice as we settled into a couple of folding chairs. They were singing a capella, many with their eyes closed, several with hands raised.

"Lord, prepare me . . . to be a sanctuary . . . pure and holy . . . tried and true . . ."

I glanced around the room, seeing a few I'd met before, and several I hadn't, all different shades of skin color. As the song drew to a close, Avis—who seemed to be leading the meeting—moved right into a prayer, asking the Holy Spirit to be present, thanking God for the privilege of coming together in the name of His Son, Jesus. "And thank You for our sister Gabby, who is visiting us tonight . . . Sisters, this is Gabrielle Fairbanks, the program director down at Manna House. We've prayed for her before—now here she is!"

I wasn't sure when Avis had stopped praying and just started talking—as if God was just another person in the room. But everyone turned to me with welcoming smiles.

"Hey there, Gabby!" said a twenty-something white girl with short, spiky hair, wearing baggy overall-shorts over a T shirt. "I'm Yo-Yo. And that's Adele"—she pointed to a large black woman with a short black natural and large hoop earrings—"who does hair an' stuff like that. An' that's Ruth"—pointing to a fiftyish white woman with rather frowsy brown hair—"who comes to Yada Yada because it's the only time she's not chasing her two-year-old twins . . ."

"Enough already, Yo-Yo," fussed the woman named Ruth. "A mouth we all have; we can introduce ourselves. I'm Ruth and my twins are adorable. One's going to be a lawyer and the other a doctor. Remember I told you so."

Everyone laughed, but then they did go around the room and introduce themselves.

Chanda, the lottery lady—she didn't say that, but I remembered the name—had a Jamaican accent like Wanda at the shelter. A lovely young Asian woman, tall and slender, spoke so softly I didn't catch her name—Moshee or Hershey or something. But the big surprise was a Hispanic woman who waggled her fingers at me and said, "*Hola*, Gabby! We've met. Delores Enriques . . . I'm the volunteer nurse who comes to the shelter on Wednesday."

"Oh, of course! I'm sorry, Delores. I'm used to seeing you in your hospital garb." I'm sure my ears were beet red, but I stumbled on: "Thank you all for letting me come tonight. Edesa has mentioned her prayer group. I didn't realize I'd already met so many of you at Manna House."

"It's all Josh and Edesa's fault," Jodi Baxter moaned. "They got involved first and kept bugging the rest of us to volunteer until we said yes. I tried to get out of it by burning the place down the first time I volunteered, but—"

This was met with more hoots of laughter. "Oh stop, Jodi," the beauty shop lady said. "Gabby's going to think you meant it."

"You mean she didn't?" I teased. The words were out of my mouth, complete with wide eyes and fake surprise, before I even realized what I was doing.

Yo-Yo snickered. "Ooo, Gabby, you all right."

Their laughter pulled me in, and I realized the friendly banter had found a chink in my armor. Like I could be the real Gabby again, just hanging out with my girlfriends, laughing and teasing and making jokes.

But a nasty little whisper in my head pulled me up short. Philip's voice, back in his office. *"Listen to yourself, Gabby . . . If you weren't so pathetic, this would be funny."*

chapter 18

I tried to shake Philip's voice out of my head. Why did I let stuff he said get to me? I tried to focus on the conversation going on around me as several of the "Yada Yada sisters" shared stuff they needed prayer for. Florida, our hostess, asked prayer for Cedric, her middle boy, who had started dressing like the gangbangers— baggy pants, crotch hanging to his knees, no shoelaces in his big, clunky gym shoes. "I know why he's doin' it, 'cause he's got that learnin' disability an' the other kids rag on him. He wants to fit in. But now, what kind of man he gonna be, all hobbled up in clothes like that. Help me, Jesus!"

Yo-Yo wagged her head. "I read ya. Pete use to dress like one o' them outlaw bikers, till he joined the army. Now they're sending him to Iraq, and gotta say, I feel guilty, all the fussin' I did over his stupid clothes." Whoever Pete was. Yo-Yo seemed way too young to have a kid old enough to join the army. "Guess I need y'all to pray for him," she went on, "'cause my kid brother still don't have much use for Jesus."

Well, that answered that.

More prayer requests. Chanda was looking for someplace to invest her lottery money. "Someting dat would help a lotta folks—an' get mi relatives off mi back!". . . . Adele said her nail girl quit and would they pray she'd find someone who didn't gossip and snap gum all day? . . . Avis read an e-mail from someone named Nony in South Africa, and from the way the others got all excited, the writer must have been one of the Yada Yadas at one time . . . And Delores, the nurse, said her husband, Ricardo, had lost his job again. "He gets so discouraged. I think he may be drinking again. He needs a miracle, sisters!"

A miracle. That would be nice. A miracle to sort out the mess that was my life. I was half-hoping these women would pray for me and half-hoping they'd forget I was there. But Estelle wasn't about to forget. "Most of you probably heard about what happened at Manna House this weekend," she started.

"What mi want to know is," Chanda jumped in, "why dat dog at de shelter in de first place! Poor t'ing."

Estelle glared. "Zip your lip, would ya, Chanda? I'm tryin' to say somethin'. An' like Avis is always sayin', anything we say at Yada Yada stays at Yada Yada. No blabbin' to the kids or the neighbors."

"Humph. What you t'ink I got, loose lips?"

A chorus of "Uh-huhs" was accompanied by nodding heads.

Chanda folded her arms over the tight blouse stretched across her ample bosom. "Humph. Jus' wanting ta know 'bout dat poor dog."

Estelle sighed. "As I was sayin', Gabby could sure use some sister-prayer because, well . . ." She looked at me. "Maybe you should say, Gabby. That way I won't be talkin' out of school."

Jodi leaned toward me. "You don't have to go into a lot of detail, Gabby. Just enough so Yada Yada has some idea how we can pray."

I nodded, feeling my armpits start to sweat. "Well . . . like Estelle said, I'd appreciate your confidentiality, because, as you've probably seen, the media is fixated on my mother's dog chasing off that intruder the other night. Jodi was nice enough to give us a place to hide out this weekend, so hopefully—"

"But—" Chanda started, then clamped her hand over her mouth.

I couldn't think what to say next, and my lip started to tremble. "Um . . ."

"Take your time, take your time," Estelle soothed.

I swallowed a couple of times. "Um, well, things aren't too good with my marriage. My mom and I are actually staying at the shelter right now, and to be honest, my, uh, husband is pretty angry at the media attention, afraid our personal stuff will end up splashed all over the TV, ruining his business chances here in Chicago . . ."

"Ooo, girl. You do need some mountain-movin' prayer!" Florida wagged her head. "You have kids?"

I nodded. "Two boys . . . in Virginia . . ." But now the tears were dangerously close to the surface.

"That's all right, Gabby," Avis said. "We don't need all the details. Why don't we pray."

"Avis? Before we pray, can I say something?" Jodi waved her hand like a timid kid in school who was embarrassed to ask for a hall pass. "Gabby, do you mind if I share what Mabel said when you first took the job at the shelter as program director?"

I shrugged, not sure where she was going with it. "I guess."

"Well, most of you have met Mabel Turner, the director at

Manna House. She's no slouch. Doesn't mince words. Also a real woman of God. And she told Gabby that from the first time they met, she had the sense that it was God who brought her to Chicago because He has a purpose for her at Manna House."

Murmurs of "All right!" and "Mm-hm, Jesus!" popped around the room. "See?" Estelle murmured.

"Now, don't laugh," Jodi said, "'cause you all know I tend to be a little skeptical about 'prophetic words' and stuff like that . . ."

Yo-Yo snickered anyway.

". . . but I've been thinking about it all day today, and I think Mabel's words to Gabby really are prophetic, and that all this stuff that's been happening, as painful as it is, isn't by accident. I think God really did bring Gabby to the shelter, and He has a purpose for her, and He's going to use it all somehow . . ."

"All right, now. Preach it, girl!" Florida said.

Edesa was nearly jumping out of her chair. "Oh, *sí*! And I told Gabby her parents gave her the right name . . . Gabrielle." She grinned at me impishly. "It means 'strong woman of God.'"

"See?" Estelle said again.

I wanted to protest, to tell them they had it all wrong, that I was a wimp, that I'd lost my children and ruined my marriage, my own mother was in a homeless shelter, and I didn't have a clue why I was at Manna House . . . but suddenly I found myself surrounded as several of the women got out of their chairs and knelt beside me, taking hold of my shaking hands, while others laid gentle hands on my shoulders. "Oh God!" someone started to pray. "Thank You for telling us in Your Word that when we are weak, that's when You are strong!" . . . "And You promised in Your Word that *all* things work together for the good of those who love You!" . . .

The prayers poured over me, pulling the stopper from the tears I'd been holding back. Someone handed me a box of tissues.

"Give our sister Gabby strength to face tomorrow!" . . . "Open her eyes to see Your purpose in her life!" . . . "Give her wisdom to meet the challenges she's facing right now!" . . . "Protect her children, Jesus, when she can't be with them!" . . .

I don't know when it happened. But somewhere in the middle of those prayers going up to God and pouring down on my head, like a river flowing two ways at the same time, a peculiar calmness settled over my body from the inside out. My hands stopped shaking. The tears dried up. My muscles relaxed, and yet . . . I felt invigorated, as if blood was surging through my body, like the time I'd treated myself to a spa treatment after Paul was born. Even the slump in my spirit seemed to straighten. It was the strangest feeling.

And that night, stretched out in my borrowed bed at the Baxters' house, I slept a dreamless sleep.

Denny Baxter offered to drive the three of us back to Manna House the next morning if that's what we wanted to do. "But really, Gabby," Jodi said, "Dandy could use a few more days of rest. I'm home most of the day now that school's out. I'd be happy to stay with your mom and Dandy while you go to work . . . the rest of the week, too, if that'd be helpful. Amanda doesn't come back till next Saturday."

It was a no-brainer as far as I was concerned. "Mom? You okay about staying here with Dandy and Jodi today? I'll be back after work. But if you want to come to the shelter with me, that's okay too," I added, feeling a bit guilty at leaving my mother in the care of strangers.

My mother scooped some kibbles into Dandy's bowl next to his bed on the back porch. The dog nosed the food and took a polite bite, then laid his head down again on the borrowed dog bed. "Dandy says he doesn't feel too good. I better stay here with him. You don't mind, do you, Celeste?"

Noticing Jodi's odd look, I whispered, "My sister. She gets confused sometimes—oh. Can I use your phone? I've got a calling card."

Hoping that P. J. hadn't left for sports camp already, I dialed the Fairbanks' number . . . and got Philip's mother. I steeled myself. "Marlene, this is Gabby. May I speak to P. J. please?"

"Where are you? I didn't recognize the caller ID."

The nerve! What business was it of hers where I was? "Please, just put P. J. on the phone."

Fortunately, Marlene Fairbanks was too much of a Southern gentlewoman to be outright nasty. I had a short but happy talk with my oldest, who promised to tell me all about the first day of lacrosse when I called that evening.

The commute on the El took twice as long from the Rogers Park neighborhood as it had from Richmond Towers, but I didn't mind. It gave me time to think about what happened at the Yada Yada prayer meeting last night.

But . . . what exactly had happened? Those women took Mabel's words seriously, even took the meaning of my name seriously, as if it all meant something. And they'd prayed for purpose, wisdom, and courage . . . not exactly the prayers I'd been praying, which mostly consisted of "Help, God! Fix it! Do something!"

Frankly, all I knew was that this morning I almost felt like a normal person. Going to work. Not scared out of my mind. Thinking about what I needed to do today. Grateful that my mom and Dandy were safe and cared for. Wishing I'd brought my umbrella because it looked like rain.

Nothing had changed. I was still homeless. Still broke. My marriage was still in the toilet. My sons were still in another state, and I missed them terribly. And yet . . . *something* had changed. As if God had stood up inside me and whispered, "I've got your back."

I laughed and got funny looks from the mute bodies standing around me in the crowded aisle of the El. Oh well. Let them think I was one of those weirdos who talked to themselves. These days it was hard to tell the weirdos from the hands-free cell phone users.

I hustled off the El at the Sheridan station and stopped in at the Emerald City Coffee Shop to pick up a coffee-with-cream-to-go from the young barista behind the counter, who wore two little rings in the side of her nose. "Hey. Aren't you the lady with the dog we saw on TV? Is he okay?"

"He's fine. Thanks." I tossed two dollars on the counter and hurried out, kicking myself for the splurge. That's what I got for pretending my life was back to normal.

At least no reporters were lurking about the shelter as I buzzed the front door, signed in at the reception desk, and sailed into the multipurpose room. Each person I met on the way to my office said practically the same thing. "Hey, Miz Gabby! Where's Gramma Shep? How's Dandy? How come you didn't bring 'em back?"

Everyone, that is, except Lucy. So far I hadn't seen the older woman on the main floor or the lower level. I double-backed to the reception cubby in the foyer. "Angela, have you seen Lucy today?"

Angela shook her black tresses. "She didn't sign out since I've been here . . . wait." The young receptionist turned the book around and flipped a couple of pages. "Don't see her on the sign-outs over the weekend either. Did you try her bunk room?"

Might as well. I ran up the stairs to the bunk room we'd been sharing. My bed and my mother's bed were still made up, and it looked like we'd added another roommate besides Tanya and Sammy.

But Lucy's bunk had been stripped, and her cart was missing.

chapter 19

I flipped the light on in my broom-closet office, feeling annoyed. Why did Lucy just take off like that? She didn't even sign out. I *told* her we'd be back in a few days. What if I'd brought Dandy back today? Hadn't she promised to help take care of him?

I sighed. Or maybe it didn't have anything to do with us. Lucy always had been unpredictable.

An envelope was leaning against my computer. A two-week paycheck and a note from Mabel:

> *Gabby,*
> *So sorry. You should have gotten this Friday, but the accountant was sick. Hope you made it through the weekend.*
> *Mabel*

> *P.S. I won't be here today. Call if you need to.*

I held the envelope against my chest. *Thank You, Lord.* This was going straight into the bank. A few more paychecks and I might have enough for a deposit on an apartment. "Not to worry, Mabel," I murmured. "God picked up the tab for my weekend."

It was true. And I wasn't going to let my frustration with Lucy ruin the feeling of peace God had given to me as an extra bonus.

The morning seemed to fly. I worked on my activities calendar, one that could be posted on every floor of the shelter to remind residents of regular classes and activities offered, as well as special program events. So far, so good . . . but I still had ideas I needed to pursue. Halfway through the morning, I left a message for Lee Boyer at Legal Aid to call, hoping to set up our next meeting. Now that I'd made a temporary decision about the boys, I was eager to find out what I needed to do next to strengthen my custody case. What else was I supposed to do before our next meeting? Oh right, the power of attorney papers he'd given me. I hadn't even looked at them yet! Well, tonight then . . .

Estelle poked her head in my door when she came in at ten thirty to do lunch. "How you doin' this mornin', sugar?"

"Good. Those prayers last night . . . I really appreciated them."

"Well, just keep 'em goin', honey. Let God do the heavy lifting. Say, I brought a bunch of material for my sewing class today. Didn't you say you had a sewing machine we could use?"

I grimaced. "Well, yeah, sorta. I mean, I said it, but it's still behind lock and key at the penthouse. And to tell you the truth, after limping out of Philip's office last Friday, I'm not feeling especially brave about calling him, much less actually going there to pick it up." I winced. "I know you all prayed for courage last night, but—"

"Nope. That's wisdom, honey. You don't need to be talking to that man right now. Hmm . . . that's the building where Harry works, right?" She tapped her teeth with a carefully manicured nail. "E-mail. The man's got e-mail, right? Tell him to leave the sewing machine at the main desk of Royal Towers or whatever it's called and someone will pick it up."

E-mail. It hadn't occurred to me to e-mail Philip. But I liked the idea. I could be brave in a note. Of course, I ran the risk that he'd just hit Delete. But he *had* agreed to me picking up the sewing machine this week . . . it was worth a try. I kept the message short. "Philip, I need to get my sewing machine this week. Please leave it at the main desk with Mr. Bentley. Someone will pick it up for me. Thanks. Gabby."

Then I hesitated . . . what was I doing? *After fifteen-plus years of marriage, I'm going to settle for just my sewing machine?!*

"Argh!" I grabbed fistfuls of my hair to keep from punching the computer . . . but a moment later I took a big breath and let it out. *No.* This was just for now. If it . . . if it actually came down to divorce, Lee Boyer would tell me how to get my fair share of our community property. Until then, I didn't want to do anything that presumed we'd never work this out. Philip's tantrum had to wear out sometime, didn't it?

Oh God, please . . .

I'd just clicked Send when I heard another knock on my door. "It's open!"

A head full of tiny black braids poked in. "Hey, Miz Gabby. How ya doin'?"

"Precious!" I jumped up, pulled her in, and gave her a tight hug. "When did you get back? Are you okay? Is Sabrina all right?"

Precious shrugged out of my embrace and sat on the corner

of my desk. "Sabrina all right. Leastwise I didn't kill her. But she ain't talkin' to me. Still, she home now. We'll get through. 'Cept . . ." The young single mom looked away.

"Except what, Precious? What's wrong?"

A big sigh escaped from her thin body, like a tire deflating. "Lost my job. Humph. I been waitressin' at the Lucky Straw almost two years. Ya'd think they'd hold it for me when I had a 'mergency, wouldn't ya?" She shook her head, the ends of her skinny braids tickling her shoulders. "But without that job . . . me an' Sabrina gonna be right back here at the shelter, back where we started."

We talked a long time. Or rather, Precious chattered and I listened. One minute she was fussing about how hard it was rais-ing a girl in today's world when all the role models on TV and the movies were rich, slutty brats, and the next minute she was cussing out the boys who couldn't keep their pants zipped. "What is *wrong* with these young people? They either smokin' they brains out with drugs, or act like havin' a little fun today is all that matters. An' we end up with all these babies ain't got no daddies and the mamas livin' off welfare. No wonder them abortion clinics do so much business. I tell you, Gabby, things gotta *stop* somewhere."

She finally sighed. "Know I shouldn't go off so hard on Sabrina. Didn't I make enough mistakes for the two of us? Just . . . makes me so mad she's not usin' the brain God gave her. What was she thinkin', runnin' off like that? That I wouldn't find out? Wouldn't come get her? Now she done cost me my job . . . Lord, I'm at my wit's end."

I reached out and took her hand. "I'm so sorry, Precious. Maybe it's not as bad as it seems. I mean, if you can find another job, maybe you won't lose your apartment."

She shook her head. "Already lost a week's pay. Even if I find a job in the next two or three weeks, it gonna be awhile till I get enough to pay for two months all in a hunk—even with Section 8. An' my landlord? Mm-mm, Lord have mercy. He got the patience of a jitterbug. What I need right now is one o' them subsidized apartments where they just take a certain percentage of your income, no matter what it is." She shook her head. "But the waitin' list for them places so long you could wrap it 'round the whole city. Maybe twice."

Precious slid off my desk. "Anyway, thanks for listenin', Miz Gabby. You wanna be my case manager if we end up back at the shelter again?" She laughed. "You'd have it easy. I know the drill. I just need someone I can yell at long enough to get the monkey off my back; then I'll get down to business . . . Okay, I'm outta here. Gonna see if Estelle needs some help with lunch."

The door closed behind her. I absently chewed on the end of a pen. That was the second time in less than a week a single mom here had talked about needing "second step" housing—a place of their own, to be a family, even before they had a job that could pay full rent. Had Manna House ever considered doing something like that? I'd have to ask Mabel. And I still hadn't told Precious that my mom and I had ended up here at the shelter ourselves . . . but that was okay. I hadn't even thought about it while Precious was unloading.

Huh. Might be the first time in a month of Sundays I hadn't been thinking about myself.

Hannah the Bored flagged me down at lunch. "So are you gonna let me do nails for the ladies or not? You *said* to give you activity ideas, an' I've axed you twice."

Had she really? Had to admit it was easy to ignore Hannah. She irritated me, just sitting around filing her nails. I made my voice light. "Hannah, you are free to do anyone's nails at any time. Go for it."

The young woman frowned. "But to do it right, I need lotsa diff'rent stuff. Cuticle cutters, nail strengthener, lots of different colors o' polish, clear coats. If you made it official, ladies could make appointments. Depends on what they want done, how long it takes. Full sets, gel overlays, French tips . . ." An excited grin lit up her face. "You should see the designs I can make— flowers an' starbursts, stuff like 'at. But it takes special brushes and paint."

I studied Hannah with new interest. Sounded like she knew what she was talking about. A crazy idea popped into my head. "Hannah, tell me, have you ever done nails professionally?"

"Ya mean like in a salon? Oh yeah. I started cosmetology school once, but my ol' man got busted an' . . . nah, never mind. Anyway, had to drop out after that. My aunt had this salon an' she gave me a job, but . . . I don't really know what happened, but she lost the salon, back taxes or somethin', an' I lost my job and ended up no place ta go. So"—the young black woman grinned flippantly—"here I am."

"But can't you get another job at a salon?"

She shrugged. "That's what I wanna do, but most of 'em want ya ta graduate cosmetology, but can't do that till I can pay for tuition, can't get a job till I get a state ID, but I'm still waiting ta get a copy of my birth certificate. Wasn't born in Chicago, so it's takin' awhile."

Whew. I never really knew Hannah's background. Who was her case manager? I knew Manna House worked on priorities and goals for each resident, and I didn't want to get the cart before the horse, but—

"Hey, Miz Fairbanks. Let me do your nails." Hannah grabbed one of my hands. "Oh, girl, they are in *bad* shape. I got a nice color, would look real good on you."

I pulled my hand back. "Oh, that's nice, Hannah, but I—"

"Aw, c'mon, Miz Fairbanks—"

"Call me Gabby, Hannah."

"Okay. Gabby. But jus' give me half an' hour, show ya what I can do."

Something Precious once said hovered at the edges of my memory. *"When you been living on the streets, a bit of pamperin' is pretty nice. Homeless women need ta feel like women, too, ya know."*

I relented. I would like to see what she could do.

By the time I left Manna House that evening, my nails glowed with a dark honey-peach nail color that did not clash with my hair. Hannah had soaked them—in a shampoo solution, but oh well—then she'd softened and rounded the cuticles, lotioned and massaged my hands, filed my nails, and painted them with an undercoat and a top coat. "My last couple bottles," she'd said. "That's why I need ta get put on the activity list, so you can get me some real supplies."

She had me convinced, but I told her I couldn't promise what the budget would be.

I had one errand to do on the way back to the Baxters'—deposit my paycheck. When I had a chance, I was going to move my household account to the branch bank near the Sheridan El. But for now, I had to get off at Berwyn and deposit it at the bank near Richmond Towers. Not likely that I'd run into Philip at this hour.

Lucy still hadn't shown up at Manna House by the time I'd left, even though there'd been brief thunderstorms off and on all day. Where did she go when she wasn't at the shelter? I'd run into her three times in the park near Richmond Towers. Should I walk over there on the off chance I'd run into her? I didn't have my umbrella, but when I came out of the bank, the sky was just overcast, so I took a chance.

No Lucy in the park. I even walked through the underpass to the beach. No sign of a purple knit hat. *Drat!* If I had my cell phone, I could call Mr. Bentley and tell him to keep a lookout when he was on the job, but . . . On a sudden impulse I headed straight for Richmond Towers and into the lobby. Mr. Bentley was holding the inside security door open for a resident whose arms were full of shopping bags from upscale stores, and his eyebrows went up like question marks when he saw me.

"Mrs. Fairbanks! Going upstairs to storm the fortress?"

I grimaced. "No, and I want to make this quick. Don't really want to run into you-know-who. Could you keep a lookout for Lucy—you know, my bag lady friend? She disappeared from the shelter this weekend, and I kind of want to find her. She wears a purple knit hat Estelle made for her—you've seen it, I'm sure. Second thing, my husband is supposed to bring my sewing machine down here to the desk for me to pick up. Either one, would you call me at the shelter and let me know? Or call Estelle, whatever's easier."

"Sure thing, Mrs. Fairbanks."

I felt a little bad at how brief I'd been with Mr. B, but at least I'd made an effort to find Lucy. Hopefully my mom wouldn't ask about her . . . but when I got to the Baxters' house, that was the first question out of her mouth. "Did Lucy send me a message? I know she's worried about Dandy. Did you tell her he's getting better and we'll be back tomorrow?"

I put her off as best I could—no, Lucy was out, but I was sure she'd be glad to see us as soon as Dandy was strong enough to go back—then collapsed on the stool in the Baxter kitchen with the glass of iced tea Jodi handed to me. "Hard day?" she asked.

I grinned at their cats, weaving in and out between her bare legs. "Actually, a good day. The prayers last night—they really made a difference, Jodi. Not sure I can explain it."

She just grinned and continued to chop vegetables for a stir fry. Patches, the calico, meowed pitifully. But Peanut, the black-and-white, hopped into my lap, knowing a sucker when he saw one.

I stroked the beautiful fur absently and was rewarded with a loud purr. "But I'm wondering if you have a phone number for the Yada Yada lady—I forget her name—who owns a beauty shop and needs a new nail girl?"

"You mean Adele Skuggs. Sure—I think her shop is open on Monday nights. You want to make an appointment? If she's got an opening, I could drive you over when Denny gets home."

I grimaced. "I should. I need a haircut. But actually, it's for somebody I know at the shelter who does nails and needs a job." I waggled my nails. "I brought home a sample. Not sure how long they'll look good, though. I'm hard on hands."

Jodi laughed. "Uh-huh. Sneaky way to get out of doing the dishes—oh, here's Denny."

The back door banged open, and Jodi's husband came in. He pecked his wife on the cheek, then handed me a plastic bag. "Something I thought you could use."

"Me?" I was so flustered, I hardly knew what to do. I pushed Peanut off my lap, reached into the bag, and pulled out a box. A cell phone. "Oh, Denny, I can't accept this. It's too much!"

He chuckled, sending those cheek dimples into big crevices. "I don't think so. It's one of those pay-ahead phones—no bells or whistles. Just a phone, but it's got decent service. You need it so you can call your boys whenever you want, and . . . whatever."

I glanced at Jodi. Was she okay with her husband giving me a gift? But she was smiling at her husband with obvious approval.

Oh dear God, I do need my own phone . . . "I—I hardly know what to say." I opened the box and took out the phone. Petite. Ice blue. A mini lifeline. And I did just get a paycheck. "Thanks, Denny. I'll pay you back."

Denny laughed and shook his head. "Uh-uh. The phone's yours, Gabby. But you can pay the monthly—the paperwork's in there. It's already charged and activated." He clapped his hands together. "Okay, enough schmaltz. What's for dinner?"

I clutched the phone to my chest and slipped out to the back porch. Might as well try it out, find out how P. J.'s first day of lacrosse camp went.

chapter 20

After supper, I spent an hour on the Baxters' back porch swing, going over the power of attorney forms with my mother. "This is just in case something happens and you can't make these decisions yourself," I assured her. Dandy, bright-eyed, seemed to enjoy our company. He'd cleaned out his food bowl, and even though it was a struggle getting out of the cushiony dog bed, he limped over and licked my toe.

My mother beamed. "See, Gabby? He's better. We can go home now."

Home. Did she mean North Dakota? . . . or Manna House? I let it go.

Mom went to bed early, but I stayed on the porch, inputting phone numbers into my new phone from the list I'd made before my old one totally lost its juice. Jodi came out and handed me a slip of paper. "Here are a few more numbers you might need—the top one is ours, then Josh's and Edesa's cells, and that one is Adele's Hair and Nails. It's almost nine—I think that's when she closes on Monday. Might be a good time to call her about your nail girl. Oh—wait a minute." She disappeared inside, then reappeared with their kitchen cordless. "Here, use our phone. Don't waste your minutes."

"Thanks, Jodi." I tapped in the number for Adele's Hair and Nails . . . but as the phone rang, I started to have second thoughts. Did I really know Hannah well enough to recommend her to—

"Jodi Baxter! Make it quick, girl. I'm trying to get out of here." The voice exploded in my ear with no introduction.

"Uh, is this Adele Skuggs? Sorry, it's not Jodi. Just using her phone. This is Gabby Fairbanks—I met you last night at your Yada prayer thing."

A deep chuckle on the other end was somewhat reassuring. "Oh, sure. I remember. What can I do for you, Gabby? Want me to do something with that white girl 'fro you've got?"

A white girl *what?* "Oh . . . my hair. Well, yeah, guess I do need a cut." Understatement. "But I was calling to ask if you still needed a nail girl."

"Why? You want the job?"

Jodi must have noticed the flustered look on my face. "Don't let her muddle you," she stage-whispered. "That's just her way."

Okay then. Two could play. "Oh, you wouldn't want me. You'd lose all your customers." I was rewarded by Adele's throaty laugh in my ear. "But actually," I hurried on, "there *is* a young woman at Manna House who's had experience in a nail salon, and she needs a job. I don't know if she's what you're looking for, but—"

"Really? Well, bring her in. I'll give her an interview. Can you . . . just a sec." I heard pages flipping. "I have a cancellation at two o'clock tomorrow. Can you bring her in? And might as well give you a cut while we're at it."

"Uh . . . sure. Two o'clock tomorrow."

I hung up and looked at Jodi, who was laughing. "You just got run over by a steamroller, didn't you? Well, that's Adele!"

Tuesday morning my mother told me Dandy was much better and she thought we all ought to go back to the shelter. "I think she's bored," Jodi murmured to me. "But I'm happy to have her stay as long as you want. She's no trouble. In fact, I'm keeping the car today and going to run some errands. Does she like to shop?"

I talked my mother into letting Dandy rest another day, privately hoping we could stay out the week until the Baxters' daughter came home. I was glad, because when I got to Manna House, a reporter and a cameraman accosted me at the front steps. "Mrs. Fairbanks! How is the Hero Dog doing? No one has seen Dandy for three days! Has he taken a turn for the worse?"

Oh good grief. "He's fine. He's resting out of the limelight and hoping all you good people will forget about him and let him return to doggy oblivion." I gave what I hoped was a friendly smile and hustled up the stairs.

"But Mrs. Fairbanks!" the reporter called after me. "What about all the donations people are sending to the shelter since Dandy caught the intruder and saved the life of one of your staff? What are you going to do with the money?"

I nearly tripped on the last step, but caught myself. I turned slowly. "I'm sorry. I don't know anything about that." I punched the buzzer, and the door clicked to let me in.

Angela Kwon looked up as I came in and waved a slip of paper at me. But I ignored the receptionist and headed straight into Mabel's office. "Money?" I demanded, even before the director looked up. "People are giving the shelter money? Mabel, we can't use Dandy to get contribu—"

"Whoa, whoa, whoa!" Mabel's face clouded. "Close the door, Gabby, and sit down."

I obeyed, stifling a groan. Why didn't those reporters just go away?

Mabel stood up behind her desk and leaned forward on her knuckles. "First of all, Gabby Fairbanks, we are not *using* Dandy to get contributions. Second, we *have* received a sudden flood of donations in the mail—unsolicited, I might add. Third, I am calling a staff meeting this morning to bring everyone up to date. What we do with the money will be a decision of the board." She sat back down with a *whump*. "Satisfied?"

I cringed. "Sorry. It's just . . . I got accosted by a reporter and a cameraman two minutes ago who were asking *me* what I was going to do with all the donations Dandy had generated for the shelter. If Philip hears about this on TV, he's going to be furious."

Mabel's expression softened. "Apology accepted. I agree; it's a bit startling. But we can talk about it at the staff meeting."

"How much—?"

"Staff meeting. Ten thirty. Now, go, Gabby." Mabel stuck on a pair of reading glasses and turned back to her computer.

Angela waved the sticky note at me as I walked back into the foyer. "Message for you, Gabby. And don't forget to sign in."

I took the note. *Lee Boyer at Legal Aid returned your call.* Oh good. And when I got to my office and booted up my computer a few minutes later, there was an e-mail reply from Philip. All it said was, *OK.*

I stared at the e-mail a long time. He was agreeing to leave my sewing machine at the lobby desk of Richmond Towers, wasn't he? So why did that "OK" make me feel crummy? So brief. Dry. Impersonal. Like . . . like being offered a thimble of water when I was dying for a long, cool drink.

No, no. Couldn't go there. I eyed the Bible on my desk. I hadn't really followed through on my resolve to read it regularly. Then again, I hadn't expected my whole life to turn upside down, like that disaster movie where the huge ship *Poseidon* got flipped over by a monster wave and everything was total chaos. A little hard to find "quiet time." Still, when I was reading the gospel of Matthew every day during our vacation in North Dakota, God had used it to speak to me, hadn't He? Maybe I should—

But maybe I should call Lee Boyer first. Hopefully he had some good news. I dialed my office phone . . . and finally got through. "Mr. Boyer? Gabby Fairbanks. I was wondering what you've been able to find out."

"*The* Gabby Fairbanks?" The male voice on the other end chuckled. "When I saw you on Friday, I didn't know you were such a celebrity."

I felt my ears turning red, glad he couldn't see me blushing. "I didn't know it either. Yeah, we had a bit of excitement here at the shelter that night, but I think it's blowing over. Hope so, anyway. My husband was livid when he saw us on TV."

Now the laughter was outright. "I can just imagine." He took a few seconds to recover. "Anyway . . . I don't think it'll hurt your case—might even help. But it'd be best if we could go over our next steps in person rather than over the phone. And bring in those power of attorney papers I gave you, if possible. Can you come in tomorrow at eleven?"

Right. The papers. I still needed to get them signed and nota-rized. "Sure. I think eleven would work."

"All right. Are you doing okay?"

His question caught me off guard. "Uh, actually, yes, I am. Some friends of the shelter took us home with them for the weekend and are actually taking care of my mother and Dandy for a few days. I almost feel like a normal person this week." I didn't mention the Yada Yada group and the impact of their prayers. Might sound a little weird.

"Atta girl. You're going to be fine. And we're going to stick it to your husband with everything we've got. You just hang in there. See you tomorrow, Gabby." *Click.*

I almost said, *"Wait! I don't want to 'stick it to my husband.' I just want my life back!"* But he was gone. And I had to admit, it was nice of him, asking if I was okay, telling me to hang in there. Calling me by my familiar name.

The phone call had definitely perked up my spirit.

I looked at my watch. Ten fifteen. Still had a little time before the staff meeting. Maybe I could get in a few minutes of Bible reading . . . wait! I had to find Hannah and tell her about the appointment at Adele's Hair and Nails! *And* find out how to get there!

Hannah went berserk when I told her she had a job interview. She threw her arms around me and practically picked me up in her excitement. "Oh, Miz Fairbanks, thank you, thank you, thank you . . . oh! What should I wear? Is my hair okay?"

I looked at her critically. She was a big girl, but not fat. Medium-brown skin, smooth, not rough and scarred like some of the women who'd been out on the streets for years. Hair was braided tight to her head, without extensions. She probably did it herself, but it was neat. "Do you have a skirt? You don't have to be fancy. But dress as businesslike as possible. Iron whatever you've got. And don't chew gum. Never, never. This woman has a thing about gum." I grinned. "Now, go. We need to leave by twelve thirty." And *I* needed to get to the staff meeting.

Only five of us—Mabel, myself, Angela, Estelle, who blew in right at ten thirty, and Stephanie Cooper, the DCFS social worker who came on Tuesdays and Thursdays for case management meetings—gathered in the schoolroom on the main floor. I expected Mabel to plunge right into the matter at hand, but we spent the first ten minutes just praying. Well, mostly it was Mabel and Estelle, but the two of them praised God for all He was doing at Manna House, for the progress many of the residents were making toward their goals, and that none of the residents or staff had been injured during the break-in over the weekend. "An' we ask You to heal sweet Dandy," Estelle added, "who risked his own safety to protect the women here. An' Your Word tells us to pray for our enemies, so guess we oughta be prayin' for that perp who broke in here. Turn him around, Lord. Clean him up and set him on the right path. An' we give You thanks that Dandy didn't hurt him too bad."

The rest of us looked at each other self-consciously as the prayers ended. Praying for the "perp" wasn't exactly at the top of the prayer list for most of us.

Mabel told the staff what the rest of Chicago already seemed to know—that good-hearted people who'd seen the TV clips about Hero Dog stopping an intruder at a local women's shelter were sending donations to Manna House. "A few are earmarked to help with Dandy's medical expenses," she said, with a nod in my direction, "but most are coming in as general donations."

Angela waggled her hand. "Like, how much?"

I was glad someone else asked. Mabel shrugged. "Right now, about two thousand dollars. But my guess is there'll be more. The reason I'm telling you now is twofold. First, we are *not* 'using' what happened to generate contributions—an accusation you may hear from some people. All contributions have been spontaneous. Second, the board will need to decide whether this goes into our general operating fund—God knows we operate on a tight budget as it is—or whether it should be deposited in a special fund for a particular project or outreach."

"We need a van." That popped out before I even thought of it.

Mabel allowed a wry smile. "Well, two thousand dollars won't go very far for a van, but Gabby preempted my next point. I'm sure the board would be willing to entertain ideas for what to do with this money—but *please*, submit them in writing." She stood up. "Okay, that's it."

"Well, hallelujah!" Estelle jumped up and was practically out the door. "I still gotta do lunch, an' I'm half an hour behind already."

Stephanie Cooper was right on her heels. "Yeah, and I need to squeeze in two case management meetings *before* lunch."

"Stephanie! Wait up!" I needed to tell the case manager about the job interview for Hannah and get a CTA pass for her.

But Mabel caught me as I started to follow. "Gabby, just a minute. Speaking of contributions, don't forget there's an awful lot of dog food and dog stuff piled up in the rec room. I'm going to let you decide what to do with it—but I want it out of here by the end of the week. *Capisce?*" She strode out the door.

Good grief. Now Mabel was beginning to sound like Sarge.

chapter 21

I went online to get directions to Adele's Hair and Nails on Clark Street, and it didn't seem too complicated. Take the Red Line north to Howard Street—the border between Chicago and Evanston—walk a couple of blocks to Clark, turn south. Easy.

Stephanie Cooper, Hannah's case manager, had worried that it might be a wasted trip since the girl didn't have her state ID yet, but she gave her a CTA one-day pass since I was going with her. "Can't hurt to try," she agreed, pushing her long bangs out of her eyes. "Let me know how it goes. And hey, why don't we set up a time on Thursday to talk about you? You and your mom are still on the bed list, right?"

I hoped. Our stay at the Baxters' was temporary at best. Made me feel funny to be treated like the other residents, but I had to admit, Stephanie had a right as case manager to talk about our "case" since we were, in fact, homeless.

When Hannah and I got off the train at Howard Street, the newish shopping center between the El station and Clark Street looked awfully familiar. "Hey, Hannah. That's the church where Edesa and Estelle go. See? In the shopping center."

She squinted and frowned. "I don't see no church. Whatchu talkin' about?"

I laughed. "That large storefront over there. See on the awning? 'SouledOut Community Church.'"

"Humph. Weird. How many more blocks we gotta walk? These shoes hurt my feet."

"Not sure. Shouldn't be far."

Wrong. How had I misjudged so badly? At ten blocks—a healthy city mile—Hannah was talking mutiny. "I ain't gonna walk this far to work ever' day! Why I let you talk me into this, I don' know. I'm so beat, I'm 'bout ready to fall over. You got any money? Can we get somethin' to drink?"

We'd passed a fruit market a ways back, but now most of the shop windows displayed a jumble of ethnic languages. Spanish. Korean. Arabic . . . I looked at my watch. We still had ten minutes, and the store numbers were getting closer. But I wasn't about to drag a disgruntled Hannah into the beauty shop. Adele Skuggs didn't seem the type of person who put up with any nonsense.

I ducked into a corner "pantry" and bought two cans of cold Pepsi. Okay, I was hot and tired, too, not to mention mad at myself for not getting better directions. But I'd gone out on a limb asking for this interview, so it was my reputation on the line too. I dangled the sweating can in front of Hannah. "I'm sure there's a closer El stop, Hannah, and if you get this job, we'll figure out a better way to get here. But if you go in there whining like a spoiled brat, you can forget going on the activity list at the shelter, too, you understand?" I handed her the can. "Now, pull yourself together. We're almost there."

A bell tinkled when we finally pushed open the door of Adele's Hair and Nails.

I glared a warning at Hannah, and she muttered, "Okay, okay."

Three beauty shop chairs lined the mirrored wall to the left just beyond a tidy waiting area. Adele Skuggs, her own hair a short salt-and-pepper 'fro, was taking pink spongy curlers out of a woman's hair in the middle chair. The shop owner gave us a brief glance. "Be with you in a minute."

A beige corduroy couch against the window and a matching love seat against the wall made an inviting waiting area. Magazines—*O* and *Essence* and *Jet* and *Newsweek*—littered a coffee table. A coffeepot and a platter of sweet rolls sat on a corner table. "Ooo, my fave," Hannah said, helping herself to a frosted twist and a napkin. Oh great, sticky fingers for her interview. But too late now.

Posters of beautiful black women with sculptured and braided hairstyles decorated the shop walls. Three "beehive" hair dryers sat across from the chairs, hidden behind the front desk counter. I didn't see anything that looked like a nail salon.

"All right, Miss Lilly. This what you wanted?" Adele gave a hand mirror to the middle-aged African-American woman in the chair. I stared. I'd expected Adele to do a comb-out or style the hair somehow, but she'd left the springy curls just as they came off the curlers, looking like fat sausages all over the woman's head. "Miss Lilly" nodded and smiled at her reflection front, side, and back as Adele took off the plastic cape.

Adele glanced our way as if sizing up Hannah, who was licking crumbs off her fingers—good grief!—but she kept talking to her client. "You in a hurry, Miss Lilly? How would you like a free

manicure and pedicure while you're here?" Adele grinned, expos-
ing a small gap between her front teeth. "I've got a new nail girl
I'm trying out, and I need a victim."

Miss Lilly laughed. "Oh, why not?" She hefted herself out of
the chair and shuffled toward the back of the shop, disappearing
around a corner. Hannah swallowed her last bite and hastily
dabbed her full lips with the napkin, her eyes wide like the proverbial deer caught in the headlights.

Adele grabbed a broom and swept up hair from around the
second chair. "Take that first chair, Gabby Fairbanks. Be with you
in a minute. Come here, girl—Hannah, is it? Mrs. Fairbanks says
you've got experience. Come on back with me . . . Wash your
hands in that sink there . . . What can you do? Full sets? French
tips?" Her voice faded as they disappeared around the corner.

By the time we left Adele's Hair and Nails at four o'clock,
Hannah had been offered a provisional job two days a week, a
four-day week if she proved responsible . . . and my wild curls had
been clipped, tamed, and freshened. "You color your hair?" Adele
had asked, blow-drying my wet tendrils.

"No. My natural color." I'd tried to keep the pride out of my
voice. "Used to be redder, but it has darkened quite a bit.
Chestnut, I guess."

"Mm. Just wondered. You don't have the freckles and green
eyes of most redheads." Adele finger-curled a few misbehaving
strands. "Hazel eyes are nice, though."

She'd charged me twenty bucks, which was certainly reasonable, though it was hard to hand over my debit card and see that
much disappear from my account. When I asked directions to the

closest El stop and Adele found out we'd walked all the way from Howard Street, her shoulders shook with silent laughter as she gave simple directions to the Loyola El station. "Six or seven blocks at most," she'd promised.

Hannah, pumped at the chance to show her stuff in a real salon, generously offered to get herself back to the shelter so I could walk to the Baxters' house from there instead of going all the way into the city and back so late in the afternoon.

By the time I dragged myself up the front porch steps of Jodi and Denny's two-flat, I was pooped. I rang the doorbell, eager to hide out in Josh's old bedroom and call my sons. And my aunt Mercy too. I needed to give her my new cell phone number and let her know where we were staying this week.

I rang the doorbell again. As I waited, it occurred to me that I hadn't talked to either one of my sisters since North Dakota, when I told them I was taking Mom back to Chicago with me "for a visit." I groaned, leaning against the doorpost. Celeste and Honor certainly had no idea Philip had kicked me out and that Mom and I were "guests" in a homeless shelter. But I needed to talk to them about the power of attorney forms the lawyer had given me for Mom. *One* of us had to do it.

Well, better late than never. I'd call tonight, maybe around nine. That would be seven o'clock in California and six in Alaska.

I frowned at the front door, still closed in my face. Strange. Finding my way around back, I found Dandy stretched out in a patch of sun in the tiny backyard. "Hey, boy. You home alone?" Mom's yellow dog jerked his head up, his mouth open in a doggy smile, pumped his tail, and struggled to get up. I squatted beside him instead. "Good boy. Easy, now . . . you doing okay? Where is everybody?"

I even climbed up the back stairs to the second-floor apartment to see if I could use the bathroom, but neither Estelle nor Stu was home either.

At about the time my bladder was threatening to burst, the Baxters' minivan pulled into the garage, and Jodi and my mother came into the yard, hauling groceries. I had to make a beeline for the bathroom the moment Jodi unlocked the back door. "Sorry!" she called after me. "I didn't know you'd be home so early!"

Back in the kitchen, much relieved, I offered to peel potatoes and carrots for the stew Jodi was making while she put groceries away. "How'd it go with my mom and Dandy today?"

"Fine. No problem . . . except your mom complained of a headache this morning. I gave her something for it and she slept, oh, a good three or four hours. That's why we ended up doing our errands late this afternoon—oh! Your hair!" Jodi reached out and pulled a curl, letting it spring back. "It looks nice, Gabby. Adele did a great job." She winked at me. "Okay, you gotta tell me about your first visit to Adele's Hair and Nails. And then I'll tell you about *my* first visit . . . when MaDear was still alive. Hoo boy, Adele's mother definitely kept things interesting!"

We had lots of time for "girl talk" that evening because Denny went to some guy meeting at Peter Douglass's house. Jodi's stories about MaDear left me bug-eyed—especially the time Adele's senile mother mistook Jodi's husband for the white man who'd lynched her older brother way back in the thirties, screaming at Denny to "Get out!" when he came to the beauty shop to pick up Jodi. I could hardly believe Jodi's husband actually asked forgiveness for the horrible deed someone else had committed just so the poor confused woman could experience some peace.

We talked so long it was ten o'clock before I remembered to make my calls, but I didn't get either sister, so I left my new cell phone number on their voice mail and told them to call me ASAP.

I was still thinking about Denny's amazing response as I was getting dressed for work the next morning. Jodi said the situation had put a real strain on their relationship with Adele, and Denny had gotten really depressed at being falsely accused. "MaDear had some kind of dementia. There was no way to make the old woman understand he didn't do it," Jodi had said. "But Denny kept reading the Bible and one day had a revelation—that Jesus had taken the death penalty for *our* sins so we could be free! That's what gave him the idea."

I grabbed my hairbrush to work on the snarls in my hair without the benefit of a mirror—didn't guys have mirrors in their bedrooms?—still chewing on what Jodi had said. *Good grief.* It was hard enough having to say I was sorry for something I *did* do wrong. Couldn't imagine asking forgiveness for something I *hadn't* done. Was sure I wasn't spiritual enough to—

I stopped brushing. A little voice niggled in my ear. *Yeah, but Gabby, aren't you always saying you're sorry for stuff Philip thinks you've done wrong when you haven't really done anything, just to keep the peace?*

chapter 22

My mind stewed on that one all the way to the shelter on the
El. My mom had insisted on coming with me that morning. "It's
Wednesday, isn't it, Celeste? Estelle needs me to help with the
knitting club."

"I'm Gabby, Mom," I'd snapped. "Not Celeste. *Gabby*, remember?" I immediately felt bad about my snitty comeback. But good
grief, why should I let her call me by the wrong name? I was tired
of being at the wrong end of everything.

At least Estelle came with us that morning, since she not only
had to put lunch together at the shelter but also supervise the
knitting club during "nurse hours." She graciously sat with my
mother on the El, leaving me holding on to a pole, alone with my
garbled thoughts.

I barely noticed as the train stopped and started, picking up
its morning glut of commuters, as I tried to grasp the difference
between what Denny Baxter had done—and even Jesus, for that
matter—and my own knee-jerk contrition. *They* had freely taken

on the burden of sin to lift it off someone else. Me, I allowed myself to swallow Philip's accusations and innuendos because . . .

Because why?

Because I was afraid.

But why was I afraid? Philip had never hit me. But somehow . . .

I stared at the backs of brick buildings flitting by, windows with shades pulled, and skinny back porches with the occasional hopeful flower box as my mind tried to make sense of my failed marriage.

Somehow . . . somehow Philip had managed to whittle away at my self-confidence, at my ideas and dreams, until I barely knew who I was . . . and I lived in fear of the real me vanishing altogether. For some reason, I had clung to Philip's version of who I was, even his negative depictions, because at least it was *something.*

"Sheridan!" the intercom squawked as the train lurched around a sharp corner and slowed at our station. I shook off my disturbing thoughts and followed as Estelle helped my mother out the doors and onto the platform. When we came out on the sidewalk below the elevated station, I suddenly remembered the papers I was supposed to bring to the lawyer at eleven.

"Estelle, wait. Do you have a minute? Mom and I have to get these power of attorney papers notarized, and we need a witness. There's a bank just up the street . . ."

"Humph," she grumbled. "If lunch is late today, I'm gonna send all the complaints to you." But Estelle accompanied us to the bank, duly witnessed my mother's and my signatures on the various forms, and even murmured, "This is good. Real good," as the notary handed the forms back to my mother.

She seemed lost in thought as we walked arm in arm with my mother the few blocks to Manna House. "Mm-mm, I wonder . . ."

"Wonder what?" I said.

"Oh. Just thinking about Harry's mom, wondering if he's taken care of this power of attorney business with her."

"Mr. Bentley's mom? You know her?"

"Oh, sure, sure. He asked me to do an assessment for her when he found out I was licensed to do home care for seniors, an' I've dropped in on her from time to time, unofficial-like. Nice lady. Real nice lady. A bit odd, but . . . she likes me." Estelle glanced sideways at me as if she'd said too much as we rounded the corner toward Manna House.

"Estelle Williams!" I whopped my friend on the arm with the back of my hand. "This is getting serious. I mean, now Mr. B's taking you home to Mama . . . oh, good grief. There's that reporter again. Don't say anything."

We hustled up the steps as the female reporter called out, "Mrs. Fairbanks! Is Dandy back at the shelter yet? We hear the residents have made him their official watchdog. So why isn't he—?"

"No comment!" I sang out, and we disappeared inside.

Where in the world was that snoopy reporter getting her information? I was tempted to call the residents and staff together then and there and insist that nobody talk to any reporters, but I forgot my snit as a happy chorus greeted us when we walked into the multipurpose room. "Hiya, Gramma Shep!" . . . "Miz Martha! We been missing you!" . . . "Where's Dandy? Thought he was comin' back!" My mother's cheeks turned pink as everyone from Carolyn the Book Maven to eight-year-old Sammy gave her warm hugs.

"Dandy needs a few more days," I said. "Don't worry, he'll be back." So what if they thought I meant a few more days to heal—which was true. But my real motive for leaving Dandy at the Baxters' as long as possible was to hopefully starve any remaining media interest in Hero Dog.

"Gramma Shep!" Hannah hustled over. "Did Miss Gabby tell you I got me a job in a beauty salon? Ooo, can I do your nails, Gramma Shep? I need the practice!"

"But where's Lucy?" My mother's face fell as she looked around the room. "I told Lucy I'd be back in a few days. Maybe she's downstairs seeing the nurse."

Carolyn caught my eye and gave a quick shake of her head.

"Come on, Mom," I said, steering my mother to a comfortable armchair near an end table. "Let Hannah give you a manicure. You have some time before the knitting club starts."

I was grateful for Hannah's offer, because I wanted to get some work done before heading out the door to make my eleven o'clock at Legal Aid. By the time I signed out and caught the southbound El for my appointment, I had a proposal on Mabel's desk to purchase a list of basic supplies to give manicures and pedicures to the residents of Manna House, using the words of Precious McGill: "Homeless women need to *feel* like women too." It wouldn't be the spa treatment, but hey, we'd do what we could do.

I arrived at the Legal Aid office on Diversey, a storefront along a strip of stores and small businesses—a medical and dental clinic, a resale shop, a real estate office, a pizza joint—with two minutes to spare, but then had to wait fifteen minutes to be called. I smoothed the wrinkles out of my cream-colored slacks and picked some stray lint off my pale green cotton knit top with the crocheted scoop neck. Did I look all right? I should've repaired my makeup before I left the shelter. Maybe they had a restroom here—

A woman with pale bug-eyes and wispy hair dyed an odd burgundy stormed out of the doorway leading to the offices, throwing dagger glances at everyone in the waiting room as she passed. "Tell me I don't got a case," she muttered. "They're gonna be sorry. Yessir, they're gonna be sorry. That woman owes me—" She jerked the front door open and disappeared.

The African-American receptionist didn't even look up from her computer screen. "Fairbanks. You're next."

Down the hall, Lee Boyer's door was half-open. "Sorry about that," the lawyer said, running a hand through his brown, salty hair, then pulling off his wire rims and cleaning them with a man's handkerchief he pulled out of his desk drawer. "Please, sit down . . . May I call you Gabby?"

I sat. "Please. 'Mrs. Fairbanks' sounds like my mother-in-law, and I'm not too happy with her at the moment."

The man laughed. "Got it. Gabby it is."

Was Lee Boyer this good-looking the last time I was here? Not Philip's kind of suave, Double-O Seven good looks that turned heads when he walked into a room. But pleasant. Open. Warm. I watched as he threw the handkerchief back into the drawer and hooked the wire rims behind his ears. "Okay, Gabby, let's get started. Let's see . . ." He studied an open folder. "Do you have the power of attorney forms?"

I pulled a business envelope out of my shoulder bag and pushed it across the desk. "Signed, sealed, and delivered."

"Excellent." He pulled out the forms and skimmed them. "We'll make copies for your files and keep these here." He then handed me a set of papers he'd drawn up to file for unlawful eviction and to regain custody of my children, which needed my signature. My skin prickled as I read, "Plaintiff—Gabrielle Fairbanks . . . Defendant—Philip Fairbanks . . ." *Oh God, is this really happening?*

But I signed.

Lee Boyer clipped the affidavits to the file folder and leaned back. "Now, anything I should know on your end? Besides you turning up on the TV news." He grinned mischievously.

I told him about the phone call with my father-in-law and the difficult decision I'd made to leave the boys where they were until I found an apartment. I didn't tell him about my ill-fated visit to Philip's office. Did it matter? But I hated looking like a fool in front of this man.

". . . know that was a hard decision," he was saying. "But all the more reason to find an apartment so we can get the boys back here with you before school starts. Have you found anything yet?"

He said *we*. "Uh, apartment . . . no. I haven't had time to look. The break-in at the shelter kind of kicked dust in my eyes. We're staying with some, uh, friends till Saturday, and then we have to come back to the shelter. With taking care of Mom and her injured dog, it's been a bit hectic. But maybe this weekend . . ."

Lee Boyer leaned forward, hands clasped on his desk. "Gabby. I understand that things are tough on you right now. But I can't emphasize enough that you need to find an apartment so your sons can come live with you, or this case could very well be thrown out. No judge is going to take two young boys out of their grandparents' home and put them in a women's shelter."

He said it kindly, but tears sprang to my eyes. I reached for a tissue from the box on his desk. "I know," I croaked. "But how can I afford—"

"Don't worry about that. You find an apartment and let me know about it. Then we'll see about supplemental funding until all this gets straightened out." The lawyer leaned back in his desk chair and chewed on the end of a pen, as if thinking about something. But all he said was, "What's the best way to get hold of you if I need to? Between meetings, I mean."

"Oh." I dug in my bag. "I have a cell phone now. A gift from my hosts." I gave him the number.

"All right." Lee Boyer consulted the calendar on his computer. "Next week? Same time good for you?" The man stood up and extended his hand. "I'll call you if anything comes up, Gabby. You do the same."

I shook his hand. To my surprise, he covered it with his other hand and held it for a nanosecond longer. Startled, I looked into his eyes—those warm, brown eyes. "It's going to be all right, Gabby," he said.

Somehow I made it out of there without blubbering. Lee Boyer wasn't anything I expected from a Legal Aid lawyer. He actually seemed to care about what had happened to me, cared about getting my boys back . . . Was that normal for a lawyer? Didn't lawyers just want their money?

Except this was Legal Aid. They didn't do it for profit.

Well, whatever. Philip could sneer all he wanted that I'd gone to Legal Aid. I was lucky to get this lawyer.

And for some reason, as I settled into a seat on the next northbound El, almost empty at this time of day, that little "we" floated into my thoughts. *So we can get the boys back here . . ."* Well, sure, as my lawyer.

But I tucked that little "we" into an empty corner of my heart.

chapter 23

Our stay at the Baxter household buoyed me up better than a week at a spa resort, a gentle oasis of ordinary family rhythms in the middle of the train wreck that was my actual life. Well, maybe not *ordinary* family rhythms, since we had no kid noses or bottoms needing to be wiped, though Dandy's "functions" and my mother's growing dependence came in a close second. Peanut—the black-and-white kitty—must have decided I was a member of the family, because he jumped into my lap whenever I sat down.

Jodi and I even played Scrabble on Thursday night after supper, just like normal people. Leslie Stuart, Estelle's housemate, came downstairs and beat us both. "And you're a teacher, Jodi!" she crowed, tossing that long, corn-silk hair back with glee.

"Yeah, but I teach third graders," Jodi protested. "My brain is stuck on third-grade spelling words, like *clean* and *could* and *cure*."

"And I'm a social worker, but you didn't see me winning with words like *caseworker* and *caseload* and *colleague*."

"No," I jumped in, "but changing *cop* to *copacetic* on a triple word score?! Who even knew that was a word?"

Stu chuckled. "Harry Bentley, that's who—my erstwhile client, your friend, and Estelle's *boyfriend,* if she'd ever admit it. He's been mourning the loss of his *copacetic* life ever since his grandson moved in with him." Which had left all three of us gasping with laughter.

But Saturday loomed when Mom and I would need to move back to the shelter. How Mabel had been able to hold beds for us, I wasn't sure. New faces appeared at the shelter every few days, and I knew our beds had been assigned temporarily to someone else Wednesday night when a major thunderstorm rolled through the city, drenching the normal haunts of the homeless. But when I checked my e-mail at work on Friday, I had two e-mails from Mabel—one an announcement to all staff and available volunteers regarding a staff meeting on Monday, the other to me saying she'd put our names back on the bed list, same room, same bunks, starting Saturday night. I stopped in at her office just before I left for the day to thank her.

"Glad you stopped in, Gabby. Shut the door and sit a minute." Mabel pulled out a file with my name on it. "Stephanie Cooper says she met with you yesterday about housing options."

I nodded, pursing my lips. That had been a little weird. The housing programs Stephanie usually worked with—Theresa's Place, Sanctuary Place, Deborah's Place, and others—typically targeted specific people groups: ex-cons trying to reenter society, addicts going through recovery, alcoholics doing AA, or the mentally challenged, though she'd also given me a list of shelters for victims of domestic violence, several out in the burbs and a couple in Wisconsin.

Mabel must have guessed my thoughts. "I know a case management meeting might feel a bit awkward, Gabby, since you're also on staff here. But neither you nor I want you here for long, right? If you and your mother are on the bed list, Stephanie needs to help you set priorities and goals for getting back on your feet. You've got a job. Now get yourself on some housing lists."

I sighed. "Yeah, I know. My lawyer is bugging me about getting an apartment, too, though he's talking about a regular apartment, not the housing programs Stephanie deals with. I don't even qualify for half of them, since I'm not an ex-con or a drug addict. And not that many take kids—just ask Tanya! The ones that do have lists from here to New York and back."

Mabel nodded, eyes sympathetic. "I know, Gabby. Look, all of us will do whatever we—"

"Why doesn't Manna House add an option like that for homeless single moms like Tanya—you know, a building with separate apartments, where women can make a real home for their kids, but with services that prepare them to make a go of it alone?" I stood up and started to pace. "Even Precious is about to lose her—"

"Gabby! Gabby." Mabel's tone pulled me up short. "That's a wonderful idea, and one of these days—years—we'd love to do something like that when some philanthropic billionaire floats us a nice fat donation. But right now, *your* reality is looking for an apartment, okay?" She came around her desk and softened her words with a quick hug.

I returned the hug. "Okay. Thanks again for putting us back on the bed list. Dandy too, right? Denny Baxter said he'd drive us down tomorrow morning, so getting Mom and Dandy squared away might take most of the day. But I'll hit the streets on Monday, I promise. *After* the staff meeting."

I left her office and almost made it out the front doors when I heard, "Oh, Gabby! One more thing." I turned, shaking my head and laughing.

Mabel was standing at her office door. "What?"

"Mabel. You always have 'one more thing.'"

"Oh. Well, I do have one more thing. All that dog food and doggy stuff, remember? It's got to go."

I had talked my mother into staying at the house with Jodi Baxter the last two days, due to a recurrence of that nasty headache during the knitting club on Wednesday. Since I was out, Estelle had helped her lie down in the multipurpose room, where she'd slept again for several hours. And when I got back to the house Friday evening, dragging from the rising humidity, Jodi said my mom had had another one that afternoon, so bad it made her cry. She was still asleep.

"When was the last time your mom saw a doctor?" Jodi asked, handing me a cold iced tea as I collapsed on their back porch swing, then settling herself on the top step leading down into the postage-stamp yard. I nudged Dandy on his dog bed with my toe, but he just flopped his tail a few times. Too hot for woman and beast alike.

"Mm . . . don't really know. She had a fall Mother's Day weekend, and my aunt Mercy took her to the hospital to get her checked out. And another fall when the boys and I were visiting her in North Dakota earlier this month. She tripped over Dandy,

and we had to ice a knot on her head, but she said she was fine."
I shrugged. "Have no idea when her last physical was."

"You might think about getting her checked out."

"Yeah, good idea, Jodi." I heard the slight sarcasm in my tone
but couldn't stop. "I don't even have a family doctor yet! And in
case you haven't noticed, my life has been a *little* crazy lately, what
with getting thrown out of my house by my own husband, losing
my sons overnight, and my mother and an injured dog dropped
in my lap!" I threw up my hands, sloshing my iced tea. "When
was I supposed to see a doctor?"

Jodi winced, but to her credit she didn't walk back into the
kitchen, leaving me to wallow in my own frustration. "I know.
Just . . . when you can."

We sat in silence for a long minute, with just the *squeak
squeak* of the swing and the drone of traffic several streets over as
background. Jodi picked up a stray nail and chipped at the loose
paint on one of the railing posts. Finally I said, "Sorry, Jodi. I
know you care. You and Denny have been super. Can't thank you
enough for hosting us this whole week and giving us a respite
from the shelter. Even dog-sitting! Not many people would do
that—especially when we were virtually strangers."

Jodi glanced up through her brown bangs, looking girlish in
her shoulder-length bob. "It's been fun, Gabby—really. It gets a
little lonely around here with the kids gone."

"Well, but Amanda will be back tomorrow, right? And she'll
be here the rest of the summer, till it's time to go back to college.
She sounds like a neat kid."

"Yeah, she is . . . when she's not driving me crazy." Jodi made
a face. "She's got this boyfriend, José, a really nice young man, but

'Manda can't decide if he's 'just a friend' or if she's in love . . . oh wait! You know his mother. Delores Enriques, the nurse at Manna House. And she's one of our Yada Yada sisters."

Delores's son? I grinned. It was fun getting "inside information" on the staff at Manna House. José and Amanda, *hmm* . . .

"Gabby." Jodi suddenly sounded serious. "I feel awful thinking about you and your mom going back to a homeless shelter. It doesn't feel . . . right. Don't get me wrong. I love Manna House, I think they do a terrific job, and I'm enjoying teaching the typing class—all two weeks of it so far. But . . . I'd hate to be living there—in a bunk room, no less. Sheesh!"

I shrugged. "It's better than some shelters I've heard about, where they've got one huge room housing thirty to sixty women, like Katrina victims wall to wall in the Superdome."

Jodi glanced at Dandy, snoring peacefully in the dog bed. "It's been nice having a dog around again. Dandy's a sweetheart—right, buddy?" She reached over and gave Dandy's ears a scratch. He rewarded her with a few more tail thumps. "Mm. Wish Amanda could meet him. She'd go bonkers! You'd have to sneak him away when she wasn't looking."

Still scratching the dog's ears, Jodi looked at me sideways. "It can't be easy having a dog at the shelter—no yard to romp in, all those stairs to climb—and he's still stiff from those stitches. What would you think about us keeping Dandy, at least until things settle down for you, you know, find a place of your own, get the boys back . . ."

I couldn't believe my ears. In a heartbeat! *Okay, God, where was this option when I really needed it, like* before *Philip got fed up with having Dandy underfoot? Don't You have Your timing a little screwed up?* But even now it would solve so many problems—like who was going to walk him if Lucy didn't come back. And the problem of getting him up and down two flights of stairs each day . . . not to mention those media hounds who were sure to sniff him out once we got back to Manna House.

The Baxters would be a perfect family for Dandy!

But I reluctantly shook my head. "My mom wouldn't hear of it. That dog means the world to her. She turned down a perfectly good retirement home I found here in Rogers Park because she couldn't keep Dandy with her."

Jodi's eyes brightened. "Well . . . your mom could stay here too! I mean, even when Amanda comes back, we still have Josh's old room. Really! She wouldn't be alone, because I'm off for the summer. And Estelle lives right upstairs. She could take her on like one of her in-home-care seniors."

I gaped at Jodi. "Are you serious?" I felt as if gold from heaven were pouring down into my lap. A safe place for my mom with people who like dogs . . . "Just until I find an apartment, though. Actually, she's got some money. We could pay, you know, for room and board."

"Oh, don't worry about that. She eats like a bird."

I was so excited, I could hardly think straight. "Oh, Jodi. This is wonderful. It's like the answers to all my prayers. Let me go talk to my mom. You think she's awake yet?"

Martha Shepherd was packing, and Martha Shepherd wouldn't budge. "No, Celeste. We have to go home. I promised Lucy that I'd be back."

"Mom! The Baxters are inviting you *and* Dandy to stay here for a while. Isn't that what you wanted? And it's just until I find an apartment for us—or until your name comes up for assisted living back in Minot. Then you can go home."

"The Baxters have been very nice, Celeste. But I promised Lu—"

"*Mom!* Lucy isn't *at* Manna House right now. She's been gone all week. Maybe she's not coming back." I hated to do it, but my mother was being totally unreasonable.

My mother calmly folded her nightgown and put it in the small suitcase. "She'll be back. She said she'd look after Dandy. And besides, I promised . . . Hand me those underthings, would you, Celeste?"

chapter 24

I tossed all night, snatching bits of sleep here and there, but waking every hour or so, wound up in the sheet. The fact that it was hot and muggy and the Baxters didn't have central air didn't help either. But mainly I was angry. The perfect solution for my mom and Dandy had been handed to me on a silver platter—and my mom said *no*?!

Argh! I mean, she "promised Lucy"? How did *that* weigh in on the grand scheme of things when I was trying to get my family back together and take care of her and Dandy too?! *Lucy* was totally unpredictable. Here today, gone tomorrow. Couldn't my mother understand that?

I kicked off the sheet, got up, and turned the fan in the window up another speed before flopping back onto the bed, my thoughts as wilted as the cotton camisole I'd worn to bed . . . Should I *make* my mother stay here? It made so much sense! She might pout a day or two, but she'd get over it, wouldn't she?

I reran my list of arguments. For one thing, there were all

those stairs. "I'm not dead yet," my mom had said, pooh-poohing my concern. "And Manna House has an elevator." Which she had yet to use.

Another thing: A homeless shelter was no place for a dog. True, they'd adopted him last weekend as their official "watchdog"— but who really cared? Lucy, maybe. Sure, she'd gotten attached to my mom and Dandy, and her disappearance was probably a royal snit because I'd whisked them away right under her nose. But I couldn't believe we'd let *Lucy*, of all people—a bag lady who'd been living on the street most of her life—determine what happened with *my* life!

I squeezed my eyes shut, remembering the day I'd first met her. Tripped over her was more like it—or rather, tripped over her cart sticking out from the bushes while I was running in the sudden rain shower, trying to get back to our penthouse before Philip showed up with his new business partner. This old bag lady came out from under the bush, hacking and coughing, with only a garbage bag for protection, fussing over *me* because I'd cut my bare foot.

I started to giggle in spite of myself just thinking about it now.

And then! The *look* on Philip's face when the two of us came in the front door of the penthouse, Lucy in her layers of mismatched clothes and smelling rather, er, stale, both of us dripping wet . . .

Ohhh! I stuffed my face into the pillow, shoulders shaking with laughter.

I finally threw off the pillow and wiped my soggy face with the sheet. Okay, Lucy had impacted my life big-time. If it wasn't for her, I never would have visited Manna House, never would have been offered a job as their program director. And I had to admit, in her own odd way, she'd been a real friend. She'd kept my mom company when I had to bring my mom to work . . . she'd taken Dandy for walks when I had to bring *him* to work . . . she'd gone hunting for Dandy when Philip "lost" the dog on purpose . . . and Lucy had found Dandy and found *me* when the tables turned and *I* was the one homeless with nowhere to go . . .

My anger slowly evaporated as the first morning light bathed the Baxters' guest bedroom in hazy blues in spite of the closed blinds and whirring fan in the window. A chest of drawers, a bookshelf, a desk—Josh Baxter's boyhood furnishings—gradually took shape in my vision.

Might as well get up. What time was it . . . five o'clock? If I could find my Bible, maybe I'd go out on the back porch, sit in the porch swing one last time, and get back to the Bible reading I'd started during my trip to North Dakota—before my life unraveled. Hadn't Jodi and the other Yada Yada sisters prayed that I'd begin to see God's purpose in my life? Prayed for wisdom to meet the challenges? That I'd have strength to face tomorrow?

Well, tomorrow was here, and I definitely needed some of that wisdom and strength. I'd already found some of it in the Matthew chapters I'd been reading a couple of weeks ago. Maybe there was more . . .

"Hey, Gabby! Wait!"

I turned to see Estelle waving at me from the upstairs porch midmorning just as we were loading up the Baxters' Dodge Caravan. The fifty-something black woman came schlepping down the outside stairs, her loose, multicolored caftan billowing in the stiff breeze off the lake, as I let Denny and Jodi walk my mother and Dandy into the garage to get them settled in the minivan.

"I'm not *leaving* leaving," I teased, setting down our suitcases. "See you Monday. Staff meeting at ten, right?"

She ignored me, gathering her pepper-and-salt, loose, kinky hair into a knot on top of her head, as if she'd been interrupted. "Humph. Harry just called. Said to tell you that your *husband*"— she dragged out the word with thinly disguised contempt—"left your sewing machine at the front desk of Richmond Towers. I say hallelujah!" She fluttered a hand at me. "You go on now. Might as well pick it up on your way. That'll come in real handy on Monday when I do my sewing class." Estelle turned away, muttering to herself as she hauled herself back up the steps. "*Mm-mm.* Maybe Mama sewed clothes by hand, but I ain't goin' back *there*. Uh-uh."

"Come on, Gabby!" Jodi yelled. "I'm teaching a typing class at eleven, remember?"

I looked at my watch. Only ten o'clock. We had plenty of time. But it was a good thing we'd left then, because traffic was heavy on Sheridan Road. "Taste of Chicago going on this weekend." Denny glanced in the mirror at me. "You ever been, Gabby?"

Jodi backhanded his arm from the passenger seat. "Don't you go getting any ideas, Denny Baxter. Last time we went, we lost a kid in that crowd, remember? And I said *never* . . ."

I was only half listening. Philip left the sewing machine as agreed. That was good. But the idea of picking up the machine *today* left a knot in the pit of my stomach. Philip said he was moving out by the end of June. Which was yesterday—Friday—but maybe he was moving out today since it was Saturday, even if it was July first. I didn't want to stop by there and risk running into him. Or maybe I did. I had Denny and Jodi Baxter and my mother with me . . . Wouldn't Philip feel like a rotten heel if we all walked in there while he was loading *our* stuff into a moving van?

"Denny, would you mind stopping by Richmond Towers a minute? There's a frontage road just off Sheridan. I need to pick up my sewing machine, and it'll be easier with a car."

I saw Jodi and Denny in the front seats glance at each other. But Denny said, "Sure. No problem."

Dandy was sitting on the floor behind the driver's seat, putting his paw in my mother's lap, trying to see out the window. As we turned onto the frontage road, I peered out the front windshield. No moving truck that I could see. Intent on the dog, my mother seemed oblivious to where we were until Denny pulled up in front of the luxury tower along the frontage road. She looked past me at the revolving door and stiffened. "This isn't Manna House." She shook her head vigorously. "No, no, won't go . . ."

"Mom, Mom. It's all right. Stay in the car. I just need to pick up something. Uh, Denny, would you mind going in with me?"

Jodi's husband turned on the hazards, got out, and we pushed through the revolving door into the lobby. Sure enough, Mr. Bentley was behind the desk, reading the newspaper, traffic through the lobby being lighter on a Saturday morning. I looked left and right. So far so good.

"Hey, Mr. B," I said. "What are you doing working the weekend?"

The doorman quickly folded the paper and jumped up, grabbing his uniform cap. "Mrs. Fairbanks! Denny, my man." He shook hands with Denny Baxter in a familiar way and grinned at me. "Oh, you know, we got a problem keepin' a weekend man on this job. So I end up with extra hours." He winked. "Don't mind the extra pay. Oh . . . here's the sewing machine Mr. Fairbanks left down here this mornin'."

Denny took the heavy case over the top of the counter. "Where's that grandson of yours today?"

Mr. Bentley chuckled. "Oh, my mama thinks she's takin' care of him, but it's actually the other way around. Just till I get off work. Then we're goin' down to the Taste. Mm-mm, can't wait to get some of Sweet Baby Ray's barbeque!" He laughed and gave Denny a high five.

Mr. B and Denny certainly seemed buddy-buddy. "You two know each other?" I wagged a finger from one to the other.

Denny grinned. "Harry's been coming to our men's group, meets on Tuesday nights. Small world." The two men laughed.

I shifted nervously, keeping an eye on the security door leading to the elevators. "Uh, Mr. B, my husband said he was moving out this weekend. Have you seen a moving truck or anything?"

Mr. Bentley shrugged. "Don't know anything about that, Mrs. Fairbanks. In fact, I'd be surprised if he's movin' out this weekend. When he brought that sewing machine down this morning, he had one of those overnight cases on wheels with him, and he headed for the parking garage. That was about . . . oh, I'd say, maybe an hour ago."

I stared. *Not moving out?* What did that mean? And if he wasn't moving out, where did he go? Had he gone to Virginia to visit the boys?

Mr. Bentley glanced about and then leaned close, as if wanting to be sure no one else heard him. "Thought you might be wantin' to go upstairs since management made him replace the original locks. I think they told him it was that or be sued for breach of contract." He straightened. "You didn't hear that from me, though. Understand?"

This news ricocheted in my head like a pinball trying to find the right hole to drop into. The locks had been changed *back*? As in, the key in my purse would actually open the door to the penthouse? I could go up the elevator, unlock the door, and—

"Denny. I—I'd like to go upstairs to our apartment for just a few minutes. Can you wait?" Was I out of my mind? What if Philip came back?

"I'll go with you." It wasn't a question. "Harry, we'll pick this up on our way out." Denny handed the sewing machine back over the counter and followed me through the security door.

Neither of us spoke as the elevator whirred its way to the thirty-second floor. The door *ping*ed open, and I stepped into the cool foyer with the beautiful ceramic floor tiles. The last time I'd been here, my clothes and personal things had been piled in a jumble of suitcases, boxes, and bags. Today the floor glistened.

Was Camila Sanchez still cleaning the penthouse on Fridays?

Quickly, before I lost my nerve, I stuck my house key into the lock and turned. The door opened noiselessly. I stepped into the cool dimness of the entryway—the "gallery," they called it—my heart beating so fast I could feel it in my chest.

The *tick-tock, tick-tock* of the old Fairbanks grandfather clock pulled me into the high-ceilinged living room with the floor-to-ceiling glass windows sweeping in a curve all along the far side. Across Lake Shore Drive, Lake Michigan sparkled under a cloudless blue sky. I felt lightheaded. I looked away.

"Wow," Denny said. Then, "Are you sure you want to be doing this, Gabby?"

I didn't answer, just started walking from room to room. Philip's den, his desk still cluttered, nothing packed . . . past the powder room on the way to the kitchen—everything fairly neat, except for a few dirty dishes in the sink . . . the dining room with its long, polished wood table, able to seat ten people . . . our Lenox wedding china—the Spring Vista pattern Marlene Fairbanks had picked out for us—still in the buffet . . .

Not a packing box in sight.

I stopped at the boys' bedrooms, side by side in the hallway leading toward the master bedroom, doors closed. Trembling, I reached out a hand and opened the door to Paul's room. The bunk bed was made up neat, but the desk and storage cubes held a jumble of CDs, action figures, games, the clothes in the closet askew . . .

The tightness in my chest squeezed so hard, I could hardly breathe. The last time I saw my sons, they'd been staying in this room together so my mother could sleep in P. J.'s room next door. When I left the house that day, I had no idea they'd be gone when I got home . . .

My breath started coming in big gulps, pain and anger rising from their hidden places like steel tendrils winding themselves around my heart. I was vaguely aware that Denny disappeared from my side, but the next minute he reappeared with a glass of water. "Gabby. Drink this. You need to sit down."

I took a couple of swallows. Then he led me to the breakfast nook in the kitchen and I sat down, my head in my hands. Jodi's husband sat opposite me. As my breath slowed, he said, "Gabby, you have every right to be here. In fact, if you want me to, I'll go get your mother and Dandy and you can move back in. But I think I should go . . . and Jodi's supposed to teach that class, remember?"

I heard the nervousness in his voice. Wasn't about Jodi's typing class either. Didn't blame him. If Philip came back right now, Denny's presence would be sorely misunderstood. Might even get ugly.

Stay? Oh, I was so tempted. I'd love for Philip to come back and find me and my mother and Dandy back in the penthouse, making ourselves at home, watching TV, soaking in the Jacuzzi, baking brownies . . .

Or would I be asking for the ugliness to start all over again? I couldn't do that to my mother—not to mention she'd flat-out refuse to come back to this house. My sweet mother could be as stubborn as a two-year-old.

Did I have the strength to face Philip alone? Mom and Dandy could stay at the shelter, and I could hunker down at the penthouse, demand my rights, lay claim to the furniture, the china, the family pictures—

"Gabby?" Denny's voice was gentle. "Your mom and Dandy are waiting in the car, and it's hot out there."

I stood up. I didn't have to make this decision right this second. I had the key. It opened the door.

But I left the water glass on the kitchen counter with my lipstick smudge.

chapter 25

Harry Bentley handed over the sewing machine on our way out of Richmond Towers but gave me a puzzled look. "What? No contraband?"

I offered a dry smile. "Not this time. But I left my calling card. Thanks, Mr. B."

When we came out of the revolving doors, we saw the mini-van had been moved to a visitor parking space. And the van was empty. "Jodi!" Denny yelled after loading the sewing machine in the back with our suitcases.

"Over here!" Jodi's voice shot back from somewhere in the park that lay between the frontage road and Lake Shore Drive in the distance, and a few moments later we saw Jodi, my mother, and Dandy making their way toward us along the jogging path—except that Jodi was having a hard time getting Dandy to cooperate. The dog kept pulling in the opposite direction, sometimes spinning her around. Denny belly laughed as the trio jerked their way toward us in stops and starts.

But we finally got my mom and Dandy in the car as Jodi collapsed in the front seat. "I don't know what happened!" she groaned. "The car was hot, so we got out and went looking for a bench . . . when all of a sudden Dandy went nuts! He darted off, and I had to run catch him; then he didn't want to come with me."

"It was Lucy," my mother announced.

I buckled her seat belt. "Uh-huh. Did you see her?"

My mother shook her head. "But it was Lucy."

"I don't know." Jodi shrugged as Denny pulled back out onto Sheridan Road. "I didn't see anybody."

I dropped it. Traffic was still heavy, but we finally drove under the Sheridan Road El station that crossed over the street a few blocks from Manna House. I glanced at my watch. "You're gonna make it, Jodi!" I sang out. "With a whole minute to spare!"

Denny rounded the corner by the Laundromat and slowed. "Uh-oh."

That pesky female reporter was hanging around the front steps of Manna House.

"Denny!" I hissed. "Back up and go around to the alley."

"Good idea—but if we back up now, she's going to guess we're the prey and run after us. I think it'd be best to just get it over with."

I was starting to panic. "But I don't want that reporter going after my mom. They don't know Dandy is her dog! But if they did, they'd start poking around and asking questions about why *she's* at the shelter—which could get messy for me real quick."

"Then you just go in with Dandy," Jodi said quickly. "We'll drive off, and nobody will follow us. We'll drive around the block and bring Martha and your stuff in the side door. Just make sure when you get inside to ask somebody to unlock it."

591

I hesitated only a nanosecond. "Okay. Come on, Dandy. Time to face the lions." I grabbed his leash as the car stopped. As quickly as I could, I opened the side door of the minivan, lifted Dandy to the ground, and walked him toward Manna House.

Immediately the reporter's voice began shouting at me. "Mrs. Fairbanks! Where has Dandy been?" The woman whipped out her cell phone. "Tony! Get your camera over here. Hero Dog is back . . . Mrs. Fairbanks! Will Dandy be staying at the shelter as official watchdog now? How did he happen to be at the shelter last weekend when—"

Even I didn't notice when the minivan pulled away.

"Girl, you too much! And I thought I had drama in my life!" Precious McGill tucked her beaded extensions under a white mesh hairnet and shook a bread knife at me from behind the kitchen counter. "When was you going to tell me about your mama's dog gettin' sliced up last weekend—not to mention you an' she takin' up space on the bed list here, just like all the rest of us po' folks?" She stuck out her lip.

"Just give me a cup of coffee, Precious. Cream, no sugar. Please?"

"You go on, Drama Queen. I gotta brew a fresh pot."

Gratefully, I unlocked my office and sank into the desk chair. The plan had worked. Hoping to pacify the reporters, I'd smiled into the cameras and made pleasant, vague comments. Yes, Dandy was much better . . . Yes, he'd been voted the official Manna House watchdog, "but we'll see" . . . We were all grateful to Chicago citizens for the outpouring of sympathy, but getting back to normal would be the best thing for all concerned.

And then I'd ducked inside. Precious, who'd turned up to do Saturday lunch on Estelle's weekend off, had been standing in the foyer, and she ran downstairs to open the side door. "Gramma Shep" and Dandy had been immediately mobbed with a spontaneous "welcome back" celebration by the residents and taken to the multipurpose room to hold court.

Given all the hullabaloo, Jodi had given up on teaching her typing class, and she and Denny were on the verge of leaving when Josh and Edesa showed up with Gracie in a back carrier, offering to take a few of the older shelter kids to the Taste of Chicago. "Dad! Mom! Didn't know you'd be here," Josh crowed. "You wanna go to the Taste with us, help chaperone the kids? Let's see, who's going?" Sammy had jumped up and down, waving his hand, along with seven-year-old Trina and her six-year-old brother, Rufino, and Keisha, a bright-eyed girl of ten. "All riiight. That would make one kid per adult, plus Gracie." He'd beamed at his parents.

Even Edesa had laid it on thick. *"Por favor?* Like a family outing, *sí?"*

Jodi knew the jig was up. Before they left, she'd given me a hug and murmured, "Invitation is still open. Think about it. And don't forget your name—'Strong Woman of God.' See you tomorrow for church?"

Now, waiting for Precious to deliver that much-needed shot of caffeine, I thought about Denny and Jodi . . . *Such nice folks.* And if Lucy didn't show up, I'd definitely lean on my mom to accept their hospitality for her and Dandy. But frankly, I was kind of relieved to leave the Baxter home. Their affectionate teasing dangled a working marriage in front of me but out of reach, like watching two lovers share a full-course meal in a fine restaurant while I stood outside the window by myself, stomach growling.

"Coffee!" Precious nudged my office door open and set down two cups of coffee, then plopped into the extra folding chair beside my desk. "Okay, no more stallin'. Whassup wit' you, girl? I want all the deets."

"Huh." I cradled the cup of hot, creamy coffee in two hands. "If I give you all the 'deets,' you'll never make lunch and we'll have a mutiny on our hands. How about the skinny version, and I'll fill you in later? Besides, I have a favor to ask you."

I'm sure Precious meant well as lunch volunteer. But bologna sandwiches on white bread—no lettuce—with mayo and mustard, potato chips, canned fruit cocktail, store-bought cookies, and a mysterious red juice that tasted like colored sugar water was definitely not in the tradition of Estelle Williams's yummy lunches. Funny thing, though. I heard no complaints from the residents, many of whom went back for seconds on those bald bologna sandwiches. Ugh.

Nutrition. I still needed to ask Edesa Baxter about doing a couple of workshops in nutrition. For everybody—not just the few in Estelle's cooking class on Thursdays. She'd be the perfect person since she was she getting her master's degree in public health.

On the pretext of taking my barely nibbled lunch into my office to work, I dumped it into the wastebasket and made a note to myself: *Ask Edesa—nutrition?*

Once the dish crew started cleanup, Precious joined me in the rec room since I'd asked her to help me decide what to do with all the dog food stacked under the Ping-Pong table, plus all the stuffed dogs, dog chews, and doggy toys we'd loaded into garbage bags last weekend. She surveyed the loot, hands on hips. "What's the problem? Keep some of the dog food for Dandy—whatchu need, three, four bags?—an' donate all the rest to the Humane Society or someplace like that. No, wait . . . I heard 'bout this group called Pet Supplies for Seniors. They give stuff free to old people who can't afford food for their pets. Call 'em up. I'm sure they'll send a truck or somethin'."

"Really? That's perfect." I held up a yellow stuffed dog with brown floppy ears. "But what about all these stuffed animals? I mean, we gave a few to the kids here at the shelter, but . . ." I swept my hand at all the garbage bags. "There must be at least a couple dozen more dogs here!"

"Keep 'em."

"What? I'm not *that* desperate for something to cuddle in my bed."

Precious cracked up. "Girl, I don't mean *you* keep 'em. I mean, store 'em someplace and give one to every kid who comes to the shelter with his or her mama, along with the basic kit. Somethin' of your own to love is lots more important than a new toothbrush to a kid who's been sleepin' in a car or just got evicted."

I liked her idea. But would Mabel? "Where in the world would we find room?"

"That, sister girl, is your problem. Look, I gotta go." Precious headed out the door of the rec room, and I followed. "Sabrina got an appointment at one o' them crisis pregnancy centers, an' I wanna make sure she goes. She kinda ridin' the fence about carryin' this baby. Pray for us, will ya, Miz Gabby?"

We paused just outside my office. Should I offer to pray with her now? Seemed like it might be the right thing to do, but—

"That your phone ringin'?" Precious darted inside my office, picked up the desk phone, listened, shrugged, and hung it up again.

"What? Oh, could be my cell." The ring was coming from a drawer in the file cabinet where I'd stored my shoulder bag. I still wasn't used to the ring on my new cell phone. My old one had the "William Tell Overture," which *always* got my attention. I finally found the phone and flipped it open, but the caller was gone.

And so was Precious.

Feeling a tad guilty that I'd let an opportunity to pray with Precious slip past me, I tapped my phone keys until I found Missed Calls. *Lee Boyer?* Why was he calling? I hit Call Back but realized I had no signal and didn't get one until I got outside on the front steps of Manna House. *Whew.* It was hot out here.

He answered on the first ring. "Lee Boyer."

Should I call him Lee? Still felt weird. I skipped it. "Hi! Gabby Fairbanks, returning your call. What's up?"

"Have you found an apartment yet?"

He was checking up on me? I tried to keep the irritation from my voice. "No. I—"

"Good. Because this real estate guy I know has an apartment for rent in a six-flat in the Wrigleyville area. Not too far from where you are now. Nice place, pretty nice area. Actually he's trying to sell the building, but that shouldn't be a problem. Buyers have to honor leases, and most are glad to keep current renters."

My irritation dissipated, replaced with . . . what? A warmth that somebody was looking out for me. "I need three bedrooms, you know." As long as my mother was with me, the boys would have to bunk up, but that's the way it was.

"That's what caught my attention. This building has both two- and three-bedroom apartments, but it's the three-bedroom on the first floor that's available. Plus it's only a couple of blocks from the Red Line—a real bonus if you don't have a car."

The first floor! No more dizzy moments just looking out the window from the thirty-second floor. As Lee Boyer spoke, I realized how overwhelmed I'd been feeling about trying to find a place to live. Where in the world would I start? I was still a Chicago tenderfoot. Could I find something big enough for me and the boys *and* my mom? And if I did, could I afford it? An actual apartment, recommended by someone who was in my corner . . . it felt almost too good to be true. "Sounds good. Could I take a look at it? Do I need to call somebody?"

"The old tenants are supposedly moving out today. But I think if I pushed, the owner would be willing to show it tomorrow, though it would still need cleaning, maybe some repairs. How about eleven? I could pick you up and take you there."

Pick me up? "Oh, Lee. You don't have to—"

"Don't mind at all. Not doing anything else. The sooner you get into an apartment, the sooner you can get your boys back. I think I've got the address of the shelter . . . See you at eleven, then."

Only after the call ended did I realize that tomorrow was Sunday. Eleven o'clock meant I couldn't take Mom to church at SouledOut.

chapter 26

My mom's face clouded when I told her the news. "But we have to go to church, Gabby. It's Sunday."

"Mom! It's just this once. My lawyer wants me to look at an apartment near here. It's important!" Did she just call me Gabby? Well, hallelujah.

"But does it have to be eleven? Couldn't you make an appointment in the afternoon?"

I tried not to roll my eyes. Actually, I'd thought of that myself after Lee hung up. Sounded like he'd just pulled eleven o'clock out of the air. But I was chicken to call him back and change the appointment. What would I tell him? *Oh, I forgot, can't do eleven; gotta go to church.* Which obviously wasn't on his agenda. Would he think I was some fundy chick?

"I'm sorry, Mom. Just this once. And they have church Sunday evenings here at Manna House, did you know that?" Couldn't remember what church group was scheduled for tomorrow, but I'd check it out.

Mom was slightly mollified by the idea that church would come to *her* . . . and by the time a youth group from Wheaton arrived at five o'clock with the makings for a taco salad supper and sides of beans and rice, I'd called the Pet Support for Seniors people and arranged for a pickup on Monday of the dog food, chews, and toys. The woman on the phone went all gaga when she realized Dandy, the "Hero Dog" of Manna House Women's Shelter, was making this donation. I barely got her off the phone.

I was antsy to call the boys. Still had time. Supper wasn't until six—but it was already six in Virginia. I had wanted to call all day but realized I'd been putting it off. Was Philip there visiting P. J. and Paul? The idea churned in my stomach. If he was, that was good . . . in a way. Would show he cared about them. They needed their dad. But they'd wonder why I hadn't come too. Would they think I didn't want to? Was too busy to make the trip? Should I tell them their father had put a lock on my finances?

Oh God, I don't want to put my boys in the middle of our mess . . .

I grabbed my cell, scurried to the main floor, and slipped outside into the warm, humid air. Several shelter guests were lounging on the front steps, having a smoke. I walked halfway down the block until I got a good, strong signal on my cell. So far, so good. No reporters lurking about.

Philip's mother answered the phone. Just my luck. "Hello, Marlene," I said evenly. "May I speak to P. J. or Paul? Actually, both."

"I'm sorry, Gabrielle. The boys are out."

And . . . ? Out where? With whom? My insides screamed, *Would it hurt to give me a little more information, mother-in-law dear?!*

I let a few beats go by while I calmed down. But I blatantly fished. "With their father?"

"With their fa—. . . with Philip? Why do you ask?"

A simple yes or no would've been nice. "He's out of town this weekend. I thought he might be visiting the boys." I loaded up my tone with sugar.

For a moment, her end of the line was silent. Then . . . "No, he's not here."

Philip isn't there? So where . . . ? The funny thing was, Marlene Fairbanks sounded startled. And offended. I wanted to laugh. The woman didn't *know* her precious Philip was out of town! Worse, he hadn't told her where he was going. Oh! I could almost hear her nose cracking out of joint over the phone.

I let Philip dangle. "So when will the boys be back? I'd like to talk to them."

"They'll be late tonight. Try tomorrow. Good-bye, Gabrielle." The line went dead.

I would've been more teed off at her rudeness, except I couldn't help but enjoy knowing Marlene didn't know any more than I did about Philip's whereabouts.

But I could take a good guess. The Horseshoe Casino in Indiana. With Henry and Mona Fenchel, who'd—

"Hey! What time ya got, Fuzz Top? Anybody take that dog out yet since ya been back this mornin'? No, 'course not. Don't know why I bother ta ask. Just wanna know if I got time 'fore supper."

I grinned as Lucy Tucker, purple knit hat perched on her head, wrestled her overloaded cart up the front steps of Manna House. "Hey yourself, Lucy. I know somebody inside who'll be mighty glad to see you."

I kicked off my sheet and sat up, careful not to bonk my head on the bunk above me. Odd. My watch already said six thirty. What happened to the usual six o'clock wake-up bell? Did they actually let the residents sleep in on Sunday morning?

I peered around the dimly lit room. The four bunks were full, top and bottom—me, my mom, Lucy, and Tanya on the bottom bunks, Tanya's boy, Sammy, above her, plus three more new lumps on the top bunks who'd been put on the bed list this past week. Must be the sweltering heat driving them in. Had hit ninety-plus yesterday.

Sliding off my bunk slowly to avoid the inevitable squeaks, I pulled on a pair of running shorts and a T-shirt, stuck my feet in my slippers, and fished under my bed for my jute carryall bag with the leather handles. Since I wasn't going to church this morning, maybe I could find someplace to read my Bible since I'd started reading the gospel of Matthew again yesterday. *Huh.* Was I just feeling guilty? Okay, maybe a little. But I really did want to find a quiet place to read and think and pray.

Dandy raised his head from the dog bed the Baxters had given him as I opened the bunk-room door, but laid it back down again as if saying, *Following you around is too much effort.* Poor dog. He still wasn't completely healed.

I slipped down the stairs to the main floor, wondering where to go. Could go to my office, but that felt too much like work . . . The chapel! Of course. It was easy to forget the small prayer room tucked behind the multipurpose room—especially since you had to pass the TV room, schoolroom, and toddler playroom first.

But this morning I peeked into the small room, with its several rows of padded folding chairs, a small lectern, and a kneeling prayer bench . . . *Drat.* Somebody was there already. I started to back out when the person turned—Liz Handley, the former director of Manna House, who'd shown up last night to do weekend night staff duty. "Gabby? Don't leave. I'm done here. Gotta go start breakfast now anyway. Wake-up bell's at seven thirty." The short woman with the mannish haircut gave me a friendly pat on the shoulder as she passed and shut the door behind her.

Well, okay. Guess I hadn't really chased her out.

I settled into a padded chair on the front row. The tiny prayer chapel didn't have the benefit of the stained-glass windows that graced the front of the building and spilled prisms of tinted light into the foyer. But warm lights of various colors embedded in the ceiling—yellow, green, rose—created a quiet mood. For several long moments, I just sat, not really thinking. Just soaking up the sense of peace.

"Come to Me . . ."

Whoa. There it was again. Jesus' words from the passage I'd read weeks ago in Matthew's gospel. The last time that Voice had tugged at my spirit with those words was the night I couldn't sleep and Dandy ended up foiling our would-be robber.

A week ago.

Okay, okay, I'm here, God. I opened my Bible and found the place I'd left off reading in Matthew's gospel, chapter 13. Oh yeah. The parable of the sower. I remembered this story from Sunday school days. Jesus telling a story about a farmer who sowed some seed. Some of it fell on the hard path, and the birds ate it . . . some seed fell on rocky ground, so it only had shallow roots . . . some seed fell among thorns and got choked when it came up . . . and some seed fell on good ground and produced a big crop.

Never really thought much about this parable. After all, people who believed in Jesus were the seed that fell on good ground, right? Been there, done that, end of story. But today I had the same question the disciples did. *What does this mean?*

I read and reread Jesus' answer. The seed was the Word of God. *Got that much.* The hard ground was like people who didn't understand it, so it never took root. *Okay, got that too.* The seed that fell on rocky places were like people who embraced God's Word at first, but when trouble came, it died, because their faith was shallow . . .

Ouch. Kinda like me when Damien dumped me, back when I was nineteen. I'd been a Christian up till then—thought I was, anyway. But at the first big bump in the road, my faith was too shallow to survive.

I kept reading. Thorns next . . . Jesus said the thorns were all the worries of this life, choking the Word of God. He said the "deceitfulness of wealth" did that too.

Oh brother. This parable had my name all over it. I'd let Fairbanks money cushion me from the pitfalls of life—until now. Huh. Always thought I didn't really care about money, but I'd let its comforts and expectations blind me to the way it'd been eating away at my marriage, numbing the person I was inside.

Or maybe, keeping me from knowing the person God wanted me to be. *Gabrielle, strong woman of God.*

I leaned forward, elbows on my knees, chin on my hands, and sat that way a long time . . .

Somewhere on the floor above, the wake-up bell was ringing. Seven thirty.

But I still didn't move. Funny that I'd found God again at a homeless shelter, of all places. Of course, if I really thought about it, God was always showing up in unlikely places. Jesus, the long-awaited Messiah—the Son of God!—had been born in a drafty, smelly cow barn, which certainly didn't look good on *His* résumé. At least I got to sleep in a room with actual people.

Except . . . if I was honest with myself, my budding faith was still choking on all my worries. Even though the prayers of the Yada Yada sisters had buoyed me up last weekend, I hadn't taken much time to pray since then. Really pray, I mean. Or listen. Most of my prayers were still talking *at* God. I let my mind get so garbled, wrestling with all my problems, that God would probably need a sledgehammer to get my attention—

Oh.

Okay, God, I get it! Back off, already!

Lucy had just snapped the leash on Dandy's collar for a morning walk when Lee Boyer pulled up in front of Manna House in a black Prius. "Just a sec!" I called out, and turned back to Lucy. "Just . . . try to keep Dandy out of sight as much as possible. Alleys or whatever. Those reporters, you know."

The old lady gave me a look. "Don't ya think I know a thing or two 'bout keepin' outta sight?" She craned her neck to look into the car. "Who's that?" Her eyes narrowed. "Not that slimeball husband o' yours, I hope."

"My lawyer, Lucy. We have an appointment." I decided not to say anything about looking for an apartment. She'd been muttering not-so-subtle digs ever since she showed up yesterday about how we'd "up and left her" last weekend. "Thanks again for walking Dandy."

I opened the car door and slid into the leather passenger seat.

"Ohh, nice." I glanced at Lee behind the wheel. His usual business attire of blue jeans and boots had given way to khaki shorts and sturdy sandals. "Don't know what I was expecting, but not such a high-tech car."

He let slip a shy grin. "Hey. When gas went over three bucks a gallon last year, I figured I'd get smart and get one of these hybrids. You all set?" He touched a button. No sound . . . until he stepped on the gas and pulled into the street.

For some reason, I was totally self-conscious of my black-and-white floral print skirt skimming my knees, freshly shaved legs—I had to sign up for the tub—and white wedgie sandals. Lee hadn't commented on what I was wearing, but was that an approving glance as I got in the car? I wished I could flip down the mirror on the visor and check my makeup once more. At least my mop head was behaving after my haircut last week.

Down, Gabby, down. Good grief. I was still a married woman. Should have worn slacks.

It seemed as if we'd only been driving for five minutes when Lee turned into a tree-lined two-way residential street and backed into a parking space. I got out and looked up and down the street. Mostly large U-shaped apartment buildings, three stories high, the kind with a courtyard with small plots of neatly cut grass and well-tended flower beds behind an iron fence. "This way," Lee said. He headed down the sidewalk and stopped in front of a narrower building—a three-story brick with a set of apartments running up either side of an entryway door. Six apartments. To my surprise, each one had an enclosed sunporch jutting out on either side of the steps leading up to the entryway door. A For Sale sign was posted in front of the six-flat next to the sidewalk.

I followed Lee up the short flight of steps, as he pulled open the glass-paned door. We stepped into the tiled entryway, and Lee poked the doorbell for 1-B. A moment later the inside door buzzer bleated, allowing us access into a small foyer. Carpeted stairs rose in front of us with a door to the left and one to the right; 1-B must be the one on the right.

Sure enough, the right door opened and a thin man with an angular face waved us in. "How ya doin', Lee?" He ran a hand through his mousy hair. "Place is more of a mess than I figured, but . . . you insisted." He shrugged. "Look around. Give me two weeks and it'll be in a lot better shape."

We walked through the apartment. I could see what he meant. Trash had been left behind in some of the rooms. Walls needed painting. The wood floors were scuffed. The stove and refrigerator in the kitchen at the back needed a good scrubbing. But I was dazzled by the high ceilings and wooden beams in the living room and dining room. It felt so spacious! Doorways and windows were framed in dark wood. And the wraparound windows on the sunporch captured mottled sunlight coming through the trees along the parkway. I peeked out the windows. The postage-stamp front yard and the sidewalk were a comfortable six feet down.

And three bedrooms with decent closets. I closed my eyes, trying to imagine the apartment filled with the happy noises of my two sons. *Could this be—?*

"It's a classic." I opened my eyes. Lee was grinning. "Could look real nice."

I swallowed. "How much?"

"Thirteen hundred a month."

And just that fast, my hopes plunged in a nosedive.

chapter 27

I got in the Prius and slammed the car door. "Lee Boyer! What are you thinking! I can't afford thirteen hundred a month."

"Easy, Gabby. Let's talk about it over lunch—Kitsch'n makes omelets to die for." He started the car with that push-button thing and pulled out.

Lee must have taken my silence for assent, because he parked a few minutes later, and we walked to a small retro restaurant that had sidewalk seating. We picked a tiny table-for-two and ordered omelets from their "Kitsch'n Sunday Brunch" menu.

Time to launch my disappointment. "Okay, guess I'm gullible. Why I thought this apartment would be a slam-dunk, I don't know. Maybe because my *lawyer* suggested it? You know my situation, Lee, know I have next to nothing. So why get my hopes up?"

"Did you like it?"

"Yes, I liked it! I mean, as far as apartments go. I'd rather have a house out in the burbs, where my kids could ride their bikes in the street, but since my reality right now doesn't include a *house* . . ." I realized I was glaring at him. "But 'liking' is beside the point. I can't afford it."

Lee leaned forward, eyes serious behind those wire rims. "I know you can't afford it—right now, anyway. But once we take your husband to court, you'll have a nice hunk of change. Thirteen hundred a month? No sweat. What do you think he's paying for that penthouse?"

I shook my head. "Lee. You don't get it. You told me yourself that could take awhile. I need an apartment *now*. I need to get my boys back here by August so I can enroll them in school. If I don't, they'll start the school year at George Washington Prep in Virginia and . . ." I grabbed a napkin and pressed it to my eyes. I did *not* want to cry in front of Lee Boyer.

I felt his hand on my arm. "Gabby. Listen. I showed you that apartment because that's what you're going to need to bring your boys here. Family-size apartment. Decent neighborhood. Not upscale, but decent. You don't *want* to live in an apartment you can 'afford' right now, believe me. You need to be thinking long-term."

I took the napkin off my eyes and blew my nose with it. "So what do I do? What about that housing subsidy you mentioned in your office—oh."

Our omelets arrived. Lee busied himself buttering hot corn bread and digging into his spinach omelet. For some reason I missed thanking God for the food—even though I'd long lost the habit after I married Philip. But it always touched me at Manna House—women who had nothing were actually grateful they had some food on their plate. Wimp that I was, I sent up an unspoken *Thank You* and dug into my omelet too. *Mmm.* Rich, moist, and cheesy. Hadn't realized how hungry I was. Cold cereal that morning and day-old pastry donated by a local bakery hadn't stayed with me long.

After a few bites Lee pointed his fork at me. "Yes, you could apply for a housing subsidy. The Housing Choice Voucher Program—used to be called Section 8—is actually a wait-list lottery. Which means, even if you qualify, your name might get pulled or not—though thousands of names each year do get vouchers."

"Like how many 'thousands'?"

"Thirty-five . . . forty."

"Oh." That sounded hopeful.

"And there are some other subsidy programs. But there might be another option, Gabby—especially with time being an issue." Lee laid down the fork. "Have you asked your mother if she can help cover the rent?"

I stopped chewing. "My mother?" I quickly swallowed the bite I was working on.

He nodded. "Weren't you looking for a retirement home or assisted living for her here in the Chicago area a couple of weeks ago? How were you going to pay for that?"

"Well, her money, of course, but—"

"How is this different? She stays with you. She can keep her dog—something she couldn't do at the places you looked at. She pays her share of the rent." Lee lifted his eyebrows at me and smiled.

"Hey, Gabby. Wanna play some Scrabble?" Carolyn caught me as I came through the multipurpose room after Lee dropped me off. In spite of it being the weekend, the room was fairly full of women just sitting, a few sleeping, several playing cards—and Hannah doing Wanda's nails.

"Would love to, Carolyn—another time, though. Got something I have to do." I spied my mother dozing in a chair with Dandy at her feet. "Try my mom—but watch out. She might beat you."

I slipped downstairs to my office. I needed someplace quiet so I could think about Lee's idea. The apartment wasn't on the market yet, he said, so I had a few days to think about it. But it made sense . . . didn't it? Still, there were some things I needed to check out.

I booted up my computer and spent the next couple of hours surfing the Net for private schools in Chicago. I had tried calling several weeks ago—before my husband decided his life would be better "unencumbered" by me—and had gotten the usual answer. "Registration is closed" or "Would you like to be on the waiting list?" Philip hadn't seemed concerned, assuming the boys would just go back to Petersburg. But it wouldn't hurt to get on some of those waiting lists. And what about public schools? Some were college-prep and magnet schools. Did any of the high schools offer lacrosse? That would be a big draw for P. J.

By the time the supper bell rang, I had a long list of schools to call, including magnet schools with a variety of fine arts emphasis, language immersion, math and science specialties, classical education, global perspective, and interdisciplinary studies. I'd better add more minutes to my cell phone.

Lucy decided Dandy *had* to go out just as folks from New Hope Missionary Baptist Church showed up to lead Sunday Evening Praise. Well, resident participation was voluntary, so I didn't say anything. I introduced my mother to Pastor Clyde

Stevens—"One of our board members," I said, smiling and shaking his hand, wondering if Mabel had filled in the board on my "adverse" circumstances. It wasn't every day a staff member ended up on the bed list. But the pastor didn't say anything about it, just proudly introduced his hugely pregnant wife to my mother as "Lady Sarah." The attractive Mrs. Stevens—glowing brown skin, hair straightened and worn short like a black cap, large gold loop earrings—looked ready to pop, but she still managed to corral three young boys all dressed in pint-size suits and ties. "Joseph! Joshua! Come here now and shake hands with Mrs. Fairbanks and Mrs. Shepherd. You too, Jeremiah! Uh-huh. I'm talking to you, young man!"

My mother beamed. "That's sweet. All Bible names." *Right.* This from a lady who'd named her daughters Celeste, Honor, and Gabrielle.

Precious waved at me and tipped her chin in the direction of her daughter, Sabrina, who looked like she'd rather be having a root canal. Mabel breezed in, trailed by her nephew C. J. The boy hunched his slender shoulders inside a Bears hoodie sweatshirt, the hood up. My heart squeezed. Had I been praying for him since his suicide attempt? No. All caught up in my own "drama," as Precious would say.

Oh, God, forgive me for being so self-centered. Help me to—

"Sister Gabby!" Edesa Baxter snuck up behind me and gave me a one-armed hug, Gracie riding on her hip. "*Hola,* Gramma Shep." She hugged my mother too. Then she plonked the Hispanic baby in my arms. "Can you hold Gracie a few minutes? Josh needs help setting up more chairs." She bustled off to help her young husband. I couldn't help grinning. The three of them looked like chocolate, vanilla, and maple cream.

Maple Cream looked up at me soberly with her dark eyes as if trying to decide if I was safe . . . and then grabbed a handful of my chestnut curls. "Aha, I knew it, you rascal." I tried to untangle her fist from my hair as a trio of African-American young men opened up the meeting, one on an electronic keyboard, another mastering a set of large bongo drums, and the third bouncing back and forth at the front of the circle of chairs, encouraging us, "Come on, come on, people! We're here to praise the *Lord!*"

New Hope had brought overheads for the words to the worship songs this time, which helped me a lot. After a few lively rounds of "Shout to the Lord" and "We Bring a Sacrifice of Praise," my mother poked me. "Don't they sing any hymns?"

Maybe she thought she had to talk loudly over the music, but she happened to speak up just as the music faded, and her voice carried. Half the residents snickered. I hid my face behind Gracie in my arms. But the young man up front, mopping the sweat from his face with a small towel, called out with a wide grin. "What hymn would you like to sing, Mother? We'll sing it just for you."

My mother got flustered, but someone else piped up, "How 'bout 'Tis So Sweet to Trust in Jesus'?" Mom nodded and smiled as the electronic keyboard gently led into the old familiar words. "'Tis so sweet to trust in Jesus, just to take Him at His Word . . ." A few of the residents sniffled as the chorus finished with "Oh for grace to trust Him more."

The words niggled at me. Was I really trusting Jesus about that apartment? About getting my sons back? How did one get that "grace" to trust Him more?

As the notes of the chorus died away, I remembered it was this group that had introduced me to the gospel song "I Go to the

Rock." Josh Baxter had actually found a CD with the song on it and had given it to me. A CD that'd been missing for two weeks, I reminded myself. But if New Hope was taking requests, maybe they'd sing it—

Too late. Pastor Stevens got up and, to my surprise, introduced his wife as tonight's speaker. "My queen, the First Lady of New Hope Missionary Baptist, Lady Sarah." All the residents clapped. A few hooted, "All right! All right, now!"

The pastor had a twinkle in his eye. "I hope you're clapping because you're going to hear this anointed woman of God speak—and not because *I'm* not."

Everybody laughed.

Mrs. Stevens—it was a little hard thinking of her as "Lady Sarah"—seemed comfortable behind the music stand that served as a lectern. "Praise the Lord, church!"

Several of the residents hollered, "Praise the Lord!" right back at her.

"How many people want that old devil to get off your back?"

"Now you're talkin'!" . . . "Preach it, sister!" I recognized Precious.

"Now, you all know John 3, verse 16, right? 'For God so loved the world . . .'" Several people joined in and finished the familiar verse. "But, ladies, I want to talk about the next verse. 'For God did not come into the world to *condemn* the world . . .' God isn't looking to condemn us for how we've messed up. No, God wants to set us *free* from that mess! But how many of you know, that's exactly what Satan is busy doing all day, all night, whispering in our ears, 'You bad. You no good. Look at you! You're just one big failure.'"

The room got very quiet.

"Or maybe he's sayin', 'Girl, you've been givin' it out on the street so long, *nobody* gon' want *you*. You're just damaged goods.' That's condemnation, sisters. Oh, that first part might be true. You've sinned. *I've* sinned. We've all sinned. Scripture is clear about that. Sin is sin and needs to be cleaned up. But *conviction*, my sisters, is different than *condemnation*. The Holy Spirit says, 'Don't carry that sin around anymore. Let me wash you clean and set you free. I made you beautiful! Don't wallow in that muck anymore.' When the Holy Spirit convicts you of your sin, it's because God wants to free you from its clutches, pick you up, and set your feet dancing!"

The young man on the keyboard played a few notes, and shouts of "Thank You!" and "Praise Jesus!" filled the room.

"All right, all right, I'm almost done here," said Lady Sarah. "Let me read you one more verse from Romans, chapter 8. 'There is therefore now *no condemnation* to them which are in Christ Jesus, who walk not after the flesh, but after the Spirit. For the law of the Spirit of life in Christ Jesus has made me free from the law of sin and death.'" She looked up, tears spilling down her cheeks. "Oh, sisters. Don't let that old devil keep you down with his condemnation. Listen to the Holy Spirit, who wants you to let go of all that old baggage, be washed in the blood of Jesus, and be *free*! Oh, glory!"

Pastor Stevens jumped up and helped his pregnant wife into a chair as the praise leader led into a song, something about being "washed in the blood of the Lamb." But I didn't even hear the words. Because as Lady Sarah spoke, I realized she'd given me the answer to my riddle—what the difference was between what Denny Baxter had done, asking forgiveness for a sin he didn't commit, and the times I'd apologized and said I was sorry when Philip accused me of stuff.

Philip's blaming made me feel condemned.

While what Denny had done had set both him and his accuser free.

chapter 28

Pastor Stevens and his wife stayed afterward to pray for a few of the residents. I noticed Lady Sarah praying for Sabrina, who was sobbing into a paper towel someone had stuffed into her hand, while Precious sat close by, praying in agreement with what was going on.

Gracie had fallen asleep in my arms. "Pray for me," I whispered to Edesa as I handed her the sleeping child. "I think I found an apartment. Just can't afford it."

"Oh, *muy bien!*" Her eyes danced, then faded. "Pray that we find an apartment too. Same problem. No money."

"Did you guys apply for a housing subsidy? Section 8 or whatever?"

Edesa grimaced. "Josh is too proud. But I'm *this* close to wrapping his pride around his neck." She lifted her eyes heavenward. *"Lo siento, Señor Dios!"*

I still had to call my boys, so I sat out on the front steps with my cell phone. Lucy came down the sidewalk with Dandy as the last New Hope people were leaving. "Nice timing, Lucy," I teased, holding open the door for her.

"Humph. He walks slow, case ya haven't noticed."

Almost eight thirty. Mom was visibly tired and complaining of another headache. I talked her into using the service elevator to the bunk room floor rather than the stairs. "For Dandy's sake," I said. Should I ask about the apartment? Maybe tell her about it, give her time to think it over?

Tanya came into the bunk room to put Sammy to bed while I was tucking my mother in. "There'd be room for P. J. and Paul, *and* Dandy and me?" Mom said.

"Yes," I whispered, wishing we were still alone.

My mother sighed . . . or was that a groan? Her head must still be hurting. I tiptoed out of the room and used the bathroom. When I came out, Tanya was curled up in one of the chairs in the small second-floor lounge, arms covering her head.

"Tanya? Are you okay?"

Her answer was muffled, and I realized she was crying. I pulled up another chair. "What's wrong?"

The young mother just shook her braided head and rocked for a few minutes, then took the tissue I handed her and blew her nose. "Are you . . . are you an' . . . Gramma Shep movin' out? I mean, didja find a place ta live?"

So that was it. "Found a place. Not sure we can afford it, though."

The tears came fresh. "Oh, Miss Gabby. Don't know what I'm gonna do. You got a place, Carolyn's got a place—"

"Carolyn?" How did I not know that?

"Yeah, yeah. Over at Deborah's Place. One o' them studios. Her name came up—she been waitin' almost a year. But she ain't got no kids. But me an' Sammy . . ."

I wrapped my arms around the girl and just let her cry. What could I say? As bad as my situation was, I had more options than Tanya did. If my mom had the money to help with the rent, we'd be out of there faster than Lucy's disappearing act. And, Lee Boyer assured me, once my court case came up, I could soak Philip's assets. One way or the other, my homelessness—and hopefully, my financial straits—were temporary.

But what about Tanya? And Precious, about to lose *her* apartment?

I got up, got another paper towel, and wet it in the bathroom sink. My reflection nodded at me from the mirror, like we were having a conversation. *So, Gabby, you're having a staff meeting tomorrow. Why don't you suggest that Manna House get an apartment building and do subsidized housing for moms with kids? . . . Huh. I tried once. Mabel pretty much shot it down. Way too expensive . . . But would it hurt to explore the idea? There have to be buildings for sale in this neighborhood—like the building you looked at today. Wasn't it for sale—?*

I felt my skin prickle.

Yeah, right. How much would a building like that cost. Half a mil? More?

I stared at the woman with the curly chestnut "mop" in the bathroom mirror and sighed. Who was I to get on some bandwagon about affordable housing? For the past fifteen years I'd managed my monthly household allowance—period. I let Mr. Big handle everything else—and look where that got me. Nowhere. Just like Tanya.

Except . . . Tanya had one thing I didn't have. I took the damp paper towel back to the girl to wipe her face. "At least you've got Sammy with you," I murmured. "He's a great kid."

I was floating a couple of inches off the floor when I headed for the staff meeting the next morning, eager to share my news. Mom's headache seemed to be gone when she woke, so I'd put the question to her. Would she be willing to share the rent for an apartment with me and the boys? "And Dandy?" she'd said. "Of course, Celeste."

Hopefully getting my name mixed up with my older sister didn't negate her positive answer. I'd called Aunt Mercy to check on Mom's Social Security and monthly annuity to be sure our two incomes could float the rent for a while. What I'd do when Mom's name came up for the assisted-living retirement home back in Minot was another "if." I couldn't take her money then.

Well, we'd jump that fissure in the plan when we got to it.

Coming into the schoolroom, I was surprised to see Peter Douglass along with the usual staff—Stephanie Cooper, Angela Kwon, Estelle Williams, Liz Handley, and Sarge. Mabel said Peter was there as president of the board. Some of the long-term volunteers—Josh Baxter, Precious McGill, and Delores Enriques, the nurse—filed in too.

Mabel started the meeting with a prayer of thanks for all God was doing at Manna House, and a few others jumped in with their own thanksgivings. I still wasn't used to this conversational-type prayer, where people talked like God was sitting with the rest of us in the circle. Didn't mean I didn't like it. I added my own silent *Thanks*.

Then Mabel got down to business. "Peter, would you like to present our first update?" A small smile played around the corners of her mouth, softening her brisk demeanor.

The African-American businessman rubbed his hands together like a kid about to dive into a chocolate cake. "You bet! As all of you know, our little incident with the intruder and Mrs. Shepherd's dog got us quite a bit of media attention a week ago." He looked over at me. "By the way, how is Dandy doing, Gabby?"

"Coming along. A little stiff. Supposed to get the stitches out on Wednesday."

"That's good. Anyway, as most of you know, it also generated some unexpected contributions . . . which have continued to come in."

Murmurs went around the circle. Last Monday Mabel had said around two thousand. Had it doubled?

Peter was grinning. He wore middle age well. Touches of gray above his ears, always in a suit and tie. I'd always thought he and Avis, who'd led the Yada Yada Prayer Group when I was there, made a handsome couple. Somebody said they'd only been married a couple of years, a second marriage for her after her first husband died of cancer.

"We don't know what the final tally will be," he was saying. "These things tend to taper off pretty quickly when the story gets old. But right now, Dandy's Fund, as we're calling it, has a little over ten thousand dollars—"

"Ten thousand!" A cheer went up. "Hallelujah!" "Praise Jesus!"

I was stunned. Right away my mind started clicking.

". . . so the board decided to act on a request that came to our attention recently, to get a fifteen-passenger van to assist our program director in—"

"Wait!"

All eyes turned on me. "Yes, Gabby?" Mabel said.

"Uh . . . uh . . . I know I requisitioned a van. Didn't really think we'd *get* one, but—"

Laughter tripped around the room. "Know whatchu sayin'," Precious hooted. "Guess the age of miracles ain't past!"

I barreled on. "But can we talk about this a little more? I mean, ten thousand dollars?! Maybe we should use it on something more substantial, like buying another building, a six-flat or something, you know, to develop some second-stage housing for moms with kids—like Tanya and Sammy, who shouldn't be staying in emergency housing for months on end, or—"

"Whoa. Slow down, Gabby." Peter Douglass frowned. "Another *building*? It took us two years to raise the funds to rebuild this one!" He spread his hands out. "I can appreciate the idea, but these contributions don't constitute that kind of funding."

"But—"

Liz Handley, the former director, jumped in. "I like Gabby's vision. I think we'd all like to see more options for homeless moms with kids . . ."

Thank you, Rev. Handley.

". . . but Peter's right. Minimum down payment on property is at least 5 percent. With ten thousand down . . ." Liz squinted, as if mentally running numbers in her head. "Biggest mortgage we could get would be $200,000." She shrugged and shook her head. "Don't think we could find even a two-flat for that. And then there'd be monthly payments."

I pressed my lips together. For one skinny moment, I'd thought we could give Tanya some hope.

"Now a van . . ." Peter Douglass eased his grin back into the fray. "Ten thousand won't buy a brand-new one, but I'm sure we can find a good used one for that."

Heads nodded all around, and Mabel moved on to the next item on her agenda. I sighed. I should be grateful. Really I should. After all, I was the one who sent a requisition to the board. With a van, I could take residents to the museums, plan trips to special events in the city, like the Taste . . .

"Wait!"

Mabel rolled her eyes. "Gabby!"

Precious guffawed. Estelle covered her mouth.

"I'm sorry to interrupt, it's just . . . is there any chance we could get that van today? I mean, tomorrow's July Fourth, and it's the last day of the Taste of Chicago. With a van I could take some of the residents and . . . what?"

Polite chuckles had turned to outright laughter. "Now, that *would* be a miracle," Sarge snorted.

Josh Baxter came to my rescue. "Even if we had a van today, you don't want to drive to the Taste, Mrs. Fairbanks. It's a parking nightmare. Take the El."

"But on Saturday . . . didn't you—?"

"Nope. We took the kids on the El and picked up my folks' minivan later." The young man grinned. "That's okay. It takes awhile to get used to Chicago."

Mabel gave me the eye. "We appreciate your enthusiasm, Gabby. Sounds like a plan. But can we move on now?"

"Okay." My head jerked up at a familiar sound. "Wait . . ."

"Gabby!" Several voices chimed together.

I held up a hand. "No, I mean it. Listen."

The room quieted . . . and then we all heard it. Dandy barking. Angry voices. I sprang for the door, pulled it open, and ran down the hall and into the multipurpose room. A knot of resident women were clustered at the open doors leading into the foyer, fussing at the top of their lungs. Pushing through them, I saw two muscular police officers, one black, one white, with blue shirts and black bulletproof vests standing in the foyer. The black officer had Dandy's leash, while the white officer held Lucy's arm in a tight grip as the old woman struggled to pull her arm away, muttering every curse word she could think of. Dandy barked and growled, while several voices behind me complained, "Leave 'er alone" and "Dumb cops," in loud voices.

"What's going on?" I demanded, startling myself with my sharp tone.

The black cop stepped up. "You in charge here, lady?"

"No. But that's my dog. What's the problem?"

The man looked down at Dandy. "Is this the Hero Dog we've been hearing about on TV?"

"Some people call him that. Is there a problem?"

The two officers cast a quick glance at each other. "Depends. We saw this, uh, derelict person here with the dog, and she tried gettin' away from us. We thought maybe she was stealing the dog. We brought them here in the squad car to check it out."

Lucy jerked her arm from the officer's grip. "I *tol'* these uniforms I'm jus' walkin' the dog, but they treatin' me like some two-bit looter, hoofin' it with hot loot."

I took the leash from the officer and handed it to Lucy. "She's right. Lucy is Dandy's caregiver."

The two officers squirmed. "So why'd she run, then?"

Mabel, followed by Peter Douglass and several other staff, now pushed through the knot at the double doors. "I'm the director of Manna House. Is there a problem, Officer?"

Grateful to be let off the hook, I laid a comforting hand on Lucy's shoulder. The old lady angrily shrugged it off and marched toward the multipurpose room with Dandy at her heels. The crowd in the doorway parted like the Red Sea, then closed after them.

The front door buzzer blatted. Good grief, it was like a zoo in the foyer. I tried to duck out, but someone yelled, "Somebody askin' for Mrs. Fairbanks!"

What *now*? Two strangers stood on the front steps, looking bewildered as the two policemen passed them. Beyond them I could see a van that said Pet Support for Seniors on the side. "Oh! Come on in. This is great. Hope it all fits in your van."

Rounding up some of the residents to help, I showed the Pet Support people where the donated dog food was stored, and they set to work. As I went back through the multipurpose room, I saw Lucy refilling Dandy's food and water dishes, which had been moved temporarily so he wouldn't have to go up and down so many stairs.

I detoured to their corner. "Lucy? Are you all right?"

"Humph," she muttered. "You the one tol' me to avoid all them reporters and people makin' a fuss over Dandy."

"I know." I hadn't meant she should run from the police, but I bit my lip.

"Them cops always pickin' on homeless folks. 'Can't be here.' 'Can't go there either.' 'Don't bother people.' 'Just go 'way.'"

"I'm so sorry, Lucy. They don't know you like we do."

Dandy finished his water, then laid down on the floor with a *whumph*. Lucy looked sideways at me from under her purple knit hat. "That true what you said?"

"What I said?"

"Yeah. 'Bout me being Dandy's caregiver."

I grinned. "True. Don't know what my mom and I would do without you." And this time she didn't push me away when I gave her a hug.

chapter 29

I waved as the Pet Support people pulled away from the curb with their van full of dog food. If I hurried, I might catch the rest of the staff meeting. Just needed to put the donation receipt on Mabel's desk—

But Mabel was back in her office.

"Everybody gone? Yikes. Sorry. Guess I missed the rest of the meeting." I handed her the receipt. "But at least all that dog stuff got taken care of—except for the cuddle toys. Precious suggested we keep those for kids who end up at the shelter with their mothers."

Mabel rubbed her forehead. "Mm. And which bunk room have you filled up with Pluto and Snoopy?"

"Uh, well, right now they're in my office. Still looking for an extra closet . . . oh. Before I forget. Do you think we can use some of the Dandy Fund to give the ladies a bit of fun at the Taste of Chicago tomorrow? Ten bucks each? And CTA passes?"

"CTA passes are for trips to the doctor or public aid office—"

"And field trips! Field trips are in the program budget, you know."

Mabel wagged her head and sighed. "You do have a way of keeping things on the edge around here, Gabby Fairbanks."

"Well, good news, then. Instead of 24/7, I'll only be here day-times. I found an apartment." I flopped down in her extra chair.

"Really?" Now Mabel looked interested. "Tell me."

I ran through the details. "My lawyer at Legal Aid told me about it." I didn't say he'd taken me to see it and we had lunch afterward. "And if Mom and I put our money together, we ought to be able to make the rent."

Mabel raised an eyebrow. "What happens when your mother's name comes up on the assisted-living list back in North Dakota?"

Gee. Couldn't she say, "That's great!" or something? Why did she always get to the sticking point? "Well, uh, hopefully by then my court case against Philip will be far enough along, I'll be able to get my fair share of assets. Or something."

Angela stuck her head in the door. "Phone call for Gabby." Mabel started to reach for her desk phone, but Angela shook her head. "It's male," she hissed.

I hid a grin. "Probably my lawyer. I'll take it in my office, Angela. Tell him to hold." Scurrying downstairs, I flipped on the light in my office and reached for the phone. Why'd he call on the Manna House phone? Had Lee lost my cell number?

"Gabby speaking." *Silence.* "Hello?"

Then his voice. "Gabrielle."

Philip! I caught my breath. Why was *he* calling?

"I see you were in the penthouse while I was out." A statement. Not a question.

"Yes." I matched his tone—crisp, level, with a slight challenge—and pressed my lips together to keep from explaining or making an excuse.

"How did you get in?"

"I still have a key to our penthouse, Philip." I dropped "our" in there.

"Why? Did you want to see me? Get something?"

"I thought you were moving this weekend. But obviously not. Where were you?"

The pause lasted a full second. "That's my business. I don't have to explain anything to you."

"Nor to your mother or your sons, it seems. No one knew you were out of town." *Oops.* I wouldn't know either if Mr. Bentley hadn't said he'd seen him leave with a suitcase.

"Who said I was out of town?" Now his tone heated. "I don't like this spying, Gabrielle."

I kept my voice even. "I'm not spying, Philip. I thought you were moving. We need to talk about our household goods. I found an apartment, and I need to furnish it." Which was true, even though I'd visited the penthouse before I knew about the apartment.

"An apartment?" He sounded off step. "How—"

"Like you said, Philip. My business."

For the first time I could remember, Philip Fairbanks didn't shoot back. And I was still standing.

I caught Estelle alone in the kitchen after lunch cleanup, making potato salad for the next day's holiday, and told her about Philip's phone call.

628

"Good for you, honey. 'Bout time you stood up to that man!"

"But it was strange, Estelle. I couldn't figure out why he called. I mean, I thought he'd really yell at me when he found that glass with my lipstick on it. But he just asked why I'd been in the penthouse."

Estelle chuckled as she cracked and peeled hard-boiled eggs under cold running water. "Humph. Probably wondered why you didn't trash the place. *He* would've, if you'd tossed *him* out." She shuffled over to the fridge, stuck the egg bowl in it, and grabbed a bag of potatoes.

"Yeah, well, that would've been stupid of me, wouldn't it? Since it's my stuff too. I told him I'm going to need my things when I get my apartment."

She looked at me sharply. "What apartment? You know somethin' I don't know?"

"Yeah, well, I was going to tell the staff this morning, but we kind of got interrupted. My lawyer found it for me." I gave her a quick rundown of Lee Boyer's call and our Sunday rendezvous.

"Hm. Who's this Lee Boyer? Sounds a bit overzealous to me."

"Oh, come on, Estelle. He's been really helpful."

"Uh-huh. *Really* helpful." She shook a potato peeler at me. "You be careful, young lady. Don't you go runnin' after the first man who sweet-talks you. You gonna need some *time* to untangle yourself from this Philip mess 'fore you be thinkin' clearly."

"Good grief, Estelle. He's just my lawyer. He knows I have to get a place to live before I can get the boys back." Was he just my lawyer? When I talked with Lee, I always felt so . . . safe. But maybe that's how a good lawyer *should* make you feel.

629

The pile of peeled potatoes was growing.

"Uh, Estelle, how much food are you making for tomorrow? You know I'm trying to pull together a trip to the Taste. If Mabel agrees to spring some of that Dandy Fund for an outing, we'll be gone most of the day. And fireworks . . . maybe we'll even stay for the fireworks."

"No you won't."

"What? What do you mean, no we won't?"

Estelle started dicing the peeled potatoes and dumping them into a pot on the big, black stove. "'Cause Chicago does its fire-works thing on July third. And I was crazy enough to let Harry talk me into goin' with him an' his cutey-pie grandson tonight. Lord, help me." She rolled her eyes and started in on a second bag of potatoes.

I grinned. Sounded like Estelle and Mr. Bentley still had a thing going on. "Why don't you just take a holiday?"

"Humph. Taste or no Taste, I'm makin' Chicago dogs with all the trimmin's an' good ol' mustard potato salad an' apple pie for my ladies. You'll see. After all that fancy-smancy food-on-a-stick at the Taste, them ladies gonna come back here an' be beggin' for my leftovers." Estelle held up a bag of onions. "You gonna just be standin' around? 'Cause if so, you can start choppin' these onions."

"Whoa, I'm outta here. Sorry! I've got calls to make!" Which was the truth. I'd barely had time to start in on my list of schools before lunch. But as I made call after call, I either got a voice message saying the office was closed because of the Fourth of July holiday, instructions to leave name and address so they could send an application, or the dreaded answer: "Fall registration is closed. However, you may apply and we'll put your child on our waiting list."

My list was growing shorter. A tinge of panic dried out my throat. What if I couldn't find a good school for P. J. and Paul? What if—

My eyes fell on the note card Edesa had left for me the second night I'd been at the shelter. I'd taped it to my computer, but now I peeled it off. The words *"I will not forget you"* and *"your sons hasten back"* leaped out at me.

Edesa had written those verses from Isaiah 49 as God's promises to me. And last night at Sunday Evening Praise we'd sung, *"Oh for grace to trust Him more."*

I took a deep breath. *Okay.* I was going to go for broke. I'd fill out every application and put P. J. and Paul on every waiting list. After that, I'd have to trust God.

To my delight, when I got the notes from the staff meeting that afternoon, Mabel had included an addendum: *CTA passes and $10 per resident approved for Taste of Chicago outing.* Quickly making a sign-up sheet, I passed it around at supper and ended up with several I knew fairly well—Hannah, Tina, Aida, Wanda, Carolyn, and Diane. I recognized a few others like Althea, the Iranian woman. A couple of names were new.

I counted the list. Only thirteen? *Hmm.* Not as much interest as I'd expected. My mother had shaken her head. "Too much walking." Well, that was true. Probably just as well. She'd been needing a nap almost every day.

Lucy's name wasn't on the list either. Was she embarrassed to just put her X? I tried to let her off the hook. "Hey, Lucy, want me to put your name down for the Taste? You get ten bucks to spend."

"Huh. Ain't got time for no gallavantin'. Dandy's stitches need to come out, and I need to stay here with him. Doc said ten days. Ten comin' up tomorrow."

I'd forgotten Dandy's stitches. "But tomorrow's a holiday! I don't even know if the animal clinic will be open on July Fourth. We can wait one more day. Dandy will be fine. Come on. It'll be fun."

"Nah. Don't like them big crowds. Dandy an' me'll stay here with Miz Martha. 'Sides, Estelle's makin' apple pie."

Well, okay. Thirteen was a good number, probably better than a huge crowd. At least I didn't have to keep track of any kids—the Baxters had taken them to the Taste on Saturday. But should we try to keep together? No, that was stupid. These were adults. They'd want to go off, do their own thing. As I understood it, the festival had music stages and other entertainment in Grant Park, besides all the food vendors.

Still, I felt kind of responsible since it was a Manna House outing. I mused about this out loud when Sarge and her college-age assistant, Susan, showed up to cover the night shift. Sarge shrugged. "Not a problem." The ex-marine grabbed Susan, who was wearing a Manna House T-shirt. "See this? Orange. Best color to stand out in a crowd. Put 'em all in Manna House T-shirts."

I grinned. "Great idea!" I had another great idea. "Sarge? Would you like to go with us tomorrow? I sure could use another staff person."

"I can go too," Susan offered. "I don't have summer school tomorrow."

Which is how sixteen of us in bright orange T-shirts that said *Manna House Volunteer* in black letters pushed our way onto the crowded Red Line El train and rode to the Loop. Once off the El, it was only a couple of blocks to Columbus Drive and Grant Park, which was teeming with the holiday crowd. After getting our food tickets at one of the ticket booths—a strip of eleven for seven bucks—and agreeing to meet at Buckingham Fountain at three o'clock, the bright Manna House T-shirts melted into the crowd like so many orange Popsicles on a hot day. Even Sarge and Susan disappeared.

But no way did I want to go solo my first time at the Taste. I felt overwhelmed at the sheer number of booths and competing smells—Thai spices, sizzling pizzas, and grills spitting out BBQ chicken and ribs. Then I spied an orange T-shirt and a familiar brown-and-gray ponytail in the line waiting at Sweet Baby Ray's booth. "Hey, Carolyn! You decided to get some ribs?" I sidled up beside her, giving the person behind her in line a "we're together" smile.

Our resident bookworm, hands stuffed in the pocket of her jeans, nodded. "But one strip of tickets isn't going to go far around here."

"Yeah, I know. Best I could do from the budget, though." The line inched forward. "Say, I heard you're leaving us. Is it true?"

Carolyn grinned, softening the plain effect of always wearing her hair pulled back in that skimpy ponytail. "Yep. My name finally came up at Deborah's Place. Been waiting a long time."

I felt a real pang. "I'm going to miss you, Carolyn. Who's going to take care of our budding libr—Oh. We're next." I squinted at the menu board. "What are you going to get?"

Five minutes later we each walked away with a boneless rib sandwich dripping a pungent red sauce. But the crowd was so thick I felt like a salmon fighting to swim upstream against a strong current. We finally stopped for a breather to watch a clown twisting long, skinny balloons into wiener dogs and giraffes, to the delight of a dozen kids and perspiring parents.

"Meant to ask you 'bout the library thing." Carolyn headed for a patch of grass where we could sit. Between bites of her sandwich, she said, "I'd like to come back to the shelter and volunteer. Didn't we talk once about doing a book club?"

I sucked some sauce off my fingers. "Carolyn! That would be wonderful! Will you have time? Won't you be getting a job or something?" Carolyn was one of the smartest women I'd met at Manna House. Mabel said she had a master's degree in literature. Had no idea why she'd ended up in a shelter.

Carolyn shook her head. "Not for a while. I'm on disability." The word hung in the air for a long moment, my unspoken *Why?* hanging there with it. Then she shrugged. "Had a nervous breakdown on the job at the public library, got really abusive, and ended up doing time in a psychiatric facility. I'm still on meds and under a doctor's care."

I stared at her. "Never would have guessed it. To me, you're one of the solid rocks at Manna House! I'll never forget you taking my boys under your wing that day and playing board games with them." I touched her arm. "Not sure what we're going to do without you."

To my surprise, the stoic Carolyn suddenly wiped the back of her hand across her eyes. "Tell you the truth, Gabby, I'm kinda scared. I want this so bad, but . . . I'm not sure if I can make it on my own."

"Oh, Carolyn." I almost added, "Sure you will," but frankly, I had no idea. Why would a talented woman like Carolyn end up in a shelter? I wished I knew how to support her on her way back to a "normal life"—whatever that was.

But who was I to help someone else? I was having a hard enough time patching my own life back together.

chapter 30

For the next couple of hours, Carolyn and I wandered around the Taste of Chicago, running into some of our orange-shirted residents in twos and threes from time to time. Some of them had pooled their leftover dollars and bought more food tickets. Carolyn and I stood in line for fresh-squeezed lemonade and ended up thirty minutes early at Buckingham Fountain, one of Chicago's breathtaking landmarks. We sat on nearby benches, gawking at security personnel riding around on Segways—those funny two-wheeled vehicles that looked like motorized pogo sticks—and little knots of Japanese tourists taking pictures of each other in front of the fountain. A menagerie of dogs on leashes trotted past.

Carolyn poked me. "Ever notice how many owners look like their dogs?" A tall, thin woman with straw-colored hair floated by behind a long-legged Saluki. I giggled right into my lemonade, snorting it up my nose and splashing it onto my tan capris and sandals . . . so it was several seconds before I realized my cell phone was ringing.

"Oh! My phone!" I snatched it out of my shoulder bag and scurried away from the fountain so I could hear better. "Hello? Hello?"

I couldn't tell if the static in my ear was from the phone or the noises all around me. But I finally heard "Gabby? Gabby? Can't hear you!"

I stuck a finger in my other ear and hunched over the phone. "Celeste? Is that you? Oh! I'm so glad you called! You got my message?"

The connection from Alaska was a little erratic, but I caught the drift. "Mother's with you in Chicago? What did you mean, Philip kicked you out? Gabby! What's going on?"

At the sound of my sister's voice, sudden tears clouded my eyes, and I had to wipe them on my orange T-shirt. I tried to bring my older sister up to date on all that had happened the past month, but it was hard. She kept saying, "What? Slow down . . ." and I had to repeat myself.

When I finally stopped to gulp a breath, Celeste blistered my ear. "I can't believe you've got Mom in a homeless shelter, Gabby. She's got a perfectly good home in Minot! You've got to take her back there."

My hackles rose. "But she can't stay alone! That's why I brought her home with me in the first place. She's had a couple falls—and left the stove on."

I could all but hear Big Sister's practical brain wheels at work. "Well, since Philip's being a jerk and you don't have a place to stay right now, why don't you just go home to Minot with Mom? That way she wouldn't be alone! Honestly, Gabby!"

Go home with Mom? That option had never occurred to me. "Can't do that, Celeste! I'm trying to get my boys back, and I need to be *here* so I . . . Celeste?" The static went dead. "Celeste? Are you still there?"

Nothing.

I closed the phone and stood at the far edge of Buckingham Fountain, feeling as if I'd just been cut loose, adrift in space. Celeste was *family*. Didn't she know I needed her right now? But Denali National Forest wasn't exactly on the cell phone highway.

If I couldn't talk to my own sister, who *could* I talk to?

Three o'clock came and went as our crew with orange T-shirts drifted to the fountain. "Will we stay to watch the fireworks?" Althea said in her careful English. "That is what you do on Independence Day, yes?"

"I'm sorry, Althea," I said. "I think the fireworks were last night."

"Yeah, too bad we missed it," Carolyn offered. "They play music to go along with the show, an' shine colored lights on the fountain, water going up and down in time to the music . . ."

Fireworks . . . we'd never missed taking P. J. and Paul to watch the fireworks back in Petersburg. It was practically unpatriotic not to celebrate the Fourth of July in the heart of historical Virginia, and we'd always made it a huge family event—grilling hot dogs and hamburgers over at the Fairbanks' grandparents' with the other relatives early in the day, then joining the throngs at Fort Lee for music, food, and the nighttime show. Were the boys doing the same thing with Philip's parents today?

Diane shook her big Afro impatiently. "I'm tired. Let's go."

I ignored Diane's whining. Our people were still straggling in. *Next year*, I thought. Next year I'd take P. J. and Paul to the Taste of Chicago on July third, and we'd stay till it got dark to watch the fountain dance as the big-city fireworks burst overhead.

We waited an extra half hour but still only counted fourteen noses. "Who's missing?" I pulled the list out of my bag. "Anyone seen Chris and Alisha?" Both were newcomers to the shelter. Late twenties or so. Hard faces. I didn't know their stories.

Aida Menéndez piped up, "*Sí*. I saw them talking to two men—tough hombres. Gold . . . *cómo se dice?*" She made necklace motions with her finger.

"Oh yeah. Loaded with gold jewelry." Sarge snorted. "You guys go on. I'll wait around and see what's going down. But those two know their way around. If they want to come back by curfew, fine. But if they came out here just to pick up some johns . . ." She drew a finger across her neck.

They'd better come back, or Mabel might dock my pay for their T-shirts. But now I was feeling impatient to get back to the shelter after my aborted call with Celeste. I still had minutes on my phone card. Maybe a land line would work better.

When we finally dragged ourselves in the front doors of Manna House, Precious McGill was at the front desk, covering for Angela, who had the day off. "You guys still hungry? Estelle left food for ya downstairs." I practically got run over in the stampede. Sure enough, the kitchen counter on the lower level was covered with a platter of watermelon, skinny slices of leftover apple pie, and a sign that said potato salad was in the fridge. I loaded my own paper plate and dug in.

Maybe we should have stuck around.

Celeste's comment about taking Mom home to Minot bugged me all night. Is that what I should do? On one hand, it made a lot of sense. I could just imagine how crazy it must sound to my sisters that Mom and I were staying in a homeless shelter. And I'd never wanted to come to Chicago in the first place!

But . . . that was before I got the job at Manna House, which was more than just a job. I really loved my work, felt as if I was doing something important for people who often got ignored. Even more important, my main priority was getting my sons back, and North Dakota seemed light-years away from Virginia. Philip *might* agree to the boys coming back to Chicago, near both of us, but he'd fight me tooth and nail if I took them to Minot.

I kicked the sheets off in the dark, stuffy bunk room. Should I pray about it? Something in me resisted. I didn't really want to ask God what He thought. What if He didn't agree with me? Besides, God gave me a brain. A mother's responsibility was to her children first . . . and Mom wasn't unhappy here. She even seemed to like it. And now we had a possibility to get a real apartment, so I could take care of my boys *and* my mom. Wasn't that God at work?

I pressed the button on my watch to make it glow . . . ten past one. Already Wednesday. I was supposed to have a meeting with Lee Boyer at Legal Aid this morning. I'd call and ask him if I could sign the contract for the apartment today.

Lucy, however, was all over me the next morning about getting Dandy back to the vet to get his stitches out. "He still ain't himself," she growled. "Lookit that; he's still all stiff. What if them cuts ain't healed right?"

"And how are we going to get him there?" I shot back at her. "I don't have a car—and I can't afford cab fare these days."

Lucy shrugged. "Call that nice cop 'at took Dandy in the first place. He gave you his card, didn't he?"

Yeah, right. I was pretty sure Chicago cops didn't do cab service.

I called Lee Boyer instead. "Lee, I have a huge favor to ask . . ."

To my surprise, Lee agreed to use my eleven o'clock appointment and his lunch hour to pick us up at Manna House and take Dandy to the vet. "And could we swing by the apartment you showed me? I'd like to bring my mom, too, see what she thinks. If she likes it, I think I'm ready to sign the rental contract."

"Great. I'll give him a call."

Lee showed up in that snazzy Prius of his, and my mom and Lucy climbed into the backseat, with Dandy between them. "Thanks, Lee. I really appreciate this."

"Hey, gotta treat my girls right . . . right, Lucy?" He tossed a grin into the back seat, then winked at me behind his wire rims.

"Humph," Lucy growled. "I ain't your girl. An' Gabby ain't your girl either. She's a married woman—even if her husband is a jerk. Humph."

My face burned, but Lee just laughed.

Dandy, as it turned out, was coming along just fine. He only whimpered a little as the stitches came out, then jumped up and licked the vet in the face. The vet laughed. "Not every day I get kissed by a celebrity." He handed me the bill. "We usually ask for payment in full at the time of service. But you can pay in installments if that'll help."

I looked at the total and winced. "Thanks. I'm going to need it." I felt a little disgruntled. All that money in the Dandy Fund, and Dandy could sure use some of it. Did I dare ask—

Lee plucked the bill out of my hand. "Let me take care of this."

"What? No, you can't do that! Give it back."

Lee held it out of my reach, dug a credit card out of his wallet, and handed both to the receptionist.

"Lee," I hissed on the way back to the car. "You can't do that. You're my *lawyer*. I'm sure it's illegal or something."

"Nothing in the rules says your lawyer can't be your friend." He looked at me sideways, that little shock of hair falling over his forehead. "I want to be your friend, Gabby."

I didn't know what to say. I felt confused. Lee *had* been more than a lawyer these last couple of weeks. When I talked with Lee, he listened. Made me feel like a real person, with valid concerns and feelings. He'd gone out of his way to go to bat for me.

Oh God, it feels so good that someone wants to be there for me.

But I wasn't ready to give up on my marriage yet, was I? What I really wanted was for Philip and me and the boys to be a family again. All of us. Together. That . . . that madman who'd thrown me out wasn't the man I'd married. If I didn't do anything rash, if I gave him some time, Philip would come to his senses, realize he'd made a big mistake, and maybe . . . maybe we could work it out.

Oh dear God! For the boys' sake, I hope so!

We rode in silence to the building with the For Sale sign in front of it. I turned to the backseat. "Mom? This is the apartment I told you about. Would you like to see it? You too, Lucy. Dandy can stay in the car."

"Nah. Don't wanna see no apartment. Leave those windows down," Lucy snapped. "Dog needs some air."

I pressed my lips together. The woman could be a real pain sometimes.

Workmen were in the apartment, scraping walls and painting, but we picked our way around the drop cloths. "See, Mom? Three bedrooms. One for you, one for the boys . . . and a nice sunroom. On the first floor too. What do you think?"

"My head hurts, Celeste."

I grimaced at Lee. "Must be the paint smell." I really did need to get my mom to a doctor and get those headaches checked out.

Fortunately, the owner hustled in, tie askew, with the contract in his briefcase. Lee had told me to bring a paycheck stub and proof of my mother's income or savings. I had a copy of her Social Security check and monthly annuity, plus her savings passbook. "We'll be sharing the apartment," I explained.

The man frowned. "Are you both signing the contract?"

I shook my head. "I'm her power of attorney. I handle her affairs."

He shrugged. "All right. But you won't be able to move in for another week and a half—maybe two weeks. Got a lot of work to do here."

"Fine with me." I needed time to work out something with Philip about household furnishings anyway.

I signed and wrote a check for the security deposit. *Ouch.*

Lee grinned and gave me a hug. "Congrats, Gabby! Now let's get those boys back to Chicago."

I hugged him back. "Thanks, Lee," I whispered. But the touch of his arms and the warm smell of his aftershave lingered as we got back in the car. I watched as he helped my mother into the backseat, buckled her seat belt, and then slid into the driver's seat in those down-home jeans and boots he always wore.

I turned my head away. *Stop it, Gabby. What do you think you're doing?* In all the years I'd been married to Philip, I had never looked at another man *that* way.

Until now.

chapter 31

I woke the next morning with Sarge's bell, realizing I'd slept the entire night without getting up once. The square of daylight framed in the one window tried to lift the dim interior, outlining the four bunks, one on each wall. Even as the other bunks creaked and feet hit the floor, I stretched and lay on my bunk a few more minutes—a disastrous decision, I knew, since the bathrooms, showers, and sinks would get more and more congested the longer I waited.

But something felt different. Different good. Like it was my birthday or something—which it wasn't.

And then I remembered . . .

I had an apartment. Or would, as soon as I delivered the deposit.

"Hallelujah!" I shouted—earning me a dirty look from Lucy, who covered her ears as she lumbered out the door with her toothbrush.

An apartment changed everything! I vaulted out of bed, my

mind spinning. If the painting and repairs to the apartment moved along, I might be able to move in by the fifteenth. That gave me a week and a half to figure out how to furnish the place—and I was going to start with Philip. He had to know that a divorce settlement would give me *at least* fifty-fifty rights to our "community property," as Lee called it—maybe more, if I got custody of the kids. Why not just divvy it up now without a big fight? Why make it difficult?

Because he can.

I shook off the little voice in my head. No! I wasn't going to go there. I would present my case in a rational way and presume we could work this out like two adults. If not . . . well, I'd cross that bridge later if I had to. In the meantime, I had a lot of work to do *besides* my Manna House workload. Filling out all those school applications for the boys, for one thing.

My mother was sitting on the edge of her bunk. "How're you doing, Mom? Come on. Let's go use the bathroom before you get dressed, okay? . . . You okay?"

My mother nodded, but she didn't really seem like herself this morning. *Rats.* The nurse had been here yesterday morning, but we were off getting Dandy's stitches out and looking at the new apartment. I really should've had Delores Enriques take a look at my mom. Next week was too far away.

I'd told myself I was going to keep up with my own Bible reading in the gospel of Matthew, but we barely got downstairs in time for group devotions at six forty-five. Susan McCall, the young night assistant, was reading short passages this week from the book of Proverbs—all those warnings about avoiding loose women and fools. Wasn't sure it really spoke to the women at

Manna House, some of whom *were* loose women and fools. But, oh well. Then Sarge read the chore list at breakfast . . . *groan.* Diane and I got assigned to clean the bathrooms and showers on the top floor. That always took more time, even with two of us. And Diane usually spent more time whining about ruining her nails than actually working.

But even scrubbing toilets couldn't dampen my spirits today. It felt like a new day. I'd turned a corner. I still had the pieces of my broken marriage to contend with. Was still separated from my children by a thousand miles. But it felt like the logjam had broken. Things could move forward.

"Thank You, Jesus," I murmured as I poured pine cleaner into the last toilet bowl. "I'm trusting You. Don't let me down now." I even started to whistle.

"What's that tune?" Diane called into the stall where I was working. "Didn't our girl Whitney sing that?"

"Yeah. It's called, 'I Go to the Rock.' I lost my CD . . . have you seen the soundtrack to *The Preacher's Wife* around anywhere?"

"Maybe. Whole buncha loose CDs kickin' around down in the multipurpose room without they covers . . . say, we got any more spray stuff for the mirrors? Then I gotta quit. Gotta meet with my case manager at ten."

Oh rats. That's right. It was Thursday again already. Last week Stephanie Cooper had said she wanted to meet with me again on Thursday, just to keep current on my goals. Well, we could make it short today. I'd found an apartment, and I planned to be off the bed list in less than two weeks.

On the way downstairs to my office, I checked on my mom,

who was sitting in the multipurpose room with an *Essence* magazine open on her lap, but not reading it. "Hi, Mom. Where's Dandy?"

She smiled up at me. "Dandy? Out in the yard, I think. Will you let him in?"

Oh dear. This wasn't good. "You mean Lucy took him for a walk?"

She nodded and smiled. "Yes, that's right."

"You okay? Or would you like to come down and sit in my office with me while I work?"

"No, no. You go on. I've got plenty to do." She patted the magazine in her lap.

I gave her a kiss, then remembered what Diane had said about "loose CDs." Sure enough, the boom box in the corner, sitting on top of the game cabinet, was surrounded with piles of CDs, half of which were out of their cases. I shuffled through them . . . and struck gold. *Aha.* My CD. Looking a little worse for wear, but maybe it would still play.

My CD player was sitting on top of the file cabinet in my office. I plugged it in, popped in the CD, booted up my computer, and started work updating the Manna House program calendar for July while the gospel songs filled the tiny room. Finally "my" song hit its groove. *"Where do I go . . . when there's no one else to turn to? . . . Who do I talk to . . . when nobody wants to listen? . . ."*

I stopped what I was doing. That was for sure. I still felt upset by my sister's phone call. She'd barely heard my story before she started jumping all over me! If we had more time to really talk or just be together, maybe she'd understand. But how *that* was supposed to happen between her log home in the middle of Denali National Forest and my broom-closet office in the basement of a homeless shelter in Chicago, I had no idea.

The song had launched into the chorus . . . *"I go to the Rock of my salvation, go to the Stone that the builders rejected . . ."* Huh. Had I heard that line before? The one about the Stone being rejected? It was talking about Jesus. Well, yeah, the Son of God had been rejected big-time. But I hadn't read that part of the gospel story since I quit church back in college. Maybe I should keep reading in Matthew until I came to the part where people turned on Jesus and killed Him. And maybe that's why I should be talking to Jesus, because He knew what it was like to be rejected . . . just like me.

I eyed my Bible and then my watch. Could I—?

No, I should get this calendar done and printed; then I had to see Stephanie. But lunchtime was coming up. I'd take a half hour then to read my Bible. And pray.

The next few days settled into an odd but not unpleasant routine. From 6 a.m. until 9, I was a Manna House resident. From 9 until 5, I was a Manna House employee. At 5, I turned into a resident again. But at least my world wasn't spinning.

Except . . . what about Philip? He was still my husband. But he had become a stranger. Was there any hope for our marriage? Didn't seem like it. Not when we weren't even talking. Maybe I should file for divorce—before he did.

Divorce. The word made me shudder. Ending up twice divorced and living single was *not* one of my life goals. And Philip and I had kids! Two beautiful boys. We were supposed to be a *family.* If we divorced, P. J. and Paul would have to choose between living with Mom or Dad. Or be split two ways during their teen years.

I shoved the question into the back of my mind. Couldn't think about that now or I might crawl back into my black hole. I had to keep moving forward. Get moved. Get the boys. Get my mother to a doctor . . .

Now, that was something I could do now. I called Delores Enriques at work on the pediatrics floor at Stroger Hospital, and she agreed it'd be good to get my mother checked out by a physician. "You could always bring her to the clinic here at County, Gabby," she said on the phone. With her Spanish accent, my name always came out *Gab-bee.* "But why don't you ask Mabel or some of the other staff who their doctor is? It's not easy to get an appointment on short notice, but if you explain that your mother's elderly, from out of town, has these symptoms, and needs to see a doctor, sometimes . . ."

Mabel agreed to call her primary doctor over at Thorek Professional Building on Mom's behalf. He was booked solid for three months, the secretary told us, but his associate, Dr. Palma, happened to have a cancellation on Friday afternoon.

I couldn't believe it! God must be listening to my prayers after all! Except, had I even prayed about getting an appointment? Well, if I did or didn't, I decided to thank God anyway. Wasn't there some verse in the Bible that said, "Before they call, I will answer"? I'd have to look it up.

Mom had another one of her headaches Friday, but she insisted on sitting in on Edesa Baxter's Bible study that morning. When Edesa heard I was borrowing Mabel's car to take Mom to the doctor after lunch, she offered to go along for moral support. "If you don't mind *la nena* too. The shelter keeps a couple of car seats for kid emergencies."

I was grateful for the company. It always helped to have

another pair of ears to hear what the doctor had to say. Lucy wanted to go, too, but frankly, I was glad I could tell her we didn't have room. As devoted as she seemed to be to my mother and Dandy, she'd been getting downright bossy when it came to either of them, and it'd been getting on my nerves.

We found the Thorek Memorial Professional Building on Irving Park Road without too much trouble, though filling out my mother's medical history for the nurse was problematic. My mother seemed confused by the questions and gave conflicting answers. And half the stuff I didn't know either. But I promised to call Mom's doctor in Minot and try to have her records sent on Monday. Hopefully Aunt Mercy could help me out.

Dr. Palma was Filipino, a pleasant young man with no trace of accent. He only had a half hour between patients, so he couldn't do a complete workup on my mother, but he seemed kind and conscientious. He listened to her heart and breathing, took a urine and blood sample, and asked gentle questions. After I helped her get dressed, I asked Edesa to take my mother into the waiting room while I talked with the doctor.

"Your mother seems reasonably healthy for her age, which is . . . what? Seventy-four? Her heart is steady—no history of heart disease?—and her lungs clear. We'll see if the urine or blood tests turn up anything unusual, but it's hard to say. She does have some early stages of dementia, but you say she's still fairly functional, though unable to live alone. As for the headaches . . ." Dr. Palma looked over the history we'd filled out. "It says here she's had several falls. Tell me about them."

I told him about Mom tripping over the dog and hitting her head. "But my aunt Mercy—she lives in the same town—said she's had a couple other falls when no one was around."

Dr. Palma frowned. "Falls are not uncommon in the elderly. I don't know if there's any relation between the falls and the headaches. But to be on the safe side, I'd like to schedule a CAT scan—the sooner the better. Hopefully early next week."

I gulped. A CAT scan? Those had to be expensive. Would Medicare cover it?

Dr. Palma shook my hand as he left the exam room. "I'll call you Monday to set up the CAT scan at Thorek Memorial—it's just next door. In the meantime, I'll give you a couple of sample bottles of a stronger headache medicine. Should give your mom some relief."

We left the office and drove back to the shelter with no real answers. In the back seat, Mom and Gracie seemed to be sharing giggles. "Well, one thing I know," I murmured to Edesa in the front seat, "staying at the shelter is better for Mom than living alone in that house of hers. She really thrives on being around people. And kids." I grinned. "Listen to those two."

My mom was doing her own version of "Creep Mousie," walking her fingers across the seat, up the side of Gracie's car seat, and tickling the eleven-month-old's neck or ear or nose. Gracie, it seemed, never got tired of it, though by the time we parked Mabel's car, I'd had enough "Creep Mousie" to last the rest of the year.

"What's that?" I said, as we came around the corner by the Laundromat. A long, white passenger van sat in front of Manna House.

Edesa giggled. "It's the van you ordered! Josh and Señor Douglass have been looking all week—and this is what they found! What do you think, *mi amiga*?"

chapter 32

Josh Baxter dangled a set of car keys as he came down the steps of the shelter. "So, Mrs. Fairbanks, what do you think of Manna House's new vehicle?" Edesa's husband kicked a tire. "All new tires, about seventy-five thousand miles on the engine, but it runs smooth enough, shocks are good, brakes ditto . . ." He slid open the side door. I peeked in. The flooring and seats were a bit worn, but all the seat belts seemed functional, and it was clean. I trusted Josh when he said everything checked out under the hood.

Josh held out the keys. "Here. Take it for a spin around the block. I'll see that Mrs. Shepherd gets safely inside." He took my mother's arm, and the little Baxter family escorted her inside as I climbed into the driver's seat. Once around the block . . . okay. But I had to admit, a fifteen-passenger van felt like driving a Mack truck as I lurched around corners, trying not to sideswipe any parked cars. Five minutes later, I pulled up to the curb in front of Manna House. So far, so good. But what if I had to parallel park the thing? I'd better practice before driving the monster on an actual outing.

At supper, which was provided by the Silver Sneakers from a Jewish senior center, I announced a contest: "Name the Van." Entries should be written on a piece of paper, I said, and given to me by supper tomorrow night, at which time we'd vote. I grinned. "Can't let our new baby go a whole weekend without a name."

Carolyn waved her hand. "I'm moving out tomorrow, so I won't be here to vote. But I have a name."

"That's great, Carolyn. Why don't you—"

"Moby Van. After Moby Dick, the big white whale in Herman Melville's novel."

"Oh, *yeah*," Diane sputtered. "That thing sure do look like a big white whale!"—which got snickers and guffaws even from women who'd probably never heard of Herman Melville.

Hannah waved her manicured hand. "No, no! Name it somethin' pretty, like Pearl or Frosty."

"Oh, be quiet," Lucy grunted. "Carolyn leavin'. Let 'er name the van."

Hannah stuck out her lip. "But Miss Gabby said we could vote."

"So? Let's vote on Carolyn's name," Lucy cut in. "Ever'body good with Moby Van?" A resounding chorus of yeahs bounced off the walls. "Nos?" Hannah just rolled her eyes.

And that was that. We even used "Moby Van" to help move Carolyn the next morning over to the apartment building sponsored by Deborah's Place on the west side. We picked up several boxes she'd stored at a friend's—dishes, a few pots and pans, a couple scatter rugs, several towels, sheets and blankets—plus two boxes of books and her clothes from the shelter. I was a bit taken aback at the tiny "studio" apartment—just one room with a refrigerator and hot plate in one corner, a single bed and dresser in another, a small table and chair by the window, and a door that led to a small bathroom with a shower stall, shared with the studio next door.

Carolyn flopped down on the narrow bed and stretched out. "Isn't this *great?* I love it! My own place!"

I was speechless, thinking about the three-bedroom apartment I'd just signed for. Could I be happy here? "Uh, well, guess it's a step up from a bunk room with roommates who snore."

"Ha!" Carolyn threw back her head and laughed. "And *that* was a step up from getting locked in my room at night up at the psychiatric facility." She rolled up to sit on the side of the bed. "I remember one of Edesa's Bible studies; she said Paul the apostle had learned to be grateful whether he had a lot of stuff or just a little. Guess I'm learning that too. The hard way."

A lot or a little . . . I qualified on that score. But had I reached grateful yet? *Huh.* I sure had a lot to learn about this business of being a Christian. Never thought my current role models would be people at a homeless shelter, though.

With a promise to come back to Manna House next week to talk about starting a book club, Carolyn gave me a hug and I headed back toward Manna House. I felt a little teary as I eased Moby Van onto the Eisenhower Expressway heading back into the Loop. People came and went from Manna House all the time. Why did Carolyn's leaving feel like such a loss?

Maybe because her story wasn't all that different from mine. Minus the husband, but still. Middle-class woman, educated, good job, whose life had suddenly spun out of control, nowhere to go. Except to God and God's people. Now she was taking her life back, one step at a time. But even Carolyn had admitted she was scared.

Me too.

As I drove through the Loop and turned onto Lake Shore Drive, I could see the huge Aon Center, which housed my husband's office, its white granite facade standing out from all the steel and glass buildings surrounding it. My last visit to Philip's office tasted like bile in my mouth. But . . . it was time to walk through my fear and get to the other side. I had a sudden urge to pull off the Drive, head for the Aon Center, and ride the elevator to the sixty-second floor. Philip and I needed to talk!

It's Saturday, nitwit. I kept driving.

As I approached the Irving Park exit, which would have taken me to Manna House within a few minutes, I drove past and took the next exit, turning right onto Montrose Harbor Drive. I parked and got out of the big van. A lot of sailboats, a few small yachts in the protected harbor. Rock wall out by the lake. Not much sand. But just being near the water felt good. Traffic noise along the Drive faded into the background as seagulls screeched overhead.

Mmm. If I missed anything about living in the penthouse at Richmond Towers, it was being able to walk through the pedestrian tunnel under Lake Shore Drive and magically be at the beach.

The penthouse . . . Why not call Philip right now and make arrangements to get some of our stuff for my apartment? I'd be able to fit quite a bit into Moby Van. Maybe I wouldn't even need to rent a truck. I sat on the rock wall, pulled my cell phone out of my shoulder bag, and punched in our "home" number.

Heard my chipper voice on the answering machine. *"Hi! You've reached the Fairbanks. Sorry we missed your call. Leave a message . . ."* Like a ghost out of my past, haunting my present. *The Fairbanks . . . we . . .* I flipped the phone closed, losing my nerve. I didn't want to leave a message on the home phone. Philip would just ignore it anyway.

Get a grip, Gabby. It was time to quit hiding from Philip. If he backed me into a corner on the phone, I could just hang up and wouldn't answer the next time. But we needed to start talking, the sooner the better. Taking a deep breath, I tried his cell. Got *his* voice mail. This time I left my new cell number and asked him to call.

But by Sunday evening I still hadn't heard back from Philip.

It had been a busy weekend. When I got back to Manna House with Moby Van after moving Carolyn, Angela was standing at the window of her cubicle, clipboard in her hand, talking testily with two women who looked vaguely familiar. "Do you want to be put on the wait list or not? As I said, the bed list is full right now."

"What about them other two, come in just 'fore us? Betcha put *them* on the bed list." The darker-skinned of the two women stabbed a finger in the direction of the multipurpose room as I tried to creep past.

"That's right." Angela was obviously trying to keep her cool. "We had two empty beds, but they came in first."

The lighter-brown-skinned woman, black hair pulled tight into a stubby ponytail, got in Angela's face. "Those beds 'sposed to be ours! Chris an' me was stayin' here just a few days ago. We left our stuff to hold our place!" The woman glowered at me. "Ain't that right? *You* 'member—we went to the Taste!"

I caught Angela's eye. *Uh-oh.* Chris and Alisha. The two who did a disappearing act at the Taste of Chicago.

"It doesn't work like that." Angela was losing patience. "You didn't come back, so we had to put your stuff in storage. I'll be *happy* to get it now." Angela came out of the cubicle and headed resolutely for the double swinging doors. "Gabby," she hissed at me, "stay with the phone."

"Yeah!" Alisha yelled after her. "You better get our stuff, Chingy Chong, an' nothin' better be missin' or I'll—" The street woman muttered a string of profanity as the doors swung closed behind Angela.

I sweated out the next five minutes, but finally the two women were gone with their "stuff" . . . without filling out the forms for the wait list. Angela blew out a breath as she took back the reception cubicle. "That was close. Look who got the last two beds." She jerked a thumb in the direction of the multipurpose room. "Thank God!"

Precious was getting herself a cup of coffee and loading it with powdered cream and sugar, surrounded by a couple of over-stuffed backpacks and a bulging black plastic bag.

"Precious! What happened? Did you get evicted?" I cried.

Precious shook her head. "Ain't gonna wait to get evicted. Uh-uh. Them sheriff's officers just dump your stuff in the street, rain or shine. I packed it up, storing some stuff at a friend's. Good timin', though. I think we got the last two beds." Precious pulled me aside. "Sabrina, though, she real upset. Don't wanna have her baby at a shelter. She threatenin' to run off again, live with the dawg who knocked her up." Precious practically spit.

"Humph. Over my dead body. She do that? Somebody's gonna die."

I followed her eyes to the black teenage girl across the room, slumped in one of the overstuffed chairs, arms folded over her voluptuous chest, her pretty features tight. How far along was Sabrina . . . three months? Four months? And now she and her mom were homeless again? She was right—a shelter was no place to have a baby! Huh. Maybe we should have taken advantage of all the media attention Dandy's "hero act" had created to raise money for another building, some second-stage apartments for homeless moms like Precious . . .

"Precious—" I wanted to say I'd do everything in my power to help them find a place to live before Sabrina's baby was born, but just then Lucy Tucker came into the multipurpose room with my mother's dog on a leash. Under the purple knit hat, the old woman's crafty eyes took in Precious, then swung across the room to Sabrina. With a shrug, she lumbered over to Sabrina's chair, unsnapped Dandy's leash, and ordered, "Sit. Stay." Dandy sat, his eyes following Lucy as she shuffled out of the room and down the stairs to the kitchen-dining area.

The whole time I was talking to Precious, Lucy didn't come back. Dandy sighed and lay down, right where he'd been put, head lying on top of Sabrina's feet. I took a step in their direction, afraid the sulking Sabrina might kick him away. But Precious grabbed my arm and turned us away, as if we weren't watching. But out of the corner of my eye, I saw Sabrina lean down and tentatively stroke Dandy's silky gold head.

"That crafty old airbag," Precious murmured. "She did that on purpose!"

Even though I felt badly for Precious and Sabrina, for some

reason my spirit lifted having Precious around. Next to Edesa and Josh Baxter—and Gracie, of course—Precious was one of the first people I'd met here at Manna House. She'd given me the official tour, with a lot of unofficial "facts" thrown in. The woman seemed to know everybody's story—and wasn't at all shy about sharing her own! "Girl," she'd told me, "somebody gonna write a book about me someday. Be a best seller! Oh Lord, what I been through."

Mom had another headache Saturday afternoon, but the new medicine Dr. Palma had given her seemed to help. After a short nap she wanted to play Scrabble and somehow talked Tina and Aida into playing with her after supper. "A good way to learn English," she scolded when Aida resisted. I wasn't so sure about that. The last time I'd played with Mom, she'd spelled several of her words backward.

But after getting the Scrabble board set up for them, I excused myself to call Aunt Mercy and bring her up to date. She totally agreed about getting the CAT scan and said she'd call Mom's doctor first thing Monday morning about getting her records sent to Dr. Palma. "But about the apartment you found, Gabrielle. Celeste called me . . ."

I knew what was coming. Now they were both going to get on my case to forget the apartment, bring Mom back to Minot, and stay with her at the house. "Aunt Mercy, look, it's more complicated than that. I'm trying to get my boys back with me, and I have to stay here in Chicago right now. But keep praying, okay? God's going to work it out somehow."

Somehow was right. I just wished He'd give me more than one clue at a time.

chapter 33

Mom insisted on going to church the next morning. "Don't want to spoil my perfect attendance," I heard her tell Precious. I decided I didn't need to remind her we'd both missed last week.

The SouledOut church service started at ten. Normally I'd allow an hour to take the Red Line up to Howard Street— especially with Mom—but at breakfast I had an inspiration. "Anybody want to go to Estelle's church this morning?" I announced. "Same church that comes here on third Sundays. If we get at least eight people, I'll drive Moby Van." Getting residents to church surely qualified as a program.

To my surprise, it wasn't hard. Precious was the first to shoot a hand up, and with Sabrina that made four. Tanya and Sammy made six. And after playing Scrabble with my mother last night, Tina and Aida had a hard time resisting when Mom sweetly asked them to go with her too. She even got a noncommittal grunt out of Lucy.

Tina, however, seemed anxious. "Señora Gabby," she hissed.

"Any Puerto Ricans at that church? Some people think we're Mexican or assume we're all *ilegal*. I get nasty comments sometimes. Don't usually go to places that are just black or white."

Big-boned Tina didn't seem the type to be intimidated, and her comment took me aback. SouledOut had seemed very multicultural to me—but come to think of it, I hadn't noticed any Latinos, though I wasn't sure. "It'll be all right, Tina. I promise." If one could promise something like that.

Lucy, however, managed to disappear with Dandy when it was time to leave. My mother wanted to wait, but I knew those two could stay out for hours. "Maybe next time, Mom. We need to go."

Driving Moby Van up to the Howard Street shopping center was easier than I'd thought—a straight shot up Sheridan Road. It was fun unloading my crew in front of SouledOut. Josh and Edesa Baxter came outside to greet us and laughed when I told them what Carolyn had named the van. "But so far I've been lucky," I confessed. "I haven't had to parallel park the Big White Whale."

A lot of people already seemed to know Precious and Sabrina, and they warmly welcomed the others. Jodi Baxter's face lit up when she saw us. "Gabby! I'm so glad you came! I want our daughter to meet you and your mom. I've told her so much about you both . . . Amanda! José! Come here a minute." In a sly undertone she murmured, "José is Delores Enriques's son . . . might be mine, too, one of these days."

Amanda Baxter had butterscotch-blonde hair caught back in a knot with an elastic hair band in that just-got-out-of-bed look of the young, and her daddy's easy smile. José's dark eyes drifted often to Amanda's face. Their fingers lightly intertwined. *Uh-huh.* I could see what Jodi meant, though neither one looked even twenty yet. "Oh, Mrs. Shepherd, I heard what happened to your dog," Amanda squealed, giving my mother a hug. "I wish I could meet Dandy. Is he all right now? Tell us about him . . ."

Across the room, I saw Mr. Bentley hovering near Estelle, so I left my mother with the young people and headed in their direction. I so badly wanted to ask my Richmond Towers doorman friend if he'd seen my husband at all that weekend, until I remembered Harry Bentley didn't usually work weekends.

"Mm-hm, what did I tell you, Harry? They just couldn't stay away from my cookin'!" Estelle lifted an eyebrow at me as I joined them. "You *are* staying for the potluck today, aren't you, Gabby girl?"

Potluck? Sure enough, right after the two-hour service, chairs were pushed back, tables set up, and food set out for a potluck meal. I felt a little anxious about staying, since we hadn't brought anything but appetites . . . but the rest of the Manna House crew obviously had no qualms, filling their plates and going back for seconds. Even Sabrina seemed to be having a good time, hanging out with Amanda, while José Enriques kept Tina and Aida laughing with his rapid Spanish.

By the time we finally climbed in the van and headed back down Sheridan Road, it was going on three o'clock, and I, for one, was peopled out.

I skipped Sunday Evening Praise that night. I saw Rev. Liz Handley come in—hers was some kind of liturgical church group, if I remembered right. But Mom seemed extra tired, barely touching her supper, so I took her upstairs early and helped her get ready for bed. Even Dandy seemed glad for an early night after staying out nearly all day with Lucy. He curled up in his borrowed dog bed and let out a long doggy sigh.

"You're a good girl, Celeste," my mom murmured, patting my hand as I tucked her into her lower bunk. "Isn't she, Dandy?" Dandy declined comment, probably thinking, *Who's Celeste?*

I kissed her cheek and gently brushed back her soft, gray hair as she fell asleep, thinking it was time for another trip to the beauty salon for a cut and set. I'd be so glad to get my mom into that apartment, to do right by her . . . maybe she wouldn't even need to go to assisted living.

One step at a time, Gabby.

By the time I turned out the light and went downstairs, the Sunday Evening Praise service was half-over. I slipped into the empty prayer chapel instead. I needed some time alone to think. And pray.

Even after the multipurpose room had cleared out and Sarge had locked the front door, I realized Philip still hadn't returned my call. I let myself out onto the front steps, making sure I had my key. The night was muggy and warm, and an almost full moon scuttled in and out of patchy clouds tinged orange from the city lights. Taking a deep breath, I tried calling the penthouse again.

Still no answer. Again I left a brief message. "Philip. This is Gabby. Please call this number. We need to talk." I bit my tongue before I said anything more. But I wanted to say, *"Are you all right? I'm worried about you."*

My cell phone rang at nine thirty the next morning . . . but the caller ID said *Palma, MD.* "Mrs. Fairbanks, can you get your mother to Thorek Memorial on Tuesday at two? Just bring her Medicare card. I've got her registered for the CAT scan."

I wrote it down. Maybe I could borrow Mabel's car again.

But still no call back from Philip. Mabel wanted to have regular staff meetings Monday mornings at ten . . . did I have enough time? I sucked up my courage and called his office. The sure place to get him. "Fairbanks and Fenchel," came the bright voice of the new secretary. "How may I direct your call?"

"Philip Fairbanks, please." I tried to sound businesslike. I didn't need to be afraid; I could live into my name, "Strong woman of God," as Jodi and Edesa had encouraged—

"I'm sorry. Mr. Fairbanks isn't in. Would you like to speak to Mr. Fenchel?"

Philip wasn't in? *What in the world*—? I hesitated. The last time I'd talked to Henry Fenchel, he'd backed off. Way off. But I heard myself say, "Yes."

A moment later a line picked up. "Fenchel speaking."

"Henry? It's Gabby."

"Gabby! Hey, are you all right? Mona and I have been worried about you."

I stifled a snort. Mona Fenchel worried about me? I doubted it. "I'm fine, Henry." Let him figure out what *fine* meant. "But I need to talk to Philip. I thought I could catch him at the office this morning, but—"

"Philip." Henry's voice got tight. "He's *supposed* to be here this morning. We've got a meeting with a key account at eleven, but I haven't seen him. He hasn't called either. If Prince Charming blows this off, I'll—"

"You mean you don't know where he is?" *Oh God, has something happened?* He hadn't gone to Virginia. At least the boys hadn't said anything about their dad when I called them on Sunday. So where—

"Humph. Didn't say I don't know where he is—or was. We did the Horseshoe Saturday night, but Mona got her, you know, female thing, and didn't feel too hot, so we came on home. But Philip decided he was on a roll, told me not to worry, he'd be here for the meeting Monday morning."

"Philip stayed at the casino by himself? Didn't you guys drive down together? He wouldn't still be there this morning, would he?"

"Huh. Meet the new Philip Fairbanks," Henry snapped. "Dashing casino man. Thinks he's got a lucky pinkie . . ." He stopped. There was an awkward pause on the other end.

"Henry?"

I heard a sigh. "Look, Gabby. Forget what I said. Buses run back and forth from Chicago to the casino all the time. He'll probably show up fresh as a daisy for the meeting, and he'd be livid if he knew I'd said anything about . . . you know."

"That's priceless, Henry. You and Mona were the ones who first took him to the Horseshoe when I was gone Mother's Day weekend, remember?"

"Yeah. Don't remind me. Didn't think he'd get so obsessed . . . But, hey, I gotta go. You sure you're okay, Gabby?"

I softened. Henry was basically a good egg, even if his wife and I had gotten along like two Brillo pads. "Yeah, Henry, I'm okay. Real good, in fact . . ." Someone was knocking at my door. "Look, Henry, I've got to go too. I'll try Philip later."

Carolyn stuck her head in and grinned. "Got time to talk about starting that book club?"

I glanced at my watch. "Uh-uh. Got a staff meeting from ten to eleven." But I grinned back at her. "It's good to see you, Carolyn. Let's talk at eleven, okay?"

Carolyn and Precious were both going through the donated books that comprised the start of our so-called library when I joined them in the multipurpose room after the staff meeting. Dandy was back from his morning walk with Lucy, bestowing wet kisses on my mom, who was supervising the activities from her usual overstuffed throne. Across the room Lucy poured out the dregs of that morning's coffee from the carafes, loading up her cup with big tablespoons of powdered cream and sugar.

"Who put all these dumb romances in here?" Carolyn frowned, waving a handful of paperbacks with similar bare-chested hunks clutching fainting damsels on the covers.

"Let me see dose!" Wanda appeared out of nowhere and snatched the paperbacks.

Precious snickered and waved her off. "At least the girl's readin'."

"Okay, ladies. Book club. Got any suggestions, Carolyn?" I sat down across from my mother, while Dandy wiggled his rump against my legs, begging for a scratch.

"Something classic—good literature. Hey, what about *Moby Dick*? You know, since we named the van and all."

I groaned. I'd barely made it through *Moby Dick* myself in school. "Might be a bit hefty to start with. What do we have already? Whatever we choose, we're going to have to get more copies." Did I have "books for book club" in my program budget?

My mother struggled up out of her chair and started rummaging through the books on the bookshelf with Precious.

"Man, what a mishmash," Precious murmured. "*Augustine's Confessions* . . . what is that? True confessions? Le's see . . . *The One*

667

Year Book of Hymns . . . huh. Never heard of some of these. Oh, what's this? *The Idiot's Guide to Grandparenting* an' *What Shall We Name the Baby?*" She pulled out the last two books and waved them in the air with a big grin. "Hey, maybe I can use these when Sabrina's baby gets here."

"This one," my mother said, pulling out a slim book. She turned and held it out to Carolyn. "I . . ." Her voice trailed off.

Carolyn tried to take the book. "Thanks, Miss Martha. Uh, I've got it; you can let go."

My mother stared at her, gripping the book. Her knuckles were turning white.

I started up off my chair. "Mom? You okay?" It was like my mother had gone into a trance. "Mom? . . . Mom!"

Dandy started barking. "Grab her before she falls!" Carolyn commanded. I leaped to her side, and the two of us lowered my mom into her chair. The dog was going nuts, barking and whining, trying to climb into the chair with my mother. Out of the corner of my eye, I saw Lucy heading this way like a runaway train.

"I think she's having a stroke!" Carolyn cried. "We need help!" She ran for the foyer.

A stroke! . . . *A stroke* . . . I'd learned ways to tell if it was happening. I crouched beside her, my heart racing. "Mom! Can you smile at me?" My mother just stared, still gripping the book. "Raise your arms! . . . What day is today?" No response, just my mother's wide eyes.

Lucy pushed her way in between us, grabbed my mother's shoulders, and shook her. "Miz Martha! Wake up, honey!" The frumpy old woman turned to me, her own eyes wide and frightened. "Do somethin', girl!"

The double doors to the multipurpose room swung open, and I saw Mabel, Angela, and Carolyn running toward us. I didn't wait. Snatching my cell phone out of my pants pocket, I flipped it open and punched 9-1-1.

chapter 34

The ambulance ride, siren wailing . . . my mother strapped to the gurney with an oxygen mask covering her face . . . the rush into the emergency room of Thorek Memorial . . . filling out forms about my mother's insurance . . . watching as they sent her frail form into the doughnut-shaped machine to do a CAT scan of her brain . . .

The last few hours blurred as I sat in the waiting room, riding a roller coaster of jumbled thoughts and emotions. *Oh God, Oh God, I don't want to lose her . . . not Mom . . . not now . . . Did I wait too long to check out those headaches? . . . I need to get hold of my sisters! . . . Should I call Aunt Mercy? . . . No, wait until I hear what the doctor has to say . . . Oh God, please don't take her . . . What if she's paralyzed? Strokes can do that . . . but didn't Dr. Palma say mom was basically healthy for her age? . . .*

Mabel, Carolyn, Precious, and Lucy had all shown up in the emergency room and waited for the doctor to come talk to me. Mabel sat beside me, her warm-brown face calm and concerned.

Carolyn paced, her pale hands nervously patting pockets, as if looking for a cigarette. Precious sat in a corner of the room, eyes closed, mouth moving, murmuring a constant stream of prayers. From time to time I heard "Jesus!" or "My Lord!" like little puffs shot into the air. Gray-haired Lucy sat slumped in the opposite corner, looking like she'd just been Dumpster diving in her sloppy pair of cropped pants, loose button-up flowered cotton shirt, purple hat jammed on her head, and ratty gym shoes, laces undone, no socks.

I was glad these new friends were here . . . but for some reason I felt terribly alone. The responsibility for my mom, the decisions to be made, felt like too much. Where was my family? Why did my sisters and I live so far apart? Even if I got hold of them today—a big "if"—there'd be no way they could get here quickly. Even if they could, what would we say to each other? It'd been years since we'd spent any time together. Since we'd really talked.

Family . . . Philip and the boys were my family. That was the biggest hole of all. Fifteen years ago, almost sixteen now, Philip and I had made vows to be there for each other through thick and thin. Times like this. I squeezed my eyes shut and tried to imagine my husband's arms around me, holding me, shielding me from the guilt and pain and what-ifs . . .

I couldn't. He'd cut me adrift. Left me alone. I didn't even know where he was.

And the boys! *They should be here! This is their grandmother!* Anger surged up through my gut and pushed hot tears down my cheeks. It was one thing for Philip to kick me out of his life. But to take my sons away—

"Mrs. Fairbanks?"

I looked up, startled. Dr. Palma stood in the doorway. For some odd reason I noticed the neat baby blue dress shirt and blue-and-black-striped tie he wore beneath his open white lab coat, a stethoscope stuffed in the coat pocket. The emergency room doctor must have called him. I quickly wiped the wetness off my cheeks and stood up. "Dr. Palma. I'm so glad to see you."

The Filipino doctor glanced at the other women, then back at me. "Would you like some privacy? We can go to a conference room." I was tempted to smile. Guess it didn't take rocket science to figure out that the other women in the room weren't exactly family members.

"We can talk here. They're with me." I sat back down and groped for Mabel's hand.

The doctor sat on the edge of the padded chair next to me and leaned forward. "Mrs. Fairbanks, your mother has suffered a massive brain hemorrhage—bleeding between the brain and the skull. Truth is, I've never seen such a large bleed."

"A hemorrhage? But why?"

"We can't be sure. Some patients have weak blood vessels that break and cause seepage into the brain. Or it can happen suddenly, without warning, as it appears to have done in your mother's case." The doctor's voice seemed to fade in and out of my head, like TV sound bites coming from another room as he listed possible causes. *High blood pressure . . . taking an anticoagulant over a long period . . . brain trauma . . . brain tumor . . . an aneurysm that burst . . .*

I forced myself to focus.

"—or possibly a combination of factors. Since I saw Mrs. Shepherd for the first time a few days ago, it's hard to tell."

I stared at him, stunned. Finally I managed, "How . . . how is she? I mean, what can you do?"

Dr. Palma shook his head. "With a smaller bleed, we might be able to do surgery, suction off the blood and try to repair the artery. But you have to understand, Mrs. Fairbanks, the hemorrhage is so massive, I'm afraid the damage has already been done."

My mouth went dry. "What does that mean?"

"It means you need to make a decision. She's in a coma now, not aware of any pain. If you want, we can put her on life support, keep her alive. Or we could make her comfortable and . . . let nature take its course."

I stared at him. "Life support? If we do that, is there a chance she'd get better?"

He shook his head. "The damage is extensive. She'd most likely be hooked to machines for the rest of her life."

"And if we don't?" My voice had dropped to a whisper.

His gray eyes were gentle, full of concern. "She might last anywhere from twelve to twenty-four hours."

My head sank into my hands. I felt Mabel's arm go around my shoulders and hold on tight. *No . . . no . . . no! Oh God, I don't want to have to make this decision alone.* I sensed Precious, Lucy, and Carolyn gathering around, like protective mother hens.

I raised my head and looked at the doctor. "Dr. Palma . . ." My voice cracked. "If she was your mother, what would you do?"

The doctor shook his head again. "I can't make this decision for you, Mrs. Fairbanks. As her family, it's yours to make. But if my mother was in this situation . . . I'd let her go naturally." He rose to his feet. "Please, think about it. Call other family if you need to. I'll come back within the hour."

He started to leave, but I ran to the door and caught him. "Dr. Palma . . ." I had to know. "The headaches. Did they have anything to do with it? If I'd brought her in sooner—?"

He shrugged slightly. "Possibly. But we're second-guessing now. As you said, the headaches only started less than two weeks ago. Not usually a cause for alarm without other symptoms. Please, don't blame yourself. You brought her in when they continued—no one could have done more."

The moment the door closed behind him, Lucy was in my face. "He sayin' jus' let 'er *die*? Ya can't do that!"

"So ya think she oughta play God?" Precious snapped. "Step in an' keep Gramma Shep goin' after her body give out? What about you? If you was in a coma, wouldja want some machine ta be doin' your breathin'? Not knowin' anything?"

"That's diff'rent."

"Why?"

"'Cause—"

"Both of you, shut up!" Carolyn grabbed Lucy's arm. "Come on, let's go get some coffee, leave Mabel and Gabby." Pushing both Lucy and Precious ahead of her, Carolyn cleared the room. The door wheezed shut after them.

I sank back into a chair, feeling as if blood was rushing through my ears. *Oh God, I should have brought Mom in sooner. But I didn't know! And everything's been so crazy. I'm trying, God, I really am. Doing the best I can, but I can't do this alone! I need You, God. I need help. Please—*

"Gabby?" Mabel's voice finally penetrated my brain. "Do you want to call your family? Your sisters?"

I started to nod—then shook my head. "Aunt Mercy first." I slowly dug out my cell phone, but just stared at it stupidly.

Mabel pried it out of my fingers, found my contact list, and a moment later she pushed the Call button, listened a brief moment, then handed the phone to me.

Aunt Mercy's voice reached across airwaves and wrapped around me like a hug. Yes, yes, she'd get on the phone right away and keep trying until she got Honor and Celeste. What hospital were we at? Did I have a medical power of attorney? Yes, it was a terrible decision to have to make. "If it was me, honey, I'd want you to let me go," she said. "But I think I have your dad and mom's living will in my files. I'll get it and fax it to you. Give me half an hour. Hang in there, Gabby."

While we waited, Mabel read the psalms to me. "'The Lord is my shepherd, I shall not be in want' . . ."

Shepherd. Funny. I'd never made that connection before. Shepherd was my maiden name and was still my mother's married name. A shepherd takes care of his sheep—feeding, protecting, comforting—like my daddy used to take care of us girls growing up. But now Daddy was gone. My sisters were gone—or might as well be. My husband was gone . . .

But Psalm 23 says God takes care of me just like a shepherd.

Mabel was still reading. "'Even though I walk through the valley of death, You are with me' . . ."

I was definitely walking through the valley of death. My marriage was dying . . . my mom was dying. But God was with me. That's what it said. Did I believe it?

As Mabel continued to read, the words of Dottie Rambo's

gospel song danced alongside the psalm in my spirit. *"Where do I go when there's nobody else to turn to? . . . Who do I talk to, when nobody wants to listen? . . . Who do I lean on, when there's no foundation stable? . . . I go to the Rock, I know He's able, I go to the Rock!"*

Tears rolled down my cheek. I wasn't alone. God was my family. After all, He had the same last name . . . *Shepherd.*

chapter 35

Martha Shepherd lay small and slight under the taut hospital sheet, her eyes closed, an oxygen mask still covering her nose and mouth, her gray hair splayed out on the pillow as her breath rose and fell. I sat in a chair beside the hospital bed, holding her left hand. My fingers played with her wedding ring, a simple gold band she'd been wearing for over fifty years. *Over fifty years . . .* Was my marriage going to end after only fifteen?

I felt so sad. As if I was treading water in a huge pool of loss.

And yet . . . I *was* treading water. I hadn't gone under. *"The Lord is my Shepherd" . . . Hold on, strong woman of God, hold on.*

Aunt Mercy had faxed my parents' living will to the hospital. No heroic measures that would simply prolong dying, it said. I felt a strange relief. My mother's decision, not mine. They moved my mother into a private room. No machines.

And now we wait . . .

Mabel had taken a distraught Lucy back to Manna House to

take care of Dandy, leaving Carolyn and Precious to sit with me and my comatose mother. But the word must have gotten around, because Josh and Edesa Baxter showed up midafternoon, and the sweet young couple held me and we cried.

I left the room long enough to call my sons. They should know. It was Monday . . . what were the boys doing at four in the afternoon? To my huge relief, Mike Fairbanks answered the phone. He swore softly under his breath when I gave him the news. "Sure am sorry to hear this, Gabby. She was a sweet lady. But, uh, the boys aren't here at the moment. Marlene went to pick up P. J. at lacrosse camp, and Paul's out riding his bike—Oh, wait. I think I hear them now. Hold on . . ."

In the background I heard muffled voices, then running feet. Paul got on the phone first. "Mom! Mom! Is Grandma Martha okay? She isn't gonna die, is she?" I heard the click of an extension pick up.

I don't know where I found the words. "It's a very bad stroke. The doctor says she won't live long . . . P. J., are you there? Would you boys like to say good-bye to Grandma? She's in a coma, so she won't be able to respond, but you'll know . . ."

Both boys were crying now. Trying to reassure them, I walked the phone back into the room and held it to my mother's ear. "Mom, it's Paul and P. J. . . ." I don't know what they said. My mother's fixed expression did not change. But when I took the phone back out into the hall, both boys were still crying.

"Mom! I wanna be with you," Paul wailed.

"Me too." P. J. sounded ten again. "I wanna say good-bye to Grandma for real."

I could barely contain the tears. "I know. I want to be with you too. I'll call you again real soon and let you know what's happening, okay? Now, let me talk to Granddad Mike again."

Mike Fairbanks must have been right there. "Gabby, have you called Philip yet?"

Philip. Was he even back in town? "No. I—I don't want him here right now."

"Humph. Don't blame you. Look, let me work it out with Philip about getting the boys there when . . . you know, the funeral and everything."

I closed the phone and leaned my forehead against the wall outside my mother's room. Odd. Philip's father was turning into my advocate—

"Gabby!" Estelle swept down the hall, wearing a bright turquoise caftan, her loose kinky hair in an untidy topknot. "Oh, baby," she murmured, folding me into a big hug. "I'm so sorry." She turned. "Harry, give that basket here. This girl needs something to eat."

Only then did I notice that a bare-domed Harry Bentley was behind her, carrying a basket that turned out to be stuffed with sandwiches and fruit. "Mr. Bentley!" I couldn't believe he'd come. I wrapped my arms around him. "Thank you for coming," I whispered. "You . . . you know you were my very first Chicago friend."

"And you, Firecracker, added some pizzazz to a very dull job." The middle-aged black man chuckled. "Not to mention that you introduced me to my lady, here."

"*Lady* is right." Estelle gave him the eye. "And don't you forget it, mister. Now, where's Lady Shepherd? She's the one we came to see." Once in the room, the large woman leaned over the bed and kissed my mother's wrinkled cheek, her glowing cinnamon face a warm contrast to my mother's pale skin against the stark-white pillow. "We're all here, Gramma Shep. Lot of people who love you. And Dandy sends his love."

Estelle straightened and shook her head at me. "If Lucy had her way, she'd be bringing that dog up in here, but Mabel put her foot down. They'll be here soon. Now . . ." She sat on the end of the hospital bed. "Tell us some stories about your mama, Gabby. You don't mind, do you, Martha?" She patted my mother's foot under the covers.

The heavy spirit in the room seemed to lift. I racked my brain for memories of my mother—but once I started, it was hard to stop. "Sundays . . . Mom always got up early to put a pot roast or chicken casserole in the oven so it'd be hot and ready after church. She usually invited someone on the spur of the moment to come home with us too."

Mr. Bentley chuckled. "Sounds like my mama. Except the guests invited themselves."

Estelle gave him a poke. "Hush. This ain't about your mama. Go on, Gabby. Tell us about Christmas."

"Oh yeah . . . One time my dad wrapped up only one new slipper for Mom's Christmas present, because only one of her old ones had a hole in it. Mom laughed so hard she got a stitch in her side! And *then* he made her hunt for its mate—can't remember where he hid it, but it took her two days to find it."

Now everyone was laughing.

"I was always bringing home pathetic stray cats and dogs—drove my dad nuts, but Mom usually stuck up for me. But seeing how much she dotes on Dandy, I realize she has a soft heart for four-legged creatures herself. Of course, that doesn't explain the snake she let me keep—"

"Snake? Whatchu talkin' 'bout snakes?" Lucy and Mabel had returned, and Lucy pushed herself in and parked herself in a chair on the other side of the bed. "Hey there, Miz Martha. It's me, Lucy. Just wantcha to know, Dandy's missin' ya real bad, so don't pay these people no mind. Just come on home."

"Lucy—" I started, but Estelle gave me a leave-it-be shake of the head. That's when I saw Jodi and Denny Baxter leaning in the doorway—Josh must have called his parents. When I started to get up to greet them, Jodi shook her head. "Go on, Gabby. We want to hear the stories."

Mom's breathing had slowed, each breath coming farther and farther apart. "Guess the thing I remember most about my mom," I murmured, stroking her hand, listening to the ragged breaths, "is all the books she read to us after supper, at bedtime, on car trips—even when we were older. I was the youngest, and one winter she read all the *Little House* books by Laura Ingalls Wilder—and Celeste and Honor would 'just happen' to hang around to hear them, too, even though they were teenagers."

Carolyn and Precious looked at each other. "That 'splains it," Precious said.

"Explains what?"

Carolyn pulled a dog-eared paperback from her backpack. "The book Miss Martha was trying to give me when she . . . you know . . ." The Manna House book maven choked up and couldn't say any more.

Precious took the book from Carolyn and held it up so we could all see the title. *Little House in the Big Woods.* My eyes watered. I'd read a lot to my boys when they were younger. That had stopped when Philip sent them to boarding school. But, I vowed, if I got them back under my roof, I'd make sure we read aloud together, even if I had to read a Harry Potter book or—

"Miz Martha!" Lucy's voice rose in alarm. "C'mon, now, breathe!"

I rose quickly and leaned close to my mother's face. A long silence—and then suddenly another long, slow breath.

"That's right. C'mon!" Lucy's wrinkled face under the purple knit hat twisted with anxiety.

The room hushed as the people who'd been family to both of us in the last few weeks seemed to hold their collective breaths. I leaned closer, my face on the pillow beside my mother's, tears sliding down my cheeks. "Mom," I whispered. "I love you. I love you so much . . ."

The silence grew . . . one minute . . . two . . .

But this time—nothing.

My mother had slipped away as gently as that last breath.

Midnight. The hospital waiting room was empty now except for Jodi Baxter and me. Bless them! Josh's parents had offered to wait with me while I finished necessary paperwork with the hospital and help make phone calls, so everyone else could go home and get some sleep. Denny had taken charge of making arrangements with a reputable funeral home to pick up my mother's body and hadn't come back.

I played with the gold wedding ring I'd gently slipped off my mother's hand. Even now, I could still hear the voices of our friends—our Chicago family—as they'd gathered around Mom's bedside, held hands, and recited the Lord's Prayer. Then Estelle began to sing "Amazing Grace." The impromptu chorus of male and female voices joining in had been tender and sweet. My mother would have loved it.

And then they'd left quietly—all except Lucy, who'd stormed out during the song, anger masking her grief.

My cell phone rang, and I snatched it. "Celeste? . . . Oh, thank God Aunt Mercy got through to you! . . . Yes, she's gone, about two hours ago . . . I'm still here at the hospital . . . I know, I know . . ." We cried together on the phone. I tried to imagine my sister, ten years older than me, whom I hadn't seen since our father's funeral two years ago. All three of us girls had cried together then, holding each other, united for the moment in our grief—Celeste's thick brunette hair pulled back, hazel eyes and freckled nose both red and running . . . Honor's bare-faced California tan under her bleached-blonde shag, looking forlorn . . . and me, the baby, feeling like Little Orphan Annie—and I don't mean the hair—once Daddy's funeral was over and we'd gone our separate ways.

Now it was our mom. After wiping my face with the back of my hand, I tried to answer Celeste's questions as best I could, but I felt on the defensive. After all, I was the one who was here, try- ing to handle everything by myself. I tried to make her understand it was a *massive* hemorrhage . . . The doctor had given no hope of recovery, even if they put her on life support . . . Yes, I had power of attorney, but Mom's living will was clear . . . Of *course* Celeste was the oldest, but it wasn't exactly easy getting in touch with her in the middle of Denali National Forest . . .

Finally we got to "what next." "Yes, I know there's a plot beside Daddy back in Minot, but . . . All right. Yes . . . Call me tomorrow, please? Maybe we can get on a three-way with Aunt Mercy to decide what to do. And try to get hold of Honor, okay? It's already after midnight here."

As I closed the phone, Jodi handed me a tissue and I blew my nose. I looked up at her through bleary eyes and sighed. "I don't know what to do, Jodi. I'm sure my mom would want to be buried beside my dad, and we already have a plot in Minot. But how do I get her there?" I ran my fingers through my tangled mop. "I *know* I can't afford to bury her in Chicago."

Jodi pulled a chair next to mine and took both my hands. "Gabby, you've done everything you can do tonight. Come home with us. Get some sleep. I'll take you back to Manna House in the morning. I'll keep the car, and we can do any running around you need to do. Okay?"

I nodded wearily and stood up. Suddenly I felt more exhausted than I'd ever felt in my life. Jodi took my arm and I let her lead me through the hallways and down the elevator until we found Denny, who said the funeral home would be there shortly. I could go tomorrow to pick out a casket and make arrangements.

Denny went for the car and picked us up at the main entrance of the hospital. Thankfully, Jodi and Denny didn't try to talk as he drove their minivan the half mile to Lake Shore Drive and turned north. I sat slumped in the seat behind Denny, gazing out the window in a half stupor. A full moon shone over the lake on the right, bathing the trees and parks along the Drive in silver gossamer, competing with the bright neon lights of the city on our left.

The lakeshore was beautiful, even at night. In spite of everything that had happened, Chicago was growing on me. Maybe when I got the apartment and the boys had settled in, we could explore the city and its wonders—

The apartment. I stiffened, coming wide awake like a jolt of caffeine as streetlights flashed by. Mom and I had been planning to share the apartment, pooling our money! That was the only way I could afford it. But now . . .

Oh God! What am I going to do now? New tears sprang to my eyes, and I started to weep silently, feeling hope drain out of my spirit. It wasn't just being homeless again, forced to stay longer at Manna House—which was about as good a place as an emergency shelter could be, even if I did have to sleep in a bunk room with four to six other women.

It was my sons.

Without an apartment where I could provide a home for them, my petition for guardianship would go down the toilet.

chapter 36

It took me a long time to fall asleep in Josh Baxter's old bedroom, but at least I wasn't awakened at six o'clock by Sarge's wake-up bell. The bedside clock said 8:36 when I finally opened my eyes, the whirring fan in the window the only noise. Reluctantly I dragged myself out of bed, clad only in the big Bulls T-shirt and pair of shorts Jodi had handed me to sleep in. Finger combing the snarls out of my hair, I wandered into the kitchen, where Amanda Baxter was perched on a tall kitchen stool wearing blue-and-orange-plaid pajama bottoms and a rumpled tank top, trying to keep the calico cat on her lap from getting into her cereal bowl.

"Oh. Mrs. Fairbanks!" she burbled, quickly swallowing her mouthful. "I'm so sorry to hear about your mom . . ." She dumped the cat and hopped off the stool to give me a hug. "I'm so glad I had a chance to meet Gramma Shep last Sunday. She reminded me of my grandma—the one in Des Moines, not New York. My dad's mom doesn't even want to be called 'Grandma,' go figure . . . Oh, Mom said to tell you she took Daddy to work, but she'll be back soon. Coffee's hot—you want some?"

I nodded, hiding a smile at Amanda's monologue as the girl poured a mug of coffee. I added milk from a jug sitting out on the counter and sipped. The hot liquid felt good going down, waking up body parts still sluggish from my five short hours of sleep.

Amanda took the elastic band out of her honey-blonde hair, shook her head, and regathered the tousled locks back into the band. She eyed me tentatively. "What's going to happen to your mom's doggy now?"

I shook my head. *Dandy* . . . just one more worry in the long list of decisions I had to make.

"Wish I could take him. Peanut and Patches are okay, but I miss having a dog. You would've liked Willie Wonka, our chocolate Lab—he was a sweetheart. But I'll be going back to U of I in August, my second year." Amanda eyed me cautiously. "But my folks might take him if you need a home."

I gave her a wan smile. "They already offered. Sweet of you to be concerned about him, Amanda. But speaking of Dandy, I need to get back to the shelter. He's probably really confused that my mom isn't—" A sudden lump in my throat cut off my words, and I scurried for the bathroom before I blubbered in front of Amanda.

Jodi was back when I reappeared in the same slacks and top that I'd worn yesterday, my hair damp and frizzled. I held up my cell phone and made a face. "Dead. I need to get back to Manna House and charge it before I can make any calls."

"Use our phone, Gabby! It's fine."

I waggled the cell. "Unfortunately, all my numbers are in here."

"Well, let's get going, then." She held up two travel cups. "Have coffee, will travel. Oh—grab that bagel and one of those bottles of juice, if you'd like."

True to her word, Jodi put both herself and their Dodge Caravan at my disposal for the day. But I wasn't really prepared for the grief-stricken faces of many of the shelter residents when we came into the multipurpose room. The women who weren't already out for the day gathered around, bombarding me with questions and comments. "What happened, Miss Gabby?" "But she wasn't sick!" "It's good, ain't it? I mean, that she didn't die of cancer or somethin' painful, right?" "Gonna miss her powerful." "Gramma Shep—can't believe she gone." "Hope I go that way—*bam*. Gone. *My* gramma got sick and was in the bed for months . . ."

Jodi finally rescued me and spirited me away to my office. She ran up to the bunk room and brought down my charger, and while the cell phone was recharging, we made a list of things I needed to do. Call Aunt Mercy. Decide what we should do about a funeral. Try to get on a conference call with my sisters. Go to the funeral home, choose a casket, make arrangements.

"What arrangements?" I wailed to Jodi. "I'm sure my sisters and Aunt Mercy want to have the funeral back home—and we have to bury her beside Daddy. But what's it going to cost to ship my mom's body all the way back to Minot? And how long would that take, Jodi?" I threw down my pen, grabbed a wad of tissues, and pressed them against my eyes to stem the tide of new tears rising to the surface.

Jodi scooted her chair close to mine. "Gabby . . . Gabby, let's stop a minute and just pray, okay? I've been trying to learn to pray first, before I get into a big stew . . . Wait. I think I hear Estelle in the kitchen. Let me get her, and the three of us can pray."

Sure enough, Estelle had come in to make lunch, but she crowded into my tiny office in her big, white apron and hairnet, shut the door, and the two of them laid hands on my head and started to pray. Jodi prayed for God-given wisdom and peace in the middle of this painful loss. Estelle prayed that God would pull everything together—all those decisions to be made, all the jagged pieces of my life—and "knit them together in a way that's *good* for Gabby and her family."

That's when I lost it. "But . . . but . . . but . . ." I tried to say, the tears coming harder. "With Mom gone, I . . . I . . . can't afford the apartment Lee—Mr. Boyer—found for me. And . . . and . . . if I don't have an apartment, I . . . I can't get my boys back!" The last words were swallowed up as my whole body shook with sobs.

The two women just held me, crooning and soothing as if I was a child. And finally my sobs quieted, and I mopped my face and blew my nose.

"Now, listen, Gabby Fairbanks," Estelle said, her voice soft but firm. "God hasn't brought you this far to leave you. If that plan for the apartment doesn't work out, it means God's got a better plan in mind. You hear? Trust Him, baby. Trust Him." She gave me another hug and slipped out of the room.

"She's right," Jodi said. "I'll call the Yada Yada sisters to pray about the apartment thing, but if you can put that aside, let it sit in Jesus' lap, let's work on the things that need to be done today." She stood up. "Why don't we go to the funeral home first and, you know, find out how it's done when somebody dies in one city but needs to be buried in another state."

I nodded, blew my nose again, and followed her out into the dining room. Then I stopped. "Wait . . . have you seen Dandy since we came in? Or Lucy?"

As it turned out, no one I asked had seen Lucy *or* Dandy all morning. At the reception desk, Angela shook her head. "But you know Lucy. Sometimes she takes the dog out and doesn't come back for hours. Just takes him along to do . . . whatever it is she does. I'm sure they'll be back eventually."

Jodi had already wandered outside. "Well," I said to Angela, pushing the front door open to follow, "if she brings Dandy in while I'm out, tell her to wait here for me. I want to spend some time with Dandy too."

Jodi was standing on the sidewalk beside the big Manna House van parked in front of the shelter, standing on tiptoe in her sandals, peeking inside. As I came up to her, she turned. "Gabby, this is going to sound funny, but . . . back there, when we were praying, I think God gave me an idea how to get your mom's body back to North Dakota."

"What do you mean?"

"Drive the casket there. Yourself. In Moby Van."

I stared at her. "In *that*? I mean, can you *do* that?"

She threw up her hands. "I don't know! But the idea just dropped into my head while we were praying about what to do, like God was giving an answer. I didn't say anything back there, because, yeah, it sounds crazy. But standing here looking at this big ol' van, I'm thinking, why not? We prayed for an answer, didn't we?" Jodi giggled nervously, as if she couldn't believe she was talking this way.

"But . . . but . . . I'm sure you'd need some special permit or something. Who in the world would we ask about something like that?" I made a face. "They'll think we're nuts."

"Probably. That's why *you're* going to ask." Jodi laughed and pulled me toward her minivan. "Come on. I'll drive you to the funeral home. Then it's up to you."

"Me! It's your idea."

"Hope not. If it works, we're gonna give God the credit."

We sat across the desk at Kirkland & Sons Funeral Home as the impeccably dressed man tapped his pen on the papers in front of him. He had sallow skin, thinning hair, and an annoying habit of pushing his horn-rims up his nose every few minutes. "I'm sorry, Mrs. Fairbanks; personal transport of a body is highly irregular. However, we *can* transport your mother's remains to . . ." He squinted at the paperwork. ". . . Minot, North Dakota, if we have the name and address of the appropriate funeral home for delivery."

"How much?"

"Well, that depends on the mode of transportation. We can arrange for air, train, or ground. When do you want the body to arrive?"

"Why, as soon as possible. A few days . . ." I glanced at the calendar on the wall. Today was Tuesday. Give a few days for my sisters to travel . . . "By this weekend?"

"Well then. We would probably need to send one of our hearses, which would run about . . ." He tapped some figures on his calculator. ". . . four thousand dollars."

I stared at the man. The "discount package" he'd already

offered added up to roughly five thousand, which included the casket—a moderately priced metal one in medium metallic blue with silver shade and a white crepe interior—and service fee for staff and facilities ("All paperwork, death and burial certificates, embalming, hairdresser, use of our chapel if you so desire, the hearse for transport . . .").

I blew out a slow breath. "Can we, uh, have someplace where my friend and I can talk in private?"

"Of course." The man politely showed us to a small "family room" with padded chairs, a coffeepot, and pitchers of ice water and closed the door behind him.

I looked at Jodi. "Jodi, I can't afford this! That's almost ten thousand dollars!"

She nodded. "I know. But the man said it was 'highly irregular.' He didn't say it was illegal. I think we ought to check it out. I'll . . . I don't know. Call the County Clerk's office or something. And maybe you should call your aunt Mercy and find out what the funeral home in Minot says."

I called Aunt Mercy at the library where she worked. She couldn't talk long, but she promised to call the funeral home that had handled everything when my dad died. "I think my brother had prepaid funeral costs here for both him and Martha. I'll call you back as soon as I find out anything . . . Oh, I finally got hold of Honor. She's pretty broken up. But she sounded like she would come for the funeral—drive, I think. I don't know about her boys. But I'll call her back as soon as we can make plans."

It was already past noon. I told the funeral director we had to talk with family and I'd be back soon. Jodi and I walked a few blocks until we found a tiny restaurant and ordered homemade vegetable soup. I wasn't sure my stomach could handle anything heavier.

My cell phone rang halfway through my soup. Aunt Mercy. She was almost laughing. "Mr. Jacobs said, 'Hogwash. Of course you can transport the body!' He said all you need is a permit from the county—which the funeral home there can get for you—and a vehicle that will hold the casket. Period."

"You're kidding!"

"I'm not, sweetheart. Here's the information you'll need to fill out the permit. And I was right; your father prepaid for a casket, embalming—everything. There might be a few extra expenses since two funeral homes are involved, but the big things are covered. Jacobs said to tell your funeral director to call him if he has any questions." I jotted down the information on a napkin, including Mr. Jacobs's phone number. "And Gabby, as soon as you decide when you can get here, let me know so I can make arrangements for a service on this end. Celeste and Honor need to know when to arrive. And there are a lot of people here who were very fond of your mom and dad."

Jodi was waiting impatiently for news, her soup getting cold. Even though she was in her forties, she whooped like a schoolkid when I told her what Aunt Mercy had said. "See? See what God can do, Gabby?" She shook her head in amazement. "To tell you the truth, I'm still surprised when God answers my prayers. Some faith, huh?"

"Well, don't stop praying yet. I haven't even asked Mabel—or the board—if I can use Moby Van for something personal like this. And that huge van must be a gas hog. Can't imagine what the gas would cost all the way to North Dakota and back."

Jodi pulled a stray strand of brown hair out of her mouth and chuckled. "A lot less than four thousand dollars, anyway!" She waved her soup spoon at me. "And I think we should go back and take apart Kirkland & Sons 'discount package' and see what it'd cost for just the things you actually need. You won't need to use their chapel, unless . . ." She stopped and looked at me funny. "Gabby? I know you're going to have a funeral service for your mom back in Minot, but there are a lot of people here who've come to know and love your mom. Especially at Manna House. Why don't we plan something here for the staff and residents? Josh and Edesa got married in the multipurpose room at Manna House. I'm sure we could do a funeral. A memorial service to celebrate Martha's life!"

I got a little teary. "I'd like that. I know Mom would like that too."

We ate our soup in silence for a minute; then I put my spoon down. "I can't do it. Can't imagine driving my mom's casket all the way to Minot by myself in that big ol' van. You gotta admit, Jodi, it's a little weird."

Jodi turned her head and gazed out the restaurant window at the misty rain that had started since we'd arrived, almost as if she hadn't heard me. Then, as if somebody had flipped her On button, she snatched up the bill for our soup and dug out a ten from her purse. She left both on the table. "You won't have to. Come on. Let's go."

I scooted out of the booth and followed her out of the restaurant. "What do you mean, I won't have to?"

She took my arm with a grin and started off down the sidewalk, ducking raindrops. "Because I'm going with you!"

chapter 37

Jodi Baxter and I came out of Mabel's office just as the supper bell was ringing. I'd reviewed with the Manna House director all the plans we were proposing. First, a celebration service for my mom's "homegoing" here at Manna House Thursday morning, open casket, everything. Followed by a repast supervised by Estelle. Then—if the board approved—loading the casket in Moby Van and driving to North Dakota, where I'd meet my sisters, have another funeral, and bury my mom beside my father in the Minot cemetery.

Mabel had been open to the idea of using the van but was noncommittal. But she was a hundred percent on board for hosting a memorial service for my mother at the shelter. "We'll all miss Martha," she'd said. "I think she fulfilled a grandmotherly role for a lot of the young women and kids the last few weeks."

I gave Jodi a tight hug in the foyer as she got ready to leave. "I don't know what I would've done without you today, Jodi. I mean, I can't believe you got the funeral home costs shaved off! That's a huge help."

She grinned. "Hey, it was fun seeing that funeral guy squirm. And don't you worry about the van, Gabby. If the board nixes the idea of using Moby, maybe we can take our Caravan if we take out all the seats. I've been wanting to go see my folks in Des Moines anyway. We could stop there the first night. It's on the way. Well . . . sorta." Jodi peeked into the multipurpose room. "So where's Dandy? I'd like to say good-bye to him. You know, Hero Dog worked his way into our hearts at the Baxter household that week you guys stayed with us."

Good question. Angela had already gone for the day, but Carolyn was babysitting the phone and the door buzzer in the reception cubicle for the evening shift. "Hey, Carolyn. Have you seen Dandy or Lucy?"

Carolyn shrugged. "Haven't seen either one."

Jodi and I looked at each other. "I'm worried," I said.

But when curfew rolled around, and Lucy still hadn't come back with my mother's dog, I started to get mad. That's when I discovered Dandy's food and water bowls, bag of kibbles, and Lucy's cart were gone too.

I wished I'd gone home with Jodi Baxter again. My mother's empty bunk—as well as Lucy's and the empty dog bed—weighed on my spirit in the night like heavy stones. I finally took my pillow and blanket, found Sarge, and asked if I could sack out on a couch in the multipurpose room, just for tonight.

Sarge shook her finger at me. "Gabby Fairbanks, you break more rules than the rest of the women on the bed list put together! I know it's tough losing your *madre*, so I'm gonna let you do it, but I'm waking you up *before* I ring the wake-up bell so nobody else gets a wise idea. *Capisce?"*

I curled up on a couch in the corner, but my mind was still spinning. I still needed to call Lee Boyer and tell him about my changed circumstances. My next appointment with him was scheduled for tomorrow at eleven, but with everything I had to do, there was no way! Hopefully we could talk by phone . . .

Celeste had called me twice that evening. I told her how things were working out on this end. Awhile later she called to say she'd gotten a flight from Juneau to Billings, Montana, would meet up with Honor flying in from Los Angeles, and the two of them would rent a car and drive to Minot, arriving sometime on Friday.

"I'm impressed you two were able to coordinate that," I'd said.

"Ha. Coordinate nothing. I bought her a ticket. *She* was talking about borrowing a car from a friend and driving straight through. I can just imagine some rattletrap with no muffler breaking down in the middle of the Mojave Desert, and we'd have to call in the state troopers to find her. Even if she didn't, she'd probably show up two days after the funeral."

That had made me laugh. Celeste wasn't that far wrong.

I'd also called Mike Fairbanks to tell him about the funeral on Thursday morning here in Chicago, and that I'd be driving my mom's body back to Minot, where we'd have a second funeral. "I wish the boys could come to the funeral in Minot, but I think they'd have to change planes, maybe even twice. I don't really feel good about that." And, I had to admit, it would probably cost more than going to Europe. Mike said okay, he'd call me back after checking flights to Chicago.

Now, as I lay staring at the ceiling fans slowing rotating over-head, I wished I'd asked if he'd spoken to Philip. I probably should call Philip myself, even if he had. *"I trust in God, why should I be afraid?"* the psalm said. Besides, shouldn't I treat Philip like I'd like to be treated? At least let him know that my mother had passed.

But I drew the line at him coming to the funeral. Not that he would. But after the way he'd treated my mother, if he tried it, I'd probably sic Dandy on him and send him to the hospital like that midnight burglar.

Sometime during the night I must've fallen asleep, because the next thing I knew, Sarge was shaking me awake and telling me to clear out of there before other residents started to come down-stairs. She also handed me the first cup of steaming coffee out of the pot, and I managed to get through that Wednesday morning on constant refills.

I called Lee Boyer first thing, told him what had happened and that I had to cancel my appointment that morning. "But this changes everything, Lee. I can't afford the apartment now . . ." I tried to steady my voice so I wouldn't break down again. "And I don't know what that means since I signed a contract. Can he sue me?"

"Now, Gabby, don't worry about the contract. I know this guy; we'll work something out. He owes me a few favors. But we do need to get you an address so we can file your custody petition with the court ASAP . . . Hey, look. Let's not try to deal with that today. You just lost your mother; that's enough to deal with. When you get back from Minot, we'll get right on it. Trust me, Gabby. I'm working this for you."

"Trust me, Gabby . . ." Why did that put a ruffle in my spirit? I felt confused about my feelings for this man. Lawyer? Friend? More than friend? But just then my call waiting beeped. The caller ID said Mike Fairbanks. "I'm sorry, Lee. Gotta take this. It's my father-in-law." I flipped over.

The call was short. Mike said he was bringing the boys to Chicago, they had a late flight that afternoon, and Philip was going to pick them up at O'Hare. "We'll be staying overnight with Philip. I'll get them to the funeral tomorrow morning, Gabby, and we'll be returning tomorrow night. That way P. J. will only have to miss one day of lacrosse."

I felt like screaming, *What does lacrosse have to do with anything?!* Even if I was leaving for North Dakota soon after the funeral, didn't Philip want the boys to stay through the weekend? They could go back to Virginia Sunday night, and P. J. would still only miss two days of camp. But I bit back my sharp retort. *Focus, Gabby, focus.* Mike was bringing the boys to their grandmother's funeral. I'd get to see my sons for those precious few hours, whether they stayed longer or not. That was all that mattered. "Thanks, Mike," I managed. "I appreciate that you're coming with them."

Blinking back tears, I hustled into Mabel's office, and we spent an hour roughing out a funeral service—Mom's favorite scriptures, music, who might participate. "Type up what you want for an obituary, Gabby," she told me, "and I'll contact Peter and Avis Douglass, see if they'd be willing to officiate. Any of the residents you'd like to include somehow in the service?"

I shrugged. "Well, Lucy—*if* she comes back, and if I don't kill her first for absconding with Dandy." I threw open my hands in helpless frustration. "Should I go look for her? Call the police? I mean, I really do want to find Dandy."

Mabel thought a moment, then fished her car keys out of her purse. "If you think you know where to look, be my guest."

I took the keys but realized it was probably a hopeless cause. Lucy could be anywhere! She was a street person, after all. It wasn't like she had a home and a workplace and a list of relatives and friends I could check out. But I did drive around the streets and through the alleys near Manna House, and even drove through Graceland Cemetery where I knew she often walked Dandy. Nothing.

Not sure why I found myself driving up Sheridan Road toward Richmond Towers, except that the park there along Lake Shore Drive was the place I'd first run into Lucy. Literally. Parking Mabel's car in the visitor parking spaces along the frontage road where Richmond Towers faced the park, I resisted the urge to peek into the lobby and say hi to Mr. Bentley. Another time.

Walking the jogging path, I veered off through the mown grass to check under some of the lush bushes. Was this the one where I'd tripped over Lucy's cart that day in the rain? I wasn't sure . . . but it was stupid anyway. Why would Lucy crawl under a bush on a breezy, warm day like today?

But I still scanned the park, following the path through the pedestrian tunnel under the Drive and coming out just north of Foster Avenue Beach. That's when I saw them . . . two familiar figures sitting on the two-tiered rock wall that led down to the strip of sand about a hundred yards to my left, a purple knit hat topping the dumpy body of Lucy Tucker, her arm draped around a yellow dog patiently sitting beside her.

I did not call to Dandy. Instead I quietly walked up beside them and sat down on the wall beside the dog. He immediately rose up, excited, licking me in the face and whimpering his greetings.

"Hey, Dandy," I said, scratching his rump. "Easy, now. How you doing, boy? . . . All right, all right, that's enough. Sit . . . sit! That's a good dog."

Dandy flopped between me and Lucy, his brow wrinkled, as if unsure what was going on or what he should do. Lucy said nothing. I, too, just sat on the wall, watching the waves stirred up by the strong breeze coming off Lake Michigan, the horizon dotted with slender, white sails. The warmth of the sun on my head and the breeze running fingers through my unruly curls swaddled me in an oddly comforting cocoon, a momentary respite from death and funerals and—

"I was goin' ta bring him back," Lucy finally muttered.

I didn't answer. Two seagulls fought over some tidbit in the shallows.

"We jus' needed some time, the two of us, what with Miz Martha dyin' off so sudden-like. Couldn't get no peace back there! Ever'body yappin' an' cryin' . . ."

Sitting there on that wall, my mad at Lucy sifted out of my spirit like so much dust. "I know. I got worried, though."

Lucy sniffled and wiped her nose with a big, faded blue handkerchief she pulled out of somewhere. "S'pose ya gotta take him back with you."

"Yeah. My boys are coming for their grandmother's funeral tomorrow, and I know they'll want to see Dandy. Paul, especially. He took care of Dandy for my mom when she was staying with us . . . kinda like you."

Lucy's head swiveled toward me. "What funeral?"

I told her our plans. A funeral at Manna House tomorrow morning, another in North Dakota, probably on Sunday. "My dad is buried there. We want to bury my mother beside him."

Lucy slid off the wall and shuffled two or three steps until she stood right in front of me, a kaleidoscope of mismatched tops and bottoms. "How you gettin' from here ta there?"

"Uh . . . driving. Mabel's asking the board if I can use Moby Van."

Lucy's rheumy eyes bored into mine. "Takin' Dandy?"

That brought me up short. I hadn't thought about what to do with Dandy. The Baxters would probably be glad to take care of him—or even Lucy—for the five or six days I'd be gone. But somehow that didn't seem right. Dandy was family, had been Mom's companion for the past ten years. And that only begged the bigger question. What was I going to do with Dandy *after* the funeral?

If I had my apartment, I'd keep him myself. That would be a big draw for the boys—well, Paul, anyway—in coming back to Chicago. His own dog.

But I didn't have an apartment. Didn't know when I would get one either.

"Well?" Lucy put her hands on her hips and stuck her face close to mine. "I *said,* are ya takin' Dandy back to Dakota ta bury your ma?"

"Yes!" I shot back. Well, why not, since we were driving.

"Okay then." Lucy hauled herself up the big step onto the grass and wrestled her cart out from under a nearby bush. "I'm goin' too."

chapter 38

Lucy would not be dissuaded. I almost hoped we'd have to take the Baxter minivan so I could honestly tell her there wouldn't be any extra seats—but when I got back to the shelter with Lucy and Dandy, Mabel had left a note for me on my desk:

Gabby—good news! The board is granting permission to use Moby Van to transport Martha Shepherd's casket, since she died while a resident of Manna House, and since there wouldn't BE a van except for Dandy. All they ask is that you cover gas and any out-of-pocket expenses. Have a safe trip!

My skin prickled. This *was* good news—so why did I feel a tinge of panic? The whole idea was crazy! Driving cross-country with a casket in the back of a van the size of a small bus. Paying for gas and expenses . . . certainly a reasonable request. But where was it going to come from? My credit cards were dead. I'd have to use my debit card, which would take money right out of my bank account. I'd just have to keep a close watch so that I didn't drain my account completely.

And now what excuse could I give to Lucy? Even if we took out enough seats to accommodate the casket, there'd still be enough room for me, Jodi, Dandy, *and* Lucy.

I grabbed the note and poked my head out the door. I'd ask Estelle what I should do. Lunch was over, but Delores Enriques was still packing up her portable medical clinic in a corner of the dining room. Two of the residents whose names I didn't know were wiping tables and sweeping the floor. Estelle was bustling around the kitchen with a larger-than-normal crew.

"*Hola*, Gabby." Delores paused her packing and scurried over to give me a hug. "I am so sorry to hear about your mother. My own mother lives in Mexico, but it's been five years since I have seen her. Now . . . I think I should go. One never knows how short life is."

I hugged her tight. "I know. Thanks, Delores. I hope you can go see your mom. The last few weeks I had with my mother were precious." I let her go, then turned back. "Say, I met your son, José, last Sunday. At SouledOut. Such a good-looking boy! He was with Amanda Bax—"

"*Sí, sí*, I know." She rolled her eyes heavenward. "Señor *Dios, por favor!* Just let him get through college before those two get any ideas . . ." The dark-eyed woman leaned close to me and lowered her voice. "José looks up to Amanda's brother, and *he* married Edesa Reyes when he'd barely turned twenty. But José is the first male in my family to even *go* to college. My Ricardo . . . oh." Delores put her hand up to her mouth. "*Perdone*. You go on, Gabby. I know you have a lot on your mind. We'll talk another time, all right?" She gave me a kiss on the cheek, then turned back to packing her stethoscope, swabs, and other instruments.

The kitchen was bustling. I leaned on the wide counter that opened into the kitchen, hoping I could get Estelle alone long enough to ask what I should do about Lucy. Althea, her hair hidden by her Middle Eastern head scarf, and Diane—took a moment for me to recognize her with that big Afro tucked into one of those ugly white hairnet caps—were both holding the big electric mixer as it went around and around, to keep it from rocking off the counter. Sammy's mom and several others from the Thursday cooking class were slicing cheese and ham, chopping vegetables, and arranging it all on a big, round tray.

"Hi, Estelle! What's happening? Your cooking class meeting early this week?"

Estelle looked up from the cutting board, where she was slicing lemons and limes. "Hey there, Gabby. You doin' okay? We just combined the knitting club and cooking class today to fix some food for the repast tomorrow after your mama's funeral. Least we can do for Gramma Shep."

"Uh-huh" . . . "That's right!" a few voices called out.

"Sheila, turn the heat down under them greens! S'posed to simmer, not boil . . . Diane! That cookie dough mixed yet? Turn that thing off! . . . Whatchu need, Tanya? Another tray?" Estelle bustled past me on the other side of the counter, giving me a quick glance. "You need somethin', honey? Can it wait a bit? We got a lot of pokers in the fire here."

I backed off with a wave. Didn't look like now was the time. Besides, I had a lot of last-minute details to wrap up for tomorrow—run to the funeral home to pick up the transport permit, call Aunt Mercy and ask how arrangements were shaping up on

that end, ask some of the residents to act as ushers, call Denny
Baxter and see if some of the guys from his men's group would
act as pallbearers, wash a load of clothes and pack for the trip,
pack up Mom's things to take back to North Dakota . . .

Everything was moving along until I got to the laundry room
tucked away behind the kitchen. All four washing machines were
busy. Good grief! I only had a load of underwear and a few necessities for my trip. Who—?

Just then Lucy lumbered in, dragging her cart. Her *empty*
cart.

"Lucy! What are you doing? Are all these yours?" I pointed at
the four machines.

"Yeah, what of it? Decided to dump it in, wash it all. Don't
know what it's like in North Dakota. Might need my winter coat
an' stuff."

"Oh, Lucy." I leaned against the wall, shaking my head.

In spite of Lucy's wash-a-thon—which, I had to admit, I'd been
hoping she'd do for a long time—I managed to get almost everything done that afternoon and evening. Sinking into my office
chair after supper, I turned on my computer and glanced at my
watch. Almost eight . . . I had time to work a little more on the
funeral program and still get to bed by lights-out.

Wait . . . Mike Fairbanks had said he and the boys were supposed to get in at O'Hare Airport around seven thirty. Philip was
going to pick them up, take them back to the penthouse, and
they'd see me tomorrow morning here at the funeral.

That meant P. J. and Paul were already here! In Chicago! How
was I supposed to wait fourteen whole hours before I saw them

tomorrow? I couldn't. I had to see them! Grabbing a pad of note-paper, I started jotting down times. Half an hour, give or take, to get their bags if they checked anything . . . maybe another sixty minutes to get to Philip's parked car and drive into the city. Add another half hour for good measure . . .

At nine thirty I got off the El at the Berwyn stop and walked briskly the two blocks to Sheridan Road and turned north. The warm night air was somewhere in the seventies, cooled by a nice breeze off the lake. I'd had to get an "emergency pass" from Sarge just to go out and come in past curfew, and she'd shaken her head when I wondered out loud whether I should take Dandy with me since it was dark. "Just *go*, Gabby Fairbanks. You want protection? Dandy and I'll walk ya to the El and you can give me a call when you want to come back. But give the poor dog a break. They don't let dogs on the El anyway."

Now Richmond Towers rose just a few blocks ahead of me, lighted windows hugging the curves of the building like a clingy dress. I hesitated as I reached the revolving doors that would take me into the lobby of the luxury high-rise, my knees suddenly going rubbery. What was I walking myself into? Philip would be there, and I hadn't been invited. *Oh God, I don't want a nasty confrontation in front of the boys . . .*

Through the glass doors I saw a familiar figure rise up from behind the semicircular desk. My rubbery knees toughened up. I pushed through the doors. "Mr. Bentley! What are you doing here at this time of night?"

The doorman's eyebrows lifted as I came up to the desk. "I could ask you the same thing, Mrs. Fairbanks. Let me guess . . . Awhile ago two young men who looked an awful lot like you went up the elevators in there"—he pointed to the glass security area that separated the lobby from the elevators—"accompanied by their father and somebody I'd guess was Mr. Granddaddy."

I nodded, relieved to hear they'd arrived safely. "Yeah. Couldn't wait until tomorrow to see them. But, well, kinda decided last minute."

Mr. Bentley pursed his lips. "In other words, they don't know you're coming." He leaned toward me over the counter. "Don't you worry, Firecracker. You've got a right to see those kids. Hold on to that. Go on. I'll buzz you in."

"Wait. Your turn. Why are you working the evening shift? Did you switch?"

Harry Bentley shook his head. "Just traded a few hours with Gomez, who covers the first night shift. So I, uh, you know . . . so I could come to your lady mother's funeral tomorrow morning."

"Oh, Mr. B." I ran around to the other side of the desk and gave the man a big hug. "You're the best. Okay, say a prayer for me. I'm going up."

Two minutes later the elevator dinged at the thirty-second floor and the door slid open. I stepped out onto the gleaming marble tile of the foyer. Ceramic urns full of silk flowers stood on either side of the penthouse door. And somewhere on the other side of the door I heard a TV going and the banter of youthful voices.

My heart thudded in my chest. But I raised my hand . . . and knocked.

An eternity passed. Then the door opened. There he stood—tall, tan, shirt collar open, a stray lock of dark hair falling over his forehead. His left eye twitched, betraying his outwardly detached demeanor.

"Hello, Philip."

"Gabrielle. What are you doing here?" My husband swiveled his head toward the front room and frowned. "Did my father—?"

"No. I knew he and the boys were flying in tonight, and . . . I just want to see P. J. and Paul for a few minutes, Philip. I don't plan to stay long."

He hesitated for a moment, then stepped aside. "Fine. They're in the front room." He disappeared in the direction of the kitchen.

I closed the door behind me and walked softly through the gallery. My heart was still tripping, and my skin prickled with excitement. P. J. and Paul were flopped on the long end of the wraparound couch, their backs to me, their grandfather Mike stationed at the other end, watching something on the plasma TV. I crept up behind them and laid one hand on P. J.'s dark-brown hair, falling over his forehead like his father's, and the other on Paul's lighter curls. "Hey."

Paul's head whirled. "Mom!" he screeched, hurling himself over the back of the couch and tangling me in an awkward hug. P. J. jumped up too, came around, and locked his arms around me. For thirty blissful seconds, I held both my big boys in my arms, laughing and crying and drinking in the familiar smell of their skin and hair.

To his credit, Mike Fairbanks shut off the TV. "Good to see you, Gabby," he said gruffly, and also disappeared toward the kitchen.

I sat on the couch, my boys snuggling on either side. Paul fired questions like a machine gun. "Why didn't you bring Dandy? Is he okay? What happened to Grandma? Grandpa Mike says you're going to bury her in North Dakota. Can we go with you?"

P. J. reached out and shoved his brother. "Can't, dork. I've still got a couple of weeks to go before lacrosse camp is over."

As best I could, I tried to fill the boys in on what had happened to their Grandmother Shepherd, assured Paul he'd get to see Dandy tomorrow, and told them I was working as hard as I could to find a place to live so we could be together again. "But P. J.'s right—you guys need to stay in Virginia until he finishes camp the end of July. Then . . . well, hopefully we'll get you back here with your dad and me as soon as possible."

Their faces had gone ashen. P. J.'s mouth tightened. "What do you mean, find place to live? Does that mean you and Dad are getting a divorce?"

I'd dreaded this moment. But I shook my head. "Nobody's said anything about divorce. But . . . your dad and I are having some problems, and we need to be apart awhile to sort things out." *Sort things out . . .* I hoped Philip was listening.

Finally scooching off the couch, I stood up. "I better go. I still have things I need to do to get ready for Grandma's funeral tomorrow." I grabbed them both in another three-way hug. "I'm so glad you came," I murmured into their hair. "I've missed you so much." Untangling myself, I found my purse and headed for the front door.

Paul ran after me into the gallery. "Mom! Don't go!" He threw his arms around me. "Can't you stay? We can go to the funeral together tomorrow morning."

I gently pried off Paul's arms and opened the door, aware that Philip had appeared in the arched doorway on the left, wiping his hands on a terry towel. "No, I can't stay, honey. But I'll see you tomorrow morning, okay?"

Paul sniffed and wiped his eyes with the back of his hand. "Okay, Mom. We'll get there early—right, Dad?"

My breath caught. Philip had stopped in midwipe, but lifted his chin and stared at me as if daring me to answer Paul's question.

I am Gabrielle . . . strong woman of God.

I held Philip's gaze, unblinking. "Sure, Paul. You boys and Granddad Mike can come as early as you like. But your father isn't coming to the funeral. He'll be going to work tomorrow."

I stepped out and pulled the door shut behind me.

chapter 39

The multipurpose room began filling early the next morning with residents and guests for the ten o'clock funeral service. The Kirkland & Sons funeral director and three of his staff had arrived at eight in their long, black hearse, unloading my mother's metal blue casket onto a wheeled cart and setting it at the front of the circle of chairs. I was surprised at the number of flower arrangements that arrived. As the funeral staff opened the casket, I busied myself looking at the cards—a large spray of pink gladiolas from the Manna House board and staff . . . red and white carnations from SouledOut Community Church . . . a mixed flower arrangement of colorful mums and daisies from Mercy Shepherd . . . a spray of white lilies with a card that said, "With sympathy, the Fairbanks Family." Probably Marlene's doing. But nice.

Another flower arrangement arrived by messenger, a huge spray of bloodred roses, which the funeral staff set up on a large stand. It took me a few moments to find the card . . . and then I couldn't believe my eyes. "With sympathy, Fairbanks & Fenchel Commercial Development Corp."

Of all the nerve!

Estelle Williams, smelling like gardenias and dressed in a black-and-white tunic over wide, silky black trousers, leaned around me and read the card. "Humph. Want me to chuck 'em for you, honey?"

Ha. I could just see them sailing out the front door and landing in the gutter. "Yeah . . . later. After the service." I didn't want any drama—for my sons' sake. Not today. But I took the card and stuck it in my pocket. No sense letting Philip "look good."

"Well, I gotta tend to some last-minute food prep. You gonna spend some time with your mama?" Estelle tipped her head toward the open casket, and I followed her gaze. My mother's face—so like her, and yet unlike her too—peeked out from the soft crepe lining of the shiny blue metal casket.

"Um, maybe when P. J. and Paul get here. Think I'll go wait for them outside." On my way to the foyer, I greeted several board members and got warm hugs from Avis and Peter Douglass, who were consulting with the female keyboard player from SouledOut about the service. Precious and Sabrina stood at the double doors, handing out the simple program and helping to seat people. "Thanks for ushering, Sabrina," I said, giving the pregnant teenager a hug. "You look beautiful today."

But I had to hide a smile as I overheard Precious send two of the residents back upstairs to "get somethin' decent on—you look like some ho. This is a funeral for a grand lady, an' don't ya forget it!"

The foyer was a beehive. Slipping around the crowd, I pushed open the oak doors and stood on the steps, my black crepe skirt blowing in the stiff breeze of another warm Chicago day. Craning my head this way and that, I was relieved to see Lucy coming up the sidewalk with Dandy, wearing a bandanna around his neck like a doggy cowboy. I'd been half-afraid she'd disappear again, and Paul would be devastated.

"Hey there, buddy." I bent down to give the dog a scratch behind the ears, his golden coat freshly brushed except for the area where the hair had not yet grown over his scars, when a familiar black Lexus SUV pulled up in front of Manna House.

I stiffened. Philip was driving.

The doors on the passenger side opened, and Mike Fairbanks and the boys piled out. Paul, unmindful of his good slacks and summer dress shirt, dashed over to Dandy, who immediately started barking and leaping all over him. Philip's father slammed the car door and hustled up the steps after P. J. My father-in-law gave me a peck on the cheek.

"What is Philip doing here?" I hissed in his ear.

Mike Fairbanks turned and jerked his thumb in a *get-moving* motion. "He's not staying. I made it clear he's not invited . . . Boys! Let's go in." They trailed Lucy and Dandy into the cool foyer.

I could have hugged him. Strange, I'd never felt that close to Philip's father, but suddenly I found him in my corner. I started to follow them inside when I saw Lee Boyer crossing the street in the middle of the block, making him pass directly in front of Philip's car. He had shed his jeans and boots for slacks, dress shirt, and tie. Stepping up onto the sidewalk, Lee peered over his wire rims at the car and driver, then at me. He raised his eyebrows . . . then came on up the steps and gave me a hug. "I'm so sorry about your mother, Gabby. You doing okay?" He followed my eyes as I lingered just long enough to make sure the SUV drove off. "Is that him?"

I nodded, not trusting myself to speak.

As we came into the multipurpose room, the young black woman from SouledOut was already playing some background music—hymns and classical pieces. Lee found a seat toward the back. People were still talking but had quieted to a low murmur, and those standing by the casket moved aside to make room for the boys and me. Mike Fairbanks crossed himself—odd, since he wasn't Catholic—then quickly sat down in the front row.

I stood at the casket, my arms around both boys, as we looked at my mom's body. A stranger lay there, hands crossed on a familiar Sunday dress. Her gray hair was done neatly, her glasses perched on her nose, but the waxy expression didn't look anything like my mother, who could in turn be sweet or stubborn—sometimes both at the same time.

To my surprise, P. J. reached out a tentative finger and gently touched my mother's hand. But as he touched the waxy skin, he recoiled, his face crumpling, and he darted to a chair next to his paternal grandfather. Paul, on the other hand, pressed himself into my side, clinging to my waist. He didn't want to leave . . . until we heard a whine at our feet. Dandy had slunk up beside us, his doggy forehead wrinkled. He sniffed the casket, whining pitifully.

Paul lost it. And so did I. We cried and hugged Dandy and each other . . . and I heard other sobbing around the room as we finally found our chairs.

Once the casket was closed and the funeral started, Avis led us in a "celebration of life." She read one of my mother's favorite psalms, and we sang "Great Is Thy Faithfulness" and "O Love

That Will Not Let Me Go." Someone had thoughtfully printed out the words and included them in the simple program. Edesa Baxter read my mom's obituary, and as she read the words I'd written, I realized what an ordinary life my mother had led, nothing terribly exciting. And yet . . . she had been a faithful and loving wife, had raised three girls who had the same genes but were as different as rain, snow, and hail, had rolled with the uncertainties of the past few years since my dad died, and took comfort in the small, everyday joys of life—puttering in her flower garden, talking to her doggy companion, going to church, and making new friends . . . even in a homeless shelter.

How many so-called celebrities could say that?

Avis invited anyone who would like to share something about Martha Shepherd to come to the front. To my surprise, Hannah was the first one up. "Even though she white, we all called her Gramma Shep, 'cause she'd sit an' listen to ya, as if you was important—*and* she let me paint her nails!" Hannah jerked a thumb toward the casket, which the funeral home staff had closed before the service started. "Jus' look in there an' see! An' if ya want your nails done, I'll—"

A chuckle went around the room as Avis Douglass cut her off. "Uh, no commercials, Hannah. We need time for others."

Carolyn got up and said it was a joy to know someone who liked to talk books and play Scrabble, followed by several other residents, staff, and volunteers—all of them giving testimony to the smiling presence of this simple, older woman who brought a bit of sunshine into the Manna House homeless shelter.

Then Lucy got up and laid a hand on the closed casket. Her rheumy eyes glistened. Dandy, who'd been lying at Paul's feet, got up and went to her, sat on his haunches, and looked up at the old woman. Lucy, dressed for the occasion in a clean but rumpled flowered skirt, white blouse, blue sweater two sizes too small, ankle socks, and sandals, didn't address the people in the chairs. She spoke to the casket.

"Miz Martha, this is Lucy." Her voice was husky. "Me an' you, we was kinda unlikely to be friends, but that's what you was—my friend. Don't have too many friends. Got one less now that you're gone. But you an' Dandy here . . ." She reached down and patted Dandy, who seemed to be hanging on every word. "You was some of the best friends I ever had. An' I really don' know what I'm gonna do now that you gone, Miz Martha . . . but if you're in that happy place they talk about 'round here, I'm thinkin' I'd like to find out how to get there, too, so we could . . ." Her voice faltered. She stood there a moment, her shoulders sagging. But then she patted the casket. "Jus' wantchu ta know, Miz Martha, you trusted me ta take care of Hero Dog, here, an' that's what I wanna do"—the old bag lady turned and gave me the eye— "though ain't nobody tol' me yet who he's gonna live with. But if Dandy needs a guardian angel down here, that's me." And she shuffled back to her seat.

Avis beckoned to me. I saw both smiles and tears in the wake of Lucy's eulogy as I faced the people who had gathered to celebrate my mother's life. I suddenly felt overwhelmed at seeing all the faces seated in the rows before me—black, white, tan . . . young, old . . . homeless women and board members . . . Mabel Turner, who'd hired me on faith and whose patience toward me was long on God's grace . . . Precious and Sabrina, Tanya and Sammy—two mothers like myself who only wanted to make a home for their children . . . Estelle Williams, who'd taken me under her wing like my own personal mother hen . . . Edesa and

Josh Baxter and baby Gracie . . . Josh's parents and sister Amanda, who'd taken in a couple of strangers . . . and even some of Jodi's Yada Yada Prayer Group sisters . . .

My mother had been in Chicago a mere four weeks—most of that spent here at Manna House—and yet the multipurpose room was full. I nodded and smiled at Harry Bentley, sitting beside Estelle, who had been *my* first friend here in Chicago. "Thank you, everyone . . . ," I started, but the lump in my throat was so big, nothing more came out.

"All right, now," Precious piped up. "Take your time, Gabby, take your time."

There was so much I wanted to say. But as I struggled for words, I saw the double doors to the foyer open—and Philip slipped in.

Mike Fairbanks must have seen the stunned look on my face, because he turned his head to follow my eyes . . . and the next minute he was out of his seat and making a beeline for the back of the room. Almost at the same moment, I saw Lee Boyer and Harry Bentley get up from different parts of the room, like a pair of white and black cops, and head for the doors as well. Seeing his father and the other two men heading for him like bouncers at a nightclub, Philip backed out of the room, followed by the three men, and the doors swung shut behind them.

I caught Avis's eye, shook my head, and fled to my chair. The pianist took her seat at the keyboard, and the next minute we were all standing and singing, "Some glad morning when this life is o'er . . . I'll fly away . . ." I turned my head and looked toward the closed doors. What was happening out there? Leaning over to my sons, I whispered, "Wait here for me, okay? I'll be right back." Hoping not to be noticed as I ducked through the standing congregation, I slipped into the foyer. Empty. I crossed to the heavy oak front doors, turned the handle of one, and pushed it open a few inches.

Through the crack I saw Philip standing down on the sidewalk, smoking a cigarette—*since when?!*—and looking off into the distance, while Mike Fairbanks, two inches shorter than my six-foot-two husband, jabbed a finger in his face. "—ashamed to call you my son! You know Gabby didn't want you here today—and I don't blame her. After what you did—"

This was my fight, and I was tired of running from it.

I stepped outside.

Mike stopped, finger in mid-jab, and all four men gaped at me.

I marched down the steps until I faced my husband. *Gabrielle . . . strong woman of God.* If that was my identity, I better start living into it—though I had to admit that the presence of my three benefactors cinched up my courage a few notches.

"You're not welcome here, Philip. You know why. You turned my mother away from your home. You treated us both like dirt. She wouldn't want you here today. I don't want you here today. The least you can do is respect that."

No hysterics, no name-calling . . . *Thank You, God, for giving me words.*

Philip took a drag on the cigarette, dropped it to the ground, and ground it out. "I'm sorry about you losing your mom, Gabby. I—" His left eye twitched, the way it always did when he was tense, and he turned his head, as if watching the El train crossing the street a couple of blocks down. "That's . . . all I wanted to say." He pushed past his father and started down the street toward his car.

Lee Boyer laid a comforting arm around my shoulder, but I was startled to hear him call out, "Fairbanks!" Philip stopped and half-turned his head. "*Sorry* isn't good enough." Lee's voice was low and tight. "We'll see you in court."

chapter 40

The repast after my mother's funeral celebration was a noisy affair, with more food than I'd seen in a long time lined up on the kitchen counter—greens, fried chicken, hot wings, sliced ham, corn bread, beans and rice, taquitos, a fruit tray, red punch, coffee . . . and three kinds of cookie bars. A regular multicultural fest. Estelle must have shanghaied her prayer group, too, because I'd seen her housemate, Stu, and several other Yada Yada sisters bringing in food as well.

The servers were all Manna House residents and volunteers, wearing clean white aprons and brightly patterned African head wraps instead of the usual ugly hairnets. Even Carolyn had her long, brownish-gray ponytail tucked up under a blue-and-gold head wrap, and her cheeks were flushed, animating her normally pale skin with a glow of color.

Dandy took advantage of the hubbub, moving from table to table, getting handouts. By popular request, Sarge retold the story of her rescue from the midnight intruder by Hero Dog and his subsequent rise to mascot and official watchdog status—omitting her ominous threats to banish him just days earlier.

P. J. and Paul remembered some of the residents from their earlier visit, and they ended up in the rec room, playing Ping-Pong with Sabrina and Hannah and some of shelter kids. But poor Mike Fairbanks seemed a little overwhelmed by it all.

It was almost one thirty by the time Jodi Baxter leaned over my shoulder and whispered, "We better get on the road before two if we want to miss traffic."

The pallbearers—Josh Baxter; his father, Denny; Harry Bentley; Peter Douglass; and the two pastors on the board—had already taken out the last three rows of seats from Moby Van and loaded my mother's casket into the back under the supervision of the funeral directors at the end of the service. Now Jodi and I added our suitcases, Dandy's bed, dishes, and a bag of dog food, and everything my mom had brought with her from North Dakota a month ago into the back alongside the casket.

"I wish I could go with you, Mom." Eleven-year-old Paul stood on the sidewalk, shoulders hunched, hands in his pants pockets, his short school haircut grown out into a mass of unruly coppery curls, not unlike my own. "Why can't I take care of Dandy till you get back?" His lip quivered. "You *are* going to bring him back, aren't you?"

"Yes. I promise." I gathered my youngest into my arms. "I wish you could go with me, too, kiddo. But . . ." My eyes blurred. "You need to stay with Granddad a little while longer. We'll be together soon. You'll see." I reached out toward P. J., who let me pull him into our good-bye hug too.

"Don't you worry about that dog none, sonny," Lucy interrupted, bouncing her overloaded wire cart down the front steps of the shelter. "I been takin' good care of him for your gramma, an' ain't gonna quit now, even though she gone."

I stared at the cart. "Lucy! You can't take that cart on this trip! I mean . . ." Frankly, I'd been hoping someone would pull Lucy aside and talk her out of going along. When was I going to learn that wishful thinking never got me anywhere?

Lucy peered into the open side door of the van, where Dandy was already sitting up on the second seat, panting in the heat. "Whatchu mean? They's plenty of room in this ol' bucket. I gotta take some clothes along. We goin' up north, ya know."

Mabel stepped in to the rescue. "Lucy, come on. We'll find you a suitcase. You can leave your cart in my office, and it'll be safe and sound till you get back. Deal?" She led Lucy back into the shelter, cart bumping behind them.

Denny Baxter hovered around the van like a regular grease monkey, checking the windshield wiper fluid, making sure oil and water were full, checking the tire pressure. "You got enough gas to get you to Des Moines? Jodi, you sure you and Gabby want to stay at your folks' place tonight? It's gotta add a couple hundred miles."

"We know." Jodi flipped her bangs back. "But it's cheap lodging. And dogs are allowed. Free breakfast too." She kissed Denny right on his dimples and climbed into the passenger seat. "Besides, if I see my folks on *this* trip, you're off the hook the rest of the summer."

I shrugged and grinned at her husband. "What can I do? I need a copilot."

Mabel and Lucy came back out, this time with an actual suitcase—the old-fashioned kind with no wheels. Still, Lucy looked embarrassed to be carrying it. "Don't feel natural," she grumbled, shoving it into the van and climbing in after it.

"Where's your hat, Lucy?" All summer she'd been wearing the purple knit hat Estelle had made for her. But now she was bareheaded, her gray hair clean but badly in need of a cut.

"Too hot. Whaddya think?"

I laughed and climbed into the van behind the wheel. "Glad you finally figured that out."

At the last minute, Estelle came rushing out with a shopping bag full of leftovers from the repast to eat on the way. Amid a chorus of good-byes from our friends and family on the sidewalk, I pulled the van away from the curb, and in five minutes we were heading south on Lake Shore Drive. I looked sideways at Jodi. "Can't believe we're doing this."

Jodi glanced over her shoulder into the second seat and then back at me, tipping her head slightly toward the rear. "Me either." In the rearview mirror I could see Dandy sitting sideways, his chin resting on the back of the seat, eyes on the blue metal casket.

Better keep your eyes straight ahead, Gabby . . .

Jodi Baxter was a good navigator. She got me off Lake Shore Drive, through the city and going west on the Eisenhower Expressway, until we picked up the I-88 toll road all the way to Iowa—a boring stretch of road if I ever saw one. Construction, cornfields, and more construction. We didn't talk much, and I was just as glad. It was the first time I'd had fifteen uninterrupted minutes since the previous Monday, when Mom had the stroke. *Only four days ago . . .*

But the images tumbling behind my eyes were less than four hours old. Philip coming into the shelter halfway through my mother's funeral. After I'd told him not to! Was he *trying* to upset me? Or—if I took what he said at face value—did he honestly feel sorry that I'd lost my mom? Was he having a crisis of conscience about what he'd done? And Lee! I hardly knew what to think about his reaction. His protective arm around me. His challenge to Philip. *"We'll see you in court!"* It felt so good to have a man stand up for me. And yet . . . why did I get this feeling Lee meant something more than lawyer-and-client by that shouted "we"? And why did I like it? Was it because I felt attracted to Lee? . . . or because I wanted to make Philip jealous?

Construction on the toll road slowed us down. I rolled down my window to save on air-conditioning as we crept along, thinking about P. J. and Paul. My time with them had been too short. Already, the memory-touch of their boyish hugs was starting to fade. P. J., in spite of his almost-fourteen stoicism, had looked so sad, as if on this trip he'd begun to understand, maybe for the first time, that his parents might actually get a divorce . . . and Paul, obviously homesick, needing his mom and dad . . . and I couldn't promise them a home to come home to.

A tear rolled down my cheek. Jodi touched my arm. "Want me to drive?"

I nodded and sniffed. "Soon as we get off this toll road."

We crossed into the Quad Cities on the Iowa-Illinois border around five o'clock, pulled into a gas station, topped off the gas tank with my debit card, and took a potty break. "Don't have to go," Lucy muttered, sliding out of the van and reaching for Dandy's leash. "I'll just walk the dog."

I snatched Dandy's leash. "Rule Number One on car trips, Lucy. You *go* every time we stop, whether you think you have to or not. Next stop might not be for another couple of hours."

Grumbling, Lucy followed Jodi into the station. But I hadn't counted on mutiny from Dandy. He wouldn't leave the van. I pulled on his leash, and he pulled back. I finally had to pick him up and carry him to a grassy area alongside the station. Even then he didn't go . . . until we got back to the van, and then he lifted his leg against a tire.

Jodi drove the rest of the way to Des Moines. The supper Estelle had packed for us—cold fried chicken, a bag of chips, fruit, and a ton of cookie bars—perked us up, and Jodi and I started singing some old camp songs to pass the time. "She'll be coming 'round the mountain when she comes, whoo! whoo!"—all the more ridiculous since the fields on either side of the road were flat as a hairbrush. I suggested "Row, row, row your boat"—no rivers or lakes in sight, either—but Jodi warbled the college prof version: "Propel, propel, propel your craft, placidly over the liquid solution . . ." By this time we were giggling like junior-high schoolgirls.

"You guys are nuts, know that?" Lucy hollered from the second seat.

It took us another three hours to drive halfway across Iowa, but it was still light when Jodi pulled Moby Van into her parents' driveway. A bald-headed man and a petite gray-haired woman who reminded me a lot of my mother came out of the house, beaming a welcome as we piled stiffly out of the vehicle. I stood back as Jodi gave her parents big hugs. "Mom, Dad . . . this is Gabby Fairbanks, the program director at Manna House. And this is Lucy, um, a friend of Gabby's mom. And this is Dandy, the Hero Dog I told you about—oh, Lucy! Don't let Dandy do that!"

Dandy was peeing on a rosebush.

"I'm so sorry," I said, flustered. "Lucy, where's his leash? . . . Oh dear, it's been awhile since we let him out."

Jodi's father chuckled. "I'm sure Dandy's not the first dog who's mistaken that bush for a fire hydrant." He held out his hand. "I'm Sidney Jennings, this is my wife, Clara, and—"

"—and I've got supper waiting for you on the table," Clara Jennings finished. "Come on, come on in."

"Oh good," Lucy muttered, stalking up the sidewalk. "Been least two hours since I last et." We trooped along after her, though I noticed that Sidney Jennings hung back and peeked in the windows of the van, as though he couldn't quite believe we were trucking my mother's casket all the way to North Dakota.

Even though I wasn't really hungry after Estelle's sack supper, the homemade chicken noodle soup was so good that I asked for seconds. Lucy had thirds. The Jenningses graciously retired at ten, knowing we needed to get to bed so we could get an early start the next morning. Lucy and a reluctant Dandy bedded down in Jodi's old bedroom, and Jodi and I got the bunk beds in her brothers' old room. "Good thing I've got lots of experience sleeping in a bunk bed," I yawned, crawling into the top bunk. "You don't snore, do you, Jodi?"

We settled down, an oscillating fan moving the night air a little in the stuffy bedroom. It had been a long day, and I was tired beyond belief . . . but I suddenly rolled over and hung my head over the side of the bunk. "Jodi?"

"Mmph . . . what?"

"I feel kinda funny."

"What do you mean?"

"I mean . . . it doesn't really feel right that we're in here together, all comfy and cozy, tucked into bed . . . and my mom is still out there in a box in the van."

Jodi stifled a screech. "No! You didn't say that . . . Oh, that's *awful.*" She grabbed her pillow and whopped my upside-down head with it, trying not to laugh, but her horrified giggles seemed to pull a plug out of the dike of pent-up emotions from the past few days, and the next thing I knew I had tumbled off the top bunk, and the two of us collapsed together on the lower bunk, pushing our faces into the covers, trying to stifle our hysterical laughter.

chapter 41

After our irrational bout of laughter had turned to tears, Jodi and I comforted each other with the reality that Mom was safe and warm in the arms of Jesus, and we fell asleep . . . and were on the road again by seven o'clock with a long twelve-hour day ahead of us. I skipped my shower—a decision I later regretted. Still in his bathrobe, Jodi's dad had insisted we eat the hot breakfast he'd prepared—bacon, scrambled eggs, wheat toast, and coffee—and her mom had packed sandwiches to take along. "I'm sorry to take Jodi away so soon, Mrs. Jennings," I said, taking the small cooler with the sandwiches she handed to me and giving her a hug, catching a whiff of lilac in her hair.

Like my mom . . .

"Never you mind," she whispered. "Her dad and I are planning a trip to Chicago for Jodi's birthday in September—but don't tell her. It's a surprise."

I almost blurted, "No, no surprises!" Parents showing up on the doorstep unannounced had had disastrous consequences in my case. But I held my tongue, realizing I had to stop seeing the world through the Fairbanks grid.

Lucy had taken Dandy for a short walk after breakfast and managed not to get lost in the unfamiliar suburb, and Jodi drove first, heading north on Route 35 toward Minnesota. From time to time, I tried to engage Lucy in conversation, but she usually answered my attempts with a grunt or one-word answer, seemingly content to hunker by the window behind the driver's seat, eyes locked on cornfields and small towns as they zipped past. And when she did talk, she talked to Dandy. "Hey, lookee there, Dandy. Ever see so many cows? Wonder who doin' all that milkin' . . ."

We'd been traveling an hour or so when I heard a familiar rumble and realized both Lucy and Dandy had zonked out, the dog's head in her lap. I shook my head, kicked off my sandals, and put my bare feet on the dash with a big sigh. "Don't know what to do about Dandy. Lucy's gotten so attached to him. Paul would really like to have a dog, which would be fine with me, once I have a place for me and the boys. But now . . ." The mental wall I'd been holding up between me and reality suddenly started to crumble.

"But now . . . what?" Jodi prodded.

It all came tumbling out, the whole fragile house of cards I'd been counting on—finding an apartment so I could get custody of my sons, getting excited about the apartment Lee Boyer had shown me, thinking I could afford it if Mom and I shared the expense. ". . . That's what!" I said between my teeth, trying not to wake up Lucy. "I can't afford that apartment by myself—and I can't shoehorn myself and two big boys into those shoeboxes that the Chicago Housing Authority subsidizes for the homeless, even if I was number one on their waiting list, which I'm not." I banged a fist on the passenger door. "Now I know how Tanya and Precious feel, stuck in a homeless shelter, dangling between nothing and nothing. And all they want is to make a home for their kid, get a job, be a family!"

Jodi nodded but said nothing, concentrating on passing a big hog transport tying up traffic in the right lane.

"Huh," I muttered. "Maybe I should play the lottery like your friend what's-her-name—"

"Chanda." Jodi pumped the speed up to seventy, glancing anxiously back at the big semi before finally pulling the van back into the right lane. "Sheesh, I keep forgetting how long this van is."

"Yeah, Chanda. If I had *her* luck, I could buy that whole building and we could all move in."

Jodi settled back against her seat, finally glancing over at me. "You don't need luck, Gabby. Remember when you came to Yada Yada a couple of Sundays ago? That was some powerful prayer we had for you—you said so yourself."

I shrugged. "Yeah, I thought so too. I've really been trying to trust God, trying to pray—and for a while, I thought God was answering my prayers. Especially when Lee Boyer said he'd found an apartment for me. But now . . . I don't know. Seems like everything's back at square one."

"Must be that God's got a better plan."

I stared at her. "*What* better plan?!"

Jodi shrugged, keeping her eyes on the road. "Don't ask me. But that's what Avis Douglass always says when one of us Yada Yadas is fussing and fuming about something not working out like we wanted it to. And believe me, Gabby, it's happened often enough—when I get enough courage to pry my fingers off my plans and ideas long enough to ask God to take over, that is—that I'm beginning to think she's right."

Lucy woke up when we pulled into a gas station outside Minneapolis about eleven. "I know, I know," she muttered, climbing stiffly out of the van. "Rule Number One. But ya fergot the rule 'afore that 'un—take care of your animals first. That's what my daddy useta say, back when we had us a farm." And she marched off to a tiny strip of grass beside the gas station with Dandy in tow, her gray hair standing up like she'd stuck her finger in a socket.

I blew a limp curl out of my eyes in the climbing heat, trying not to watch as the little numbers whirled upward on the gas pump. Like Jodi said, at least it was cheaper than shipping my mom's casket, and a *lot* cheaper than buying a cemetery plot in Chicago. *Guess I should be thanking You about that,* I prayed silently as I hung up the gas hose and screwed the gas cap back on. *But, Jesus, if You've got a better plan for what happens next, I'd sure like to know what it is.*

Lucy and Jodi were coming out of the restroom as I came in. I took one look in the mirror over the sink and grimaced. My curly hair hung limp, the color dull, my face bare of makeup. *Ouch. Should've gotten up fifteen minutes earlier for a shower.*

I splashed my face and freshened up as best I could, and when I got back to the van, Jodi and Lucy had the back doors of the van open. "Them flowers is wiltin'," Lucy announced as she hauled herself awkwardly into the van and inspected the casket in the back. "Here." She handed two flower arrangements out to Jodi and me. "Go find some water."

Jodi stifled a grin. "Bossy, isn't she?" she murmured as we found a water hose and wet the green floral foam and containers holding the flower sprays.

Behind us, Dandy suddenly starting barking furiously. I whirled and saw a couple of lanky teenage boys pointing and laughing at the open doors of the van. Before Jodi and I could get the flower arrangements back to the van, a larger crowd had gathered—a mother and half a dozen kids from a minivan gassing up at the next pump, a couple of hefty, bearded guys who'd driven up in a dirty pickup, and one of the gas station attendants who came out to see what the ruckus was about.

I sucked in my breath. "Uh-oh . . . look at Dandy."

My mother's yellow dog was standing on top of the metal-blue casket, facing the open doors, barking and showing his teeth. Lucy stood at the back of the van, arms crossed, eyes narrowed as if daring anybody to get within punching range.

"You got a real dead body in there?" one of the teenagers snickered.

"Whatcha do, steal it from a graveyard?" The two boys thought that was real funny, slapping each other on the back. Even the pickup truck guys chuckled.

Sudden rage burned behind my eyes. *How dare they!* "Okay, show's over, you meatheads!" I yelled as Jodi and I pushed past Lucy and set our armload of flowers into the van. "Lucy!" I hissed in her ear. "Close the doors and get in the van. Now!"

I'd never seen Lucy move so fast. Slamming the back doors, the old lady hustled to the side of the van, climbed in, and slammed that door shut too. I got in the driver's seat, turned the ignition, and started the van while Jodi was still pulling her door shut. "Gabby!" she screeched. I slowed for a nanosecond, but

Dandy was still on top of the casket, barking and snapping at the windows as we lurched past the finger-pointing gawkers.

A glance in the rearview mirror as I took the on ramp for Route 94 heading west caught Lucy climbing over suitcases, boxes, and bags to get to the back doors. She punched the lock; then I heard her coaxing Dandy down from the casket. "Come 'ere, Dandy, it's okay . . . They was just jerks . . . Good dog . . . Miz Martha would be proud of you." Another glance in the rearview, and I realized Lucy and Dandy must be sitting on the floor with the casket and the luggage, because I could no longer see them.

It took me a good half hour to calm down, and Jodi had to point out that I was riding the accelerator ten miles over the speed limit. She finally coaxed Lucy back into the second-row seat and made her put on her seat belt, passed out the sandwiches her mother had packed, all the while cheerfully pointing out the picturesque farms, lush fields, and little lakes tucked into the rolling hills as we sailed down the highway.

I finally grinned at her. "You'd make a good Jewish mother, Jodi."

She laughed. "Well, I've got a good role model. Remember Ruth in my prayer group—the one who had twins at fifty? . . ." Pretty soon she had me laughing about the escapades of the two-year-old Garfield twins, running circles around their midlife-plus parents. Then she dug out some music CDs and filled the van with some good gospel, singing along and clapping and waving at other drivers who looked at us funny.

"If there's one thing I've been learning, Gabby," Jodi said, grinning at me, "it's that praise is *not* Satan's working conditions.

When the enemy throws something at you like what happened back there?—it's *praise* that changes the battle lines."

I wanted to hug her, but I kept my hands on the wheel. How long had it been since I'd had a friend who'd talk to me like that?

We traded drivers at Sauk Center, Minnesota, and again at Fargo as we crossed into North Dakota about midafternoon. We tanked up on Cokes to keep us awake, but my butt was beginning to hurt from the long hours driving. And we still had 250 miles to go!

"Hey!" Lucy called out. "What happened to all the trees and green stuff?"

It was true. The topography had drastically changed to grazing land and sagebrush country, with the occasional wheat field stretching clear to the horizon. I grinned in the rearview. "This is where I grew up, Lucy."

I saw her roll her eyes. "Humph. Look like this place never pulled through the Dust Bowl."

Jodi had just taken over the driving again when my cell phone rang. I scrambled to find my purse and snatched out the phone. "Probably one of the boys . . . Hello? Hello? . . . Oh! Hi, Lee . . ." I felt my face flush, and I turned toward the window.

Several minutes later I flipped the phone closed and dropped it back into my purse. "Uh, just my lawyer."

"Uh-huh. Does your face always get red when you talk to your lawyer?"

"He's sweet on her!" Lucy hollered from the backseat.

"Oh, stop it, Lucy. We're just friends. He's concerned, that's all." I assumed a nonchalant slouch as Jodi drove straight toward the sun slipping down the western sky, grateful for the wrap-around sunglasses hiding the telltale confusion in my eyes.

Familiar fast-food icons were harder to find once we left the main highway and headed north on a two-lane toward Minot, but we finally spied a Hiway Drive-In just as we turned onto Route 52. We ordered hamburgers, fries, and milk shakes to go—and to my surprise, Lucy shoved some crumpled dollar bills into my hand to pay for hers.

Once we'd finished eating, we all fell silent, opening the windows and enjoying the cooling air as the sun slipped toward the horizon. I couldn't help thinking about the last time I'd driven this road with Paul and P. J., going to visit my mom a mere month and a half ago. So much had happened since then . . .

I called Aunt Mercy when we were about an hour out and asked if she'd heard from Celeste and Honor. "They should be at the house by the time you get here," she said. "I'll meet you there too."

The setting sun had streaked the western sky with golden, orange, and brilliant red clouds when I finally pulled Moby Van into the parking lot of Minot's family-owned funeral home. Jodi and Lucy waited in the van while I went inside, signed the necessary papers to transfer my mother's casket, and walked out with the director and a couple of his staff pushing a rolling cart. Dandy whined as my mother's casket was loaded onto the cart and wheeled inside, but Lucy kept a tight hold on his collar.

The funeral director handed me a folder with my copies of all the papers. "I believe your aunt, Mercy Shepherd, suggested a family viewing tomorrow afternoon at four, and then a service in our chapel on Sunday at two, with the burial immediately following. Does that sound right to you, Mrs. Fairbanks?"

I nodded, shook his hand, and climbed back into the van, not really thinking about what he'd said. I was thinking about meeting my sisters after two years, showing up in my mother's driveway with a monster van that said "Manna House Shelter for Women" along the side, our mother's dog with still-visible scars on his shoulder, and two strangers, one of whom was a crusty old bag lady in a rumpled flower skirt and ankle socks.

chapter 42

I pulled Moby Van into the driveway of my mother's house, right behind a silver Chevy compact with a rental car sticker. *Home.* The yard had been mowed—Aunt Mercy must have hired a neighborhood kid—but my mother's beloved flower garden across the front was thick with weeds.

No, no, can't let the weeds take over! Heading straight for the flower bed, I started yanking weeds right and left.

Dandy tumbled out of the driver's side door I'd left open and ran all around the yard, sniffing and whining. "He knows he's home," Jodi murmured, climbing rather stiffly out of the front seat and sliding the side door open so Lucy could get out.

The front door opened. "You made it!" Aunt Mercy beamed. Her silver-rinsed hair was cut in its usual youthful pixie cut. "Quit pulling those weeds, Gabby Fairbanks, and come give me a hug . . . Oh, oh, Dandy, yes, yes, you can come in too . . ." She turned and called into the house. "Celeste! Honor! Gabby is here!"

My oldest sister appeared two seconds later, suntanned and

freckled, wavy brunette hair caught at the back of her neck with a wooden barrette, wearing a black tank top and khaki cargo pants cropped at the knee. She gave me a quick hug. "Hey there, Gabby. Talk about timing. We just got here thirty minutes ago . . . Oh! Who's this?" Celeste's hazel eyes looked over my shoulder, and I realized Jodi and Lucy were still standing on the front walk.

Uh-oh. Didn't I tell my sisters I wasn't driving alone? "Come on up here, you guys. Celeste, this is Jodi Baxter, my friend who graciously offered to help me drive the van from Chicago . . . and, uh, Lucy Tucker, a friend of Mom's who's been taking care of Dandy—kind of a long story. Jodi and Lucy, this is my dad's baby sister, Aunt Mercy, and my sister Celeste . . . Say, where's Honor?"

Celeste nodded a mute greeting to my guests and jerked a thumb inward. "Living room. Kinda broken up."

Aunt Mercy, bless her, rose to the occasion. "Well, come in, come in, girls. We've got the air on; it's cooler inside. Did you all eat? Because I've got a pasta salad in the refrigerator and garlic bread in the oven. Would you all like some iced tea?"

"Oh, good," I heard Lucy mumble, as we trailed my aunt inside. "Been a couple hours since I et."

I let Aunt Mercy herd Jodi and Lucy into the kitchen at the back of the house, while I detoured into the living room. My sister Honor was curled up on the couch, her face a blotchy red, a pile of tissues in her lap. Her screaming blonde hair, complete with green and red streaks, was even longer than the last time I'd seen her. She'd added skinny braids hanging down in front of her ears with tiny feathers and beads tied at the ends. A graceful blue dolphin tattoo dove from the top of her shoulder halfway down her bare upper arm. Probably had some mystical meaning. I wanted to shake my head. She looked like a cross between an aging hippie and a runaway kid on Rush Street in Chicago.

"Oh, Gabby," Honor wailed, throwing both arms around my neck as I bent down. "Can you bear it, coming home, and Mama not being here?"

I endured Honor's awkward hug for half a minute, then untangled myself. I could hear Dandy's nails clicking on the wood floors, going from room to room, whining, then scrambling upstairs to the second floor. At that moment, I felt worse for Dandy's loss than I did for me and my sisters.

"We've got company," Celeste informed Honor, raising an eyebrow at me reproachfully.

Honor's red-rimmed eyes flew open. "Who?"

I tipped my chin up defensively. "I couldn't drive Mom's casket all the way from Chicago by myself."

Celeste flopped in an easy chair, frowning. "But who's the old lady? I mean, she looks like something you found on the street."

I almost laughed. *Bingo*. "It's a long story. But please, be kind—"

We heard the dog scrambling back down the stairs, and then he appeared in the living room, staring up at me, brow wrinkled, whimpering. "Oh!" Honor gasped. "What happened to Dandy? Where'd those long scars come from?"

I sighed, settled down on the carpet with my back against Celeste's easy chair, and pulled Dandy down beside me. "Like I said, it's a really long story."

We talked until midnight, my sisters and I—me doing most of the talking as I tried to tell my far-flung siblings what had happened since I'd realized Mom couldn't stay alone any longer and had taken her back to Chicago with me for an indefinite visit.

Aunt Mercy graciously entertained Jodi and Lucy while we talked, put Lucy in the small "summer bedroom" off the back porch, made up the pull-out couch in my dad's study upstairs for Jodi, leaving the two bedrooms we girls had shared growing up for Celeste, Honor, and me. "I'll be back in the morning," she'd whispered, poking her head into the living room to explain the sleeping arrangements. I heard Lucy calling Dandy, and the dog disappeared. I wondered if he'd sleep in my mom's bedroom, as he'd always done before, or with Lucy.

I bet on Lucy tonight.

"Wish you had let us know what was going on." Celeste's scowl was in danger of becoming a permanent fixture. "It's bad enough that Philip threw you out, but *Mom* . . . !" She cocked an imaginary rifle and "aimed" it at a picture on the wall. "I think I want to kill him."

I gaped at her. "Let you know?! Not like I didn't try. Neither of you guys is very good at returning phone calls. Or living within reach of a cell phone signal."

"Mom was really staying in a homeless shelter?" Honor said it like she'd just driven out of the fog. "That's . . . that's *awful*. You should have sent her to live with me, or . . . or something."

I grabbed a throw pillow and smacked my California-dreaming sister with it. "Hey! I tried to get both of you out here in June for a family reunion. If you'd made half an effort, we could have made a decision about Mom together. But that didn't work out, did it? So quit blaming me. I did what I had to do." I folded my arms tight across my chest. Both my sisters stared at me. The wall clock ticked in the silence that followed. Finally I let my arms fall to my lap, along with the tears I'd been pushing down all evening. "Didn't know my whole life was going to unravel."

Our emotions spent, we finally flicked off lights and crept upstairs to our bedrooms—Celeste to her old room with the double bed that she'd earned as the "eldest" child, Honor and me to our old bedroom with the single beds and matching faded bedspreads. It had been a really, really long day . . . but somehow all the frayed and frazzled ends of my life felt tucked in for the moment, like the loose ends of yarn my mother used to tuck into her knitting.

Aunt Mercy showed up at ten the next morning with a manila folder tucked under her arm. "Hope you girls got a chance to sleep in." She poured herself a cup of coffee, pulled out a chair at the kitchen table where Honor, Celeste, and I sat in the rumpled T-shirts and shorts we'd slept in, and pushed the folder toward us. "Your parents' will. Your dad left a copy with me, and I suppose the lawyer has the original. I made an appointment for you girls at his office on Monday at ten." She looked from one to the other of us. "Hope no one has to leave before then."

Honor groaned. "My plane leaves from Billings late Tuesday afternoon, and it took us eight hours to drive from the airport—right, Celeste?"

Celeste nodded and picked up the manila envelope. "Yeah, but we can leave early Tuesday. Monday's fine."

"Oh, brother," I muttered, rolling my eyes. "It's going to take longer than that to deal with"—I waved my hand in a big circle that took in the whole house—"all this stuff."

"It's only Saturday, Gabby. That's practically three days." Celeste frowned. "Where are your city buddies? They could help, you know."

"They *are* helping! Who do you think made the coffee before we came down? And they've taken Dandy . . . somewhere. Probably to stay out of our way."

"Girls." Aunt Mercy eyed us. "You should look at the will. You will have some decisions to make."

Celeste slid the will out of the folder. "Okay, they named me executor when Mom died—but I understand you've got power of attorney, Gabby?" She frowned at me. "How does that work?"

"Don't worry, Celeste. That was just because of Mom's dementia." I sighed. "Just read the will. The lawyer can figure it out."

The will held no surprises. Divide everything equally three ways after paying any outstanding bills and funeral expenses. That sounded hopeful. Maybe my account could get reimbursed for the trip after all. I could sure use that.

Celeste stuffed the simple form back in the envelope. "Mom had . . . what? An annuity she was living on? Maybe some savings . . ." Her eyes roved around the house. "The big thing will be selling the house. Can't do *that* in a day."

Honor stuck out her lip. "Wish I could buy it. Seems like it oughta stay in the family."

Celeste and I both stared at her. "You buy it? Would you really move back to Minot?"

Honor shrugged. "Maybe. River and Ryan . . . I dunno. They've been hanging with a pretty fast crowd—River especially. He'll be a junior next year, Ryan a sophomore. Maybe they could finish high school here. But . . ." She shrugged again.

It was hard to imagine my tattooed middle sister, with her green-and-red-streaked hair and feather-and-beads, skinny braids, fitting back into small-town life in North Dakota. But it was a moot point. She couldn't afford the house anyway. Me either. And Celeste wasn't about to trade her log cabin outpost and park ranger husband in Denali National Forest for an old, two-story frame house in sagebrush country.

We spent the rest of the day making an inventory of furniture and household stuff. It felt weird, trying to decide what to leave with the house—we could sell it furnished—and what to divide between us. As long as Mom and Dad were alive, it had been sweet to come home to this house full of childhood memories. But, no, I didn't want to move back to Minot. I'd been gone too long. Besides, we *had* to sell it. Closest thing to an inheritance we three girls had.

I felt a tad guilty wishing we could sell it tomorrow. But, I told Jodi later, as she helped me count the china, glassware, and ironed tablecloths in the dining room hutch, I could sure use my third to help me rent that apartment in Wrigleyville and get back on my feet. My ticket to getting an actual address to prop up my custody petition.

Lucy shut herself into the downstairs bathroom and scrubbed it until floor, sink, tub, and wall tiles sparkled, then repeated the process in the second-floor bathroom—which seemed odd to me, since the Lucy I first met had been living under a bush, and housekeeping wasn't exactly a necessity. But it knocked the chips off my sisters' shoulders, and they started warming up to Lucy in little ways—a smile, a nod, an invitation to "come sit down, we're making some lemonade . . . want some?"

Four o'clock rolled around much too soon, when we were

supposed to go to the funeral home for the family viewing. "You go on," Jodi said, when Aunt Mercy invited her and Lucy to go along. "This is your time." I wished I could stay home too. I'd been through this once before at the funeral at Manna House. The memory was bittersweet, sad but satisfying, too, and I didn't really want to go through it again. But this was the first time for Celeste and Honor, so I climbed into Aunt Mercy's car.

The viewing room at the funeral home felt like a different planet from the multipurpose room at Manna House. Piped-in organ music instead of SouledOut's electronic keyboard. The funeral home staff talking in discreet, low tones instead of Precious loudly scolding the girls wearing low-cut tops and tight skirts. Tomorrow at the funeral, church folks and former patrons of Dad's carpet store would come to pay their respects, their faces pale or sunburned instead of the black, brown, and tan skin tones that populated Manna House. And we'd all speak North Dakota's flat, Midwestern English, instead of the street slang peppering most conversations at the shelter, with bits of Spanish, Italian, Asian, and Jamaican patois thrown in.

Still, standing with Aunt Mercy and my sisters beside the open casket, looking at the still, peaceful form that was our mother, we melded, sharing tissues and hugs. The tears came, fresh and cleansing. I was glad I came for this sacred moment . . . just us. Celeste and Honor and I had been apart too long—not just in distance and lifestyles, but letting our everyday lives and thoughts and care for one another drift further and further apart, like flotsam at sea.

I wanted my sisters back. I needed all the family I could get. I didn't know how to tell them, but I reached out my arms and slid one around each sister's waist as I made a silent vow. *Mom, I'm going to do whatever I can to keep our family together, I promise—*

"What is *that?*" Honor suddenly spluttered, pulling away from my embrace. She reached into the casket under the folds of my mother's pastel flower-print Sunday dress and pulled out a wadded-up purple knit hat with a crocheted flower bobbing on the brim.

Lucy's hat.

Her final gift to her friend.

I collapsed in a chair and laughed. And then I cried. And then I made my sisters put the hat back in the casket again, tucked beneath the folds of Mom's dress.

chapter 43

We picked up some Chinese takeout on the way back to the house, only to find out that Jodi had found a package of frozen chicken in Mom's basement freezer and had a pan of honey-baked chicken in the oven. "Told you you'd make a good Jewish mother," I teased, giving her a hug. I pulled her aside and told her about the purple knit hat, making her promise not to tell Lucy we'd discovered it.

All of us were too beat to do any more sorting or packing up of Mom's things, and we actually ended up playing a ruthless game of Monopoly all evening—well, we three sisters and Jodi, that is. Lucy and Dandy disappeared outside for their evening walk, and Aunt Mercy announced that her Monopoly days were long gone, and she'd see us tomorrow for church.

I looked at my sisters. They looked at me. I cleared my throat. "I think we'll take a pass, Aunt Mercy. The funeral and burial are tomorrow afternoon. I think we need the morning to keep sorting Mom's stuff. We don't have that much time."

Which turned out to be true. The next morning Jodi packed most of Mom's clothes in large plastic bags to take to Goodwill— none of us sisters could bear to do it—though she asked permission to let Lucy pick out some things as a keepsake. I knew Mom's dresses, skirts, and slacks would never fit Lucy's ample behind, but the old lady almost reverently picked out some silky head scarves and took all of Mom's socks.

The day seemed to pass in a blur. At one point, Lucy asked where she could find a shovel, and I sent her to the garage, too distracted to wonder what she wanted a shovel for. Outside, the sky was clear and the heat index hovered somewhere up in the nineties. "Thought it was s'posed ta be cold up here in the North," Lucy grumbled as the five of us climbed into Moby Van to meet Aunt Mercy for the two o'clock funeral. None of us answered, willing the AC in the van to hurry up before we all sweated our good clothes. Jodi had ironed Lucy's flower print skirt that she'd worn to Mom's funeral at Manna House and even tried to style her choppy hair a little, but to little avail. The old lady had been wearing the purple knit hat for so long, I hadn't realized what a squirrel's nest had grown underneath.

I could only imagine what the good folks of Minot were thinking when Lucy plonked herself down in a front-row seat at the funeral home.

Aunt Mercy had printed a nice program with a picture of Mom on the front and the obituary I'd written on the inside. Several new flower arrangements from my parents' church and some of Dad's old employees flanked the casket, open once again for a half hour before the service, then closed for the last time.

But the funeral service had almost no meaning for me. It lacked the life and celebration of the service we had at Manna

House, though people were kind, said how good it was to see the three Shepherd girls home again, what wonderful people Noble and Martha Shepherd were, the town was going to miss them . . .

The burial, however, was a different story. The white-haired pastor of the little stone church my parents had attended in recent years read the Twenty-third Psalm as we three girls and Aunt Mercy sat in folding chairs by the open graveside, which had been dug right beside my father's grave. A final prayer, and then several people pulled flowers out of the arrangements standing nearby, placed them on top of the casket poised over the open grave, and turned to go.

"Wait a minnit!"

I winced at Lucy's gravelly voice behind me. Heads turned. The old lady pushed her way through the small crowd until she stood right beside the grave. She was carrying the shovel, which she must have put in the van. "We ain't done yet! Look at that— they even got the pile o' dirt all covered up with that fake grassy stuff . . . whatchu call it? That sure ain't how it's done back where I come from."

Celeste started to rise up out of her seat, but I put out an arm to stop her. "It's all right," I said, loud enough for the others to hear. "This is Lucy, my mother's friend from Chicago." I got up and stood beside her. "Do you want to say something, Lucy?"

"Yeah. I ain't got any fancy words, but ever since we brought Miz Martha back home here, it's been eatin' at me. I met this lady here"—she patted the casket—"at a homeless shelter back in Chicago, where we was both stayin' . . ."

Celeste and Honor squirmed, and glances passed between folks in the crowd.

". . . an' then I come here and see that Miz Martha has a real nice house, just like a picture in a magazine. Not big an' fancy, but comfortable, nice place ta raise a family, nice place ta grow old in. *Lot* better than a homeless shelter, even if Manna House is one o' the better ones 'round Chicago."

Jodi slipped up and stood on the other side of Lucy, as if owning what Lucy was trying to say. A smile passed between us.

"An' yet she came to Chicago and stayed in a shelter, and ever'body called her Gramma Shep . . ." That got a chuckle from a few folks in the crowd. "An' she loved on the little 'uns 'at didn't have no home, an' read 'em stories, an' let Hannah paint her nails, an' let me take care o' her dog, when I ain't never had no dog of my own . . ."

Now tears were spilling down Lucy's cheeks. I saw a few other tears on the faces around the grave, too, before my own eyes blurred up.

"Just gotta say . . . kinda reminds me of all that Jesus talk I hear at the shelter, 'bout how He left heaven and came down to earth to live with all us riffraff." She sniffed and wiped her wet face with a big handkerchief she pulled out of somewhere. "That's all I wanna say. 'Cept"—she waved the shovel—"I don't plan on walkin' off till I see this good woman to her final restin' place. Now, you there . . ." She pointed at the funeral home staff. "Get that fake grass stuff off that pile of dirt, put the casket in the ground, and let's finish this up right."

Later that night I sat on the foldout couch with Jodi, and we laughed and cried, remembering the stunned looks on my sisters' faces as Lucy shoveled dirt on top of my mom's casket and then handed the shovel to me. But in the end Celeste and Honor had shoveled, too, and not a soul left without taking a turn shoveling that good, brown earth on top of the metal-blue casket. Someone even started to sing a hymn, as if decorum was being buried, and we'd all relaxed, witnesses to the natural cycle of life.

"And I'll bet your mom was looking down from heaven, enjoying the whole thing," Jodi murmured, pulling her knees up under Denny's extra-large Bulls T-shirt she usually slept in.

I giggled. "Yeah. Who ever thought we'd hear Lucy, of all people, preaching about the Incarnation!" Which set both of us off once more, laughing and crying.

But in fact, Lucy's little homily stayed with me all that night and into the next day, making me realize something I'd never really thought about before . . . just how much Jesus really *did* know about how I felt, because it all happened to Him—being rejected, scoffed at, homeless, no money, unappreciated . . .

For some reason I just wanted to sing and praise God the next morning, so while Jodi was making us all some breakfast, I got her gospel CDs out of the van and riffled through them. To my delight, I discovered she had the same CD her son, Josh, had given to me, the one with "my" song on it. I dusted off my mom's CD player—had she ever used the thing?—and turned up the volume.

Where do I go . . . when there's no one else to turn to?

Who do I talk to . . . when nobody wants to listen? . . .

I stood in the middle of Mom's living room, letting the words flow over me. *Yeah, that's why I can talk to God, because Jesus understands what I'm going through—*

"Hey!" Lucy poked her head into the living room. "Howza

body s'posed ta sleep when you makin' such a racket? 'Sides, Miz Jodi says it's time ta eat."

My sisters and I barely had time to eat Jodi's breakfast, get dressed, and pile into their rental car for our appointment with Mom's lawyer. Aunt Mercy, who'd taken the day off from work, threw up her hands in relief when we walked in at two minutes past ten. "This man charges by the *minute*," she hissed at us. "Get in there."

We made Aunt Mercy come in too—she was family, after all—and we all sat across the table from the lean man with hawk-like eyes. He peered at us over a pair of reading glasses perched on his nose, as if uncertain we were all related. "I'm Frank Putnam, senior partner of Putnam, Fields, and Pederson. Which one of you is Celeste? . . . Ah, all right. You've been named executor of the estate, as you probably know."

In a rather perfunctory manner, Mr. Putnam read through the will, which, he said, was fairly routine. "Bottom line, all assets should be divided equally between you three siblings, *after* paying any remaining costs surrounding Mrs. Shepherd's last illness, outstanding bills, and funeral expenses. Which are . . . ?"

Aunt Mercy handed over statements from Mom's bank and a handful of bills that had come in the mail since Mom had been in Chicago. I had brought the death certificate and receipts from the funeral home in Chicago. "I don't have the doctor and hospital bills yet from the past two weeks."

"All right . . ." The lawyer paged through a number of papers. "Your mother had Social Security and an annuity, both of which, of course, are cancelled at her death. But according to her bank statements, her checking and savings account amount to . . ." He punched numbers on his calculator. ". . . a few thousand dollars, which I recommend you leave in her account to cover any out-standing bills. As for the rest of her assets, there is, of course, the house—"

"How much do you think it's worth?" Celeste interrupted.

"Well, good news there. Your mother paid off the rest of the mortgage with your father's life insurance policy when he passed, which means you'll realize the full value of the house when it sells—minus any taxes and insurance due, of course. However, the real—"

"How much?" Honor's skinny, multicolored braids fell over her shoulders as she leaned forward. "Like, how much do houses sell for around here?"

Putnam shrugged. "I haven't seen your mother's home, but—"

"Your mother had it assessed not long ago," Aunt Mercy broke in. "Similar houses in this area are going for anywhere from one-twenty-five to a hundred seventy-five thousand."

The three of us sisters looked at one another with probably the same thought. We might realize a hundred fifty thousand from the house—fifty thousand each. My heart started to trip double-time. *That* would be a nice nest egg to enable me to start over again. Even rent that nice apartment in the Wrigleyville area. Except . . . how long would it take the house to sell? My heart started to sink again. Probably not soon enough to rent that apartment—or *any* apartment—before school started for my sons.

I was so engrossed in my thoughts, I didn't catch what the lawyer was saying until Honor gasped, *"What?!"*

The lawyer did all but roll his eyes. "I *said*, after paying off the house, your mother used the rest of the money from your father's life insurance policy to buy a simple term life insurance policy—which, I told her at the time, wasn't the wisest thing. A cash value policy would have also given her cash to invest or use to enjoy her retirement, go on a cruise, visit the grandchildren whenever she wanted, but"—he shrugged—"she insisted. Small premiums for her, its only value a benefit to her survivors."

Mr. Putnam handed a fat business envelope to Celeste. "Here it is—a term life insurance policy worth six hundred thousand dollars, to be divided equally between the three of you. With the death certificate, you should be able to cash it in fairly quickly. If you want, I can handle that for you and mail you each a check."

Our mouths hung open. Six hundred thousand dollars? Six. Hundred. Thousand. Dollars. Divided three ways? I couldn't breathe. That was two hundred thousand each . . .

No one spoke . . . until Honor screeched. "I—I could buy the house! With my share! And—and still have fifty grand left over!"

"Plus your third of the house sale," the lawyer said. "If that's what you want to do."

Celeste turned to her. "Do you want to? I mean really, Honor?"

"Yes! . . . I think." Her forehead scrunched. She chewed on one of her skinny decorative braids. "Or maybe not. I mean, it's cold here in the winter. River and Ryan would probably refuse to leave California . . . oh, I don't know!"

Mr. Putnam cleared his throat. "Uh, ladies. I have some papers here I need you to sign. You no doubt have some decisions to make, but I think we're done here. If you have any further questions, feel free to call my office. And, Ms. Shepherd"—he gave a short nod at Honor—"Putnam, Fields, and Pederson would be happy to handle the real estate transaction, if that's your decision." He stood up and shook hands all around.

I walked out the office door with my stupefied sisters, my mouth dry. I could hardly think what this meant. Except I kept hearing Jodi Baxter's off-the-cuff remark as we were driving here in the van: *"God must have a better plan . . ."*

I wanted to scream. Dance a jig and shout hallelujah! With two hundred fifty grand, I could afford an apartment! Get a real address! Bring my boys home! Maybe afford private school for them if I needed to!

Except . . . my heart twisted at the same time. *God, did my mother have to die for me to get back on my feet? Wish there'd been some other way.*

chapter 44

✸ ✸ ✸

Aunt Mercy had said little during our visit to the lawyer's office, but when we got out to the parking lot, she asked me to ride with her to the house. "Gabby, I want to tell you something, but I don't want Honor to know . . . yet, anyway. Let her make her decision about whether to buy the house. If she wants to buy it, fine, don't say anything about this. But . . ." She glanced at me as we followed my sister's compact Chevy rental back to the house. "Noble and I grew up in that house. It has sweet memories for me too. If Honor decides not to buy it, I'd like to. I'm only sixty-two; I've got a few years before I have to pack it in." She grinned and turned her eyes back to the street.

"Oh, Aunt Mercy," I breathed. "Could you do that?"

She nodded. "What else am I going to do with my money, an old maid like me! I've been doing the research. A hundred-fifty thousand would be a fair price. Actually, I was going to say something to you girls, once your mom's name came up on the list for assisted living. But now . . ." She reached out and patted my knee.

"I'm so sorry you've lost your mom, Gabby. Sorry for everything that's happened to you the past few months. Please, I . . . I hope you'll let me be mama to you, whenever you need me. You and your sisters. You're all the family I've got."

Both of us were blubbering by the time we got back to the house. I grabbed her arm before she got out of the car. "Aunt Mercy, I think you ought to tell Celeste and Honor that you'd be willing to buy the house if Honor chooses not to. Frankly, I don't think Honor really wants to move back to Minot. I just think she's grasping at something to hold on to, now that Mom is gone. But if we had a home to come home to sometimes, a place to be together . . ."

Which turned out to be exactly the case. We sat around the kitchen table, eating a chicken Caesar salad we'd picked up at Marketplace Foods and downing copious amounts of iced tea as we sorted out "what's next." Honor was giddy with relief that the house could stay in the family, but that she didn't have to actually *buy* it and move back here. "Maybe in twenty years I'll be sick of California—or California will be sick of me—and I could buy it then," she giggled . . . and then realized what she'd said. "Oh! Aunt Mercy, I didn't mean I want you to *die* or anything in twenty years. But if you want to move into a retirement home or something . . ." She actually turned red under that California tan of hers.

Aunt Mercy laughed. "Hey, missy, you'll be *my* age in twenty years . . ." She put her silver pixie-cut alongside Honor's long tresses. "What do you think, girls? Can you imagine Honor at sixty-two?"

Celeste and I cracked up. "Yeah, sure," I gasped. "Spitting image—except she'll be sixty-two with that permanent dolphin tattoo."

"Yeah, yeah. You laugh. But believe me, there are already a lot of sixty-somethings in California walking around with tattoos. But hey—what about Mom's Galaxy? I could use a car. Could drive it back now."

As a matter of fact, I'd been thinking the same thing. I needed a car now, didn't I?

Celeste frowned. "What about your plane ticket? We got round-trip."

"Goose. So I lose a few hundred. That's cheap for a car. Or . . . should I pay you guys for it or something?"

We all decided Honor should take the car. I had the van to drive back anyway. Aunt Mercy said she'd see Putnam about the title change.

A load seemed to have lifted off the pressure to get everything done that Monday afternoon. With Aunt Mercy buying the house, we decided to leave most of the furniture, since Aunt Mercy's condo was a lot smaller and wouldn't fill this house. "But if any of you girls want something down the road, and have a way to get it, just tell me," Aunt Mercy said.

Celeste reached out a hand and gently untangled a few of my unruly curls. "What about you, Gabby? Aren't you going to need something to put in that apartment when you get it? Might as well take some of the family stuff now since you got that empty monster van out there in the driveway. *We* don't really need anything"—she nailed Honor with a look—"do we, Honor?"

"Ah . . . nope." Honor shook her head. "Couldn't take it on the plane anyway. I'd like some of Mom's jewelry, though. That old-fashioned stuff is funky right now."

I looked at my sisters—these virtual strangers Mom's death had catapulted back into my life. My oldest sister's gentle touch as she untangled my rebellious curls had conveyed more affection than I'd experienced from her in a long time. And their encouragement to take what I needed from our family home to fill an empty apartment somehow seemed so much more than that—a step toward filling my empty life with a promise to care for one another once again . . .

I started to weep. And suddenly Celeste and Honor and I were in each other's arms. Grief and loss, love and hope all mixed up in our tears.

A last round of hugs with promises to call at least once a week—Honor still didn't have e-mail—and my sisters set out early Tuesday morning, driving in caravan to Billings, Montana, where Celeste would catch her plane for Anchorage, and Honor would just keep going, driving the Galaxy to Los Angeles. It had cooled off during the night but promised to be another sky-blue scorcher.

All six of us had spent the previous afternoon loading Moby Van with my old single bed, which we'd taken apart, and several boxes of dishes, silverware, pots and pans, blankets, sheets, and towels—most of which had seen better days, but hey, at this point in my life, something was better than nothing. We even squeezed in Mom's favorite wingback upholstered rocker and the Oriental rug from the dining room. "You need *something* to sit on in your new apartment," Aunt Mercy had insisted.

Celeste had had the brilliant idea of making Aunt Mercy the power of attorney for Mom's estate, even though she—Celeste—was still technically the executor, so we stopped packing long enough to drive back over to Mr. Putnam's law office to fill out the necessary forms, sign our names, and get them notarized. The man's secretary got a bit flustered when we piled into the law office with no appointment, but given the circumstances, Mr. Putnam agreed to stay an extra hour to squeeze us in.

"Huh. Probably charged us extra too," Honor grumbled on our way out.

Aunt Mercy had come over early Tuesday morning to say good-bye to all of us before going to work at the library. "I'll move this real estate transaction along as quickly as possible, Gabby," she whispered in my ear just before I climbed into the driver's seat. "I know you need the money to get on your feet and get your boys back. Now go before my mascara runs and I look like a raccoon when I show up for work." I felt a pang as I backed Moby Van out of the driveway and waved wildly to my aunt out the window, yelling good-bye, which got Dandy all excited, barking until the house and Aunt Mercy disappeared from sight.

With the van loaded to the gills, we left Minot behind and headed down the two-lane highway, intent on taking I-94 all the way back to Chicago. Jodi and I decided we'd split the cost of a motel room somewhere around Minneapolis—if we could find one that allowed pets—and get back at a decent time the next day. "You sure?" I asked. "That was an awful short visit with your parents. We could go back through Des Moines, same way we came."

Jodi shook her head. "Uh-uh. Right now I'd rather get home to Denny." She looked at me a little doe-eyed. "This is the longest we've been apart since Denny and the kids drove to New York to see *his* folks a couple of years ago. I had to stay home because I'd been sick all spring, and cases of SARS were cropping up everywhere . . ."

We talked a lot, Jodi and I, on the way back to Chicago. But I steered away from saying anything about the breakdown between Philip and me until I heard Lucy snoring in the backseat after we ate the sack lunch Aunt Mercy had packed for us. Jodi had taken over the driving, her shoulder-length brown hair caught back with an elastic band to keep it off her neck. She was a few years older than I, but somehow managed to look younger. Her face was relaxed, her eyes alive. The look of a woman who knows she's loved.

"I'm jealous, you know."

Jodi glanced at me, startled, then looked back at the highway. "What do you mean?"

"You and Denny. You guys ought to clone your relationship, sell it on eBay. You'd make a ton."

She slipped a small grin. "Yeah, well, we have our moments. Me, I'm a terrible nag. And Denny can be *so* dense."

I shrugged. "Maybe. But it's obvious you guys love each other. Philip and I were that way once. Crazy about each other. Gosh, Jodi, the man's so gorgeous I used to melt like chocolate on a hot day whenever he came in the room. We laughed at his mother's objections to our 'mismatch'—almost like marrying me was his rebellion against their snooty conventions. He was going to be the rising star in the commercial development business, and I . . ." I grabbed my T-shirt and dabbed at my eyes. "I tried, Jodi, I really tried to be the good corporate wife. But somewhere along the way, I lost myself. Lost Philip too . . ."

I leaned against the passenger-side window, watching the Minnesota hills rolling past. "It's like I don't even recognize him anymore . . . couldn't relax and be myself when he was around . . . everything I did was wrong. But"—I felt heat in my chest—"I still can't believe he just kicked me out, kicked my mother out, even kicked the dog out! I mean, who *is* that man?!"

My voice had risen, and I glanced into the backseat to be sure Lucy was still sleeping. "He even started gambling," I muttered darkly. "Practically every weekend! Last time I talked to Henry Fenchel, it sounded like Philip's new love affair with the dice was starting to affect their business partnership."

We rode in silence for a few minutes. Then Jodi glanced at me. "Do you pray for Philip, Gabby?"

I gaped at her. Pray for *Philip*? I'd certainly done a lot of praying *about* Philip. Or ranting at God about Philip. But pray *for* him? "Not really," I said slowly. "I've been too mad."

"Maybe you should. He sounds lost."

We found a motel just across the Minnesota-Wisconsin state line that allowed pets for a ten-dollar fee. Lucy complained about stopping, said she could sleep in the car just as well. "Maybe *you* can," I muttered. "*We* need a bed." The room had two queen beds, and Lucy claimed the one farthest from the door—after double-locking the door and jamming the desk chair under the handle. She didn't bother to undress either. I shrugged at Jodi. *Go figure.*

I was used to sleeping with Lucy's snores back in the bunk room at Manna House, but I don't know if Jodi got very much sleep. At one point, I got up and rolled Lucy over onto her side, and we managed to fall asleep before she moved again.

In the morning we treated ourselves to breakfast at a nearby pancake house before hitting the road again. Couldn't believe how many pancakes Lucy was able to put away. I asked if she'd like to sit up front for a while, but the old lady shook her head. "Nah, me an' Dandy is all settled back here. 'Sides, can't keep up with all that chitchattin' you two doin'. Ain't got no kids to talk about, ain't got no husband, ain't been anywhere, ain't got nuthin' to say."

I laughed and glanced in the rearview, still not used to seeing Lucy without her purple hat. "Okay, just one question, Lucy," I said over my shoulder, "and then we'll leave you out of the chit-chatting. Where did you learn how to clean a bathroom like you did at my mom's house? You even folded the ends of the toilet paper in that cute little hotel style too. I think you've been living a secret life."

"Humph. Ain't got no secret life. Got this job as a hotel maid when I first come to Chicago, but . . ." Her voice drifted off. "Let's jus' say, cleanin' bathrooms wasn't the only thing I learned on that job. All sorts o' people gonna take advantage of ya any way they can, 'specially if they think you ignorant. Decided it was safer out on the streets. Been makin' my own way ever since. Just . . . lonely sometimes." A long pause. "Gonna miss Miz Martha."

Jodi and I looked at each other. That might explain the triple door-locking last night. Still, there was a lot of story left out of that two-bit summary. But at least it was more than she'd ever given up before. "Thanks, Lucy."

"Yeah? Thanks fer what?"

"For being a good friend. I think you were the best friend my mother ever had."

Lucy made a funny noise. "Just . . . shut up an' drive, will ya?"

We laughed and settled down for the final day of our trip. Jodi studied the road atlas. "Gee, it's not that far. We oughta be home in six hours or so."

Home . . . For the first time in weeks, I let myself think about what that meant. I was still pretty broke, but within a few days or weeks, I'd have real money in my bank account. "Can't believe my mom actually left us an inheritance," I murmured. "Paid off the house when my dad died, bought that term life insurance . . ." The reality of it all was beginning to sink in. I might even have enough to buy a house one of these days—but that would have to wait. I had more immediate goals. "Can you believe it, Jodi? I'm going to be able to rent that apartment, get my boys back here in time for school—"

"Buy the whole building if ya want!" Lucy quipped from the backseat.

A big semi thundered past us, making the van shudder. I gripped the steering wheel, wondering if I'd heard right. I looked over at Jodi. She was staring at me. "Gabby! What Lucy just said."

"Buy the—?" Now a shudder did ripple through my insides. I shook my head. "Oh, no, no, I don't think so. I don't have *that* much . . ."

"How much? I mean, how much are they selling it for? You might have enough for a down payment."

"Yeah, buy the building," Lucy growled. "I might even move in. Or visit ya."

I kept shaking my head. "You guys are crazy, you know that?"

Jodi laughed. "Yeah, I know. God is crazy too—look at how He answered our prayer about how to get your mom's body back to North Dakota for burial! But Gabby, think about it! Josh and Edesa told me you wanted Manna House to use the Dandy Fund to buy a building for second-stage housing for mothers with children, but—"

My ears got red. "Yeah, what did I know? We're riding in the Dandy Fund."

Jodi was practically bouncing in her seat. "Gabby! Listen to me! What did Mabel Turner say to you when you applied for the job at Manna House? You told me yourself! *She* believes God brought you to Chicago because He has a purpose for you at Manna House."

My mind was tumbling even as she spoke. *A six-flat . . . not far from Manna House . . . up for sale . . . Precious and Sabrina . . . Tanya and Sammy . . .*

Jodi punched me on the shoulder. "Maybe this is it."

chapter 45

The idea of buying that six-flat was flat-out crazy, probably impossible . . . but it grew on me like a second skin. Dozens of questions tumbled through my thoughts, and I jabbered at Jodi like a set of wind-up chatty teeth all the way back to Chicago. Was a building for second-stage housing a good idea? Mabel had thought so, just not yet. Did I even want to live in Chicago? Well, yeah, because I loved my job—more than that, if Mabel was right, God had called me to it—and it made sense to live close by. Would my boys want to live there? Moot point. *I* was going to live there, even if I just rented the first-floor apartment, and they were going to live with me, because Lee Boyer said I had a slam-dunk custody case. But what about Philip? What if we got back together? There was always that possibility, wasn't there? Buying a building was a really big leap to take by myself. What would he think? Was it a smart thing to do with my money? Good question. Probably should invest it. But what about investing in the lives of women like Precious and Tanya? How would buying a building work with Manna House? I had no idea. Would my inheritance even make a dent in the asking price for the building? Probably not . . .

"Well, *duh!*" Jodi said. "Pull over. Let me drive, and you can call your lawyer friend and ask what they're asking! That'd be a start anyway. Look, there's an exit up there with a Wendy's. Time for lunch anyway."

We made a pit stop for hamburgers and fries, fed and watered Dandy, filled the gas-guzzler on my debit card, stretched our road-weary muscles, and climbed back in the van for the last leg of our trip, with Jodi behind the wheel.

"Step on it," Lucy grumbled. "I'm tired. Me an' Dandy 'bout ready to get out an' walk."

"Just a few more hours, Lucy," I said, twisting in my seat. "Don't blame you. But you and Dandy have been good travelers. I'm glad you came."

"The phone, Gabby," Jodi reminded me as she pulled onto the interstate. "Call the lawyer guy."

"You *are* a nag, you know that?" But I dutifully dug out my cell phone, found Lee's number, and pushed the Call button. "He's going to think I'm nuts . . . Lee? Hi, it's Gabby."

"Gabby!" Lee Boyer's voice crackled in my ear. "I was hoping to hear from you. Where are you? How'd it go driving the casket back to, uh, North Dakota, right?"

"Yeah. Minot. Real good. We're still on the road, almost to the Illinois border, though. But, hey, today's Wednesday, I think I missed my eleven o'clock appointment, so thought I'd check in."

He chuckled in my ear. "Yeah, I bill double for missed appointments."

Jodi was making *hurry-up* signs. I waved her off. "Well, just wanted to let you know it's going to work out for me to rent that apartment after all. You didn't call the guy to cancel my contract or anything, did you?"

"No, no, I said we'd deal with that when you got back. But that's good, real good! What happened?"

"Just . . . well, I got some inheritance money I didn't expect. I'll explain more when I see you. But I have another question." I held my hand up to stop Jodi's impatient gestures. "Do you happen to know the asking price for the whole building?"

There was a brief hesitation at the other end of the phone. "The *building*? I think he's asking six hundred. Why, are you—"

"Six hundred thousand?" I repeated for Jodi's sake. "Really? I thought it'd be even more."

"Are you thinking of buying? That must be some inheritance."

I laughed, feeling a bit giddy. "Not that much. But I might have enough for a down payment. Manna House needs a six-flat for homeless mothers with children, and I thought—"

"Gabby. Gabby! Whoa, slow down. Don't go making any rash decisions! Hey, promise me? One thing at a time. You need to be smart about this."

I felt a prickle of irritation. But what did I expect? It was a wild idea. "Well, don't worry. I don't even have the money yet. What I do have is a van full of furniture and household stuff for my new apartment. Can I get in yet? Is Mr. What's-his-name done with the refurbishing?"

Lee said he'd check it out and let me know when I could get the key. "Glad you're back, Gabby. Glad the apartment is working out for you too. Now we can move on the custody petition ASAP. As for the other . . . well, let's talk."

"Okay. Thanks, Lee." I closed the phone. "He thinks it's crazy."

Jodi grinned. "It *is* crazy. The question is, is it *God's* crazy idea? If it is, it doesn't matter what Mr. Lawyer thinks."

As we came into the city on the expressway, Lee called back on my cell and said I could get the key the next day—Thursday—and move in any time after that. "Well, at least we won't have to unload the van tonight," I told Jodi. "Hope no one needs it before tomorrow night."

"Denny and I'll come down and help you unload," Jodi said as she turned off the expressway and headed for her Rogers Park neighborhood on city streets.

"You don't have to do that, Jodi."

She grinned. "Oh yes I do. I want to see this building you're moving into, want to see just how crazy this idea of yours is, and"—her grin widened—"maybe even pray over the building too. You know, claim it for God." Now she laughed. "That's what the Yada Yada sisters would do, anyway."

I sighed. "I like that. Hope some of their faith rubs off on me."

We dropped Jodi off at her two-flat in Rogers Park, our good-bye hugs wrapped with the realization that our week together on the road had deepened our new friendship for both of us. Lucy even let Jodi give her a hug—not her usual MO. Back in the driver's seat, I drove south on Sheridan Road, under the Red Line El tracks that crossed over just north of Wrigleyville, and pulled up a few blocks later in front of Manna House.

"Home again . . . more or less," I told Lucy, shutting off the motor. I closed my eyes a weary moment, my heart full. *God, thank You for keeping us safe, for . . . for everything You've done the past few—*

"My butt's sore," Lucy grumbled. "Can you unlock these doors or what?"

So much for prayers. We straggled in the front doors of the shelter—even Dandy was limping, stiff from lack of exercise—and got a welcome screech from Angela Kwon in the receptionist cubicle. Mabel came out of her office to see what all the noise was about, and Lucy immediately insisted on trading in the borrowed suitcase for her wire cart. I left her busily rearranging her belongings in the foyer. Dandy and I tried to navigate our way through the multipurpose room but were cornered by a handful of shelter kids who fell on Dandy with hugs and kisses, which Dandy was happy to return.

I snuck off to unpack and clean up before supper, which was brought in that night by a service group from a local Kiwanis Club. The men, mostly middle-aged, looked pretty funny in the white hairnets required of all food workers, but they took the kidding with good humor. All the residents hooted and clapped when Mabel announced that Hero Dog was back. "Oh yes, and Lucy and Gabby too," the director teased. "If you two don't mind, why don't we have coffee and dessert up in the multipurpose room after supper to hear about your trip and Grandma Shep's burial? Estelle baked brownies to celebrate your return and said to give you both a hug."

Lucy shrugged off Mabel's attempt to pass on Estelle's hug. "Aw, c'mon, none o' that mushy stuff. But them brownies sound good."

"I'll take two hugs then," I grinned, holding my arms open.

Mabel gave me a warm hug, using the occasion to whisper in my ear, "And how about a meeting in my office tomorrow morning? Ten o'clock good?"

I woke the next morning in the bunk room before Sarge's wake-up bell and lay there a few moments as my new reality sunk in. *This could be my last time waking up here in the shelter . . .* I propped myself up on my elbow. Dandy's bed had been moved alongside Lucy's bunk. The bunk my mother had occupied had been filled with a new resident, a scrawny white woman with several missing teeth who'd raised a ruckus when she learned she'd be sharing a room with a dog.

"Tough," Sarge had sniffed. "It's a warm night. You can sleep here in *Dandy's room,* or outside. Your choice." The new woman stayed, turning her back on all of us.

I lay down again and closed my eyes. Maybe I should stay a day or two and move on Saturday. I still didn't know what to do about Dandy. Take him with me? Paul would be happy . . . but what about Lucy? Maybe I should leave him here at the shelter, since they'd dubbed him their official watchdog. But who would be responsible for him—Lucy? This was an emergency shelter, not a permanent residence . . .

I hadn't told anyone I was moving out yet. I wanted to bring Mabel up to date first. And I felt a bit guilty, having everything work out for me, while Precious and Tanya felt stuck here at the shelter with their kids. Should I tell them my hope? Or was it too soon to talk about a House of Hope—

My eyes flew open. That's what we would call it! The House of Hope.

I wanted to bounce out of bed and call Jodi. Tell *somebody*. But it wasn't even 6 a.m. yet. I squeezed my eyes shut again. *Oh God, is this idea for the House of Hope really from You? Or am I going out on a limb here? Show me the path, Lord! And I could use some patience too. But I do want to thank You, Jesus! Thank You for helping me get an apartment so I can bring my sons back. Thank You for my mother, for her sacrificial love, her sacrificial gift* . . . My heart was so full, my prayers poured out in the silence, praying for Celeste and Honor, for Aunt Mercy, for P. J. and Paul having to deal with their parents' separation . . .

Suddenly remembering what Jodi had said, I added, *Guess I ought to pray for Philip too. That's kinda hard, God, 'cause . . . 'cause he's hurt me so much . . . I don't even know what to pray for him. Shake him up! Do something! But . . . I guess You know better than I do—*

Sarge's wake-up bell and familiar bark shattered the silence. Bodies rolled off the bunks, and the morning routine started. Jostling for space at the sinks in the bathroom . . . trying to pay attention during the obligatory morning devotions . . . breakfast of cold cereal, bananas, toast and jam, hot coffee . . . getting chore assignments for that day . . .

Dandy didn't seem like his usual lively self—missing Mom, no doubt—so I let him curl up in my office while I tried to re-orient myself by reading staff meeting minutes and a board report I'd missed while I was away. And I took him with me to the main floor when ten o'clock rolled around—bumping into a perspiring Estelle in the foyer as she came bustling in with her usual haul of bulging grocery bags for that day's lunch.

I was immediately swallowed up in her sweaty hug. "Oh, baby, baby . . . Jodi told me you're going to be able to get your apartment. Ain't that just like God? Making a way out of no way!

Mm-mm, praise Jesus!" And then she was gone through the swinging doors as suddenly as she'd appeared, but not before she tossed over her shoulder, "Harry and I'll come help you unload that van tonight. I want to see the apartment!"

Whew. I needed to tell the residents I was moving before Estelle did all my announcing for me. But at least Jodi had been circumspect and didn't say anything about our crazy idea about buying the whole building.

But after bringing Mabel Turner up to date on everything that had happened since my mom's funeral at Manna House, including the inheritance that made it possible for me to get an apartment and bring my sons back from Virginia, I leaned forward in my chair, resting my forearms on my side of Mabel's desk. "And . . . there's something else. Don't laugh, and just hear me out, okay? I don't know how to make this happen, and I don't have a proposal to present to the Manna House Board yet. I—I just want you to pray about this with me." And in a big rush, I spilled out the crazy idea of using my inheritance money to put a down payment on the six-flat I was moving into, to create a House of Hope for moms like Precious and Tanya.

To Mabel's credit, she didn't laugh—though she did smile and wag her head. "So you've already got a name for this housing project of yours, hm? Well, it certainly won't hurt to pray about it. I'm happy to do that much." And she did, reaching across the desk, taking my hands, and praying in that wise and winsome way that was Mabel's special gift. "God, if this is just a wacky scheme percolating under the cap of curls sitting in front of me, protect Gabby from making a big mistake. But if this wild and wonderful idea belongs to You, we know nothing is going to stop it, and help us to know how to get on board."

I was stunned by Mabel's prayer. I even wrote it down as soon as I got back to my office so I could pray the same way. She'd called it a "wild and wonderful idea" . . . along with that "if," of course. But she was right. I didn't want this to be just my idea. Huh! If it was, it'd fall flat faster than it took me to trip over Lucy's cart. If it was from God, I had to give it back to God, because it was going to take God's help to pull it together.

But my heart was tripping a little that evening as I pulled Moby Van up in front of the six-flat, which turned out to be a mere five minutes from Manna House—I timed it. Lee Boyer was there with the keys, his light-brown eyes twinkling behind those wire rims of his. A few minutes later Jodi and Denny Baxter pulled up in their Dodge Caravan with Edesa and Josh, minus little Gracie this time, followed by Mr. Bentley's RAV4 with Harry Bentley, Estelle, and that cute grandson of Harry's, DeShawn.

Looking at all my friends, I wasn't sure if I was going to laugh or cry. "With all this help, it'll take us about ten minutes." Which was almost true, though once the van was unloaded, Estelle dragged me into the kitchen and insisted on opening the boxes of kitchen stuff and putting them into the newly refinished maple cupboards.

"Know you got a lot on your mind," Estelle murmured as she unwrapped a box of glasses stuffed with newspaper and handed them to me. "But want you to keep Harry in your prayers."

I looked at her sharply. "What's wrong with Mr. B?"

"Don't think he knows. But he been complaining about a blind spot in one of his eyes. I keep tellin' him ta see a good eye doctor, but you know Harry. Too busy with DeShawn these days. An' just between you an' me, I actually think he's scared. But don't say anything. Just pray."

"Sure." My heart squeezed a little. "Harry the doorman" had been my first real friend here in Chicago—and now he was so much more. But had I actually ever prayed for him? A blind spot in his eye! What did that mean? *God,* I prayed silently as I lined up the assorted odd glasses in a cupboard near the sink, *don't let me be so consumed with my own problems that I forget to pray for Harry . . . and Precious, and Tanya, and all my other friends who need You too.*

When Estelle and I had emptied the last box and wandered back to the others, Denny and Josh had already put my old single bed together, and Jodi had made it up, while Mr. Bentley and DeShawn had rolled out the Oriental rug in the living room and brought in the wingback rocker. We had all worked up a sweat in the muggy July heat, and I made a mental note to buy some fans and at least one window air conditioner.

I was about to thank everybody when Jodi whispered something to Estelle and Edesa, and the next thing I knew they were gathering everybody into the living room to pray over my new apartment—"and the whole building," Jodi slipped in. Everybody except Lee Boyer, that is. He disappeared, saying something about an evening appointment and he'd be in touch. The rest of us joined hands, even Harry's nine-year-old grandson, and several took turns praying for God's provision and protection, and that God would make this a true home for me and my sons . . . "and everyone else who takes up residence here," Jodi added, squeezing my hand.

Oh, Jodi was good.

As people climbed back into their cars and pulled away, calling out congratulations and waving good-bye, Jodi and I still stood on the sidewalk, arm in arm, looking at the front of the brick building. I pointed out the wide stone lintel above the doorway. "Don't you think 'House of Hope' would look good up there?"

Jodi grinned and squeezed my arm as I told her about the name that had popped into my head early that morning, and then about Mabel's prayer. Then I sighed. "But I can't think about that right now. Even with all the stuff we brought back from my mother's house, the apartment is still pretty empty. I'm going to need beds for the boys, a TV, more furniture . . . what?"

Jodi had pulled away and looked me in the eye, her face scrunched into a puzzled frown. "Gabby Fairbanks. I don't get it. You have all that good furniture sitting up there unused in that penthouse. It's *yours too*, Gabby. Didn't you tell me Philip had to put the original locks back? You still have a key. Just go get it, for goodness' sake! Why should Philip get it all? A judge will make you divide it up anyway."

I stared at Jodi. *Just go get it?*

Jodi blew her bangs off her damp forehead and grinned. "Want me to round up another moving crew?"

chapter 46

The rented U-Haul truck driven by Josh Baxter backed into the service lane of the parking garage at Richmond Towers and lined up with the wide doors leading into the security area. Mr. Bentley wasn't on duty on Saturday, but he showed up to make sure everything went smoothly getting the truck into the garage, letting the moving crew into the security area, and up the elevators to the thirty-second floor.

Penthouse.

I had arrived an hour earlier, let myself into the penthouse that had been my home for a mere two and a half months, and marked the furniture and items to be moved with large, lime-green sticky notes. I felt uncomfortable being there without Philip's knowledge and permission, but God knew I had tried.

I'd called his office Friday morning and asked to speak to Philip Fairbanks. I had planned to tell him—not ask his permission—that I was coming Saturday with a moving crew and taking enough stuff to make my apartment functional. I had no plans to rob him blind, just take a fair share.

But it was Henry Fenchel who came on the line. "He's out of town, Gabby," his partner said flatly. "Didn't tell me where, just said he was taking Friday off, and he'd be back in the office Monday morning. But I can guess. He—"

"But it's very important that I get hold of him, Henry," I interrupted, not really wanting to hear another rant from Henry Fenchel.

Henry snorted in my ear. "Well, you can try his cell phone, but I've tried that on weekends, and he usually turns it off when he's gaming. I tell you, Gabby, something's not right. First he dumps you, dumps his own kids, and spends nearly every weekend in Indiana at the Horseshoe. The accounts aren't adding up here in the office either. I'm calling in an accountant to—"

I'd hurriedly said good-bye and hung up. Philip siphoning business monies to support his gambling? Did he have debts he couldn't cover? No, no, I wasn't going to believe that about Philip . . . though there were a lot of things that had happened recently I never would have believed about Philip.

I did try his cell phone, got his voice mail, and left my message.

I never got a call back.

Now the volunteer moving crew—Denny and Jodi Baxter, Josh and Edesa Baxter, Estelle Williams and her housemate, Leslie Stuart, and Carl and Florida Hickman and their two husky boys—hauled in boxes, packed up the boys' rooms, and moved out the things I had marked. Everything from the boys' bedrooms, including their small TV. My bedroom dresser and mirror and an upholstered reading chair. Some scatter rugs. I left the master bath as it was, but I cleaned out the powder room and the second bath—towels, cleaning supplies, shampoo, and lotions. I put neon-lime *Take Me* notes on the square kitchen table and its four chairs, leaving the expensive dining room set and the bar stools in the kitchen for Philip. I'd brought a lot of kitchen stuff from my mom's house already. The only piece I took from the living room was another upholstered chair—now the boys and I all had a place to sit. I left Philip's office untouched, except for the family photo albums and children's books I'd collected over the years. Those went in a box and out to the truck.

Mr. Bentley stayed out of the penthouse, doing no more than directing traffic on the lower floor. Maybe that eye was bothering him more than he let on. Still, it was for the best. I didn't want Philip or anybody else to make him lose his job over "conflict of interest" with a resident. But his grandson DeShawn wanted to be where the action was, especially since the older Hickman teens, Chris and Cedric, were doing a man's job hauling chairs and boxes, and kept saying, "Hey, DeShawn, you take that end" or "Get that box, will ya?" The youngster beamed.

"What about the big bed, Gabby?" Denny Baxter asked, standing in the master bedroom.

I shook my head. That was my marriage bed . . . and right now I didn't have a marriage. Sleeping in it alone would be too painful.

My throat tightened. Would Philip and I ever sleep together in that bed again—husband and wife . . . lovers . . . friends? Or was it really over?

Denny must have seen me brush tears from my eyes because he quickly left the room, but I lingered a few moments longer, picking up a framed photo from the top of Philip's dresser. The four of us two years ago in a candid snapshot, arms around each other, wide grins. Philip's dark head was next to my "mop top," as he often called it, the boys laughing as if they were being tickled.

The way we were . . .

I slipped the framed photo into my backpack.

"All done?" Jodi said as I came into the kitchen, where Estelle had managed to produce lemonade and paper cups. "Should we swing back by the shelter to pick up Dandy?"

I shook my head. "I, um, gave him to Lucy yesterday. Just couldn't bring myself to separate them. There are enough bags of dog food left at Manna House to last her at least six months. I made her promise that she'd take shelter in the winter—Manna House is probably the only shelter that's going to let her come back with a dog. And if she couldn't take care of him, I'd take him back." I grimaced. "Don't know if it was the right thing to do. She and Dandy disappeared last night. Her bunk was empty and her cart was gone. Dandy's bed too."

"Oh, Gabby." Jodi gave me a hug. "What about Paul?"

I shrugged. "I'll get him another dog, maybe a puppy. It'll be okay. But speaking of Paul, could you excuse me a minute? I'll meet you downstairs. I have a call to make."

The moving crew tromped through the gallery and out into the foyer, chatting with each other as they waited for the elevator. And then all was quiet.

I stood a few feet back from the wraparound floor-to-ceiling windows, looking out—not down—at Lake Michigan sparkling a deep azure blue in the midday July sun. Lake Shore Drive was bustling and alive . . . but silent up here behind the thick windows. To the south, Chicago's skyline rose into the air, a thousand stories walking the streets. And now, my story was one of them.

Strange. I would not miss this penthouse. Most of the memories here had been painful ones. But Chicago . . .

I pulled out my cell phone, made the call, and waited until I heard the voices of both my sons on the phone. "P. J.? Paul? It's Mom. It's time to come home."

Reading Group Guide

A note from the author . . .

Okay, okay! I've heard from enough faithful readers who were disappointed that *Where Do I Go?* (Book #1 in the **Yada Yada House of Hope** series) ended on a "cliff-hanger" without a clear resolution, that I feel compelled to share some background . . .

After including the Manna House Women's Shelter in the last two books of the **Yada Yada Prayer Group** series, I realized I knew zilch about homeless shelters or why people become homeless, so I began volunteering once a week at Breakthrough Urban Ministries women's shelter here in Chicago (www.breakthroughministries. com). I learned there are numerous reasons people end up homeless, and I began to feel a burden to tell some of these stories—and the fictional Manna House was the perfect segue.

But Gabby Fairbank's story got so deep, I found it impossible to wrap everything up nice and tidy by the end of the first book. I don't blame you if you were distressed over the ending. But my primary purpose was to bring Gabby to a place where she realized that when her whole life felt as if it were falling apart, she could turn to "the Rock" of her salvation, just as the song says—*even without the promise that life would turn out rosy.*

But I share your pain! I'm a person who wants hope and redemption in my stories—which is why Gabby's story picks up right where it left off in this second installment. I'm delighted that you've hung in there with the **House of Hope** series and read Book 2, *Who Do I Talk To?* So let's dig in and talk about it!

1. Even though Gabby Fairbanks' situation might seem extreme, what kind of life situations / experiences / circumstances can create that "end of the world" feeling? Even though your circumstances might not be the same, have you or someone in your family experienced a life-altering event where it seemed that nothing would ever be the same? What were the initial feelings you had to cope with?

2. What were the seeds of hope that Gabby clung to as this book opened, even though everything looked hopeless? What are the seeds of hope you or your family clung to when faced with a seemingly hopeless situation?

3. In Gabby's case, her anguish was exacerbated because someone deliberately "did something" that caused her pain (as opposed to an accident or natural disaster). **Read Psalm 37:1–17.** What phrases stand out to you that might give *comfort* in such a situation? What *guidance* does the psalmist give to help deal with hurts caused by other people?

4. A number of people come alongside Gabby during this crisis, but in different ways. What role does each of

the following play in helping Gabby to stand up and be strong? *Edesa . . . Mabel . . . Estelle . . . Harry Bentley . . . Lee Boyer . . . Lucy . . . Sarge . . . Mike Fairbanks . . . Jodi Baxter.* (Anyone else?) What (or who) do you think was most helpful to Gabby in changing her perspective?

5. How does Dandy the Hero Dog impact this story—and the various people in the story—beyond just stopping a nighttime burglar? *(Gabby? Her mom? Lucy? The shelter women? Any others?)* Why do you think dogs or other pets often play an important role in times of emotional stress and difficulty?

6. How do you feel about Gabby's difficult decision to leave her boys in Virginia (chapter 12)? Can you think of any other alternative? What does this show about Gabby's character?

7. In Book 1, Mabel Turner said she thought God had brought Gabby to Chicago and to Manna House "for a purpose." How does that "prophetic word" continue to impact Gabby in Book 2? What do you think that purpose is? How does knowing (discovering) God's purpose for our lives impact how we deal with our particular life situation and the people around us?

8. In what ways do you see Gabby growing and changing in this book? In what areas do you still want to shake her and tell her _____ ?

9. The death of Gabby's mother—Martha Shepherd— seemed to also be the death of Gabby's patchwork plan to get an apartment and get her boys back. First Estelle, then Jodi says, "God must have a better plan." Has anyone ever said that to you when things fell apart with

your own plans? How did it make you feel? Was it true? Or did it seem like "spiritual mumbo-jumbo"?

10. Philip Fairbanks . . . we all hate him. (At least you've told me you do!) Why do you think he showed up at Martha Shepherd's funeral? How did you feel about that? What do you think is going on with Philip? Is he redeemable? What do *you* think is going to happen with Philip? Why? How?

11. How realistic is Gabby's dream to create a "House of Hope"? She's well-meaning but . . . is she equipped? Is this the right time? What problems do you foresee? How do *we* know when to let go of our unrealistic dreams, and when it's important to hold onto those dreams?

12. Gabby muses at the end Book 2, "There are thousands of stories walking the streets of Chicago—and mine is one of them." Why is it important to realize that every person we meet "has a story"—even the homeless person or panhandler we meet on the street? How might that change how we relate to that person?

P.S. To my readers . . .

Wish I could be a fly on the wall to hear your discussion! Thanks for being such faithful readers of the **Yada Yada House of Hope** *series. I appreciate each one of you!*

Until then . . . be blessed!

785

who do i
lean on?

BOOK 3

A
yada yada
HOUSE *of* HOPE
Novel

To Pam
My ministry partner
My "Avis," my sistah, my friend
For putting up with me on all our travels
Speaking words of encouragement when I falter
Praying God's Word to keep our focus
Laughing about all our bloopers
Correcting me when I need it
And doing it all
In love

prologue

Philip Fairbanks watched stoically as the young man in the gold brocade vest and gold bow tie snapped cards out of the automatic shuffler and dealt two cards facedown in front of each player. But feeling his left eye beginning to twitch, he glanced around the poker room, already busy this early on a Friday afternoon. Wouldn't do to give the other players a clue that he was nervous. He took it all in—the hum of activity at the other tables, the chandeliers glittering overhead, the clink of glasses as pretty young things in revealing black teddies brought drinks from the bar—trying to recapture the thrill he'd felt when he first came to the casino "just for fun" with his business partner. But today, the atmosphere seemed to be closing in on him. Like a cloying silk blanket generating static electricity, waiting to spark.

He turned back. The opening bid was already on the table. Two hundred each. Leaning forward, Philip casually picked up the two cards he'd been dealt. *Two tens*. A pair of dimes . . . He had to do better than that.

"There you are!" Two young women moving through the poker room of the Horseshoe Casino made a beeline toward them, stopping by two frat-types who helped make up Philip's table. "Crystal and I've been looking all over for you! What are you playing?"

"Texas Hold 'Em," said one frat boy with a blond buzz cut. "The game I was telling you about. Can you wait? We've already started, but it goes fast."

Philip put his cards facedown. He didn't like spectators. The girls were too close. Distracting. He could smell a faint whiff of gardenia perfume. Too heavy. He felt like telling the girls to beat it. No, he just had to focus. He raised an eyebrow at the middle-aged guy to the left of the dealer. Was the man going to fold, or . . . ?

The bald man frowned at his hand. "I'll raise it three hundred." He pushed his chips forward. Philip shrugged as if bored, stacked the same number of chips, and pushed them into the pile. The two college kids each matched the first bid.

All right. It was starting to look interesting. Two thousand on the table. He needed twice that to cover the business account before Henry Fenchel got the company's bank statement next week. Shouldn't be a problem. After all, the Fairbanks and Fenchel Commercial Development Firm was his brainchild. His money as much as Henry's. He'd just been off his game last weekend—having his sons show up in Chicago for their grandmother's funeral had distracted him. And his new credit cards had only arrived two days ago, after he'd frozen his personal cards to keep his wife from using them. Why it had taken so long was beyond irritating.

Still, he wasn't too worried. If he had a few good games this weekend, he would make up the money he'd borrowed from the business account . . . plus gravy.

Philip watched, impassive, as the dealer burned the top card and then flipped the next three cards faceup on the table. The community cards, called the "flop." *A jack . . . another ten . . . a six.* All different suits. But that ten would give him three of a kind. Philip studied the faces of the other three players. Nothing. Well, the bet would tell.

The big guy shook his head and passed. *Ah, good.* Now it was up to Philip to bet. He could simply check, see what the other two would do . . . no. He'd push it. Maybe they'd fold. Could he win with three of a kind? Not a great hand, but he'd won with less. Still, he shouldn't appear overconfident.

"I'll raise two hundred."

The twentysomething to his left pursed his lips. Philip wanted to smile but didn't. The kid had to match, raise, or fold. The girls standing behind them whispered something, gave Philip a flirty glance, and giggled. Philip wished they'd go away. Bad for concentration. Half a minute ticked by. The young man shrugged and matched the bid. So did his friend.

Back to the bald-headed guy. Sweat glistened on his forehead. Philip didn't think he'd raise it after passing the bet when he had a chance. But now it was either match or fold. *Don't sweat it, buddy. You've only got five hundred in the pot. Go ahead. Fold—*

The man pushed chips worth a matching two hundred into the pot.

Well, okay. The pot was now twenty-eight hundred. Maybe he'd make up the four thousand he owed Fairbanks and Fenchel on the first game. Sweet.

The dealer burned the top card, then flipped a single card faceup next to the original flop of three. *An eight of hearts*. That made two hearts on the table—the eight and the six. It didn't help Philip. His best hand was still only three of a kind. Maybe he should get out, take his losses, and try again. He'd only be out seven hundred. He'd still have the rest of the four thousand to play, and the night was young.

The older guy checked again. Philip tried to read him. The guy couldn't have a good hand, or he would've bet right out of the gate. He was leaving it to Philip to make the call—reacting rather than taking the initiative. *Chump*. Philip waited a good thirty seconds and then raised the pot another two hundred.

The whispering continued. Philip glared at the young women. They backed off, still whispering and laughing.

One of the college kids folded; the other matched Philip's bet. That made a pot of thirty-two hundred. Back to the bald guy. What would he do?

The man chewed his lip. Took out a handkerchief and mopped the back of his neck. Shaking his head, he matched the bid, moving his chips to the center of the table.

Was the fool bluffing? If so, he was taking it too far.

Last play. Philip watched as the dealer burned the top card of the deck and flipped the next card faceup next to the other four. The final card. Sometimes called "Fifth Street," sometimes "the river." Philip's heart pumped. *Another ten!* With two on the table and two in his hand, he could make *four* of a kind. Not bad . . . not bad at all!

The bald guy looked at his cards. Looked at the five community cards on the table. Each player could use any three from the table to make his five-card final hand. The only unknowns were the two cards each player was holding. Philip tried to picture what the guy could possibly use. The new ten made three hearts—ten, eight, six. Maybe the guy had a pair, or even two . . . or an ace, hoping to take the pot with a single high card.

None of which would win over his four of a kind.

The guy suddenly moved all his chips into the center of the table. *What—?* Those chips were worth another thousand! Philip recalculated. The guy probably had two hearts in his hand—a flush, five cards in the same suit.

A decent hand. But his four of a kind would beat it.

What the heck. This is what made it fun. Philip matched the man's thousand and sat back.

Fifty-four hundred in the pot.

The second kid threw up his hands. "I fold. You guys are nuts."

"That's it?" the dealer said. "Lay down your hands."

Breaking into a wide smile, the bald guy laid down two hearts—a nine and a seven. *Humph, a flush. Just what I thought.* Philip gave the guy five seconds to enjoy his "victory," then laid down his tens. "Four of a kind beats your flush," he said, finally allowing a small smile. *Ohh, that was easy.* He mentally added the pot to the twenty-one hundred in chips he still had. *Seventy-five hundred.* Not bad for a twenty-minute game. Even after he repaid the four thousand he'd borrowed from the business account—Henry none the wiser—he'd still have thirty-five hundred in cool profit . . .

"Not a flush. A *straight* flush, buddy! Lookit that. Six, seven, eight, nine, ten—all hearts! Beats *your* four of a kind. Ha ha!"

The bald guy started raking in the pile of chips from the middle of the table.

Philip stared. Why hadn't he seen it? He felt his face redden. Now he felt like a fool. Worse than seeing his winnings evaporate.

Well, he wasn't going to let this chump get the best of him. He still had twenty-one hundred to work some magic. He looked up at the dealer. "I'm in again. What's the minimum bid?"

Philip pulled the Lexus into his space in the parking garage at Richmond Towers on Monday morning and turned off the motor. He sat for several long minutes before opening the car door, a sense of dread pooling in his gut. The weekend at the casino had gone badly. He should've pulled out while his losses were minimal. But it would have been so easy to make it all right! Just one good win and he could've covered the withdrawal from the business account *and* made a profit. But it didn't go down that way. He'd taken out a couple thousand from his personal account, sure his luck would turn . . . and then had to do it a few more times. Now he'd lost ten thousand of his own money, and he still had four thousand to pay back to Fairbanks and Fenchel.

He got out of the car and retrieved his overnight bag from the trunk. Well, he'd take care of the business account and worry about the rest later. He'd make the transfer with his personal debit card and hope Henry wouldn't notice the withdrawal and deposit if the balance was good. Even if he did, he'd smooth

Henry's feathers, just tell him it was an emergency. What was the problem if he put it back?

But now he was out nearly fifteen grand. He never meant to let his losses get that high.

Philip slid his security card through the keypad that let him into the residential elevators. He should have come home Sunday—maybe even Saturday—before he'd lost so much money. But the penthouse was so empty these days without Gabby and the boys . . . no, he couldn't go there. *Don't look back, Philip. What's done is done. It wasn't working.*

Stepping into an empty elevator, he punched the button for the thirty-second floor. Still, he spent as little time as possible in the penthouse. Everywhere he turned, it was like he expected to see them—the boys tussling over the remote . . . Gabby's mop of auburn curls on the pillow next to him . . .

It wasn't supposed to turn out this way! Gabby had gone off her rocker—dragging that smelly old bag lady home the first time Fenchel and his wife had come to dinner. Then she took that charity job at the homeless shelter without even discussing it with him! It was like she'd forgotten why they came to Chicago in the first place. Just decided to dance to her own music, never mind that it clashed with his.

But bringing her elderly mother and the mutt to stay at the penthouse had been the last straw . . . No, costing him the deal with a potential client—*that* was the last straw. He blamed Fenchel for that. Henry should have known better than to trust Gabby to deliver a phone message with sensitive information related to the business. She was so clueless about business protocol, she was like a loose cannon on a pitching ship.

The elevator dinged at the top floor of Richmond Towers, and the door slid open. Kicking her out had been drastic, but the situation had gotten intolerable. Maybe a few months on her own would knock some sense into her. She'd gotten a lawyer—some do-gooder from Legal Aid—but he knew Gabby. She wouldn't want a divorce. If he didn't rush things, if he worked stuff out with the boys, she'd come around. Let it pinch for a while.

Philip glanced at his Rolex as he crossed the marble foyer and pulled out his keys. He still had time to get a quick shower, change his clothes, and do the money transfer online before he headed to the office. Monday morning traffic into the city from Indiana hadn't been too bad. If he hustled, he could still get to the office by ten.

Intent on a quick in-and-out, Philip headed down the hallway to the master bedroom—but stopped as he entered. Something was wrong here. He scanned the room.

Gabby's dresser was missing.

He tossed his overnight bag on the bed and scanned the room once more. What else was missing? Had she said something about this? He flipped open his cell phone and scrolled down through recent calls. There . . . Gabby's new cell phone ID, dated last Friday. He hadn't bothered to listen to the message or return the call. Figured whatever it was could wait. But had she just—?

He turned on his heel and strode back down the hallway, jerking doors open as he went. Half the linens and towels from the linen closet—gone. Both the boys' bedrooms—cleaned out. In the kitchen, the breakfast nook table and chairs had disappeared. He opened the cupboards. Most of the dishes, pots and pans, and utensils still seemed to be there. Hard to tell. At least she'd left enough for him to function.

Philip crossed to the dining room . . . it looked untouched. Even their wedding china was still in the china cabinet. *Huh.* Why didn't she just clean him out while she was at it? Go figure.

Wait. His study. *She better not have touched my study!* Practically breaking into a run, Philip threw open the door to his inner sanctum. But everything looked just as he'd left it . . . no, wait. The bookshelves had been disturbed. The family photo albums were gone. And a bunch of books. And a file drawer was open. The one that usually held their medical records, the boys' school records—personal stuff.

He stood in the middle of the room. His computer, his papers, untouched. But something else seemed missing . . . what was it? His eyes roved the room, then settled on an empty spot on one of his bookshelves and realized what it was.

The framed photo of the two of them on their fifth wedding anniversary, cake smudges on their noses, Gabby's hair a halo of red-gold curls, laughing up at him mischievously.

That photo. Happier times . . . Why had she taken it? Or had she thrown it away? A quick check of the wastebasket in the study and the kitchen trash can yielded nothing. But somehow the photo's absence yawned larger than the rest of the missing items put together.

Philip walked slowly into the living room. As far as he could tell, only one easy chair was missing, plus some framed photographs from the walls. That was it.

Running a hand through his dark hair, he stood by the floor-to-ceiling windows looking out over Lake Shore Drive and Lake

Michigan beyond, battling his emotions. Gabby had more *chutz-pah* than he'd given her credit for. She'd been in the penthouse once before when he wasn't there—had left a glass with her lipstick on it as a calling card. *Huh.* He should've been warned. In spite of himself, a tiny smile curled one edge of his mouth. This raid was like the old Gabby—impetuous, daring—like the girl in the photo.

The tiny smile died. Now she was gone, along with her stuff. It wasn't the things she'd taken that bothered him so much, but what it meant. He hadn't thought it would go this far! Was it too late to turn things around? She'd not only taken her stuff but everything that belonged to P.J. and Paul too!

An unexpected wave of loss swept over him . . . but it was drowned a moment later by a larger surge of anger. *No!* No way was she going to just take the boys away from him. He swore under his breath. Where were the boys supposed to sleep when they came to visit? And now he was fifteen grand in the hole! He couldn't just go out and buy new furniture for their bedrooms, not to mention CD players, clothes, sports equipment—all the stuff it took to keep two preteens housed and entertained. He didn't have time for this crap—

A vaguely familiar figure caught his eye thirty-two stories below in the narrow park that created a verdant buffer between the luxury high-rise and Lake Shore Drive. Looked kind of like the old bag lady Gabby had run into, the one who'd started this whole mess. She had a yellow dog with her this time . . . *Wait.* Philip leaned closer to the wraparound window and squinted. Not just any yellow dog. That was Dandy! His mother-in-law's dog—or Gabby's dog now that her mother had passed. What was that old woman doing with Gabby's dog? Stupid question. She probably stole him while Gabby was out in North Dakota burying her mother. Give those thieving street people a dime, and they'd rob you blind.

Well, the old bag wasn't going to get away with it!

With a reckless energy that surprised even Philip after his short night at the casino hotel, he strode out of the penthouse and back into the elevator . . . and a few minutes later he was half-running across the frontage road between Richmond Towers and the park. "Hey, you!" he yelled. What was her name? Couldn't remember it. "You with the dog!"

The old lady had sat down on a bench, but she looked up as he ran toward her. The dog made a low guttural noise. Philip stopped. "Is that Dandy? Martha Shepherd's dog?"

She looked him up and down, narrow eyes glittering between sagging folds of skin. "Was."

So she was going to play games. He wanted to shake her. "Okay, so you know Mrs. Shepherd died a week ago. But that dog belongs to my wife now. Our son Paul is crazy about that dog. You—whatever your name is—you stole him. Give him back—*now*." He thrust a hand out, ready to jerk the leash out of her hand if she didn't give it up.

The old woman stood up. "Well! Don't that just rot my socks. You sayin' you want the dog?" She took a menacing step in his direction. Dandy growled again, his top lip curling over his canines. Philip pulled his hand back. "*You?*" she hissed. "Mister high-an'-mighty Philip Fairbanks? Who don't even have the decency to give food an' shelter to that *wife* you mentioned two breaths ago. You kicked her out on the street, left her no place to go. Now you want a *dog?*"

She stabbed a finger in his chest so hard it hurt. Startled, Philip took a step backward. "And if'n I got my facts straight, you don't even have time ta take care o' them two boys o' yours. Just packed 'em off to they grandfolks. Guess you thinkin' this dog can take their place."

Philip felt his face flush. She had no right—

"Oh yeah. Almost fergot. You kicked poor Miss Martha outta your fancy digs too. But, hey." The old lady shrugged. "Guess you figgered if ol' Lucy here could live out in the street, must be good enough for your wife and her ol' lady too. Why, I'm kinda flattered—for about half a second."

She punched that stubby finger in his chest again. "But I *feel* for ya, Mister Fairbanks. Now that you don' got no wife, no kids, no mother-in-law ta take care of, must get kinda lonely up there in the sky. Guess you be needin' a *dog* to take care of. Ain't so hard. Just gotta take him for a walk mornin' an' evenin', and pick up his poops—they got a law, see, says ya hafta clean up after ya dog. Sign's right over there." She jerked a thumb somewhere behind her. "So . . . here." She held out the leash in her clawlike hand. "Guess he's yours. Go on. Take him."

Philip stared at the old woman . . . *Lucy*, that was her name. The old bag was nuts! He suddenly felt foolish. What had he intended to do? Return the dog to Gabby, like a peace offering? Maybe . . . but mostly, he'd just been angry. Angry at everything. Nothing was going right.

He threw up his hands. "Look. I can't take the dog now. I have to go to work. But you . . ." He shook a finger at her, trying to regain the upper hand. "You have no business with that dog. An old lady like you can't take care of a dog living out on the streets. Just take the dog back to Gabrielle, wherever she is. If I see you around here again with Dandy, I'll . . . I'll call the police."

Philip wheeled and walked stiffly back toward Richmond Towers. He gave a fierce shake of his head, but Lucy's words still burned in his ears.

chapter 1

For the umpteenth time, my twelve-year-old jumped up from the living room floor where he and his older brother had been squabbling over last Sunday's newspaper comics and peered out the front bay window. "Mom! When's Dad coming? He said six and it's already six thirty!"

"Yeah, and wherever we're going for supper, it better be air-conditioned." His older brother's voice rode the edge between whining and wilting. "All that fan's doing is moving hot air around, Mom."

I'd been hanging around the living room for the past half hour, rearranging books in the built-in bookcase on either side of the painted brick gas fireplace and watering the new houseplants my coworkers at the Manna House Women's Shelter had given me as housewarming gifts, not wanting to miss even one minute of precious time with Paul and P.J. before their dad came to pick

them up. I bit back the first words that rushed to my mouth—
"Ask *him* why he's late!"—and instead chirped, "He'll be here any
minute, I'm sure. Friday night traffic can be a beast, you know."

Like a prophecy fulfilled, we heard two short honks outside.
"See? There he is."

Both Paul and P.J. grabbed their duffel bags and scurried for
the front door. I followed them outside, trying to imprint the
backs of their heads in my mind to last me for the next twenty-
four hours until Philip returned them. Free from boarding school
regulations, Paul's hair had grown back into the tousled chestnut-
red curls that reminded me of my own at that age. P.J.'s hair was
dark and straight like his dad's, but the two inches he'd added
over the summer were still a startling revelation, as if his new
height had been attached to his fourteenth birthday—the birthday I'd missed.

I'd missed Paul's birthday too, for that matter. But that was
going to change this weekend.

"Hey!" I called after them. "I need a good-bye hug."

"Oh yeah! Sorry, Mom." Paul did an about-face, ran back
to give me a smack, then disappeared into the backseat of the
Lexus. P.J. waited until I caught up to him on the sidewalk and let
me give him a hug, then he opened the front passenger door and
lowered his lanky body inside.

I gave a little wave as the car pulled away, a lump crowding
into my throat.

So this is my new reality.

I should be in that car too, all of us going out together for
pizza, or whatever they were going to do tonight.

Instead, I turned and looked at the three-story six-flat that was now my home. A classic Chicago brick with bay windows at the front of each apartment. Late afternoon sun—still muggy and warm—trickled through the leaves of the trees lining the mostly residential street, casting speckled light and shadows dancing on the brick facade. My new apartment was on the first floor—a gift I gratefully embraced every time I looked out the front windows and saw the ground only seven feet down. No more dizzying heights.

I brushed a damp curl off my forehead. No use moping. I had more phone calls to make if I was going to pull off this welcome-home-birthday-party surprise that Jodi Baxter and I'd been cooking up. The boys had arrived last weekend from Virginia, where they'd been staying with Philip's parents the last six weeks, but I'd wanted to give them a week to get adjusted to the new apartment and the new situation between Philip and me before I invited people over to celebrate. Frankly, as hard as it was to let the boys out of my sight, Philip's taking the boys for tonight and tomorrow gave me time to make party food and do some shopping. I'd better get to it.

I ran up the six wide steps leading into the building and into the small foyer with its six gleaming mailboxes, three on each side—and stopped. I'd come out without my keys! The inside foyer door was locked—and there was no one in my apartment to buzz me in.

Stupid, stupid, stupid!

I peered through the glass panels of the foyer door. My apartment door to the right stood open. Well, that was half the battle. If I could get through the foyer door, I was in. The only thing standing between me and getting inside were the glass windowpanes in the door. *Huh.* All I had to do was break one, reach inside, and open the handle—

Nope. A broken windowpane in the door would be an open invitation for any stray Tom, Dick, or Harry to walk into the building too.

I walked back outside and looked at my bay windows. The fan sat in the open window closest to the steps—but would still be a long reach, even if I got up on the wide cement "arms" of the low wall on either side of the outside landing where I stood. Even if I could reach it, I'd have to find a way to take the screen out first. If only I had something sturdy to stand on so I could reach it from below.

Rats! I sat down on the top step and buried my face in my hands. This was so . . . so *stupid!* How in the world was I going to get in? Even my cell phone was inside the apartment—but a lot of good it'd do me, even if I had it. Anybody I called wouldn't have a key to my place anyway. Guess I'd have to sit here until one of the other residents in the building came home, and—

Wait a minute! I stood up, went back inside the foyer, and pushed the buzzer of the apartment above me. I waited thirty seconds—no response. I pushed the third-floor buzzer. Still no response. *Oh, please, please, somebody be home.* I crossed to the other side of the foyer and pushed the buzzer for the other third-floor apartment and waited. Suddenly the intercom crackled.

"Yeah?"

"It's Gabby Fairbanks in the first-floor apartment! I—"

"Who?"

"Gabby Fairbanks! First-floor apartment! I—"

"You got the wrong apartment. No Fairbanks up here."

"No, wait—" The intercom went dead.

I pushed the buzzer again and leaned on it this time.

The intercom came alive. *"What?"*

"I'm locked out! Can you let me in?"

"Oh. Wait a minnit . . ." The intercom went dead.

I waited a good five minutes, but finally a black dude in a big T-shirt, baggy jeans, and bare feet came down the stairs and pulled open the foyer door. "Thank you so much," I gushed, slipping inside before he changed his mind. "Gotta remember to take my keys. So sorry to bother you."

The young man, maybe late twenties, jerked his head at my open door. "That your apartment?"

"Yes. I just moved in a few weeks ago. My name's Gabby. You are . . . ?"

"Cinco. My brother lives up on third. He's letting me crash there."

"Oh. Nice to meet you. Thanks for helping me out." I held out my hand and he shook it awkwardly, then I slipped into my apartment and let out a long breath. I really should get to know my neighbors in the building.

Although I'd have to hurry up, because if my dream came true, I might have new neighbors before long.

chapter 2

Jodi Baxter showed up at my apartment at noon the next day, juggling a cake carrier and two shopping bags. "The keyboard's in the van," she huffed, dumping her armload on the living room floor. Then she clamped her hand over her mouth. "Paul's not here, is he?" she whispered.

I shook my head with a laugh. "Told you, the boys are with their dad today. The stuff for P.J. came too, right?"

My friend nodded. "Yeah, but it's going to take two of us to get those boxes in. Whew! It's hot in here. You got enough fans?"

"Not really. I've got three. We just move them around." *Oh, for central air.* I propped open the foyer door with a wastebasket and followed her into the sultry steam bath outside—my house keys safely hooked to a belt loop on my jeans as added insurance—and the two of us carried in the long, heavy box from the back of the Baxter minivan. On the second trip we brought in the other box, not as heavy but big and square. We set them on the wooden window seat in front of the open bay windows in the sunroom just off the living room. One fan on the highest setting moved the muggy air around.

"Wow." I ran my hand along the length of the long box. "I hope Paul likes it. Thanks for letting me have it sent to your house. I didn't want to risk the UPS guy showing up here when I was at work—or worse, when the boys were here."

"No problem. Oh, by the way . . ." Jodi dug into one of her shopping bags. "I snatched a couple of sandwich plates from Manna House instead of staying for lunch after the typing class. Tuna on white bread, chips, and potato salad. Figured you'd be busy cooking for tonight, but we need lunch, right?"

I grinned as I took the paper plates she handed to me, neatly wrapped in aluminum foil, and headed down the long hallway that led to the kitchen in the back. "You'd make a good Jewish mother, Jodi Baxter," I tossed over my shoulder. "How'd the typing class at the shelter go today?"

Jodi lugged her bags down the hallway right after me. "It was okay. Althea wasn't there. Somebody said she's no longer on the bed list. But Kim and Wanda are still coming—Kim's been practicing on the computer, I can tell—and a new girl I hadn't met before . . . Tawny or something like that. Real young. What's *her* story?"

I peeled the foil from the paper plates, poured two glasses of apple juice from the fridge, and set them on the breakfast nook table—the one I'd hauled away from the penthouse at Richmond Towers. "Don't know." I shrugged, plopping into a chair. "She's only been at the shelter two or three days." I started to bite into the tuna sandwich and then looked guiltily at Jodi. "You, um, wanna pray for the food?"

Jodi laughed. "Sure." She closed her eyes and was quiet a moment. I watched her through half-closed lids, her brown shoulder-length hair swinging forward as she bowed her head. Maybe she was just going to give thanks silently—but then she started to pray aloud, so I closed my eyes.

"Thanks, Jesus, for being present with us today. Thanks for this food You provided for the ladies at Manna House—and for us." She giggled a little. "And thank You for the special occasions we're celebrating today—Paul and P.J. being back home with their mom, and for their birthdays Gabby didn't get to celebrate a few weeks ago. *And* that we can celebrate a birthday for little Gracie, who was born sometime in this month a year ago. Oh, God! You have done so much in such a short time for that precious little girl . . ."

Jodi stopped. I opened my eyes. She was fishing for a tissue but coming up short. I handed her a paper napkin.

"Sorry." She blew her nose. "Had a flash about the first time I saw Gracie and her birth mom, huddled in a doorway last November. Hoo boy." Jodi shook her head. "Had no idea when Denny and I took them to the shelter that Carmelita was a drug addict—or that my *son* and his fiancée would end up adopting her baby when she died. But now look at us—celebrating Gracie's first birthday." Jodi eyed me sideways. "Even though I'm waaay too young to be a grandmother."

I laughed. "Not to mention your Josh is waaay too young to be a daddy. What is he, twenty?"

"Almost twenty-two. But it feels like he just graduated from high school. Uh . . . did I ever say amen? Amen, Lord." "Grandma Jodi" took a bite of her sandwich and wrinkled her nose at it. "Ugh, kind of soggy. Sorry."

Soggy or not, we were both hungry. As we scarfed down our lunch from the shelter, I thought about what Jodi had said about Gracie. From what little I knew, Gracie's short life had been nothing short of a miracle. After Carmelita was discovered in a drug house dead of an overdose, the staff at Manna House had found a note among her things saying if anything ever happened to her, she wanted Edesa Reyes, one of the shelter volunteers, to keep her baby. Edesa, a young black woman in the U.S. on a student visa from Honduras, spoke fluent Spanish and had bonded quickly with Carmelita. But when Carmelita died, Edesa's fiancé, Josh Baxter, pushed up their wedding date so Carmelita's orphaned baby could have a mom *and* a dad.

And now it was August. Nine months since Gracie's mother had died. Eight months after Josh and Edesa Baxter's Christmas wedding. Four months since Philip and I moved to Chicago chasing Philip's ambitions. Three and a half months since I tripped over a homeless woman and ended up with a job at the Manna House Women's Shelter. Two months since my husband said I wasn't the "corporate wife" he needed . . . since he'd kicked me out and sent our sons away, and I'd ended up on the shelter's bed list myself.

Three short weeks since I'd moved into this apartment and could finally bring my sons home . . .

"Guess we better get busy." Jodi jumped up and tossed her paper plate in the kitchen wastebasket, interrupting my thoughts. "You're making a separate cake for your boys, right? I don't think they'd appreciate this teddy bear cake I'm trying to decorate for Gracie. Ha. It's been so long since I've put together one of these things, it might look like a mud-covered snowman by the time I'm done." She mopped perspiration off her face with a paper napkin. "Say, any chance you could move all three of those fans in here?"

By the time five o'clock rolled around, we had two cakes on the counter and two kinds of pasta salad in the fridge. The other guests were supposed to bring food too.

Jodi's teddy bear cake had turned out perfect: chocolate icing "fur," Oreo cookie ears, chocolate mint eyes and nose, licorice rope mouth, a white icing tummy with a heart-shaped "red hot" for a belly button. "Too cute," I murmured. "Hope P.J. and Paul don't mind a plain old layer cake."

"Mind?! It's three layers of chocolate fudge! Besides, you've got those trick candles—" The front door buzzer sounded. "Whoops. Somebody's here. Want me to get that?"

But I was already halfway down the hall. "Yikes! Hope it's not the boys already. I told Philip six!" Instead of buzzing the intercom, I opened the front door a crack and peeked out. "Oh good! It's Estelle and Harry. And DaShawn!" I flung the door wide.

That was the nice thing about a first-floor apartment—I could actually see who was standing in the outer foyer beyond the glass-paneled door. I crossed the hall and pulled it open. Estelle Williams—one of my coworkers at Manna House and my personal "mother hen"—swept right past me in a loose yellow caftan. "Too hot for a hug, honey. I'll make it up to you this winter. C'mon, Harry. You too, DaShawn. Bring in those wings and stick 'em in the oven."

Harry Bentley, his brown dome shining with perspiration, gave me a wink and obediently followed his ladylove into the apartment with the aluminum pan he was carrying. His grandson trailed behind with an identical pan. "Hi, Miz Fairbanks. Your kids here?"

I shook my head. "Not yet. We want all the guests to get here first." As the trio disappeared toward the kitchen, I wondered how Mr. Bentley was adjusting to suddenly having custody of the nine-year-old grandson he hadn't even known existed until a few months ago. So far so good, as far as I could tell.

The Baxter crew was next to arrive. Denny Baxter, Jodi's husband, lugged two shopping bags into the apartment and mopped his face with a handkerchief. "Uh, tell me again how Jodi got to drive the minivan by *herself*, while the four of us"—he tipped his head at Josh and Edesa coming in behind him, wrestling Gracie's stroller into the apartment—"had to take the El and walk . . . how many blocks?"

Jodi swooped Gracie out of the stroller and gave the tiny girl a big cuddle. "Tell your grandpa he helped me load those boxes for Gabby's boys himself, so he *knows* I had to get them here early." She handed Gracie to me and motioned to Edesa to follow her back to the kitchen.

The buzzer rang again. "C'mon, Gracie," I murmured to the sweet-smelling toddler in my arms. "Let's go see who's coming to your party." With my free hand I opened the foyer door for Mabel Turner, the director of the Manna House Women's Shelter—a woman with steel nerves covered in brown velvet. "Oh, hey, C.J." I beamed at her fourteen-year-old nephew, whose tight cornrows all over his head didn't do much to toughen his "pretty boy" features.

The boy hunched his shoulders, not meeting my eyes. "I go by Jermaine now," he mumbled. "My real name."

"Oh! So the *J* in C.J. stands for Jermaine. What does—?" But C.J. had already disappeared inside before I found out what *C* stood for.

"Don't close that door!" someone hollered. I peeked out to see Precious and her daughter Sabrina—sixteen and pregnant—climbing out of Mabel's car, along with Tanya and her eight-year-old Sammy. Both moms and their offspring were long-term "guests" at the Manna House shelter.

"Get in here quick! Paul and P.J. might get back any minute—ouch! Let go of my hair, sweetie." The toddler in my arms had grabbed a fistful of my corkscrew curls and squealed.

"*Oomph*. Sabrina don't do quick anymore." Precious practically pushed her gorgeous teenager—too cute for her own good, according to Precious—up the short flight of steps. "An' she only five and a half months gone. Girl, I'm gonna need a wheelbarrow for you by the time that baby gonna pop."

Sabrina arched her eyebrows in that exaggerated patience teens reserve for their parents, but she coyly held her arms out to Gracie as the knot of new arrivals came into the apartment building. The baby let go of my hair and willingly threw herself into the girl's arms. I shooed Tanya and Sammy inside, but hung back with Precious. Waving my hand at the building, I dropped my voice. "What do you think?"

"What do *I* think?" Precious practically snorted. "Sista girl, if these apartments have a hot shower an' a front door and a back door I can lock, they beautiful. What I want to know is what *you* thinkin'. You gonna buy this building or not? When can we move in?"

"That's what I want to do, Precious. But the boys just came back this week. I've been busy getting them registered for school and haven't had a chance to talk to my lawyer. Or the Manna House board. Hopefully next week, though. Just . . . pray, okay?"

"Pray? Gabby girl, my knees got dents in 'em from all the hours I been spendin' praying 'bout this crazy idea of yours."

"You haven't said anything to Tanya yet, have you?" Tanya had been a teen mother herself, and she and Sammy had never had a home of their own.

Precious tossed her head full of tiny twists. "Whatchu think I am? You ask me not to say nothin', so nothin' is what I'm sayin'. 'Cept to God, of course. *He* gettin' an earful."

A familiar car turned the corner. "Quick, get inside. There's Philip with the boys." We hustled inside. "They're here, they're here, everybody! Come out of the sunporch, away from those windows, okay? . . . Where's Jodi? Oh, there you are. Jodi, you take care of the apartment door, okay? When they buzz the intercom, I'll go out and let them in from the foyer, but when the boys get to the apartment door, you pull it open and everybody yell 'Surprise!' Okay?"

Laughing and jostling, my guests obediently crowded into the not-too-big living room while we waited for the front door buzzer. A hot minute went by. Then two. What in the world was taking the boys so—

Blaaaaaat.

"Quiet! Quiet. I'm going out." I slipped out the front door. *Rats!* What was Philip doing in the foyer? He was supposed to just let the boys out and drive off, wasn't he?

I hesitated, but the mirage didn't disappear, so I pulled the foyer door open partway. "Uh, hi, guys!"

"What's the matter, Mom? Doesn't the buzzer work? You could've just buzzed us in." P.J. shouldered his way past me.

"Uh, yeah, it's fine. It's just . . . well, since the apartment is right here on the first floor, it's almost as easy to—"

Paul squeezed past me next, so I had to step back and open the door wider. I shot a glance over their heads at their father with a *what-are-you-doing-here* frown.

Philip Fairbanks, cool and debonair as always in his aviator sunglasses, held up two mammoth plastic shopping bags. "Got some gear for the boys—belated birthday gifts, you know."

My eyes widened in panic. The Sports Authority logo splashed across the bags in big bold script. *Double rats!* If Philip had pre-empted my birthday gifts, I'd . . . but I couldn't go there right now. I had to get rid of Philip.

"Uh, I can take those." I reached for the bags. "Thanks for bringing the boys back on time. We—"

"No problem. They're heavy. I'll take them in." Philip pushed past me with the bags. "The boys want me to see their 'new digs' anyway, as they say."

At that exact moment, the front door swung wide open and a chorus of voices from inside yelled, "Surprise!" . . . "Happy birthday!" . . . "Welcome home!"

The boys looked startled but slowly advanced into the front room, where they were mobbed with handshakes and hugs. Philip stopped just short of the open doorway and looked at me. "What's this?"

I stepped in front of him, barring his way. "A surprise birthday party for Paul and P.J. obviously. Now, please—"

The corners of Philip's handsome mouth tipped up. "So . . . am I invited?"

I glared at my estranged husband. What in the world was he

thinking?! But before I could tell him to disappear and take his Lexus with him, his quip must have carried into the living room, because Paul suddenly darted between us. "Oh, could Dad stay too? Please, Mom? That'd be great! Please?"

My mouth hung open as my brain synapses ricocheted inside my skull, searching for the right words that would make Philip leave—*now*—but not hurt Paul, who was already confused by our separation. But my silence, which couldn't have lasted more than two seconds, must have been interpreted as permission, because Paul grabbed his father by the arm and dragged him past me into the party.

My party. My party for *my* sons.

chapter 3

❀ ❀ ❀

As the tall figure of my husband and Paul stepped inside, the jolly living room buzz hiccoughed and disappeared, as if sucked up by an invisible vacuum cleaner. Suppressing the urge to pull out fistfuls of my Orphan Annie hair and scream like a two-year-old, I hustled after them—but did not close the door. "Uh, everyone, this is Philip, the boys' dad. Paul, uh, wanted him to stay for a few minutes."

Get that, Philip? A few minutes!

Flustered, I tried to make introductions. "P.J. and Paul, you remember my boss, Ms. Turner, the director of Manna House. And this is her nephew, uh . . . Jermaine. He's starting ninth grade at Lane Tech too, same as you, P.J. Thought you might like to meet a few kids before you start school."

The slender black boy gave a hopeful nod, but P.J. didn't react.

Estelle's lips were pressed together as though barely restraining brickbats she'd like to rain down on Philip's head, so I skipped her for the moment and rushed on. "And you boys remember Mr.

Bentley, the doorman at Richmond Towers . . ." I almost added, ". . . where your dad lives," but wisdom said don't make a point of it. "And this handsome young man is his grandson, DaShawn."

DaShawn was all sunshine. "You dudes got a cool crib here. Thanks for inviting us to your party!" The boy looked up at his grandfather and stage whispered, "We gonna eat soon, Grandpa? I'm hungry!"

That broke the ice and people laughed. *Bless DaShawn.* "You're right, DaShawn. The rest of you can introduce yourselves. Food will be in the dining room in five minutes." I beckoned to Jodi, eager to flee.

"I'll do it." Estelle brushed past me. "You stay here and play hostess. C'mon, Jodi."

Oh, thanks a lot, Estelle. But I couldn't blame my friend for weaseling out of the situation. What in the world was I going to do with an uninvited guest who just happened to be the man who'd kicked me out of house and home barely two months ago?

Correction. The penthouse at Richmond Towers had been a house, but certainly not a home.

I turned back to my hostess duties in time to hear Philip say, "Bentley. Haven't seen you around the past couple of weeks. You working the night shift now?"

"No, Fairbanks," Mr. Bentley said evenly. "I quit the job. Now that I've got custody of my grandson here, I want to spend more time with him before school starts."

I covered my mouth to keep from laughing. On the job at Richmond Towers, Harry Bentley had *always* called Philip "Mr. Fairbanks." *Oh, Mr. B, you got him good.* Still, I was surprised by the news.

"Mr. Bentley! You quit your job? How—" I stopped. Maybe it was rude to ask how he was going to support both himself *and* a kid.

But the middle-aged black man winked at me as if he knew what was on my mind. "It was just a job to supplement my retirement anyway."

Retired? Mr. Bentley was pushing sixty, but he didn't look old enough to be retired yet. But before I could satisfy my curiosity, he said, "By the way, DaShawn and I are going to go to the zoo and some of the museums before school starts. Was going to ask if P.J. and Paul might want to come along too."

I almost forgot Philip was standing right there. "Oh, Mr. B! That would be great! I'm only working half time at Manna House until school starts—maybe we could go together."

Estelle appeared in the doorway. "Food's ready. Somebody want to say a blessing over the food and over our birthday boys?"

"It's Gracie's birthday too, don't forget!" Precious piped up.

"That's right, and you just volunteered to say the blessing. C'mon now, everybody join hands."

Join hands? Did the woman know what she was doing? I ducked into a space between Mr. Bentley and DaShawn, so I wouldn't be forced to hold hands with Philip. But who would? Everybody here knew our story, and Philip's name might as well be Mud. But Paul and P.J. crowded on either side of their dad—oh my, God's angels must be working overtime in the neighborhood—not exactly holding hands, but at least filling a chink in the ragged circle.

I lowered my eyelids but peeked through my lashes as Precious grabbed Gracie's small hand—still in Sabrina's arms—and raised her other hand like a Pentecostal preacher. "Precious *Jesus*! Thanks be to God! This is a mighty good day, and we give You *all* the glory. Bless this bunch, every one of 'em, an' especially bless Paul and P.J. on they birthdays, even though the days is past, an' bless lil' Gracie, this precious baby girl You've given to all of us, who's got a birthday sometime here in August even if we don't know the exact—"

"Precious," growled Estelle. "Bless the *food*."

"—day," Precious rolled right on, "'cause You got our days numbered, Jesus, an' that's all that matters. Now we thank You for the food we're about to eat, an' remove all impurities so nobody gets sick. *Aaaa . . .*"—Precious opened her eyes and simpered at Estelle—". . . *men!*"

With grins and chuckles, the party threaded through the long hallway to the dining area in the back, where the pasta salads, a pot of smoky greens, hot wings, enchiladas, crusty bread, bowls of chips, and lemonade were set out on one of my mother's flowered tablecloths. I knew no one in this crew would mind the makeshift table beneath the cloth, made from a plywood board sitting on two sawhorses I'd found in the basement—but that was before Philip invited himself. *Rats.* I steeled myself for a joke about decorating the place in "Early Alley" or something. But Philip just filled his plate and took a tour of the boys' bedrooms along the hallway. At least those rooms were filled with the good maple beds and dressers I'd hauled out of the penthouse.

I avoided Philip as much as I could, but I was distracted out of my mind by his presence. *Why is he still here?!* I noticed Denny Baxter talking to him in the living room—bless that man. Had

Jodi snapped up the only decent husband in the universe? The two men could have been cut from *Sports Afield* and *GQ*. Denny, midforties, rugged-looking, salt-and-pepper brown hair, school T-shirt, shorts, gym shoes, very much the high school coach or athletic director—whichever—but with two amazing dimples that creased his cheeks whenever he smiled, making me want to go "kitchy koo" under his chin. Philip stood half a head taller, tan and slender beneath his polo shirt, slacks creased, dark brown hair combed back, though it sometimes fell over his forehead in a boyish moment, brown eyes and dark lashes that could melt my insides like butter in the sun.

Denny—casual. Philip—cultured.

Why is my heart pounding?

Why is Philip here?

Why is he being so . . . decent?

"Time for birthday cake!" Estelle hollered into the living room. "Gabby, get in here and light those candles before this heat melts the frosting. Everybody else, give us one minute!"

The woman had taken over my house. She probably noticed that I was a complete zombie, needing my buttons pushed like an obedient robot.

Jodi Baxter was sticking a big candle "1" in the teddy bear cake's stomach.

"I'm sorry, Estelle. You and Jodi are doing all the work."

"Humph." Estelle handed me the kitchen matches. "You better be glad we are. Otherwise I might just punch that man's lights out. Lord, help me!"

I grinned, struck a kitchen match, and lit the fourteen skinny sparkler candles on the triple-layer chocolate fudge cake I'd made for my boys, which was starting to lean in the heat. I knew Estelle was just sputtering, but I kinda wished she'd go ahead.

"Y'all get in here!" Estelle called again, and the noisy guests once more crowded into the small dining room.

"Look at the teddy bear cake, Gracie!" cooed Grandpa Denny.

Sammy bounced excitedly. "Two cakes, Mama! Can I have a piece of each?"

"Who's got a camera?"

Somebody started a ragtag version of "Happy Birthday," and we managed to get *P.J.-Paul-and-Gracieeeee* in there in one breath before Precious screeched, "C'mon, blow out those candles 'fore that chocolate tower topples over!"

Paul huffed and puffed, but the sparkler candles wouldn't blow out, of course.

"Ha, I got it." Smirking, P.J. snatched them out of the cake and doused them in a glass of lemonade.

Estelle handed P.J. a knife. "At least there's a *real* cake under all that frosting, young man—unlike a certain birthday cake that shall go unmentioned." She leveled a tattletale eye at Harry Bentley to the knowing chuckles of guests from Manna House.

DaShawn hooted. "Yeah! My grandpa fooled Miss Estelle with a foam pillow cake on her birthday. He better watch out. She aimin' to get him back."

"Really, Mr. Bentley?" Young Paul was obviously impressed, seeing a new side of the unflappable doorman. "Cool. You want some real cake, Miss Estelle?"

"No, no." Mr. Bentley threw up his hands. "She's not safe around cake. I got the last one dumped on my head. Here, let me cut that cake. How big a piece you want?"

By now, everyone was laughing. As Harry Bentley handed out wide pieces of triple layer cake, I grinned happily. My sons were enjoying themselves. My sons were home. This party was a great idea, surrounded by our new friends. If only—

I glanced at Philip, cake in hand, head tilted as he listened to Paul, who was talking to his dad with his mouth full. Like a blip on a radar screen, my heart caught. This was how it should be—the four of us celebrating the boys' birthdays, together with friends. I had wanted so much for Philip to get to know my new friends and coworkers at the Manna House shelter. But our worlds here in Chicago had spun into different orbits, until they'd collided like meteors in space, reducing my sphere into jagged hunks of debris.

At least it felt that way, until God started to put my world back together again. There was still a big hole where that meteor hit, but at least I was functional again. Moving forward.

So why now? Maybe I should be glad Philip stayed for the party. Maybe he was realizing the penthouse wasn't a pie in the sky after all, up there by himself. Glad he could see so much life and love closer to the ground.

The blip got stronger. *Was he having second thoughts about us?* Not that I would ask him straight out! The party was drifting back down the hallway to the living room again, but on impulse I planted myself in front of Philip before he followed. "Hey. Thought you were only going to stay a few minutes."

He looked at me. Those eyes. "I didn't say that. You said that."

"But this is *my* party for the boys, Philip. You had them since yesterday; now this is my time. What's going on?"

He took a last bite of chocolate fudge cake, chewed,

swallowed, and then set his paper plate on the makeshift table. The look on his face . . . he almost seemed wistful. "Nothing's 'going on,' Gabby. This birthday party for the boys—our boys—is nice. Real nice. Just wish you'd let me know about it. Paul obviously wanted both his parents to be here. P.J. too. Even if things aren't working for us right now, we can—"

"Mom? Dad?" Paul, his curls damp on his forehead with the humidity, appeared in the doorway. "They're letting the baby open her presents. Can we open ours? Those boxes on the window seat are for us, aren't they, Mom?"

But Philip's words were still echoing in my ears. He'd called me Gabby. And did he really say *"right now"*? Meaning what?

"Mom?"

"Yes. Yes, of course, honey. Coming."

Paul disappeared again. I sighed. "Might as well stay while they open gifts," I said over my shoulder as I followed our youngest down the hall. This was so . . . awkward. Frankly, I wished the floor would open up and swallow Philip. Or me.

But it was hard to stay morose while Gracie was gleefully tearing paper off her packages. First a sorting toy, then a cute squeezable doll, a stuffed penguin, cute pink overalls, and pink tights with ruffles on the rump. Josh and Edesa opened the last few, because by this time Gracie was happily playing with the wrapping paper and the boxes.

Denny Baxter rubbed his hands together. "Okay! So who gets those big boxes on the window seat in the sunroom? Do we draw straws?"

"Back off, bud." Jodi backhanded her husband on the arm. "This is Gabby's show."

Jodi and I had managed to "wrap" the boxes in brown paper from grocery bags to hide the contents, and I'd stuck a big red bow on the top of each. Trying to ignore the big plastic bags sitting nearby with the Sports Authority logo, I said, "P.J., your birthday was first. The square one is yours."

For a moment, I saw P.J.'s fourteen-year-old cool veneer slip, and he also ripped off the brown paper and packing tape with gusto. Digging through inflated plastic padding, he lifted out a gleaming blue-and-gold lacrosse helmet, and matching gloves and shoulder pads. Lane Tech colors. "Uh . . ." He looked at his father. "Dad just got us some lacrosse equipment—and some shoes too."

Huh. Figured. I'd steeled myself for this.

"Well, guess we both know what you like," I said brightly. "Don't worry. We'll exchange it for some other gear."

"Can I keep the stuff Dad got? He let me pick out what I wanted. He got Paul some too, so we can practice together."

It was getting harder to maintain brightness. "We'll work it out, honey . . . Paul? You want to open the long box? No duplicates this time." My laugh fell flat.

Paul didn't seem to notice. "Yeah! You wanna help me, DaShawn?" Paul and Harry Bentley's grandson tore off the brown paper, then Paul stepped back, reading the box, his eyes big. "Mom! A Casio keyboard?! Awriiiight! Anyone got a knife? I wanna open it!"

Josh Baxter produced a pocketknife, and a few moments later Paul slid out the gleaming keyboard. "Wow, Mom! Just what I wanted! Can we set it up?"

I didn't know anything about keyboards, but Josh seemed to

know a great deal, and before long had it set up on the window seat, plugged in, and Paul was running his hands over the keys.

"Josh used to run the soundboard at SouledOut Community Church," Jodi murmured to me. "He had to set up a lot of keyboards!"

I was glad but already distracted by what was happening at the window seat. "Look at Jermaine."

Mabel's nephew had drawn alongside Paul, reverently touching the panel of buttons. "You play?" he asked Paul.

"Yeah. Some. Mostly my own stuff. Do you?"

The older boy's face was alight. "Yeah. Wanna do some stuff?"

"Sure!" Paul, on his knees in front of the keyboard, scooted over, and within moments Jermaine was pounding out something on the bass keys while Paul trilled a tune on the treble keys. Soon people were crowding around, listening and clapping as jazzy music filled the apartment.

Satisfaction seeped deep into my spirit. Well, one bull's-eye out of two tries wasn't bad. But just then I smelled Philip's familiar Armani aftershave and heard a whisper in my ear. "Good heavens, Gabrielle. Don't you realize that skinny black kid is a fairy? I don't want Paul hanging out with a sissy!"

"*Philip!*" I snapped, anxiously looking around to see who might have heard.

"Okay, okay." Philip put up his hands as if backing off. "I'm just saying . . ."

chapter 4

A fly droned in my ear. I brushed it away, unwilling to own that it was Monday already. Moving air from the window fan felt cool after the oppressive humidity that had hung over the city all weekend. Morning light filtered through the miniblinds, but the sun rose how early? Surely it couldn't be time to get up yet.

I cracked an eyelid. The digital alarm said 5:56. *Ahh.* A good half hour before the alarm. I curled my arms around my pillow, willing myself to fall asleep again. After all, once Monday started—

The fly came back, louder than the fan . . . then stopped.

Argh! I sat up straight and frantically ran fingers through my tangled cap of natural curls. All my life I'd lived with the morbid fear that one day a fly or mosquito or bee would crawl into the reddish-brown corkscrews that haloed my head and hide there. Make a nest. Raise a family.

People with sleek, straight hair didn't have to worry about that.

The fly had to go.

Turning on the bedroom light, I slid out of bed, grabbed a slipper, and stood stock-still. Zzzzzzz. There. I waited until the little bugger landed on the wall . . .

Swat!

Success.

But now I was wide-awake. Wrapping a thin kimono around my silky black boy-shorts-and-tank-top sleepwear, I padded out of my tiny bedroom at the rear of the apartment into the kitchen and started the coffee. After an inch had dripped into the pot, I poured a first cup, added milk from the fridge, and sat down at the little kitchen table while the rest of the pot was filling.

Monday already. It should have been a good weekend, except Philip's stupid comment about Mabel's nephew had upset me to no end. What if Mabel had overheard? Or Jermaine? Sure, the boy was a bit effeminate, but that didn't mean anything. Not at fourteen—did it? So what if he had a passion for music instead of football! I thought it was neat that Paul had found a kid who shared his creative genius, even if Jermaine was a couple of years older. Couldn't Philip see that?

I should talk with my boys about this, before Philip's mind-set poisoned their attitudes too.

Still, the welcome-home-birthday-party combo on Saturday had been fun . . . well, if I hadn't been so distracted by Philip inviting himself in when he brought the boys back. And ruining my birthday surprise for P.J. by buying similar stuff at the Sports Authority. At least Paul had been ecstatic about the Casio keyboard. A splurge on my part. Had nearly wiped out my last check from Manna House. But the life insurance money from my mother should arrive any day now. She would've approved of the keyboard for Paul.

Sunday was good too. I thought the boys had enjoyed their first visit to SouledOut Community Church. *"Start now, baby,"* Estelle had told me. *"Take 'em to church every Sunday. Tell 'em it's part of the package. They'll get used to it."* I hoped so. We'd been sporadic attenders at best back in Virginia, mostly for Christmas, Easter, weddings, and funerals. It helped that the boys already knew some of the folks at SouledOut, since half the people who had come to their party were members there. Well, maybe Mr. Bentley wasn't a member, but he'd been pretty regular since he'd started romancing Estelle Williams. Such beautiful people at SouledOut, a lovely mix of brown and black and white and tan. And even one redhead lately. Me.

Now it was Monday. P.J. started cross-country practice at Lane Tech today. Had to get him there by nine and pick him up at ten thirty—which meant I had to leave staff meeting a little early. I had a rental car for now until I could buy a car, but he'd have to learn how to take the bus sooner or later. The kids still had three weeks until school started, but fall sports practices started early. Lacrosse was a spring sport, so P.J. had signed up for cross-country to help him stay in condition. But, oh, Lord, I was so lucky to get the boys registered for school last week! Lane Tech College Prep for P.J.—just a day school, praise God—and Sunnyside Magnet School for Paul, a K-through-eight school right in our neighborhood. No, not luck. An answer to a lot of prayer. *Thank You, thank You, Lord . . .*

Getting the boys in school had been first on my agenda when

their grandfather arrived in Chicago a week ago with the boys. After P.J.'s summer lacrosse camp was over at the end of July, Mike Fairbanks had decided to drive their big Suburban from Petersburg, Virginia, in order to bring the boys' bikes too. Over Nana Marlene's protests, no doubt. Philip's mother still clung to the belief that P.J. and Paul were returning—*must* return—to George Washington College Prep boarding school in the fall because, well, that's what the Virginia Fairbanks males *did*. In fact, Philip had left the boys' bikes with his parents when we'd moved to Chicago last spring, assuming the same thing. *"They'll need them when they go back to school, Gabrielle."*

But now the bikes were here, courtesy of Philip's father. Locked in the basement of this six-flat. A symbolic reality that Chicago was now home for P.J. and Paul too. *Bless Mike Fairbanks, God.* Why was it only now, when my marriage with Philip was falling apart, that his father had become my advocate?

I refilled my coffee cup and let the hot liquid do its magic on my recalcitrant brain cells. *Staff meeting* . . . Should I bring up the idea about buying this six-flat and turning it into second-stage housing for homeless moms like Precious and Tanya? So far I'd only mentioned my crazy idea to Mabel. And my lawyer. Barely. But I needed some idea of what I was going to do when that check from my mother's insurance arrived—

"Mom?" Paul's sleepy voice made me jump. My twelve-year-old stood in the kitchen doorway in his pajama bottoms and skinny, bare torso.

"Hey, kiddo. What are you doing up? I was going to let you sleep in a bit longer."

"I'm thirsty."

"Okay. You want water or some O.J.?"

"Just water." Paul plopped into a kitchen chair, elbows on the table, chin in his hands. "Mom, how come you gave Grandma's dog to that old bag lady—Lucy what's-her-face? It's not fair. Dandy's like family!" He stuck out his lip, ignoring the glass of water I put in front of him.

Ah. Dandy. Knew I'd have to answer for that sooner or later. "You really want a dog, don't you, bud." A stall, I knew.

"Yeah. But we already had a dog . . . well, kinda. When Grandma—" The corner of his mouth curled into a small smile. "Did the homeless people at the shelter really call her 'Gramma Shep'?"

I smiled. "Sure did."

He sighed. "Cool. Anyway, when Grandma died, I thought Dandy would come live with us! I would've taken care of him."

I laid a hand on his arm. "I know you would, bud. But your dad, well, he didn't want a dog in the penthouse, you know that."

"Yeah, but . . . since you guys . . . I mean, since you . . ." Suddenly Paul's face took on the stricken look of a child who had just backed into the elephant in the middle of the room. His lip trembled. Before I could say anything, he tore out of the kitchen, tipping the chair over in the process, and slammed the door of his bedroom. I grabbed the glass of water before it tipped over too, waited thirty long seconds, and then padded quietly to his bedroom and opened the door.

Paul was sprawled on his bottom bunk, face in the pillow, shoulders shaking. "Aw, honey . . ." I sat on the edge of the bed and gathered him into my arms. "I know, kiddo, I know. It hurts."

We sat that way for several minutes, while he cried in my lap. Then he sniffed and sat up, glaring at me reproachfully. "Why do you guys want to get divorced anyway? What about P.J. and me?"

Divorce. Had Philip used that word around the boys? I swallowed. "I . . . we haven't said anything about divorce, honey. Just . . . we need some time apart right now. To work things out." *Oh, God. Am I getting his hopes up? After what Philip did, do I even want to work things out? Help me, Lord. I don't know what to say!*

There I was again, jumping right into the "help me!" prayers. But sometimes that's all I knew what to pray.

I drove the gray Nissan I'd rented into the parking lot of Lane Tech. The high school campus sprawled on the southwest corner of Addison and Western Avenue. Wide front lawn, classic brick building with several wings, athletic field, outdoor stadium, surrounded by city on all sides. Definitely a change from George Washington Prep, with its white-pillared campus tucked into the rolling countryside around Petersburg.

No uniforms or blazers here. Instead, the kids spilling out of other cars with their gym bags looked like a regular United Nations. Unlike other neighborhood high schools, Lane Tech College Prep took applications from all over the city and had a long waiting list. Fortunately, P.J.'s lacrosse camp this summer had helped shoehorn him into the list this fall. Lane Tech had an up-and-coming lacrosse team.

"Do you know where to go, kiddo? Want me to go with you?"

"No, Mom! I'll find it." P.J. piled out of the Nissan with his gym bag, wearing running shoes, shorts, and a T-shirt. Where did he get that confidence? New city. New school. Didn't know a soul. First year of high school, no less. When I'd started high school in Minot, North Dakota, I knew half the kids already from middle school.

Must be his dad's genes. Well.

I rolled down the passenger side window. "P.J., wait! Remember, I've got a ten o'clock staff meeting. I'll leave early, but it might be eleven by the time I get here. Meet me right here in the lot, okay?"

"I'll be fine, Mom. See ya." P.J. trotted off, gym bag over his shoulder.

A voice piped up from the backseat. "Can I ride up front with you, Mom? I'm twelve now."

I glanced at Paul in the rearview. "Sorry, bud. I checked it out. Backseat for *twelve and under*, not *under twelve*."

Scowling, Paul flipped his seat belt buckle and slid over behind me, where I couldn't see him. "Seat belt," I reminded, waiting until I heard it click before jockeying the car out of the lot. I'd given my just-twelve-year-old the choice of staying at the apartment and playing with his keyboard until I got home at two, or coming with me to the shelter. To my relief, he chose to come. And the shelter had a rec room with a Ping-Pong table, a TV, and games.

We rode in silence for a mile or so as traffic moved in starts and stops along Addison. Suddenly Paul said, "Hey! Is that Wrigley Field? Where we went that time to see the Cubs?"

The huge ballpark loomed in the distance like a poignant

memory. *Memorial Day weekend. Our first weekend together as a family after picking the boys up from school in Virginia. Still full of hopes and dreams for our new life in Chicago.* "That's it. That was a fun day, wasn't it?"

No answer. But I turned my head just enough to catch his face pressed against the window behind me, watching the curved walls of Wrigley Field slide past as I turned the corner by the Addison El station and headed north. I knew what was going on in his mind. *Would we ever have a fun day like that again, all of us together?*

A few blocks north of the ballpark, the Manna House shelter was tucked into a neighborhood known as Wrigleyville North. I parked on a side street, leaving plenty of exit room between me and the next parked car. I'd gotten blocked in once when I drove Philip's Lexus to work and had to leave it on the street overnight.

Another one of my so-called sins that contributed to the downfall of my marriage. Well, maybe not, but it didn't help.

"How come the shelter looks so much like a church?" Paul gazed up at the building as we waited at the top of the wide steps to be buzzed in. The brick building was less than a year old, and at its peak the wooden beams of a cross stretched top to bottom and side to side inside a circular stained-glass window.

"Because the old church that used to house the shelter burned down, so they rebuilt it along the lines of the original building— oh! Here we go." As the buzzer sounded, I pulled open the big oak door. "Hi, Angela!" I waved at the young receptionist in the glassed-in cubicle as we crossed the foyer. "Will you sign me in? And you remember my son Paul, don't you? He's here with me today."

"Sure! Hi, Paul. Nice to have a man about the place." The pretty olive-skinned girl winked at Paul beneath her sleek black bangs, then grabbed the phone as it rang.

Huh. I pulled open the double doors into the multipurpose room. *She doesn't have to worry about some ol' fly making a nest in that straight silky hair.* A distinct advantage of Asian parentage.

The multipurpose room was abuzz, not untypical for Monday morning. "Sarge," the shelter's no-nonsense night manager, was still on site, arguing with Wanda, a rather verbose Jamaican woman—one of the few who managed to stand up to Sarge's Italian toughness. Someone was sleeping on one of the couches with a jacket over her head, couldn't tell who. A couple of unfamiliar faces glanced our way as we came in and looked away, just sitting, not doing anything. Must have come in over the weekend. Sheila, a heavy-chested black woman who usually kept to herself, was vacuuming the various rugs that carpeted the room in a patchwork, one of the many chores residents did daily. I still didn't know her very well, even though I'd been a resident here myself for several weeks this summer. I really should—

"Paul!" A childish voice greeted us from across the large open room. Sammy came running. "I didn't know you was gonna come with your mom today. You wanna play with me an' Keisha? We just started Monopoly, but it's funner with more."

Paul shrugged. "I guess. Okay, Mom?"

"Sure. I'll be downstairs in my office if you need me." *Perfect.* Keisha was ten, the oldest of the few children currently at the shelter—well, not counting sixteen-year-old Sabrina, who qualified as a "child" because she was here with her mother. Keisha's grandmother, Celia, a vacant-eyed woman in her fifties, seemed to be her guardian, though I didn't know their story. Thank goodness Paul didn't mind playing with younger kids. Monopoly would keep him busy until staff meeting was over at least, if the kids didn't end up fighting.

Manna House was designed for homeless women, not families, and didn't have enough kids to develop a full-blown youth program, but the shelter occasionally took in moms with young children if there was bed space. And residents like Precious McGill and Tanya—I didn't even know her last name—felt it keenly, not being able to make a home for their kids.

Which was exactly why my "House of Hope" idea stuck like peanut butter to the roof of my spirit.

I scurried downstairs to the lower level, which housed the shelter's dining room, kitchen, laundry facilities, rec room— and my office. A former broom closet. Still, I got a rush every time I unlocked the door with the nameplate: Gabby Fairbanks, Program Director.

Except—the door was already unlocked. And a ribbon of light shone from beneath the door of the windowless room. *What?* Had I left it unlocked all weekend, and the light on too? Or . . .

I tentatively pushed the door open, unsure what I'd find.

A yellow furball explosion nearly knocked me over. As I protected myself from the excited wriggling dog, I saw a familiar craggy face under a cap of thinning gray hair grinning at me from my desk chair.

Lucy!

chapter 5

"Lucy Tucker, you goose! You scared the bejeebers out of me."
I bent down and gave the wriggling yellow dog with her a good
scratch on the rump. "Okay, okay, glad to see you too, Dandy.
Where have you two been the last couple of weeks?"

"Around." Lucy's standard answer. Don't know why I bothered to ask.

I hadn't seen Lucy but once since we'd come back from North
Dakota in July, when she'd ridden along with my mom's casket in
the Manna House van to bury my mother. What a strange friendship they'd formed! Lucy, the streetwise "bag lady," and Martha
Shepherd, my slightly demented mother, who had spent most
of her life in a small town on the Western prairie. Both of them
in their seventies—actually, that was a guess in Lucy's case—but
there the similarity ended.

I brought my mother to Chicago when it was obvious she
could no longer live alone. Brought her to work with me at the
shelter so she didn't have to stay alone at the penthouse. Until my

husband gave his ultimatum: find another place for Grandma or send her home. According to Philip, the penthouse just wasn't big enough for a family of four *and* a mother-in-law *and* her rambunctious mutt.

For Lucy it was simple. Martha should stay at Manna House. "She homeless, ain't she?"

My mother became "Gramma Shep" to the other residents—happy to just sit in the multipurpose room while drama bustled around her, patiently listening to anyone who wanted to talk or vent, tickled to read a story to a whiny kid. Streetwise Lucy, who normally only came to the shelter when she had to ("Too many rules!"), took over care for Dandy, walking him every day, something my mother could no longer do—especially not in Chicago. A responsibility that bonded Lucy to my mother and Dandy in a special way I didn't have the heart to break.

Which is why I gave Dandy to Lucy when my mother died.

Something I still needed to explain to my youngest son.

I dumped my purse and tote bag on the desk. "You two doing all right?"

"We doin' okay. Dandy makin' friends with half the city. But I stopped by ta pick up some more dog food from that stash ya got here—ya know, when he was Hero Dog."

Oh yes, Hero Dog. The night Dandy had scared off a midnight intruder. When the media got hold of the story, Chicagoans smothered "Hero Dog" with bags of food, chew toys, and stuffed animals. And checks for the shelter. Which was how we got that big whale of a white passenger van the residents dubbed "Moby Van." Most of the other stuff got donated to an organization that helped fixed-income seniors care for their pets, except for six months' worth of dog food we kept stashed here for Dandy.

"No problem. You got room in your cart for a whole bag?" Lucy's cart stood in a corner of my office, relatively empty, considering. "Uh, where's all your stuff?"

"In the wash. Didn't have no quarters for the Laundromat. Angela said I could use the machines if nobody else had 'em signed up. That's why I came early. Me an' Dandy been here since breakfast."

"Well, I'm glad to see you both." Definitely glad to see Dandy looking fit and healthy. I couldn't help worrying how he'd fare as a "street dog." Cold weather, though . . . that would be a different story, something we needed to talk about.

But not now. "Hey, I know somebody upstairs who'd love to see Dandy. My boys are back, Lucy. I got them registered for school and everything. Paul's here today. You mind taking Dandy upstairs to see him? I've got work to do before staff meeting anyway."

"Okay by me." The old lady hefted herself out of my desk chair, dressed as usual in several layers of mismatched clothes. "If you think your kid's nose ain't gonna get outta joint 'cause Dandy's with me."

Ah. Very astute. Maybe I should leave well enough alone. Paul was probably immersed in the Monopoly game by now, but if he saw Dandy . . .

No. What if he found out Dandy had been here and he didn't get to see him? He'd *really* feel like he'd been cut out of Dandy's life.

"Mm. He might. But I still think he'd love to see Dandy. Go on . . . and thanks. You can leave your cart here if you want."

Lucy pondered. She rarely went anywhere without that cart. "Well, okay. If you gonna be here the whole time. C'mon, Dandy." She lumbered through the door, Dandy at her heels, but before they disappeared I heard her holler, "Hiya, Estelle! Whatchu makin' for lunch today?"

I shut the door, isolating my cocoon. If I got started talking to Estelle, staff meeting would be here and I wouldn't have gotten a thing done!

I was startled by a knock at my door. Estelle Williams poked her head in. "You comin' to staff meeting, girl?"

"What—? Oh, thanks, Estelle." Where had the time gone? I'd been trying to take five or ten minutes to pray before starting my workday—how hard should that be?—but it was still a struggle not to check my e-mail first to see if there was anything urgent and plunge right back into work I'd left undone on Friday. Especially since I'd cut back to half time for the next few weeks until the boys started school. Fewer hours. Same amount of work.

But I grabbed a pad of paper and a couple of folders and scurried up the stairs behind the shelter's lunch cook, who was still wearing her white net cap and big white apron over wide navy blue slacks and a rumpled white blouse. "You go on, Estelle," I huffed at the top of the stairs. "I need to check on Paul and try to catch Mabel before the meeting."

"Then, girl, you shoulda come up ten minutes ago. I'll save you a seat." Estelle had a mild way of scolding me, like she'd dripped honey all over a prickly pear.

Mabel was striding across the multipurpose room, professional as always, notebook in hand, makeup perfectly blended with her creamy walnut skin, talking to Stephanie Cooper, a thirtysomething social worker with straight, straw-colored hair and wearing jeans, who worked two days a week at the shelter as a case manager. "Mabel!" I called. "Can I see you a sec? Oh wait . . ." I glanced around the multipurpose room. No kids. "Oh no! Anybody seen Paul and Sammy and Keisha?"

"They wanted to take the dog for a walk," one of the couch-sitters offered.

"Not by themselves!" I shrieked. All I got was a shrug. "Sorry, Mabel," I called over my shoulder. "Gotta find Paul." I dashed into the foyer, where Angela was turning over phone duty to one of the residents for the next hour. "Angela, did you see the kids go out with Dandy? Was Lucy with them?"

"Yeah, I saw them. Not Lucy though. But I think Hannah went with them—no, wait. It was Tanya."

At Hannah's name, I was about to bolt out the door, staff meeting or no staff meeting. The wannabe cosmetician was barely twenty, and not the brightest crayon in the box. But if Tanya had gone with them, it was probably okay. Sammy's mom was a real sweetie, one of the young women I was hoping to recruit for the House of Hope, if it ever materialized.

But now . . . Oh no! I'd wanted to check with Mabel about bringing up the House of Hope idea at staff meeting! Could I catch her before—?

I ran back through the multipurpose room, past the TV room and toddler playroom to the "schoolroom," which boasted four computers, several school desks, and assorted chairs. Mabel was already praying over a circle of bowed heads crowned with Stephanie's straw-colored hair, all varieties of black hair—straight, straightened, kinky, and salt-and-pepper—and now my mop of auburn curls as I slipped into the chair next to Estelle.

Rats! I didn't get a chance to ask Mabel first.

"... praise You, Lord, for Your hand of protection over each resident in this house. You are the Creator and Sustainer of every woman who comes through our doors, each one precious in Your sight. You are a gracious and merciful God, patient with all our shortcomings ..."

Mabel's prayers still took some getting used to. I expected staff prayers to dive into the long list of needs we had at the shelter— more volunteer church groups to cook the evening meal ... someone to cover night duty for Sarge, who wanted to take a week of vacation ... how to help the residents over fifty, whose possibilities for job training and finding a job were almost nil ... the used-up girl who came in off the street last week, desperately wanting help to kick her habit and to get away from her pimp, but who only managed to stay half a day before the drug-induced hunger in her body drove her back out to her old life. The needs at the shelter were all more or less desperate. But Mabel always started meetings with "just lovin' on God," as Estelle called it.

As Mabel breathed out her last murmur of worship and opened her notebook to read that day's agenda, I quickly scribbled a note and passed it to her. *I'd like to bring up the House of Hope idea, get some feedback from the staff. What do you think?—G*

She glanced at the note, tucked it in her notebook, and continued reading her agenda. A report from Sarge about the fight in the second-floor shower over the weekend. Reviewing the new residents who had come in the past week, their case management assignments, any special needs. Gabby's new schedule for the next few weeks. Need for more case managers by the time cold weather filled up the shelter. Suggestion from residents for renaming the multipurpose room . . .

I tried to catch Mabel's eye, pointing to my note. Calling on Sarge to make her weekly report, Mabel pulled out my note, wrote something on the bottom, folded it, and passed it back to me. I opened the note. *Not today. Let's go to the board with it first. Is Saturday good?*

The board? I knew I'd need to talk to the board at some point. But . . . Saturday? I wasn't ready for something that official! I'd been hoping to brainstorm the idea with some of the staff and my friends here at the shelter to get their ideas. Besides, it was going to be hard keeping it under my hat another whole week. I really wanted—needed—to talk about it. Was it a good idea? Or just out-and-out crazy?

Well, at least I had an appointment with Lee Boyer, my Legal Aid lawyer, on Wednesday. I definitely needed to talk to him about my options. He'd been the one who went out of his way to get me out of the shelter and into an apartment so I could prove to a judge I was capable of providing for my boys in the custody suit he planned to file on my behalf. Once I had my own apartment it'd be a "slam dunk," according to Lee.

Funny thing, Philip hadn't even protested once I got the ball rolling. I'd expected all kinds of delays and roadblocks to bringing the boys back. Maybe he'd been counting on his parents joining his fight to keep the boys in Virginia—"for school," of course. Frankly, I'd expected an uphill battle with all the Fairbanks. But to my surprise, Mike Fairbanks had sided with me when Philip dumped me. Said he'd bring the boys back as soon as I had a place to live. And he was as good as his word.

". . . and Tawny," Mabel was saying. "Bright young thing. Got dumped out of the foster-care system when she turned eighteen last month, has been staying with different friends until she came here a few days ago. She seems very motivated to finish her GED, get a job, and go on to college."

I'd only been paying half attention until I heard the name. "Tawny? Yeah, Jodi Baxter said she showed up for the typing class Saturday morning." I'd no sooner joined the conversation than the hands of the schoolroom clock caught my eye. Almost 10:45! I jumped up. "Oops. I have to pick up P.J. at Lane Tech. Sorry. It's only for a few weeks until school starts." I inched apologetically toward the door. "I'll check in when I get back to see what I missed."

Mabel nodded. "Okay. We only have a few more items. We'll table the discussion about a new name for the multipurpose room. I think you'll want to be here for that, Gabby. Some of the residents think we ought to rename it in memory of Gramma Shep—but we can talk about it next week."

I almost sat down again. Name the multipurpose room after my mom? Of course I wanted to be here for that discussion! Maybe—

But I made myself slip out and run for the car.

Still no Paul that I could see—inside or outside the shelter.

Oh, that boy! He was going to be grounded big time for not telling me he was going out!

But even as I jumped into the rental car and peeled rubber

going around the first corner, I knew I only had myself to blame. Why did I think I could handle this superwoman single mom stuff—program director for a shelter full of aimless homeless women, sole wage earner, solo parent most of the week, chauffeur, shopper, entertainer, housekeeper, cook, prospective real estate investor—when for the past fifteen years I'd basically traded my aspirations and a stiff backbone for the comfort of Southern charm and old money . . . like Esau in the Sunday school stories I'd grown up with, trading his birthright for a pot of savory stew.

chapter 6

The parking lot at Lane Tech was virtually empty by the time I pulled in at 10:59. P.J. was waiting at the same spot where I'd let him out, except his T-shirt was wet around the neck and armpits, and his dark hair lay damp on his forehead. "Sorry, kiddo," I said as he jumped into the front seat. "Did you have to wait long?"

He shrugged.

"Put on your seat belt . . . How did it go? Looks like the coach worked you hard."

"Yeah." He turned his head toward the window, but not before I caught the hint of a grin playing the corner of his mouth.

I hooted. "You rascal. Did you run? I bet you came in first the very first day."

He shook his head. "Not really." But the grin widened. "But I kept up with the front group. Coach called me out, said, 'Good job, Fairbanks.'"

I reached over and rumpled his damp hair. "Well, I second that, *Fairbanks*. Good job! Why don't you call your dad?" I handed

P.J. my cell phone. "He'd like to hear how your first day of practice went, I'm sure." A self-righteous amicability smothered the
angst I'd been feeling just fifteen minutes ago. Yeah, I could be the
mature single-again mom, generously keeping the jerk father in the
picture, refusing to make my sons choose between their parents.

But he shrugged and handed the phone back. "Maybe later."

I dropped P.J. off at the apartment, telling him I'd be off work
at two and to stay put. The rest of the afternoon, we'd do whatever he wanted. When I got back to the shelter, the dog walkers
had returned and Paul was triumphantly purchasing another tiny
plastic house with Monopoly money to put on Park Place. Still
feeling magnanimous, I decided to wait until we were alone to
talk with him about leaving the premises. I knocked on Mabel's
office door instead.

"Sorry I had to leave staff meeting early. What'd I miss?"

Mabel turned from her computer. "I was just typing up the
minutes. But sit down, Gabby. Let's talk about this transitional
housing idea of yours. If you want to bring it to the board on
Saturday, we need a proposal—description of the property, how
it's going to be financed, how to partner with city resources . . ."

I sat, nodding my head as the director listed things the board
would want to know. When she finished, I drew in a big breath
and then blew it out again. "Um, write up a proposal. You're
right. Definitely right. Except . . . I don't *know* how it could
work! That's why I need help, brainstorming with people who do
know this kind of stuff. I mean, what if I gave Manna House two
hundred thousand for a down payment? A donation, you know,
earmarked for purchase of the building. Could Manna House pay
the monthly mortgage?"

Mabel just looked at me for a long moment or two, tapping the eraser end of a pencil on her desk. Then her eyebrows—those perfectly plucked arches—went up, and her dark eyes widened just a fraction. "A donation. That's a pretty hefty donation for someone who was penniless a few weeks ago. Is that wise? Would you have anything left to live on? Besides your *huge* salary for part-time work here at Manna House, of course." Her full lips parted in a teasing smile.

"I don't know. I mean, yeah, I'd have something left. Not a whole lot, but something." Something like fifty grand. Which I was counting on to help meet expenses for the boys, and I'd need a hunk of it pretty soon to get a car.

Mabel tapped the pencil eraser a few more times and then put it down. "Have you talked to your lawyer? You're still working with Lee Boyer at Legal Aid, aren't you?"

I nodded. "Yes. I mean, he's the one filing the custody petition for me. But no, I haven't had time to really discuss this idea with him." Not for lack of Lee's persistence. He'd called me several times the past few weeks, but I was feeling confused about Lee Boyer. Was he my lawyer? My friend? Both? Or . . . more? I'd cancelled my last two appointments to give myself some space. "Just until I get the boys settled," I'd told him.

"Well, talk to your lawyer, Gabby. You need to get your own finances squared away and make some decisions about your situation. You and Philip have only been separated . . . what? Less than two months? And you just lost your mother. That's a lot of change and a lot of stress. Might not be the best time to make a major decision like this."

I blinked back sudden tears. "But I really think this is God's idea, Mabel." My voice croaked. "Jodi Baxter thinks so too. I don't know how it all fits together, but—"

How could I explain what the shelter meant to me? It was here I'd met God again, discovered He'd been whispering my name and calling me to "come" all those years I'd left Him behind. But I couldn't hear Him until I'd lost everything. Now I wanted to give something back. I didn't want to forget what it felt like to be in Precious's and Tanya's shoes, with no home for my children.

I felt Mabel's hand on mine. "Gabby." Her voice was gentle. "If this is God's idea, then it's going to happen. God's timing is perfect. You don't have to rush it."

"I know." I fished for a tissue and blotted my eyes. Probably raccoon eyes by now.

Mabel's hand left mine and she sat back. "But tell you what. Talk to Boyer, get his legal advice, and maybe he can recommend a financial adviser. And write down your vision for this House of Hope idea, wild as it may sound. Plus as many facts as you can—cost of the building, purchase requirements, repairs needed, whatever you can pull together. Put it down on paper. Meanwhile, I'll do some fact-finding on current city and federal resources for rent subsidies—something I've been wanting to do anyway. We'll put it on the agenda for Saturday . . . but we can always take it off, Gabby, if you decide not to pursue it right now, or just need more time."

"Thanks, Mabel. I really appreciate this."

"And one more thing."

A grin tickled my mouth. With Mabel, there was always "one more thing."

"Pray about it. The psalmist said, 'Unless the Lord builds the house, its builders labor in vain.' That would definitely apply to *this* house. Do you have a prayer partner?"

"Uh . . . not exactly."

"Find one. Estelle, Edesa, Jodi Baxter . . . someone. Pray about it together. I'll be praying about it too."

"I'd like that." I stood up to go. "Thanks again, Mabel."

"Oh—and one more thing."

Now I laughed aloud.

"Okay, okay, never mind." She waved me off and turned to her computer, pretending to work.

"Mabel! What?"

She whirled her desk chair to face me. "Your Paul seems to get along well with the kids here. The last few weeks before school starts are likely to be nuts around here, since city summer camps are over and we don't really have any activities for the kids going on. Do you think he'd want to volunteer a few days a week? During the time you're here? Just play with the kids, be a big brother. We could give him a volunteer T-shirt."

My feet wanted to dance. "*Yes!* I mean, I'll have to ask him. No, better yet, *you* ask him. Make it official. Give me ten minutes to disappear, though. Don't want him to think it was my idea." I darted out the door—and two seconds later poked my head back in. "Oh, one more thing," I snickered. "He already has a T-shirt. You gave one to both boys the first time they visited."

Still grinning, I slipped through the multipurpose room and down the stairs without Paul noticing me. I'd been worried about finding something for the boys to do until school started, even with my shortened hours. But look at God! He'd answered my prayer before I'd even prayed about it.

"Yeah," I overhead Paul telling P.J. in the backseat as we headed for Foster Avenue Beach later that afternoon. "Ms. Turner asked if I'd be a volunteer at the shelter, helping out with the little kids. She gave me another T-shirt since I've worn that other one a lot. I'm supposed to wear it so the kids know I'm the boss."

"Ha!" P.J. snorted. "Did you tell her you used the first one to clean your bicycle after you greased the wheels?"

I stifled a laugh and stayed out of it. Younger brothers always lived in their older siblings' shadows. But Mabel's volunteer job offer had definitely raised Paul's status. His big brother couldn't tease him for "playing with the little kids" if it was a *job*.

Foster Avenue Beach was within sight of Richmond Towers, but the boys had already been there a few times earlier in the summer, and this is where they'd swim when they were with their dad, so familiarity and consistency had points in their favor. I spread my beach towel so my back was to the row of luxury high-rises in the distance. P.J. and Paul were both good swimmers and the beach had several lifeguards on duty, so I let my mind and body relax, watching the boys dash for the shoreline.

It didn't get much better than this . . . except for the hole in my heart. But I stuffed Philip's rejection underneath the pleasure of the moment, smothering the nagging pain with the warmth of the sun on my skin, the breeze running gentle fingers through my tangled curls, and the sheer joy of watching P.J. and Paul cavort in the water.

And the long envelope from Putnam, Fields, and Pederson that was in the mailbox when Paul and I got home from the shelter the next day definitely buoyed my spirits. A check for two hundred thousand dollars, my share of my mother's term life insurance policy.

I turned right around and drove to the little branch bank near Manna House where I'd opened a new account and put it all in my checking account. For now. And then I walked a few yards to the Emerald City Coffee Shop underneath the Sheridan El Station, ordered the Kona Mocha—maxi-size—and two of their to-die-for buttery pumpkin cookies, settled back on one of their cushiony couches near the front window . . . and started to cry with sheer thankfulness.

"Mom!" Paul accosted me just as I was heading out the door of the shelter at ten thirty on Wednesday to pick up P.J. from his third day of cross-country practice. After taking him home, I needed to go straight to Legal Aid for my eleven o'clock appointment with Lee Boyer. "Mom! Why don't we take Sammy and Keisha swimming with us at Foster Beach this afternoon? They never get to go swimming!"

Keisha and Sammy? No way would that be relaxing! I doubted if either of them knew how to swim, and I'd have to keep an eagle eye on them. I opened my mouth to say no, and then hesitated. Here I was taking time off for a personal appointment from my already shortened day, and even though Mabel was generous with flexible hours for doctor's appointments and the like, I still felt I should make up the time somehow. Taking Keisha and Sammy swimming with my boys this afternoon would certainly fall under my job description of program director for the shelter.

"Good idea, buddy. But it has to be after my appointment at Legal Aid, and they need to ask their moms. You work it out, okay? I'll be back to pick you up after lunch—and if they don't have swimsuits, tell them to bring an extra pair of shorts and a T-shirt!"

I smiled as Paul ran off in his orange-and-black T-shirt that said "Manna House Volunteer" across the front, with "I'm part of God's miracle" in small letters beneath. The week was settling into a workable routine. P.J. seemed just as glad to chill out at the apartment after his sweaty workout with the Lane Tech cross-country team, and by two o'clock when I got off work, we were all ready to do something together. The beach. Grocery shopping. Maybe the bike trail along the lake one day—though I had to get a bicycle first. And Mr. Bentley was picking us up to go to the zoo on Thursday.

After all the pain and uncertainty of the first part of the summer, these few weeks felt like being rocked in God's lap. *Thank You, Jesus. Thank You . . .*

I was still basking in the blessings of God when I walked into Lee Boyer's office at eleven. "Hey, Gabby!" he said, jumping up from his desk and giving me a quick hug and big smile. A professional hug, I told myself. "Glad you didn't cancel another appointment. I've got good news! We've got a court date to hear your petitions on"—he glanced at some papers—"September eighth. That's three weeks from Friday. I figured you'd want time to get P.J. and Paul settled in school." He looked up and grinned again. "I'm eager to hear how it's going since your boys got back."

Lee Boyer. Dressed in his usual jeans, Birkenstock sandals, open-necked short-sleeved dress shirt, brown hair with gold flecks brushed neatly to one side, and friendly light brown eyes behind retro wire-rims. He was such a down-home guy. I'd liked him from the first time I'd made an appointment at Legal Aid, and he'd certainly gone out of his way to help me find a place to live so I could get custody of my sons. He seemed to like me too . . . which got a little confusing at times.

Like now. I hadn't come for a personal chat. "I . . . the boys are fine . . . but I really need some legal advice about money."

"Ah. The inheritance your folks left you. That's good, that's good, Gabby. Now that you've got an apartment and a nest egg in the bank, that can only strengthen our case for getting custody of the boys. Not that I have any doubt that a judge will rule in your favor." He smiled and leaned back in his desk chair. "I suppose you want to set up some kind of trust fund for the boys?"

I licked my lips. "Well, not exactly. I have an idea, something I want to talk to you about. The building where I live . . . it's still for sale, right?"

Lee peered at me over the top of his wire rims. "As far as I know. But if you're thinking of buying property, don't you want to look at some single family homes? Or a condo here in the city? You don't have to jump into anything right away. The apartment you're renting is sufficient as far as your legal case is—"

"It's not about my custody case." I squirmed a bit in my

chair. "It's that building. I want to buy a six-flat. And live in the building. It's all part of this idea . . ." Taking a deep breath, I told Lee about my idea of purchasing a building that would provide second-stage housing for some of the homeless moms at Manna House, real apartments where they could be a family with their kids, not sharing bunk rooms in an emergency shelter. "I even have a name for it. The House of Hope." I grinned. Just saying the name triggered goose bumps up my arms.

Lee blew out a breath. "Whew. When you get an idea, you don't waste any time jumping out of the starting gate, do you!" He leaned forward, his eyes searching mine. "Gabby, it's okay to take some time to get yourself squared away before jumping into such a big financial commitment." He cocked his head. "How much are we talking about here anyway? Your inheritance, I mean."

"Uh, well, my share of my parents' life insurance is two hundred thousand, plus another fifty when the sale on their house closes—and that's after Mom's attorney pays the inheritance taxes. My aunt is buying the house, so it's a sure thing."

His eyebrows went up. "Two hundred fifty thousand? That's it?"

"Well, yes. Of course I wouldn't put all of it toward the building. But that's why I need some financial advice. How much would I need for a down payment? And what would be the best way to do something like that? I mean, should I just make a major donation to Manna House, earmarked for purchase of this building? Seems like that would save me a lot on taxes. Or should I use my money as a down payment on the building and buy it myself? I mean, two hundred thousand would be a substantial down payment, wouldn't it?"

Lee threw up his hands. "Whoa, whoa, whoa. Gabby, slow down. Look, I'm not a financial adviser, but as your lawyer, I would *not* advise you to give away the major portion of your inheritance like that. Really, you need some sound financial advice, someone who can help you invest your money, make it work for you. That's not a large inheritance—it's nice, but it doesn't put you on easy street."

I stared at him. Words rushed to the tip of my tongue, like foot soldiers defending my idea, but I pushed them back, afraid my voice would quiver.

Lee's voice softened. "Gabby, I'm not just speaking as your lawyer, but as your friend. I really care about what happens to you and your boys. And this . . . this idea just doesn't seem wise. Noble, yes. But let's get things settled with the custody case, follow through on your divorce, give yourself some time. And as I said before, the divorce settlement could give you a nice financial footing as well."

Divorce. Why did he keep bringing that up? As for time . . . "No, there's not plenty of time," I said, tipping my chin up. "Not if someone else buys the six-flat in the meantime. I don't think you understand. This House of Hope is very important to me. It has to be that building. I'm already living there. It's close to Manna House. It's for sale. I'm going to be talking to the Manna House board on Saturday, and I wanted your advice how best to go about it. But if you're just going to shoot it down . . ." I stood up. "Maybe I'd better go."

"Gabby, wait." Lee got up and came around his desk. "Please sit."

I slowly sat back down as he perched on the edge of his desk.

"Okay. I hear you. This idea is important to you. If you are determined to go ahead, then my advice is, buy the building yourself. Property is a good investment. Pay the mortgage payments with rent from the other apartments. I don't know how that would work with subsidized housing—but the board of Manna House should be able to figure that out. I'm pretty sure there's a Low-Income Housing Trust Fund that works with a number of landlords to provide subsidized rents."

I nodded. "All right. That makes sense. I don't want to do something foolish. But . . ." How could I explain to Lee that this wasn't just my idea, but an idea that God had dropped into my spirit?

Lee reached out and took one of my hands in his. "There is one more thing we need to talk about. With this inheritance you've just received, you don't exactly qualify for Legal Aid any more." He grinned mischievously. "I think I can make a case for following through on the petitions we've already started on your custody case. But you're going to need to hire another lawyer to handle things beyond that."

I stared at my hand in his, his touch sending tiny waves of heat all the way up my arm and making my heart jackhammer. "But I don't want another lawyer. You've been a great help to me, Lee. I mean, you understand my situation. I don't want to start all over again with someone else."

He smiled gently. "Well, look at it this way. If I'm not your lawyer, that doesn't mean I can't keep on being your friend. In fact, if we end our professional relationship, it opens the door to other possibilities . . . and I'd like that, Gabby. Very much."

chapter 7

Open the door to what other possibilities?

All the way back to the shelter, Lee's quip replayed itself in my brain like an LED advertising billboard. A dozen reactions sprang to the tip of my tongue—*Of course we can be friends . . . Don't cut me loose now; I need you! . . . I'm still married, so back off, buddy!*—but for the life of me, I couldn't remember what I said in return. I'd stammered something, said I really had to go, could he recommend a financial adviser, told him I'd call. I think. Or had I bumbled out of there like a tongue-tied idiot?

I wasn't ready for that kind of friend.

And yet . . . the memory of Lee's touch sent heat into my cheeks again. I liked that he found me attractive at the ripe old age of thirty-nine. And I couldn't deny I found *him* attractive. Even more, he made me feel safe. At ease in a way I never had been with Philip. I liked that he had stood up for me in front of Philip the day of my mom's funeral. He seemed to like me for who I was—even though he'd met me at my messy worst. Most of all, he believed in me. Made me feel like a real person.

But divorce Philip? I still kept thinking I was going to wake up from a bad dream. That Philip would show up, realize what he'd done, beg me to forgive him, and say he wanted us to be a family again. After all, we had two sons—growing boys who needed both their parents. Philip and I had been in love once. Surely there was a spark somewhere under all the debris from our wrecked marriage that could be fanned once more into a flame.

And if there was, I didn't want to do anything to snuff it out forever.

Parking the rental, I managed to dash into Manna House while lunch was still being served, eat Estelle's midweek offering of sloppy joes and mustard potato salad, assure Sammy's mom and Keisha's grandmother that the beach was safe and I'd have the kids back to the shelter by five, and herd Paul and his charges out of there by two o'clock—all without raising Estelle's suspicions that I was feeling like a teenager who'd just been asked out on her first date. I had to totally avoid her to do that, though. Didn't know how she did it, but Estelle seemed to read me like Gandalf the Wizard reading his crystal ball.

Both Sammy and Keisha were afraid to wade into the lake farther than their knees, but they found plenty to do digging in the wet sand with a plastic Big Gulp cup someone had left behind. Soon Paul was showing them how to pack the wet sand into walls and forts, decorated with rocks and sticks. Even P.J. got involved, scooping out an inlet that captured Lake Michigan's small tide creeping up the sand—who knew the Great Lakes had tides?—into their man-made moat.

"Can we go to the beach tomorrow, Miss Gabby?" Keisha begged, hanging on to me for dear life when I brought them back to Manna House.

I shook my head. Mr. Bentley had invited the boys and me to go to the zoo with him and DaShawn. "Maybe next week, okay?" I should have known that was as good as a promise as far as Sammy and Keisha were concerned.

Mr. Bentley picked us up at two thirty sharp the next day in his RAV4.

P.J. had balked that morning when I reminded the boys we had a date for the zoo that afternoon. "Aw, Mom, do I hafta go? I mean, a zoo's a zoo, I've seen a gazillion of them." Hardly true, though Philip and I had taken the boys to the Metro Richmond Zoo numerous times when they were small. "And it's not like we're going with someone my age," he fussed. "DaShawn's just a little kid." Which *was* true, though DaShawn would surely protest the label. And then the zinger. "Don't you know any white kids my age? We didn't have to hang out with black kids back in Petersburg."

Half a dozen snapbacks fought for airtime as I whisked breakfast dishes through the sudsy dishwater, my back to P.J. so he couldn't read my face. What was going on here? Was I raising a teenage bigot? But hanging around people like my boss, who calmly dealt with several crises every week at the shelter, must've been having a good effect on me because I maintained my composure and decided not to make it a big deal.

"I'd really like it if you came with us, P.J. It's supposed to rain tomorrow—this'll give us something to do together while the weather's nice. We won't have time to explore the city once you've got homework every day and cross-country meets on the weekends. I'm sure you'll make friends your age once school starts. But until you make your own friends, guess you're stuck hanging out with mine." Mustering a grin, I grabbed a dish towel, whirled it into a rope, and snapped him with it.

"Okay, okay," he said, backing off. "Just don't expect me to entertain the twerps."

As we piled into Mr. Bentley's compact SUV later that day, I almost offered to sit in the back with the "twerps," but Mr. B gallantly held the front passenger door open for me, so I let the boys sort out the seating arrangement for themselves. Once we hit Lake Shore Drive, it didn't take long to find ourselves at Lincoln Park Zoo, situated at the south end of Lincoln Park, which ran alongside the Drive going toward the Loop. As Mr. B pulled up to the entry booth and fished for his wallet, I dove for my purse. "I thought you said the zoo was free!"

"It is." Mr. Bentley winked at me. "They just gouge you for the parking . . . Now you put that away. This is my treat. It'd be the same for the car whether it was just DaShawn an' me, or a carful."

"Hm. Maybe we ought to ride bikes next time—right, boys?"

Only groans from the backseat. But I was half-serious. A bike trail ran the full length of Chicago's lakeshore. It'd be fun to bike it one of these days.

We got zoo maps and let the boys pick what areas they

wanted to see. "Gorillas!" DaShawn shouted. Paul voted for "big animals like giraffes and stuff." P.J. shrugged and managed to look bored. But I noticed that Mr. Bentley shut one eye and squinted with the other, holding the map at different distances, as if he was having difficulty reading it.

He caught me watching him and quickly stuffed the map in his pants pocket. "Okay! Big animals first. They're at the north end, and if we're lucky, the polar bears might be swimming. Then we can work our way down to the Gorilla House." Before DaShawn could complain, he herded the boys over to one of the food vendors and bought hot dogs and lemonade for everybody.

As we trailed the boys past the rhinos, ostriches, and camels, I decided to just out with it. "Are you having trouble with your eyes, Mr. B?"

"Nah. It's nothing. Just got this weird blind spot in my left eye."

"A blind spot! You should get it checked out. An ophthalmologist might be able to do something before it gets worse."

He shrugged. "Yeah, already did. Doctor's hoping it'll just go away. Me too!"

"Grandpa! Grandpa!" DaShawn was yelling at us from the bottom of a ramp that led to an underwater window in the polar bear exhibit. "Come see!"

Sure enough, one of the polar bears was in the water, his massive body passing by the underwater window like a silent surge of raw power. A crowd quickly gathered, but we held our front row places, mouths open, as the big brute turned and swam past again and again, paws as big as dinner plates, long gray-white fur rippling.

"Beautiful," I breathed.

Nothing else in the zoo quite matched the polar bear water dance, since most of the other animals lay comatose in the muggy August heat or hid away in their dens, but we dutifully wandered toward the south end of the park, taking in the Gorilla House and some of the other indoor exhibits. P.J. actually forgot to be bored when we ducked into a building that featured snakes, bats, and other creepy, crawly things.

My feet were tired, and I was glad when the boys caught sight of paddleboats for rent on the lagoon at the far end of the zoo. "*My* treat," I insisted. "You guys go." Anything for a chance to sit down for a while.

Even though the paddleboats were four-seaters, Mr. Bentley waved the boys off and stayed with me. "Whoo-ee," he huffed, sinking down onto a bench. "I must be crazy thinking I can raise a nine-year-old." He tipped his chin toward the paddleboat, where P.J. and Paul were pedaling furiously in the front two seats and DaShawn was squealing with delight behind them. "How you doin' with the single-parent thing, Firecracker?"

I sighed. "I don't know. I'm afraid I let Philip take care of a lot of things, never thinking I'd have to know stuff—like how to buy a car. And I need one, like, yesterday! But a savvy car salesman could sniff out in two seconds that I'm a sucker." I looked at him hopefully. "You got any advice?"

Mr. Bentley chuckled.

"You really askin'? Buy used. Just a year or two old can save you some big bucks, and it'll still have a lot of miles left on it. Less of an invitation to car thieves too. But you gotta know what to check out so you don't get a lemon."

I deliberately raised my eyes upward at the treetops waving in the slight breeze coming off the lake across Lake Shore Drive, tempering the muggy heat . . . and cleared my throat. "You know what I'm going to ask you, right?"

I drove the rental to work the next morning under cloudy skies with Mr. Bentley's promise to help me look for a good used car this weekend. But before then, I had to write up a proposal to present at the Manna House board meeting on Saturday morning—and it was already Friday! Decided I'd have to miss Edesa's weekly Bible study today, even though she was starting something new—something about *Bad Girls of the Bible*. Ought to tickle the curiosity of our cast of shady characters coming off the streets anyway.

Armed with a cup of coffee from the coffee cart in the multipurpose room, I unlocked my office door, dumped my bag on the desk, and pulled the desk phone toward me. Lee Boyer had left phone numbers on my voice mail for the real estate agent handling the sale of the six-flat I lived in, as well as a number for the current owner. I needed some hard facts for my proposal, and time was running out.

But before I could make my first call, the door opened and Sammy peeked in. "Didn't Paul come today, Miss Gabby?" The door swung wider, revealing three more anxious faces—siblings Trina and Rufino, ages seven and six respectively, and ten-year-old Keisha.

"Sorry, kids." Paul had elected to stay home that morning to play around on his new keyboard. "Paul is practicing his music today. But he'll be back next week." I hoped. It *was* a volunteer job, after all. I hoped Paul's enthusiasm for entertaining the younger kids at the shelter hadn't run out yet. "Keisha, you know how to work the DVD player in the rec room, don't you? Why don't you put on some of those VeggieTales movies we got last week?" Someone had donated a whole shopping bag full of DVDs, some of which were so violent and R-rated, I had to trash them. But I pulled out the good ones, including some VeggieTales that should keep the kids entertained for a while.

An hour later I heard the familiar banging of pots that announced Estelle Williams had arrived and lunch-making was in the works. Grinning, I came out of my office and leaned across the counter dividing dining room and kitchen. "Guess what we did yesterday?"

Estelle, dressed in her usual hairnet and roomy apron covering a loose white blouse and black baggy Capri pants, dumped large cans of tomato soup into a big pot on the stove. "Don't have to guess. You went to the zoo. And didn't invite me."

I blinked. That hadn't even occurred to me. "Oh, Estelle. I'm sorry. Mr. Bentley invited the boys and me . . . I mean, we were his guests, so it didn't occur to me to invite someone else."

"Humph. Not blaming you. But *Mister* Harry Bentley could've invited me."

"Wait a minute. Yesterday was Thursday. Didn't you start a cooking class on Thursday afternoons?" I scooted over to the activity sheet posted on the wall beside the counter and hooted. "Yes, there it is! You couldn't have come anyway, so what are you fussing about?"

"Humph. Doesn't matter. He could've *asked*. Then I could've said no."

I laughed out loud. "Estelle Williams! You usually bend over backward to deny any romantic interest going on between you two—which doesn't fool anyone, by the way. But here you are, pouting like a jilted lover that Mr. B took us to the zoo without you."

"Am not." *Bang.* Another pot went on the stove.

"Besides, his car only seats five."

"Well." But she looked sideways at me and her tone changed. "Did he say anything about me yesterday?"

"Uh . . . nope. Nothing."

"Humph."

"But I asked him about his eyes."

Now she stopped completely. "You didn't tell him *I* told you anything, did you?"

"Didn't have to. He was squinting and holding the zoo's visitor guide at all angles. I just asked. And he said the doctor hopes it'll go away."

"*Go away?*" A cloud passed over her face. "It's been weeks, and Harry's not tellin' me much of anything anymore. Stubborn old goat. I'm worried about him. Gotta help me pray, Gabby."

"I will. And I've got something for you to help *me* pray about." I handed her the proposal I'd just printed out.

Wiping her hands on a dish towel, Estelle leaned on her elbows on the counter and read through my proposal. Her eyes widened. "Girl! You full of surprises. What's this House of Hope idea? You want to *buy* the building you livin' in and turn it into apartments for some of our single moms here?"

I looked around to make sure we were alone and lowered my voice, hardly able to contain my excitement. "And look what I found out. Somebody in 3A is moving out the end of August, which means Tanya and Sammy—or Precious and Sabrina, whoever needs it most—could move in September first! Well"—I backed off—"maybe not September first. I think all the apartments need some repairs and refurbishing. And the board has to agree to help get rent subsidies from the city."

Estelle started to laugh, her shoulders shaking as she handed back my proposal. "Gabby Fairbanks. This idea is so crazy, it's gotta have God's hand all over it."

I grinned. "That's exactly what Jodi Baxter said."

But the moment I said her name, I clapped my hand over my mouth. *Jodi Baxter!* Mabel told me I needed a prayer partner, and Jodi had been part of this House of Hope idea from day one. Here I was telling Estelle, and I hadn't even told Jodi about the board meeting tomorrow morning!

I made a beeline for my office. What made me think this crazy idea was going to fly without prayer?

chapter 8

Jodi Baxter picked up on the first ring. "Gabby! I was just think-ing about calling you. Haven't talked to you since the birthday party last weekend. Oh, guess I saw you at church on Sunday. What's going on? Everything okay?"

"Yeah, it's been a good week." I gave her a quick rundown of how I'd been keeping the boys busy. "But I called to ask you something."

"Sure. Fire away."

"Well." I took a big breath. "I talked to Mabel about our House of Hope idea, *and* she's actually letting me present a pro-posal to the board tomorrow morning."

"Oh, Gabby! That's wonderful. I'll definitely be praying. What time is the board meeting?"

"Ten. But, uh, that's what I'm calling about. Mabel encour-aged me to find a prayer partner to pray with me about this, and I'm wondering if you—"

"Of course! Oh, Gabby, I'd love to be your prayer partner! On one condition. That we make it a two-way street. I mean, if you'll pray for me too."

I wasn't sure what to say. I mean, that made sense. "I'm not sure exactly how prayer partners work, but—"

"Well, one thing I've learned by praying with the Yada Yada Prayer Group. Praying *for* someone or for their requests is all well and good, but there's nothing like praying *with* each other. So . . . hm. Tell you what. Denny and I are driving Amanda down to Champaign on Saturday afternoon, but I've already told them I can't leave until after I teach my typing class there at the shelter. Why don't I just come early, say . . . nine thirty? That'll give us half an hour to pray before the board meeting at ten. Sound okay?"

"Oh, Jodi. Could you? I wasn't going to ask you to make a special trip. Just thought we'd pray, you know, over the phone or something. But I'd really love to see you before the board meeting. I could show you my proposal too. Except your class doesn't start until eleven. You'll be there a whole hour and a half before your typing class."

She snickered. "Don't worry about that. That'll get me out of Amanda's hair tomorrow morning. Otherwise I'll be nagging her about what she's packing or fussing because of all the last-minute stuff she'll just then be 'remembering' she has to have in her dorm room. Know what I mean? So, see you tomorrow . . . Oh, wait a sec."

Jodi must have muffled the speaker, though I still heard two voices in the background. Then she was back. "Amanda wants to know how Dandy is."

"Dandy? I presume he's okay. Lucy stopped by with him on

Monday, and he was fine. Almost his old self. But I haven't seen either of them since."

Jodi turned away from the phone, but I heard, "Gabby says he's fine. He's still with Lucy . . . I know, honey, but I'm sure Gabby knows what she's doing." Her voice came back to my ear with a slight chuckle. "Amanda disapproves of you giving Gramma Shep's dog to Lucy, in case you haven't figured that out. But I think it was a very kind thing."

"Well, tell her she's not alone. My Paul is upset about it too. Can't blame him. I have my own doubts about the wisdom of it, especially when it's raining. And I presume it's going to get cold in a few months."

Jodi laughed. "That's right. You haven't been here for a Chicago winter yet. But I'm sure Lucy will figure it out. She's been on the streets a long time."

I glanced at my watch. "Yikes! I've got to go pick up P.J. See you tomorrow at nine thirty . . . and thanks, Jodi."

I'd meant to tell Jodi about my conversation with Lee Boyer but decided it could wait until tomorrow. That'd be a good thing to pray about anyway. Who was I going to get for a lawyer now? Even more, I wanted to tell her about him wanting to take our friendship to another level. At least, that's what I thought he meant . . .

I'd managed to set aside my conversation with Lee for the past two days. But all day Friday it distracted me so much that when the apartment door buzzer rang later that day and I pulled the door open to see Philip standing in the outer foyer to pick up the boys for their overnight, I felt guilty. Caught red-handed. A married woman thinking about another man.

I left him standing in the foyer, called for the boys, and headed back to the kitchen. But a moment later I heard Paul saying, "Dad! Dad! Come in and listen to the song I wrote!"

Oh great. Why can't they just leave? I didn't want to talk to Philip just then. But a few moments later I heard Paul on the electronic keyboard, playing a jazzy little number he'd created that morning. I couldn't help but smile. He'd played it for me as soon as I got home after work. It was good.

Five minutes later P.J. poked his head into the kitchen. "Bye, Mom. We're leaving now. No surprise parties when we get back tomorrow, okay?"

I grinned at him. "Promise." I headed for the front room to say good-bye to Paul too. But as I came into the room, I saw Philip standing by the window seat in front of the bay windows in the sunroom reading a sheet of paper he held in his hand. My heart somersaulted into my throat. *The proposal!* When I got home from work, Paul had been so eager for me to hear the song he'd made up, I'd dumped my stuff on the window seat and sat down to listen . . . and never put it away.

In four giant strides, I snatched the paper out of Philip's hand. "Nosy, aren't you?"

"It was lying right here. Couldn't help seeing it." His eyebrows lifted curiously. "I see you're planning to buy this building. Where'd you get that kind of money?"

I gritted my teeth and barely hissed the words, not wanting the boys to hear. "None of your business."

"Grandma left Mom and her sisters a bunch of money when she died," Paul piped up helpfully from the living room, where he was struggling to put on his backpack stuffed with clothes for his overnight.

"Ah."

That's all Philip said. And when they were gone, I leaned against the front door and banged my head against it. The last person in this world I wanted to know about my proposal to buy this building and create a House of Hope was Philip Fairbanks.

When I met Jodi Baxter at Manna House the next morning, I vented. "He saw the proposal, Jodi! He knows I want to buy the building! What am I going to do?"

"Is that bad?"

I stared at her. "Yes! I mean . . . sure, he'd find out eventually, but I'd rather he found out when it was a done deal instead of just an idea. He . . . I don't know, what if he tries to buy it himself just to throw a monkey wrench in my plans?"

Now it was her turn to stare at me. "He'd do that? Just to be mean?"

"I don't know! I wouldn't have thought so a couple of months ago. But the way he's been acting . . . it's all crazy. I just . . . I just wish he didn't know about it yet." I covered my face with my hands and moaned.

"Gabby." Jodi took my hands away from my face and held them. "Gabby, we're here to pray about this proposal, and that's still what we're going to do. Remember, if this is God's plan, if

God is in it, then nothing Philip does will be able to thwart it. You need to trust God with this. Here, let me read you something." She grabbed my Bible sitting on the desk and flipped pages. "Here it is, Proverbs three, five and six. 'Trust in the Lord with all your heart and lean not on your own understanding; in all your ways'—including this House of Hope proposal—'acknowledge Him, and He will make your paths straight.'" She closed the Bible. "See? It's a promise!"

I wagged my head. "I wish I had your faith, Jodi."

She gave a short laugh. "Well, I give you permission to quote me the next time I'm fussing and worrying about something. It's usually easier for me to trust God for other people's problems than it is for my own. But that's why it's good to have a prayer partner or a group of praying sisters, Gabby. To hold up our shaky faith, to remind us of God's promises, to stand with us when we don't feel so strong by ourselves."

I nodded and sniffed, grabbing for a tissue from my desk. "Well, that's what I need right now. For you to pray with me about this proposal, because I'm definitely quaking in my shoes right now."

Twenty minutes later, fortified by the prayer time with Jodi, I took my stack of proposals—a copy for each board member—and made my way to the schoolroom on the main floor, where Mabel was arranging chairs in a circle. Within minutes, the board members trickled in, a diverse assortment of professional men and women. Besides Mabel, two others were women—Rev. Liz Handley, the former director of Manna House, now retired, and Stephanie Cooper, a social worker for the city's Department of Child and Family Services, both of whom doubled as case managers here at the shelter. Two were local pastors, Pastor Stevens and Rev. Álvarez, whose churches—New Hope Missionary Baptist and Iglesia Cristiana Evangélica—led Sunday Evening Praise on various weeks here at the shelter. The board member I knew best was Peter Douglass, an African-American businessman who sold computer software, better known among my Yada Yada Prayer Group friends as "Avis's new husband."

Mabel asked Rev. Handley to open with prayer, which she did, short and to the point. I hid a grin. The shelter's former director and its current one couldn't be more different—even besides the fact that Liz was white and Mabel was black. Mabel's prayers, even in a staff meeting, were straight from the heart and often long. Rev. Handley's prayer sounded formal, as if she'd memorized it. Mabel's face had a classic mature beauty, her warm brown skin always perfectly made up, and she wore her clothes well. Liz Handley was more of a "character"—squat and dumpy, salt-and-pepper hair cut as short as a man's, a round face with twinkling eyes and a hearty laugh.

But my thoughts were interrupted when Peter Douglass, the board chair, spoke my name. "—Fairbanks has joined us with a housing proposal she'd like us to consider. We have a number of items on our agenda today, but since Gabby is here, let's move this item to number one. Gabby?"

I glanced at Mabel, hoping she'd go first and introduce the board to my idea for second-stage housing, and I'd follow with my specific proposal about a building. But she just gave me an encouraging smile to go ahead. So I took a deep breath and launched into my story.

"I think all of you know that, um, my mother and I found

ourselves suddenly homeless this summer, and we spent several weeks here at Manna House as residents." I allowed a self-conscious grin. "Actually, I might recommend the experience for all staff personnel and board members—it gives one a whole new perspective."

A few chuckles around the room helped put me at ease, so I continued. "Since I was separated from my children and couldn't get them back until I found suitable housing, I became painfully aware how desperately some of our single moms need to find a place to live where they can be a real family. But the process is often tediously slow, given the long waiting lists for some of the subsidized housing in the city. I know I'm fairly new to the staff here, but I . . . um, I think I have an idea for how Manna House could provide that kind of environment . . ." I stopped, feeling flustered. "Actually, my proposal only concerns one aspect of this idea, and that's how to obtain a building. After that, well, I need your expertise and ideas how to make this a vital part of Manna House's ministry to some of our residents."

I handed out the proposal I'd written and gave time for the board members to read it, sweating profusely in the lightweight pantsuit I'd worn to be suitably dressed to speak to the board. I saw a few heads nodding and heard murmurs around the circle.

"Mm, 'House of Hope' . . . nice concept."

"Not a bad price for a six-flat."

"On-site staff living in one of the apartments . . . that's good."

"I suppose rent from the apartments would cover the monthly mortgage? But—"

To my relief, Mabel jumped in. She'd been doing research on Chicago's Low-Income Housing Trust Fund, which provided rent subsidies to the poor. I didn't understand all the agencies and examples she mentioned, but the gist was clear: renters who qualify pay 30 percent of whatever income they have—zero if they have no income—and the trust fund pays the rest. "The program actually requires a three-party arrangement," she said, a smile playing on the corners of her mouth. "The city, via the Trust Fund. A housing provider or private landlord—which is what Gabby's proposal is about. And a service provider. In our case, that would be Manna House."

For a brief moment silence fell on the group circled in the schoolroom of the Manna House Women's Shelter. And then a gasp—mine—as the weight of what she'd just said sank into my heart. "Oh. Oh! Then . . . it's really possible?"

chapter 9

A lively discussion about "possible" followed that took my breath away. The board was really trying to figure out how to make this House of Hope work! But the discussion was pulled up abruptly by a knock at the door of the schoolroom, followed by Jodi Baxter poking her head in. "Sorry to interrupt, but it's almost eleven and I'm supposed to teach typing in the schoolroom here. You know, using the computers. Should we, uh, cancel class today?"

"Oh, no, no, Jodi, we thought we'd be done by eleven." Mabel looked around at the group. "Should we table the rest of the agenda until next month? Or—"

Rev. Handley heaved herself up out of her chair. "No, I'd rather keep going as long as we're here. How about the chapel? It's usually empty this time of day." The former director marched out the door, but not before giving me an encouraging squeeze on the shoulder. "Hang in there, Gabby. You've got some spitfire under that mop of yours."

The board members trailed out of the schoolroom—so named in hopes of having a full-blown afterschool program one of these days—some of them still talking among themselves about how to apply to the city's trust fund and what the criteria should be for House of Hope applicants.

Jodi stared after their retreating backs and then turned to me, her mouth hanging open. "Did they . . . did I just hear . . . ?"

I nodded, feeling as if my grin was going to reach both ears.

"Whoa!" Jodi sat down with a plop in one of the chairs. "Why am I always so surprised when God answers our prayers?"

I laughed nervously. "Yeah, me too. But you said if it was God's idea, it could happen even if it looked impossible."

She eyed me sideways. "Yeah, I know what I *said*. But believe me, this faith business takes a *lot* of faith sometimes! Oh—I gotta go tell Kim and the others they can come in now before they get sucked into some blithering talk show in the TV room. But call me later! I want to hear all about the meeting."

I left Jodi to her typing class and ran downstairs to my office to get my things, mentally running through the list of tasks I wanted to get done the rest of the day before Philip brought the boys back that evening. Did I have time to call my sisters before Mr. Bentley came to pick me up to go car hunting at one o'clock? Celeste and Honor and I were still trying to find a time all three of us could talk on a conference call in three different time zones.

Still planning my to-do list, I headed out the front door—and ran right into Lucy Tucker bumping her wire cart up the front steps of Manna House.

"Hey, hey, hey! Watch where ya goin', Fuzz Top." Lucy glared at me as she pointed at Dandy's food bowl that had bounced out of the cart and was clattering down the steps. Her head was wrapped in a scarf that looked like one of my mother's, one of several we'd given her from my mother's things.

"Sorry, Lucy!" I scurried down the steps to pick up the bowl, stopping to shower some love on my mom's dog, who was running circles around my ankles until I sat down on the steps and gave him a good scratch on the rump. "What are you guys doing here?"

"Humph," Lucy snorted. "Gotta fill my bucket with some more dog food." She pointed at a bright yellow plastic cat litter bucket tucked down in her cart among her usual assortment of plastic bags. "Dog eats more'n I do, an' he only half my size."

I stifled a grin. A third her size or less was more like it. "You filled it up just last Monday. Why don't you take a whole bag of dog food, Lucy? There's a twenty-five-pound bag stored in my office." *And I'd love to get it out of there.*

She looked at me as if I were crazy. "Don't you know *nuthin'* 'bout livin' on the street, Miss Gabby? Gotta keep *ever'thing* in plastic. Otherwise, one good rain soak it all. An' how you think I'm gonna fit that big bag in here? Humph." The old lady bumped her cart up the last step and rang the doorbell. "Some people don't use the brains they was born with."

I waved good-bye as the door opened and Lucy and Dandy disappeared inside the shelter. "Must be a bad hair day," I chuckled to myself, though as long as I'd known Lucy, I couldn't actually remember a good hair day. Even when it got washed—which was seldom enough—Lucy's hair still looked like a gray squirrel's nest.

I was still smiling when I pulled up in front of the six-flat in my rental car, thinking about Lucy's head wrapped in one of my mother's head scarves—a replacement for the purple knit hat she used to wear, which had disappeared the day of my mom's Manna House funeral. Just before the burial back home in North Dakota, I'd found the hat hidden inside my mom's casket. I never told Lucy I'd found her sacrificial gift. *So. Mom has Lucy's purple hat, and Lucy has my mom's scarves.* As far as Lucy was concerned, wearing those scarves probably had nothing to do with a bad hair day.

As I got out of the car, I stood on the sidewalk looking at the wide stone lintel above the outer doorway of the six-flat. New excitement flickered in my chest as I tried to imagine how we could put House of Hope on that lintel in big letters. Chisel it in? Paint it on? Wooden letters?

"Huh! First things first, Gabby!" I told myself, using my keys to let myself into the building and then into apartment 1B. *Like buying the building.* I dumped my bag and tossed my keys into the basket on the hallway table. *And, yikes, coordinating that with Manna House and the city so I'm not stuck with empty apartments and paying a hefty mortgage . . .*

That last prospect unnerved me, so I reheated a cup of cold breakfast coffee in the microwave and sank into a chair at the kitchen table. Suddenly "possible" looked a lot more complicated than it had an hour ago. Not to mention that the coffee tasted terrible. I made a new pot, and while it dripped, leaned my elbows on the table and pressed my fingers to my eyes. *God, I know I can't do this on my own! Please, if it's Your idea, if this is something You want to use to bless single moms like Precious and Tanya and even me when they find themselves homeless, help me to trust You to work out the details and the timing and . . . and everything!*

The coffee timer dinged. Smelled wonderful. And I was proud of myself for obeying Rule One about prayer, according to Jodi Baxter: *Pray first*.

My conference call to my sisters only half worked. I tried at noon Chicago time and got Celeste on her landline at the ranger station in Denali National Park. It was only nine o'clock there, but her husband, Tom, was already out chasing down a report of campers trying to feed bears. "And then they wonder why somebody gets mauled!" Celeste fumed.

At least I didn't have to deal with *bears* here in Chicago. I put Celeste on hold and dialed Honor's cell in Los Angeles, but only got her voice mail. "Huh. You think she's out already or still in bed?" I asked Celeste when I got her back on the line. Our middle sister was a tad unpredictable.

"Who knows? She's doing that jewelry thing, you know. Maybe she's got an art fair or something. We can try again tomorrow. How are you doing, Gabby? Did P.J. and Paul get the package I sent them for their birthdays? What's up with Philip these days?"

We commiserated for nearly an hour until Mr. Bentley rang my door buzzer, and a few minutes later I hopped into the front seat of his RAV4. I still wasn't used to seeing Mr. B in his "civvies," but that tweedy slouch cap really did suit his shaved head. "What are you grinning about, Firecracker?" he asked, glancing at me sideways as he pulled out.

"Just feeling glad. I talked to my sister in Alaska. We're trying to keep in touch better since Mom died. It feels good to have family right now." A sudden lump caught in my throat. Oh dear, Mr. B was going to think I was an emotional yo-yo, up one minute, down the next. But talking to my sisters again after years of emotional distance was like a miracle. I blinked back some happy tears. "And," I rushed on, "I met with the Manna House board this morning, and guess what?" I spilled it all—the crazy idea Jodi and I had come up with for me to buy the six-flat and turn it into a House of Hope for homeless single moms. "In partnership with Manna House, of course."

Mr. Bentley stared at me so long, I was afraid he was going to run a stop sign or something. Finally he wagged his head. "Young lady, do you know what you're doing?"

I snorted. "No. Not really." But I was still grinning.

Mr. B threw back his head and laughed. "Good! You might just have a chance with this crazy scheme if you realize that." And he chuckled all the way to the Toyota dealership, where he said we wanted to look at the pre-owned Subaru wagon they'd advertised online. "But let me do the talking," he murmured as the salesman led us past the new Toyotas—my eyes lingered on a silver Prius like the one Lee Boyer had—to the cars they took as trade-ins.

The Subaru Forester wasn't bad. Only three years old with twenty-seven thousand miles on it. Sticker price said $16,999. A nice burgundy red, clean inside, automatic transmission, fairly roomy space behind the second seat, even a rollback luggage cover to keep the area nice and neat. Mr. Bentley spent a long time looking under the hood, inspecting the tires, even getting down and looking under the chassis while I wandered a bit, looking at some of the other, sportier cars on the lot. I was tempted by the new Toyotas . . . I mean, why not? Wouldn't have to be a Prius. Some of those Camrys were really nice—sunroof, leather seats . . .

"Come on, Gabby!" Mr. Bentley called. "Let's take it for a drive."

I drove. It handled pretty nice. When I tried to say something, Mr. B held up his hand for silence, as if he was listening to the motor or something.

I felt a little annoyed. Sure, I'd asked him to help me look for a car. But what if I didn't want to buy a pre-owned? Someone got rid of it for a reason, right? Maybe I'd just be buying someone else's problems.

We drove it back onto the lot. Mr. Bentley steered me away from the salesman and pretended to look at some of the other cars. "It's a steal, Gabby. Good, solid car. I know a mechanic who can check it out for you, to be sure. But as far as I can tell, somebody probably just wanted to upgrade. A lot of people do that, even though the car they got is still perfectly good."

I got stubborn. "But shouldn't we look at some of the new Toyotas? You drive a RAV4 and like it. Wouldn't a new car be smart in the long run?"

He scratched the horseshoe-shaped beard along his jawline. "Well, sure, if that's really what you want to do. But a new car in the Wrigleyville neighborhood . . . well, just more of a temptation for car thieves. You'll spend a whole lot less on a pre-owned and still get a good car for you and your boys. No shame in that. All my cars are at least a year old when I buy—even the RAV4. And pardon me saying so, but you're on your own now, Gabby girl. Doesn't hurt to cut your expenses where you can."

My face heated. Mr. B was right. Sure, I had Mom's insurance money right now, but it was going to have to go a mighty long way—especially if I was going to take a leap of faith and buy an honest-to-goodness Chicago six-flat! I sighed. "You're right. Guess I got a little greedy. Should I—?" I dug my checkbook out of my purse.

"Put that away! No way are you going to pay that sticker price. C'mon, let's go talk to that baby-faced salesman, who's probably only been on the job a month." Harry Bentley chuckled. "He ain't had to deal with Harry Bentley before!"

Don't know how Harry finagled it, but we drove the Subaru to a mechanic friend of his, who gave the Forester a once-over and a clean bill of health. "'Cept the coolant in the air conditioner is low. We can recharge it, but there might be a leak that could be expensive. Can't tell without running a pressure test. You'd want to get that fixed, 'specially in this hot weather."

Mr. B told him to hold off on recharging, and once back at the dealer, used what the mechanic found to knock down the price a cool thousand. I paid cash, drove the wagon home, and parked it in front of the six-flat with Mr. B tailing me. I walked back to his RAV4, and he rolled down the passenger side window. "Take that in next week, have my guy recharge it, see what happens. He'll do right by you."

"Thanks, Mr. B. Don't know what I'd do without you." He shrugged it off, as I knew he would. "The boys will be home soon. You want to stay for supper or something?"

"Can't. Gotta pick up DaShawn. My former partner—a great gal named Cindy—took him to a Cubs game today." He grinned as he started the car. "Radio just said they beat the Cardinals, 5 to 4. Go Cubbies!"

I was stuck back on this great gal named Cindy. "Your former partner? What do you mean, partner?" I tried to imagine Mr. Bentley, former doorman at Richmond Towers, with a side business that needed a partner . . . named *Cindy*?

"You know . . . partner. Two to a car, got my back, all that stuff. She was the best on the force. Still is. I'm a retired Chicago cop, Firecracker. Didn't you know that?"

chapter 10

✿ ✿ ✿

Know that? I stared at the spare tire mounted on the back of the black-and-silver RAV4 as it disappeared around the corner. How could I not know something as important as that? To be honest, I'd just assumed Mr. Bentley had been a doorman all his life.

Mercy! A retired Chicago cop.

I felt embarrassed. Stupid me. What else didn't I know about Harry Bentley? Or about his ladylove, Estelle Williams, for that matter? Still didn't know why she'd once been a resident at Manna House. She never said. On the other hand, I had never asked her either.

That was going to change.

I was locking my "new" burgundy red Subaru and wondering if the rental car place could come pick up their car today so I wouldn't have to wait until Monday and pay for another two days, when Philip's big black SUV came down the street and pulled up to the curb. P.J. and Paul piled out. "What's that, Mom? A new car?" Paul ran a circle around it. "Kinda small for an SUV, isn't it?"

"Big enough." I kept my voice light. "Yep, just drove it home."
I snatched him as he whirled past. "C'mere, kiddo. I need a hug."
He let me hug him long enough for him to snatch the car keys
out of my hand, unlock the car, and crawl in, inspecting the travel
cup holders, the pockets on the back of the front seats, and figur-
ing out how to work the rollback cover over the luggage space in
back. Even P.J. got into the driver's seat, checking out the dash
and console. I had to smile when he adjusted the rearview mirror
to check out his hair and wraparound sunglasses.

I was so distracted watching the boys that I didn't realize
Philip had gotten out of the Lexus until I heard his voice right
beside me. "So. You got a used car."

I looked up. *Gosh.* With the wraparound sunglasses P.J. was
wearing, the two looked like spitting images of each other. The
fact kind of unnerved me—or maybe because I didn't know what
Philip really meant. Did he approve? Disapprove? Did he think a
secondhand car wasn't good enough for his boys?

"Yes," I said—and bit my tongue, realizing how easy it would
be for me to blather on making excuses for why I got a pre-owned
car, trying to convince Philip it was a good deal.

He was dressed in neatly pressed tan slacks, dress shoes, and
an open-necked short-sleeved black silk shirt that looked good
against his tan skin and dark hair. Dressy casual, like he was
going somewhere. Not exactly knockabout clothes like he'd
been hanging out with the boys at some city fest or down at the
lakefront.

"You're a half hour early," I said. "You got somewhere to
go?" *Ouch.* I knew Philip didn't like me asking personal questions
about his comings and goings. It just popped out. But why not, if

he was going to bring the boys back early? What if I hadn't been here?

Wasn't surprised that he didn't answer. He just walked over to the Subaru and inspected a tiny dent in the rear fender, then walked around the car giving it the eye, and came back to me. "Looks okay for a 2003. Hope you had a mechanic check it out. They give you decent financing?"

He was fishing. No way was I going to tell him I paid cash. "Mm." I took a few steps to the Subaru and knocked on the windows. "Come on, guys! I've got to call the rental car place to pick up the car before they close!"

Philip was still standing on the curb. "Is it far? If you want to drop it off, I could follow you over and give you a lift back."

I stared at him. Had Philip Fairbanks just offered to do me a favor? I opened my mouth but stumbled over the words. "Uh . . . no, thanks anyway. This place picks up and delivers. You, uh, look like you're headed someplace. Don't want to make you late." I raised my voice. "Boys! Come on! Lock up the car!"

Philip shrugged and headed for the Lexus. Then he turned. "Maybe you and I could get together next week sometime, talk over some stuff."

What—? "About the boys, you mean?"

"Well, yes, that too. But maybe we should talk about us. Think we could do that?"

The boys dashed past, grabbing their duffel bags off the sidewalk and bounding up the low steps to the front door, Paul jangling my keys. "We got a new movie, Mom!" P.J. hollered over his shoulder. "Can we watch it tonight?"

I was glad for the momentary distraction. Philip wanted to

talk? In person? The two of us? Sudden anger . . . confusion . . . longing . . . all pounded on the doors in my heart where I'd locked them all away, begging to come spewing out.

Don't, Gabby, don't. You don't have to respond right now. Breathe, Gabby . . .

"Um, let me call you about that, okay? I gotta run." And I did, escaping into the foyer of the six-flat as the big black Lexus pulled away with a squeal of its tires.

"Mo-om!" P.J. yelled from the living room while I was putting together a quick taco salad to eat while we watched their new DVD. "I thought you were going to get an air conditioner this weekend!"

"I tried!" I yelled back. Well, I had called one store. "They're out. Everything's for fall now—leaf blowers and stuff like that." Which was a bummer. I'd hoped to get two or three end-of-the-season air conditioners at a rock-bottom price. At least I'd be prepared for next summer. Hadn't figured they'd all be gone.

Well, the three fans would have to do for a few more weeks. While waiting for the hamburger to fry, I called Jodi Baxter. No answer. She'd said to call her, hadn't she? Then I remembered. She and Denny were going to drive Amanda down to Champaign-Urbana that afternoon to get her settled for her second year at the University of Illinois. How long a drive was it? Three hours? Three down . . . three back . . . it would probably be late by the time they got in.

Shoot! I had to talk to Jodi! Somebody! What was I going to do about Philip's request?

The boys had bought one of their favorite movies, *Secondhand Lions* with Robert Duvall and Michael Caine, even though we'd seen it at least two times already, and it kept us laughing the third time around despite the lingering August heat and the noise from the fans trying to keep the air moving. Curled up in my mom's wingback rocker, I relished just hanging out with my boys having simple fun—but felt guilty about it too. Was I too easily slipping into "just me and the boys" mode, too easily giving up on my marriage, giving up hope that it could be the four of us again?

Philip said he wanted to talk about "us." What did he mean by that? I hadn't filed for divorce yet—even though Lee said it would be a slam dunk—but I *had* filed for unlawful eviction and custody of the boys. Wouldn't he have said something if he'd gotten those papers in the mail? Lee said we had a court date now.

So what did Philip want to talk about? Getting a divorce? Or . . .

My heart constricted. Was he having second thoughts about our separation?

Taking a deep breath to loosen my chest, I gathered up the empty taco salad bowl, bag of corn chips, and dirty dishes, and stole out of the room while the boys were cheering for the two old brothers running off the conniving scoundrels who only wanted their money. Dumping the dirty dishes into the dishwasher, I tried Jodi's number again. Still no answer. *Rats.* I'd have to wait until tomorrow at church.

Which I did. I pulled the Subaru into the big parking lot of the shopping center on Howard Street the next morning, which marked the city limit between Chicago and Evanston, its first suburban neighbor to the north. The large storefront hosting SouledOut Community Church would be hard to miss, the name painted in bold red script across the wide windows. The large open room, painted in bright blue and coral colors that reminded me of a Mexican restaurant, was rapidly filling up as P.J., Paul, and I came through the double-glass doors.

The boys had grumbled as usual about going to church on Sunday morning, but I held fast to Estelle's no-nonsense approach. *"Just tell 'em that's the way it is."* And I suspected they found the lively service a lot more interesting than they let on.

I looked around for familiar faces, but didn't see Estelle or Mr. B that morning. However, the Baxter's Dodge Caravan pulled up outside, and Jodi came in, followed by Edesa and Josh carrying little Gracie while Denny drove off to park the car. Jodi immediately came over to me. "Oh, Gabby. I saw that you called a couple of times last night. I'm so sorry, but we didn't get home until close to midnight. We decided to go out for dinner after getting Amanda settled in the dorm, and . . ." Jodi got all puppy-dog faced. "For some reason, it feels harder letting her go this year than the first time."

"Uh-oh. You mean it doesn't get any easier? Don't worry about not calling. I just wanted to—"

"Oh, look! Pastor Clark is back!" Jodi interrupted. "Let's talk later, okay, Gabby? I promise!" And she scurried off to join others welcoming the tall, thin white man who was one of SouledOut's pastors. I vaguely remembered the church praying for Pastor Clark about two months ago when he'd gone to the hospital with chest pains, but that was the Sunday before *my* life ended up in the "critically ill" ward, and I had to admit I hadn't given poor Pastor Clark a single thought since then.

I was glad to see Avis Douglass leading worship this morning—she was my favorite worship leader on the team—and she called the church to worship this morning with a call-and-response based on Psalm 103, basically giving thanks to God for restoring Pastor Clark to the congregation after his heart attack. The poor man still looked frail to me, but I noticed happy tears trickling down his face, seeming glad just to be there as the congregation worshipped with song after song.

When the kids and teens had been dismissed to their Sunday school classes, Pastor Cobbs, the other pastor—a short, African-American man with energy to spare—was all over the low platform that morning, preaching on a verse from 2 Corinthians, chapter 12, saying that "God's grace is sufficient, brothers and sisters, *sufficient* all by itself—"

"Say it, pastor!" a woman called. Sounded like Florida, one of the Yada Yada Prayer Group sisters.

"—because His 'power is made *perfect*' . . . Do you hear that, brothers and sisters? Made *perfect* in our weakness."

"Well," someone else said.

"And I want you all to know that this brother here"—Pastor Cobbs stepped off the platform, walked over to Pastor Clark, and laid his hand on the tall man's bony shoulder—"This brother here has been *weak*, laid up in a hospital room, poked full of tubes, hooked up to all kinds of fancy machines. And yet the power of God was so evident on this man, all kinds of hospital staff kept coming into his room just to be in the Presence. And you may be thinkin' that Pastor Clark was takin' a sabbatical from ministry these past many weeks, but I don't think there was a doctor, a nurse, a PT or PA or food service person who came into that hospital room that this man didn't pray for. Not quietly either. He asked, 'How can I pray for you, son? How can I pray for you, daughter?' And they'd tell him. And he'd hold their hands and pray. Pastor Clark here had his own congregation goin' on up there on that hospital floor!"

By this time, everyone was clapping and shouting and saying, "Hallelujah!" Which of course led into some more praise singing and prayer that each of us, when we're feeling weak, would remember this man's example and realize that God's power working in us isn't dependent on us feeling strong and confident and all that. "In fact," Pastor Cobbs ended, "sometimes God needs to take us down so He can remind us of the Power Source who changes lives. Amen?"

"Amen!" people shouted back, and the word seemed to still resound in the air even when the service ended and everyone gathered around the coffee table, consuming sweet rolls and coffee and lemonade.

"I don't see Estelle or Mr. Bentley or DaShawn today," I mused aloud to Jodi as I slipped cream into my coffee. "Mr. B helped me buy a car yesterday, but he didn't say anything about not coming to church. Do you know where they are?"

Jodi shook her head, picking out a sweet roll. "Not for sure. Estelle and Stu were leaving just as we were coming out to get in the car, and Stu said she was taking Estelle to check on her son—something like that."

"Her son?"

"That's what she said." Jodi grimaced. "To tell the truth, I didn't know she had a son."

"Huh. That makes two of us." At least I wasn't the only one in the dark. "And Mr. B?"

"I don't know. Maybe he went with them." Jodi balanced her sweet roll on top of her cup of coffee. "But, hey, what's this about a new car? And I still want to hear more about what the board said about your proposal! Do you have time now?"

P.J. and Paul were hanging out with some of the other SouledOut teens, so I followed her to a couple of chairs in a corner. "But that's not all I need to talk to you about. It's . . . Philip."

chapter 11

Jodi's eyebrows shot up when I told her about Philip wanting to talk. "You're kidding."

I snorted. "Would I kid about something like that?"

"What did you say?"

"Nothing! Just . . . I'd call him later. Actually can't remember exactly what I said. It was like he'd thrown marbles under my feet and I couldn't get my balance! I mean, he barely returns my calls when we have to make a decision about the boys—and now he wants to talk? Doesn't that just rot your socks?"

Jodi giggled. "Now you sound like Lucy." Then she sobered up. "He actually said he wanted to talk about you two? Not the boys?"

I made a face. "Huh. Even talking about the boys would have been a big deal. We haven't had an actual conversation since—" I felt color rise into my face. Not since the disastrous day I'd ignored everybody's advice and confronted Philip in his office about kicking me out of the penthouse. But he'd whittled me down good, made me feel like he'd done me a favor kicking me out and putting me on the street where I belonged. "Anyway," I finished lamely, "he said not just the boys, but about us."

"Whew." Jodi blew out a long breath, staring into her Styrofoam cup of coffee. "Wonder what he'll say when you talk to him."

"*If* I talk to him."

Her head jerked up. "Gabby! What do you mean, *if*? What if your husband wants to—"

"*Ex*-husband." My voice was as cold as the coffee. I tossed the remains of my cup into the closest potted plant.

A long silence sat between us. I studied my nails. Badly in need of a manicure. I should go back to Adele's Hair and Nails and give Hannah the nail girl some business. Especially if I was going to talk to Philip for longer than two minutes. He'd notice if I had ragged nails.

Finally Jodi spoke, her voice soft. "Gabby. I know you've been through a lot . . . no, I take that back. I *don't* know what you've been through, but it sounds awful from what you've told me. But what if Philip wants to talk about getting back together? Maybe he's willing to work on the relationship. Isn't that what you want?"

"I don't know," I mumbled. "Don't know what I want. I guess, in one way, yeah. I'd like us to be a family again, especially for the boys' sake. But . . ." I didn't want to say it, but Jodi— whose own husband adored her—couldn't possibly understand the stress I felt just being around Philip, who knew all the right buttons to push to reduce me to pulp. Talk? Did we even know how? I shrugged. "He probably just wants to talk about getting a divorce. Probably wants to talk me into a 'no-fault' or something, no alimony or child support. Might as well just let our lawyers talk."

"Oh, Gabby." Jodi laid a hand gently on mine. "There's only one way to find out. And that's to talk to him. That's all I'm saying. Just talk. But I'm not in your shoes. You're the one who has to decide, and it's got to be hard. Do you want to pray about it?"

I jerked my hand away and stood up. "No. Not now. I—I'm sorry, Jodi. I need to get the boys home." Which was a pathetic lie, but I was close to tears and wanted to get out of there. I didn't want to pray about it! Didn't want Jodi or God or anyone else to tell me I "should" talk to Philip.

I was miserable as I drove home from SouledOut. How could I treat my friend like that? Jodi Baxter, of all people! Hadn't she listened patiently to me spilling my guts the past month and a half about the breakup of my marriage? Hadn't I asked her to be my prayer partner? So why had I gotten all riled up when she wanted to pray with me about this latest wrinkle?

The boys—bored as usual on a Sunday afternoon—wanted to do something. Me, I just wanted to pull the blinds, turn on the fan, and take a long nap. "Look, Mom." P.J. shoved *The Chicago Guide to Summer Festivals* in my face. It listed a Greek festival going on that weekend in the Lincoln Square neighborhood. "They've got *souvlaki* or whatever you call it and a bunch of other neat Greek foods. And live music and dancing and lots of stuff. It's not that far. See?" P.J. spread a Chicago city map out on our makeshift dining room table and found the Lincoln Square neighborhood north of us where the Greek Orthodox Church hosting the festival was located.

I gave the map a cursory glance. "I don't know, guys. Parking could be a nightmare." Lame excuse. But I let it hang there, hoping it might carry the day and I could crawl into my cocoon.

P.J. snatched up the brochure and the map and stomped out of the room. "Fine," he tossed over his shoulder. "Paul and I can go by ourselves if you don't want to. I can figure out how to get there by bus."

That did it. They probably could get there by themselves—I saw lots of teenagers using the El and buses to get around town. But I knew if P.J. and Paul were out and about, navigating a still-strange city by themselves, I could forget a nap even if I stayed home in the bed with the covers over my head. I sighed and picked up my purse. "Okay, okay! You guys win. Let's go."

As it turned out, I said to Estelle the next day, leaning over the kitchen counter at Manna House, the Greek Festival was noisy and fun and took my mind off stewing about Philip. "I even got talked into trying one of the traditional line dances by a fifty-something Greek gentleman with dark twinkly eyes." I giggled. "Much to the embarrassment of my sons." I held out my arms to the side shoulder-high and did a few steps with a line of imaginary partners. *"Dum de dum de dum . . . Opa!"*

"Uh-huh." Estelle poured two cups of fresh coffee, added cream to one, and passed it over the kitchen counter. "You gotta watch out for those fifty-something Romeos who can dance your feet off. Next thing you know they gonna be down on their knee promising undying love."

I stopped dancing. "Estelle! Did Harry Bentley ask you—?"

She cut me off with a look. "Now, don't you go readin' more into that than just good advice, girl! I'm just sayin'." She snatched up the required hairnet to cover her topknot and took a tray of hamburger patties out of the freezer to thaw.

I hid a grin. It was definitely true that Estelle had been swept off her feet by Mr. Harry Bentley dancing the Mashed Potato at Manna House's first-ever Fun Night. But something else niggled at my brain . . .

"Um, speaking of Harry, I missed you guys at church yesterday. Jodi said something about you needing to check up on your son." I stirred some more powdered creamer into my coffee, trying to be casual. "I didn't realize you had a son. Is everything okay?"

For a few moments, Estelle busied herself banging trays around and pulling condiments out of the refrigerator. Then she sighed and came back to her coffee. "Oh, he's grown. Usually takes care of himself. But he's . . . where's that sugar?" She dumped twice as much sugar into her coffee as she normally used.

"What's his name?" I prompted.

"Leroy. After his daddy. But his daddy left when the doctors diagnosed the boy as schizophrenic *and* bipolar." She reached for the sugar again, but I grabbed her hand. "Oh, right," she said. "Already did that." Estelle's chest rose and fell as she heaved a big sigh.

"So . . . is he okay?"

She shrugged. "As long as he takes his meds. But he's on disability and can't work. So he has too much time on his hands. Sometimes he gets rebellious, doesn't take his meds, and then . . . well." She wagged her head. "Just help me pray for Leroy, Gabby."

I wasn't going to let her off that easily. "And yesterday?"

She gave me a look. "You sure are nosy this morning."

"Ha. Got a right to be. You know all *my* business, but turns out there's a whole lot about Estelle Williams I don't know. Like why you ended up here at Manna House in the first place."

"Sometimes," she murmured, "you just gotta keep goin' forward, not lookin' back . . ."

My own eyes caught the wall clock behind her head. "Rats! It's ten already. Staff meeting!" I grabbed my coffee and headed for the stairs. "You coming?"

Unlike the Manna House board meeting, where the pastors and businesspeople sat in a neat circle of chairs, the staff—both paid and volunteer—were sitting helter-skelter on any available surface in the schoolroom. I squeezed into a school desk. Josh Baxter jumped up and offered his chair to Estelle and leaned against the computer table. I saw him wink at Edesa across the room.

Huh. Newlyweds.

Attendance at the Monday staff meeting usually fluctuated, depending on who was around that day. Today the room was surprisingly full—even Sarge, the blustery night manager who usually left when Mabel arrived, had stayed. When I raised my eyebrows at her, she threw up her hands. "Got to put in my two bits about the name for the multipurpose room, no?"

Naming the multipurpose room! I'd forgotten that was coming up today.

"Which is first on the agenda today," Mabel said. "Everybody here?" She offered an opening prayer, surprisingly short for Mabel, and got down to business. "As you all know from last week, several people have suggested we name the multipurpose room in memory of Martha Shepherd, known to most of our residents as 'Gramma Shep.'"

Chuckles and nods skipped around the room.

"Do I take that as agreement for naming the room in memory of Gabby's mother?" Mabel asked.

This time there was a chorus of "Aye!" and "Yes!" Precious, there as a volunteer, piped up, "Better be, or we gonna have a mutiny on our hands among the residents." Everyone laughed.

"All right. Suggestions for the actual name?"

Ideas flew. Everyone liked the idea of including my mom's last name—*Shepherd*—in the name, because of its double meaning of Jesus being the Good Shepherd. But then the discussion got sticky. *The Martha Shepherd Room*? Too formal. "What about Shepherd's Crook?" Precious said. "Ain't that the stick thing the Good Shepherd carries, ya know, with that hook thing on the end?"

Estelle wagged her head. "Uh-uh. You know whatever name we come up with, it's gonna get shortened to something. You want us to be calling that room 'The Crook'?"

That got a laugh.

"Could call it The Crook an' Cranny," Sarged quipped.

"That's how we shoehorn people in here, into every crook and cranny!"

"That's 'Nook and Cranny,' Sarge," someone snickered, amid general laughter.

Shepherd's Nook? Some people liked that one. "It sounds cozy," Angela Kwon said, twirling a lock of straight black hair around a finger. Others protested that "Nook" didn't have any connection to "Shepherd."

"What about Shepherd's Fold, then?" Edesa Baxter suggested. "*Mi tío*—my uncle—in Honduras raises sheep. That is what he calls the sheds where he pens the sheep safely for the night. Kind of like a shelter."

I liked that. A shelter for the sheep. So did several others—though "The Fold" for short didn't have the snappy ring to it that "The Nook" did.

A few other suggestions were made, but we kept coming back to Shepherd's Fold. Josh raised his hand. "We could have a little plaque on the wall that says, 'Shepherd's Fold . . . In Memory of Martha Shepherd' or something."

Heads nodded. Mabel said, "Everyone agreed?"

"*Bueno! Bueno!*" Sarge gloated. "Though could somebody get me one of those shepherd's crooks to use on the pesky stragglers that keep comin' in at ten past eight every night. *Capiche?*"

The room broke into laughter. But my eyes misted as Mabel prayed a prayer of blessing on the new name for the multipurpose room. I couldn't wait to tell Aunt Mercy and my sisters. I hoped my sisters would be pleased. I knew my mother would be.

Mabel stood after her "Amen." "I hope you all don't mind cutting staff meeting short today. I have a dentist appointment."

She made a face and pointed to her cheek. "Cracked my tooth yesterday eating caramel corn with Jermaine."

"Works for me." I wiggled my way out of the tight school desk. "I have to go pick up P.J. at Lane Tech. But this is the next-to-last time, I promise! School starts in two weeks!"

I managed to get out the door right on the heels of Mabel and Estelle just before traffic snarled behind me as everyone tried to scoot out the schoolroom door at the same time. But that's how I overheard Mabel murmur to Estelle, "Is Leroy all right? Did the fire damage your house too much?"

chapter 12

Fire? At Estelle's house? Estelle had a house?

I had to run out to pick up P.J., or I would have followed Estelle then and there. What was Mabel talking about? None of this computed. If Estelle had a house, why had she ended up a resident at Manna House? And now she was sharing an apartment with Leslie Stuart on the second floor of the Baxters' two-flat.

I hurried back to the shelter after picking up P.J. from cross-country practice, hoping to talk to Estelle before the lunch crunch hit. But by the time I checked on Paul, who was doing his volunteer thing playing Ping-Pong with a handful of kids in the rec room, Estelle was hollering orders at her two assistants who had pulled lunch prep on the residents' chore chart. "Tawny! Turn those burgers over! No, no, not with a fork . . . Wanda, show that girl where the spatula is!"

"Mi? Mi? How do mi know where dat ting is? . . . Ohh. *Dat* ting."

Decided this wasn't a good time to have a heart-to-heart with

Estelle. I'd catch her later. But I felt a tad sorry for the new girl, Tawny, who scurried like a mouse trying to stay out of the way of the big cats. Both Wanda and Estelle were large women, and Wanda's Jamaican *patois* wasn't so easy to understand.

Unlocking my office door, I glanced back at the girl in the kitchen, now flipping burgers on the hot stove-top grill. *Tawny . . .* she'd been aptly named. The teenager's skin was fawn-colored, her long bushy hair—barely covered by the ugly hairnet—a fusion of brown, tan, and gold rivulets. Hard to tell what her ethnicity was. Mabel said she'd been dumped out of the foster-care system when she turned eighteen, even though she didn't have her high school diploma yet. But the girl had *chutzpah*, turning up at Jodi's typing class twice now, saying she wanted to get her GED, maybe even go to college.

I slipped into my office and turned on the computer. *Still, she's just a kid . . . a kid with no home, no parents apparently . . .* As I waited for the computer to boot up, I looked around at the excess of stuffed toy dogs still piled on every available surface in my office, left at the shelter after Dandy had made himself a "hero dog" by attacking a burglar and getting himself knife-wounded in the process. Chicago loved heroes, even dog heroes. We'd given away most of the stuff left by well-wishers, but kept the stuffed animals to give to children who ended up in the shelter.

I picked up a soft black dog with floppy ears and a pink ribbon around its neck. *Would Tawny . . . ?*

I never did get a chance to talk to Estelle that Monday. Forgot she taught a sewing class on Mondays, even though I'd donated my one and only sewing machine to the effort. She was busy at the far end of the dining room helping the three ladies who showed up how to lay out a pattern for a simple apron when I left with Paul at two o'clock. And I took the boys shopping that afternoon for school clothes at Woodfield Mall, "Chicago's Largest Shopping Center." I figured a big mall with lots of stores would be a safe bet to find what the boys needed for school, and we'd be back in time for supper and a quiet evening when I could call Estelle.

What I didn't figure on was just how long it took to get to "Chicago's Largest Shopping Center" from the north side. Schaumberg, it turned out, was way out past O'Hare Airport, past a half-dozen suburbs, past a huge forest preserve, and traffic on I-90 was already starting to creep with homebound traffic. It was almost four o'clock by the time we parked and found our way around the mall.

As far as I was concerned, one big department store should've been able to cough up the necessary gym shoes, socks, jeans, shirts, and underwear for two boys. But no, they wanted to check out all the specialty teen shops too. P.J. had shot up at least three inches in the past year, faster than he could wear out his clothes. They'd probably be just right for Paul, I mused, as the boys tried on the latest Gap jeans . . . but it didn't seem fair for P.J. to get all the new clothes while Paul wore hand-me-downs. And both boys were going to need winter jackets and boots, though I held off on those. Good grief, it was still eighty degrees outside! Chicago's deep freeze would definitely be different from Virginia's mild winters, but maybe Philip could help buy some of the big-ticket items for the boys. Something to talk about when we talked . . .

If we talked.

Which reminded me, maybe I should talk to Estelle about Philip, get a second opinion about whether I should talk to him. Then maybe I wouldn't seem so nosy if I said, oh by the way, I heard Mabel say something about your son and a fire at your house?

I parked myself on a bench when the boys got diverted by a video game arcade and called Estelle's cell, but only got voice mail and had to leave a brief message.

The boys wanted to eat at the Rainforest Cafe at the mall, billed as "A Wild Place to Shop & Eat." It was wild all right, and I don't mean just the simulated rainstorms with thunder, lightning, rainbows, and animated wildlife in the "trees" hanging over the tables that punctuated our supper of Lava Nachos, Rainforest Burgers (the boys), Rasta Pasta (me), and lemonade. A gazillion other families must have had the same idea to "shop Woodfield" that day, and the place was full of kids on too much sugar.

By the time we got back to the car with our bulging packages, I had a splitting headache and a bulging balance on my new Visa card. The light was blinking on the answering machine when we walked in the door of the apartment, but I didn't bother to listen to the messages before falling into bed. Probably Estelle calling back. Right now I didn't want to talk about Philip or anything. Whatever it was could wait.

I should have listened to the messages.

Prying my eyes open with my first cup of coffee the next

morning, I pushed the Play button and got the first beep. "Hey, Gabby. Jodi here. Just checking in to see if you're okay. I want you to know I'm praying for wisdom about you-know-what. And a sense of peace too. Love you!" *Sweet*. At least she wasn't mad at me for walking out on her at church on Sunday. And smart enough not to mention what she was praying about in case the boys checked the messages before I did. I should've called her first . . . well, I'd do it today.

Philip's voice caught me up short as the next message beeped. "Gabrielle, please pick up if you're there. Can we get together like I mentioned last Saturday? What about four o'clock this Friday? Before I pick up the boys. Can we meet somewhere? Let me know."

Now my eyes were wide open. I quickly glanced at the boys' bedroom doors that opened on the hallway, hoping they hadn't heard. Both still closed. I hit Delete before the next message played. Didn't want the boys to know Philip had asked me to talk in case I decided not to. What did he *want*? He was polite enough on the phone message. Actually, he'd been pretty decent when he dropped the boys off on Saturday. Even offered to follow me so I could take the rental car back and have a ride home. Or was that a first attempt to have "the talk"? Just him and me in the Lexus on the way back from the rental car place—

Third beep. "Gabby? It's Mabel. Call me tonight if you get this. Estelle won't be in tomorrow. She had a family emergency. I need you to put together a lunch team for tomorrow, maybe the next day too. Let me know what you can do."

Oh no! Another emergency? Mabel said "family emergency," so it had to be about Estelle's son . . . Leroy, she said his name was. Poor Estelle. Was this related to the fire at Estelle's house over the weekend? Hopefully this wasn't something worse. But whatever it was, I needed to hustle if I was going to put together a lunch team for *today*, or I'd be cooking lunch by myself.

I managed to get the boys up and moving and P.J. dropped off at cross-country practice in time to get to work ten minutes early that morning. I headed straight for Mabel's office, leaving Paul to sign us in and figure out his volunteer activities by himself. "Mabel!" I burst in without knocking. "What—?"

Mabel was on the phone. She held up a manicured finger. "Yes, yes . . . Thanks, Harry. Tell her not to worry. We'll cover things here . . . Okay. Keep us posted." She hung up and turned to me, rubbing worry lines out of her usually smooth forehead.

"Was that Mr. Bentley?" I asked. "Sorry I didn't call back last night . . . didn't get the message until this morning. What's wrong? Is Estelle okay?"

Mabel nodded. "Yes, that was Mr. Bentley and yes, Estelle is okay." She sighed and absently tucked her straightened bob behind one ear. "It's her son, Leroy. He's in the burn unit at the county hospital with third-degree burns over a third of his body."

I gasped and sank into a chair. "But what happened? You said something yesterday about a fire, but Estelle didn't seem all that upset. So how—?"

Mabel held up a hand. "Two different episodes. Estelle came in yesterday, said there'd been a minor kitchen fire at the house. Leroy was okay, but she was worried that he'd caused the fire—on purpose or accidentally, she didn't know. She hadn't heard from him for several days . . . happens when he doesn't take his meds. He has a long history of mental problems, you know."

I was about to say, "I didn't even know Estelle *had* a son until yesterday!" but Mabel didn't stop for my little snit.

"She told me yesterday maybe she should put Leroy in a mental health facility before he hurt himself. She'd been resisting that idea for years. Then . . . well, I don't know all the details. Harry was listening to his police scanner, heard the address of a major house fire yesterday afternoon and recognized it as Estelle's house—the family home, I mean, where Leroy lives. Harry called Estelle right away, but by the time they got there, the house was basically a total loss, and an ambulance had already taken Leroy to Stroger Hospital. Estelle's with him now, of course. And she's all over herself for letting Leroy stay in the house on his own too long."

I could hardly speak. "Is he . . . is her son badly burned?" Just burning my hand on the stove was painful. I could hardly imagine how Estelle must feel, knowing her son was in terrible pain.

Mabel shook her head. "Don't know." She straightened and pushed back from her desk, all business again. "Well. Main thing we need to do is put together some lunch teams to cover for Estelle. Can you work on that this morning? Start with Precious—she's done it before. But someone will need to check on the menus and food supplies on hand. Estelle usually takes care of all that."

And now it was in my lap. Which was okay . . . though I wanted to ask Mabel why Leroy was living alone. Why didn't Estelle live with him—it was her house, wasn't it? And how come she ended up here at Manna House a couple of years ago? But Mabel was already back on the phone.

I found Precious in the schoolroom, trying to update her

résumé. But before I could say what I'd come for, she pounced. "Girl, you just the sistah I need to see. Can you proofread this for me? I gotta find a job an' soon. Money I had is all run out, and Sabrina gettin' bigger all the time. That baby gonna be here 'fore we know it." The thin, strappy woman eyed me sideways from beneath the fall of short kinky twists that fell across her forehead. "An' I don't mean ta ride on ya, but anything happenin' 'bout this grand idea of yours ta turn that building into a place for us single moms? Me an' Sabrina, we gonna need someplace ta live, an' quick, 'fore that baby gets here."

I ran my fingers through my own mop of red curls, my head spinning. Yes, I needed to get moving on the next steps for the House of Hope, but I wasn't even sure what came first—buying the building or approaching the city? And in the meantime, Philip had thrown me off center asking to talk . . . and now Estelle was out of commission and I was supposed to make sure Manna House served lunch to the fifteen or twenty residents who weren't out for the day, plus staff . . .

I blew out my pent-up frustration. "Uh, Precious, we've got a situation." I quickly filled her in on Estelle's absence and the need to put together a lunch team. "You know your way around that kitchen better than I do. Can you help me put together a lunch team today? If you'll find a couple extra hands—"

Precious was already halfway out the door. "No, *you* go find the warm bodies. You think they gonna listen to me if I tell them they gotta cook today? You're on staff. They'll listen to you. *I'll* go hunt up Estelle's menu and see if we got the goods."

chapter 13

Estelle didn't come back until Thursday, and in that time Pluto had been demoted as a planet and Precious and I managed to pull off two halfway decent lunches for twenty-five folks. The former was big news on CNN and for the astronomy junkies at Chicago's Adler Planetarium, but for me, filling Estelle's shoes in the Manna House kitchen and getting only two complaints—and that was because we ran out of watermelon the second day—should have been right up there with CNN's top stories.

When I'd gone looking for helpers, I'd spied the stuffed animal dogs I'd secretly placed on Tawny's and Sabrina's bunks sitting on their pillows like spoiled show dogs, and Sarge told me on the sly that both teenagers had gone to sleep hugging their new comfort friends. Which gave me the courage to ask Tawny if she'd mind doing lunch prep again—"Since you know your way around the kitchen better than I do"—after her stint on Monday. Okay, maybe I stretched the truth a little, but she deserved some encouragement after surviving kitchen duty bouncing back and forth between Estelle and Wanda. Besides, it gave me a chance to get to know the girl a little.

But I sure was glad to see Estelle come sweeping through the double doors into the multipurpose room—correction, Shepherd's Fold—on Thursday morning, shaking water off her umbrella as an early thunderstorm shook the building. Her hair had been pulled into a no-nonsense topknot and she looked like she hadn't slept much the past few days. Against my selfish instincts—I didn't really want to "do lunch" again—I trailed her downstairs to the kitchen. "Are you sure you should be back at work? You look like you could use some R & R."

She stowed her carryall bag under the counter and tied on a big apron. "Don't need sleep. Need to get back to work. Only so much bedside-sittin' a body can do." She cast a critical eye over the counters, stove, and appliances. "Hm. Not bad. Everything looks clean. And praise Jesus, somebody made coffee." She raised an eyebrow at me. "You?"

"Heard you were coming back today. Thought you might need it." I grabbed the pot, poured two cups, and headed for the nearest table in the dining room. "Estelle, please, take a minute to sit down. I want to hear how your son is doing. Mabel said he has third-degree burns. That sounds terribly painful. Is he going to be all right?"

Estelle hesitated and then gave in, easing herself into a folding chair while I brought sugar for her, creamer for me, and a couple of spoons. She stirred absently and heaved a big sigh. "Hard for me to tell. They've got him in a sterile environment, pouring all kinds of intravenous fluids into him, antibiotics and all that. And he's pretty knocked out on morphine to cut the pain." Her dark eyes teared a little. "He's got burns on a third of his body, mostly along his left side—his left arm, part of his torso and back, and his left leg. They started skin treatment yesterday, putting moist dressings on the burns, then taking them off . . . Lord, Lord, couldn't stand to watch it." She shuddered.

"But, what happened? Mabel said your house is a total loss from the fire. He was living in your house?"

"Mm." Estelle seemed lost in thought.

I waited, but when nothing more was forthcoming, I said bluntly, "Estelle, I don't understand. If you have a house, why were you a resident here at Manna House a couple of years ago? I mean, why is your son living in your house and not you?"

She allowed a sad smile. "Kind of a long story. Told you the other day Leroy has mental problems. One day he's gentle as a lamb, other days . . . well. He lived with me a long time, held odd jobs in construction. But sometimes he'd get upset, wouldn't take his meds. Then . . . well. All hell would break loose. Got so we couldn't live together."

I stared at her. "What are you saying? He got violent? I mean, did he hurt you?"

She didn't answer.

"So *you* moved out and let Leroy stay there? That doesn't make any sense!"

"Not to you, maybe. Did to me." Her eyes got soft. "If I'd kicked him out, where could he go? He would've just ended up in some institution."

"But *you* ended up in a homeless shelter! Seems upside down to me."

"Maybe, maybe not. But what mother can kick out her own child from the only home he knows? He's family!"

Family. The irony was not lost on me. That hadn't stopped Philip from kicking *me* out. But I kept my mouth shut. Estelle's son was in the hospital with serious burns and her house was a total loss. Kind of put my woes in perspective.

"Oh, Estelle, I'm so terribly sorry. Is there anything I can do?"

Estelle shook her head. "Can't talk about it anymore. I'm too tired." Then she frowned at me. "I think you called me a couple of days ago and left a message, something about Philip. Didn't get it until yesterday. What's going on?"

"Oh, just . . . Philip said he wants to talk. About us. But I—"

"What's he want to talk about?" Estelle's frown deepened.

I felt guilty diverting attention from Estelle's big crisis to my petty marital problems. "I don't know! But as you well know, talking 'about us' isn't our strong point. Usually turns out to be Philip talking at me, and me mentally bouncing around trying to figure out how to keep the Fairbanks boat from rocking."

"Humph. Told you before, don't talk to that man alone. Look what happened when you ignored Mama Estelle's advice and sailed into his office, like a curly-headed pigeon flying into a skeet shoot."

I groaned. "Don't remind me. I haven't said I'd meet him. Don't really want to talk to him at all."

"Oh, you have to talk to him, Gabby girl."

"What?" *Not* what I expected from Estelle.

"He wants to talk. That's new. Could be anything. Might be good, might be bad. Only way to find out is to talk to him. Or ask him straight up what it's about. All I'm sayin' is, ain't real smart to go it alone. That's all I'm sayin'." Estelle pushed herself up from the table. "Gotta get to work. Hang in there, Gabby."

I kicked myself later for bringing up the stuff with Philip. Hadn't asked Estelle how the fire started, or what was going to happen now that her house was gone. On the other hand, those topics might be a little touchy. Maybe it was just as well.

By the time Paul and I left Manna House that afternoon, the morning rain had moved out over the lake, replaced by a hazy sky and muggy air. Dropping Paul off at the apartment, I decided it was as good a time as any to take the car to Mr. B's mechanic and get the air conditioner fixed. He even said he'd fix it while I waited. "Harry told me to take good care of you," the mechanic said. "He's always brought me his business. Glad I can return the favor."

By the time the car was fixed, I was wilting from the heat. "Dad called a few minutes ago," P.J. said, not looking up from the video game he was playing as I came in the door. "I told him you'd call him back . . . aha! *Zam zam! Gotcha!*"

Oh, thanks a lot, buddy. I rolled my eyes at P.J. behind his back and headed for the kitchen, where I stuck my head into the fridge . . . *Darn it!* Who drank all the cold pop? Stupid question. All I could find in the pantry were a couple of cans of warm, generic lemon-lime soda. Did I buy that? Oh well. I poured the contents of a can over ice, crushed the can, and went out onto the back porch to toss it into the plastic wastebasket I used for recyclables . . . which was overflowing. I'd forgotten to empty it into the big recycle bin out by the Dumpster. Which got me thinking . . . Did the city pay for that Dumpster and recycle bin? Or the landlord? If I bought the building, would I have to pay for services like that? I had an hour to kill before the boys and I took in the 5:30 movie at the Broadway Theater—our plan for this Thursday. Maybe I should do some more research on the responsibilities of owning a six-flat in Chicago . . .

I let the screen door slam behind me. I was stalling and I knew it. This was the third time this week Philip had left a message, and I still hadn't returned his calls. Had to admit, that in itself was enough to annoy any normal person, me included.

Okay, I'd call him back—but first I dialed Jodi Baxter's number. She sounded a bit breathless when she answered.

"Hey, Jodi. It's Gabby. Philip's been calling. He wants to meet tomorrow before he picks up the boys. I still haven't called him back. Thought I could use that prayer we talked about . . . and, uh, I have a favor to ask."

"A favor? Sure, if I—hey, hey, hey! Isaac! Don't bang that on Havah's head! That is not a toy! Gabby? Hang on a minute . . ." Jodi put the phone down, and I could hear the screeching of some little kids and Jodi's teacher voice sounding as if she was distracting them with something. Then she was back. "Sorry. I'm babysitting Ruth Garfield's twins while she gets her hair done at Adele's. Cute little buggers, but hoo boy. Mischief is their middle name. Now, what were you saying about needing a favor?"

I told her I'd decided to talk to Philip, probably tomorrow, but Estelle didn't think I should talk to him alone. Would she consider going with me?

Jodi didn't answer right away.

"I mean, if you can't, I understand," I blathered. "Estelle just said—"

"No, no, it's not that. I was just trying to think. If Denny and I were having a problem and he wanted to talk, he'd shut up like a clam if I showed up with someone else. Would Philip be willing to talk to you if I came along?"

Denny and Philip. *Huh*. That was like trying to compare Chicago hot dogs and *fois de gras*. Still, maybe they had a few guy things in common. I sighed. "Probably not. In fact, highly unlikely. But . . ." I was grasping. "What if you 'just happened' to drop by wherever we decide to go, act all surprised, say hi and go sit somewhere else?"

"Mm. I don't know, Gabby. He'd see through that in a minute. Look, why don't you just call him and ask what this is about. If he wants to talk divorce or legal stuff about the kids, tell him you want your lawyer present. Otherwise . . ." Her voice trailed off.

"Otherwise what?"

Jodi gave a short laugh. "Otherwise, we better pray! Because I've run out of my half-baked wisdom and I think we need to ask God for some of His!"

Jodi's prayer calmed my spirit. Didn't God have my back? She prayed those words from Psalm 56: "When I am afraid, I will trust in You . . . in God I trust; I will not be afraid." And it was true. In the past few months, when I'd trusted God for the things

I didn't understand or when I didn't know what to do, God always came through. Somehow.

I made sure the boys were busy, went outside to sit on the flat cement "arms" that hugged the outside landing and front steps, and called Philip on his cell. Couldn't believe it when he answered. "Gabrielle! I've left several messages. Why—"

"I know, Philip. I should have called before now. But I don't know if I want to talk about us. Can you tell me what this is about?"

A brief silence. "It's . . . personal. I'd rather talk face-to-face."

Take the initiative, Gabby. "Look, if it's about our legal situation"—ouch, why didn't I just say "divorce"?—"I think I'd like to have my lawyer present."

"Don't need our lawyers. Like I said, it's personal. Can we just talk? You name the place. I'll meet you there. Like five o'clock tomorrow? I'm supposed to pick the boys up at six. Just one hour, Gabby."

He called me Gabby. I let a moment of silence go by. Then . . . "All right. I'll meet you at the Emerald City Coffee Shop. It's right under the Sheridan El Station, a few blocks north of Wrigley Field."

The wall clocks at Manna House seemed to crawl on Friday. Nine hours until my meeting with Philip . . . eight and a half . . . eight . . .

This was stupid! You'd think I was in a hurry to talk to him . . . No, that wasn't it. I was in a hurry to get it over with.

I'd wanted to sit in on Edesa Baxter's Bible study she'd started on *Bad Girls of the Bible*, using a book by Liz Curtis Higgs. The ladies who attended last week, I'd been told, had eaten it up like chocolate. But I only caught the tail end of her study about Lot's wife and the consequences of momentary disobedience after doing my midmorning run to get P.J. from Lane Tech. Maybe Edesa would loan me the book and I could catch up.

I concentrated on work to make the time go faster. Getting the afterschool program up and running by the time school started was the main priority right now. Kids whose lives had been uprooted needed a lot of extra help to not fall through the cracks at school. Avis Douglass, Jodi's principal at Bethune Elementary, had sent us some helpful math and reading materials for grades one through five. But I needed at least two volunteers to be here daily . . . and so far I only had Precious, who'd be great with the younger kids. She only had a high school education herself, but she was the queen of trivia—what's new in NASA's space program . . . who just got traded in the NBA . . . the latest squabble at Chicago's city council . . . the sorry state of bridges in the U.S.— you name it, Precious had the latest facts. Or opinions, anyway.

But her daughter Sabrina had two more years of high school, and the girl would need a *lot* of help with schoolwork once that baby got here. Had to be someone besides her mother—*wait*. What about Carolyn? She'd been at the shelter when I first came and only recently got her own apartment. But Carolyn had been a lit major and former librarian, for goodness' sake! She said she wanted to come back to Manna House to volunteer and we'd been talking about starting a book club . . . why not ask her to put together an honest-to-goodness afterschool program *and* tutor Sabrina? For that matter, why didn't we run our own GED program for our residents? Seemed like half of the adult women hadn't finished high school.

Two o'clock—my quitting time until the boys went back to school—galloped across the finish line before I knew it. I'd managed to get hold of Carolyn and she agreed to come in Monday to talk about it. I gathered up my things, collared Paul—whose enthusiasm for entertaining half a dozen bored kids seemed to be fading—and took P.J. and Paul out for ice cream and a swim at Foster Avenue Beach. When we got home, they flopped in front of the TV and the fans and didn't seem the least bit curious when I said I had to go "out" at quarter to five.

"Don't forget to pack your duffel bags with a change of clothes and underwear," I reminded them, freshening my lipstick and giving my auburn curls a comb-through in front of the hallway mirror. "Your dad will be here to pick you up at six."

On the dot. Philip had one hour to underwhelm me.

chapter 14

I arrived at the coffee shop ten minutes early. No way did I want to arrive late and apologetic. I ordered an iced latte and looked around for a seat. The couch by the window? No, too cozy. But most of the small tables were occupied. *Rats.* Maybe I should have suggested something like that funky retro place Lee Boyer had taken me to after he showed me the six-flat . . . *no, no, no.* Meet Philip at the same place I'd been with Lee? Too weird. This would have to do.

A middle-aged guy with a shock of uncombed hair packed up his computer, stuffed it in a messenger bag, and vacated a tiny table by the opposite window. I zipped over and claimed the space, swiping crumbs off the table with a napkin he'd left.

I sipped my latte, letting the creamy cold coffee soothe my nerves. Philip's black Lexus slowed outside just as an El train rattled into the station overhead, unloaded and loaded, and pulled out again. New customers fresh off the train trailed in. The Lexus disappeared from sight . . . but a few minutes later Philip pushed open the door and walked in.

Several heads turned as he entered. The glances of the females lingered. Couldn't blame them. Even at forty-one, Philip Fairbanks had movie-star good looks. Tall and slender, his dark hair and tan skin complemented the pale green dress shirt he wore with an open collar, topping a neat pair of black slacks and black loafers.

Two twentysomethings at a nearby table wearing Gap-inspired wrinkle-look tops, short skirts, and flip-flops gave each other *gosh-darn-it* looks when Philip headed for my table and sat down across from me. For a nanosecond, a smug smile tugged at the corner of my mouth—that age-old rivalry when The Man chooses The Alpha Woman over the other females in the herd. I'd dressed carefully—white slacks, russet cotton top that complemented my reddish-gold auburn hair, russet-colored beaded earrings that dangled, and gold strap sandals. But reality snuffed out the smug smile. *If they only knew.* I had to stifle the urge to toss out, *"You want him? You can have him!"*

"Thanks for meeting me, Gabrielle." Philip took off his wrap-around sunglasses and slipped them into his shirt pocket.

How did we start this talk anyway? "Do you want to get a coffee? Something to drink?"

He shook his head. "I'm fine. Everything okay with the boys this week? Do they have everything they need to start school?"

Okay, safe start. Talk about the boys. "Pretty much. They still need backpacks. Might need some sports equipment, depending on what they sign up for. And winter coats and boots when the time comes."

"Okay."

"Okay what? Are you offering to get that stuff for the boys?"

"Yeah, yeah, sure."

I wanted to say, *"See? We should have met with our lawyers to iron out all the child support stuff, get it down on paper."* But I sipped my iced latte to keep from filling up space with empty chatter.

"I—" Philip glanced out the window a moment, then back at me. "I know this might sound phony after everything that's happened, but I really am sorry about your mother, Gabrielle. Sorry she died staying in a shelter. I, uh . . ." He cleared his throat. "At the time, I thought it'd be better for everyone if she had her own place, a retirement home or something. Didn't think you'd put her in the shelter. It's just . . . everything felt out of control—summer plans for the boys falling through, losing an important client at work, the house suddenly crowded . . ."

I didn't trust myself to speak. What was he saying? Was he apologizing for kicking my mother out? Not really. Sorry things worked out the way they did? I was supposed to feel sorry for him because things felt out of control?

My hand holding the tall latte started to shake. I set it down and put my hands in my lap.

Philip actually kept eye contact. "It's been a rough time for all of us. But in the long run, you seem to be doing good, Gabby. The money from your folks . . . that was a surprise. Who would have thought? I'm glad things are working out for you."

I hardly knew how to respond. He actually sounded glad—relieved?—I'd gotten myself together. But I still didn't trust myself to speak. Or maybe I didn't trust what he was saying.

He glanced at the tables near us and lowered his voice. "But to be honest, things haven't been going too well on my end. The business . . . well, a start-up company has its highs and lows. Just can't sustain too many lows. And personally . . . I'll be frank. I've gotten myself in kind of a jam. Which is why I wanted to talk to you."

I all but snorted. Philip—confident, bold, over-the-top, I-can-do-anything Philip Fairbanks—was actually admitting things weren't going well? If the business was floundering, what did that have to do with me?

But my thoughts must have been plastered all over my face because he held up both hands, palms out, as if begging for patience. "Just hear me out, Gabby. I need a loan—a personal loan. I've got a debt I need to pay off, and—"

"A *loan*?" I found my voice. So *that's* what this was about! "You want *me* to give you a loan? Good grief, Philip, you've got all kinds of credit! Just ask the bank for a loan."

He shook his head. "It's not that easy. Uh, things have gotten complicated. I've let business and personal stuff overlap . . . when you own the company, it's easy to do, you know. Anyway, while that's getting sorted out, a loan the size I need would take a whole lot of paperwork and collateral I can't afford right now. And time. Time is an issue. I need this loan right away."

My eyes narrowed. "It's a gambling debt, isn't it?"

He threw open his hands. "I've made some mistakes. Right now I just want to take care of my debts and get back on track."

"Mistakes. Uh-huh. Exactly what size loan are you talking about?"

He tried to be casual. "Twenty-five thousand. Fifty would be better. Would get me back on track faster. Just need to get over this hump."

I wanted to laugh. Hysterically. "Philip Fairbanks! This is ridiculous. I work for a homeless shelter, for heaven's sake. Part time, I might add, until the boys go back to school. You've got a commercial real estate company that's capable of pulling in big bucks. Why ask me?"

"I told you, the company's had some rough times lately. And, well, this is personal. I'd rather not involve Henry. I know you got some money from your folks. I don't know how much, but an inheritance usually comes in a lump sum. I'm talking about a short-term loan. Short-term, Gabrielle. I'll pay it back. I just need to put things straight, get back on track. You know I'm good for it."

I started shaking my head the moment he said *"money from your folks."* "I need that money, Philip. And you know it. I'm starting from scratch, thanks to you." A well of emotion threatened to push through the plug I'd stuck in it. I stood up, bumping the table and almost sending my half-empty latte onto the floor. But I grabbed it in time and stalked to the counter to get a glass of water. This was why we met in a public place or I might have gone off on Philip right about then.

I was tempted to head out the door without even finishing the conversation. But I took my ice water back to the table and sat down. "Besides," I said, as if I hadn't left, "I have plans for that money."

A small smile tugged at his mouth. "I know. You'd like to buy that building. Which seems like a big risk, Gabby. I'd hate to see you get in over your head—"

"I don't believe this! You've got a *gambling* debt, and you're talking to me about risk?"

He put up his hands again. "Okay, point taken. But even if you go ahead with that plan, unless you're signing papers today, you won't need a down payment for another couple of weeks, right? And by then I'll have the money back to you. With interest. I promise. And . . ." His voice trailed off, and he started to draw circles on the table with his finger.

I waited. *I really should just get up and walk out the door.* But he seemed to be struggling to say something. Morbid curiosity got the better of me. "And?"

The circles stopped and he looked up, his brown eyes searching mine. "Once I'm out from under this cloud, Gabby, maybe we could sit down and talk about where we go from here. You and me, I mean. And the boys. Maybe . . . maybe it's not too late to repair the damage."

It was like he knocked the breath out of me. What did he just say? *Repair the damage?* Did he really say that?

I stood up, not looking at him, reaching for my purse. "It's almost six. The boys are waiting for you."

He followed me out to the sidewalk. "Will you consider the loan, Gabby?"

Another El train lurched and groaned into the station overhead.

"When?" I shouted over the din.

"When?" Philip grimaced. "Well, yesterday would be good."

I headed for my car without replying but heard him call after me, "Just think about it, Gabrielle. Please?"

chapter 15

The black SUV with Philip and the boys was barely out of sight before I ran back into the apartment, grabbed the phone, and called Jodi Baxter. "The nerve of that man!" I exploded in her ear, not even taking time to identify myself. "He wants a *loan*, Jodi! Can you believe it? He's asking me for a loan!"

"You're kidding! . . . You're not kidding."

"I am not kidding. He's got a gambling debt—don't know how much or who he owes money to. The casino? Do they give credit? But he said something about his business being in trouble too. Anyway, he asked for twenty-five thousand—" I heard a gasp at the other end. "Ha. You think that's bad? He said fifty would be even better, would help him get 'back on track' faster. And *then*—"

"Whoa. Slow down, Gabby. I better sit." I heard their screen door slam in the background and the creaking of the back porch swing. "Now, start at the beginning. Because I don't believe Philip walked in and said right off, 'Hi, Gabby, will you loan me twenty-five thousand bucks?'"

"Okay, okay," I muttered. "Give me a sec . . ." I plumped up a couple of fat throw pillows on the window seat in the sunporch, set a fan in one of the open windows, and made myself comfy. Then I told Jodi as best I could the gist of my conversation with Philip barely an hour ago, starting with his pseudo sympathy for the loss of my mom . . .

"But that's not all," I said when I'd covered most of it. "He got all weird at the end, kind of emotional. Said once he was out from under this 'cloud'—paying off his debt, I guess—he wanted to talk about how we could 'repair the damage' to our marriage."

"No! He actually said he wanted to repair the damage to your marriage?"

"Well, what he said was, he wanted us to talk about 'where we go from here.' And 'Maybe it's not too late to repair the damage.'"

"Oh. My. Goodness. Gabby, that's huge! What did you say?"

"Uh . . . nothing. I was so taken aback, I just got up and left. It was time to leave anyway."

"You just left."

Why was Jodi repeating everything I said? "Yes! I just left . . . no, take that back. When we got outside I asked, 'When'—like, how soon did he need the loan. He tried to joke, said he needed it yesterday. But he meant as soon as possible." Even as the words came out of my mouth, I wished I *had* just left without saying anything else. "Oh, Jodi, do you think by asking when he needed the money, it sounded like I was going to give it to him?"

The squeaking from the swing on the Baxters' back porch stopped, as if Jodi was pondering my question. "I don't know. Maybe. But don't worry, Gabby. You haven't committed yourself to anything. I'm just . . . I dunno. Kind of flabbergasted he even suggested that maybe it wasn't too late to repair the damage to the marriage."

"Except . . ." How could I put into words what I was feeling right now? Or not feeling might be more like it.

"Except what?" Jodi finally asked.

"Maybe it is too late."

Sitting on the beach near Montrose Harbor an hour later, I dug my toes into the warm sand and hugged my knees. After the phone call with Jodi, I'd grabbed my car keys and got out of the house. Didn't even change clothes. So what if I still had my white slacks on. Lucy wasn't around to give me what for. I chuckled, remembering the time the frumpy bag lady had lectured me on not wearing my good clothes to the beach. Frankly, I wished Lucy and Dandy would turn up about now. I could use a little down-to-earth distraction after my weird talk with Philip and trying to field Jodi Baxter's fixation on my estranged husband's "repair the damage" comment.

Jodi meant well. After all, *she* had a marriage worth saving. And of course there was a lot of stuff in the Bible about honoring marriage vows. But Estelle! I laughed to myself again. Estelle made no bones about saying she'd like to "put down her religion" long enough to give Philip a good whack upside his head!

A puff of warm wind off the lake stirred up my mop of curls as erratic thoughts tumbled inside my head. But now . . . Would everyone get all excited if I said Philip wanted to work on our marriage? Was he serious? Or just buttering me up to make me consider giving him that loan?

Wouldn't put it past him.

But even if he was serious . . . why didn't I feel anything? Didn't I want us to be a family again? Even though the boys seemed to be adjusting to our separation, I knew they were still hurting. They'd probably like nothing better than to see Mom and Dad get together again.

I dug my toes deeper into the sand. And what about me? Didn't I get lonely? Stupid question. Crawling into a single bed every night made me feel like the last kitty in the litter, no one to snuggle with. Didn't I struggle with feeling rejected, like an old shoe tossed into the garbage? Like every day. Wouldn't I rather be married than a single mom, eking out a living on my own? Yes . . . maybe.

And that was the rub. I *had* been rejected, tossed out, left to claw my way out of a pit. But now I was standing on my own two feet. And I had plans. Good plans. Okay, maybe impossible plans, but plans that made me feel like the real Gabby.

And Philip wasn't part of them.

My answering machine light winked at me when hunger drove me in from the beach. I punched the Play button as I pulled out some leftover chicken salad and ate it cold, straight from the plastic container. "Gabby? It's Jodi. I realize we didn't really talk about that loan Philip wants, much less pray about it. Some prayer partner I am! Sorry I got off track. I'll be praying you get some good advice about that. Maybe you should talk to your lawyer—or a financial wizard, if you've got one. Though I realize it's not just a money thing. More like a wisdom thing. Okay. I'm blathering. Just wanted to apologize. Don't sit up all night worrying. Or if you do, call me and we'll pray on the phone. Bye!"

Couldn't help smiling. I loved that Jodi, I really did. When I first met her, she'd seemed so together—perfect family, perfect husband, perfect church attendance, perfect Christian . . . but on our road trip to North Dakota with my mom's casket in the back of the shelter van, she admitted she'd done the "good Christian girl" thing so long, she didn't even realize how judgmental and self-righteous she'd become until she got involved with the Yada Yada bunch.

"Remember Yo-Yo, the girl in our prayer group who wears overalls all the time? She wasn't brought up in church," Jodi had told me somewhere on that long drag through the Midwestern plains, "so she makes me explain myself whenever I use churchy clichés. 'Why didn't ya just say so!' she huffs. And Florida? She's got antennas fine-tuned to pick up on any self-righteous, better-than-thou Pharisee stuff. Whew, she can take me down quicker than I can say hallelujah."

That had cracked me up, made me wish I could be part of a group of praying sisters like that, women who were real. The one time Jodi had taken me to the Yada Yada Prayer Group, they'd prayed for me so powerfully that I would "live into the meaning of my name"—which Edesa Baxter said meant "Strong woman of God"—that I went back to the shelter with renewed hope that God had not forgotten me and my mom, that He would give me the strength to get through the mess my life had become.

And He had. So far anyway. It had to be God's doing, because

I never would have dreamed I'd be able to stand on my own two feet without Philip. Or in spite of Philip. And *never* in a million years did I imagine Philip would come crawling to me, asking for a *loan*.

It was almost pathetic.

I dumped the empty leftover container into the sink and started to reach for the phone. I should call Jodi back, pray with her about what I should do . . . but I hesitated. What if God wanted me to give him that loan? Give him the benefit of the doubt? Help him "get over this hump" so we could move on and talk about where we go from here?

Instead I called Lee Boyer's cell. After all, Jodi said I should get some wise advice. What was a lawyer for if not to get advice about something as big as a twenty-five-thousand-dollar loan?

We met for breakfast the next morning at Kitsch'ns in the Roscoe neighborhood south of Wrigleyville, the same funky place Lee had taken me to before. "Gabby!" he said, sliding into the chair opposite me at the wobbly sidewalk table outside the tiny restaurant. "I'm so glad you called me. What the heck is this about? Philip is asking you for a *loan*?—Wait. Let's order, then I want to hear all about it."

Lee was wearing Birkenstocks, rusty-tan cargo shorts, and a short-sleeve T-shirt that showed off the freckles on his tan arms. Quite a contrast to my "dress for success" husband—which was one of the things that endeared Lee to me. While waiting for our omelets, I told him the whole story. All except the part about

Philip saying once he got over this hump, he wanted to talk about "where do we go from here."

The look on Lee's face behind his wire rims was priceless. He laughed aloud. "Unbelievable! Look, I'm sorry. Don't mean to laugh at a guy who's down on his luck, but this is beautiful. You're on your way up; he's unraveling. Definitely works in your favor when we see the judge about your custody petition."

A waiter in jeans made the rounds of the sidewalk tables and refilled our coffee. I waited until he was gone. "I don't think Philip is going to give me a problem about custody. The boys are with me now, and he agreed to have them just Friday night and Saturday. Works with his schedule, I think."

Lee wagged his head. "Don't take anything for granted, Gabby girl. I won't feel easy until you have it court-approved and in writing. As for the loan?" Lee leaned toward me, tapping a finger on the table for emphasis. "Don't . . . do . . . it. That would be a huge mistake. *You* need that money, every penny. It'll look good—real good—on your bank statement when you go before the judge to prove you have the means to support the boys. And if you're serious about buying the six-flat you're living in . . . say, by the way, I called the realtor handling the building. He seemed very interested when I told him I had a reliable client who already lived in the building. I'll make an appointment for you next week if you want to move on it."

"My lawyer says don't do it," I told my sisters on the phone. Celeste, Honor, and I had actually managed to pull off our

Saturday three-way call this time—noon my time, ten in California, nine in Alaska.

"I guess not!" Celeste barked. "That's Mom's money. And after the way he treated her? She'd turn over in her grave if you loaned that money to him."

I let that go. Our mom never had been one to hold grudges. If Martha Shepherd thought her son-in-law was trying to quit gambling and do right by his family, she'd probably forgive him and *give* him the money. Though come to think of it, he never did admit he needed help as a problem gambler. Just that he'd "made some mistakes."

"But Gabby said she didn't tell her lawyer what Philip said about wanting to work on their marriage," Honor said, talking to Celeste as if I wasn't on the line. "Doesn't that make a difference? Maybe loaning him the money would show good faith on Gabby's part that—"

"Honor Shepherd!" Celeste practically yelled in our ears. "Are you high on something? He just said that to make her think he's turned around. But did he say he was sorry? Unless I missed something, I didn't hear 'sorry' in there. I'm with the lawyer, Gabby. Don't do it."

"Well, I think she could loan him *something*. He said he'd pay it back."

"And you believe him? That's the trouble with you, Honor. That's why you're raising River and Ryan in a trailer park, because you believed all the nonsense their loser father kept promising."

"And what's wrong with a trailer park? We got a nice double-wide now with our share of the inheritance money—nicer than that log cabin you and Tom live in, up there in that godforsaken wilderness they call a national forest."

"How would you know, Honor? You've never been here. We happen to *like*—"

"Celeste! Honor!" I butted in. "I'm losing you! I'm just getting static . . . sorry . . . we'll talk next week, okay? Love you! Bye!" I put the phone down like a hot potato. *Good grief.* What was up with those two?

I glanced at the kitchen clock. Yikes, Philip would be bringing the boys back in a few hours and I still needed to do the grocery shopping. And, drat, I'd wanted to go looking for a decent dining room table to replace the ridiculous plywood-on-sawhorses sitting under that linen tablecloth. Well, forget the table. No time for that now. The boys still had one week to go until school started, which meant they'd be in the house eating all day.

But even as I grabbed the scrawled grocery list off the refrigerator door, I realized a lot more than restocking my pantry had to be in place by six o'clock.

Philip, no doubt, would be expecting my answer by then.

chapter 16

Well, so what? I told myself, lugging the last of the grocery bags into the house a couple of hours later. I had my answer, didn't I? At least my lawyer and my big sister agreed with my first, second, and third inclinations—don't give Philip a loan. *In fact*, I thought, stuffing the freezer with frozen waffles and Tombstone pizzas, *he has a lot of nerve, asking me for money after he cut me off without a dime!* I got hot just thinking about it. As far as I was concerned, it served him right to be suffering financial loss just like he'd made me suffer—

The loud door buzzer down the hall rattled my interior monologue. *What?* I glanced at the clock. Only five o'clock! Was Philip back early? *Oh no. Oh, God, I don't feel ready.* Ignoring the intercom as I ran down the hall, I opened the front door a crack and peeked into the outer foyer . . . and breathed a sigh of relief. Estelle Williams, dressed in a bright yellow-and-black caftan, was fanning herself with a piece of junk mail on the other side of the glass-paneled door while Harry's grandson gleefully pressed my doorbell as if it were dispensing free gum balls.

I stepped into the outer hall and pulled open the locked door. "Estelle! You must really be desperate to show up on my doorstep, because you *know* I don't have central air. Where's . . . Oh, hi, Mr. B." Harry Bentley backed into the foyer still trying to lock his car with the remote key. I waved the trio inside. "Come in, come in. Did you go to the hospital today? Is Leroy doing okay?"

Estelle heaved a sigh. "So-so. Gonna be a long haul. We stopped by the house too—what's left of it—to see what we could salvage. Not much. Lord, have mercy. What a mess."

Harry pulled a large handkerchief from his back pocket and mopped sweat from his shaved head, glistening like a brown bowling ball. "I decided to get her out of that burned-up mess and do something fun to take her mind off it—"

"We gonna see fireworks tonight—from a boat!" DaShawn blurted, bouncing up and down. "Grandpa got free tickets! Can P.J. and Paul come too?"

Harry grinned sheepishly. "Like the boy said. You know, one of those Chicago lakefront cruises. The department gets these complimentary tickets to give out all the time. My partner— ex-partner, sorry—thought we could use a bunch." He pulled out a handful of tickets. "We've got enough for the Fairbanks Musketeers—you too, Firecracker."

"Oh, Harry, that sounds like fun. I'm sure the boys would love it. But they're still out with their dad, won't be home for another hour . . . You want to play with that, DaShawn?" The boy had pounced on P.J.'s Nintendo, which was still hooked up to the TV. "Sure, go ahead. You all want some ice water or something?" I started for the kitchen.

Estelle stopped fanning and perked up. "The boys aren't here? Good. Was hopin' we could talk private-like." She was right on my heels and plopped herself at my kitchen table, waving Harry into a chair. "Don't worry about no ice water, girl. I wanna know did you talk to Philip? Did you take somebody with you? What did he want?"

I got the water anyway and joined Estelle and Harry at the tiny table. "Yes, I did. I mean, yes, I talked to him. No, I didn't take anybody with me, because . . ." I filled her in on Jodi's point of view when a guy says he wants to talk. Alone.

"Smart girl, that Jodi," Harry smirked. "Listen and learn, Estelle."

"Humph. Don't remember askin' you. Go on, Gabby."

"Okay. Maybe you guys can give me some advice about what I should do . . ."

Even as I retold what had transpired between Philip and me at the Emerald City Coffee Shop, I thought, *What am I doing? Haven't I already made up my mind how to answer Philip?* But something still nettled me. I wanted to feel more confident that I was doing the right thing. I was pretty sure Estelle would agree with me. But I'd like to know what Mr. Bentley thought about the whole thing. He'd been around the block a few times and he'd always given me good advice.

"Lord, have mercy!" Estelle said, rolling her eyes when I'd told my story. "That man must be in a heap o' trouble for him to come askin' *you* for a loan. You told him to go soak his head, right?"

I laughed. "Not yet. I told myself I didn't have to respond to anything right then, so I just listened and left. Frankly, why should I rescue him after what he did? That's what everybody is telling me. Don't do it."

Mr. B's cell phone rang. He glanced at the caller ID and got up. "Sorry. Gotta take this. Be back in a minute." He disappeared into the dining room.

Estelle was right back on our conversation. "Everybody who?"

"Well . . ." I told her about my conversations with Lee Boyer and my sisters.

"You said you talked to Jodi? What did she say?"

"She didn't really give me her opinion about the loan. Just offered to pray with me about it."

"Did you?"

I squirmed. "Uh, not really. Haven't really had ti—"

"Uh-huh. I figured."

I frowned. "What do you mean? Estelle! *You* don't think I should give him the money, do you?"

"You kidding? I happen to agree with you and Mister Lawyer and your big sis. But can't say my reasons are all that holy. Yours either, for that matter. Oh, Harry's back . . . Everything okay?"

Mr. Bentley sank back into his chair, a smug grin on his face. "Yep. That was Cindy. They've picked up our man. Indictment came out this morning."

"Oh, praise Jesus!" Estelle said. "I'm glad that dirty cop is off the street."

Mr. Bentley grunted. "For about a minute. He'll pay his bond and be out tomorrow. But at least they'll put him on leave from the force till the trial."

"Hello-o." I waved my hand in their faces. "What are you guys talking about?"

"Sorry. Just some old police business. What'd I miss while I was out?"

"Gabby says everybody tellin' her don't go givin' Philip a loan. But she wants to know what *you're* thinkin'."

Mr. B pursed his lips and scratched his beard. "Sounds to me like Fairbanks is a classic 'problem gambler.' I've seen it take down guys on the force again and again. He's addicted, just like a drug addict. Doesn't know when to stop. Even if you did loan him money out of the kindness of your heart, you wouldn't be doing him a favor. He'd just gamble it away. And you'd just be enabling a bad habit."

Don't know why I stuck up for Philip. "He promised to pay it back. I think he honestly realizes—"

Harry shook his head. "Maybe your husband thinks he sees the light, even promises himself he won't do it anymore. I don't much care for the man, but I'd be the first one to cheer if he actually got some help, turned things around, decided to treat you right. But throwing money at a gambling problem is the worst thing you can do. If you care for your husband at all, don't loan him that money. Any money."

Estelle rolled her eyes heavenward and wagged her head. "Mm-mm-mm. Outta the mouth o' babes an' old men. Now *that* sounds like a God-reason to say no. Now that we got our petty little selves outta the way, maybe we're ready to pray 'bout this? What do you say, honey?"

For some reason, tears rolled down my face as Estelle prayed. A sense of peace replaced my anxiety as I held hands with Estelle and Harry. Saying no felt right now. Not out of vengeance. Not because it was Mom's money. Not even because it was mine and I needed it. But because it was the right thing for Philip's sake.

The door buzzer rang while we were still praying. "I'll get it!" DaShawn yelled.

Estelle, Harry, and I looked at each other. "It's okay," I said, starting toward the front of the apartment. "I'm glad you guys came. Go ahead and ask the boys if they'd like to go on the fireworks cruise—" Which was a moot point, because by the time we got to the living room, DaShawn was already begging P.J. and Paul to go with them.

"Can we, Mom? Huh? Can we?" Paul bounced on his feet. Even P.J. looked interested as DaShawn showed them the brochure of Windy City Cruises.

Philip had come in with the boys, not just let them out as he usually did. I noticed he was dressed basically in the same clothes he'd worn yesterday, and he didn't look happy to see me with company. "Bentley," he acknowledged with a stiff nod. "And Miss . . . I'm sorry. I've forgotten your name."

"Haven't forgotten yours," Estelle quipped. "Estelle Williams, chief cook and bottle washer at Manna House Women's Shelter, friend of sinners and friend of your wife."

Philip seemed taken aback. He frowned. "Uh . . . I was hoping you and I could talk, Gabrielle."

"Estelle and Harry were just leaving," I said, more breezily than I felt. "Boys! Would you like to go on this boat cruise with DaShawn's grandpa and Miss Estelle? You'd have to go now."

"What about supper?" P.J. wanted to know.

"Don't worry, we'll feed you." Harry grinned.

Within a few minutes, P.J. and Paul had scrambled into the backseat of Harry's RAV4 with DaShawn and were fighting over whose seat belt was whose.

"Are you sure you want to talk to Philip by yourself, baby?" Estelle murmured to me as she got in the front seat. "You could just tell him the answer is no and come with us. You don't have to explain yourself."

"I know, Estelle. But I'll be okay. Thanks for taking the boys. This works out for the best. I was wondering how we were going to talk with them around."

I watched until Harry's car turned the corner, and then went back into the house. Philip was sitting forward on the upholstered chair I'd taken from the penthouse, elbows on the padded arms, hands together in front of his face. He looked up as I came in. "Did you think about my request, Gabrielle?"

"I did." I sat down in the rocking chair I'd brought from my mom's house, crossing my legs at the ankle, hoping my mascara hadn't run when I got teary during our prayer time. "The answer is no, Philip. I'm not going to give you a loan."

His jaw clenched. "Why? I need this, Gabrielle! I said I'd pay you back. You've got the money—more than enough, right? How would it hurt you to help me out for a couple of weeks?"

"It would hurt you, Philip. You need more than money. You need to get some help. Your gambling has obviously become a big problem."

"Yeah, yeah." He snorted and leaned back in the chair. "Fine. I'll get some help. But first I need to get out from under this debt. *That's* the problem."

"No, your problem is you've become somebody I don't even recognize anymore. What you did to my mother and me? That's not the Philip Fairbanks I married."

Philip looked at me sharply. "So that's what this is about. I figured as much. This is payback, isn't it?" He suddenly stood up and stabbed a finger at me. "Well, let me tell you something, Gabrielle Fairbanks. You *owe* me! You owe me a whole lot more than twenty-five or even fifty grand."

I nearly fell out of the rocker. "I *owe* you? What are you talking about?"

"How long have we been married? Fifteen, sixteen years? How much income did you contribute to our family during that time? *Nada*. Oh, oh, I take that back. You had that sweet little job playing games with the old folks at the nursing home, which gave you a little spending money for . . . what? One year? Two? Meanwhile, who was paying the real bills? I was. Gave you a beautiful home. Gave you two closets full of clothes. Put food on the table—a Belfort Signature table, I might add. Paid for the boys' school, their sports, vacations to the ocean . . . Add *that* up, Gabrielle. Add up sixteen years of marriage in dollars and cents, and you'll see what I'm asking you for is peanuts! Peanuts!"

By this time, Philip was pacing back and forth, running a hand down the back of his head. I was so furious I couldn't say anything for a few moments. But then I found my feet and my voice. I stood up. "How *dare* you reduce our marriage to dollars and cents, to who owes who what?" My voice was shaking. "I won't play that game, Philip. My answer is still no. You'll have to find the money somewhere else."

I crossed the room and opened the front door. "I want you to go. Go!"

Philip glared at me for several moments, and then strode to the door. But at the door he turned, only inches from my face. I could smell his Armani aftershave. "You think you are so holy, so self-righteous, Gabrielle. Going to church now, helping out the homeless. You've told everybody you know—and probably the media too—your pathetic sob story, how I'm the villain who tore our marriage apart. But get one thing straight, Gabby! You walked out of our marriage the day we moved to Chicago. You think I'm not the person you married? I could say the same thing about you!"

chapter 17

The outer door had barely closed behind Philip when I grabbed the closest thing at hand and threw it across the room. "I *owe* him?!" I screeched at the empty house. "I *owe* him?"

Unfortunately, I'd grabbed a glass candle jar off an end table and it smashed against the painted brick gas fireplace on the other side of the room, scattering glass and broken candle wax in a dozen directions.

I stalked down the hallway, then back again with a broom from the pantry. "He thinks I owe *him*?" I muttered to myself as I swept shards of glass into a pile. Hadn't I read somewhere that if everything an at-home mom did had to be hired out—*ha! Including sex?*—it would exceed most paychecks their husbands brought home.

In the middle of my rant, Estelle called to say they had the time wrong and the fireworks cruise didn't start until nine thirty, so they'd be late getting home. "Fine," I said and hung up before she could ask how my talk with Philip went. I was so upset by Philip's accusations—he thought *I* had walked out on the marriage? What kind of baloney was that?!—I didn't want to talk to anybody. I watched a dumb movie on TV, and then used the fact that the boys didn't get home until almost midnight as an excuse to let them sleep in Sunday morning and not go to church.

The boys nixed my suggestion about going for a bike ride along the lakefront that afternoon and instead wandered over to the playground to shoot baskets at the school where Paul would be starting in another week. I stayed home and did laundry, ignoring the phone. Lee Boyer left a message that he'd made an appointment with the realtor for eleven on Tuesday and he'd see me then. And Jodi Baxter left a message saying she didn't see me at church and was I okay?

No, I was not okay, but I didn't feel like talking about it either.

Monday's gray gloom and dripping skies matched my mood as I squished into the shelter. I'd dropped off P.J. at Lane Tech for his last week of preseason practice—rain or shine, the coach said—and talked Paul into coming to the shelter at least a couple of days this final week, but frankly, I didn't want to be there either. *What's wrong with me?* I wondered as I signed in. I'd felt such peace about saying no to Philip after the prayer time with Estelle and Harry. Now I just hoped I wouldn't snarl at the first person who talked to me . . .

"Mom!" I heard Paul squeal from beyond the double doors. "It's Dandy and Lucy!"

Sure enough, Lucy Tucker was sprawled on one of the couches in the newly named Shepherd's Fold, her damp hair plastered against her head, grinning as the yellow dog practically break-danced around Paul, who was down on his knees trying to keep from being bowled over. "Look, Mom, you can hardly see where the stitches are anymore."

It was true. Dandy's hair had grown out over the long knife cut over his shoulder, but overall his hair looked rather matted and dirty, which made me wince. "Hi, Lucy." I plopped down on the couch beside the old lady. "You dropping in for your weekly spa treatment?" *Ha ha*. My hint that a shower and hair wash would be in order. Which gave me an idea. "Hey, Paul, why don't you give Dandy a bath and a blow-dry this morning? Is that okay with you, Lucy?"

The older woman shrugged. "Guess so. Though he jus' gonna get dirty again on a day like this, mud everywhere."

"Why don't you stay a few days until the weather dries out? Weather guy said rain today and tomorrow. Want me to see if there's a bed available?"

Lucy shrugged again, which struck me as odd. She usually had a definite opinion one way or the other. I told Paul to round up Sammy and Keisha—he was going to need the two older kids to help—and I'd set things up for them in the laundry room downstairs. Mabel's office was empty, but a quick look at the bed list at the reception desk showed me there were two beds left. They'd be gone by evening if this rain kept up. I signed Lucy's name for two days and told Angela I'd work it out with Mabel later if there was a problem.

"What's that?" Lucy pointed to the handmade poster on the double doors with scrawled bubble letters: *Shepherd's Fold*.

"That's the new name for the multipurpose room. You know,

Shepherd was my mom's last name, and a Shepherd's Fold is where the shepherd keeps his sheep safe and secure."

"Whatchu think I am, stupid? I *know* what it means an' I know it's named after Miss Martha. What I wanna know is, where's the bronze plaque? That stupid poster gotta go. It's an insult to her memory. We gotta put that name up on a nice, big bronze plaque that says, 'In memory of Miss Martha Shepherd' or somethin' decent. Maybe frame her picture too."

I barely had time to assure Lucy that I'd take her suggestion to the staff meeting that morning when Carolyn showed up to talk about the afterschool program. The shelter's former book maven still looked the same as the day she'd moved out—brownish-gray hair slicked back into a long ponytail, no makeup, and forty extra pounds. But frankly, I thought my idea to ask Carolyn to oversee the afterschool program was brilliant—a lot better use of her talents than just leading a book club once a week. It had taken me a few weeks after I started working at Manna House to realize that the dumpy middle-aged woman had a master's degree in literature. Still on disability after an emotional breakdown and time spent first in a psychiatric facility and then here at the shelter, she'd finally gotten a tiny two-room apartment at Deborah's Place.

But I'd missed her everyday presence, missed seeing that straggly ponytail hunched over a Scrabble board or game of chess. As far as I was concerned, Carolyn and I had a lot in common—two educated women who never thought they'd end up in a homeless shelter. But we had.

The two of us hunkered down in my office to put together a rough plan we could take to the staff meeting at ten. Squeals and doggy whines from the laundry room punctuated our work for about twenty minutes, but shouts of, "Come back, Dandy!" drew both of us out of my office in time to see a sudsy Dandy escape up the stairs to the main floor. By the time we caught the dog, wrestled him back into the laundry room tub, and got him rinsed and dried off, it was already time for staff meeting.

Our damp, rumpled clothes raised a few eyebrows and grins when Carolyn and I joined the others in the schoolroom. I was glad to see Edesa and Josh Baxter there. Regular volunteers were always welcome to attend staff meetings whenever they could. Estelle caught my eye, and I knew she wanted to know what went down when I talked to Philip the other night, but I just mouthed, "*Later.*"

As we plunged into that week's agenda—a new social work intern to assist Sarge at night starting in September, a slug fight over the weekend involving two of the residents, and my proposal that Carolyn take on the afterschool program—I realized my spirit had lifted from the cloud of gloom I'd been under all weekend. That's what I needed, to just keep busy, immerse myself in the work here, forget about Philip. After all, I'd given him my answer and I had a good reason for saying no. What had I expected, that he'd say, "*Sure, I understand. Thanks anyway*"?

". . . classes start this week at UIC," Josh was saying, "so we don't have as much time to look for an apartment. So far we haven't found anything we can afford, and we're starting to feel desperate. If anyone hears of anything for rent in this area, let us know."

Mabel, of course, suggested we stop and pray about that right then, but I had to leave in the middle of her prayer to pick up P.J. and drop him off at home, and by the time I got back, the staff meeting was over. I poked my head into Mabel's office, where she was talking to Josh and Edesa. "Oops, sorry," I said. "Just wondered if you've got any time today. Couple of things I need to talk about . . ."

Mabel peered at me over the top of her reading glasses, then at her appointment book. "I'm free at two. See you then."

I gulped but nodded. Paul and I were supposed to leave at two. But if I was going to talk with the realtor tomorrow, I'd really like to know if things were moving ahead with the city on this second-stage housing idea before I signed on the dotted line. Owning a building just to rent out apartments to any Tom, Dick, or Henrietta wasn't exactly what I had in mind.

Carolyn had stayed after the staff meeting to do more work on the afterschool plans, and bless her, she agreed to challenge Paul to a game of chess to keep him occupied during my meeting. Estelle, of course, tried to corner me after lunch and pry out of me what happened when I talked to Philip, but all I said was that I'd told him no, like she and Harry advised, and of course he wasn't happy about it, but what did we expect?

She gave me a real funny look and muttered, "You and me gonna have a talk, girlfriend. Somethin' don't smell right."

I escaped saying I had a meeting with Mabel, promised Paul I'd try to make it short, and knocked on the director's door right at two o'clock.

"So," she said, as I sank into the sturdy armchair beside her desk. "What's up?"

I let slip a wry smile. Mabel was one of the most attractive, mature African-American women I'd ever met. She definitely had pleasant features, but it was more than that. Her unlined face, framed by her straightened bob, radiated calm. "What's up is I want to be like you when I grow up, Mabel. I come in here, and all my ragtag ends flying every which way just seem to sew themselves up like a quilted baby blanket."

Mabel almost laughed. Almost. "If there's peace in this office, Gabby girl, all the credit goes to God, because I've got a few ragtag ends myself. Jermaine, for one. He starts high school next week—well, you know that, since P.J. is starting Lane Tech too—and I'm on my knees a couple of hours every night praying he won't get picked on like he did last year."

I'd almost forgotten that Mabel's nephew, who suffered a lot of teasing by the more macho types, had tried to commit suicide just months ago. "Oh, Mabel, I'm sorry. I didn't mean to imply you don't have any troubles. It's just . . . how do you keep so peaceful in the midst of all the craziness around here? Like that new woman messing with Tina. Whew! Glad I wasn't here." Sarge's description of the fistfight that started over "get your stuff off my bunk" had all the earmarks of a street feud.

Mabel tapped the Bible she kept on her desk. "Just have to stay in the Word. Stay in the Word . . . because it's not enough to believe *in* God, Gabby. You have to *believe God*. He's a mighty big God, if we let Him *be* God in all our messy situations."

I squirmed. Couldn't say I'd managed to "stay in the Word" the past few weeks since the boys had returned. But if that's what it took to be like Mabel, I needed to make the time. I actually made a note in my notebook—*Pick up where I left off in Matthew's gospel*—then looked up. "Speaking of P.J. and Jermaine, do you want to work out some kind of ride sharing? I'd like to increase my hours again once school starts, but if I could work eight to four, I'd be glad to pick them up after school if you want to do the morning run."

Now Mabel did smile. "Great idea. I'd like to be sure Jermaine gets to school and home again in one piece, at least for the first few weeks. Tell you what, I'll pick up P.J. at your apartment at 7:45 on . . . hm, Monday is Labor Day . . . so next Tuesday." She looked up from her calendar. "Speaking of Labor Day weekend, how about a picnic for the residents at one of the forest preserves or something? This is the first Labor Day since Manna House was rebuilt. Might be a nice tradition to start."

I made another note: *Plan Labor Day picnic ASAP.* Then I brought up the House of Hope proposal and felt encouraged. Mabel had already made contact with the city's Department of Housing and Urban Development, which funded the Low-Income Housing Trust Fund and had started the application process for Manna House to be the service provider. "There will be papers you'll need to sign, Gabby, as the housing provider once you actually own the building. So I'd encourage you to go ahead as quickly as possible—*if* you're still clear this is what you want to do."

I nodded, both excited and anxious. "How long is this going to take? Sabrina's baby is due in November, I think, and I know that girl doesn't want her baby born in a shelter."

Mabel shrugged. "I don't know . . . thirty days minimum if we're lucky. Could be sixty or even ninety days. Depends on several things—how quickly you can get a mortgage, how fast HUD processes the paperwork . . . you know what I'm talking about."

I sagged a bit into my chair. "Yeah, I know. I just wish it

was done already so we could move Precious and Tanya in next weekend."

Mabel just nodded and looked at me thoughtfully. "One other thing . . . you've got your boys back living with you and seeing their father on the weekend. But what's happening with you and your husband? You told me you've filed for custody and redress for unlawful eviction . . . but you haven't mentioned divorce. Are you hoping that you and Philip can reconcile? How does buying this six-flat fit into that?"

I looked down at my lap and then reached for a tissue on her desk. The next thing I knew I was telling her all about Philip "wanting to talk," and how he ended up asking me for a loan to bail him out of his gambling debt, even saying that once he was out from under this cloud, he wanted to talk about "what's next" and that maybe it wasn't too late to "repair the damage."

Mabel listened without speaking up to that point, but then she actually whistled. "Praise God, Gabby. That's amazing! What a breakthrough. But . . . I don't know if loaning him the money would be wise. He—"

"Huh!" I interrupted. "Don't praise God yet. Wait until you hear what happened when I told him I *wasn't* going to loan him the money." The anger I'd been dealing with all weekend crept into my voice as I told her what he'd said, that I "owed" him that money. "And then . . . Mabel, he actually had the audacity to tell me that the failure of our marriage was my fault! That I'd 'left the marriage' when we moved here to Chicago. Can you believe it? I gave up my job, gave up living near my children, gave up my beautiful Southern home with a porch and a yard to follow him here to Chicago! And now he's trying to blame *me!*"

Mabel sat for a long minute with her eyes closed, as if deep in thought. Finally she opened her eyes and gazed at me with a tender, pained expression that almost hurt to see. "There's something to that, you know," she said quietly.

chapter 18

That couldn't be what she said.

For a moment I just sat there, my face stinging as if she'd slapped me. *"What?* Are you saying he's *right?"*

Mabel picked up a pen, rolled it in her fingers, and then put it down again. "No. Believe me, from the little I know, Philip seems like a first-class jerk. I just mean that the breakdown of your marriage isn't all Philip's fault. You bear some responsibility too."

I felt my back stiffen, as if a line had just been drawn in the sand and Mabel had stepped over to the other side. "What exactly are you saying, Mabel?" My voice was tight, holding back the things I wanted to yell, like, *"What do you know, Mabel Turner? Are you forgetting he threw me out and stole my kids?!"*

"All I'm saying, Gabby, is that if you and Philip do talk about repairing the damage to your relationship, it will be important for you to take responsibility for some stuff. I'm not blaming you, or saying it's your fault or that he had any right to kick you out. It's just that . . . I've been troubled by some things that have happened since I've known you."

Hot tears sprang to the back of my eyes, but I was determined not to cry. I gritted my teeth. "Like what?"

Mabel grew thoughtful. "When I offered you the job as program director, you didn't go home and talk it over with your husband. You interviewed, accepted the job, and then told him it was a done deal."

"I was afraid he'd squash the idea!" I cried. "You know that!"

"I realize you had your reasons. But I was concerned that no marriage can tolerate that kind of behind-the-back decision making for long, especially for something that affects a family as much as a job."

Angry tears finally spilled over. I grabbed at the tissue box on her desk again. "This isn't fair, Mabel! You . . . you said yourself that you believed God brought me to Manna House for a special purpose! But *now* . . . oh, now you're saying I should've got down on my knees like a wimp and *asked* my Almighty Husband for permission to take this job—and you *know* if I'd done that, that would've been the end. No job. The last you'd have seen of me."

She waited while I blew my nose. Then she said, "Maybe. Maybe not."

I narrowed my eyes. "What do you mean by that?"

"You're absolutely right. I did say I believed God brought you to Manna House for a special purpose, and I still believe that—"

"Then why are you blaming me for taking the job? I don't understand you, Mabel!"

"Let me finish, Gabby. If we believe God has a purpose for bringing you here, then we can also trust Him to make it happen.

But you were afraid—afraid if you talked it over with your husband, he'd say no. So you took it into your own hands to make it happen, rather than trust God to work it out. But what if you had included Philip in this decision? What if—"

But I had started shaking my head. "You don't understand," I said fiercely. "Philip never would have agreed to me taking this job. He was down on me even coming here to visit! It didn't enhance my image as a 'good corporate wife' and all that."

"That may be so. I don't know. But our timing isn't always God's timing. Maybe you wouldn't have been able to start right away. Maybe there were steps in between that would have helped change Philip's perspective. But my guess is that your choice to move ahead without Philip's agreement put a major stress on your relationship." She tipped her head to the side. "True?"

A tension headache had started to screw its way into the back of my head. I stood up abruptly. "I . . . I can't do this right now. I'm sorry, Mabel. I need to go . . . take Paul home. Maybe we can, you know, talk later . . ." I stalked out of her office, poked my head into the multipurpose room—yeah, yeah, the Fold—and yelled in the direction of the chess game, "Paul! We gotta go!"

"Wait a sec, Mom! I'm winning!"

"*Now*, Paul!"

I was pretty much a basket case the rest of the day. The boys decided I was in a "mood" and stayed out of my way. So what if they watched TV all afternoon—it was a rainy day and school would start next week anyway. Wouldn't rot their brains for just one day.

But I felt . . . betrayed. By Mabel, of all people! And I'd thought I could count on her to be in my corner through all this mess. She'd always bent over backward to give me time off to see the lawyer, let me use the phone to work on getting the boys back, gave me flex time in my schedule when I needed it—like the past few weeks, when I had to pick up P.J. midmorning . . . which, I had to admit, still counted for something.

So why was she turning things around now? Dumping the blame for my failed marriage into *my* lap?

Stewing over our conversation made my head hurt the rest of the day, and I went to bed early. Briefly thought about calling Jodi Baxter, just to have *someone* to lean on, then remembered she'd gone all wide-eyed about that maybe-it's-not-too-late-to-repair-the-damage nonsense Philip had fed me. *Huh.* I doubted very much he intended to talk about "what's next for us" after I'd said I wasn't going to give him any money.

But lying on my bed in the back bedroom wide-awake, staring into the dim light of Chicago's long evening, I felt as if I was going nuts. I wanted to talk to somebody . . . but who? My sisters? Not Honor. Maybe Celeste. She'd stick up for me. Or maybe Lee Boyer . . . *he* had absolutely no sympathy for Philip. And not just that, he had a lot of feelings for me. A man who really cared—and would care more if I gave him any encouragement.

I suddenly wanted to talk to Lee very much. See him. Closing my eyes, I could almost feel his touch as he laid his hand over mine in his office. I tried to imagine how it would feel to lean into his embrace, feel his arms around me . . .

Fishing for my cell, I rang his number, but all I got was his voice mail. That threw me. "Uh . . . Hi, Lee. It's Gabby. Call me if you get this . . . on second thought, don't call. I'm going to bed. Guess I'll see you tomorrow at the realtor's office."

So much for Lee always being there to lean on.

I cried myself to sleep.

Paul showed up for breakfast in his pajamas saying he didn't want to volunteer at the shelter today, maybe tomorrow if it stopped raining and we could take the kids to the beach in the afternoon. I didn't push him. Frankly, I didn't feel much like going to work either, but I sucked it up like a big girl and sailed into the Manna House foyer only five minutes late after dropping off P.J. at the high school.

Mabel came to her office door as I was signing in. "You all right, Gabby?"

I put on a bright smile. "Sure, Mabel. Sorry I got a little emotional yesterday. I'll be fine. Oh . . . I've got an eleven o'clock appointment with the realtor. I'll let you know how it goes."

That's right, Gabby, just move on. Don't let Philip's rants goad you—or even Mabel's opinion of what went wrong in your marriage. After all, that was in the past. What's done was done. Good things were happening now—the House of Hope idea was still afloat, I was moving ahead on buying the building, I'd be seeing Lee in a matter of hours . . .

Lee was waiting for me at the realtor's office, wearing a white short-sleeved shirt with open collar, khaki jeans, and boots. His version of business casual. He gave me a quick hug—the professional kind, sorta sideways, since we were standing in the waiting room of Coldwell Banker realty. "Gabby! Sorry I didn't get your message last night. My cell phone battery died and I didn't realize it until later. Are you all right?"

I nodded, realizing his warm concern could easily pull the plug I'd stuck in my emotional dike. "Just cold feet, I guess. I realize I don't have a clue how to navigate this thing. Glad you're here." All of which was true . . . just not why I'd called last night.

His light brown eyes crinkled behind his wire rims. "Don't worry. I'm not a real estate lawyer, but I think I can get us through this. And I happen to know the owner would much rather get a deal now than have that building sit on the market for six months waiting for his asking price."

I let Lee do most of the talking. Twice the agent representing the building stepped into another office and made a call to the owner . . . but when it was over, the owner had accepted our offer, which was less than the asking price, because I was willing to put 30 percent down instead of the usual 5 or 10 percent.

There was one glitch. Two of the tenants—not one—were moving out on Labor Day weekend, just days away. The apartments needed to be rented—but I didn't want new tenants in there, since I had plans for the building. Normally, the apartments would stand empty for a few weeks while they were refurbished for new tenants, but the current owner didn't want to put out the expense now that I'd signed the first papers. And I didn't legally own the building until the closing date, which had to wait for a title search, application for mortgage, all the red tape.

We finally agreed on a rider that I could do basic cleanup and painting—at my expense—but no structural changes or major repairs before the closing date in case the sale fell through for some reason.

The rain had stopped. Outside the realtor's office, Lee grabbed me and swung me around. "Wahoo! This calls for a celebration, don't you think? Let's do lunch. On me."

I laughed, grabbing for his arm to keep the world from spinning. "It's always on you, Lee. Maybe this one should be on me—as thanks for being a great tugboat."

"Hey! Who are you calling a tugboat? Okay, you can pay, but let's take my car. I'll bring you back to get yours."

Lunch at Hing Wang Restaurant for Chinese was giddy, and we laughed a lot. Which was good, since I avoided dragging up my last fiasco with Philip and yesterday's shocker with Mabel. Until we were back in Lee's Prius, that is.

"Say, what happened when you turned down Philip's request for a loan? You *did* tell him no, right, Gabby? . . . Hey, watch it, buddy." He blew his horn at a pizza delivery van that cut in front of us.

I nodded, hoping that would suffice, but Lee had his eyes on errant traffic. So I said, "Yep. Told him no. Thanks for the good advice."

"And . . . ?" Lee glanced over at me.

I turned my face toward the window, but a tear escaped and slid down my cheek.

"Hey, hey . . . what's wrong, baby?" Lee pulled out of traffic and into a No Parking space along Broadway. He reached for me and pulled me into his arms. "What did that bully do that's making you cry?"

So there it was. Lee's safe arms around me. The plug came out, and I ended up blubbering all over his white shirt. Bit by bit he drew out of me what Philip had said when I gave him my answer to his request for a loan.

"Don't cry, Gabby," he murmured into my hair, pulling me closer. "Don't let him mess with you. You don't owe him anything! And as for that other crap—that's just what it is. Don't let it get to you."

Tell that to Mabel, I thought. Should I tell Lee what she said?

I opened my mouth, but Lee murmured, "Shh . . . shh . . ." and laid a finger on my lips. Then he turned my face up, touching my lips softly with his.

And I let him.

chapter 19

I was still slightly giddy when I finally got back to the shelter. Precious was manning the reception desk and Mabel's office was empty, which meant people were still at lunch.

"You missed lunch," Precious said, handing me the logbook. "Taco salad."

"Oh, I ate out . . . You got a pen?" I hummed a little non-tune.

Precious eyed me suspiciously from beneath the row of kinky twists that fell over her forehead. "What you all hum-happy 'bout?"

"Oh, nothing much . . ." The memory of Lee's kiss still tingled on my lips. Still humming, I made a pretense of paging through the logbook. "Except, oh yes, we did make an offer on the six-flat, and—"

Precious snatched the logbook away. "And *what?*"

I grinned at her. "*And* the owner accepted our offer!"

"Praise *Jesus!*" Precious threw her hands in the air. "Hallelujah!

Look at God, movin' that mighty mountain. So when can me an'
Sabrina move in?"

Voices were rising on the other side of the double doors. I
lowered mine. "Not until we close. We have to apply for a mortgage, and they've got to do a credit check and a title search, all
that stuff. Not sure how long it'll take. And meantime, Mabel's
got to work it out with the city how you apply for the rent subsidy. She's going to handle that end of it."

Precious stuck a lip out. "I knew it. That baby gonna come
out and we *still* gonna be here at the shelter. Can't we hurry this
along a little?"

"Don't think so. Oh! There is one thing we can do." I beamed
at her. "A couple of tenants are moving out Labor Day weekend,
and Lee worked it out so we can fix up those apartments before
closing. How about a painting party? Want to help choose the
colors?"

"Wait a minute. Lee who? And what's all this 'we' and 'our'
business? I thought *you* was the one buyin' this building."

I felt my face color. "Uh, I am. Lee is just my lawyer. Lee
Boyer. You know."

"Don't know nothin' 'bout no Lee Lawyer." She eyed me
closely. "That why you missed lunch?"

"I told you. We ate out. A little celebration." I could feel
the tips of my ears getting hot—and was relieved when Mabel
came through the double doors talking to two women I didn't
recognize, but who had the depleted look of "just off the street."
Must've come in this morning. I used the interruption to escape
through Shepherd's Fold and down to my office . . . only to run
into Estelle bossing the cleanup crew.

"There you are! Saved you some taco salad. In the fridge. An' you got—"

"Oh. Thanks anyway, Estelle. I ate out." And I zipped toward my broom-closet office.

But before I could unlock the door, Estelle hollered after me. "—a visitor in there. And ain't you s'posed to tell me when you not gonna be here for lunch? I gotta plan these things, ya know."

My "visitor" turned out to be Dandy, wiggling his rump and bestowing wet kisses on whatever bare skin he could find. Fending him off, I poked my head back out. "I'm sorry, Estelle. I didn't know ahead of time. I'll be sure to let you know next time. And what's Dandy doing in here?"

"Don't ask me! Lucy just said to tell you she had to go someplace and could you take care of Dandy for a couple of days."

A couple of *days*? That's when I noticed she'd left his dog dishes and the bucket of food. Huh! She could've at least *asked*.

I blew out a long breath. Well, Paul would be happy about it anyway.

I was tempted to tell Estelle about my meeting with the realtor—she was one of the few who knew about my House of Hope idea outside of the board—but getting into *any* conversation with Estelle was likely to lead to questions about my talk with Philip, and I just didn't want to talk about it with her. Or Jodi. Or anyone at Manna House, for that matter. Not after Mabel jumped all over me about "taking responsibility" for my part in the marriage bust-up. Once was enough.

My eye caught my Bible sitting on the desk. But I left it there. Didn't really feel like talking to God about it either.

But Dandy? Now there was a good listener with no opinions.

"Hey there, Dandy. Good dog," I murmured as I scratched his rump. "Remember that guy who kicked you out of the penthouse? Well, he's still being his same jerk self . . ."

To my relief, Mabel didn't try to follow up on our conversation from Monday. In fact, my mood brightened with the sun peeking through the clouds on Wednesday. Paul had been ecstatic when I brought Dandy home for a visit and willingly came to the shelter with me and Dandy when I promised one last "beach day" with the shelter kids.

It felt good to stay busy. I went to the bank and applied for a mortgage. Carolyn showed up twice more that week to work with me on the afterschool program. And I started calling forest preserves to see if I could get a picnic permit for a group of thirty or forty folks for Labor Day.

Not a chance. Seemed like every group-size picnic site in the Chicago area had been booked for months. *Huh. Maybe I should book one now for next year.* But Friday morning I finally found one—though only available Sunday, not Monday—at a forest preserve called Sunset Bridge Meadow along the Des Plaines River, which wound its way through a whole string of forest preserves just west of the city. Some family reunion had cancelled at the last minute—their loss, our gain. Sunset Bridge had a large picnic shelter, restrooms, an open meadow surrounded by woods, and the river running through it. Perfect.

But a picnic meant food, which meant I had to talk to Estelle. She didn't usually work weekends—and this was a holiday weekend at that. We hadn't spoken much that week, but I could always plead "busy."

Estelle came in about ten. I waited until she had tied on her apron and stuffed her loose topknot under the required poufy cap, then popped out of my tiny office and leaned casually over the counter between kitchen and dining room. "Hi, Estelle! I've got a big favor to ask you."

The older woman eyed me, and then dumped a large sack of corn on the cob on the counter in front of me. "If you gonna lean on me for a favor, you can start shuckin'."

I obediently picked up an ear of corn and started pulling off the husk. "I'm trying to put together a Labor Day picnic for the ladies, but the only day I could find a picnic site is Sunday. And obviously we need food. I'm wondering—"

"Nope." She shucked two ears of corn to my one. "Not Sunday. I don't work on Sunday. That's the Lord's Day."

I was taken aback. And got huffy. "Well, *somebody* has to work on Sunday, don't they? Because these ladies have to eat on the *Lord's Day* too. But don't get your tail in a knot. I was just asking. I'll find somebody else." I tossed my stripped-down ear of corn on the pile, turned on my heel, and stalked back to my office.

Dandy got up and wiggled a welcome like I'd been gone five hours instead of five minutes. "Move, dog," I snarled. Where was Lucy anyway? She'd been gone three days already. I plonked myself down in the desk chair and pressed my fingers to my eyes. I wanted to be mad . . . but instead I started to cry. How did Estelle and I get to be at odds?

I heard my door open and knew it was Estelle. Reaching for

969

a tissue, I blotted my eyes and blew my nose before looking up. "What do you want?"

She sank into the folding chair beside my desk. "To say I'm sorry. Look, Gabby. I know when somebody's been avoiding me. Just got my goat that you came askin' for a favor after blowin' me off all week. But eye for an eye wasn't called for. What you doin' for the ladies is real nice. They'll enjoy getting out . . . Tell you what. I'll put together some picnic food on Saturday—shouldn't be too hard. Mostly shopping for a couple of melons, brats and buns, some deli potato salad, lemonade—stuff like that. I'll leave it in the fridge and you can take it in the coolers we got back there. Sound okay?"

I nodded, but now the tears started up again. Gag, I hated being such a crybaby! I grabbed for another wad of tissues . . . but found myself wrapped in Estelle's arms and my head on her ample bosom. "Come on, now, Gabby girl," she murmured, "what's goin' on? Somethin' happened when you talked to Philip, didn't it? Come on, now, you can tell Mama Estelle. I ain't gonna bite you."

For a few minutes, all I could do was cry. Wasn't even sure why. I'd gotten beyond Philip's mean words, hadn't I? The New Gabby wasn't going to be blown away every time the man who'd kicked me out tried to kick me again. He'd done his worst and I'd survived, hadn't I? I had my boys back, we had a nice apartment, they were starting school here in Chicago soon, the House of Hope idea was moving ahead . . . So what was the big deal?

But Estelle had put her finger on it. I'd been avoiding her . . . and Jodi . . . and everyone who'd become my friend. And I felt so alone. Why? Why was I afraid to tell them what Philip had said to me? Afraid to tell anybody about my conversation with Mabel? Why? Why?

Because I was afraid it might be true.

chapter 20

I finally got hold of myself long enough to give Estelle a brief rundown of what Philip had dumped on me when I gave him my "no" answer. "I'm s-sorry I've been avoiding you, Estelle. Just didn't want to talk about it." I blew my nose and reluctantly reached for my car keys. "There's more, but I've gotta run—P.J.'s last day of preseason practice."

"Hm." Estelle hefted herself out of the folding chair. "Just remember one thing, honey. *The truth will always set you free*. But there are a lot of things masquerading as truth these days, an' Satan, he's whisperin' a lotta nonsense in our ears he'd like us to believe 'bout ourselves an' other people. But there's only one place to get your truth. Here, look this up an' read it when you got some time." She scrawled something on a scrap of paper and stuck it in my Bible. "Now, shoo, get on outta here so I can get cookin'."

I was halfway up the stairs to the main floor when she hollered after me. "An' since you gonna pick up P.J., bring him on back to the shelter for lunch. I'm fixin' a surprise back-to-school lunch for all the kids of residents an' staff."

My spirit felt lighter after crying on Estelle's shoulder, even though I didn't quite tell her everything, like what Mabel had said. *It wasn't intentional*, I told myself as I pulled into the Lane Tech parking lot. *I just ran out of time.*

"How'd it go, kiddo?" I asked as P.J. jumped into the front seat of the Subaru.

"Good." My oldest fiddled with the radio until he found a pop station and hiked up the volume. "We find out next week who Coach is putting on the varsity team, but there's a good chance I'll make it. The first meet on home turf is coming up in a few weeks, September something." He glanced at me sideways. "Will you and Dad come?"

"Absolutely—but only if you turn that thing *down* twenty decibels! . . . Ahh, thanks, that's better. As for your dad, you'll have to ask him. Might depend on when it is. But you'll see him tonight, right?"

P.J. shrugged. "Guess so. He hasn't called all week."

Which was true. I'd been just as glad, figured Philip was mad at me for turning him down—and I had *nothing* to say to him since he made that stupid "you owe me" remark. But it hurt knowing stuff between us was hurting the boys too.

"Be patient, kiddo. Your dad's going through a hard time right now . . . Hey, is it okay if we go back to the shelter? Estelle's making a special back-to-school lunch for everybody—staff kids too."

P.J. didn't answer, just pumped up the music again and turned his head away.

True to her word, Estelle had made a special kid-friendly lunch—hamburgers, chips, corn on the cob, and ice-cream bars. Harry showed up with his grandson and Mabel's nephew. I noticed Jermaine put his food tray down across from P.J., but there was no interaction between the two until Paul plopped his tray down beside Jermaine and started jabbering away. Probably talking music.

Mabel surprised Paul by naming him "Volunteer of the Month" and presenting him with a poster that had a photo of Paul in his volunteer T-shirt with all the shelter kids. Sammy, Keisha, Trina, and Rufino wanted to sign the poster, and even Dessa and Bam-Bam, the toddlers, added their scribbles. Paul covered his embarrassment by acting the clown, but I knew he was pleased.

The second surprise was a backpack filled with school supplies for each kid, donated by one of the big insurance agencies in the city—the company logo boldly emblazoned on the bag, of course. Sammy and the other schoolkids excitedly dug through the contents. P.J. and Paul, however, looked at the bags and then at each other. I could read the look between them: *"No way."* Sabrina didn't take one either.

I made an announcement about the Labor Day picnic—"On Sunday, not Monday!"—and said whoever wanted to go should sign up today and I'd be back tomorrow to pick up the list so I could work out transportation. I started the list with my name and my boys, and then handed the clipboard to Harry Bentley. "You and DaShawn are invited too, Mr. B." I lowered my voice and teased, "You used to be a cop, right? We could use some security."

"Might just do that." Harry signed, and I chuckled. He obviously hadn't checked with Estelle, who didn't *do* Sundays.

Lucy still hadn't come back to pick up Dandy. "I think Lucy should just give him back to us," Paul pouted as he packed his duffel bag for the overnight with their dad. "Maybe she's never coming back. He's practically my dog anyway . . . hey! Can he come with us to Dad's?"

I lifted a knowing eyebrow at Paul.

"Oh, right. Well, will you promise to feed him? And walk him?"

Assuring Paul I would, I hustled the boys so they'd be ready by six o'clock when Philip usually picked them up. But six came and went, then six thirty . . .

I didn't particularly want to talk to Philip, but I dialed his cell phone and got his voice mail. But when he hadn't shown up by seven, I tried again. Again I got voice mail—but this time he called back just as I was telling him what I thought of a father who stood up his own kids.

"Gabby, I can't talk right now . . . Look, can I call you back?"

"Philip! It's seven o'clock! The boys have been waiting for you for an hour." The background on his end was noisy. Other voices. Some music.

"I know. I thought I'd be done here. Something got delayed."

"Something-*what* got delayed? Something more important than your kids?"

"Just some . . . business I had to attend to. And no, it couldn't wait." Philip's tone got tight. "I wouldn't have to do this if you had—" In the background I heard someone yell his name. He tried to muffle the phone, but I heard him say, "I *said*, just give me a minute, Fagan." Then he came back on. "Look, Gabby, I have to go. I *will* pick up the boys. Just ask them to sit tight." The phone went dead.

Irked, I went ahead and fed the boys some boxed macaroni and cheese and hot dogs, but I had a hard time trying to cover for their dad. I was mad, and the boys knew it. Finally the front door buzzer sounded at eight o'clock. Philip was already back in the car when the boys clomped out the front door and down the steps. "See you tomorrow night, guys," I called after them, watching P.J.'s dark hair and Paul's red-gold curls disappear into the backseat of the Lexus.

Only after I went back inside did I realize the significance of *both* boys climbing into the backseat.

Well, good. Philip needed to know the boys had feelings too. What kind of business was he doing, anyway, on a Friday night? *Huh.* Probably out drinking with Henry Fenchel and some business client, Fagan-somebody. Except, what did he mean he wouldn't have to do this if I had . . . if I had what? Given him the loan? Was he getting a loan from somebody else? Well, let him. It wasn't my responsibility.

"Come on, Dandy; guess it's just you and me." The yellow dog flopped by my feet as I tried to watch TV, but another Friday night by myself made me feel depressed. Turning it off, I curled up on the window seat in the sunroom at the front of the apartment and stared at the streetlights shining through the trees. Holding two fingers together, I touched my mouth, trying to remember Lee's soft kiss . . .

Good grief! If Lee felt that way about me, why didn't he ask me out on a date? I'd love to see a movie or go out to dinner or . . . or even bowling! What did Lee like to do on weekends? I had no idea. Why had I let him kiss me when I still hardly knew the guy!

Well, I wasn't going to call him and whine. It was almost ten. I should just walk Dandy and go to bed. Would it be safe? I got the dog's leash and stepped outside, glad to see at least two other dog walkers. The night air was mild. Warm, not hot. Nice for September first. But it'd soon be fall, with winter not far behind. "What are you and Lucy going to do then, huh, boy?" I murmured to Dandy, as he lifted his leg for the tenth time, marking every tree along the sidewalk.

As we returned to the six-flat, I saw bright lights in the first- and third-floor apartments on the left side of the building. Windows open. I could hear loud voices from the third floor. An argument. Those were the people moving out tomorrow.

My spirit revived a notch or two. It'd be fun to fix up those apartments for Precious and Tanya and their kids. Maybe I could get a work party together on Monday. "Labor Day," I snickered at Dandy as he curled up on the scatter rug beside my bed. "Get it? Labor . . . work . . ."

I was just about to turn off the light when I spied my Bible I'd brought home from my office and realized I hadn't read the note Estelle had stuck in it. I pulled it out. All she'd scrawled was a Bible verse: *John 8:31–32*. Plumping up my pillows, I found the Bible passage and read it aloud to Dandy. "Then Jesus said to those Jews who believed Him, 'If you abide in My word, you are My disciples indeed. And you shall know the truth, and the truth shall make you free.'"

Huh. That's what Estelle had said to me . . . *"The truth will set you free."* What was she trying to tell me? Something about Satan telling us lies about who we are and who other people are. And the only place to get the truth was God's Word—just like these verses said. I read them again. *"If you abide in My word"*—hmm, definitely hadn't been doing much "abiding" in God's Word lately—*"you shall know the truth, and the truth shall make you free."*

I shut the Bible, turned out the bedside light, and slid down beneath the sheet. "God," I whispered into the inky darkness, "I've been kind of afraid to know what You think about all this mess with Philip. Afraid maybe You'll end up on Philip's side and I'll be the person in the wrong again. But if the truth sets us free, guess I shouldn't be afraid, right? I'm sorry I've been avoiding You. Not wanting to pray, not reading my Bible. You've done a lot already to free up my spirit, now that I found You again at Manna House. I want to be Your disciple, Lord, like it says in those verses. So I'm going to try to be a little more faithful about 'abiding' in Your Word . . ."

As sleep overtook me, I found myself wondering what "abide" meant. *Funny word . . . kinda archaic . . . My kids would say, "Huh?" . . . Maybe it just means "hanging out" with God . . . no, more than that. Soaking in His words? Soaking, that was it . . .*

I woke up to thumps out in the stairwell and voices cursing. Moving day. Standing by the open back door with my coffee, I winced as I saw broken furniture, an old box spring, and bags of trash get dumped out in back by the alley. Who was going to pick *that* up? Shuddering at the prospect of being the future owner and having to deal with all that, I decided to get out of there until the move was over.

Top on my list of things to do was picking up the picnic list and making sure we had enough transportation. I drove to the shelter—and ran into Jodi Baxter on the front steps, just about to ring the doorbell. Right on time for her typing class. She was wearing a denim skirt and had pulled her brown shoulder-length hair into a short ponytail. "Hey," I said and fumbled for my Manna House key. "I can let you in."

"Hey, yourself." Jodi didn't move, even when I got the door open. "I was hoping I'd see you. I left a couple of messages this week but you haven't returned my phone calls. Did I . . . I mean, are you upset with me for some reason?"

I let the door wheeze shut again and sighed. "No . . . well, yeah, kind of." I sank down onto the top step. She sat down beside me. "But not just you. Just ask Estelle. I've been avoiding her too. Avoiding everybody, I guess. Even the Big Man Upstairs." I rolled my eyes heavenward and made Jodi smile. "I'm sorry, Jodi. You're a good friend. And a good prayer partner. It's just . . . you got so excited about Philip and me 'fixing' our marriage, I didn't feel like you were really listening to me."

She winced. "Ouch. Okay. I'm listening now."

We sat outside for several minutes while I tried to tell Jodi everything that had happened since I told Philip I wouldn't give him the loan. It came out all in a jumble, but she put her arm around me and pulled me close. "Oh, Gabby, I'm so sorry. You're right. I was too quick to jump ahead, hoping things could get resolved between you and Philip, and didn't take time to put myself in your shoes." She glanced at her watch. "Ack, I'm late. The ladies are probably waiting on me for class, if they haven't given up already. But I really do want to hear more. I promise to shut up and listen this time." She gave me another hug and stood up. "I'm glad we bumped into each other. I've really missed you, my friend."

I stood up too. "Yeah, missed you too . . . Uh, by the way, what are you and Denny doing tomorrow?"

"Tomorrow? Besides church you mean?" She squinted as if reading her schedule on the bright sky. "Nothing much, far as I know."

"You guys want to go on a picnic? Can we borrow your grill . . . and your Caravan?"

chapter 21

Not counting people who had their own cars—Harry Bentley and the Baxters and Mabel—twenty-five ladies had signed up for the Labor Day picnic. "Your minivan won't be enough," I moaned to Jodi before she left. "And Moby Van only holds fifteen."

"Talk to Josh," she suggested. "Maybe he can borrow the SouledOut van."

I didn't tell Josh his mother had suggested it—but he seemed excited about bringing Edesa and Gracie to the picnic when I got him on the phone. "Sounds like fun. Don't know of any reason we couldn't use the church van. I'll let you know."

"You're a prince, Josh," I gushed. Frankly, having another man on hand made me feel more secure herding a large group of streetwise females, many of whom, I was told, had never been to a forest preserve. I didn't want to lose anybody in the river.

I did my grocery shopping, stopped by the dry cleaners, and got my nails done. By the time I got back to the six-flat in late afternoon, both moving trucks were gone. Curious, I tried the door to the first-floor apartment across the hall from me. Locked. *Drat*. I'd have to get the key to do any painting. But the third-floor apartment door was open.

I peeked into the empty apartment . . . "empty" being a relative term. Trash still littered the front room—a stained carpet, a broken lamp, old newspapers, even some clothes. I heard my front door buzzer while I was still in the apartment. Almost six . . . had to be the boys. I located the intercom and buzzed them in, then yelled down the stairwell, "I'm up here!"

The boys thundered up the stairs. P.J. stopped at the front door. "Whoa. What a mess." But Paul came on in and ran down the hall, opening doors and looking in every room. "Hey, can we play up here?"

"Sure," I said, grabbing him and knuckling the top of his head. "We can play drag-the-carpet-out-to-the-garbage, and then—"

"Aw, that's not what I meant."

"Well, let's not waste a trip down. Here, help me roll up this rug . . ."

It took all three of us to heave the old carpet into the Dumpster in the alley. If the first-floor apartment was in similar shape, I'd need a cleaning crew before we could do any painting.

Back in our own apartment, I stuck a frozen pizza into the oven. "Wash your hands, guys. This won't take long. You have fun with Dad?"

P.J. ran his hands under the kitchen faucet and wiped them on his shorts. "I dunno. Kinda boring. Dad took us out for breakfast this morning, but then he spent most of the day in his office."

"Yeah," Paul piped up. "We played video games all morning, then he let us go swimming at Foster Beach."

"He didn't go with you?"

Paul shook his head. "Nah. But it was okay. They've got a lifeguard there."

I zipped my lip. No, it was not okay. Wasn't the whole point for Philip to spend time with his sons?

I did get the boys up in time to go to church at SouledOut, even though they griped about not getting to sleep in. Frankly, I was sorely tempted to let them sleep so I could get to work on the empty apartments, but I couldn't very well ask to use the church van today and miss another Sunday.

And I was so glad we went. I'd pretty much taken going to church for granted growing up. But today, singing "We come rejoicing into His presence" and seeing arms lifted all over the room was almost a tribal experience for me. The congregation was such a mishmash of colors and cultures—where else would people who might not have much in common come together and sing with such abandon? For that moment I felt part of a family— a sense of belonging that made me feel connected to people all over the world who were together worshiping God today.

If only it would last.

I'm so sorry, God, I prayed as the youth were finally dismissed for Sunday school. *How easily I gave this up in Virginia, traded it in for a few extra hours to eat a lazy breakfast and read the Sunday paper . . .*

Out of the corner of my eye I saw P.J. and Paul leave the

building with the other teens and climb into the church van. "Where are they going?" I whispered to Jodi.

"The lake," she whispered back. "Pastor Cobbs asked Josh to teach the teens a series on Sea of Galilee stories from the Gospels, and Josh being Josh, he thought taking the teens to the lake might make it seem more real and relevant—though I'd like to know what he's going to do about Jesus telling Peter to get out of the boat and walk on the water. Half the teens might just try it!" Jodi started to giggle and we both had to stifle it when Pastor Cobbs—the younger pastor of the two-man pastoral team at SouledOut—got up to preach.

The van came back while the rest of us were enjoying coffee and sweet rolls after the worship service. P.J. and Paul both hung around Josh with some of the other teens, talking and horsing around. "Aw, Mom!" P.J. whined when I told them I needed to leave to get ready for the Manna House picnic. "Do I hafta go?"

"What?" Josh overheard us and feigned horror. "Your mom's making me drive! You're not going to leave me alone with all those women, are you? Hey—make you a deal. Why don't you guys stay here and ride with me in the church van? What time do you want us there to load up, Mrs. Fairbanks—two thirty?"

The boys were already in cargo shorts, T-shirts, and gym shoes—typical teen garb even for church these days—so I said fine, a bit amused at this sudden bonding between my sons and Josh Baxter.

"Bring Dandy!" Paul yelled after me as I headed for the Subaru in the parking lot.

True to his word, Josh pulled up with my two boys and his wife and baby in the SouledOut van right at two thirty, followed a few moments later by the senior Baxters and their Dodge Caravan. Most of the women and shelter kids were already waiting outside on the front steps, and I noticed we'd picked up a few more strays. No problem. With the shelter van, too, we'd get everybody in.

Edesa helped me pack two large food coolers with the picnic stuff Estelle had left in the refrigerator, and Josh and Denny Baxter loaded them in the Caravan with their grill. Paul wanted Dandy to ride in the SouledOut van with him and P.J., but I didn't want Josh and Edesa to have to be responsible for ten women, my two sons, *and* the dog, so I said Dandy had to ride with me in Moby Van. To my surprise, Paul hopped out of the church van and climbed in behind me with Dandy.

"Where's Mabel?" Precious yelled from the back. "She was on the list!"

"Going to meet us there! Everybody buckled up? All right, let's go."

I waved at Josh behind me and had just started to pull out into the street, when I heard someone yelling, "Hey! Hey, wait for me, dagnabit!" Stomping on the brake, I glanced in my rearview mirror, trying to see who we'd left. Someone was knocking on the windows of the passenger side. Then the side door slid back.

"Where y'all goin'?" said a gravelly voice. "Hey, there he is! Hiya, Dandy boy! Didya miss me? I'm back!"

"Aw, Mom!" Paul hissed in my ear. "It's Lucy!"

Ignoring groans and complaints from the already crowded van, Lucy dragged her cart into the van and parked her ample behind on the seat next to Paul while Dandy joyfully gave the old lady a hero's welcome. Twisting in my seat, I could see Paul smoldering next to the window. But Lucy rummaged in her cart and handed him something wrapped in a plastic bread bag. "Got somethin' for ya, Paul," she said. "Little thank-ya present for takin' such good care of Dandy. Share 'em with your maw."

Paul handed me the bag and I peeked inside.

Big, fat blueberries.

Paul was sullen the whole trip. I told myself I'd find a time at the picnic when we could talk through his feelings about having to share Dandy. But when we pulled into the parking lot at Sunset Bridge Meadow, I saw we had a bigger problem than Lucy showing up. Another group was using the picnic shelter.

Bikers.

At least fifteen Harleys filled the lot, all leather and chrome. My heart sank . . . and then I saw Harry Bentley's car at the end of the row of bikes—*Oh, hallelujah*—and Harry himself over at the rustic shelter talking to one of the bikers. "Hang on, ladies," I said, climbing out. "Don't get out yet."

Yeah, right. I was only halfway across the meadow when I realized all the ladies in Moby Van were right behind me, including Paul holding on to Dandy's leash. And then the SouledOut van pulled into the lot, followed by the Baxters' minivan.

Mr. Bentley was mopping his brown dome with a big hand-kerchief, surrounded by a dozen or more muscular white dudes in red kerchiefs, sporting a variety of beards, earrings, and leather vests. "I told these fellows you have a permit for this picnic grove, Gabby." Underneath Mr. B's tone I heard, *"I sure hope you have one!"*

By now we were surrounded by a swarm of Manna House residents and a handful of staff, volunteers, and kids. "Uh, sure, right here." I pulled out the permit that had been faxed to me on Friday—a concession because we were a social service agency— and handed it to the guy Harry had been talking to.

Mr. Leather Pants took the permit and grunted as he looked it over. "Manna House . . . is that like 'manna from heaven' from the Bible?"

"Uh, I think so." Mabel would know but she wasn't here. "It's a Christian homeless shelter for women."

"A *Christian* shelter." Precious sniffed.

"Hey, wait a minnit!" Lucy elbowed her way to the front of the Manna House crowd and looked Mr. Leather Pants up and down. "Ain't you the guy gave me a ride on that big bike t'other day in Michigan?"

I stared at Lucy. She'd been in *Michigan*? And this biker dude had given her a *ride*?

The bearded man broke into a wide grin and waggled a finger at her. "Lucy Tucker, right? Yeah! You was hoofin' it along that two-lane road, tryin' ta find the bus station. I see ya made it back to Chi-Town okay."

Lucy turned to Mr. Bentley and me, cackling like an old hen. "Heh, heh, heh. You guys don't hafta worry. These dudes are all right. They just a bunch of Jesus freaks on wheels."

The big guy grinned, revealing a gold tooth. "Show 'em, fellas!" He turned around, along with the rest of his motley crew—and there, emblazoned in big red stitching on the back of their black leather vests, were the words GOD SQUAD and beneath them, CHRISTIAN MOTORCYCLE CLUB.

"Hey! That's fantastic!" Josh said, stepping forward and extending his hand. Within moments, the group of leather-clad bikers were shaking hands and greeting the women from Manna House, some of whom still looked frightened at all these tough-looking men.

"Well, now, isn't this a pretty how-d'ya-do," murmured a familiar voice in my ear. "Wonder which group is gonna turn the other cheek?"

I turned. "Estelle! What are you doing here? I thought you didn't do picnics on Sundays!"

"I said I don't *cook* on Sundays. Didn't say I don't *come* to picnics. Besides, you got Harry to sign up. What was I s'posed to do? Sit home an' twiddle my thumbs?"

"Ma'am?" Big Dude interrupted. "Sorry me an' the boys took your spot. We're travelin' from Michigan to a Christian Biker Rally and needed a place to eat our lunch. We'll be movin' on since you got a permit an' all that."

"Well, now, what's the big problem?" Precious butted in. "Lookit this shelter. 'Nuff picnic tables for a hunnerd folks or more, an' what we got? Forty . . . maybe fifty all together? We all God's children, ain't we? Well . . ." She glanced around at the Manna House residents. "Well, maybe not all of us, but enough to count. Jesus said if two or three folks get together in His name, He shows up too. So to my way of figurin', we all just one big family. I'm gettin' hungry, so I say let's eat!"

Big Guy looked at me. I shrugged. Not exactly what I'd planned, but . . .

chapter 22

Turned out the picnic was a blast. The bikers were downright gentlemanly, helping us set up the Baxters' grill, adding their sandwiches and bags of chips and coolers of colas to the feast. One of the bikers—a smaller guy who actually wore a safety helmet—even hopped on his bike and roared down the highway, and by the time the coals were ready he was back with more hot dogs and buns to throw on the grill.

I cornered Lucy. "What were you doing in Michigan? I mean, you just up and disappeared! What did that biker mean, you got tired of picking? Blueberries?"

"Humph. Grew up pickin'. Gotta make some money somehow to see me through the winter, don'tcha know. Now, how 'bout another slice of that melon. I gotta go sit with Dandy so Paul can play some ball."

Josh had produced a couple of bats, a softball, and mitts—he'd been thinking of the kids—and we ended up with two rowdy teams made up of both bikers and "maidens," as our residents had been dubbed by the God Squad. Since the picnic and ballgame were no longer mostly female, the boys—even Paul—looked like they were having a great time.

"Look at God," Estelle murmured to Jodi and me as we cleaned up paper plates, leftover buns, and searched for missing caps to the plastic containers of catsup and mustard. "We make our plans, but God comes up with an even better idea."

I decided not to comment on Estelle *cleaning up* on a Sunday. "Yeah, and I was worried about security, you know, all these women out here in the middle of nowhere, with only a few guys to stick up for us if anything happened."

Jodi swooped up Gracie, who had discovered a bag of marshmallows. "Oh no, sweetie. Let Grammy get those out of your mouth—"

"Look, look, Gracie!" I screeched. "Your mama just knocked a home run! Way to go, Edesa!"

We clapped and hooted from the picnic shelter as Jodi's daughter-in-law rounded third base, which consisted of somebody's T-shirt. As the pretty Honduran girl slid into home plate—another T-shirt—Jodi sighed. "Please keep praying for Edesa and Josh. Things are really stressful for them with you-know-who in that tiny apartment. Can't even call it an apartment, it's so small!" She nuzzled Gracie's loose curls, then looked at Estelle, who'd resumed cleanup. "Speaking of our grown kids, Harry said you guys weren't at church this morning because you went to visit Leroy. How's he doing?"

Estelle shook her head. "Humph. They say he's doing good, but it ain't a pretty sight for a mother to see her boy suffer like that." The older woman heaved a sigh and sat down on one of the picnic table benches. "Gotta pray for me, sisters. I don't know what I'm gonna do with him when he does get better, now that he done burned the house down. Jus' never wanted to put him in an institution. But . . ."

"Oh, Estelle," Jodi said. "Of course we'll pray. All the Yada Yada sisters are praying already. In fact, let's pray right now." Jodi looked at me. "How about you, Gabby? How can we pray for you? Yesterday you said Philip was late picking up the boys. Do you think he did that on purpose since you told him you wouldn't loan him any money?"

Another cheer went up from the makeshift ball field. Mabel's nephew had hit the ball and was heading for first base. The outfield fumbled it, and I heard P.J. yell, "Run to second, you wuss!" But others yelled, "Stay there! Stay there!" Jermaine looked confused, ran, and got tagged out.

I winced, trying to remember Jodi's question. "No-o, I don't think Philip would deliberately take it out on the boys like that. But it was kind of weird. When I got him on his cell phone, he said he got stuck with a business client, somebody named Fagan, I think, who—"

Estelle's head snapped up. "Stop. Gabby, did you say *Fagan*?"

"Well, yeah, I think that's what he said. Don't know if it was a first name or last name. But somebody told him to hurry up on the phone and Philip said something like, 'Just a minute, Fagan!'"

Estelle got to her feet faster than I'd ever seen her move. "Girl, if that's the Fagan I think it is, that man of yours is in real trouble now. I gotta tell Harry."

I didn't know what had gotten Estelle's tail in a knot, but whoever Philip's client was, he wasn't my problem. I had all I could handle getting everyone to clean up the picnic grounds and get the vans loaded for our trip back home. The "God Squad" escorted our vans halfway back to the city, much to the delight of the shelter residents and kids, then peeled off when the highway signs pointed north to Wisconsin.

Once we got back to Manna House, Lucy marched off with Dandy and her wire cart, and I noticed Paul sulking on the front steps. I sat down beside him. "I know you feel sad, kiddo. But maybe it's just as well. You're starting school in two days and Dandy would be alone all day. At least with Lucy, he's got a companion twenty-four/seven." Paul got up and stomped off, hands jammed in the pockets of his cargo shorts. Didn't blame him. My words sounded hollow even to my own ears.

What Paul needed was his own dog.

As for P.J. . . . that boy was going to hear from me about calling Jermaine a "wuss" in front of everyone.

However, it turned out to be serendipity that we had our picnic on Sunday, because the Monday holiday woke up cloudy and wet. I made coffee and took it back to bed, curling up with my Bible. A good time to make good on my promise to God to "abide" in His Word, since I didn't have to go in to work that day. I actually read several more chapters in Matthew's gospel before my phone rang at eight o'clock.

Jodi was on the line. "Didn't you say you could use a work crew over there in those two empty apartments? We were going to barbecue today with Josh and Edesa, but with weather like this—ha. I don't think so! Can you use some help?" She laughed. "After all, it's *Labor* Day!"

No way was I going to turn down a volunteer work crew. I

called over to Manna House and talked to Precious, told her we weren't ready to paint yet but could use a cleaning crew.

"You talk to Tanya yet?" she asked.

"Uh, no. Kinda wanted this House of Hope idea to be a sure thing before I got her hopes up. Mabel's not there today, is she?"

"Nope. But Tanya's a big girl, Gabby. She could use a little hope right now. Want me to talk to her? I'm sure she an' Sammy would love to come help out."

We finally decided Precious would recruit Tanya, I'd pick them up in an hour, and once we got back here to the six-flat, then I'd tell her my dream for the House of Hope. We didn't even ask Sabrina, since we were starting on the third-floor apartment, and Precious said no way was she going to push that girl and her big tummy up all those stairs.

When I pulled up in front of the six-flat, Precious wisely disappeared inside with Sammy, but I held Tanya back to tell her about my dream of developing this building as second-stage housing for homeless single moms. "You and Precious are first on our list if it all comes through," I said. "But we're still working on it, so don't tell Sammy yet."

The next thing I knew, Tanya had thrown her arms around my neck and started to cry. "Oh, Miss Gabby," she sniffled, her braided head tucked tight next to my auburn mop. "That would be the answer to my prayers."

I held her for a few moments, and then untangled myself from her hug. "Don't stop praying yet, Tanya. We've still got a few hurdles. Come on, I've got to wake up my boys if Sammy hasn't done it already."

P.J. and Paul complained at first about having to work on

a holiday, but when the Baxter clan showed up at ten o'clock, it started to feel like a party. Jodi had brought a whole slew of cleaning supplies—buckets, a mop, rags, and several different kinds of cleaners—so with what I also rustled up, we assigned tasks and set to work. Edesa, Precious, and Tanya tackled the filthy kitchen on the third floor, Jodi volunteered to do the bathroom, and I put all three boys to work with garbage bags just collecting all the trash left in the various rooms and on the back porch. Denny Baxter had brought his toolbox, and he and Josh went room to room repairing windows that wouldn't stay open, the dripping kitchen faucet, sagging rods in the closets, and who knew what else.

Repairs I'd never thought of that would need to be done in every apartment as they became available.

"Oh, brother," I sighed, sinking down on the closed toilet seat in the bathroom where Jodi was scrubbing the gritty ring around the bathtub. "I think I'm in over my head. Painting the apartments is one thing. But seeing Denny and Josh doing all that fix-it stuff, I realize the owner of a building is responsible for all kinds of repairs! Electrical wiring gone bad . . . rusted pipes . . . broken fixtures . . . rotting porch railings . . . *aagh!* I can't do that stuff!"

"Well"—*scrub, scrub, scrub*—"just ask Denny or Josh to help you out when you need it. Or hire somebody."

"Oh yeah, right. What were we thinking, Jodi—six apartments full of women and kids? We need a man!"

Jodi blew a stray lock of hair out of her face and grinned up at me. "We? You're the one who . . ." Jodi's voice trailed off and she got a funny look on her face. "Wait a minute. You need a man, and I know a certain man who needs an apartment." She rolled her eyes and tipped her head "out there" toward the rest of the apartment.

My mouth dropped open. "You mean . . . Josh and Edesa? But . . ." My mind did cartwheels. "But the whole idea is to turn the building into second-stage housing for homeless single moms."

Jodi popped up and sat on the edge of the tub. "Sure. But you're the owner and you live in the building, kind of like a housemother. And you just said yourself you need a property manager—someone to do all that stuff you can't do and would have to hire out. Why not Josh? He's pretty good at that stuff."

Good grief. Why hadn't I thought of this before? Having Josh and Edesa Baxter living in the building would be a godsend! Still, hurdles kept rising up in my mind like an animated obstacle course. "But, Jodi! There are only two available apartments right now, and I promised Precious and Tanya they were tops on the list. *Especially* Precious, because Sabrina's baby is due in a couple of months."

"Gabby Fairbanks." Jodi closed the bathroom door and lowered her voice. "Have you really thought this through? I mean, does Tanya need a three-bedroom apartment? It's just her and Sammy! Now Precious and Sabrina could probably use one after the baby comes—but even that is more than most families are able to afford. Maybe Precious and Tanya could share an apartment for the time being until another one opens up. It's still a whole lot better than a bunk room at the shelter."

I ran a hand through my hair, absently untangling a few snarls as I tried to "think this through," as Jodi said. "What about the rent? Could Josh and Edesa afford it? It's ridiculous—thirteen hundred a month! But I'll need the rent from all the apartments—one way or the other—to cover my mortgage. Though I should probably reduce it in exchange for the work he'd do."

Jodi got back down on her knees by the tub and turned the water on to rinse the scrubbing she'd been doing. "Yeah, well, the rent's a good question. You'd have to talk to Josh and Edesa about that. In fact"—she grimaced at me guiltily—"I think I need to drop out of this conversation. I'm a little biased about wanting them to find a bigger place to live. Sorry. I probably misspoke."

"No, no, it's a good idea, Jodi. Makes a lot of sense all the way around. I really do need a property manager, and the fact that Josh and Edesa are also volunteers at the shelter makes them perfect candidates! But I don't quite know what to do next."

Jodi turned off the water. "Well, we could pray about it. Want to? Right now?"

So there we sat, on the toilet and the tub, praying about whether to ask Josh and Edesa to be property managers for the new House of Hope, when someone pounded at the door. "Mom? You in there?" P.J. hollered from the other side of the door. "It's past lunchtime! You want me to order some pizza?"

chapter 23

Tanked up on Gino's pizza and root beer, my volunteer cleaning crew had made Apartment 3A look fairly presentable when Lee Boyer showed up with the keys to the two empty apartments. It was the first time I'd seen him since he'd kissed me, and I felt a flutter of panic. At least my heart was tripping double time. He gave me a wink when no one was looking, but otherwise he was a model of decorum. "Hm. Nice," he said, glancing around 3A. But as he was leaving, he pulled me aside. "Gabby. I'm not sure you should put in all this work until you actually own the building. What if—"

"Have some faith, Lee!" I gave him my brightest smile and a wave, then turned to the tired crew and held up the keys to 1A. "Ta-da! Who wants to take a look?"

Nobody moved. I heard a few groans. "Huh! If that apartment downstairs be a big mess like this one? . . . uh-uh." Precious shook the tiny twists covering her head. "My joints already hurtin' after all this scrubbin'."

"Okay, okay. We don't have to clean it today. Just look." Though I knew I wouldn't have the nerve to ask this volunteer crew to come back a second time.

But I was pleasantly surprised. Apartment 1A had been completely cleared out, floors had been swept, and both the bathroom and kitchen were basically clean. "Ready to paint, I'd say," Jodi said happily, rubbing hand cream into her water-wrinkled fingers.

Her husband gave her a look. "Right. *After* preparing the walls, filling in the nail holes, taping the wood trim, and"—he jiggled the light switch in the living room, which did nothing— "repairing this light."

"Oh, stop it, Denny." Jodi backhanded his arm. "Don't discourage Gabby. It's probably just a burned-out bulb."

"Maybe." Denny wandered off to check out the other room lights.

Jodi winked at me and murmured, "Or maybe just confirmation that you need a maintenance person *on site.*"

"Shh!" I hissed back at her. "Don't say anything to Josh and Edesa until I have a chance to talk to Mabel in private. It, um, might be a little sticky." I tipped my head toward Precious and Tanya, who were already arguing about who got the first-floor apartment.

I was just as glad we didn't have a big cleaning job in that apartment, because as soon as everyone left, I had to focus on the other "big job" at hand—getting the boys ready for their first day of school the next day. Book bags, jeans, new underwear and T-shirts laid out, and bag lunches made and in the fridge . . . though the next morning I wondered why I bothered. P.J. showed up for breakfast in an old T-shirt ("You want me to look like a twinky new kid?" he growled), and after Mabel picked him up, I discovered his lunch still sitting in the fridge.

Well, let him go hungry. He wouldn't forget tomorrow.

Scattered clouds dotted the sky over Chicago, but the temperature was a pleasant seventy degrees as Paul and I walked toward Sunnyside Magnet School. Suddenly my heart felt so full, I felt like doing a little jig right there on the sidewalk . . . but I settled for giving Paul a sudden sideways hug.

"Mo-om!" My twelve-year-old pulled away, looking around in a panic. "What if somebody sees you?"

"Sorry, kiddo." I meekly resumed walking straight ahead, but couldn't help the big grin on my face. "I'm just so . . . so grateful that you're here, that I get a chance to walk you to school today, that I might just burst—and then you'll have a big mess to clean up right here on the sidewalk." I laughed and he rolled his eyes, but I was rewarded with a grin as he shook his head at his hopeless mother.

"Hey, Paul!" a youthful voice yelled. "Wait up!"

We turned to see Sammy and Tanya hurrying to catch up with us a block from the school. Sammy was so excited he ran at the mouth. "I didn't know you was goin' to Sunnyside too! What grade you in? Man, I hope I don't get ol' Bean Face for anything this year—she the strictest P.E. teacher ever. You probably on the third floor with the older kids. You gonna do band? I wanna do band, but they don't let you start till sixth grade . . ."

The two boys walked ahead of us, then Paul turned and waved us off. Tanya and I stopped and let them go into the school yard alone. "Oh, Miss Gabby," Tanya breathed. "If we get to move into your building like you say, maybe Paul can walk

Sammy to school every day. That would make me so happy . . . mm-mm. Jesus, Jesus! Thank You, Jesus!" Tanya gave me a spontaneous hug. "Things be lookin' up for us now, Miss Gabby. I just know it."

Yes, thank You, Jesus. Even as I waved good-bye to my young friend from the shelter and walked home to get my car—I'd need it later that day to pick up P.J. and Jermaine at Lane Tech as Mabel and I had agreed—I was convicted by Tanya's spontaneous thanksgiving to God. I felt so grateful to have a home for my sons, so glad they were with me and enrolled in school here in Chicago instead of a thousand miles away in Virginia, so excited about the future of the House of Hope . . . but was I giving thanks to God for how far He'd brought us in the past two months? For how far we'd come from those first few terrible weeks after Philip had abandoned me?

Philip . . . A messy stew of anger, confusion, and sadness threatened to boil up and consume my glad heart. He'd gotten so *weird* lately, almost as if he'd forgotten that he'd kicked me out of house and home, and was wrestling with some monkey on his back. And what in the world did Estelle mean by saying, "That man of yours is in real trouble now!" when I mentioned Philip's meeting with Fagan-somebody. She'd taken off like a shot to tell Harry, of all people. Why would they care who his clients were?

I put a lid on the stew. I didn't want to think about Philip. Today was a happy day and I wanted to sing some praises to God, like Jodi Baxter and Edesa and their Yada Yada sisters did. I stuck a CD in the player of the Subaru as I drove the few blocks between my six-flat and Manna House, and there it was. My song. The song that had been a spiritual lifeboat to me in those first dark days at the shelter. I belted it out along with the CD . . .

Where do I go . . . when the storms of life are raging?

Who do I talk to . . . when nobody wants to listen?

Who do I lean on . . . when there's no foundation stable?

I go to the Rock I know that's able, I go to the Rock! . . .

I was still humming and doing a white-girl jive to the gospel song as I came into the shelter. Angela Kwon eyed me suspiciously as I signed in at the receptionist's cubby. "What are you all happy about, Mrs. Curly Top?"

"First day of school." I grinned.

"Oh yeah. No kids. Maybe it'll be quieter around here during the day now."

"Nope, that's not the reason. I'm just thankful that God"—*there, I said it!*—"gave my kids back to me and I got them into decent schools!" I swiveled my head. "Is Mabel in yet?"

At Angela's nod, I crossed the foyer and knocked at the office door, still humming. But when I heard the director's familiar, "Come!" the song in my heart suddenly twitched and died, replaced by an uneasy misgiving. Mabel and I hadn't actually talked since a week ago, when she'd suddenly turned tables on me and said I bore some responsibility for the demise of my marriage. We'd both backed off the touchy subject, but I'd basically avoided getting into another actual conversation.

Still, I opened the door and peeked in. "Got a minute? I have something I want to run by you regarding the House of Hope plans."

Mabel looked up. "Yes. I need to talk to you too."

Uh-oh. Feeling even more uneasy, I closed the door behind

me and sat down in the chair beside her desk. "Oh. Okay. What's up?"

"About our conversation last week . . ."

I squirmed. I really did *not* want to talk about Philip and me right now, especially if she was going to dump more guilt into my lap.

"I think I owe you an apology."

I blinked. "What do you mean?"

"I . . . well, for one thing, I let my concern about you not telling your husband about this job simmer way too long without saying anything. So when I did say something—after he'd kicked you out and disappeared with your boys—it sounded like I was blaming you for *that*, as if it was your fault. I'm sorry for that." She sighed.

I didn't trust myself to speak right then. She'd sounded so . . . so "righteous" the last time we talked. What brought about this revelation?

Almost as if she read my mind, a corner of Mabel's mouth tipped in a wry grimace. "I was listening to 1390 on the radio a few days ago—you know, the gospel music station—and a Christian counselor was saying we in the church too often blame the victim in our rush to find a 'quick fix' for hurting marriages. True, I was concerned about the communication breakdown between you two. But no one *deserves* the kind of emotional abuse you've experienced, Gabby. Especially the constant belittling that made you afraid to talk to your own husband about this job."

I swallowed past the lump in my throat. "Thank you." The words came out husky and I fished for a tissue. Why did I always end up crying in Mabel's office? I quickly pushed away the niggling notion that there might be some truth in what she'd said last week. She'd apologized, hadn't she?

Mabel picked up a pencil and rolled it between the fingers of both hands. "Uh . . . but there is something else I need to talk about."

I dabbed at my eyes. *Now* what?

"About P.J. and Jermaine."

"Oh." I tensed up again. I was pretty sure what was coming. The picnic—

"I don't think it's going to work out for P.J. and Jermaine to ride together to school."

"Why? P.J. was ready on time this morning when you came by. And I plan to pick them up—"

"It's not that. P.J. didn't talk to Jermaine the whole way to school—which I can deal with. We can't force the boys to be friends. But two blocks away from the school, P.J. suddenly ordered me to stop. He wanted out, said he'd walk the rest of the way. I refused. It wasn't safe. There was no good place to pull over, not with rush-hour traffic at that time of the morning. Besides, you and I had agreed on a drop-off and pick-up spot, and I wasn't about to change that without discussion. So I pulled into the parking lot . . . but then P.J. wouldn't get out of the car until Jermaine got out and walked away. Then he got out and ran past him, but I could tell he said something snotty in passing. And after hearing what he called Jermaine at the picnic, I have a pretty good idea."

My heart sank like a lead weight into my belly. "Oh, Mabel. I'm so sorry. I'll talk to P.J. I don't know why he's—"

She held up her hand like a stop sign. "Fine. But I don't want

Jermaine getting hurt while P.J. is learning how to behave like a decent human being. That boy is already fragile. He's been called names all his life by other kids because he's more effeminate—might as well say it—than the average boy. But I'm not going to put him into a situation where he's going to be belittled before he even starts his school day." Mabel leaned forward and said softly, "You of all people ought to understand what I'm saying, Gabby."

chapter 24

Mabel was ready to scrap our plan to share rides then and there, but I begged her to let me pick up both boys today as we'd planned, and I would make sure P.J. acted decently toward Jermaine. "We don't want to let P.J. think his rude behavior got him what he wanted, do we? Not riding with Jermaine, I mean."

She pursed her lips for a moment or two, and then reluctantly agreed. Maybe because she'd backed off from last week's conversation, I suddenly got up and gave my boss a hug. "I'm with you one hundred percent on this, Mabel," I whispered in her ear, "even though it hurts that it's *my* son who's acting like a jerk." This time Mabel was the one who reached for the tissue box.

I headed for the door, but almost belched a hysterical laugh when I heard Mabel say, "Oh, one more thing, Gabby . . . didn't you say you had something you wanted to talk about when you first came in?"

I started to wave her off, thinking I'd had enough of talking with Mabel for one session. Then decided I should act like an adult. I turned and sat down again. "Well, this might sound crazy, but . . ."

She listened while I ran through Jodi's and my new idea for the House of Hope. Two of our best volunteers—Josh and Edesa Baxter—desperately needed a larger apartment. The House of Hope could use a property manager on site, and we already knew Josh was pretty handy around the shelter. "I could reduce their rent or something in exchange for helping me keep up the property."

A slow grin lit up Mabel's face. "What a wonderful idea, Gabby! Why not? It's up to the property owner, not the city, to say how many apartments are available for second-stage housing. I put down five on the application to the Housing Trust Fund, but changing it to four is no problem. And"—her smile got bigger— "isn't that just like God to make a way out of no way for His children? How long have Josh and Edesa been looking for a bigger apartment? Could be they haven't found anything because God had something better in mind than just finding an apartment! And to tell you the truth, it makes your crazy House of Hope idea a lot more viable to have more staff on site."

I was so excited by her response I wanted to call Josh and Edesa on the spot with the proposal. And then I remembered. "There's, uh, just one hitch. Precious and Tanya. I've told both of them they're at the top of the list to get an apartment when we sign the final papers with the city. But there are only two apartments available."

Mabel leaned forward, all professional again. "Gabby. There's no way Tanya and Sammy need a *three*-bedroom apartment. Or even Precious and Sabrina! It's perfectly legit to offer them a shared apartment. A lot of second-stage housing units are shared. There's one in the city for single women, and each apartment is shared by three women. It's still an apartment with all the amenities of home—living room, dining room, kitchen . . . and closets!" She smiled. "Believe me, sometimes I think that's what shelter women miss most. Having their own closet."

I wanted to believe her. "But if Precious and Tanya are expecting their own place . . ."

"Make it temporary if you want to. When another apartment comes available, you can shuffle things around if that seems right." She leaned forward again. "Gabby, the important thing is to make sure you're listening to God and asking the Holy Spirit to guide you in these decisions. Are you prayed up about this? Even the best idea can fall flat if God's not in it. The Bible says, 'Unless the Lord builds the house—'"

"'—its builders labor in vain,'" I finished. "I know, I know. Haven't really prayed about this—it just came up yesterday when the Baxters were helping me clean up one of the empty apartments."

"Well then. Now's as good a time as any." Mabel reached across her desk and took both my hands in hers. "Lord," she said, squeezing her eyes shut, "I've got Gabby Fairbanks by the hand and we're coming to You with another one of her crazy, wonderful ideas . . ."

I spent most of the morning working with Carolyn getting the schoolroom ready to start the afterschool program that afternoon. She'd been haunting garage sales all weekend and showed up with two boxes of kid books to use as readers. I sorted through them, taping the ones with loose covers or torn pages. "Oh, wow, these take me back." I laughed, holding up a handful of thin paperbacks about the Berenstain Bears. "And all these Scholastic Junior Classics! *Robin Hood . . . Wind in the Willows . . . Alice in Wonderland . . .*" I set aside a couple that needed mending. "This is great, Carolyn."

"Yeah, couldn't believe I found them at a garage sale. Too bad we only have four kids in the afterschool program. I'd love to give a whole passel of kids the love of reading." She sighed and opened the next box. "Should've been a teacher instead of a librarian."

I stared at her. "Carolyn! You just gave me an idea. Maybe we should open up our afterschool program to neighborhood kids too! I bet there are a lot of kids around here whose parents don't have time to help them with homework."

Carolyn's pale eyes glittered. "You mean it?"

"Sure! But we'd need more volunteers." The idea bounced around in my head like a pinball—we'd need more computers, I'd have to write up a proposal for the board, find more volunteers, budget for more supplies—and got hung up on a reality check. "Okay, okay, maybe we're getting ahead of ourselves here. We're just getting this program started . . . We should probably wade in the water for a month or so, get our feet wet with the few kids we've already got before we expand the program."

"Yeah, guess you're right." Carolyn shrugged and started sorting another stack of books.

I reached over and grabbed her hand. "I still think it's a great idea, though. Why don't we pray about it—you and me?"

"Guess so." She shrugged again. "That your cell phone ringing?"

Sure enough. I dug it out of my bag and flipped it open long enough to see who was calling—Lee Boyer—and closed it again. "I mean pray right now." *After all, like Mabel said, unless the Lord builds the house . . .*

Carolyn let me do most of the praying, though she offered a hearty, "Amen!" Then I excused myself and took my cell phone outside where I could get a stronger signal, though I had to walk down the sidewalk to get away from the residents having a smoke on the front steps. "Lee? It's me, Gabby. You called?"

"Yeah. Just wanted to remind you that we've got a date in court this Friday for a judge to rule on your petitions. Philip and his lawyer got notices too."

My petitions. One for unlawful eviction and the other for custody of my sons.

"Lee . . ." I said slowly. "What happens if I win the one about unlawful eviction? I don't want to go back to the penthouse."

"Don't worry about it. We'll request compensation, damages—some kind of financial settlement to help with your current housing."

"But—" Given Philip's current gambling debts, I doubted I'd ever see a penny in damages.

"The important thing, Gabby, is to not let him get away with what he did. It's unconscionable! Personally, I can't wait to hear the judge ream him out."

Somehow my own fantasies about "payback" had lost their glitter—especially since Estelle and Harry had prayed with me about doing what was right for me, the boys, *and* for Philip. "Lee, all I really want is legal custody of my sons."

"I know. It's going to be all right. I'll see you Friday at the

Richard J. Daley Center in the Loop. Got something to take down the address and courtroom number?"

I didn't but ran back inside and grabbed some notepaper from the reception cubby. I was scribbling the address for the Daley Plaza when the front door buzzer went off and Angela buzzed the person in.

Josh Baxter, all lanky and sweaty, a book bag slung over his shoulder, backed through the door saying to someone outside, "Sorry . . . sorry, don't have a light. Nope, don't smoke." He swung around. "Oh, hi, Mrs. Fairbanks. Thought I'd stop in and make sure all the computer programs for the afterschool program are loaded and working before I head to class. Today's the first day, right?"

I grinned. Just the man I wanted to see. "Carolyn will be delighted. But, um, before you do that, could I talk to you a minute in my office?"

His perpetual grin faded. "Uh-oh. What'd I do?"

I laughed. He was still such a kid. "Nothing! Just an idea I want to throw your way."

As we came out of my office ten minutes later, Estelle Williams leaned over the kitchen counter and watched Josh take the stairs back up to the main floor two at a time. "Now, what's that boy so happy about?"

I peered around the kitchen looking for other ears. "Where's your help?"

"You tell me. Mabel didn't post a new chore chart, so of

course nobody showed up." She gave me a wicked grin. "Except you. Grab a hairnet and a peeler, Firecracker." She shoved a two-pound bag of carrots at me.

"I . . . oh, all right." Josh Baxter was now helping Carolyn in the schoolroom. I guessed I could spare half an hour to help Estelle get lunch out. I picked up the vegetable peeler and double-checked for stray ears. "Can you keep a secret?"

"Ha," she snorted. "Question is, can *you* keep a secret? You're just dying to tell me." Estelle snapped a hairnet over my curls and snickered. "Now you look like a white turnip instead of a head of escarole."

Ignoring her teasing, I eagerly rehearsed the possibility of Josh and Edesa renting one of the apartments in my six-flat in exchange for becoming part-time property managers for the House of Hope. "He's going to talk to Edesa, and we'll have to figure out a fair exchange of hours-for-rent, but . . . oh, Estelle. Wouldn't that be wonderful? Not to mention"—another perk fell into my spirit like a shooting star—"having Josh around as a 'big brother' would be wonderful for my boys. You know, since their dad isn't around that much."

"Mm. Yes." But Estelle gave me a funny look.

"What?"

She frowned. "What you said about the boys' dad. If that man ain't careful, he won't be around at all."

"Estelle! What are you talking about? What does Philip have to do with this?—Wait a minute. Does this have anything to do with you going bonkers when I mentioned that client Philip was talking to? That Fagan person? Why? Do you know him? Does Harry?"

Footsteps clattered down the stairs. Tawny, the "new kid" who'd landed at Manna House after DCFS washed its hands of her, and a thirtysomething black woman with a hard face I'd noticed smoking outside with some of the others this morning, sidled up to the counter. "Mabel said we're on lunch today," Tawny said. "This is—what's your name, lady? . . . Oh yeah, Bertie. Whatchu want us to do, Estelle?"

"Humph. Wash your hands at that sink back there and get you both a clean apron and hairnet. I'll be back in five." Estelle took me by the elbow and propelled me toward my office, shutting the door behind us. "Sit," she ordered, plopping into my desk chair.

I sat in the extra folding chair. "What's this about?"

Estelle shook her head. "Don't know yet. But Harry's trying to find out. Because if this Fagan person is who we think he is, Philip has got himself in a heap o' trouble."

"But who is he?"

"Rogue cop, got himself indicted by Internal Affairs of the police department." Estelle shook her head and clucked her tongue. "From what Harry's told me, you don't want to mess with Matty Fagan."

chapter 25

What Estelle said didn't make sense to me. Why would Philip do business with some cop who was being indicted by the Chicago Police Department?

Had to be some other guy named Fagan.

But I felt uneasy the rest of the day. In spite of everything, Philip was my sons' dad and I didn't want them to suffer any more drama than they had already. I pulled out one of my "desperate Gabby" prayers and kept it going all afternoon: "Please, God, don't let Philip get mixed up in any mess with this Fagan character—for P.J. and Paul's sake at least."

At three o'clock, I walked to Sunnyside with Tanya and the other shelter moms to pick up our kids since it was the first day, but realized the kids could soon walk back to Manna House as a group in a few days—including Paul. Seemed like a win-win situation to me. Paul could hang out where I worked after school, could even get help with his homework from Carolyn in the afterschool program if he wanted to—and there was always Ping-Pong, board games, and the DVD player when he got done. I made a mental note to mention this when I went for my custody hearing on Friday.

I poked my head into the rec room when it was time to pick up P.J. and Jermaine at five, but Paul and ten-year-old Keisha were doing battle with the foosball paddles and he waved me off. "Pick me up on your way home! . . . Ha! You just knocked the ball into my goal, Keisha!"

Fine with me. I'd rather not have Paul along if I had to deal with any mess involving P.J. and Jermaine. I pulled into the parking lot at 4:55 and waited at the designated spot for the boys. P.J. had cross-country practice after school, and Mabel said Jermaine would either be using the library to study or signing up for one of the afterschool clubs.

Jermaine was the first one to show up, wearing skinny jeans and a Lane Tech T-shirt, his head neatly braided in tiny cornrows with short braids-and-beads hanging down the back of his neck. I waved at him and leaned over to open the front passenger door. "Hi! Get in!"

Jermaine hesitated and leaned down, peering at me through the open door. "That's okay, Mrs. Fairbanks. P.J.'s gonna want to sit in front."

"It's fine, Jermaine. You got here first." I gave the boy a warm smile.

Somewhat reluctantly, Mabel's nephew lowered himself into the front seat. He had such big eyes, as pretty as a girl's. I started to ask if he'd signed up for any clubs when I spotted P.J. coming across the wide front lawn toward the parking lot, walking with a handful of other lanky boys, all wearing baggy shorts with gym bags slung over their shoulders. *Good.* He was beginning to make some friends. I resisted tapping on the horn, sure that he'd seen the red Subaru. *Don't embarrass him, Gabby,* I told myself.

P.J. stopped a good twenty feet away from the car and stood talking to the other kids. Once his eyes darted our way, but he quickly looked away.

That rascal. He's pretending he doesn't see us. What's he waiting for?

I got out of the car and stood with the door open. I was just about to shout, "P.J.! Over here!" when he glanced over his shoulder once more, caught my eye . . . then deliberately turned his back to us, moving slowly in the opposite direction, almost as if he was herding the knot of kids away.

A shot of anger surged through my body like a lit fuse. I opened my mouth to screech, "P.J. Fairbanks, get over here right now!"—but I shut it again, got back in the car, and turned on the ignition. Enough of this nonsense! Whatever Philip Fairbanks, Jr., thought was going to happen—maybe wait until his buddies got picked up and he could hop in the car unnoticed by anybody that mattered—he had another thing coming.

Wheeling out of the parking lot, I turned onto Addison and headed east toward the lake. Jermaine stared at me, wide-eyed and open-mouthed. "You just gonna leave P.J. back there?"

"Mm-hm," I murmured through gritted teeth. And no, I was *not* going to go back and get him on a second run.

"But . . . it's okay, Mrs. Fairbanks. I don't mind waitin'."

"*I* mind. He's being rude." I took a slug from the water bottle in the cup holder to douse the fuse still sparking in my spirit. "So." I glanced at Jermaine as I slowed for a red light and put on a smile. "Did you find any clubs you're interested in?"

I listened with half a mind as Jermaine told me about signing up for the drama club, though he'd really like to join the jazz ensemble and play keyboard, but designing sets for the school plays sounded like fun. The other half of my mind spun like a top. How *was* P.J. going to get home? Take the bus? He had money. I'd given both boys five bucks "just in case." Or walk. Couldn't be more than a mile and a half, maybe two to our apartment. Would he be safe? It was still light for several more hours, and Addison was a main street . . .

I dropped Jermaine off at the shelter—Mabel's car was still parked across the street—and asked him to send Paul out. I left the car running, my resolve starting to waver. *Maybe I should go back. Maybe leaving him standing there was enough to teach him not to mess with me* . . . when my cell phone rang. I didn't recognize the caller ID.

"Mom!" P.J. shouted in my ear. "You just drove off and left me! How am I s'posed to get home?" He must have borrowed another kid's cell.

My resolve resumed its backbone. "You figure it out, kiddo." I flipped the phone closed just as Paul ran down the Manna House steps and hopped into the backseat.

"Where's P.J.?" Paul leaned forward to peer into the front seat. "Thought you went to pick him up."

I second-guessed myself the whole time I put together the hamburger roll-ups—a kid-friendly recipe Jodi had given me—for supper. Was I doing the right thing? What if P.J. didn't get home soon? I wouldn't even know where to start looking for him!

I had just sent Paul outside with the garbage and taken the hamburger-filled pastries out of the oven when I heard banging out in the front hallway and a muffled voice yelling, "Let me in!" What in the world—was there something wrong with the buzzer?

I ran down the hall and opened the door a crack. P.J.! "Thank You, Jesus!" I breathed and flung the door wider.

That's when I saw two figures out in the foyer. P.J. *and* Philip. *Oh no, P.J.! You didn't . . .*

I crossed the hall and pulled open the glass-paneled door. "Hey! What's with the banging? Did you try the buzzer?"

"Been punchin' it for five minutes. Why didn't you answer it?"

"But it didn't—" Before I had a chance to finish, P.J. brushed past me and stomped into the apartment, followed by the slamming of his bedroom door.

Philip—suit coat off, tie loosened—frowned at me. "What's the meaning of this, Gabrielle? P.J. called me at the office, said you left him standing in the parking lot and he didn't have a ride home from school. Called *me* wanting me to pick him up!"

I stepped into the foyer, letting the door close behind me. I folded my arms and lifted my chin. "Guess he forgot to tell you I was there waiting for him, and he refused to get in the car."

"He said he was just talking to his friends and you drove off!"

"No, he was talking to his friends so he wouldn't have to get in the car. Because he didn't want to be seen with another kid I was taking home."

Philip snorted. "Who? That wuss you invited to the boys' birthday party?"

It was all I could do not to haul off and slap him. "*Wuss?* Where do you get off insulting Jermaine that way! He's Mabel's nephew, and we agreed to share rides taking the boys to and from school. P.J. was very rude to Mabel and Jermaine when she drove them this morning. I wasn't going to let him get away with it again!"

"Good grief. Give the kid a break, Gabby. It was the first day of school. He's the new kid, trying to make a good impression."

"All the freshmen are new. Besides, that doesn't excuse being rude."

It was like Philip hadn't heard me. "He said he didn't have any lunch either."

I snorted. "He forgot it."

"And why did he have to pound on the door? Can't get into his own house?"

"He *has* a key. Must've forgotten that too." I rolled my eyes. "Just . . . leave, Philip."

Philip ran his hand through his hair in that boyish way I used to find endearing. But I was angry—angry that P.J. had called his dad and dragged him into this. So much for the "tough love" lesson I was trying to teach the kid.

"Fine." Philip pointed a finger at me. "But a judge may have second thoughts about giving you *custody* when he hears you left your own kid high and dry on the first day of school."

A long finger of ice down my spine froze me to the spot as Philip pulled open the outer door and hustled down the steps to his car. He was threatening me?

Shaken, I turned the door handle and pushed on the inside foyer door. It had clicked shut. I fished in the pocket of my jeans for the key . . . no key. *Dang!* I kicked the door—and winced, realizing I only had sandals on. I eyed the buzzer—was it working or not? I pressed the button under the mailbox that said "Fairbanks" and heard . . . nothing.

Paul finally heard me banging on the foyer door and let me in. "Why didn't you ring the buzzer?" he griped, following me back to the kitchen. "I'm hungry. Is supper ready?"

I didn't trust myself to speak, just flopped hamburger roll-ups on three plates and sent him to get P.J. for supper. I decided to say nothing to P.J. about his behavior until we'd both cooled off a little and got some food under our belts.

But my "talk" with P.J. later that evening didn't go too well. I made it clear that his rude behavior about riding with Jermaine was unacceptable, though I got a halfhearted shrug when I asked if he understood. Finally I told him that if he conducted himself decently with our current plan for the rest of the week, *then* we'd talk about him taking the city bus.

It wasn't just P.J.'s sullen demeanor during our talk; the kid was fourteen, after all. Not even the fact that he'd referred to Jermaine as a "wuss" at the picnic—though I told him he'd be grounded for a week if I ever heard him use insulting labels like that to refer to *anybody*, and I didn't *care* if his father had said it first.

What really rattled me were his parting words as I left his bedroom. "Why can't I live with Dad? *He* wouldn't make me ride with some loser like Jermaine. Don't know why you brought us to Chicago anyway. If you and Dad aren't gonna get it together, Paul and I oughta at least get some say about where we're going to live!"

chapter 26

I woke early the next morning . . . with P.J.'s last words ringing loudly in my ears. I burrowed my face into the pillow, fighting back tears. *Oh, God, I really don't know what to do. I'm trying to trust You with my kids, but I'm so scared I'll lose them again . . .*

I was still feeling rattled when I got to work. It was Wednesday—Nurse Day—and I had to thread my way through a dozen or more residents in the dining room waiting to see Delores Enriquez, the county hospital nurse who donated her time one morning a week to take care of basic medical problems. Locking myself into my broom-closet office, I tried to shut out the noisy chatter outside and get to work. But my talk with P.J. ate away at me, like a big slug of Drano corroding my insides.

I stared at the cursor blinking from the computer screen as P.J.'s words mocked me. *Why can't I live with Dad? If you and Dad aren't gonna get it together . . .*

"Oh, God," I moaned, leaning my elbows on the desk and pressing my fingers against my skull. "I can't do this. I don't want to lose my kids!" Had P.J. told his dad he wanted to live with him? Philip hadn't said anything last night . . . except that threat about telling the judge I'd "abandoned" my kid in the parking lot on his first day of high school.

Stupid, stupid, stupid . . .

Lee Boyer had assured me my custody petition was a slam dunk. But what if it wasn't? What if Philip challenged it? What if the judge gave the boys a choice where they wanted to live? What if . . . what if P.J. said he wanted to go back to Virginia and live with Nana and Grandad, so he could continue going to George Washington Prep with all his old friends? Would the judge let him?

Nausea swept over me and I pulled the wastebasket within upchuck distance. The feeling passed, but now all my nerves felt as if they were going to jump out of my skin. I paced back and forth in the tiny office—five steps this way, five steps back—running a hand through my snarly curls. *I should've just ignored P.J.'s snit and made the best of it, waited it out. Standing up for Jermaine isn't worth starting a landslide that might take my kids away from me.*

I immediately winced at my selfish thought and sank back into my desk chair. "Oh, God," I moaned again. "I need some help here. I feel like I'm going crazy!"

Come to Me . . .

I made myself sit still. Those were the words that kept coming to me when I'd started reading the gospel of Matthew, even before Philip kicked me out. That's what Jesus said. *"Come to Me . . . and I will give you rest."*

I sat quietly for a few minutes. What did it mean to "come to God and find rest" when I was on the verge of being a nervous wreck? I needed someone to pray with me. That's what a prayer partner was for, wasn't it? I picked up the phone and dialed Jodi Baxter's number—and got her voice mail. Of course. School had started and she was teaching a room full of squirrelly third graders at Bethune Elementary.

Well, I could pray with Estelle. I opened my office door and peeked outside. Estelle usually came in early on Wednesday to help Delores with sign-ups and teach her knitting group. But . . . no Estelle. Only Precious and Diane-of-the-Big-Afro behind the kitchen counter, banging a few pots and pans. I slipped up to the counter. "Where's Estelle?"

Precious pulled a plastic container from the refrigerator and plopped it on the counter. "What do I know? Mabel just said Estelle had an emergency doctor's appointment—eye doc or something—and could I throw some food together for the lunch crew. Huh. How come I always end up coverin' lunch when Estelle don't show up? Don't nobody blame me if it's Leftover Surprise today."

Emergency doctor's appointment? Eye doctor? For herself or Harry?

Well, okay. Guess I needed to "get my own prayers on," as Precious would say—when she was in a better mood anyway. But I had to get out of my office. Felt as if the walls were closing in on me. And I had an idea how to stop my mind from spinning like a Tilt-A-Whirl and get focused.

Five minutes later I was sitting in my red Subaru, parked—hallelujah—under a leafy locust tree along the side street around the corner from Manna House, windows open to a slight breeze, listening to the gospel CD Josh Baxter had given me:

. . . The earth all around me is sinking sand
On Christ the Solid Rock I stand
When I need a shelter, when I need a friend
I go to the Rock . . .

Listening to the CD and spending some time praying helped calm my spirit enough that I was able to get through the day. I even worked up the courage to step into Mabel's office at one point and ask, "How'd it go this morning?"

The director gave me a little smile. "Okay. Good, actually. P.J. got in the car and said, 'Hi, Miss Turner. Hi, Jermaine.' Didn't say anything the rest of the way, but we'll take what we can get, right? Oh—he also said, 'Thanks' when he got out."

My spirit hiked up a notch. That was more than I expected out of P.J., given our bum talk the night before. And he did get into the car when I drove into the school parking lot at five that afternoon, sliding into the front seat and turning on the radio full blast. We waited five minutes for Jermaine, who climbed wordlessly into the back. The radio filled the car, negating the need for any conversation and I let it alone.

But I did call Jodi that evening and asked her to pray with me about the whole Jermaine-P.J.-ride-to-school-live-with-me-or-Philip-custody-hearing-coming-up stew mushing around in my spirit. "Sheesh," she said. "I'm the same way, Gabby. I let the what-ifs get me all in a panic, when nothing has happened yet. Remember that verse we talked about? 'Trust in the Lord with all your heart—'"

"Yeah, I've got it taped on the kitchen cupboard. It's that part about 'lean not on your own understanding' I need to work on."

She sighed. "Me too." But she prayed over the phone, thanking God "that Gabby can trust You to make her paths straight like the verses in Proverbs promise."

"Thanks, Jodi," I said when she'd finished. "By the way, Estelle didn't come to work today. Do you know anything about an emergency eye doctor's appointment?" I figured Jodi might know since Estelle and her housemate, Stu, lived on the second floor of the Baxter's two-flat.

"Really? No, but come to think of it, I haven't seen her this evening. I'll run upstairs and ask Stu what's up and call you back."

Jodi called back in ten minutes. "Stu doesn't know much either—but it's not Estelle. It's Harry. Stu says he called Estelle this morning before she was even out of bed, like six or something, and the next thing she knew, Estelle was throwing her clothes on and muttering, 'I told that man to get himself to the eye specialist, but did he go? No, the stubborn old goat'—or something like that."

I couldn't help but laugh. I could just see Estelle stomping around, telling Harry a thing or two even if he wasn't there. But my laugh quickly died. "Sounds like it might be serious. She still isn't back? I wonder if we should call her, find out what's wrong."

"Good idea. But let's pray for her and Harry first, okay?"

I called Estelle's cell phone two times that night and left a message both times, but didn't get a call back. Both boys already had homework—and I hadn't been able to convince Paul to use the afterschool time to get his done and earn a free evening—so I spent most of the evening making sure they were doing their work and not getting distracted by their iPods or the TV. Couldn't believe it, though, when the house phone rang and it was for P.J.—from a girl. Good grief, school had just started two days ago and girls were calling him already?

"Can you believe it?" I told Angela when I signed in at the reception desk the next morning. "P.J. got a call from a *girl* last night. He's only been at school two days. And since when do the girls call the boys?"

Angela laughed and handed me a couple of messages. "Oh, Gabby. You're showing your age. Girls call guys all the time these days, even make the first move. Equal opportunity, you know! And besides, that P.J. is pretty cute. Give him a few years and he'll be breaking hearts right and left." She winked and answered the incessant phone. "Manna House. Can I help you?"

I pushed that image—a trail of broken hearts in P.J.'s wake—out of my head before it sent me into a deep depression and glanced at the messages as I headed downstairs to my office. A phone call from Peter Douglass, asking if the shelter could use a couple more computers. And a handwritten note from Sarge, saying a newbie had come in last night and asked for me by name. I squinted at the name: Naomi Jackson.

Naomi . . . Naomi Jackson. I vaguely remembered a girl by that name. By the time I got to my office, I remembered. White girl, tangled brown hair with blonde streaks under a brown felt cap. Pierced nose—maybe her lip too, couldn't remember—and high as a kite on something! I'd only been working at the shelter a few days and did her intake, shaking in my shoes because I had no idea what I was doing. Mabel had been out, but took over when she came back, and I'd been impressed how straightforward she'd treated Naomi—no-nonsense, firm, kind.

But the kid had only stayed one day. The craving for a fix had been too strong.

That was almost three months ago. The staff had wondered if she'd come back. I was glad she had—but why in the world was she asking for me?

I went looking for her and found her curled up in an over-stuffed chair in Shepherd's Fold, sound asleep. I gently shook her arm. "Naomi?"

The girl opened her eyes, seemingly confused about where she was. She still had the same stud in her nose—none in her lip, though—and streaked brown-and-blonde hair pushed up haphazardly under the same brown felt cap. But this time a black eye and facial bruise ran halfway down her cheek.

But she wasn't high. Recognition lighted her eyes and she half-smiled—only half because the swollen cheek hindered a full one. "Hey, Mrs. Fairbanks. You 'member me?"

I sat down in the chair next to her. "I do. I'm glad to see you came back, Naomi."

"Yeah." She wagged her head. "Shoulda come back sooner, but . . ."

"What happened to your face? Who beat you, Naomi?"

"Aw, it ain't nothin'. My pimp, he got a little excited when I told him I was leavin'—but I mean it this time, Mrs. Fairbanks. I gotta get off the streets." She grabbed a throw pillow and hugged it to her chest, rocking it like a rag doll. "Them streets gonna kill me if I don' get off that smack."

I watched her for a few moments, feeling helpless. How did one help a girl as far gone as Naomi? But I wanted to—wanted to gather her in my arms and hold her, rock her, kiss her hair, tell her it was going to be all right. But what did I know? I was the program director. Not a case manager or social worker. Not her mother either.

"I got a note from Sarge saying you wanted to see me. I'm surprised you remembered my name."

The girl blushed. "Aw, that's 'cause you was the first person I met when I came here the last time. I remembered that. You talked to me like I was a real person."

I had? All I could remember was being scared to death because she was high on drugs and might do something. "I'm glad . . ." I said, distracted momentarily by the double doors swinging open and Estelle coming in. I stood up, hoping to catch her. "Be strong, Naomi. It might be tough for a while to stick it out—but you'll be glad you did. I've seen some mighty big miracles happen here. Including me."

The girl squinted up at me. "You? Naw. You look like a good person—not like me."

"You don't have to be good to have God do a miracle in your life," I murmured—and suddenly bent and kissed her on the forehead. Probably not kosher. But I didn't care. How long had it been since she'd had a kiss from someone who wasn't trying to get something from her?

chapter 27

Estelle had stopped to pour herself a cup of coffee from the coffee cart and thumped the carafe down when a mere few drops leaked into her cup. "Humph, can't even get a decent cup of coffee," she snapped, gathering up her bags again as I arrived.

"I'll make you some fresh," I said, quickly snatching up the empty carafes and following in her wake down the stairs to the kitchen. Within minutes I had a pot dripping and the rich, nutty aroma wafted through the kitchen like a lazy genie. I poured two steaming cups and doctored them with milk (for me) and sugar (for Estelle).

"Gimme that," she said and added another heaping tablespoon of sugar. "Why you always so stingy with the sweet stuff?"

I steered her to a nearby table and waited until she'd taken a few long sips. "So tell me what's going on with Harry. What's this emergency with his eyes? I'm worried."

Estelle sighed. "You should be. Don't know if I understand it myself—but he started seeing flashes of light in his eye during the night, scared him silly. I got myself over to his apartment and tried to calm him down until we could call the Medical Center at U of I and get him in to see an eye specialist." She wagged her head, both hands gripping her coffee cup. "He went last week and they did some laser treatment to pin down a retinal tear. Harry said it hurt like heck, but now they saying he's got a retinal detachment. They patched up both eyes and told him to stay still till they can get him in for surgery later tomorrow."

"What? They patched up *both* eyes? How's he supposed to see? And what about DaShawn?"

Estelle snorted. "That's just it. He can't see nothin', not supposed to do nothin' either. We took DaShawn to school before heading to the Medical Center and Jodi brought him home with her till we got back. You know he's goin' to Bethune Elementary where Jodi teaches, right? Anyway, after I got Harry back home and settled, I picked up DaShawn and kept him with me for the night. Jodi took the boy to school this morning. I told Harry he can stay with me till he gets this eye thing taken care of. Between Stu an' me an' the Baxters, I think we can work things out for DaShawn."

"But what about Mr. B?" This was worse than I'd imagined. "How's *he* supposed to manage?"

Estelle's eyes suddenly filled up and she fished for a tissue somewhere in the folds of her roomy tunic. "I don't know, Gabby. He needs somebody with him, that's what. Otherwise he gonna be liftin' off those bandages an' peekin', just to get around. But the doc said he has to totally rest his eyes so those retinal tears don't get worse." She blew her nose and stood up. "That's why I'm gonna put lunch together an' get myself outta here. Who's on lunch duty today? I could use some extra help . . . What day's today anyway?"

"Thursday." I headed for the chore chart Mabel posted on the dining room bulletin board each morning. "Uh, it's Kim and Wanda."

"Mm, Kim and Wanda. Okay . . . wait. Thursday?" Estelle slapped her forehead. "I'm s'posed to teach cooking class this afternoon too! Well, I can't do it. *Somebody's* got to go sit with Harry. Denny Baxter's comin' this evening to hang out with Harry so I can go see Leroy. I been readin' to my boy from the Bible—seems to calm him some."

No wonder Estelle was edgy, with the two men in her life *both* laid up. I assured her I'd take care of cancelling her class and hurried off to find Kim and Wanda and ask if they could come early to help Estelle with lunch. As I came into Shepherd's Fold, I spotted Wanda standing with Precious and several other residents in the center of the room, clapping and laughing. A gospel CD had been turned up loud on the CD player and the object of their amusement was soon apparent—little Gracie Baxter was gyrating and bouncing to the music like a toddler version of *American Idol*, egged on by the attention of her circle of "aunties."

Her mom must be around somewhere . . . which suddenly gave me an idea. I touched Wanda's shoulder. "Is Edesa here?"

"Mi t'ink she talkin' to Mabel . . . Now look at dat lil gal. She de cutest ting."

Gracie was cute, but I had other things on my mind. "Estelle is in a bind and needs some extra help. Can you find Kim and go a little early to help with lunch?"

The big Jamaican woman shrugged. "No problem." She

sidled off, but first she gave Gracie a tickle under her chin, which set off a ripple of giggles.

I was just about to go off in search of Edesa, when Gracie's adoptive mother came through the swinging double doors, sized up the situation, and swept the one-year-old into her arms. "*Niña, niña*, are you showing off again?" She clucked reprovingly at the grinning women. "*Por favor*, don't encourage her. She gets too much attention as it is."

"Pooh," said Precious. "If we can't spoil Gracie, who will? Besides, if a girl gotta dance, she gotta dance!" Precious shimmied her shoulders and hips from side to side with a "Mmm-mm-mm" as the knot of women drifted.

I grinned at her antics but beckoned to Edesa. "Can I talk to you a minute? I need a favor." I'd been meaning to ask her about teaching a class on nutrition for our residents from her Public Health studies. If she had time, maybe she could cover Estelle's cooking class today!

"*Sí*." Edesa jiggled Gracie on her hip. "But, oh, Gabby! *Muchas gracias* for offering one of your apartments to our little *familia*! I could hardly believe it when Josh told me! What a blessing that will be. When do you think we can move?"

Even as the words spilled from Edesa's mouth, I saw Precious freeze in midshimmy and stare at us. Stare at me, rather—a startled look that took only a nanosecond to turn from question to accusation.

As the moment froze, I felt caught in a time warp, kicking myself that I hadn't talked to Precious and Tanya yet about the new plan. I gave Precious a pleading look, but she turned and marched out of the room.

Edesa hesitated. "Did I say something wrong, *mi amiga?*"

I shook my head. "No, no . . . It's my fault. I'll explain . . . but give me a minute, will you?" I ran after Precious, but no one was in the hall and the stairs were empty. Where had she gone? I ran up the stairs and peeked in each of the bunkrooms, but still no Precious. Then I heard a flush, and a moment later Precious came out of the bathrooms into the small lounge. She stopped when she saw me.

"Precious—" I said.

She folded her thin arms across her chest. "So. When was you gonna tell us you promised one of them apartments to somebody else?"

"I'm sorry, Precious. I meant to talk with you and Tanya this week. It's just that I realized how much work it's going to take to maintain the building, and Josh is pretty handy, and they've been looking for a bigger place, so I thought—"

"Yeah, yeah, I feel ya. Your heart all bleedin' for that poor little family, all crunched up in that tiny little apartment which, by the way, *they live in by they own selves*. But"—Precious shook a finger in my face—"you promised me an' Sabrina were top of your list for this so-called House of Hope. Tanya an' her Sammy too. But, hm, lemme see . . ." The arms crossed again and her chin went up. ". . . that's *two* apartments an' *three* families you done promised can move in. So. Which one of us was you gonna bump to make room for them Baxters?"

I sank down on one of the threadbare couches in the upper lounge. This had all made sense when Mabel and I talked about it in her office, but now I felt like a certifiable jerk. "You and Tanya are still at the top of my list, Precious. I was . . . I was going to ask you and Tanya if you'd be willing to share an apartment to start with—at least until another apartment opens up. And ask Josh and Edesa to move into the House of Hope as property manager. But"—my voice cracked—"I can see I went about this all wrong. I should have talked to you and Tanya before I said anything to Josh and Edesa. I'm so sorry." I wagged my head miserably.

Precious just stood in front of me, arms still crossed. Finally she spoke. "But you didn't. So . . . what we s'posed to do now?"

I didn't know what to say. I'd done it again—running ahead of God with my "good idea." When was I going to learn to "lean not on my own understanding" like those verses in Proverbs said? Mabel always said if my "good idea" was part of God's plan, it was going to work out in His time and in His way. I didn't have to rush it.

I looked up at Precious and heaved a sigh. "I think I need to go back to Josh and Edesa and tell them I spoke out of turn. That I'd already promised that apartment to someone else."

Precious sat down on the couch beside me. "You'd do that?"

Suddenly it seemed simple. Just own up to my mistake. Start over. I nodded. "I could tell them they're first in line for the next apartment that opens up."

"An' when would that be?"

I shook my head. "I don't know. I'll try to find out."

We just sat on the couch not saying anything for several minutes, but I could feel the tension dissolving between us. Then she said, "You serious about makin' this right?"

I nodded.

"Okay. Then this is the way it's gonna go down. Step one. You got this big idea how to stretch two apartments an' fix everybody's problems. Step two. You talk to me an' Tanya about it—though right now you talkin' to me an' *I'm* gonna go talk to Tanya. She don't have to know you already jumped the gun and talked to the Baxters. Step three. Tanya an' me gonna talk about it and decide if we *like* the idea of sharin' an apartment—which gonna be five people in three bedrooms once Sabrina's baby get here."

"I know. I—"

"Zip it, Miss Gabby. I'm talkin' here. Step four. Tanya an' me will tell you what we think of your big idea. Then you'll know what ya gotta say to Josh and Edesa. Maybe nothin' if we take you up on it."

I felt confused. "What do you mean? I was going to go downstairs right now and tell Edesa I can't offer the apartment after all."

"An' I'm tellin' you I just want a chance to be part of the decision—since you first off made me an' Tanya think we each gettin' our own place."

Now it was my turn to stare at Precious. Who *was* this woman who had accumulated more spiritual wisdom in her streetwise noggin than I had in all my "churchy" years growing up? Was she really willing to consider this idea after I'd changed the plan without telling her? Finally I spoke. "I . . . I hardly know what to say. Just promise you'll be honest with me, even if the answer is no. And if it is no, the sooner I can say something to Josh and Edesa, the better."

Precious snorted and stood up. "Since when has Precious McGill ever shied away from speakin' my mind? Now let me go find Tanya and tell her about this big idea. Gonna be easier for her to be honest 'bout how she feel if you're not there."

chapter 28

It was hard for me to talk to Edesa about filling in for Estelle's cooking class today and not say anything about the problem with the apartment. But she seemed excited about teaching some nutrition basics even on short notice and the apartment didn't come up again. "This is what I want to do when I graduate, Gabby," she said, her dark eyes dancing. "I can wing it today—but next time, give me more notice so I can prepare properly!" She laughed, her face breaking into that wide Edesa-smile that seemed to turn on highlights from within her warm mahogany skin.

Lunchtime came and went, but Precious and Tanya didn't show. I set aside two plates for them with the baked chicken, green beans, and macaroni on the lunch menu. Estelle had disappeared as soon as food was on the counter, leaving Wanda in charge of supervising serving and cleanup.

After lunch, Edesa put Gracie down for a nap in one of the beanbag chairs in the empty rec room and used the time before the two o'clock class to prepare some notes. When I peeked out my office door at two thirty, she was using that day's menu to illustrate the five basic food groups. ". . . and the cheese sauce in the mac 'n cheese counts as protein from the dairy group. But if you look at the basic food groups on the paper I passed out, what was missing? . . . Tawny?" I closed my door with a smile. Edesa seemed as happy as if she had a class of thirty instead of just the five who showed up.

But still no sign of Precious and Tanya. I started to feel anxious. Should I go look for them? I didn't want to make them feel pressured. But if I had to tell Edesa that the apartment offer was off, I wanted to do it before she left. Otherwise I'd feel like a wimp doing it over the phone.

I picked up one of the stuffed dogs still stacked around my office and glared at its mopey face, beginning to regret I'd let hurt feelings get tangled up in the decision. If I backed out on Josh and Edesa now, I could hardly blame them if they got tired of waiting and rented something else—and that would be the end of my good idea. A property manager and his family right on the premises, a couple I knew and trusted and who were already volunteers at Manna House . . . it would've been so perfect!

Rats! I threw the stuffed dog into a corner with more force than necessary. *I* was the one buying the building, the one offering most of the apartments for second-stage housing. Didn't I have the right to do what I thought best? And like Mabel said, most women who qualified for second-stage housing didn't end up with their own three-bedroom apartments! But no, I was trying to please everybody.

Double rats! Why did I—

A light tap at my office door was followed immediately by

Precious and Tanya slipping into my office, momentarily allowing chatter from the class outside to slip in with them. Precious
jerked a thumb in that direction. "Since when did Edesa start
teaching healthy eatin'? I shoulda put Sabrina in that class! That
girl carryin' a baby and eatin' like a teenager with pizza on the
brain."

I tried to read their faces but got nowhere. "Edesa's just filling
in for Estelle. Long story. Besides, Sabrina's at school. Don't they
talk about the importance of nutrition in her birthing classes at
the hospital?"

"Huh. Don't get me started. She's missed so many of those
classes—"

"Precious!" Tanya hissed. "That ain't what we came to talk
about."

"Oh. Right." Precious gazed somewhere over my head. "We
gonna do it."

I looked cautiously from one to the other. "Do what?"

Tanya giggled. "Share the apartment—if we can have the
first floor, you know, 'cause Sabrina ain't gonna be walkin' up no
three flights of stairs."

I hardly dared breathe. "You . . . really? You're okay with sharing an apartment?"

Tanya nodded. "To tell you the truth, Miss Gabby, I was
kinda scared thinkin' about Sammy and me alone in one of those
big ol' apartments. How would I ever get enough furniture to fill
it up? And Sammy an' me don't need three bedrooms—in fact, he
sleeps better if he's in the same room as me. 'Course it's different
for Precious an' Sabrina . . ."

Precious made a face. "Got that right. I been relishin' the

thought of havin' a whole bedroom to myself, an' one for Sabrina—that girl drives me nuts, the way she throws her clothes around—and a baby room we could fix up with teddy bears or Winnie-the-Pooh or somethin'."

"But I told Precious if we're housemates, we can help each other with the cookin' and cleanin' an' babysittin' too!"

I still was having a hard time believing what I was hearing. "And the bedroom situation?"

Precious shrugged. "Like she said, Tanya an' Sammy would just as soon share a bedroom—for now anyway—so she's cool if Sabrina an' me have the other two. An' I'm thinkin' it might be better for the baby to sleep in Sabrina's room anyway, help her remember she's a mama now. If that baby had a room all its own, Sabrina is likely to sleep right through its nighttime feedings, an I'd be the one gettin' up at 2 a.m. Uh-uh. Been there, done *that*." She shook her head, sending her twists swinging.

"Besides." Tanya smiled shyly. "I like the idea of Mr. Josh an' Miss Edesa livin' there too. My Sammy don't know his daddy, an', well, it'll just be nice to have a young man like Mr. Josh around the place. He's good with all the kids. An' we all love Miss Edesa and little Gracie. It'll kinda be like . . ." She seemed embarrassed. "Kinda like the family we never had."

Long after Precious and Tanya had slipped out of the room, I sat at my desk talking to God. *Oh, God, forgive me. I nearly made a mess of things—but just look at You, God. You took it away from me and then gave it back, better than before! Giving Precious and Tanya a chance to own the new plan is so much better than me getting all self-righteous about my "rights." Oh, Jesus! Help me to trust You more . . .*

Another tap at my door interrupted my scattered thought-prayer. Edesa stuck her head in. "I'm leaving now. Got studying to do. But any chance Josh and I can come over to the apartment this weekend and maybe do some painting? Or, knowing Josh, he's going to want to prep the walls. I know you haven't closed on the building yet, but . . ."

I grinned at her. "That'd be great. Just one thing . . . I forgot to tell Josh which apartment. It's the third floor. Tanya and Precious will be sharing the one on the first floor. Is that going to work for you?"

"*Sí, sí!* I like being on the top floor. No little footsteps running back and forth overhead—oh, I hear Gracie fussing. Can you believe it? She slept through the whole class." The vivacious young woman gave me a quick hug. "And *gracias* again, *mi amiga*. A larger apartment will look very, very good next time we meet with our social worker about Gracie's adoption. *Dios es bueno!*" Laughing, she shut the door behind her, but her sweet presence seemed to linger. I still wasn't used to a Spanish-speaking woman who looked African-American—her "African-Honduran" heritage, she'd told me. Edesa seemed at once exotic and earthy, sweet and salty. No wonder Josh Baxter, three years her junior, had fallen in love with her.

My spirit was nearly bursting with joy at how things were turning out. *If I trust in the Lord, He promised to make my paths straight*. Amen to that!

I turned back to my computer, looking forward to having Josh and Edesa pop over while the boys were with their dad this weekend. It got lonely when they were gone. Did I have anything else scheduled this weekend?

I clicked on the icon for my computer calendar, which

popped up instantly on the screen. My next appointment leaped out at me: *Friday, Sept. 8. Court date. 1:00 p.m.* Tomorrow. My buoyant spirit suddenly sank under the weight of Philip's last words to me: *"A judge may have second thoughts about giving you custody when he hears you left your own kid high and dry on the first day of school."*

I tried to swallow but my mouth had gone dry. Was he going to challenge my custody petition?

I wanted to talk with the boys about their dad and me going to court the following day, but it seemed like the phone rang all evening. Lee called to give me a few tips about tomorrow: Arrive early. Dress professionally but conservatively. Don't bring a big purse—keep it simple, easy for the security personnel to see what's in it. Nothing metal or sharp. Let the lawyers do the talking unless the judge specifically addresses me . . .

Estelle called from Harry's house, saying she had to drive Harry to the Medical Center tomorrow and she wouldn't be at work. She'd already told Mabel, but wanted to let me know and ask me to pray. I started to ask her to pray about my court case tomorrow, but she was off the phone already.

I called Jodi Baxter to pray about my custody petition, and she said Avis Douglass and several of the other Yada Yada sisters were at her house praying for Harry Bentley, and they'd be glad to pray for my custody case as well. "You doing okay, Gabby? Do you need somebody to go with you?"

Yes! I wanted to screech. But what was she going to do, take a personal day off from teaching? Sounded like a bad idea. "I'm all right. I'll be fine. Just pray, okay? One o'clock."

The boys would be going to bed soon. I made a couple of smoothies out of some leftover strawberries, two overripe bananas, and the last of the orange juice, and told the boys I had a couple of things I needed to talk to them about. P.J. looked wary, but joined Paul and me on the window seat in the sunroom just off the living room. The evening was still pleasant, somewhere in the seventies, and I opened the windows to catch the breeze coming off the lake a mile away. Underneath our windows, a cricket orchestra sawed away as the boys sucked the straws in their smoothies.

Just start, Gabby. No matter how I did this, it wasn't going to be easy. I blew out the breath I'd been holding. "You both know your dad and I worked out an informal agreement about where you'd live and when you'd spend time with him after you came back to Chicago."

P.J. shrugged. "Yeah. So?"

"Well, I filed a petition for temporary custody, and the court date is tomorrow. I just wanted you boys to—"

"Why?" P.J.'s eyes sparked. "I mean, why do you have to go to court and do all that stuff? Why can't you just leave it like it is? You said yourself that you and Dad agreed how to work it out."

Paul seemed preoccupied, blowing bubbles through his straw back into his smoothie.

I chose my words carefully. "Because earlier this summer, your dad took you back to Virginia and left you there without telling me. You just . . . disappeared, and I didn't even know where you were." My voice wobbled slightly. "I'm filing for custody so that can't happen again."

Paul blew more bubbles. P.J. glowered at him. "Stop it, squirt!" Paul noisily sucked up the last of the smoothie and slumped against the throw pillows on the window seat, kicking his legs against the baseboard.

P.J. wasn't through. "Shouldn't we go to court too? We're not babies. Maybe the judge wants to ask us where we want to live."

"I don't wanna go to court," Paul piped up. "Let Mom and Dad figure it out."

"Paul's right. This is something your dad and I have to figure out." I tried to soften my voice. "But even if I have legal custody, we can still talk about how much time you spend with your dad and make changes if we all agree."

P.J. still glowered. "Don't see why you moved out in the first place," he muttered.

Why I moved out?! Anger spiked through my body so strongly, I half expected sparks to shoot from my hair and fingertips, like some electrified humanoid. Is *that* what Philip had told the boys? I stood up, my back to the boys, and counted to ten before turning to face them. "P.J. and Paul, look at me. Whatever your father told you, I want you to know that I did *not* move out." *Locked out, thrown out was more like it!* "I would *never, ever* leave you, especially not without saying a word." Hot tears threatened to spill over.

"So he lied, then."

Yes! I wanted to scream. *He lied! He stole you away from me!* But P.J. seemed to be fishing for something. I needed to be careful, not to tear Philip apart in front of his sons, to stick to my side of things. I breathed deeply and sat back down on the window seat, trying to calm down. "I don't know what he said or why he said it. Your dad and I had a . . . a huge misunderstanding. I came home from work and discovered I'd been locked out and you were gone. I didn't know where! I was frantic!"

"But you called us at Nana and Grandad's. And told us to stay there."

"I guessed that's where you might be, and I was right. And it took me awhile to find a place to live so I could bring you back. But I didn't leave you, and I never will." I reached for both boys, pulling them close. "I love you too much to do that."

Paul suddenly crumpled into my lap and burst into tears. I cradled him as his shoulders shook, and to my surprise, P.J. let me pull him close as the three of us rocked together there on the window seat.

As Paul's sobs subsided, I let him sit up but kept my arms around both boys. "Hey, you know what? I have some good news."

"What?" Paul sniffed. "Is it about Dandy?"

"Mm, no. But I think you'll like it. Guess who's going to move into the House of Hope with us?"

"Ha, I know *that*," Paul scoffed, wiping his nose and eyes on his T-shirt sleeve. "Sammy told me. He and his mom, and that big girl Sabrina and her mom."

"She's big, all right." P.J. snickered and stuck out his stomach. "Big with baby."

"Well, that's true. They're going to share the first-floor apartment. But somebody else too."

P.J. looked at me sideways. "Not Miss Turner and that Jermaine kid?"

I let that pass. "No. Our new mystery neighbor taught your Sunday school class at the lake last week and he's also a pretty good baseball player."

"You mean Josh Baxter?" P.J. actually sounded interested.

I grinned. "*And* his wife, Edesa, and little Gracie, of course. Josh is going to be the property manager for this building—you know, fix stuff that gets broken, keep the furnace running, make sure the building stays up to code, stuff like that. In fact, Josh and Edesa are going to come this weekend to prep the walls and start painting the third-floor apartment, getting it ready to move in."

"But we'll be with Dad." Disappointment clouded P.J.'s face. "Wish we could help paint. That'd be fun."

I couldn't help but smile. "Don't you have a cross-country meet on Saturday? Like, waaay out in Wauconda?"

P.J. made a face. "Yeah. Buses leave from the school real early. Like six thirty."

I almost laughed. Poor Philip. "Well, the next meet that's within spitting distance, let me know. I want to see you run." I gave my oldest a teasing sock on the arm, which he shrugged off. But I could tell he was pleased.

"Okay, off to bed, you two. Tomorrow's a school day. Shoo!"

But fifteen minutes later I slipped into Paul's bedroom and sat on the edge of his lower bunk. "What about you, Paul? Think you'll like having the Baxters living here?" I tousled his curly head on the pillow, so like mine, except with a boy cut.

He snuggled under the light blanket. "Yeah, that's cool. But I'd like it even better if Jermaine and his Aunt Mabel could move in."

I hid my surprise. "And why is that?"

"'Cause"—he yawned—"then Jermaine and I could play music together whenever we wanted to . . ."

chapter 29

I didn't know what time Mr. Bentley's eye surgery was on Friday, but Mabel called a short prayer meeting in Shepherd's Fold before Edesa's Bible study for anyone who wanted to pray for "Mr. Harry." As the small group gathered, I worked up the courage to say, "I could also use prayer for my custody hearing this afternoon" without offering any details—and was humbled when two of the women who'd lost custody of their own children when they were drugged out on the street spoke up and prayed for me.

"Rev'rend Liz" Handley, the former-director-now-board-member of Manna House, showed up to cover lunch prep in Estelle's absence. I had to chuckle seeing her bustle around the kitchen, because Liz Handley and Estelle Williams were as different as chalk and cheese. Liz was short, white, and fairly round in the face, with blue eyes and short, steel-gray hair. Estelle was a large black woman, but tall and solid, her dark hair streaked with silver and usually piled in a bun on top of her head. But she could also wear it down and wavy—I suspected Mr. B liked it that way—very womanly.

Then again, those white hairnets and big white aprons had a way of swallowing everyone's "distinctives" and turning them into look-alike kitchen blobs.

Whatever Liz was making smelled good, but I couldn't stay for lunch because my custody hearing was scheduled for one o'clock at the Circuit Court of Cook County, which had its offices in the Richard J. Daley Center in the Loop, and Lee had told me to arrive early. My stomach was in such a knot, I didn't think I could eat anyway.

Rather than hassle with parking, I took the Red Line, which had an El stop a mere two blocks from Daley Plaza. Passing in the shadow of the towering Picasso sculpture—which looked like a skinny iron horse head wearing two winglike ponytails to me—I merged with the stream of people flowing into the Daley Center and lining up at the security checkpoints. I tried not to stare, but the mix of humanity was eye-popping. Orthodox Jews with long beards and tassels hanging beneath their suit coats rubbed elbows with guys in dreadlocks and pants barely hanging on below their butts. Men in traditional suits and ties stood in line with ethnic women—Muslim?—wearing black head scarves that covered all but the face. *What if somebody showed up swathed in a burka? A person could hide almost anything under that.* Some people with ID tags were allowed to go through a special gate, avoiding the security check. Lucky them.

The rest of us inched forward. "Empty your pockets, put everything in the bin . . . Put all purses and bags on the moving belt . . . Sir, sir? You can't take that pocketknife in . . . I don't *care* if your granddaddy gave it to you, you can't take it in . . . Well, I'm sorry. You'll have to leave it in the sheriff's holding room or get out of line . . . Next!"

I made it through security and took the elevator to the eighth floor. I had to ask two different people where to find the room number Lee had given me, but I finally found it with ten minutes to spare. Peeking through the small square window in the door, I saw the back of Lee's head. Relieved, I pulled the door open.

Lee Boyer stood up as I approached the table where he sat, giving my black skirt, black shell with an ivory embroidered cardigan, small earrings, and low heels a quick once-over and smiled his approval. "Glad you're early. Philip isn't here yet." He pulled out a chair for me.

The smallish room helped my racing heart slow down. A desk for the judge, two small tables facing it for the respective parties and their lawyers, a few chairs behind them in two short rows. No jury box. Clearly a room for a hearing, not a trial.

Philip and his lawyer came into the room with one minute to spare. He didn't look at me, just sat down at the other table, whispering to his lawyer. A door at the side of the room opened and a white woman entered, brown hair drawn back into a neat bun at the nape of her neck, reading glasses perched on her nose. A young male clerk scurried behind her and sat down with a transcription machine. That made six of us in the room. We started to stand—don't they say, "All rise" or something?—but the judge waved us back into our seats. For a few moments she didn't say anything, just studied some papers in a folder.

Finally she looked up. "I presume," she said, looking at Lee, "you are representing Mrs. Gabrielle Fairbanks, concerning two petitions"—she glanced again at the folders—"one for unlawful eviction, the other for temporary custody of the couple's two sons?"

Lee stood. "I am, Your Honor. Lee Boyer." For the first time I noticed he was actually wearing a suit and tie. Well, slacks, sport coat, and tie.

"And Mr. Hoffman"—she eyed the other table—"you are representing Mr. Philip Fairbanks?"

Philip's lawyer, a big man with wavy silver hair and a Florida tan, also stood. "Yes. Your Honor, my client would like to—"

The judge interrupted. "I will give you time to present your client's wishes. But I haven't said my piece. Sit down." Mr. Hoffman sat.

The judge peered over her reading glasses in our direction. "Mr. Boyer. This is a custody hearing, yet you have asked that both petitions be considered simultaneously. Why?"

Lee had remained standing. "Thank you, Your Honor. The two petitions are relevant to each other. It is because of the unlawful eviction and subsequent disappearance of the couple's two children that my client is requesting custody."

The judge leaned back in her chair, took off her reading glasses, and chewed on one of the earpieces, looking not at me, but at Philip. It might have been only thirty seconds, but I felt as if I was holding my breath for thirty minutes. Finally . . . "Mr. Hoffman. *What* was your client thinking, locking his wife and her elderly *mother* out of the house—a luxury penthouse, I see—and skipping town with their sons without her knowledge?"

I smiled inwardly. *Thank you, Judge!* But Philip's lawyer must have been prepared for the question because he stood, clearing his throat. "Your Honor, this is not an unusual happenstance when couples quarrel, though it is usually the wife who throws her husband out, along with his clothes and golf clubs, and no one thinks it strange that she has sent him packing. Just because in this case the roles were reversed"—he cleared his throat again, more for emphasis than anything else—"doesn't make it any more heinous."

The judge leaned forward. "Says who? Mrs. Fairbanks has a right to be in her own home. If Mr. Fairbanks doesn't want to live with his wife, *he* can move out."

I cast an anxious glance upward at Lee. I didn't want to move back into the penthouse! He gave me a subtle signal with his hand to be patient. Philip and his lawyer were rapidly conferring. Finally Mr. Hoffman straightened up. "Your Honor, may my client speak in his behalf?"

The judge shrugged. "Of course." But she said it in the tone that P.J. used when he said, "Whatever."

Philip stood up. Even as I tensed, dreading what he might say, I realized he seemed . . . vulnerable somehow. As usual, his handsome features were easy on the eyes, his clothes—slacks, open-necked silk shirt, summer-weight suit coat—just right. I couldn't put my finger on it—the way his eye twitched? the new stress lines in his face?—but he didn't seem his usual relaxed, confident self. "Uh, Your Honor, I know what it looks like from the outside. But the situation in our home had become untenable. My wife brought her mother and a dog into the home without consulting me, which overcrowded our space. She also took a job that prevented her from caring for our sons during their summer vacation, and otherwise burdened the household with her unwise choices. I know what I did was drastic, but I did it to make a point. Something had to change."

He sounded so reasonable, so persuasive, I felt like crawling under the table. He made me sound like a totally unfit wife and mother.

The judge frowned. "But block her credit cards? Cancel her cell phone? I understand from what it says here"—she waved the petition—"that you left her virtually destitute with no means of support, and she ended up in a homeless shelter. A *homeless shelter*, Mr. Fairbanks."

Philip swallowed. He looked uncomfortable. "She is employed at that shelter, Your Honor. It was natural that that was the first place she turned."

The judge shook her head. Clearly she wasn't buying it. "Thank you, Mr. Fairbanks. I'm sure you think you had your reasons. But I am ruling in favor of the petitioner that she has been unlawfully removed from her home and may return immediately."

I scribbled a furious note for Lee. *No!*

Lee spoke up. "Your Honor, my client has since been able to find alternative and adequate housing for herself and her children, and has no desire to return to her former place of residence. We are requesting a financial settlement instead to help cover her alternative housing expenses."

I was watching Philip. He seemed to flinch.

The judge considered. "Hm. Do you have a statement of expenses?"

"We do." Lee strode forward with a financial statement that

included my meager salary and monthly rent for the apartment in the six-flat. The judge looked it over.

"Your Honor!" protested Mr. Hoffman. "Mrs. Fairbanks has recently come into a family inheritance that is allowing her to purchase the whole building! I hardly think she needs financial assistance—"

The judge glanced up at Lee, who was still standing by her desk. "Is this true?"

Lee nodded. "Yes. We have included that on the financial statement . . . there, on the bottom. However, Mrs. Fairbanks is still currently renting, and legally, her family inheritance—which she knew nothing about at the time of her unlawful eviction— has nothing to do with this case. The fact is, Philip Fairbanks unlawfully removed his wife from her place of residence, and in lieu of returning to that residence, she deserves financial assistance to maintain an alternative residence for herself and her children."

Lee returned to our table. I smiled at him. *Good job*. I'd managed to get by, even without Mom's life insurance, but it was the principle of the thing, wasn't it?

The judge studied the sheet of paper she'd been given. Finally she said, "I agree. I will decide the financial amount after we deal with the custody petition, since this case involves residence for the children." She took up a second folder. "I understand Mr. and Mrs. Fairbanks have worked out a mutual agreement that their two children"—she consulted the folder—"Philip, Jr., age fourteen, and Paul, age twelve, should reside primarily with their mother with weekly overnight visitation with their father. Is this correct?"

"Yes, Your Honor." Both lawyers spoke together, like Siamese twins. But Mr. Hoffman plowed on. "Which puzzles my client," he said, "why a Petition for Temporary Custody is necessary. He has agreed to his wife's wishes in this matter and the boys are currently living with their mother with weekend visits to their father."

"But as you can see, Your Honor," Lee countered, "at the time that Mrs. Fairbanks was unlawfully evicted from their home, her husband disappeared with the children, their whereabouts unknown to their mother. It is against the possibility of that occurrence happening again that my client is requesting temporary custody."

Mr. Hoffman threw out his hands. "My client simply took the boys to their grandparents, where, I might add, they had been staying previously when Mr. and Mrs. Fairbanks first moved to Chicago in order to finish out their school year. Mrs. Fairbanks was not prohibited from communicating with her sons at any time."

Sudden tears threatened to undo me. The fear and desperation I'd felt when I didn't know where they were in that first twenty-four hours rose to the surface like boils about to pop. Sensing I might break down, Lee laid a reassuring hand on my shoulder. I took a deep breath and let it out slowly. *Breathe, Gabby . . . breathe.*

Out of the corner of my eye, I saw Philip conferring with his lawyer. Was he going to bring up me leaving P.J. in the school parking lot? After a long minute, Mr. Hoffman straightened. "Your Honor, my client agrees to 'no contest' to the custody petition—provided that the financial settlement for the, uh, 'unlawful eviction' is waived."

The judge shook her head, as if she couldn't believe what she was hearing. But I motioned to Lee. "Tell the judge we accept!" I whispered. "I don't want his money. I want custody. Do it!"

"But, Gabby—"

"Just do it, Lee!"

chapter 30

Too rattled to go back to work, I went straight to my car after getting off the El at the Sheridan station, picked up Paul from Sunnyside, and took him out to McDonald's for burgers and shakes. I said, "Uh-huh" and "Really?" as Paul burbled nonstop about an annoying kid who played first-chair trumpet in the band, but I kept seeing Philip's face as we left the courtroom. For a split second, our eyes had met. He could have been gloating—Lee was angry about the deal we'd made, letting Philip get off scot-free financially—but to me, Philip seemed . . . tired. Sad.

But hanging out with Paul managed to keep me distracted until it was time to pick up P.J. and Jermaine. Paul scooted over in the backseat to make room for Jermaine and bombarded him with questions. "Hey, 'member that smokin' piece you played at my birthday party? Could you teach those chords to me? What else you been doin'?"

P.J. said nothing in the front seat, but he did look my way, questions in his eyes about the custody hearing. I tried to give him a reassuring smile. "It's all okay," I murmured. "Nothing has changed."

Philip pulled up right at six to pick up the boys, giving a quick toot of the horn outside. I was just as glad he didn't come to the door. We hadn't spoken at the hearing either. What was there to say? The judge had given me custody of our sons and Philip had pleaded "no contest" in exchange for "no consequences" for kicking me out. Who won? I did, I guess. Except . . . for some reason, I wanted to cry.

Which I did on and off all that evening, using up the last box of tissues and half a roll of toilet paper, feeling that something was terribly wrong. I'd just secured legal custody of the boys— "temporary custody," the judge reminded me, since we were just separated, not divorced—and yet here I was, alone, the rest of my family off doing something without me. Lee had tried to ask me out, wanted to take me to dinner "to celebrate," he said, but I'd turned him down. What was there to celebrate? My marriage was in the pits, my sons had to straddle two households, had to divide themselves between mom and dad, and whatever had been good about my marriage with Philip had somehow been lost in a tsunami of . . . of what? Each of us pulling our own way until the bond that held us together had stretched too far and snapped.

Jodi Baxter called to find out how it went and said, "Praise God!" when I told her the judge had granted both petitions. So why didn't I feel like praising God?

Between sniffles, I managed to sort the boys' dirty laundry and lug it down to the basement where two ancient washing machines and one beat-up dryer sat mostly unused, but I didn't feel like going out to the Laundromat. Even as I stuffed jeans and towels into the largest top-loader, Philip's complaint to the judge and Mabel's concerns she'd shared in her office seemed to drip down on me from the musty walls. *"Without consulting me"* . . . *"You didn't talk it over with your husband"* . . . *"No marriage can tolerate that kind of behind-the-back decision making for long."*

Frustrated, I poured laundry detergent on top of the clothes without bothering to measure and banged the washer lid down as it started to fill. Hadn't Mabel apologized for making me feel I was to blame for ending up in the shelter? And she'd called Philip's actions "emotional abuse."

But a quiet Voice somewhere in my spirit whispered, *That doesn't make her concerns any less true.*

I couldn't deal with this! Pawing through the boys' collection of DVDs in the living room, I stuck *Napoleon Dynamite* into the DVD player and zoned out in front of the TV . . . at least until I went downstairs to switch laundry loads, only to find suds had poured out of the washer and all over the floor, and the load had shut down somewhere in the middle of the rinse cycle.

Loud knocking in the front foyer the next morning sent me scurrying into the building hallway wondering who was making such a racket at eight in the morning. But I had to grin seeing Josh and Edesa Baxter on the other side of the glass-paneled door, loaded down with cans of primer and spackle, sandpaper, spackling tape, and paint rollers and brushes. I yanked the door open. "Sorry! The buzzer doesn't seem to work. Aren't you guys up kinda early?"

Josh dumped his armload in the hallway. "Unnh. Gracie woke up at five . . . Do I smell fresh coffee? Make you a deal. I'll look at what's wrong with the buzzer if you'll bring me a really big mug of joe—just black." He propped open the foyer door with a can of primer. "Do the other buzzers work?"

"I think so—at least for the two empty apartments." I headed for the kitchen, Edesa on my heels. "Wait until I tell him I flooded the washing machine in the basement," I murmured, pulling out two more mugs. "Maybe he won't want this job as property manager after all . . . Where's Gracie?"

"Grandma Jodi agreed to babysit so we could actually get some work done. She and Denny are taking care of DaShawn too. Gracie adores DaShawn! Hopefully she'll keep him distracted so he doesn't worry about his Grandpa Harry too much."

Harry! I'd almost forgotten about his eye surgery. I poured the coffee. "How's Mr. B doing? Did his procedure go okay?"

Edesa shrugged. "*Sí*, I think so. I don't really understand what they did. I just know he has to lie still for several more days—on his side, I think—and it's driving him *loco*." She circled her finger in the air. "Or maybe he's driving Estelle *loco*, not sure which."

I laughed. "I can just imagine . . . Wait a sec, let me take Josh his coffee."

Josh had the buzzer assembly dismantled, peering into the tangle of wires, and only grunted when I set his coffee on the floor, so I turned to go. But he called me back. "Mrs. Fairbanks? I was just thinking . . . if Precious and Tanya would like to come over today, I could get them started spackling the walls in the first-floor apartment too. I think we've got enough to do both apartments."

"Which I need to reimburse you for, by the way. I'll call Manna House and see if they can come over. But when are you going to stop calling me Mrs. Fairbanks? Edesa calls me Gabby, why not you?"

Josh actually blushed. "Ah, see, it's a little awkward for me, because you're my *mother's* friend, and she always taught me . . . well, you know, it's rude to call adults by their first name. And I'm still in college, you know. But Edesa got to know my mom in that Yada Yada Prayer Group, so Edesa has always called her Jodi . . ."

I laughed. "You are so funny, Josh Baxter. You're a married man and a daddy—I think that qualifies you as an adult, college or no college. So call me Gabby, okay?"

He shrugged, giving me a shy grin. "Okay. I'll try. And thanks for the coffee." He took his first sip gratefully. "*Some*body needs to tell the Little People that the Big People want to sleep in on weekends—especially when *this* Big People had to stay up late last night writing a paper."

I left him to tinker with the buzzer . . . but that's how I ended up driving over to Manna House and picking up Precious and Tanya, who were eager to get to work on their apartment. I tied a big bandana over my hair and joined in, at which point we all decided to work on the third-floor apartment first, and then all work together on the first-floor apartment, since Precious, Tanya, and I didn't really know what we were doing, though I remembered hating the sanding part the time Philip and I repainted our big old house back in Petersburg.

I made sandwiches for everybody at noon, and then excused myself for an hour or so after lunch to go see how Harry Bentley was doing. "By the time you get back, the spackle will be dry enough for sanding," Josh teased.

"Oh great. My favorite part," I moaned, wondering if I should change my clothes, then deciding it wasn't worth the effort to change back again.

I didn't plan to stay long visiting Mr. B—frankly, I'd never been to his apartment before and it felt a little strange to get this intimate look behind the man I'd first known as the doorman of Richmond Towers—but I was surprised to hear laughter and childish voices when Estelle opened the door. "Jodi and Denny brought Gracie and DaShawn over," she explained, but put her finger to her mouth as she led me into the small living room. "Shh, the kids are doing a 'smelling game' for Harry."

"A what?" Mr. Bentley sat on the old-fashioned couch, head bowed forward, chin on his chest. White gauze patches covered both eyes. For the first time it hit me what it must be like for him not to be able to see a thing . . . no, on second thought, I couldn't really imagine it, only knew it must be frightening.

But at the moment, the retired cop was grinning as DaShawn held a jar lid under his nose. "Guess what this one is, Grandpa!"

"Uhh . . . cinnamon?"

"Aw, that was too easy. You'll never guess this one!" DaShawn picked another lid out of a box and waved it under his grandfather's nose.

Jodi sidled up to me, a big smile on her face. "Isn't that cute? DaShawn invented this smelling game since his grandpa can't see, spent all morning at our house putting it together."

"What all does he have in those lids?" I whispered.

"Well, Harry did *not* guess Estelle's lilac perfume—he's in the doghouse over *that* one—but so far he guessed garlic and coffee grounds and bacon grease. And the cinnamon. Not sure what's left . . . oh, apple shampoo is another one. Can't remember the rest."

"Okay, kids, that's all." Estelle clapped her hands like a schoolteacher. "Mr. Harry's got another visitor, so why don't we go out to the kitchen and get a snack. Jodi girl, bring that baby with you. Harry's probably got pickled pigs' feet up in there somewhere . . . you like pickled pigs' feet, DaShawn?"

"Yuck!" the boy yelled as they disappeared out of the room.

"Don't let her pull your leg, DaShawn!" Harry hollered after them from the couch. Then, "Did she say I've got another visitor?"

"Right here, Mr. B."

"That you, Firecracker? Come here." The man reached out, feeling the air.

I pulled up a hassock next to the couch and put my hand in his. "I'm really sorry about all this eye stuff you're going through. What did they—"

"Never mind that. I gotta ask what you know about your man Philip's association with Matty Fagan."

I was taken aback. "I—I don't really know, Mr. B. Just that one time when he was on the phone, I heard him talking in the background to some guy named Fagan. That's it."

"Humph," he muttered. "It's never just 'one time' with Fagan." He suddenly swore under his breath and almost got up, then sagged back down on the couch. "Sorry, Gabby. I'm just so *frustrated* to be laid up with these stupid eye patches right now. If this Fagan is who I think he is, whatever's going down with Philip can't be good—and could be downright dangerous. The man's always got some racket going on."

"But who is he, Mr. B?"

I couldn't believe it when Mr. Bentley told me Matty Fagan used to be his boss in the elite Anti-Drug and Gang Unit of the Chicago Police Department. Harry had blown the whistle on Fagan and his cronies a year or so ago for shaking down drug dealers and gangbangers, then reselling the drugs and weapons they'd confiscated back on the street. Internal Affairs had suggested Harry quietly retire early—he already had more than twenty years on the force—until they'd built a solid case and brought an indictment against Fagan. "Which they did several weeks ago," Harry said, "but of course he posted bail and is out on bond until time for his trial. But knowing Fagan, that wouldn't stop him from finding some other marks to go after. You think your husband is using?"

"Using? You mean drugs? No!" Whatever Philip was, he wasn't a druggie. "Only vice I know about is his gambling, which I told you about, and now he's in debt up to his eyeballs. That's why he came to me, trying to borrow money to pay it off . . ."

I suddenly had an awful thought—and it must've occurred to Mr. Bentley at the same moment, because he grabbed for my wrist and said, "That's it."

"Oh, Mr. Bentley, you don't think—!"

"That's exactly what I think. Fagan's got himself a new racket, loaning easy money to people like your husband—upstanding business types who've got themselves in trouble at the gaming tables."

"But where would this Matty Fagan get that kind of money?"

Mr. Bentley snorted a mirthless laugh. "Ha. You'd be surprised how easy it is for someone like Fagan to get his hands on fifty grand, even a hundred or two hundred—mostly payoffs from the big drug dealers in exchange for his cops looking the other way. And you can be sure the 'interest' he's charging will set your man back even more."

"So why would Philip do that?"

"Quick money, no questions asked, no check into assets, all the stuff that banks do. But it's risky, because Fagan doesn't take kindly to people who cross him."

I was dumbfounded. Should I warn Philip about this Fagan guy? Did he know the man was under indictment by a grand jury for fraud and illegal sale of weapons and stuff?

My skin crawled, not wanting to think about what Philip had gotten himself into. If Mr. Bentley was right, no wonder he'd looked so stressed at the courthouse yesterday. "But if Philip pays it back . . ."

"I hope he does, Firecracker, I truly hope he does. Because Fagan isn't a patient man."

chapter 31

For some reason, I felt all shook up after I left Harry's apartment. Not that I knew for sure what was really going down with Philip and this Fagan person, or even if it was the same Matty Fagan that used to be Harry's boss at the police department, but I had a feeling Harry's gut instincts were right on the money—pun intended.

I got back to the six-flat in time to do my share of sanding—*ugh*—but it was fun working with Precious and Tanya . . . until they got into an argument about what color to paint the living room, that is.

"I once saw an apartment painted all red an' black," Tanya said, dreamily sitting on the floor in the middle of the empty room, her dark hair and skin covered with a fine coat of "Tinkerbell" dust, "an' I tol' myself, if I ever get my own place, I'm gonna paint it red an' black!"

Precious nearly fell off her step stool. "Girl, ain't no way I'm gonna live in an apartment that looks like one o' them serial killers been here." She waved her hand at the walls. "We should do somethin' classy, like silver wallpaper—ya know, the kind with fuzzy designs on it. An' paint all the trim gold . . . they got gold paint, don't they, Gabby?"

I made a strangled noise.

"Well, red an' black for the kitchen, then."

"Girl, you got red an' black for brains."

"The bathroom?"

"Hold it," I broke in. "Tell you what, since I'm the landlord—"

"Landlady," Tanya broke in.

"Landlady, then." Which sounded ridiculous, but I wasn't going to argue the point. "Since I'm the land*lady*, and since I have to pay for the paint, how about if we go with some nice muted colors in the common rooms, and you can do whatever you want for your personal bedrooms. Deal?"

Precious looked dubious. "Whatchu mean, 'muted'?"

I opened my mouth to suggest "sea-foam green" or "morning mist blue" when I glanced out the window and saw Philip's black Lexus pull up. Was it six o'clock already? "Excuse me," I said and ran outside.

P.J. climbed out of the SUV still in his green-and-gold running clothes, his sport duffel bag slung over one shoulder. I gave him a hug. "How'd it go, buddy? Did Dad just pick you up?"

"Yeah. Went okay . . . We got any orange Coke?" He took the outside steps two at a time and disappeared inside. I smiled at his back. All soft drinks were "Coke" to a Southerner. My inability to remember that back in Virginia always gave me away as an outsider. How many funny looks would it take for my boys to learn most Chicagoans called it "pop"?

Paul slid out of the backseat, squinting at the open windows on the first and third floors. "Hi, Mom! People still working? I'm gonna go see what they got done."

"Don't forget your duffel bag!" his father called through the open windows. Paul turned and grabbed a bag from the rear seat. "Not that one . . . Paul! Watch what you're doing."

Paul grabbed his own bag, slammed the car door, and ran up the walk. I started to follow, but Philip called me back. "Gabrielle? You got a minute?"

I hesitated. Wasn't sure I wanted to talk to Philip. The last time we had a "talk," I'd ended up throwing things. But I screwed up my courage and stepped to the passenger side window. "Maybe a minute. I'm in the middle of something."

Philip's eye twitched. "Just wanted to say I was, uh, out of line . . . you know, how I reacted when you turned down my request for a loan. I was just frustrated."

I hardly knew how to respond. Was Philip Fairbanks actually apologizing for saying "you owe me"? Finally I said, "Yeah, that was pretty ugly."

He looked away and the moment hung there awkwardly, like a clothesline of bras and undies flapping in the breeze. Then he cleared his throat. "Something else we need to talk about. My time with the boys. I barely saw P.J. this weekend. Had to have him at the high school at six thirty this morning, and he didn't get back until an hour ago! I didn't realize this cross-country business would be all day on Saturdays."

A flicker of irritation started at the base of my skull. My legal custody was barely twenty-four hours old, and already he wanted to change the visitation plan? But he had a point. And he'd just apologized, hadn't he? "Well . . . okay. You want to talk now?"

Philip reached for his aviator sunglasses sitting on the dash and slid them on, hiding his eyes behind the dark, curved lenses once more. "Can't right now. I'm headed somewhere. But think about it. I'll call you, maybe Monday."

I glanced into the back. Philip's overnight bag sat on the seat. My gut tightened. "Another weekend at the casino?"

His mouth got tight, but he said nothing, just put the car in gear and started to pull away from the curb.

I don't know what got into me—my talk with Harry, anxiety, fear—but I ran alongside. "Philip! Please don't go. You're in over your head and it's only going to get worse!"

But the Lexus sped up and disappeared around the far corner, leaving me standing in the middle of the street.

Philip's request to change his time with the boys nettled me all weekend. I talked to my sisters that evening and got an earful of *their* opinions. When I took the boys to SouledOut Community Church the next morning, I realized if we moved their time with their dad—say, from Saturday evening until Sunday evening instead—they wouldn't be able to go to church with me anymore. Unless Philip would bring them . . . and that was as likely as the Cubs winning the pennant, Harry Bentley would probably say.

Speaking of Harry, I didn't see him or Estelle at church again, though I did see his grandson sitting with Jodi and Denny Baxter. Which meant Harry was probably still at home with his eyes bandaged, and Estelle was still on his case like a Secret Service Mother Hen.

They should just get married. I chuckled silently. We all knew it was inevitable. The two of them just hadn't figured it out yet.

I corralled my thoughts and focused on the worship, letting the song the music group was singing wash over me. "The steadfast love of the Lord never ceases . . ."

Ah, a familiar song! Used to sing this one growing up in North Dakota. But the worship leader just said the song was based on a passage in the third chapter of Lamentations. Really? I grabbed my Bible, looked in the index, found Lamentations, and ran my finger down the verses . . .

Seeing the words in Scripture as the music group sang made the words seem fresh and new: *"The faithful love of the Lord never ends . . ."* It was true! God had slowly and steadily been putting my feet back on solid ground, in spite of my spiritual neglect for most of my marriage, in spite of my husband's love growing cold.

". . . His mercies never cease . . ."

Yes, oh yes! I had received a great deal of mercy in recent days. A new home, custody of my sons, a dream coming true in the House of Hope . . .

". . . His mercies begin afresh every morning . . ."

Which meant I could count on His mercy for all the loose ends still in my life! As the congregation sang, I found myself praying for something to work out about the boys' visits with their dad. I even prayed for Philip, that God would somehow untangle the mess he'd gotten himself into, gambling himself into debt and now getting mixed up with this Fagan person . . .

"*. . . Great is His faithfulness . . .*"

The song came to an end and the music group moved right into another. But the song and the Scripture still played in my heart. I'd come a long way back to faith since I'd stumbled over Lucy Tucker in the park and we'd both ended up sheltered at Manna House. But I couldn't take any credit for it. It was all God's faithfulness, never giving up on me.

My eyes got misty. Something in me wanted to kneel down and renew my vows to the Lord, like I'd done at camp one summer as a kid, giving my heart to Jesus. And suddenly it occurred to me there was something I could do—I could join this church, become a member, as a way of marking my return to faith, taking my stand publicly with the people of God in this place.

My heart beat faster with a childlike excitement. I'd speak to Pastor Clark or Pastor Cobbs as soon as the service was over.

"Gabby! That's wonderful!" Jodi said, when I told her I'd spoken to Pastor Cobbs about becoming a member of SouledOut Community Church. "Did he say when?"

"Two Sundays from now, the last Sunday in September. If I don't get cold feet before then. He gave me some papers to read about the church and a copy of the membership questions I'd be asked." I was already wondering if I'd been too impetuous. Church membership at SouledOut definitely meant something more than it had at Briarwood, where we stayed on the church membership roll even though Philip and I had only shown up three or four times a year. Even the name—*SouledOut*, for goodness sake!—made me feel as if I was taking holy vows.

Jodi gave me a sympathetic hug. "You won't. This is definitely the right thing to do. Everyone who follows Jesus is part of the body of Christ on Earth—but those 'body parts' are a lot more effective when they're connected with the other 'body parts'!" She laughed. "Me, I'm a toe—but the foot needs me and I need the foot. We all need each other!"

I rolled my eyes, though I couldn't help grinning at Jodi's "theology." "Well, if you're a toe, maybe I'm a toenail."

"See? That's exactly it! Just think where we'd be without toenails!"

I did think about it that afternoon as I wandered through the apartments across the hall from ours on the first and third floor while the boys did homework. A lot of wall prep had gotten done just in one day with a bunch of us working together. My heart seemed to crowd into my throat. *God, I know the House of Hope wouldn't be happening if I were trying to do this on my own. Thanks for giving me other parts of the body to—*

"Yo! You de lady who buyin' de building?"

I jumped at the unfamiliar voice, a thick Island accent. A tall thin figure, dark skin, long dreadlocks caught back in a fat ponytail, poked his head into the third-floor apartment. How stupid of me to be up here by myself with the door unlocked! I tried not to let my apprehension show, even as I moved quickly to the door and squeezed past the man into the hallway, where I could yell if need be. The door across the hall was open. Reggae music bounced within. Now that we were standing face-to-face,

I realized I'd seen the man going in and out of the building, but had never actually spoken to him before.

"Yes, I'm the new owner." The sign out front said Under Contract, even though I hadn't closed yet. "And you are . . . ?"

The man jerked a thumb at the apartment across the way. "Mi livin' dere wit me woman and me mada. Yuh still be renting dese apartments or going condo?"

I began to relax. Just a tenant wanting to know what was happening. I shook my head as I locked the door of the empty apartment. "Neither. I'm working with a shelter program . . ." It would be hard to explain. *Just cut to the chase, Gabby. You know what he wants to know.* "I'm sorry. I won't be renewing any leases. When will your lease be up?"

The man's face fell. "January." It sounded like *Jan-oo-wary*. "Dat not a good time to be wit'out a place to live."

I suddenly realized this man and his family were being put out by my plans for the House of Hope. Could I make it easier somehow?

Impulsively I said, "Tell you what. If you find a place to move sooner, you can move out without having to sublet the apartment or breaking your contract." That would work both ways, wouldn't it? It would give more options to the remaining tenants, as well as make the apartments available sooner to the House of Hope.

Or leave me with empty apartments and having a hard time paying the mortgage.

But I'd said it. And I would keep my word—to this man anyway.

The man nodded and turned to go. But I stuck out my hand. "My name is Gabby Fairbanks. You are . . ."

He shook my hand, his hand sinewy and thin. "Campbell. Maddox Campbell." Then he pointed to my hair—which was probably a frizzy mess, since it had rained as we came out of church and caught me unprepared—and for the first time a slow grin spread over his face. "Dat be a heap of curly hair—like de poodle dog."

I didn't know whether to be offended at being compared to a poodle or pleased that he was being friendly. I chose friendly. I laughed. "Yes. But did you ever see a *red* poodle?"

Now he laughed, *heh heh heh*, as he moved back into his apartment and I started down the stairs. But as soon as I got inside my apartment, I called Lee Boyer. "If the current tenants know I'm not going to renew their leases, can I allow them to leave earlier without having to sublet?"

"What are you up to now, Miss Moppet?"

I told him about my interaction with Maddox Campbell and Lee promised to do a little research. "I don't want you to get stuck with a lot of empty apartments before you're ready to fill them with your House of Hope tenants." I could just imagine him shaking his head. "You can't save the whole world, Gabby. But you *could* save a lonely guy from eating takeout again. How about dinner tonight?"

I was definitely tempted. And I'd already turned him down on Friday after the custody hearing. But . . . "I'm sorry, Lee. It sounds great. But it's a school night for the boys and I want to spend some time with them. Rain check?"

Short pause. "Is that a promise?"

I laughed. "You sound pathetic. Yes, it's a promise. Next Friday? The boys will be with their dad." I hoped. If the plan hadn't changed by then.

I'd promised the boys we could watch a movie if they got their homework done by seven, so we made popcorn, drank "orange Cokes," and watched *The Pink Panther*—the Steve Martin version—with a pile of blankets and pillows since I didn't have an actual couch yet. We laughed ourselves silly, though I winced at some of the crude humor, and ended with a pillow fight. But once they'd gotten ready for bed, I stopped in P.J.'s room to say good night. "You figure out where to catch the bus tomorrow? Better give yourself extra time. It's going to take longer."

"I'm good, Mom. It's just a straight shot down Addison." He rolled over.

I leaned over the bed and kissed the back of his head. Smooth dark hair, so like Philip's. "Good night. Love you." *Take care of him tomorrow, dear God . . .*

Next stop, Paul's room. He was propped up in the bottom bunk with a book. I sat down on the edge of the bed. "Hey, kiddo. What are you reading?" He held it up for me to see. "*Dog Stories?*" Uh-oh. I could see where this was heading.

"Yeah. Got it from the school library."

"You'd really like to have a dog, wouldn't you?"

He shrugged. "Yeah, but . . . not just any dog." He hugged the book. "Wish you hadn't given Dandy away. He was practically like my dog."

"I know, kiddo." What else could I say? We'd been through the why-I-gave-Dandy-to-Lucy scenario before. I gently took the book and turned out the reading light as Paul slid under the covers.

"I see him, you know."

"What do you mean?"

"When I go to Dad's. When I look out the penthouse window, I can see Dandy and Lucy down in the park. Sometimes she's looking up at the penthouse. Seems like it anyway."

"Really?" That was curious.

"Yeah. Why is she always in that park? I mean, it's not that close to Manna House. Doesn't she stay at the shelter too?"

"Sometimes. Usually when the weather's bad. Maybe that park is where she's used to hanging out. That's where I first met her, you know." "Met" being a rather loose term for how I'd run into her cart sticking out from under a bush, smack-dab in the rain, me crashing onto the muddy ground and ending up with a bloody foot . . .

"Yeah, I know. But when I saw her and Dandy this weekend, I went right down the elevator and ran outside to see Dandy—but I couldn't find them. It was like they just disappeared . . ." I heard a sniffle in the darkness. ". . . or didn't want me to know they were there."

chapter 32

True to his word, P.J. left the apartment fifteen minutes earlier the next morning to catch the bus that would take him to Lane Tech. He even remembered to take his lunch. *Well, good for him. He wants to make this work.* I tried not to think too much about the reason he'd rather take the bus than get a ride. His attitude would work itself out if I didn't make a big honking deal about it.

I hoped.

Mabel seemed a little put out now that she had to take Jermaine to school *and* pick him up, though she agreed that if P.J. didn't want to ride together, it was for the best.

I drove Paul to Sunnyside, reviewing the plan we'd made for him to walk Sammy and Keisha back to Manna House after school. He seemed upbeat, in spite of his "doggy mood" the night before. "What about Trina and Rufino?" he wanted to know. "I could walk them, since they have to go back to the shelter too."

"Yes, but they're still pretty little, you know." Trina was in second grade and Rufino just starting first. Their mother, Cordelia

Soto, had been at the shelter for a couple of months, but was hoping to move in with her brother in the Little Village neighborhood, home to many Mexican and other Spanish-speaking Americans—which would mean having to change schools. A lot of upheaval for little ones. "Their mom wants to walk with them for a while."

Much to my relief, frankly. It was one thing for Paul to walk back to the shelter with Sammy and Keisha, who were older. But round up and keep four kids out of the street? Two of whom were only six and seven? That was a lot of responsibility for a twelve-year-old.

I thought the shelter would be a bit quieter with the kids at school, but Angela rolled her eyes as I came in. "The day has barely started and already Sarge had to throw two women out who started a fight," she muttered, pushing the sign in/out book at me.

I signed in. "Over what?"

"Who knows? Somebody dissin' somebody over something."

"It wasn't Naomi Jackson, I hope." If Naomi was still here, it meant the young girl had managed to stay off the street—and off drugs—for five whole days so far.

"No, a couple of cats who came in over the weekend. I think I remember the one named Alisha from before."

I snorted. "Right. Bet it was Chris and Alisha. Figures." The two women had been on the bed list at least twice since my sojourn at Manna House—streetwise prostitutes who tended to show up whenever there was a crackdown on the "business" by the cops. But they always seemed to kick up dust, staying out past curfew or breaking some other shelter rule, then raising a ruckus when they got tossed out. They were usually told they had to stay away at least thirty days before trying again.

"Well, at least they won't be back for another month." I gave Angela a thumbs-up and pushed through the double doors into Shepherd's Fold, hoping there would be some fresh coffee in the carafes . . . and then stopped. Naomi Jackson was curled up in one of the overstuffed chairs in the big room, arms wrapped around her knees, head down, her shoulders shaking. Tawny was crouched by her side, saying, "Hey, hey. What's wrong, girl?" but getting no response.

I walked over and touched Tawny on the arm. "Thanks, Tawny. I'll talk to her."

At my voice, Naomi jerked her head up, her face wet, her nose running, eyes accusing. "How come you ain't been around?!"

I sat down on the arm of the overstuffed chair. "Because I don't work on the weekend, Naomi. What's wrong?"

She wiped her face on her T-shirt. "Nothin' . . . I mean, ever'thing. You don't know what it's like . . ."

That was true. I didn't. "But you're still here. That's a good thing."

"I dunno," she said dully. "Dunno if I can make it. That Sarge! See, one of my homegirls—name Alisha—was here, an' felt sorry for me, was gonna give me a joint to help calm my nerves . . . but that Sarge yelled bloody murder an' threw her out." Naomi sniffed. "She was jus' tryin' to help me."

"Oh, Naomi. You don't need that kind of help." I was sure of that, but what kind of help did she need? "Who's your case manager? Are you going to see her today?"

Naomi shrugged. "That Cooper lady—but I don't got an

appointment till tomorrow." She looked up at me hopefully. "Can I hang out with you today?"

I was taken aback. I had a couple of proposals for new activities I wanted to work on before the weekly staff meeting at ten, but . . . oh, why not. "I've got work to do, but if you want to hang out in my office, that's fine with me. You got a book to read or something?"

Naomi's weepy eyes actually got bright. "For real? Don't read much, but I like to draw sometimes . . . you got some paper an' stuff?"

"Paper and stuff" I could manage. I headed for my office with Naomi on my heels. I wished I didn't feel so ignorant about how to help someone like this girl. Now Tawny . . . that girl was going to make it, in spite of her circumstances. But Naomi?

Maybe I should ask in staff meeting what kind of training I'd need to become a case manager . . . Huh! Like I needed something else to do!

It felt good to be back into the normal swing of things now that school had started—if "normal" could be used to describe a job where the clientele included prostitutes, older teens abandoned by DCFS, women trying to kick drug addictions, even the occasional professional with a college degree . . . Where three or four different languages or dialects peppered mealtimes, and the "décor" in my broom-closet office included a couple dozen stuffed-animal dogs donated by the people of Chicago . . . Where a retired female army sergeant ruled the roost at night, and

Estelle Williams—soul-food cook extraordinaire and the love of my friend Harry's life—ruled the kitchen by day.

Yes, Estelle was back, banging pots and pans with her usual abandon. Which meant Harry must be doing better.

To top off my "normal" day, Paul showed up at the shelter with his two charges right on time after school and even asked Carolyn for some help with his Algebra. And P.J. showed up at home before supper without getting lost or mugged.

But the *coup de grâce* was the call from the bank Tuesday morning, saying my mortgage loan had been approved. I was so excited, I did a Snoopy-dance in the dining room outside my office—to the snickers of several residents who'd come downstairs to "nuke" their coffee and fulfill chore duty by washing sheets from the bunkrooms.

"Normal" took a sharp right turn on Tuesday afternoon, however, when a couple of Sunnyside parents got wind of the afterschool program Carolyn was doing at the shelter, and they showed up in Mabel's office wanting to know if the program was open to the neighborhood.

After taking their names and saying we'd have to run the possibility by the Manna House board, I heard loud "music" coming from the lower level as I headed back to my office. Following the sound to the rec room, I stuck my head in the door to see Jermaine Turner's fingers flying over his electronic keyboard and Paul drumming with two drumsticks on an upended plastic bucket to the adoring audience of Dessa and Bam-Bam, Manna House's youngest residents.

"Mom!" Paul jumped up. "Look who's here! Jermaine doesn't have anything going on after school on Tuesdays and Thursdays, so he's gonna come here. Isn't that cool?—Oh! Can you bring my keyboard to work with you Thursday? We wanna work on some music together."

Philip didn't call on Monday or Tuesday about changing the boys' schedule. But just in case, I tried to think it through as I breaded some fish to fry for supper Tuesday night. Did we even have any other options? Sunday through Thursday were school nights, and they wouldn't give Philip any more time with P.J. I was reluctant to suggest Saturday evening through Sunday evening, because then they'd miss church and the boys seemed to be enjoying SouledOut—once they got there anyway. And most of the complaining about having to get up on Sunday morning wasn't any worse than having to get up and go to school.

Holding a spatula in one hand, I stared at the kitchen wall calendar. Maybe I could offer to let the boys stay longer Saturday evening on the weekends P.J. had cross-country meets. *Which were . . . ?*

I was looking at the schedule of cross-country meets when I heard the front door slam and P.J. hollering down the hallway toward the back of the apartment. "I'm home!" A few moments later he appeared in the kitchen. "Supper ready? I'm starving! Coach worked us real hard today because we're hosting our division meet tomorrow after school. All the freshmen and varsity teams are running." P.J. grabbed a fork and speared a hunk of watermelon I'd planned to serve as a fruit salad, stuffing it into his mouth. "Can you come?" he asked with his mouth full, melon juice squirting six different ways.

I'd just noticed the midweek "Lane Tech Invitational" on the schedule. "If I can. What time?"

My oldest speared another hunk of watermelon and shrugged. "I dunno, four o'clock I think. Hey! I'm gonna call Dad, see if he can come too."

I almost told P.J. his father probably couldn't since it was a workday, not wanting the boy to be disappointed. But I bit my tongue and served up the golden-brown catfish, some plain rice, a heap of hot peas, and the rest of the watermelon while P.J. was on the phone. By the time I'd corralled Paul and got him to the kitchen table, P.J. was off the phone, a grin on his face. "Yeah, he's coming."

"Coming where?" Paul asked. "Can I come too?"

I almost forgot to pray a blessing on our supper. *Well! This ought to be interesting. The whole family . . .*

Paul and I drove around behind the high school and found a parking space on the backstreet that ran alongside the Chicago River as we'd been instructed. The street was filling rapidly with cars pulling in between an assortment of buses from other schools. An early-morning thunderstorm had given way to a cool fall day, neither hot nor cold, the air clean and fresh. An open field lay between the backstreet and the narrow river, which was hidden in a low channel and flanked by a thick wall of trees.

We followed the general drift of parents and siblings across the field, passing numerous canopies set up by each school. Lanky teenage boys and girls in all shapes and sizes and school colors swarmed everywhere. I tried to read the names of the schools on the sweatshirts and athletic tank tops as groups of runners warmed up. Loyola Academy . . . Whitney Young . . . Payton Prep . . . Latin School . . . Von Stueben . . . Lakeview . . .

"Oh my goodness," I muttered, "we'll never find him."

But somehow P.J. found us, running toward us in his silky green shorts and gold tank top. "Hey! You made it. Girls race first. My race is second." P.J. punched Paul playfully on the shoulder. "Wanna race me, squirt?"

Paul shrugged him off and peeled paper off a stick of gum.

"I didn't know there'd be so many people here! How'd you find us?"

P.J. snickered. "Your *hair*, Mom. I just told my teammates to look for Little Orphan Annie, and they pointed you out."

Figures. It was great to see P.J. in such a good mood. Had he grown a couple of inches since last night? Why did he look so tall and muscular all of a sudden? Like a high school athlete instead of a kid. He twisted his head around, his eyes darting here and there at the crowd of spectators. "Have you seen Dad?"

I shook my head. "Not yet. But if he said he'd be here, I'm sure he will."

"Well, just look for my number . . . 29! See ya!" P.J. ran off, rejoining the sea of green-and-gold doing warm-ups.

The girls from the different schools soon lined up, the gun went off, and their teammates cheered them on as the pack started around the field, angled onto the path alongside the river, and then disappeared into the wooded area at the far end. For P.J.'s sake, I was glad his race wasn't first. Maybe Philip would still get there in time.

Three times around the course, I was told. The first of the girl runners were just coming out of the woods across the finish line when I heard . . .

"There you are."

I turned at Philip's familiar voice. He was smiling. Gosh, he looked so . . . fine. A lock of dark hair fell over his forehead, complementing the casual tweed sport coat he was wearing over an open-necked white shirt, khaki Dockers, and the ever-present aviator sunglasses.

"Hey, Dad!"

"Hey yourself." He knuckled Paul's head. "Where's P.J.?"

"He's over there warming up with the Lane Tech team. Number 29." I kept my voice neutral. "He'll be glad you came."

"Yeah, well, traffic was a hitch as usual. What's the schedule?"

"His race is next. See?"

The Lane Tech boys' team was lining up with the teams from the other schools—four runners from each school—and a few moments later the starting gun cut the air. "I see P.J.!" Paul yelled. "Go 29!"

We kept them in sight for about two minutes, and then they swung through the stand of trees at the end of the field and disappeared. It would be several minutes before the first runners came around the course and off again on the second leg. But the crowd of parents and fans faded from my awareness, and I was acutely conscious of Philip's presence, his familiar height and maleness, even that slight whiff of the Armani shaving lotion he liked. The one I'd given him for his last birthday.

"Uh . . ." I needed to fill the silence. "You wanted to talk about changing the boys' schedule?"

He didn't reply, but patted his back pocket, then pulled out his wallet and removed a five. "Paul! Go get us some Cokes, will you? Anything."

"Cool!" Paul took the money and ran off to look for a vendor.

Philip took off his sunglasses and slipped them into his coat pocket. "Guess I was thinking about the same schedule, just twenty-four hours later. Saturday evening until Sunday evening. Except . . ."

I was all set to give my objections about church, but caught myself. "Except what?"

"I . . . well, I go out of town sometimes, might be hard to get back right at six on Saturday night."

"Oh, sure. If you're having a good run at the card tables, why in the world would you want to come home in time to be with your sons?" I turned my head away.

I expected a comeback to my sarcasm, but he said nothing for a moment or two, and when he did, he actually sounded regretful. "I know what you're thinking, but it's . . . it's not like that, Gabby."

I turned back, feeling sparks behind my eyes. "Then what *is* it like, Philip?"

The crowd around us started yelling. The string of runners came out of the woods, around the field, and disappeared again. We cheered and waved at P.J., but he was concentrating on his run.

As P.J. disappeared from sight once more, Philip shoved his hands in his pants pockets and hunched his shoulders. "I told you. I'm in a jam. Trying to work my way out of it. But I was able to get a loan . . . I just need time."

The sparks sizzled and died. I stood there, looking at the man who'd been my husband for almost sixteen years. And suddenly I felt afraid—not for me, but for him. A jumble of scenarios rushed to the front of my brain. The night he was late picking up the boys . . . the phone call where he'd called out Fagan's name . . . Estelle's alarm when she heard it . . . the things Harry Bentley had said about Matty Fagan . . .

Impulsively I put my hand on Philip's arm. "This man you borrowed money from . . ." I knew I was jumping off a cliff here. This was the first time he'd mentioned that he'd gotten a loan, and how would I know it was a person and not a bank or credit union? But I plunged on. "Is his name Matty Fagan?"

Philip looked at me sharply. *Bull's-eye.* He stiffened and pulled his arm away from my hand. "It's really none of your business, Gabrielle."

"Philip! Listen to me." I was pleading now. "I don't know how you know him, or how much he loaned you, but Matty Fagan is a rogue cop who's been indicted by Internal Affairs for misconduct, fraud, shaking down pimps and drug dealers, selling drugs and weapons back on the street—you name it!"

Philip frowned. "How do you know anything about Matty Fagan? Who's been telling you a lot of scary stuff? He came recommended."

"He used to be part of the same police task force with Harry Bentley! Didn't you know Harry is a retired cop? You can find out yourself by calling the Chicago Police Department. But he's dangerous, Philip. If you can't pay him back . . . I don't know, but I've heard stories. I'm afraid for you. Please—"

"Here are the Cokes!" Paul pushed in between us, juggling

three cans of pop. "All the guy had was root beer and cream soda. Hope that's okay—hey, look! Some of the first runners are coming in! Do you see P.J.? Look for number 29!"

chapter 33

We never did decide on a workable change in the visitation schedule. Philip got tight-lipped and left soon after congratulating P.J. on a good run, even though the team from Whitney Young won the boys' race. Paul and I hung around for two more races until P.J.'s coach released the Lane Tech teams, but the unfinished conversation about Matty Fagan weighed heavily on my spirit all the way home.

Josh and Edesa were at the six-flat when we got back from the meet, trying to finish up the sanding and wall prep on the first-floor apartment, while Gracie toddled around banging a wooden stir stick on buckets, ladders, and windowsills to test their percussive qualities.

"Let me take her." I laughed, picking up the hefty toddler, who immediately went for my hair. "Ouch! Let go, Gracie . . . Anyway, she can eat supper with us. How about you guys?"

"Oh, Sister Gabby!" Edesa sighed gratefully, looking cute as a bug with her corkscrew curls tied up in a bandana. "That would be *bueno* . . . but do not worry about us. We can eat something later."

"It's not a worry. Look at all the work you're doing! Will we be ready to paint on Saturday? We need a trip to Home Depot."

"*Sí!* We could go Friday night. We already picked up some color strips."

"Sounds good! . . . Oh, wait." I'd promised Lee I'd go out with him Friday. "Uh, no, can't do it Friday. How about tomorrow night?"

By now Gracie was squealing to be put down, so I whisked her across the hall to our apartment and let her bang on some pots and pans while I fried ground beef and chopped lettuce, onions, and tomatoes for a quick taco meal. "Mom!" Paul groused from the dining room table, where he was reluctantly tackling his algebra. "Does Gracie have to bang on those pans?"

I poked my head around the door. "Hey, if you add Gracie's drumming to your jazz duo, you'd practically have a band."

Paul made a face. "Not funny. Just don't forget my keyboard tomorrow."

I called Josh and Edesa to join us when I had the taco makings on the makeshift dining room table—I really needed to go furniture shopping!—and it was fun having spur-of-the-moment guests. As the boys teased Gracie, who was trying to mimic everything they did, I suddenly realized that living in the same building would make sharing meals like this easy to do.

For a moment the loneliness I lived with every day evaporated just a little.

"Are you okay, *mi amiga*?" Edesa asked, helping me clear the table afterward.

I nodded, but realized it wasn't true. After making sure the boys were out of earshot, I spilled my worry about Philip. "At first I was just upset about his gambling. But I think he's gotten desperate about this debt hanging over his head. Not sure why he can't just get a bank loan and pay it back the regular way, but I think he's trying to take a shortcut, some shady loan shark. I tried to warn him, but—"

"Oh, Gabby." Edesa pulled me into a chair and held my hands across the small kitchen table. "We need to pray for him. You did a good thing to try to warn Philip, but now you must leave him in God's hands." Squeezing her eyes shut, the young black woman began praying in Spanish, and then translating for my sake.

Leave him in God's hands . . . Put Philip in God's hands . . .

It felt strange to pray for Philip that way. But it felt good too. It was hard to be angry with someone I was praying for.

Lee called the next day to ask what time he should pick me up on Friday night and to tell me we finally had a closing date. "That's two weeks from today!" I squealed. "Maybe by then we'll have the apartments painted and our first House of Hope residents can move in that weekend!" I grabbed the calendar and wrote "Moving Day!" on the last Saturday in September.

Lee was quiet a moment. "I sure hope you know what you're doing, Gabby. I just don't want you getting in over your head or getting hurt."

I closed my eyes, imagining the look in his gray eyes. Gentle, concerned. "I know. I appreciate that, Lee. It's just . . . sometimes you have to take risks to do something important. This is something I really want to do."

"Yeah, well, that's my Gabby. Just don't get so focused on saving the world that you don't save some time for me."

When we hung up I felt all a-jumble. Did he really say *"my Gabby"*? Those words made me feel warm and delicious, like eating sweet cinnamon rolls right out of the oven. At the same time I felt annoyed. Did he want me to drop everything that was meaningful to me just to spend time with him?

That had an echo of Philip to it.

Or maybe I was being oversensitive.

I shook off my annoyance and decided to work on a letter to the remaining tenants, explaining that I was the new owner, that I would not be renewing any leases, and if anyone wanted to move before their lease was up, to talk to me and we would work something out. That was being reasonable, wasn't it?

I remembered to bring Paul's keyboard to work with me on Thursday, and he and Jermaine had a "jam session" after school. I wasn't a huge jazz fan, but I had to admit they were pretty good for a couple of kids. A few of the residents complained about the noise and Carolyn had a hard time keeping Sammy and Keisha focused on their work in the schoolroom, so I had to insist that the boys close the door to the rec room and turn down the volume.

"Maybe we need to add music appreciation to the afterschool program," Carolyn said wryly, as she dragged the kids back upstairs—but I could tell she was more amused than upset.

I had borrowed the sample color strips from Josh and Edesa, and before leaving Manna House on Thursday I sat down with Precious and Tanya to choose paint for the first-floor apartment. Tanya was mesmerized by the shades of greens and blues, yellows and reds, turquoise and melon colors, leaning toward the brightest colors at the ends of the strips. "Uh, remember, Tanya," I cautioned, "a little color goes a long way on a wall."

The young mother finally chose "Strawberry Red" for one wall of her bedroom with a pale tint version of the same color for the other walls, and agreed to white for the window trim after I suggested she could paint her bedroom furniture black if she wanted. Precious chose a "Goldenrod" yellow for her bedroom with something called "Green Tea" for trim. I insisted on ivory for the long windowless hallway to lighten it up, but agreed on a couple of blue shades for the bathroom, an orangey "Melon" for the kitchen, and some pretty greens and ivory for the living and dining rooms.

But I felt wrung out at the end of our paint-color session. Was I going to have to go through this with the rest of the apartments and their new residents?

At the hardware store that evening, I left Josh and Edesa to pick out their own colors for the third-floor apartment, while I piled my cart full of the paint for the first floor. I saw Josh and Edesa arguing at one point and realized their different cultural backgrounds—not to mention the whole male-female thing—were probably clashing no less than me with Precious and Tanya. Chuckling, I pushed my overloaded cart to the paint mixing area. For some reason it made me feel better.

Until the clerk rang up both carts full of paint, that is. I had no idea it would cost so much! *Oh, Lord, help!* I silently sent up a heavenly SOS as I handed over my credit card. *Maybe this is dumb to paint before closing on the six-flat—but I'm stepping out in faith here, believing this House of Hope has Your blessing. You know Josh and Edesa are hoping to move sooner rather than later, and the same with Precious and Tanya. But*—I gulped as the clerk handed me the twenty-inch long register tape—*I know I have a bad habit of running ahead of You, Lord . . .*

We stuffed the paint cans, thinner, brushes, rollers, and metal paint trays into the Subaru, leaving hardly any room for Edesa to squeeze into the backseat while Josh and I climbed into the front. Then we reversed the process when we got to the six-flat, unloading it all into the first-floor apartment. But I picked up my prayer again when I finally collapsed into bed.

. . . So if I'm wrong here, God, I'm asking for a little mercy. Please, just get us through the closing without any major pitfalls!

I finally got to attend one of Edesa's *Bad Girls of the Bible* studies Friday morning. About seven residents, including some of the younger ones like Aida, Tawny, and Naomi, had pulled chairs into a circle in Shepherd's Fold and were listening as Edesa read verses from the Bible about Michal, the daughter of King Saul and wife of the future King David, when I slipped into a chair off to the side. I'd always heard David the shepherd boy, the giant-killer, the psalmist, and second king of Israel taught in glowing terms. But, Edesa said, the author of this study—Liz Curtis Higgs—had a different take when it came to Michal. She was crazy in love with the popular young man, but to David, she was mostly a political move, a way to make Daddy Saul happy.

I listened as Edesa summarized the story that was only vaguely familiar—the story of Michal wasn't exactly Sunday school material—how she helped David escape when her daddy was trying to kill him . . . how King Daddy had declared her marriage null and void and given her to another guy . . . how years later David, now the king, had demanded her back . . . and finally, how she'd watched him worshiping God and dancing with joy as he brought the Ark of God back to Jerusalem—and despised him for acting like a fool.

"So that makes her a 'bad girl'?" Tawny spluttered. "Who can blame her? He treated her pretty bad."

Ditto that, I thought. Pretty Boy David reminded me a lot of a certain man in my life who looked like a good catch at first, but wasn't exactly Mr. Charming at home. Not lately, anyhow.

The conversation got pretty hot, but Edesa was able to make a few points from the story. "*Sí*, we agree, *mi amigas*, Michal had good reason to feel abandoned and hurt—but she had let the *hombres* in her life define her, rather than leaning on God to lift her above her circumstances. And she had developed a critical spirit, which not only caused her to ridicule David but to reject the God he was worshiping."

Humph. The analogy to Philip broke down at this point, because the proper Philip Fairbanks was definitely *not* a worshiper, dancing or otherwise. But I squirmed a little at Edesa's comment that Michal had let the men in her life define her. The failure of my teenage marriage to Damien Spencer—my "Romeo" church youth group leader—had sent me running away from God. Then marriage to suave and sophisticated Philip Fairbanks had made me decide God was irrelevant to our good life.

Only when the bottom fell out of my life did I realize God wanted to put His arms around me and pick me up . . . .

For some reason I started to weep—silently, hoping the women sitting in the circle wouldn't notice. But a few moments later I felt a pair of slender arms slide around me from behind. "Oh, Miss Gabby! What's wrong? *You* can't cry. You gotta be strong so I don't cry . . ."

I wept all the harder. I knew that voice.

Naomi Jackson.

chapter 34

After Philip picked up the boys Friday evening, I felt a little guilty skipping out with Lee, leaving the young married Baxters still doing the final prep on the walls for the "paint party" the next day. But I was so glad to be whisked away in Lee's Prius—away from homeless girls like Naomi Jackson, barely out of their teens and already wasted by drugs . . . away from reminders of my own current marriage mess . . . away from a three-story building that would soon be *my* financial responsibility . . .

"You okay, Gabby?" Lee glanced over at me as he drove down Lake Shore Drive into the city. "You're kind of quiet."

"Mm, I'm fine." I leaned my head back on the seat rest, closed my eyes, and let the wind from the open windows whip my auburn curls into a welcome frenzy. "Just blowing the cobwebs out."

I heard him chuckle. "Know what you mean. I had several clients this week that made me seriously consider burning my law license."

We rode down the Drive in comfortable silence except for the country-western music sniveling from the radio speakers. The September evening was perfect, the air balmy, the sky overhead mottled with clouds outlined in brilliant pinks and oranges from the setting sun somewhere beyond the city, the choppy lake to our left dotted with sailboats making the most of the offshore breeze. I wished we could just keep driving . . .

But when Lee finally turned off the Drive and pulled into an underground parking garage, I stuck my fingers into my hair trying to detangle my wind-whipped curls. "Ouch," I groaned, jerking at another snarl. "Now I'm paying for my wild life."

"Don't worry." Lee grinned, coming around to open my car door and help me out. "No one but you knows about those snarls. It still looks the same."

"Oh, thanks. With friends like you, who needs a mother?"

He laughed. "Hey, I like the tousled look."

I hustled to keep up with Lee, even though he had me by the hand as we climbed the stairs out of the subterranean garage. He'd told me to dress "nice but comfy" so I'd worn a flowered peasant skirt, tank top and light sweater, and flat sling-backs. "Where are we going anyway?"

"Ah. Wait and see."

We ended topside at Chicago's new Millennium Park, eating at the Park Grill, which was a lot fancier than the name implied. We started with a yummy garlic and tomato hummus, dipping baby artichoke leaves, grape tomatoes, and pita bread, followed by a chilled melon gazpacho soup to die for. I wasn't sure I had room for the main course, but ordered the rich, cheesy fettuccine while Lee had the cedar-planked lake trout.

"No, no, absolutely don't have room for dessert," I protested an hour later, so Lee paid the bill and we wandered outside to look at the Cloud Gate sculpture—otherwise known as "The Bean" because of its shape—created by its artist to reflect the sky and lights of the city. Daylight had disappeared, but the city skyline was brilliant, creating its own stunning architectural design against the night sky.

Funny thing, it suddenly made me wonder what the Celestial City in heaven might look like. I'd never tried to imagine it before, but it had to be at least as beautiful as this night . . . only more so! A million lights sparkling like diamonds? The streets full of people singing and dancing? An atmosphere of excitement and joy and expectancy because King Jesus was in town?

I almost blurted out my thoughts. Almost. Would Lee think I was weird to say I was starting to sense God everywhere? He never mentioned God or anything spiritual. So I just breathed, "It's beautiful," as we walked hand-in-hand along the promenade.

"So are you," Lee murmured, slipping an arm around my waist and pulling me closer.

I let my head rest on his shoulder as we walked, but when we came to the Crown Fountain with its two rectangular towers projecting the faces of people who spouted water out of their mouths into a shallow pool, I couldn't resist slipping off my shoes and wading into the pool. "Come on in, silly!"

"Who, me silly? Only when I'm with you." Lee tugged off his boots and socks and rolled up his pant legs, and we splashed in the pool, along with twenty or so others waiting for the spouting mouths—at which time half of the waders ran under the streams of water, laughing as they got soaking wet. Lee pulled me over to the stone benches, murmuring, "We're too old and smart to get a soaking at ten at night, right? Here, use my sock to dry your feet"—which made me laugh so hard I nearly fell off the bench back into the wading pool.

The Prius pulled up in front of the six-flat about eleven. "Guess Josh and Edesa aren't pulling an all-nighter," I murmured, glancing at the dark windows of both the first- and third-floor apartments. "They've done a lot of work, though. We're planning to paint tomorrow." *What now? Should I get out? Let him walk me to the door?*

Dating was awkward after you'd been married for fifteen years.

Lee came around to my side of the car, opened the door, and we walked up the sidewalk together. "It's still early," he said as I fumbled in my shoulder bag for the house key. "You got any coffee? Beer? A nice red wine? Dry socks?"

"Just coffee and dry socks." I grinned, pulling out my keys. He wasn't being very subtle. I was tempted to extend our pleasant evening . . . what would a cup of coffee hurt?

But I knew good and well coffee wasn't what Lee had in mind. He'd been attentive and affectionate all evening—holding hands, walking with his arm around me, kissing me in the middle of the wading pool. Taking our relationship to the next level . . . which was what, exactly?

Impulsively I rose on my tiptoes and brushed his cheek with my lips. "Good night, Lee."

"Gabby, wait." He grabbed my arm as I pushed open the foyer door. "I'd like to come in. The boys are gone tonight, right? What's the problem?"

I turned my head away, blinking to hold back sudden tears. Yes, the boys were gone. Friday nights always yawned empty. Why not fill the house and my bed with someone who loved me? It wasn't like I was still married—well, technically, yes, but not really. Not "two shall be one" married . . .

That was the problem. Lee and I weren't "two shall be one" married either.

"I'm sorry, Lee. I . . . can't. Please . . ." I pulled my arm away and let the foyer door wheeze shut between us, leaving him on the steps outside. My hands were shaking so badly, I could hardly fit my key into the inner door. By the time I finally got inside my apartment, tears were sliding down my face.

I didn't sleep well, waking up early with the top sheet knotted around me as if I'd been wrestling it all night. *Ugh.* I'd forgotten to brush my teeth before falling into bed and could taste my bad breath. Swishing my mouth with mouthwash, I stared in the bathroom mirror at the bags under my eyes. *So where did it get you, Gabby, being a self-righteous prude?* Another lonely night in the single bed I'd brought from my parents' home in North Dakota, that's what.

But as I put on the coffee, I noticed the index card I'd taped to the cupboard with the verse from Proverbs I'd been memorizing, paraphrased to make it personal. "I will trust in the Lord with all my heart," I murmured, reading the card, "and will not lean on my own understanding. In everything I do and say, I will acknowledge that I'm following God, and He will show me which path to take."

I sighed, poured the first cup of coffee that dripped into the pot, and took it to the window seat in the little sunroom at the front of the apartment. Sunlight filtered through the leaves of the trees along the parkway, birds flitted here and there chirping a welcome to the day . . . and gradually the pity party I'd been having all night began to dissipate like the dew on the patch of grass outside.

"Okay, God," I sighed, "maybe I didn't exactly acknowledge You last night, but You did show me the right path. It's just . . . hard, You know? I really like Lee, and I get so lonely sometimes. I need You to walk with me and show me the way, because it's not always easy to recognize the right path."

Hide My Word in your heart, Gabby. Then you'll know the way. The words seemed so clear, I felt startled, and for a nanosecond wondered if someone else was in the room. But then I realized it was the same quiet Voice that had whispered in my spirit, *Come to Me.*

Hide My Word . . . well, I had to read it first. Fortified with my Bible and two more cups of coffee and cream, I was still curled up on the window seat in my silk lounging pants and chemise when the Baxter minivan pulled up in front of the six-flat and the whole Baxter tribe piled out, along with Estelle and her housemate, Stu. "Good morning!" I yelled out the open window. "Looks like a painting party! Give me five minutes and I'll join you!"

By the time I pulled on some old sweats and a paint-spattered T-shirt and joined the crew, more help had arrived, bringing additional brushes, rollers, and paint pans. I recognized several of the "sisters" from Jodi's Yada Yada Prayer Group . . . the spiky-haired girl they called Yo-Yo, the couple Josh and Edesa were currently renting their tiny studio from—Florida and Carl Hickman—and the single mom who'd won all that money in the Illinois Lottery. Candy or Chancy or Chanda, something like that.

Josh took off in his folks' minivan. "Where's he going?" I asked Jodi, staggering up the stairs with a couple of buckets of paint in each hand.

"Going to pick up some of the youth group from SouledOut who said they'd be willing to help out."

Shoot. I wished P.J. and Paul were here, but even if they weren't with their dad, P.J. had another meet out west some-where—Peoria? As soon as we got the paint distributed to the right rooms, I was going to go pick up Tanya and Precious from Manna House. I was sure they didn't want to miss *this* party.

Most of the painting crew left by suppertime, but Josh and Edesa and the senior Baxters were back Sunday afternoon after church, in spite of some threatening thunderstorms. "We can only stay a couple of hours," Jodi said, "because SouledOut is doing the Sunday Evening Praise at Manna House this evening— every third Sunday, you know."

I nodded. But to tell the truth, I hadn't been back to Sunday Evening Praise since I'd moved out of the shelter and gotten my sons back. Getting them to church on Sunday morning was a major accomplishment as it was.

Josh sweet-talked P.J. and Paul into helping him paint the long hallway in 1A, and a few curious questions got P.J. chatting almost nonstop about the cross-country meet in Peoria the day before. I grabbed a roller and worked with them, too, just to be with the boys and eavesdrop on their conversation.

"So what do you do at a meet on a day like today—you know, rain and thunderstorms?" Josh asked.

P.J. dipped his roller in the pan of ivory paint and rolled every which way. "If it's just rain, we run anyway. But I think they call it off if it's a lightning storm. Which would have been a bummer yesterday, since it took three hours to get there!"

With four of us painting the hallway, we got it done in record time and the boys moseyed back to our apartment while Josh and I cleaned brushes in the bathtub of the empty apartment. Suddenly he stopped, listened, and turned off the spigot. "What's that?"

I chuckled. "Just Paul playing around on his keyboard."

I started to turn on the gushing water once more, but Josh held up his hand. "Wait." He listened some more and then grinned. "He's good."

"Yeah. I guess. He and Jermaine started practicing after school at Manna House."

"Really?" Josh got a funny look on his face.

As soon as we finished cleaning the rollers, brushes, and paint pans, he made a beeline for our apartment and I followed. "Hey, Paul, you're pretty good," Josh said. "You want a gig, like tonight?"

Paul just stared at him, confused.

Josh laughed. "SouledOut is doing Sunday Evening Praise at Manna House tonight and our keyboardist got sick. You want the job?"

Paul shook his head. "Aw, I don't know church music. I just fool around."

"Do you play by ear? I mean, pick up tunes you hear?"

"Well, sure. I do that all the time."

"Well, you're my man, then! We have a guitarist who can play the chords, and singers who carry the tune. You can just pick it up."

Paul was staring at Josh wide-eyed. "Uh, could I call Jermaine Turner? I mean, he's real good. Maybe between the two of us . . ."

"Sure." Josh grinned at me. "Can you get Paul there by quarter to six?"

I'd been listening to this conversation trying to keep my jaw from dropping. But it looked like we'd be going to church again tonight.

chapter 35

I couldn't believe Paul and Jermaine. With each new song sung by SouledOut's praise team, the young teens developed more confidence, catching the right key and playing along with the melody at least half the time. The residents loved it, clapping to the music and giving shouts of encouragement! Most of them knew the boys or had seen them around Manna House often enough.

A heavy thunderstorm let loose right in the middle of the service, drowning out the music. But I did hear the front door buzzer and ran to let in whoever it was before they got caught in the deluge—and nearly got bowled over by a wet, yellow furball jumping all over me, whining and licking my face, followed by Lucy Tucker pulling her dripping wire cart into the foyer.

"*Oof!* Get down, Dandy! Hey there, Lucy," I gasped, trying to keep my voice hushed in the foyer. "Ohh, you're all muddy, Dandy. Get down!"

"Whaddya 'spect when it's rainin' buckets out there?" Lucy dug around in her wire cart. "Got a towel in here someplace . . ."

She rummaged in a black trash bag and pulled out a large towel that had definitely seen better days. "Here, why don'tcha dry him off while I get somethin' dry on."

"Lucy, wait! They're doing Sunday Evening Pra—"

Too late. She'd already pushed through the double doors pulling the cart behind her. A male voice was speaking—maybe one of the praise team, giving a testimony or something—but I still heard Lucy mumbling and her cart squeaking as they crossed the big room. I wasn't surprised when Paul came dashing through the double doors into the foyer to see Dandy—and the jumping and whining and licking started all over again.

"Paul! Shhh. Here . . ." I handed him the ragged towel. "Dry him off, okay?"

Somehow we got Dandy dried off and most of the wet mud on the tile floor mopped up. As the three of us slipped back into Shepherd's Fold, Dandy seemed content to just lie on Paul's feet at the back of the room as the testimonies and short teaching followed. When the praise team got up to do one last song, Jermaine beckoned wildly for Paul to come back and join him at the keyboards.

When Sunday Evening Praise was over, the shelter residents and guests from SouledOut gathered around the coffee cart helping themselves to store-bought cookies and lemonade. Denny Baxter and one of the SouledOut couples—Carl and Florida Hickman, who'd been at the six-flat yesterday helping to paint—were pushing chairs and couches back into place when Lucy came back in, dressed in a different layering of ill-fitting clothing, but at least these were dry. Coming to a halt in the middle of the room, the gray-haired bag lady squinted her eyes and swiveled her head as if looking for something. "Where is it?" she demanded.

"Where's what?" Precious helped herself to another Oreo cookie and popped it into her mouth.

"Martha's plaque! A big mural on the wall! The name in lights . . . *somethin'*!" Lucy planted her fists on her hips. "This room got a new name, ain't it? But I don't see *nothin'* yet sayin' ya named it after Martha Shepherd."

"Oh, Lucy," I broke in. "It's only been a few weeks since we chose the name. We haven't had time—"

"Somebody say somethin' about needin' a mural on the wall?" Florida, Jodi's Yada Yada friend, poked her head into the group. The African-American woman was maybe ten years older than Precious, who was thirty, but she had the same in-your-face way of talking, as well as a scar running down the side of her face. The woman had been around.

"Well, Lucy was just wanting something in this room to let people know why we named it Shepherd's Fold," I said.

"Which was . . . ?" Florida pressed, simultaneously calling out, "Hey, Jodi, any more of that lemonade left?"

So I found myself explaining why Manna House had renamed the multipurpose room after my mother, as Precious and Lucy and several of the other residents chimed in bits and pieces of the story.

"Hm. Plaque would be nice with the lady's name an' all, but . . ." Florida Hickman surveyed the room, much as Lucy had done. "That wall there." She waved a hand at the wall opposite the double doors leading into the foyer. "As people come in, it'd be real nice to have a mural of the Good Shepherd, don'tcha think?"

"Uh-huh" . . . "That's it" . . . "You talkin' now, girl," murmured several of the residents.

Florida turned to Jodi and smirked. "You thinkin' what I'm thinkin'?"

"That's the trouble 'round here," Lucy grumbled, jerking her cart out of the circle that had formed around her. "People do too much thinkin' an' not enough doin' . . . Where's Dandy?" She stalked over to where Paul was brushing the dog's matted coat with a plastic brush from the Lost and Found. "Hey, now, that looks real good."

I followed, realizing leaving Dandy behind when we went home wasn't going to be easy for Paul. It never was.

He looked up at Lucy, his eyes challenging. "I saw you, you know."

"Did ya now!" Lucy said.

"Yeah. Saw you last week, saw you again yesterday in the park outside Richmond Towers where my dad lives. Like you're spying on us or something."

"Paul!" I gasped.

Lucy held up a hand before I could say anything else. "You got a real smart kid there, Miss Gabby. Real smart . . . C'mon, Dandy. Time fer us ta be goin'."

To my surprise, Dandy obediently got up, gave Paul a lick on the face, and followed Lucy out into the front foyer. When we left the shelter five minutes later, the rain had stopped and Lucy and Dandy were nowhere to be seen.

Paul was triumphant. "Did you hear that, Mom? Lucy didn't deny it! She even called me a smart boy, maybe 'cause I figured it out."

"Nonsense." I assured Paul that Lucy wasn't "spying" on them. Why would she? It was actually a rude thing to say, did he think of that? She probably thought his accusation was so far-fetched it wasn't worth responding to . . . but Paul had his mind made up, so I finally dropped it.

Boys!

That third week of September started to feel like fall, as the temperature dipped into the forties at night and the rain continued off and on for a couple of days. Both boys were settling into their school and homework routines—not to mention Paul and Jermaine seemed determined to practice music on Tuesday and Thursday afternoons in the shelter's rec room. It tickled me to hear snatches of the praise songs from Sunday night in their growing repertoire.

The bed list at Manna House also began to fill up because of the change in weather, meaning a new crop of residents to introduce to the various activities we were already offering—and now that fall was here, definitely time to initiate some new ones. I told the staff I wanted to schedule another brainstorming session to hear needs and ideas from the residents, and started making calls to get some field trips on the calendar. The Shedd Aquarium . . . Adler Planetarium . . . Field Museum of Natural History . . .

"Don't forget all those requests to open up the afterschool program to the neighborhood kids," Carolyn reminded me.

Expand Afterschool Program, I wrote on my to-do list. This

Saturday was the monthly Manna House board meeting. I'd try to get it on their agenda. And good grief! Had they gotten the go-ahead yet from the city for HUD's Supportive Housing partnership between Manna House and "Gabby the Landlady" to create this fledgling House of Hope? My closing was next week and people wanted to move in!

Definitely needed to meet with the board this weekend.

Estelle was back on deck for all her activities this week, including her knitting club during the nurse's visit on Wednesday morning. "Harry doing okay?" I asked, bringing her a fresh cup of sweetened coffee while she juggled the task of picking up somebody's dropped stitches while handling the clipboard with sign-ups of residents waiting to see Delores Enriquez behind the portable partition. "And how's your son?"

"Both of 'em comin' along, comin' along—if they'd both just do what they're supposed to do. *Humph.* What I got are *two* immature boys trying to be tough guys . . . Here ya go, honey." She handed a wad of knitting back to one of the new residents, and then picked up her own crocheting from the bulging yarn bag.

"What are you making?"

"Another hat for Lucy. I figure the first one is *definitely* gone and buried." She grinned at me and I grinned back. Lucy had tucked her original Estelle-creation into my mother's casket as a final farewell gift to her friend.

"So what's this?" I picked up a finished crocheted hat sticking out of her bag made of multicolored yarn with a cute wavy brim and crocheted flower on the side.

"Made that for Jodi Baxter. Her birthday was yesterday, but Yada Yada isn't goin' to celebrate it till we meet next Sunday—Oh, hey there, Delores. You ready for the next sign-up?" Estelle looked at the clipboard. "Sunny Davis! You're up!"

I moved back toward my office to let Estelle do her job. Jodi's birthday was *yesterday*? How did I not know that? Some friend I was.

I called Jodi that night. "Happy belated birthday, you sneaky thing you. Why didn't you tell me it was your birthday?"

She groaned in my ear. "When you're closer to fifty than to forty, you're not exactly announcing it to the world. Can't believe I'm forty-seven. Sheesh."

"That's not so old. I'm going to be forty next month . . . oh, you're right. That does sound really old! Still, look at it this way— you've earned a celebration!"

"Well, Josh and Edesa and Gracie came over last night with Chinese takeout and Denny picked up a pie at Baker's Square. At least I didn't have to cook."

"Sounds like nobody cooked."

She laughed. "Hey, been meaning to ask, what's going on with Philip? Last I heard you were pretty worried he was mixed up with a loan shark or something."

"Don't know. Haven't heard from him since we talked a week ago at P.J.'s cross-country meet. Maybe I overreacted. It's probably okay. He hasn't said anything more about changing the visitation schedule either, so I'm presuming he's dropped it."

"Okay. But don't stop praying for him, Gabby. God knows what's happening, even if we don't."

I sighed. "Yeah. Thanks. Guess I need that reminder. Doesn't come natural to me to pray *for* Philip . . . but you're right. God knows."

"Oh. Meant to tell you I have to cancel my typing class at the shelter this Saturday. I've got a parent open house at school I've got to get ready for. But I'll see you on Sunday—you *are* still becoming a member at SouledOut this Sunday, right?"

"Yes—if I don't chicken out. Every time I think about getting up in front of everybody, I get jelly knees. Hey . . . will you stand up with me?"

Jodi laughed. "You're not getting married!"

"Feels like it. Please?"

"Sure. Of course I will. See you then!"

Josh Baxter showed up at the six-flat Thursday evening to do some trim work and said they were cooking up another painting party on Saturday to finish up the two apartments. "But I was wondering . . . is Paul home? I want to ask him something."

"Sure. Come on in. The boys are doing homework in the dining room. Paul! Josh Baxter wants to talk to you!"

"Thanks. This won't take long."

I hovered in the kitchen, making a snack while Josh grabbed a chair and straddled it backward, chatting with P.J. and Paul for a few minutes. Then I heard . . . "You guys coming to the Youth Jam this Saturday night at SouledOut?"

"Yeah, guess so," P.J. said. "Mom? Okay with you?"

I stuck my head around the door. "Sure. They announced it last Sunday, right? Kind of an outreach party to neighborhood kids?"

Josh nodded. "Yep. And I've got a favor to ask, Paul. You and

Jermaine did a great job last Sunday at the Sunday Evening Praise at Manna House. So I wondered if you wanted to play for the Youth Jam."

Paul seemed speechless. P.J. snorted. "You've *got* to be kidding. The electronic twins here? Oh brother."

Josh grinned. "I'm not kidding. We want as many kids involved as possible running the show. Whaddya think, Paul?"

"Well . . . sure," Paul sputtered. "But only if Jermaine can do it too. He and his Aunt Mabel don't come to SouledOut, you know."

"Doesn't matter. Lots of kids will be there whose folks don't attend SouledOut." Josh unstraddled the chair with his long legs. "Okay! I'll call Jermaine and let you know if it's a go. Bye, Mrs. Fairbanks . . . um, Gabby. See you guys Saturday night."

P.J. rolled his eyes. "I forgot. I think I'm busy Saturday."

The phone rang as I started after Josh to let him out. "Get that, would you, P.J.?" At the front door I said, "Ignore P.J. He's got a burr under his saddle."

Josh just grinned. "No problem. Maybe I'll keep him busy on the soundboard. He's a smart kid—he'll pick it up real fast."

When I got back to the dining room, both boys looked glum. "What's the matter? Who was on the phone?"

"Dad." P.J. shrugged, playing with his pen. "Says he can't pick us up this weekend, something 'important' came up."

"What?" I couldn't believe it. "He's been wanting to spend more time with you, and you don't have a cross-country meet this weekend!"

"Yeah." P.J. flipped a pen across the room. "But . . . who cares?"

chapter 36

Honestly, I considered calling Philip back and cussing him out. What was so important that he couldn't spend even twenty-four hours with his two sons this—

Jodi's voice popped into my head, urging, *"Don't stop praying for him, Gabby. God knows what's happening, even if we don't."*

Pray for Philip? *Huh.* What I wanted to do was rip Philip apart verbally for blowing off his kids, especially the one weekend this month when no cross-country meets were scheduled . . . but instead I counted to ten—slowly—and gave both boys hugs. "I'm so sorry, guys. You know your dad loves you. He must have a good reason." Though I didn't believe the "good reason" bit for a minute.

After promising we'd do a movie or something together tomorrow night, I left the boys to finish their homework at the dining room table and curled up on the window seat in the front sunroom, lights off, only a few flickering candles on the windowsills. The rain of the previous days had left the air clean and sweet-smelling and I opened a window, even though it was chilly enough to need one of my mom's afghans wrapped around me.

Pray for Philip? Well, I could try . . .

"God," I whispered, "You know what's going on with Philip. I don't understand it, Lord. But if it has anything to do with that Fagan guy, I—I don't want him to get hurt. The boys need their dad. And Philip needs You. All he's got is himself, and he's finding out that's not enough . . ."

I surprised myself at the words that popped out of my mouth. That was the prayer I needed to pray for Philip. That he would find God, or that God would find him. Whatever it took. Because it was going to take a big, big miracle to get Philip out of the massive mess he'd created.

The cell phone vibrating in my pocket interrupted my candle-light prayers. I looked at the caller ID. *Lee Boyer.* But I had an idea what he was calling for, so I let the call go to voice mail and listened to it later. *Would I like to go out Friday night to dinner and a movie?* My heart tugged. We'd had such a good time last week . . .

I waited until the next day to call him back and got his voice mail, so I left a message. "Sorry, Lee. Philip can't take the boys this weekend, so I need to do the movie-thing with the kids tonight. But I'd love a rain check; maybe next weekend?" I don't know *what* possessed me, but heard myself adding, "I'm becoming a member at SouledOut Community Church this Sunday. Do you want to come?"

Mabel put me on the agenda for Saturday's board meeting and told me to show up at ten o'clock so I could be first and wouldn't have to stay for the whole thing. I felt a little guilty skipping out on the painting party again, but left two "hostages" in my place under Josh Baxter's supervision. The boys needed something to do anyway.

When I showed up at Manna House, the double doors into the multipurpose room were blocked with bright yellow construction tape and a ladder lying crossways in front of the door. A hand-lettered sign said, "Keep Out! Work in progress."

I poked my head into Mabel's office. "What's going on? Where's the board meeting?"

"There you are. We have to meet somewhere else. Had to schedule some last-minute work in the main room. The, uh, contractor could only come in on the weekend." The director grabbed her purse, took me by the arm, and practically pulled me out the front door and down the steps. "The rest of the board is meeting at the Emerald City Coffee Shop. Knew you wouldn't mind."

"But I left the afterschool proposal in my office! Maybe I could get in through the side door—"

"I have the copy you gave me and made copies for the board. Don't worry about it." Mabel set off for the Sheridan El Station at a good pace, dressed today in jeans, a light sweatshirt, and gym shoes.

This was so unlike Mabel Turner that I wanted to laugh. But, hey, it was good for all of us, even Mabel, to loosen up from time to time. I scurried to keep up. "What do you think about Jermaine and Paul playing for the Youth Jam at SouledOut tonight?"

"I'm glad. Really glad. I just hope . . ." Mabel's voice trailed off. "I worry about him, Gabby. He's my sister's boy, but I've raised him from the time he was five. She . . . never mind. Long story. But I worry every time he's with a new group of kids. He's different, you know. And kids can be so mean."

I wanted to give Mabel a hug, but we were crossing the street and the coffee shop was in sight. "It'll be okay. Josh Baxter is one of the youth group leaders, and I'm pretty sure Edesa will be there tonight too. They'll look out for him. This might be just the ticket for Jermaine anyway—you know, playing 'gigs' is a big deal for someone his age. Other kids will be impressed."

We pushed open the door of the coffee shop under the El tracks and sure enough, most of the Manna House board members were there already. An assortment of chairs had been pulled into a circle near one of the front windows. Mabel and I got coffee and joined the group. I wondered if I had last night's pizza in my teeth because everyone seemed to be grinning at me.

"What?" I said.

Peter Douglass, the board chair, ignored my question and asked Reverend Alvarez to begin the meeting in prayer, which he did in a strong accented voice with no regard for the fact that we were meeting in a public place. I peeked through half-closed eyelids, embarrassed to see several people in the coffee shop frowning at us. ". . . And *gracias*, *Señor Dios*, that You have cut through the red tape and given us the city's blessing on the new House of Hope . . ."

I screeched. "Oh! Oh, sorry. I'm so sorry, but did they—? I mean, is it all—?"

". . . Amen!" boomed Reverend Alvarez. Everyone laughed. And then Mabel and Peter Douglass were both talking at once, showing me the signed papers making Manna House the official service provider for the Supportive Housing Program, along with "Gabrielle Fairbanks, Proprietor," providing housing in the six-flat at such-and-such address, and the HUD Trust Fund subsidizing rent monies . . .

I was so excited, I almost forgot to present the proposal for expanding the afterschool program, but when I did, the board decided to take it under advisement, realizing we needed time to add more volunteer staff, equipment, and supplies, as well as look into the legalities. "Start slow, Gabby," Reverend Liz Handley advised. "You've got good ideas, but it's better to build up a program slowly and have it stick than move too fast."

Did she know me that well in such a short time? "At least I didn't go looking for this idea," I said in my defense. "It came knocking at the shelter door."

Josh managed to entice P.J. into coming to the Youth Jam in spite of the fact that his kid brother was going to play keyboard by saying they needed someone else who could learn to work the soundboard. So I picked up Jermaine and drove all three boys to SouledOut Saturday evening, and then I went to the Baxters' house to hang out until it was time to pick them up again. Denny was at the church as "designated bouncer" in case any of the neighborhood kids mouthed off or got too rough, so Jodi and I had the house to ourselves. We curled up on their couch, each of us with a cat on our lap and a big bowl of popcorn between us, and watched a golden oldie, *The Princess Bride*, laughing ourselves silly every time Vizzini lisped, "Inconthievable!"

As the credits rolled, I jumped up, dumping the calico kitty off my lap. "Sorry, Patches. Gotta pick up the boys." I headed for the door. "Thanks for letting me hang out, Jodi. Too bad the Youth Jam wasn't Sunday night; then I could've brought the boys and stayed for your Yada Yada Prayer Group"—I almost said, *"since they're celebrating your birthday,"* but realized that might be a surprise. So I just said, "I could use a lot of prayer this coming week. The closing is on Thursday, and hopefully the new tenants"—I winked at her—"can move in on Saturday."

Jodi, still holding the black-and-white kitty in her arms, followed me to the front door. "Wait a sec, Gabby. Can't you come to Yada Yada anyway? After all, this is a real answer to our prayers for Josh and Edesa to find a larger place to live, and it'd be so neat for the Yadas to hear about it from you, and pray for you *and* for Edesa . . . Hey!" Her brown eyes danced. "Maybe you and Edesa could start a Yada Yada Prayer Group at the House of Hope since you'll be living in the same building. Think about it!" She gave me a hug—giving Peanut a perfect opportunity to take a swipe with claws extended at a stray curl bouncing in his face, but the cat missed and caught my cheek instead.

"Ow!" My hand flew to my face. Blood.

"Oh, Gabby!" Jodi dumped the cat and grabbed a tissue to dab at my cheek. "I'm so sorry. Are you okay? We should clean that with hydrogen peroxide or something."

I looked in the mirror in their little hallway and groaned. "I'm fine . . . I'm just going to look terrific doing that membership thing tomorrow."

And I'd invited Lee to come, of all the stupid things.

I guess the Youth Jam was a success because the boys jabbered about it all the way home. "How'd they do?" I whispered to P.J., who was sitting in the front seat with me, casting my eyes toward the back where Jermaine and Paul were still "playing" imaginary keyboards on their knees and making "da da de da" noises.

P.J. shrugged. "Okay, I guess. Some of the kids like that kind of jamming."

I smiled to myself. *"Okay, I guess"* was pretty high praise coming from P.J.

The boys didn't even seem to notice the long scratch on my face, but I was pretty self-conscious about it when we walked into SouledOut the next morning for Sunday worship—especially when Harry Bentley, wearing a black patch on one eye, looked me over with his good eye and mused, "So what does the other guy look like, Firecracker?"

"Ha! You should talk, Mr. B. Where'd you get the pirate outfit? It's not even Halloween yet." Then I relented. "Are you okay?"

"Oh, yeah, yeah, I'm fine. If Estelle would just give me back my car keys. That woman! Thinks I can't drive with one eye." He moved off, muttering.

I hadn't heard from Lee whether he was going to come today or not, but I kept looking around during the first part of worship when the whole congregation was standing and singing, half-hoping he'd show up and half-hoping he wouldn't. Then I didn't have time to worry anymore because Pastor Cobbs announced they were going to receive new members into SouledOut's fellowship that morning and would Gabrielle Fairbanks and Harry Bentley please come forward?

Did the pastor say Harry? We both made our way to the six-inch high platform at the front of the wide half circle of chairs that made up SouledOut's "sanctuary." "You didn't tell me!" I whispered to him as we met at the front.

"You didn't ask!" he whispered back, but gave me a big grin.

Jodi joined me on the platform, giving me an encouraging hug, but I was surprised to see her husband, Denny, come up and stand alongside Harry. *Not Estelle?* Okay, maybe that would have been too obvious.

SouledOut's pastoral team stood together, smiling broadly at Harry and me. I tried not to think of Jodi's offhand comment once that the two men reminded her of the "Mutt and Jeff" cartoons—Pastor Cobbs, short and sturdy, Pastor Clark, tall and gangly—and made myself pay attention to Pastor Clark's homily on the meaning of church membership.

"Just as baptism," the older man was saying, "is a public declaration of one's personal faith, receiving fellow believers into church membership is not only a recognition that this brother and this sister are members of the worldwide body of Christ, but they are an essential part of *this* church family—similar in many ways to a family adopting children, who become just as much part of the family as anyone else. And as the apostle Paul tells us in his first letter to the church in Corinth, the family of God is made up of many different kinds of members, with different gifts and different roles, but *all* the parts need each other."

He picked up a hammer, grinning mischievously. "And as we know, the different parts of the human body are organically interconnected. I hit my thumb with this hammer the other day"—he held up a bruised thumb—"and you better believe the rest of my body knew about it!" The congregation laughed. "Same when I eat a really good piece of April Simmons's chocolate cake—the rest of me is *really* happy." More laughter.

Pastor Clark was beaming now, full of spirit in spite of his wrinkles and thinning hair. "So Sister Gabrielle and Brother Harry, we are excited that you have both decided to become members of SouledOut Community Church. We pray that God will meet you here and that you will grow closer to Him—because in the end, it's about Jesus, not us. But we also want you to know that you're family now. When you cry, we will cry with you, and when you're happy, we will laugh with you, not at you . . . Let's pray."

I barely made it through the rest of the membership service without blubbering. Pastor Cobbs took over and asked each of us questions, affirming our faith in Jesus Christ as Savior and Lord, confessing and receiving God's forgiveness for our sins, and inviting the Holy Spirit to release our spiritual gifts in service to others . . .

The membership questions replayed themselves over and over in my mind the rest of that day, sinking deep into my spirit. I had "accepted Jesus into my heart" at an early age back at Minot Evangelical Church—it pleased my parents to no end—but I'd drifted so far from Him after the failure of my teenage marriage. Since coming to Chicago and falling into the arms of Manna House, both as staff and as a resident, my faith had been fanned back into a burning ember in my soul.

But it felt so good to *say it*. To say it publicly! *Yes! I believe! I'm taking my stand with God's people, a follower of Jesus!* It felt so good, I wanted to celebrate my new relationship with "God's people" somehow, to end the day with a bang, not a whimper.

And I knew just the thing.

Grabbing the phone, I pushed a speed-dial number. "Jodi? . . . Yeah, it's me, Gabby. Is it still okay to show up at your Yada Yada Prayer Group tonight?"

chapter 37

Jodi gave me directions how to get to Ruth Garfield's house where the Yada Yada Prayer Group was meeting that night. "Don't worry if you're a little late," she assured me. "I'm so glad you're coming! Everyone will be so excited to see you."

I left the boys with money for a pizza and strict instructions to finish their homework before watching TV or playing video games, and then stopped at Dominick's to pick up a mixed bouquet of gerbera daisies, tinted carnations, and fall leaves for Jodi's birthday. For some reason, the yellow, orange, and red colors of the sturdy flowers made me smile—they were so like Jodi. Down-to-earth, bright, seemingly ordinary but comforting just by being there. And the colors would complement her brunette coloring . . . which didn't work for *my* reddish hair and fair skin, even though I had a fall birthday too. *Next month.*

My smile turned to a grimace as I headed up Lincoln Avenue toward Ruth's address. *Mercy!* Philip had thought it was such a hoot to put thirty-nine candles on my cake last year and light all of them. Now I was going to turn forty . . . forty and newly single.

I hadn't seen it coming.

Get a grip, Gabby, I scolded myself. *This is a glad day! You're going to the Yada Yada Prayer Group to celebrate your new spiritual family.* Yes, my life had felt like a train wreck only a few months ago, but I'd somehow come through having found myself—and God—again.

Ruth's house turned out to be a classic Chicago bungalow—a tidy one-story brick with a tiny front yard and a neat flower bed of mums beneath the two bay windows on either side of the two-stair stoop. No porch. I rang the bell, and a moment later Ruth Garfield appeared at the door, dark hair dyed and frowzsy. "A guest, it had to be," she announced, waving me in. "Everybody else just walks in. Oh! Flowers . . . very sweet of you." Beaming, she reached for my bouquet.

I held on. "Uh, they're for Jodi. I thought . . . I mean, Estelle said—"

"Well, of *course* they're for Jodi." Ruth dropped her voice to a stage whisper. "But leave them here in the foyer until we bring in the cake."

I wasn't sure if she'd been kidding or just covered up her little blooper, but I carefully stuck the bouquet in the umbrella stand and followed my hostess into the compact living room, which was alive with chatter.

"Yay, Gabby! You made it!" Jodi Baxter jumped up from where she'd been sitting on the arm of the overstuffed sofa and glanced around for an empty seat. The small room was crowded, with every chair and couch seat taken. Several of the welcoming faces I knew well—Edesa and Estelle and Jodi—and most of the others I'd met at one time or another—Estelle's roommate, Stu, and Adele the beauty-shop lady—or recognized from when I'd visited the group once before.

The twentysomething white girl with spiky hair and wearing overalls—Yo-Yo, that was her name, I remembered—jumped up from a folding chair and said, "I'm good." She plopped down cross-legged on the floor.

"Sit! Sit!" Ruth urged me. "And you two—out! Out!"

Bewildered, I wondered who she was talking to—then saw two round, impish faces peeking into the living room from the doorway. Ah, Ruth's three-year-old twins. Some of the women laughed and I heard a familiar voice call out, "Isaac! Havah! Come give Auntie Estelle a goodnight kiss."

The two children ran into the room, dressed in matching yellow-and-green footed pajamas, and jumped into Estelle's lap. Isaac, I noticed, had a large, strawberry birthmark on his face.

Ruth rolled her eyes. "Kids, schmids, their mother they ignore and obey total strangers. Ben! . . . Ben? Where *is* that man?" Huffing, Ruth disappeared to look for the mysterious Ben.

By now, the twins were scooting from lap to lap, getting good night kisses . . . until they got to me. Then they just stood like Dr. Seuss drawings of Thing One and Thing Two, staring at me. The little girl—Havah, I presumed—pointed an accusing finger at my hair. "Is that a clown wig?"

Estelle chortled right out loud. Taking my cue, I grinned too, and pretty soon everyone was chuckling. "Yep," I teased. "I just forgot my clown suit. Sorry."

The twins' eyes got big—but just then an older man with

silvery hair and a rather bulbous nose scurried into the room, scooped up a twin under each arm, and hustled out again. Their father? If so, the twins must have been "late-in-life blessings."

I didn't have time to figure out the family dynamics, because Avis Douglass was saying, "All right, sisters, we need to get started. It's already five thirty. We want to have enough time to hear praise reports and prayer requests—but first let's worship our awesome Savior, just for Who He is . . . Oh, Jesus, You are wonderful! We're so glad to just sit at Your feet and be in Your presence . . ."

And just like that, Avis slid into talking to God as though He'd come walking through the door. Others joined in, sometimes several at once, murmuring prayers of thanks and praise. I closed my eyes and drank in the atmosphere of these women worshiping together, not asking God for anything, just focusing on being grateful for His love and faithfulness.

Someone started singing, "O come let us adore Him . . ." —which surprised me, because I'd only thought of that song as a Christmas carol—but I loved the fact that the chorus was so simple, I didn't need to look at any words, I could just let my heart sing. Then people added other phrases: "For You alone are worthy" . . . "We give You love and honor" . . . and back to "O come let us adore Him . . ."

The song died away and Avis finally opened the conversation for praise reports and prayer requests. Edesa was the first. "Oh, *mi amigas*, I am so excited. God has answered your prayers for me and Josh and Gracie in a mighty way! Not just for a bigger place to live, but—" She suddenly turned to me. "Sister Gabby, *you* tell them. Because God answered both our prayers!"

All eyes turned to me. I shrank slightly into my chair. I'd wanted to come tonight to share the good things God had been doing in my life with these sisters, but I'd hoped to listen to others first. "Uh, that's okay, Edesa. Go ahead."

To my relief, Edesa burbled on, telling the Yada sisters how the new House of Hope needed a property manager on site and how I'd offered the job to Josh, and what a wonderful answer to prayer it was since it meant living on the premises.

"What's dis 'House of Hope'?" the Jamaican woman named Chanda demanded. "How come all you talking tings mi not hear about?"

"Humph," Yo-Yo snorted. "If you'd stay put 'stead of flyin' to Jamaica or Waikiki to lie in the sun, you woulda heard about it too."

Realizing some of the women hadn't heard the whole story, I started at the beginning and told how the idea for the House of Hope had come to be, with Jodi and Edesa jumping in from time to time to fill in details. "But I've got more good news!" I said, grinning with excitement. "I met with the Manna House board on Saturday, supposedly to bring a proposal about an expanded afterschool program, and—"

"Wait a minute," Florida Hickman interrupted, frowning. "You met with the Manna House board on *Saturday*? At Manna House?" She glanced anxiously at Jodi and Jodi returned a slight shrug and shake of her head.

"Well, no . . . not *at* Manna House. Some kind of construction was going on, so we met at a coffee shop nearby. Why?"

A grin replaced Florida's frown. "Oh . . . no reason. Now what was you sayin'?"

What was *that* all about? *Weird.* But I went on, telling how the board casually let slip that the city of Chicago had approved the House of Hope as part of their Supportive Housing Program, with the HUD Trust Fund subsidizing rent monies and Manna House providing the needed social services. "The House of Hope is now official! Well, as soon as we close on the building this Thursday," I added. "Which I'd like prayer about, that we wouldn't run into any hitches. If all goes well, Edesa and Josh and the first two moms from Manna House can move in this coming weekend."

The room erupted into a joyous cacophony of clapping, "hallelujahs," and laughter. After a few minutes of congratulations and happy tears from Edesa, Jodi piped up, "And that's not all the good news! As some of you know already, this morning our sister Gabby, here, became a member of SouledOut Community Church!"

"And Harry too!" Estelle said. "An' I'm not talkin' 'bout no 'transfer of membership' neither. For both Harry and Gabby, we're talkin' 'bout two people comin' back to God after a long time out in the cold. Am I right, Gabby girl?"

By this time, I was all choked up and couldn't speak, but I nodded . . . and Florida just started thanking God for "our new sister in Christ" while Jodi pressed a tissue into my hand to take care of the tears and my runny nose.

After the prayer, Chanda crossed her arms across her chest, looking puzzled. "Mi know mi been gone a few weeks, but, Sister Gabby, you keep saying 'we' when you talking 'bout closing on dat building. Is 'we' you an' dat husband of yours? You two back together again?"

The room went silent and some of the Yadas looked at one another as if embarrassed by her question.

"Uh, well, I guess I said *we* because my friend, Lee Boyer—my lawyer, I mean—has been helping me with this whole process. He's really been there for me." I could feel myself blushing, remembering that kiss . . .

"Uh-huh." Chanda looked at me critically. "So what happened wit de husband? You still married?"

"Good grief. Shut up, Chanda," Yo-Yo muttered from her spot on the floor. "So what if she is? The jerk kicked her out, left her high and dry. Ain't like she's really got a husband anymore. Heck, if this Lee guy wants to be her friend or her boyfriend or whatever, I say more power to him!"

"Mi just asking," Chanda protested. "You all be on *mi* case when mi be wit a man mi not married to. Mi jus' trying to figure it out, what be okay walking de Jesus walk and not just de Jesus talk."

I squirmed helplessly. Fortunately, Avis spoke up, her voice calm but authoritative. "That's a good thing to think about, Chanda. Our actions *should* line up with the Word of God—walk the talk, as you say. But Gabby's situation might be better shared with some of the sisters she knows personally. However, we can certainly pray . . . Gabby, are there some things you'd like us to specifically pray about?"

I nodded, grateful to be off the hot seat. "Uh, well, just what I already mentioned, the closing on the six-flat this coming week. That's the last step to making the House of Hope a reality. And"—I decided to claim some high ground—"I do want prayer for my, um, husband, Philip. He's gotten himself into a lot of debt gambling at the Horseshoe, and I'm afraid he's trying to fix it in ways that only make the situation worse. To be honest, I'm really concerned about him. In spite of everything, he *is* my kids' dad and I don't want him to get in trouble."

Avis nodded, and even though there were others who still needed to share, she suggested they pray right then about the closing on the six-flat, and then she prayed for Philip. "Lord Jesus, You know everything about this man—his past, his present, his future. From our point of view, it's easy to be angry at what he's done, kicking Gabby out of her home and basically abandoning her. But You died for all our sins, including Philip's. You know his heart, his hurts, his weaknesses—and right now, we're praying that You will touch his heart and bring him to his knees. Help him to realize that what he needs is You. Protect him from the evil one, who is using him not only to hurt Gabby and his family but himself . . ."

I could hardly believe Avis's prayer. It seemed so . . . right. She admitted being angry at what Philip had done, as if God really understood, and still prayed that God would "touch his heart" and "protect him from the evil one."

When others had had a chance to share and pray—Estelle did a short update on her son, Leroy, who was still in the burn unit at the county hospital, and asked the sisters to keep praying that she'd know what to do with him once he got released—Ruth bustled into the room with a pineapple upside-down cake and a tray of hot tea and lemonade while everyone sang "Happy Birthday" to Jodi. When Estelle gave Jodi the crocheted hat she made, I rescued my flowers from the umbrella stand and gave them to her.

"Oh, Gabby. They're perfect!" Jodi grabbed me in a hug. "I'm so glad you came tonight. The things you shared, your membership at SouledOut this morning—those are the real things to celebrate. But . . ." She pulled me away from the others into the front hallway, lowering her voice to a whisper. "Do you want to talk about Lee sometime? I'm sure it can be confusing where another guy fits when you're separated but still married. I promise I'll listen and not jump in with instant answers. But I *am* your prayer partner, remember?" She smiled. "It might help to pray together."

I nodded and gave her a wordless hug. Yes, yes, yes, I needed to talk about Lee. And pray. About Lee and me. About how to "walk the talk" when things felt so mixed up right now.

Sunday had been such an amazing day, I was still grinning when I pulled open the big oak doors of Manna House the next morning and walked into the cool foyer, with the stained glass reflections falling on the floor in sparkling colors. "Hi, Angela!" I beamed at the young Asian receptionist as I signed in. "Good morning, Mabel!" I called into the director's office, whose door stood open. "Great day, isn't it?"

I barely noticed when Angela came out of her cubby and Mabel stood up from her desk to follow me as I pushed open the double swinging doors into the next room, and I was halfway across the room before I saw it . . .

A large, colorful mural had been painted on the wall directly across from the doors. The figure of Jesus the Good Shepherd was surrounded by a flock of sheep that He was bringing into a sturdy enclosure, a long staff in one hand and a tiny lamb tucked into the crook of His other arm. Over the top of the mural flew a long open scroll with bright blue script lettering that said, "Shepherd's Fold."

I felt as if the breath had been knocked out of me. Slowly I walked closer to the mural, hardly aware that many of the residents were standing around the room in little clusters, because no one was talking. As I stood looking up at the mural, I noticed that the sheep weren't the fat, wooly kind populating most biblical pictures, but they were all different colors and shades of white, brown, and tan, some with scraggly, dirty wool, some thin and starved looking, some with bleeding or bandaged wounds. But the look on the Shepherd's face was pure love.

"Who did this?" I croaked.

Mabel came up alongside me. "Florida Hickman's son, Chris—he's an art major over at Columbia University. Got his 'training' tagging walls and underpasses around the city before the law caught up with him. Now . . . well, you can see for yourself."

I smiled. So this was the "work" being done over the weekend behind the yellow construction-taped doors. No wonder Florida had almost freaked out last night when she thought I'd met with the board here over the weekend.

Only then did I see a little brass plaque over to one side. I bent closer to read it:

In memory of Martha Shepherd,
fondly known as "Gramma Shep."
A resident of Manna House
from June 19—July 10, 2006.

Tears streamed down my face. "Lucy should see this," was all I could say.

chapter 38

Speaking of Lucy, she showed up during lunch and it wasn't even raining.

"Wonkers!" she said, appearing in the dining room on the lower level with Dandy in tow. "Now *that's* more like it." Her gray eyes glittered as she jerked her thumb upward toward Shepherd's Fold.

The tables erupted in clapping and whistles. "Ya shoulda seen Miss Gabby's face when *she* came in this mornin'!" Hannah laughed. I had to smile. I rarely thought of the young woman as Hannah the Bored any more, because Adele's Hair and Nails had increased her afternoon hours to four days a week, Wednesday through Saturday.

Lucy loaded up a plate with Caribbean rice and beans and Mexican sausage at the lunch counter and sat down with an *"Oomph!"* at the table where Mabel, Estelle, and I were sitting. "So who done it?" She grabbed the bottle of hot sauce on the table and liberally sprinkled her rice and beans. "That wall thing, I mean."

Mabel told her about Florida Hickman overhearing her complaint after Sunday Evening Praise a week ago—

"I seen the lady. Who is she?"

"One of my Yada Yada prayer sisters," Estelle put in. "Her family's been renting half their second floor to Josh and Edesa, place no bigger'n a shoebox. Guess Flo was here when SouledOut came to Sunday Evening Praise last week."

"Yeah, yeah, yada, yada . . . whatever. Go on." Lucy poured on more hot sauce.

Mabel picked up the story. "So that's when Florida got the idea to ask her son, Chris, about doing a mural for Shepherd's Fold. The young man is in a special art program for talented teens at Columbia College and he jumped at the chance."

Lucy guffawed when she heard the boy had first used his artistic talent "tagging" the walls of buildings and elevated train underpasses . . . but Estelle jumped in with even more juicy details. Even Mabel hadn't heard the story of Jodi Baxter volunteering to be a drama coach at the Juvenile Detention Center when the regular JDC English teacher got sick, which is where she saw Chris's talent come alive painting the large backdrop for a dramatic piece the kids wrote themselves and acted for staff and parents.

That was the first time the Hickmans realized their son had *real* talent, since up to that point all it had gotten him was doing time at the JDC.

"That's a fantastic story," I murmured when Mabel and Estelle were done. "I hope we get a chance to thank this young man in person one of these days."

Lucy shoveled more rice and beans into her mouth. "Well, maybe we oughta have some kinda dedication or somethin' for Shepherd's Fold, now that ya got a decent plaque an' ever'thing."

"Good idea, Lucy. A *really* good idea." I slipped my last bite of sausage under the table to Dandy, who was parked by my knees, collected my empty dishes, and started to get up. "Well, time to get back to work."

"Hey, don't run off, Fuzz Top. You the one me an' Dandy come here to see. Just got sidetracked by that mural thing upstairs." The old woman pointed her fork at me. "You an' me gotta talk. But somewhere private like."

I raised an eyebrow at her. What in the world was this about? "Well, okay. When you're done, just come into my office." But by the time I'd scraped my dirty dishes and sorted them into the heavy plastic dishwasher bins, Lucy and Dandy were already parked in my office.

I closed the door and sat down at my desk. "So what's up?"

Lucy narrowed her eyes. "Your boys okay? I didn't see 'em up at Richmond Towers all weekend. Not their dad, neither."

Now I raised both eyebrows. "You *are* spying on them!"

Lucy pulled herself up indignantly. "So? Just makin' sure they all right when they not with you. Can't seem to forget how I found you that night when that mister of yours kicked you out, cryin' your eyes out on that park bench . . . an' don't forget who found Dandy here, wanderin' 'round the park after bein' lost all night an' all day. So you got a problem with me keepin' an eye on your boys? Huh?"

I shook my head with a rueful smile. "No . . . no, I'm grateful, Lucy, really I am. But I think it freaked Paul out a little. He doesn't know why you're 'spying' on them."

Lucy leaned forward. "Well . . . I ain't tellin' you the whole truth, neither. Fact is, I been seein' some strange characters hangin' around Richmond Towers, overheerd 'em askin' 'bout the mister, where he lives an' stuff."

My breath caught. "What kind of strange characters?"

She shrugged. "Don't belong there is all. One was an under-cover cop, 'nother was a man in a suit . . .'"

I blew out my breath. Why would a cop and a man in a suit be asking around about Philip? Had he done something illegal? "How do you know it was an *undercover* cop? I thought the whole point was not to look like a cop."

Lucy snorted. "Huh. When you live on the street long as I have, you can smell an undercover a block away."

I frowned. "Are you sure they were looking for Philip? Though I suppose it could be one of Philip's creditors trying to find him. He's, uh, run up some big debts. But I appreciate you keeping an eye on my boys."

"Yeah, well . . ." Lucy pushed herself out of the chair. "Mostly wanted to know the boys was okay since I didn't see 'em this weekend up at the Tower."

"That's because they stayed with me this weekend. They're okay." I grabbed a pen and scribbled on a notepad. "But here are my phone numbers—both home and cell phones. Call me if you're concerned about anything, okay?" I held out the note.

"Now, Fuzz Top, whatcha think I'm gonna do with that? You know I ain't got no cell phone."

"Just take it, Lucy. If you need to call me, you'll find a way."

When Paul showed up at the shelter after school, I told him he was right after all, Lucy and Dandy *were* keeping an eye on them when they were staying at Richmond Towers, just wanting to make sure they were okay. When I said Lucy *and Dandy* were keeping an eye on them, he seemed to feel better about it. But I made a mental note that I should probably talk to Philip about the "strange men" Lucy had seen. Who were they? What did they want? Or was she just imagining things?

But it seemed as if Thursday showed up on the calendar before I even had time to blink. Closing day! I was so nervous Mabel told me not to bother coming in to work that day until it was over, because I'd be virtually useless. Lee had called me at work several times during the week to let me know what to expect at closing and to make sure I brought the necessary bank draft to cover the down payment, title fee, and other expenses. *Whew*. Taking out that bank draft sent my savings account plummeting to a low water mark. I'd be barely wading in my inheritance money now instead of swimming.

As many times as we'd talked that week, I thought it was strange that Lee didn't say anything about my invitation to come to church last Sunday, so I finally asked if he'd gotten my message. "Oh gosh, Gabby. I'm sorry. I did, but I thought . . . well, obviously I didn't make it. To be honest, I'm not really a church kind of guy. But I hope it was everything you wanted it to be."

"What do you mean, you're not a church kind of guy? I wasn't asking you to join the church, just come to something that was meaningful to me."

"Hey, down, girl. Don't jump all over me. It sounded like an afterthought when you turned down *my* invitation to go out to dinner last Friday. I didn't think it was that big a deal."

I'd hesitated. "You're right. It was an afterthought. But it was a big deal—to me anyway. Becoming a member of the church, I mean. But . . . never mind. What's the address of the title company where we're doing the closing? Eleven o'clock, right?"

"Don't worry about finding it. I'll pick you up at your house."

After we hung up, I'd picked up one of the floppy stuffed dogs still hanging around my office and went nose to nose with it. "Hey. Remind me next time not to mix business with pleasure. There're probably plenty of blogs out there about not getting romantically involved with your lawyer."

Still, I was glad it was Lee who sat beside me at the big conference table at the title office Thursday morning at eleven. He squeezed my hand before the owner of the building and his attorney and the title company rep came in, giving me an encouraging smile. I squeezed back. Lee Boyer had helped me through one of the roughest periods of my life, and the fact that he knew it all and still thought I was special, well . . .

An hour later we all shook hands, the attorneys and title guys packed up their briefcases, and we headed out into the parking lot to go our different ways. I started to lean against Lee's Prius to regain my equilibrium, but it set off his car alarm and I leaped away in shock as the horn began blaring. Grinning, Lee used his clicker to shut off the alarm and then we both collapsed against the car.

"Uh, Lee? Did I just hand over a check for two hundred grand?"

"More. All those fees, remember?"

"And all those papers I signed. You read them, I hope."

"Uh, they're pretty standard. I have read them at one time or another."

"Uh-huh. And now I own a very large building."

"Mm. Medium I'd say. Just a six-flat. But if you want, now you can move out to the suburbs and join the fine tradition of Chicago's absentee slumlords—ow!" He threw up his hands to defend himself against another slug on the arm. "Just kidding."

I looked at him sideways. His easy grin, wire-rim glasses, and brown hair falling over his forehead gave him a perpetually boyish look that made me feel like kicking off my shoes and running barefoot in the grass—except the parking lot was concrete.

"Let's go buy a kite," I said suddenly.

"What?" Now he started laughing.

"I feel like flying a kite! Come on!"

"You're crazy, Gabby Fairbanks, you know that?"

I was still glowing and windblown when I finally got back to Manna House at three o'clock. We almost didn't find a kite, since all the stores were already stocked with Halloween costumes and Thanksgiving decorations. But we finally found a big, black bat-shaped kite in the Halloween section of a discount store and took it to Lincoln Park along the lakefront. The wind off Lake Michigan had been nippy, but it sent the kite flying high and gave us rosy cheeks and red noses.

"Friday?" Lee said hopefully when he dropped me off at the shelter.

For some reason Chanda's snippy comment at Sunday's Yada Yada meeting niggled at me. *"Just trying to figure out how to walk the talk . . ."* But I'd already blown Lee off last weekend. What could it hurt? "Sure, Friday," I promised and ran up the steps.

Precious and Tanya took one look at the grin on my face when I came in the door and started screeching with joy. "We can move! We can move!" . . . "We got us a real apartment! Oh, thank You, Jesus!" They both grabbed me and dragged me down the stairs to the lower level. "C'mon—Estelle's got somethin' for ya!"

"Something" turned out to be a large sheet cake Estelle and her Thursday afternoon cooking class had made and decorated with "Congratulations!" The cake and fresh coffee brewing drew residents and staff from all corners of the building, and by the time the schoolkids joined us, we had a regular party going. Even eye-rolling, pregnant Sabrina finally seemed excited that she was going to have her own bedroom at last.

I called Josh and Edesa on their cell phones and told them the move was a "go" on Saturday. But it wasn't until the boys were climbing into their dad's Lexus at six o'clock Friday evening that I realized I hadn't called Philip about Lucy's report of "strange men" hanging around Richmond Towers. I didn't want to say anything in front of the boys, so I just asked Philip to call me later that evening when he had a chance.

His call came when Lee and I were slow-dancing to a live band at one of the popular country-western venues around the city. *Okaay, this is awkward,* I thought, trying to find a corner of the room farthest from the band. Plugging one ear I held the cell phone to the other. "Philip? Thanks for calling. Just wanted to tell you that, uh, Lucy Tucker said she's seen some strange men hanging around Richmond Towers asking for you. She wanted me to tell you." I felt silly even as I relayed the message.

"Lucy? The old lady who's got your mom's dog?" I heard him snort in my ear. "What's *she* doing snooping around here? Look, tell her to mind her own business . . . Where are you anyway? I can hardly hear you with all that racket in the background."

"Good-bye, Philip." I flipped the phone closed and moved back across the dance floor to where Lee was waiting for me, a welcoming grin on his face.

It wasn't any of Philip's business where I was.

The second call came at six thirty the next morning.

I almost didn't hear the phone ring, because I'd left the cell in my shoulder bag, which I'd tossed in a corner of the bedroom. But consciousness finally dawned and I scrambled out of bed, snatched up the purse, dumping the contents out on the bed to find the phone. "Uhh . . . hello?"

"Gabby." The voice was scratchy. Gruff. "Get over here and pick up your boys."

I was suddenly wide-awake. "Wha—? Lucy? Is that you? What's going on?"

"Dandy an' I found your mister beat up in the walkin' tunnel under Lake Shore Drive—"

"The boys! Lucy, where are they?"

"Up in that penthouse sleepin', far as I know. Your man was out joggin' early is my guess—"

"Did you say beat up? How bad is he? Did you call 9-1-1?"

I could hear Dandy barking in the background, and Lucy's voice pulled away. "Dagnabit! I'll give it back to ya. Just a minnit!" Then she was back on. "Yeah, I called 9-1-1. Now this jogger guy wants his phone back."

I could hear faint sirens in the distance on Lucy's end of the phone. I pinched the bridge of my nose and squeezed my eyes shut. I couldn't believe this. "How bad, Lucy?"

"Pretty bad, Fuzz Top. He's unconscious. Lotta blood, but still breathin' . . ."

"Stay there, Lucy. I'm coming. Just find out where they're going to take him."

chapter 39

The boys and I huddled in the waiting room of the ER. Why wasn't someone coming out to tell us how badly Philip was hurt? Lucy had gone outside to walk Dandy, who didn't understand why he couldn't come inside too . . .

The frumpy bag lady and yellow dog had been waiting for me just outside Richmond Towers when I came screeching into the frontage road and pulled the Subaru into a Visitor Parking space. She said the ambulance had left just five minutes ago and was taking "the mister" to Weiss Memorial Hospital.

"Do the boys know their dad's hurt?"

She wagged her head. "Don't think so. He was wearing them fancy jogging clothes—ya know, them silky shorts an' matchin' jacket—like he'd gone out early for a run while they was still sleepin'."

"Don't disappear, Lucy," I commanded. "I want to know what happened—but right now I've got to get my boys. I'll be back as soon as I can."

Muttering thanks to God that I still had my security pass and keys to the penthouse—once management had insisted that Philip replace the original locks—I rode the elevator to the thirty-second floor and let myself in. All was quiet. Trying to ignore the schizophrenic feeling of walking around in the high-priced penthouse that used to be my home, I found the boys sprawled in discount store twin beds in one of the bedrooms, dead to the world. Waking them gently, I told them to get dressed quickly. We had to go to the hospital . . .

I couldn't answer any of their questions. Lucy rode in the front seat with me, Dandy between the boys in the back. "Now tell me, Lucy! What happened?"

"Like I said . . ." She and Dandy were taking their early morning walk in the park, staying close to Richmond Towers. As they came through the lighted pedestrian tunnel that gave joggers and residents of the luxury high-rises along Lake Shore Drive access to the beach, Dandy suddenly started to whine and pull on his leash. A man was crumpled on the ground in the tunnel. "Thought at first it was just a wino passed out on the ground. But when I saw them fancy jogging clothes, I knew this wasn't no wino." Then Dandy had stiffened and started to growl. The light wasn't that good in the tunnel, but when Lucy got close, she realized who it was.

"Another jogger came along an' let me use his cell phone, so I called 9-1-1, then I called you." She'd snorted in disgust. "The guy didn't want to wait around till the ambulance got there. Had to finish his run. Made me give the phone back."

"Did the paramedics tell you *anything* about how badly Philip was hurt?"

"Nope. Cops came, asked me a couple of questions since I was the one who found 'im. Never let on I knew who he was, though."

When we came flying into the emergency room, I'd rushed to the desk and asked if a Philip Fairbanks had been brought in by ambulance. The receptionist looked at a clipboard. "Relation to the patient?"

I hesitated a nanosecond, then blurted, "His wife. These are his children."

"Have a seat."

Now we sat in the waiting room . . . waiting. Two uniformed policemen came out of the double doors marked Hospital Personnel Only and spoke to the receptionist, who nodded at me. They wanted to know what I knew about what happened. I shook my head. "Nothing! We're . . . separated. Someone called me, told me he'd been found beaten unconscious while he was out jogging. I . . . the boys were with him this weekend. I picked them up from their dad's place and came here."

The police treated it as a routine mugging, jotted a few notes. Left.

Who to call? I should call somebody! I called Jodi Baxter . . . Wondered if I should call Philip's parents but decided to wait until we knew something about his condition. I asked the boys if they'd like to get something to eat. Both of them shook their heads. The clock's second hand labored toward 7:40 . . . 8:05 . . . 8:30 . . .

The move. My new tenants were supposed to be moving into the six-flat this morning. But I just sat. They'd have to figure it out for themselves.

Jodi and Denny Baxter pushed through the revolving doors

into the ER waiting room at nine o'clock. "Gabby! What happened? Is he going to be all right?"

I shook my head. "Don't know yet . . . Oh."

A young doctor in a white coat flapping open to show his pale blue shirt and blue striped tie, stethoscope sticking out of one coat pocket, came through the double doors and looked at our little group, the only people standing. "Mrs. Fairbanks?"

I nodded. The doctor motioned us into a nearby conference room, and I insisted that the boys and the Baxters come too.

"We've done our preliminary exam. Whoever worked him over did a bang-up job." I winced and glanced at my boys. A crude choice of words. "Your husband has several broken ribs, a broken arm, possible internal injuries from being punched in the stomach, a severe laceration on his head caused by striking concrete, a badly broken nose that will cause a lot of bruising, a possible concussion . . . but the good news is, none of it is life-threatening. We need to do more tests to determine the extent of any internal injuries, and he'll have to be hospitalized for several days. Maybe a week. But"—the young doc actually smiled—"he's going to be fine."

Paul drew his legs up onto the chair with his arms, put his head down on his knees, and started to cry. P.J. put his arms around his brother and murmured, "Hey, hey. It's okay. He's gonna be okay, didn't you hear?"

"Thank you," I said to the doctor. The words barely came out in a whisper.

Jodi and Denny took the boys to the hospital cafeteria to get some breakfast and brought me a bagel and a large coffee. "With cream," she pointed out with a sweet smile. Then she and Denny left, taking Lucy and Dandy with them, to check on the move.

"They should just go ahead," I told them. "Josh has the building keys. They've waited long enough."

It was almost three before Philip was moved to a private room. They'd sedated him to set the broken bones and deal with the pain, so he wasn't aware when the boys and I tiptoed into the room to sit with him. He seemed swathed in bandages—his rib cage was bound, his right arm had been set and was held away from his bruised body with some kind of contraption, and his head had been shaved and was wrapped in bandages except for his face, which was a mess—swollen nose and eye, scrapes and cuts.

He looked awful.

Estelle Williams and Harry Bentley peeked into the room. "We're not stayin', honey," Estelle said, sweeping me into a big hug. "Just wanted to let you know there are a whole lot of people prayin' for Philip right now. An' if you need anything—*anything*— you let us know, you hear?"

I blubbered into her soft bosom and nodded, even though I could hardly breathe, she was hugging me so tight.

Harry motioned me out into the hall. "You know who did this, don't you?"

I shook my head . . . then slowly nodded. "If you're right about Matty Fagan." I fished for a tissue and blew my nose.

"I know I'm right. What's it been . . . four weeks since Philip met with Fagan? Fagan never gives anybody that long to pay back what he loaned 'em. I've got my ex-partner on the case, seeing what she can find out." Harry shook his head. "The sooner Internal Affairs gets that rogue off the streets, the better for everybody."

Harry and Estelle left. We sat some more. "Look, Mom!" P.J. cried. "His eyes are open!"

Philip's eyes were mere slits. I leaned close. "Philip? It's me, Gabby. And the boys are here."

"What . . . where am I? . . . What happened?" he croaked.

I told him briefly. He closed his eyes and seemed to think about it a long while. Then he opened them again. "Are . . . boys okay? I—I left them alone, just going for a short run . . ."

"We're fine, Dad." P.J. bent close into Philip's line of vision. "Don't worry about us. You're going to be fine too. Doctor said."

Philip raised his left hand and crooked a finger at me to come close. I bent over him. "I don't . . . want . . . boys . . . here. Don't want them . . . to see me like . . . this."

Too late for that. But I nodded. "They're going home soon."

Jodi and Denny Baxter returned later that afternoon and said the move was done—including picking up household and personal things Precious had stored here and there with friends. But everyone was worried about her and the boys and Philip. The Baxters offered to take the boys back to our apartment and stay with them until I came home. "Not a hardship for us," Jodi assured me. "After all, Josh and Edesa and Gracie are right upstairs now! I'm sure they can use some more help getting settled. But . . . why don't you come home for the night? Get some sleep. You can come back tomorrow."

We were standing out in the hallway. I looked back into the room where Philip lay on the hospital bed attached to all kinds of wires and tubes and IVs. I shook my head. "No. Think I'll stay here tonight."

Jodi looked ready to argue, but I held up my hand.

"The thing is, Jodi, he doesn't have anyone right now . . . except me."

chapter 40

I dreaded making the call but couldn't wait any longer. Once the boys had left with the Baxters, I found a family waiting room and dialed the Fairbanks' number in Virginia. Marlene Fairbanks went ballistic when she heard we'd been at the hospital since early that morning and I was just now calling them.

"I'm sorry, Marlene. We didn't know for a long time what his injuries were, and I knew you'd want to know. The boys needed my attention; they're upset, of course, and—"

I don't think she heard me, because she was still calling me every name she could think of while telling me this was all my fault.

"Get off the phone, Marlene!" snapped Philip's father. I heard the senior Fairbanks arguing, then one extension went dead and Mike Fairbanks came back on the phone. "Now. Tell me again what happened, Gabby. He got mugged while jogging? Of all the—!" Mike Fairbanks let loose with a few choice expletives, and then checked himself. "Sorry. But I *told* that bull-headed son of mine not to move to Chicago. So, what are the doctors saying?"

When I finished rehashing the doctor's report, Mike just said, "Look, we'll get the earliest flight we can, be there sometime tomorrow." Then his voice softened. "Thanks for being there, Gabby . . . after, you know, everything."

After we hung up, I pinched the bridge of my nose, trying to stave off a wicked headache threatening the back of my head. There was another call I needed to make—to Henry Fenchel, Philip's business partner in the commercial real estate firm they'd established together last spring. He wouldn't be expecting Philip to come in until Monday . . . maybe I could wait until late Sunday. By that time Philip's parents would be here and *they* could deal with Henry and Mona Fenchel . . .

I sighed. No, better to let Henry know sooner rather than later that Philip was going to be laid up awhile. That was only fair. Henry would have to cancel meetings, follow up on clients, fill in for Philip—whatever it was the two of them did during a week to keep Fairbanks and Fenchel Development Corp running.

Sucking up my courage, I dialed Henry's cell, but only got his voice mail. Not surprising on a weekend. I left a brief message, saying Philip had had an accident and was at Weiss Memorial, and to call me as soon as possible.

I looked at my watch. I'd been out of Philip's room half an hour already. Should probably get back soon. He was basically helpless right now if he needed ice chips or lost the call button for the nurse. But there was one more call I wanted to make before I lost the battery on my cell phone . . .

I called Lee.

I sat in the recliner in Philip's hospital room the rest of that day, listening to the beeps and ticking of the half-dozen machines attached to his body, wondering what in the world I was doing there. I wished I had somebody to talk to! But all I got when I called Lee was his voice mail. Frustrated, I'd left a cryptic message and hung up. Where was he when I needed him?

Maybe it was just as well. He'd tell me Philip had brought this down on his own head—which was probably true, if Mr. B was right about that guy Fagan—and I should just go home. Still, I knew, somehow, I'd made the right decision to stay. I turned on the TV and watched some mindless reality show so I wouldn't have to think, and actually welcomed the parade of nursing aides who came in and out to check Philip's vitals, change his IVs, and give him more pain meds, which kept him zoned out most of the time.

But I was surprised when Pastor Joe Cobbs and his wife, Rose, from SouledOut came by that evening, bringing a tote bag Jodi Baxter had packed for me with some of my toiletries, a few sandwiches and fruit, my Bible . . . and my cell phone charger. "You know Jodi." Rose Cobbs smiled. "Thinking of everything." The African-American couple didn't stay long, but Pastor Cobbs did pray for Philip in his strong voice that I'm sure carried down the hall clear to the nursing station.

When they left, Philip muttered through his swollen lips, "Who was that?"

I was startled to hear his voice. He'd seemed basically out of it when they were here. "My, um, pastor and his wife."

A long silence. "You asked him to come?"

"No. They just came."

"What? Uh . . . Whole world knows I'm laid up here?" He winced with pain.

I decided not to answer. "You're hurting. I'll call the nurse—it's probably time for more pain meds."

I reached for the call button, but Philip grabbed my hand with his one good one. "Just . . . don't tell my parents. Or Fenchel."

I gently pried my hand from his grip. "I'm sorry, Philip. They needed to know." I tensed, expecting him to get angry—but all I heard was a groan escaping his dry and swollen lips.

I had dozed off in the chair when my cell phone rang. I squinted at the caller ID: *Henry Fenchel.* Slipping out of the room, I closed the door and hit Talk. "Hello?"

"Gabby! What's this about an accident? What kind of accident?" I'd expected Henry to be worried, concerned, anxious. But his words slammed through the phone like a challenge. I told him briefly. "How bad?" he demanded.

Again I kept the details brief. "They need to monitor him for a while. Could be a week."

Henry spat out a curse word. "Gabby, this is the last straw!" He was practically shouting into the phone. "Philip has taken money from the business account to cover his gambling debts, thinks I don't know because he transfers money to cover it from . . . *somewhere*, who knows! He's distracted, he comes in late on Monday, he's missed some important meetings with clients . . . Ever since you left him, Gabby, he's been going downhill. Now this. How are we supposed to run a business, tell me that!"

"Since I left him? Since *I* left *him*? Henry Fenchel, you know good and well—!"

"Whatever. Since the two of you broke up. But I've had it! I'm going to sue him, break off the partnership. You tell him that, Gabby!" And the phone went dead.

My heart was pounding so hard I had to lean against the wall to get my breath. When I finally went back into the room and saw Philip lying there looking like a wreck, knowing it was going to get worse—a lot worse—before it got better, I fell into the chair and put my head in my hands. *Oh, Jesus! You're the only one who's going to be able to turn this around for Philip. Please, God . . .*

The night was long, but I must have finally fallen asleep, because when I woke up sunlight was slipping long fingers through the blinds, making pretty patterns all around the stark hospital room. I looked over at Philip . . . and realized he was staring at me.

"You're awake," I said.

He just looked at me for a long moment. Then he croaked, "You've . . . been here all night. Why did you . . . stay?"

Good question. Wasn't sure I could answer it. I pushed off the blanket the nurse had given me and got out of the recliner, standing uncertainly at the end of the bed. But finally I took a deep breath and blew it out. "Because, Philip, I'm still your wife and you needed me."

He kept staring at me. I could hardly stand to look at his bruised and battered face and looked away . . . but when I looked back, tears were running down his face. "Oh, Gabby . . ." he moaned. And then he started to weep, big deep sobs racking his body, mixed with pain with every move. His sobs sounded almost animal-like, a guttural wail I'd never heard before. I didn't know what to do. What was going on?

I almost reached for the call button to call the nurse, but his free hand flailed, motioning to me to come closer. Tentatively, I moved around to the side of the bed and he grabbed my hand. "Gabby!" he gasped. "Gabby, I've . . . I've messed everything up so bad. I don't know what to do! You . . . you were the best thing that ever happened to me, and I . . . I drove you away. Please . . . please, don't leave me. You have every right to . . . to walk out of here, but . . . can you forgive me? I'm begging you! Please . . ."

Out of the corner of my eye, I saw the door open slightly and a man's face appeared for a moment, and then disappeared again.

Lee Boyer!

I gently slid my hand out of Philip's grasp. "Just a minute. Someone's here."

"Gabby, please . . ."

"I said just a minute."

I hurried out of the room into the hall, closing the door behind me. Lee Boyer had walked several yards away, but he turned back when he heard the door close. His eyes flashed and his body was rigid.

"Lee?"

He strode toward me, almost shaking with anger. "I heard. Heard everything that—that con man was saying to you! You know it's all a lie, don't you? He'll say anything right now, because he's in trouble. What are you doing here anyway, Gabby? I called your house and they said you were still here at the hospital."

The absurdity of the situation made me want to laugh—or cry—or something. I could still hear Philip's voice in my head— *"Can you forgive me? I'm begging you!"*—and now Lee was hissing at me between clenched teeth, *"It's all a lie!"* But for some reason a strange calm settled over me, like standing in the eye of a storm with the two men in my life swirling like hurricanes around me.

Lee threw his hands out in frustration. "You don't owe that man anything, Gabby Fairbanks. I . . . I love you, don't you know that? We could have a good life, you and me. We're the same kind of people. We get along great. We like the same things . . ."

For the life of me, I don't know why I said it. "Except church. And God."

I don't think I could have startled him more if I'd slapped Lee in the face. His mouth dropped open and his eyes widened behind his wire rims. Then he found his voice. "Church? God? What do church and God have to do with *us*?"

A sudden sadness settled over me. "Maybe . . . everything."

Lee looked totally bewildered. Then the anger rose in his voice again and he pointed a shaking finger toward Philip's hospital room. "And you think that . . . that self-centered jerk in there is your churchgoing, God-praying type?"

I shook my head. "No, that's not what I meant." The sadness weighed heavily on me. Part of me wanted to fling myself into Lee's arms and run away with him, disappear from this hospital and leave Philip to wallow in his own mess. I had no idea what to say or do, but the strange calm seemed to surround me and hold me up.

Lee's diatribe finally ran out. He paced back and forth a few steps, then stopped. "Gabby, I don't know what's going on here.

But I want to know if you feel for me what I feel for you . . . because if you do, then come with me. Don't listen to him. But if you go back in there, we might as well call it quits."

"Lee. Don't make me choose. Not now. This isn't the time."

"Yes it is. Leave him. Come with me." He held out his hand.

My calm threatened to shatter into little pieces, to be sucked into the hurricanes swirling around me in that hospital hallway and the room just steps away.

I wanted to go.

But I couldn't.

My eyes filled with tears. "I'm sorry, Lee," I whispered. I slowly turned, opened the door to Philip's room, and shut it behind me.

chapter 41

I slipped into the bathroom of Philip's private room and cried silently into a skimpy white towel. *What have I done?* Lee said he loved me! But to insist that I leave with him now when Philip was hurt and broken, to say if I stayed we might as well call it quits . . . it was so unfair!

I heard a nurse come into Philip's room. "Well, look who's awake already. How are we feeling this morning? . . . Let's see, which thigh did they use to give you the Heparin shot last night? . . . Okay, turn over, we'll do the other thigh this morning."

Turning on the faucet in the sink, I let the water run so she'd know I was in there. What would I say to Philip when I came out? *"I forgive you"?* No, no . . . it wasn't that simple! He'd nearly destroyed me! Was saying he was sorry just a big lie to get my sympathy, like Lee said?

But . . . what if he really was sorry?

That possibility was so beyond comprehension, it would have to be a miracle. But I'd seen some pretty impossible miracles in my own life the past few months. What if God hadn't given up on Philip yet? What if . . . what if God had allowed Philip's life to spin out of control to get his attention, like Avis had prayed at Yada Yada? Was Philip paying attention? What he'd said to me not fifteen minutes ago wasn't the self-confident man I'd married, or the cruel egomaniac who'd washed his hands of me.

He'd sounded like a broken man. A Humpty Dumpty who'd had a great fall . . .

But if God was working on Philip, where did I fit into the picture? Was I ready to take responsibility for my part in our broken communication? To ask Philip to forgive *me*?

Oh, God, I groaned. *I can't do this. I need time. Time to think. Time to pray. Time to talk to someone who isn't going to give me an ultimatum.*

Washing my face, I took several deep breaths and came out of the bathroom. The nurse was exchanging the IV bag and doing readouts from the machines. She smiled pleasantly and said the doctor would be doing rounds shortly, they'd probably want to do more tests to determine the extent of internal injuries . . . and then she was gone, leaving Philip and me to deal with our unfinished conversation, like a sticky spider's web filling the room.

His head was turned away, his face still twisted in misery. But as I approached the bed, that Voice seemed to speak to my spirit. *Gabby, take the time you need. You don't have to figure it all out right now. Can you trust Me with all your heart? Can you lean on Me instead of your own understanding?*

Startled, I stopped beside the bed. Was God telling me that promise I'd been memorizing was for *now*? This moment? I *didn't* understand how all this craziness was going to work out—so it might as well be now. I took a big breath, then breathed out a silent prayer . . . *Okay, God, I'm going to trust You. But I'm going to need a lot of help.* But even as I prayed, the "sticky spider's web" seemed to shrivel and disappear, and the anxious knot in my stomach began to loosen.

I laid a hand on Philip's leg covered by the thin blankets. "Philip? I'm still here. But I can't answer you right now. I need time to think . . . and pray."

He turned his head toward me and his tortured eyes met mine. He nodded slowly. "I know."

I finally left the hospital late that afternoon, after Philip's parents arrived. They hadn't been able to get a direct flight to Chicago and had to wait for a connecting flight in New York. Marlene Fairbanks had rushed into the room crying, "Oh, my poor baby. Who did this to you?!" ignoring me completely.

I'd greeted Mike Fairbanks briefly, gathered up my things, and slipped out as unobtrusively as possible. As I walked to my car in the parking garage, I felt as if someone pulled a plug from the bottom of my feet and all my energy drained out. I couldn't wait to get home, crawl into my bed, and take a long nap.

Except . . . I'd promised P.J. and Paul I'd bring them back to the hospital this evening after their grandparents arrived. They'd called that morning, wanting to spend the day hanging out at the hospital, but I'd told them their dad had been taken to radiology for some tests and I didn't know how long it would be. "You can come this evening, I promise."

Paul had seemed alarmed. "Nana and Grandad are coming all the way from Virginia? Dad's not going to die, is he?"

"No, no. Didn't you hear the doctor? Once his injuries heal, he'll be fine."

"So why are they coming?"

"Because he's their son and they love him." I thought about this and realized it was true. "If *you* lived in another city and got hurt, I'd come to see you in a heartbeat."

"Oh." I could almost hear Paul smile. "Okay. But I miss you, Mom. When are you coming home?"

Now, buddy. I'm on my way.

Turning south on Sheridan Road after pulling out of the parking garage, my mind drifted to the way God's Spirit had spoken to me in that hospital room. And I realized I'd been right to tell Lee that my relationship with God and my decision to become a member of SouledOut did have everything to do with my relationship with him—and with Philip too. The second part of that promise in Proverbs was that if I kept on putting God *first* in the decisions I had to make, He *would* lead me in the right path.

That was His promise.

As tired as I was, a smile crept onto my face as I turned into my new neighborhood. In the thirty-five hours since I'd rushed out of the apartment Saturday morning, the six-flat had surely gone through a transformation. Josh and Edesa and little Gracie would be settling in on the third floor . . . Precious and Tanya and their children would be right across the hall . . . and when Sabrina delivered, there'd be a new baby to fuss over!

And that was only the beginning. In the next several months, the other tenants would move out and more Manna House moms would be assigned to the House of Hope so they could create a home for their children . . .

"Oh, Jesus," I murmured aloud. "What have we started here?" I knew I was in over my head—waaay over—but a sense of excitement and expectancy pushed my weariness aside and I hiked up my speed a few notches, eager to get home and see the beginning of the dream come true.

As I turned the corner onto my street, I saw a cluster of people gathered outside the six-flat, some standing or sitting on the steps, others on the flat concrete "arms" that hugged the steps leading up to the front door. What was going on?

I pulled the Subaru into a parking space along the curb, sorting out faces. Jodi and Denny Baxter sat on the steps, holding their granddaughter Gracie . . . Josh and Edesa Baxter had their arms around each other, laughing about something with P.J. . . . oh my goodness, there was Harry Bentley and his grandson . . . couldn't miss Estelle, sitting on the "arm" in her latest home-made caftan, braiding Sabrina's hair . . . and Mabel Turner, of all people, talking with Precious and Tanya . . . and was that Lucy Tucker?! The elderly woman sat like a boulder in the middle of the steps while Paul and Tanya's Sammy chased a yellow dog in circles around her . . .

Paul spotted me first. "There she is!" he yelled, galloping toward the car, Dandy fast on his heels, tongue lolling.

I climbed out of the Subaru laughing as Paul grabbed my hand and started pulling me up the walk toward the building, while the rest of the crowd started clapping and cheering. "Look up, Mom! Look up!"

"Look up where?" I said . . . and then I saw it.

A large, curved wooden sign had been fitted over the stone arch above the doorway of the six-flat. In twelve-inch high wooden letters, it said . . .

HOUSE OF HOPE

Tears sprang to my eyes. "Who . . . ? How . . . ?" I gasped.

Jodi Baxter came to my side and slipped her arm through mine as I stood looking up. "Denny and Josh made it—been working on it a couple of weeks. I tried to get them to call it The Yada Yada House of Hope—to remind the moms who come to live here that God knows everything about them, like Psalm 139 says—but I was voted down. 'Three words is enough!' Denny told me." She shrugged and laughed. "That's okay. *We* know it's a 'yada yada' thing, don't we, Gabby?"

"Hey!" Lucy yelled from the steps. "Ya gonna stand there all day? Some of us got stuff to do, places to go!"

The people around her cracked up. "She's right!" Precious waved me in. "Come on! See what the House of Hope looks like from the inside, now that some of us be livin' in hope again!"

With Paul hanging on one hand and Jodi on the other, I moved through the grinning crowd of friends and family, up the broad steps and through the front door that Harry Bentley—ex-doorman but never ex-friend—held open for me.

And I knew I was coming home.

reading group guide

1. In chapter 6, Gabby's lawyer, Lee Boyer, tells her the House of Hope idea, while noble, doesn't seem like a wise use of her inheritance money while she's in the middle of a custody case and possible divorce. What do you think—is she being impetuous? Acting in faith? How can we tell the difference in our own lives?

2. In the same chapter, Mabel Turner says, "If this [House of Hope] is God's idea, then it's going to happen. God's timing is perfect. You don't have to rush it." How do we know when something is "God's idea"? If we run into roadblocks, how do we know when that's the work of Satan trying to stop it and we should press on—or God allowing circumstances to show us it's *our* idea, not His?

3. In chapter 17, what did Mabel mean when she says it's not enough to "believe in God," you have to *"believe God"*? What would it mean for you to *believe God* for something in your life situation today?

4. Do you think Gabby contributed to the downfall of her marriage as Mabel suggested in chapter 18? Why or why not? Why does Gabby have such a difficult time hearing what Mabel said? How do you understand Mabel's apology in chapter 23? Do you think "taking responsibility" for mutual problems in a marriage helps or hinders when one is dealing with emotional abuse?

5. In chapter 27, Gabby offered one of the available apartments in the House of Hope to Josh and Edesa Baxter before talking it over with Precious and Tanya (to whom she'd already promised the two apartments). In what way was she "leaning on her own understanding" (see Prov. 3:5–6)? Now she's in a bind! . . . What are the implications for Josh and Edesa if she tells them they can't move in after all? For Tanya and Precious if they do? For Gabby either way?

6. Are you sometimes tempted to "run ahead of God" with *your* good ideas? What kind of pitfalls have you fallen into?

7. Gabby's solution to the above fiasco: "Suddenly it seemed simple: Just own up to my mistake. Start over." How would Gabby's solution help in *your* situation?

8. Why do you think Gabby held back from telling her sons the stark, bald truth when P.J. implied that his mom was the one who "moved out" (chapter 28)? Do you agree with her reasoning for not vilifying Philip? How would you have responded in that instance?

9. Do you think Gabby did the right thing not making "a big honking deal" out of P.J.'s negative attitude toward Jermaine (chapter 32)? What is she hoping to accomplish? How would you handle a similar situation?

10. Gabby gradually changed her prayers from praying *about* Philip to praying *for* him. In chapter 33, she said, "It was hard to be angry with someone I was praying for." Is there someone you're angry with right now? Have you thought about praying *for* this person (not just *about* him or her)? What would your prayer be for this person?

11. On her date with Lee Boyer in chapter 34, Gabby was starting to "sense God everywhere." Has that happened to you? Where or when was the last time an experience or place made you actively aware of God or spiritual reality (outside of church or reading your Bible)?

12. When Gabby attended the Yada Yada Prayer Group in chapter 37, Chanda challenged her about her relationship with Lee while still married to Philip. What do you think about the way Avis handled the awkward situation? How would you have handled that situation? What do *you* think about Gabby's relationship with Lee?

13. After Philip is mugged and ends up in the hospital, do you believe he is sincere when he asks Gabby to forgive him? Why or why not? If you were Gabby, how would you have responded to the choice Lee presented to her at the hospital?

14. Do you think there is any hope for Gabby and Philip's marriage in the future? What would you like to see happen with Philip? With Lee? Why?

15. What are your thoughts and feelings about emotional abuse in marriage? How can sisters support one another when some form of emotional abuse takes place in a marriage? How can the church be more active in addressing this often hidden problem?

Challenges. Prayers. Friendship. Hope.
It all comes together for an inspiring
finale in . . .

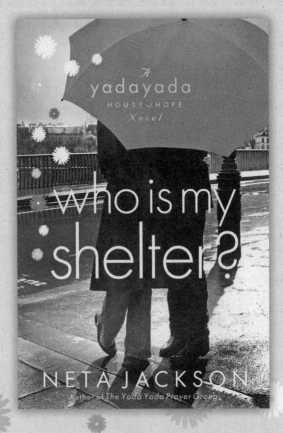